Cloud Native Java

*Designing Resilient Systems with Spring Boot,
Spring Cloud, and Cloud Foundry*

Josh Long and Kenny Bastani

Beijing · Boston · Farnham · Sebastopol · Tokyo

Cloud Native Java

by Josh Long and Kenny Bastani

Published by O'Reilly Media, Inc., 1005 Gravenstein Highway North, Sebastopol, CA 95472.

O'Reilly books may be purchased for educational, business, or sales promotional use. Online editions are also available for most titles (*http://oreilly.com/safari*). For more information, contact our corporate/institutional sales department: 800-998-9938 or *corporate@oreilly.com*.

Editors: Nan Barber and Brian Foster	**Indexer:** Ellen Troutman-Zaig
Production Editor: Melanie Yarbrough	**Interior Designer:** David Futato
Copyeditor: Molly Brower	**Cover Designer:** Karen Montgomery
Proofreader: Sonia Saruba	**Illustrator:** Rebecca Demarest

August 2017:   First Edition

Revision History for the First Edition
2017-08-10:   First Release

See *http://oreilly.com/catalog/errata.csp?isbn=9781449374648* for release details.

978-1-449-37464-8

[LSI]

To Eva and Makani with love from Uncle Josh.

To my grandfather Abbas, who waited 100 years to see his name on the cover of a book.
—Kenny

Table of Contents

Part II. Web Services

Foreword (James Watters)

You could not step twice into the same river.
   —Heraclitus

Sitting next to Josh Long at a coffee shop in Venice Beach in the summer of 2015, I knew we were at the start of something big. His travel schedule was packed as developers demanded to learn about our new technology—Spring Boot. Our cloud native platform, Pivotal Cloud Foundry, was quickly becoming the popular runtime for cloud native apps. With Spring Boot already popular, the arrival of Spring Cloud promised to be explosive. "This is going to be big buddy—this is happening," I offered.

The forces at work were enormous. Spring Boot offered a microservice and DevOps friendly approach to enterprise development at the moment that CIOs were desperately seeking developer productivity gains. The increasing integration between Spring Boot and PCF made production deployments a simple pipeline and API call away, Spring Cloud delivered the world's first microservices mesh, and a standard Cloud Native approach to Java was born.

Far from a superficial change in development fashion, the unique combination of these technologies changed the delivery structure of large organizations. For too long developers were prevented from deploying to production by the operational complexity of legacy Java application servers and patterns. Customer horror stories of multiday deployments were common. We knew our platform would change their lives. Clients began writing us fan mail describing updates to production in minutes versus months when adopting Spring Boot on PCF.

Since 2015, the results are now in and organizations migrating to this approach observe at least a 50% improvement in developer/feature velocity, more than halving their MTTR/downtime, and operating tens of thousands of JVMs with small platform teams. Most importantly, organizations that have adopted Cloud Native Java are investing more time thinking about their customers and markets, and significantly less time worrying about development and operational complexity.

Page by page, this book delivers a detailed exposition of the most important patterns in modern enterprise software design. Josh and Kenny's hard-won and hands-on experience working with many of the world's top enterprises in production shines through in the many examples.

I encourage every developer and IT leader ready to exploit the power of adaptability and resilience in their organization to enjoy this work.

— James Watters, SVP of Pivotal Cloud
Foundry, Pivotal, @wattersjames

Foreword (Rod Johnson)

We are in the midst of one of the farthest-reaching transformations in our industry's history: the move from legacy architectures to the cloud, and from the traditional division of development and operational concerns to unified "DevOps." *Cloud Native Java* tackles this transformation head-on, explaining the opportunities and challenges of writing cloud native applications and providing clear guidance as to how to succeed in doing so.

Transformations don't happen overnight. One of the strongest points of this book is its emphasis on how to get to the cloud from where you may be today, building on your existing experience. The section on "achieving service parity," in particular, provides an outstanding resource on how to move from legacy enterprise practices to cloud-friendly ones.

This book offers an excellent balance of theory and practice, explaining both the architectural principles of modern applications and effective, proven ways of implementing them. Practice requires making choices: not merely of programming language, but of primary open source framework, as modern applications are invariably built on top of proven open source solutions to generic problems. If you've chosen Java—or are open-minded about language—this is your book.

> The report of my death was an exaggeration.
>
> —Mark Twain

A few years ago, reports of Java's death were commonplace. Today, Java is thriving, and this book is a reminder of why. Java has gained a new lease on life, partly because Java technologies have led the way to building modern, cloud-ready applications. Two crucial factors have been Netflix open source projects and Spring. *Cloud Native Java* does an excellent job of covering both.

Initially conceived to simplify a bygone era of Java EE complexity, the core ideas of Spring have stood the test of time and proven a perfect basis for cloud applications. More than a decade ago, we used to talk about the "Spring triangle": Dependency

Injection, Portable Service Abstractions, and AOP. All are equally relevant today, when cleanly decoupling business logic from its environment is more important than ever.

The heart of this book is its coverage of Spring Boot: a new way of using Spring for the microservice era that is deservedly experiencing a groundswell of adoption. Spring Boot makes it easy to create new Spring services of any granularity, and to deploy them in a modern, containerized environment. Whereas a traditional "enterprise" Java application was a monolith running on an still larger application server, Spring Boot reverses things for simplicity and efficiency: the service rightly becomes the focal unit, and is deployed with just enough server to run it.

This book's up-to-the minute coverage showcases the latest work from the Spring team: for example, Spring Cloud Stream and improved integration testing support, as well as the evolving integration with Netflix open source projects.

I'm delighted to see Spring's continued innovation and focus on simplifying things for developers. Although for the last five years I've interacted with Spring only as a user, it's a joy to see it prosper and conquer new sources of complexity. Today I'm continuing that simplifying mission at Atomist, where we aim to do for development teams and the development process what Spring did for Java applications, through providing the ability to automate everything that matters. Spring provides a simple, productive structure and abstraction for working with everything a Java developer cares about; Atomist aims to do the same for project source code, build system, issue tracker, deployed environment, etc., enabling powerful development automation, from creating new projects to enhancing team collaboration via Slack and observing deployment events.

A fundamental building block of automation is testing. I particularly enjoyed *Cloud Native Java*'s thorough coverage of testing, which shines valuable light on the challenging issues around testing microservices. I also enjoyed the many code listings with thorough annotations—a strength of the proven O'Reilly format, well-used by the authors.

It's a pleasure to write a foreword for a book written by friends about technology I love. As those fortunate enough to have heard him in action know, Josh is a great communicator. He is as good on the printed page as he is at live coding. Josh and Kenny are passionate, curious, and well-informed guides, and it's a pleasure to take this journey with them. I learnt a lot along the way and I'm sure you will, too.

— Rod Johnson, Creator, Spring Framework CEO, Atomist, @springrod

Preface

Faster! Faster! Faster!! Everybody wants to go faster but few know how. The demands of the marketplace are accelerating and the size of the opportunity increasing but some of us are just not able to keep up! What separates the traditional enterprise from the likes of Amazon, Netflix and Etsy? We know that these companies have grown to insane scale and yet, somehow, they still retain their competitive edge and stay well ahead of the competition. How?

It takes a lot of work to move an idea from concept to customer. To see an idea evolve to the point of utility, of value. Work moves through a lot of different stations on its way to production, from product management to user experience to developers, testing, and then over to operations. Historically, work slows at every one of these stations. Over time, as a community, we've optimized different parts of the process. We have cloud computing, so no longer need to rack-and-stack services. We use test-driven development and continuous integration to automate testing. We release software in small batches—microservices—to reduce the scope of change and the cost of change. We embrace the ideas behind devops—*weaponized empathy*—to foster a holistic perspective of the system and a sense of camaraderie between developers and operations, reducing the agonizing cost of misaligned priorities. Any of these things in of themselves is interesting, and an improvement over what they replace. But taken together, these things let us isolate everything in the value chain that matters. Taken together, these things are what we mean by *cloud native*.

As members of an industry and practitioners of a discipline, software developers are at an amazing juncture today. There are reliable, open-source, stable, and self-service solutions for infrastructure, testing, middleware, continuous integration and delivery, development frameworks and cloud platforms. These primitives let organizations focus on cheaply delivering higher order value and at larger scale.

Who Should Read This Book

This book is aimed primarily at Java/JVM developers who are looking to build better software, faster, using Spring Boot, Spring Cloud and Cloud Foundry. You've heard the buzz around microservices. Perhaps you've seen the stratospheric rise of Spring Boot, and wondered why most enterprises today are using Cloud Foundry. If this matches you, then this book is for you.

Why We Wrote This Book

At Pivotal, we help our customers transform into digital-first organizations by teaching them continuous delivery and using Cloud Foundry, Spring Boot and Spring Cloud. We've seen what works (and what doesn't) and we wanted to capture the state-of-the-art as defined by our customers, and informed by our experiences. We don't purport to cover every possible angle, but we've tried to touch upon key concepts - corners of the cloud native world that you're going to run into - and introduce them cleanly.

Navigating This Book

This book is organized as follows:

- Chapters 1 and 2 introduce the motivations for cloud native thinking and then provide an introduction to Spring Boot and Cloud Foundry

- 3 introduces how to configure a Spring Boot application. This is a skill we'll lean on almost everywhere.

- 4 looks at the how to test Spring applications, from the simplest components to distributed systems.

- 5 introduces soft-touch refactorings that you can do to move an application to a cloud platform like Cloud Foundry, so that you get some value out of the platform.

- 6 looks at building HTTP and RESTful services with Spring. You'll do this a lot in an API and domain-driven world.

- 7 looks at common ways to control the ingress and egress of requests in a distributed system.

- 8 looks at how to build services that act as the first port of call for requests coming in from the outside world.

- 9 looks at how to manage data in Spring using Spring Data. This sets the foundation for domain-driven thinking.

- 10 looks at how to integrate distributed services and data using Spring's support for event-driven, messaging-centric architectures.

- 11 looks at how to leverage the scale of a cloud platform like Cloud Foundry to handle long-lived workloads.

- 12 looks at some ways to manage state in a distributed system.

- 13 looks at how to build systems that support observability and operations.

- 14 looks at how to build a service broker for platforms like Cloud Foundry. Service brokers connect stateful services like message queues, databases, and caches - to the cloud platform.

- 15 looks at the big ideas behind continuous delivery. This may be the last chapter, but it's just the beginning of your journey.

If you're like us, you don't read books from front to back. If you're really like us, you usually don't read the Preface at all. However, on the off chance that you see this in time, here are a fw suggestions:

- No matter what you do, read Chapters 1 and 2. They will lay the foundations for how to consume the rest of the book. All technical discussions are pointless absent the motivations and business context established in Chapter 1. All technical discussions depend on the foundations established in Chapter 2.

- Chapters 3 through 6 introduce things that any Spring developer should be aware of. These concepts apply to older Spring apps and new ones. Chapter 5, in fact, is about how to set older applications, Spring or otherwise, on the course to being a new one.

- Chapters 7 and 8 introduce concepts that are useful in an HTTP-based microservices system, including security and routing.

- Chapters 9 through 12 help you better manage and process data in distribution.

- Chapter 13 is, really, a core concept and would've been included in the discussion of core concepts and testing, much earlier in the book, except that it depends on technical concepts not introduced until later. Operationalized applications are observable. Read this chapter early if you can. If you know the basics then it might be enough. Otherwise, try it again as you get to it in its natural order.

- Chapter 14 introduces using Spring, a cloud native development framework, to build components for the platform, the cloud. The discussion in this chapter is particularly poignant in light of the open service broker efforts.

- Finally, Chapter 15 refines the discussion around continuous delivery. This entire book is written in terms of continuous delivery, and it's so fundamental to what we're trying to do that we save the discussion of it for our conclusion. Read this first, and then last.

Online Resources

There are a lot of great resources online to further your research and help you on your journey:

- The code for this book is available in its own GitHub repository (*http:// github.com/cloud-native-java/*).

- The Spring website (*http://spring.io/*) is your one stop shop for all things Spring, including the documentation, technical question-and-answer forums, and so much more.

- The Cloud Foundry website (*http://cloudfoundry.org*) is the center of gravity for work being done by all the contributors to the Cloud Foundry foundation. You'll find videos, tutorials, news, and so much more.

Conventions Used in This Book

The following typographical conventions are used in this book:

Italic
> Indicates new terms, URLs, email addresses, filenames, and file extensions.

`Constant width`
> Used for program listings, as well as within paragraphs to refer to program elements such as variable or function names, databases, data types, environment variables, statements, and keywords.

`Constant width bold`
> Shows commands or other text that should be typed literally by the user.

`Constant width italic`
> Shows text that should be replaced with user-supplied values or by values determined by context.

 This element signifies a tip or suggestion.

This element signifies a general note.

 This element indicates a warning or caution.

Using Code Examples

Supplemental material (code examples, exercises, etc.) is available for download at *http://github.com/Cloud-Native-Java*.

This book is here to help you get your job done. In general, if example code is offered with this book, you may use it in your programs and documentation. You do not need to contact us for permission unless you're reproducing a significant portion of the code. For example, writing a program that uses several chunks of code from this book does not require permission. Selling or distributing a CD-ROM of examples from O'Reilly books does require permission. Answering a question by citing this book and quoting example code does not require permission. Incorporating a significant amount of example code from this book into your product's documentation does require permission.

We appreciate, but do not require, attribution. An attribution usually includes the title, author, publisher, and ISBN. For example: "*Book Title* by Josh Long and Kenny Bastani (O'Reilly). Copyright 2017 Josh Long, Kenny Bastani, 978-1-449-37464-8."

If you feel your use of code examples falls outside fair use or the permission given above, feel free to contact us at *permissions@oreilly.com*.

O'Reilly Safari

 *Safari* (formerly Safari Books Online) is a membership-based training and reference platform for enterprise, government, educators, and individuals.

Members have access to thousands of books, training videos, Learning Paths, interactive tutorials, and curated playlists from over 250 publishers, including O'Reilly Media, Harvard Business Review, Prentice Hall Professional, Addison-Wesley Professional, Microsoft Press, Sams, Que, Peachpit Press, Adobe, Focal Press, Cisco Press, John Wiley & Sons, Syngress, Morgan Kaufmann, IBM Redbooks, Packt, Adobe

Press, FT Press, Apress, Manning, New Riders, McGraw-Hill, Jones & Bartlett, and Course Technology, among others.

For more information, please visit *http://oreilly.com/safari*.

How to Contact Us

Please address comments and questions concerning this book to the publisher:

O'Reilly Media, Inc.
1005 Gravenstein Highway North
Sebastopol, CA 95472
800-998-9938 (in the United States or Canada)
707-829-0515 (international or local)
707-829-0104 (fax)

We have a web page for this book, where we list errata, examples, and any additional information. You can access this page at *http://bit.ly/cloud-native-java*.

To comment or ask technical questions about this book, send email to *bookquestions@oreilly.com*.

For more information about our books, courses, conferences, and news, see our website at *http://www.oreilly.com*.

Find us on Facebook: *http://facebook.com/oreilly*

Follow us on Twitter: *http://twitter.com/oreillymedia*

Watch us on YouTube: *http://www.youtube.com/oreillymedia*

Acknowledgments

First, we would like to thank our incredibly patient and supportive editors at O'Reilly media, Nan Barber and Brian Foster.

To all the reviewers and people who gave us insights, ideas, and inspiration. To Pivotal and its ecosystem at large: thank you so very much for supporting us. Special thanks to each reviewer who provided technical feedback, which includes Brian Dussault, Dr. Dave Syer, Andrew Clay Shafer, Rob Winch, Mark Fisher, Dr. Mark Pollack, Utkarsh Nadkarni, Sabby Anandan, Michael Hunger, Bridget Kromhout, Russ Miles, Mark Heckler, Marten Deinum, Nathaniel Schutta, Patrick Crocker, and so many more. Thank you!

Last but not least, we'd like to thank Rod Johnson and James Watters. With your generosity, you have both owed us nothing while giving us everything. Thank you very much for your forewords, feedback, and inspiration.

This book was written using the Asciidoctor toolchain, which is led by Dan Allen (*http://twitter.com/mojavelinux*) and (more sensible) design partner Sarah White (*http://twitter.com/carbonfray*) of OpenDevise. The source code for all the examples is managed on GitHub (*http://github.com*) in public repositories. The code was continuously integrated on Travis CI (*https://travis-ci.org/cloud-native-java*). The build artifacts were stored and managed on a hosted Artifactory repository account graciously donated to us by JFrog (*https://www.jfrog.com*). All the examples ran on Pivotal Web Services, a hosted Cloud Foundry instance managed by Pivotal. These tools, without which writing this book would have been very difficult, are either open source or run by community-minded companies and so cost us nothing. Thank you very much! We hope you'll consider them for your next projects and support them as they have supported us.

To the Spring team (*http://spring.io/team*) and the Cloud Foundry teams (*http://cloudfoundry.org*): thank you very much for all the code you wrote, tested, and support so that we don't have to.

Josh Long

I want to thank my coauthor, Kenny, for joining me on this adventure! I want to thank O'Reilly for the opportunity to work with them and their incredible indulgence as deadlines slipped as we scrambled to keep on top of the ever-expanding Pivotal ecosystem. Thank you Dr. Dave Syer (*https://twitter.com/david_syer*) for your kind words for the book and for being my spirit animal. I code myself into corners in between cities, time zones, countries, and continents, and the Spring and Cloud Foundry teams at Pivotal have always been helpful, regardless of the day or hour—thank you!

Kenny Bastani

I want to first thank my friend, mentor, and colleague, Michael Hunger, who first instilled in me a passion for writing and speaking about open source software. I would also like to thank my immensely talented coauthor Josh Long, who invited me to write this book with him while I was putting my first Spring Boot microservices into production over two years ago. It has been an incredible adventure writing this book with him. From the time that Josh and I first put words on paper, we've seen Spring Boot grow to become one of the most successful open source projects ever created. Today, this growth represents almost 13 million downloads of Spring Boot per month, consisting of a mix of new applications and a continuous stream of production deployments. For all of this success, the Spring Engineering team has grown to fewer than 50 full-time engineers. For this modest number, the Spring team maintains over 100 open source projects—which includes framework components, sample applications, and documentation—all under the wing of its gracious sponsor, Pivotal. Everything that we've accomplished in this book would not be possible without the tremendous dedication of this staff to support a community of developers who are currently generating around 3 million new production-ready Spring Boot applications every year.

From 2004 to 2017, the Spring Framework project alone has seen 381 open source Java contributors create 36,412 commits, which represents roughly 339 years of combined human effort.

## PART I

Basics

## CHAPTER 1

The Cloud Native Application

The patterns for how we develop software, both in teams and as individuals, are always evolving. The open source software movement has provided the software industry with somewhat of a Cambrian explosion of tools, frameworks, platforms, and operating systems—all with an increasing focus on flexibility and automation. A majority of today's most popular open source tools focus on features that give software teams the ability to continuously deliver software faster than ever before possible, at every level, from development to operations.

Amazon's Story

In the span of two decades, starting in the early '90s, an online bookstore headquartered in Seattle called Amazon.com grew into the world's largest online retailer. Known today simply as *Amazon*, the company now sells far more than just books. In 2015, Amazon surpassed Walmart as the most valuable retailer in the United States. The most interesting part of Amazon's story of unparalleled growth can be summarized in one simple question: how did a website that started out as a simple online bookstore transform into one of the largest retailers in the world—without ever opening a single retail location?

It's not hard to see how the world of commerce has been shifted and reshaped around digital connectivity, catalyzed by ever-increasing access to the internet from every corner of the globe. As personal computers became smaller, morphing into the ubiquitous smartphones, tablets, and watches we use today, we've experienced an exponential increase in accessibility to distribution channels that are transforming the way the world does commerce.

Amazon's CTO, Werner Vogels, oversaw the technical evolution of Amazon from a hugely successful online bookstore into one of the world's most valuable technology companies and product retailers. In June 2006, Vogels was interviewed in a piece for the computer magazine *ACM Queue* on the rapid evolution of the technology choices that powered Amazon's growth. In the interview, Vogels talks about the core driver behind it.

> A large part of Amazon.com's technology evolution has been driven to enable this continuing growth, **to be ultra-scalable while maintaining availability and performance**.
>
> —Werner Vogels, *"A Conversation with Werner Vogels," ACM Queue 4, no. 4 (2006): 14–22.*

Vogels goes on to state that for Amazon to achieve ultrascalability, it needed to move toward a different pattern of software architecture. He mentions that Amazon.com started as a monolithic application. Over time, as more and more teams operated on the same application, the boundaries of ownership of the codebase began to blur. "There was no isolation and, as a result, no clear ownership," said Vogels.

Vogels pinpoints that shared resources such as databases made it difficult to scale out the overall business. The greater the number of shared resources, whether application servers or databases, the less control teams had when delivering features into production.

> You build it, you run it.
>
> —Werner Vogels, *CTO, Amazon*

Vogels touches on a common theme that cloud native applications share: the idea that teams own what they are building. He goes on to say that "the traditional model is that you take your software to the wall that separates development and operations, and throw it over and then forget about it. Not at Amazon. *You build it, you run it.*"

In what has been one of the most reused quotes by prominent keynote speakers at some of the world's premier software conferences, the words *"you build it, you run it"* would later become a slogan of a popular movement we know today simply as *DevOps*.

Many of the practices that Vogels spoke about in 2006 were seeds for popular software movements that are thriving today. Practices such as *DevOps* and *microservices* can be tied back to the ideas that Vogels introduced over a decade ago. While ideas like these were being developed at large internet companies similar to Amazon, the tooling around these ideas would take years to develop and mature into a service offering.

In 2006 Amazon launched a new product named Amazon Web Services (AWS). The idea behind AWS was to provide a platform, the same platform Amazon used internally, and release it as a service to the public. Amazon was keen to see the opportunity to commoditize the ideas and tooling behind that platform. Many of the ideas that Vogels introduced were already built into the Amazon.com platform; by releasing the platform as a service to the public, Amazon would enter a new market called the *public cloud*.

The ideas behind the public cloud were sound. Virtual resources could be provisioned on-demand without needing to worry about the underlying infrastructure. Developers could simply rent a virtual machine to house their applications without needing to purchase or manage the infrastructure. This approach was a low-risk self-service option that would help to grow the appeal of the public cloud, with AWS leading the way in adoption.

It would take years before AWS would mature into a set of services and patterns for building and running applications that are designed to be operated on a public cloud. While many developers flocked to these services for building new applications, many companies with existing applications still had concerns with migrations. Existing applications were not designed for portability. Also, many applications were still dependent on legacy workloads that were not compatible with the public cloud.

In order for most large companies to take advantage of the public cloud, they would need to make changes in the way they developed their applications.

The Promise of a Platform

Platform is an overused word today.

When we talk about platforms in computing, we are generally talking about a set of capabilities that help us to either build or run applications. Platforms are best summarized by the nature in which they impose constraints on how developers build applications.

Platforms are able to automate tasks that are not essential to supporting the business requirements of an application. This makes development teams more agile in the way they are able to support only the features that help differentiate value for the business.

Any team that has written shell scripts or stamped containers or virtual machines to automate deployment has built a platform, of sorts. The question is: what promises can that platform keep? How much work would it take to support the majority (or even all) of the requirements for continuously delivering new software?

When we build platforms, we are creating a tool that automates a set of repeatable practices. Practices are formulated from a set of constraints that translate valuable ideas into a plan.

- **Ideas**: What are our core ideas of the platform and why are they valuable?
- **Constraints**: What are the constraints necessary to transform our ideas into practices?

- **Practices**: How do we automate constraints into a set of repeatable practices?

At the core of every platform are simple ideas that, when realized, increase differentiated business value through the use of an automated tool.

Let's take for example the Amazon.com platform. Werner Vogels stated that by increasing isolation between software components, teams would have more control over features they delivered into production.

Ideas:

- *By increasing isolation between software components, we are able to deliver parts of the system both rapidly and independently.*

By using this idea as the platform's foundation, we are able to fashion it into a set of constraints. Constraints take the form of an opinion about how a core ideal will create value when automated into a practice. The following statements are opinionated constraints about how isolation of components can be increased.

Constraints:

- *Software components are to be built as independently deployable services.*
- *All business logic in a service is encapsulated with the data it operates on.*
- *There is no direct access to a database from outside of a service.*
- *Services are to publish a web interface that allows access to its business logic from other services.*

With these constraints, we have taken an opinionated view on how isolation of software components will be increased in practice. The promises of these constraints, when automated into practices, will provide teams with more control over how features are delivered to production. The next step is to describe how these constraints can be captured into a set of repeatable practices.

Practices that are derived from these constraints should be stated as a collection of promises. By stating practices as promises, we maintain an expectation with the platform's users of how they will build and operate their applications.

Practices:

- *A self-service interface is provided to teams that allows for the provisioning of infrastructure required to operate applications.*
- *Applications are packaged as a bundled artifact and deployed to an environment using the self-service interface.*
- *Databases are provided to applications in the form of a service, and are to be provisioned using the self-service interface.*

- *An application is provided with credentials to a database as environment variables, but only after declaring an explicit relationship to the database as a service binding.*
- *Each application is provided with a service registry that is used as a manifest of where to locate external service dependencies.*

Each of the practices listed above takes on the form of a promise to the user. In this way, the intent of the ideas at the core of the platform are realized as constraints imposed on applications.

Cloud native applications are built on a set of constraints that reduce the time spent doing undifferentiated heavy lifting.

When AWS was first released to the public, Amazon did not force its users to adhere to the same constraints that they used internally for Amazon.com. Staying true to the name *Amazon Web Services*, AWS is not itself a cloud *platform*, but rather a collection of independent infrastructure services that can be composed into automated tooling resembling a platform of promises. Years after the first release of AWS, Amazon began offering a collection of managed platform services, with use cases ranging from IoT (Internet of Things) to machine learning.

If every company needs to build its own platform from scratch, the amount of time delivering value in applications is delayed until the platform is fully assembled. Companies that were early adopters of AWS would have needed to assemble together some form of automation resembling a platform. Each company would have had to bake in a set of promises that captured the core ideas of how to develop and deliver software into production.

More recently, the software industry has converged on the idea that there is a basic set of common promises that every cloud platform should make. These promises will be explored throughout this book using the open source *Platform as a Service* (PaaS) Cloud Foundry. The core motivation behind Cloud Foundry is to provide a platform that encapsulates a set of common promises for quickly building and operating. Cloud Foundry makes these promises while still providing portability between multiple different cloud infrastructure providers.

The subject of much of this book is how to build cloud native Java applications. We'll focus largely on tools and frameworks that help reduce undifferentiated heavy lifting, by taking advantage of the benefits and promises of a cloud native platform.

The Patterns

New patterns for how we develop software enable us to think more about the behavior of our applications in production. Both developers and operators, together, are placing more emphasis on understanding how their applications will behave in production, with fewer assurances of how complexity will unravel in the event of a failure.

As was the case with Amazon.com, software architectures are beginning to move away from large monolithic applications. Architectures are now focused on achieving ultra-scalability without sacrificing performance and availability. By breaking apart components of a monolith, engineering organizations are taking efforts to decentralize change management, providing teams with more control over how features make their way to production. By increasing isolation between components, software teams are starting to enter the world of distributed systems development, with a focus on building smaller, more singularly focused services with independent release cycles.

Cloud native applications take advantage of a set of patterns that make teams more agile in the way they deliver features to production. As applications become more distributed (a result of increasing isolation necessary to provide more control to the teams that own applications), the chance of failure in the way application components communicate becomes an important concern. As software applications turn into complex distributed systems, operational failures become an inevitable result.

Cloud native application architectures provide the benefit of ultra-scalability while still maintaining guarantees about overall availability and performance of applications. While companies like Amazon reaped the benefits of ultra-scalability in the cloud, widely available tooling for building cloud-native applications had yet to surface. The tooling and platform would eventually surface as a collection of open source projects maintained by an early pioneer of the public cloud: Netflix.

Scalability

To develop software faster, we are required to think about scale at all levels. *Scale*, in a most general sense, is a function of cost that produces value. The level of unpredictability that reduces that value is called *risk*. We are forced to frame scale in this context because building software is fraught with risks. The risks created by software developers are not always known to operators. By demanding that developers deliver features to production at a faster pace, we are adding to the risks of its operation without having a sense of empathy for its operators.

The result of this is that operators grow distrustful of the software that developers produce. The lack of trust between developers and operators creates a blame culture: people point fingers instead of looking at systemic problems that lead to, or at least precipitate, problems that negatively impact the business.

To alleviate the strain that is put on traditional structures of an IT organization, we need to rethink how software delivery and operations teams communicate. Communication between operations and developers can affect our ability to scale, as the goals of each party tend to become misaligned over time. To succeed at this requires a shift toward a more reliable kind of software development—one that puts emphasis on the experience of an operations team inside the software development process; one that fosters shared learning and improvement.

Reliability

The expectations that are created between teams (development, operations, user experience, etc.) are contracts. The contracts that are created between teams imply that some level of service is provided or consumed. By looking at how teams provide services to one another in the process of developing software, we can better understand how failures in communication can introduce risk that leads to failures down the road.

Service agreements between teams are created in order to reduce the risk of unexpected behavior in the overall functions of scale that produce value for a business. A service agreement between teams is made explicit in order to guarantee that behaviors are consistent with the expected cost of operations. In this way, services enable units of a business to maximize its total output. The goal here for a software business is to reliably predict the creation of value through cost—what we call *reliability*.

The service model for a business is the same model we use when we build software. This is how we guarantee the reliability of a system, whether in the software we produce to automate a business function or in the people we train to perform a manual operation.

Agility

We are beginning to find that there is no longer only one way to develop and operate software. Driven by the adoption of agile methodologies and a move towards *Software as a Service* (SaaS) business models, the enterprise application stack is becoming increasingly distributed. Developing distributed systems is a complex undertaking. The move toward a more distributed application architecture for companies is fueled by the need to deliver software faster and with less risk of failure.

We can hear you exclaiming, "Agile? Isn't agile dead?? (*https:// www.linkedin.com/pulse/agile-dead-matthew-kern*)" *Agile*, as we use it, refers both to a wholistic, organization-wide fervor for delivering new value, *and* to the idea of responding quickly. We're talking about little-a agile; we don't talk about it in terms of a management practice. There are a lot of roads that lead to production, and we don't care what management practice you embrace to get there. The key is to understand that *agile* is a value, not a destination.

The modern-day software-defined business seeks to restructure its development processes to enable faster delivery of software projects and continuous deployment of applications into production. Not only are companies wanting to increase the rate at which they develop software applications, but also to increase the number of software applications they create and operate to serve an organization's various business units.

Software is increasingly becoming a competitive advantage for companies. Better and better tools are enabling business experts to open up new sources of revenue, or to optimize business functions in ways that lead to rapid innovation.

At the heart of this movement is *the cloud*. When we talk about the cloud, we are talking about a very specific set of technologies that enable developers and operators to take advantage of web services that exist to provision and manage virtualized computing infrastructure.

Companies are starting to move out of the data center and into public clouds. One such company is the popular subscription-based streaming media company Netflix.

Netflix's Story

Today, Netflix is one of the world's largest on-demand streaming media services, operating its online services in the cloud. Netflix was founded in 1997 in Scotts Valley, California, by Reed Hastings and Marc Randolph. Originally, Netflix provided an online DVD rental service that allowed customers to pay a flat-fee subscription each month for unlimited movie rentals without late fees. Customers were shipped DVDs by mail after selecting tiles from a list and placing them in a queue, using the Netflix website.

In 2008, Netflix experienced a major database corruption that prevented the company from shipping any DVDs to its customers. At the time, Netflix was just starting to deploy its streaming video services to customers. The streaming team at Netflix realized that a similar kind of outage in streaming would be devastating to the future of its business. As a result, Netflix made a critical decision: it would move to a different way of developing and operating its software, one that ensured that its services would always be available to its customers.

As a part of Netflix's decision to prevent failures in its online services, it decided that it must move away from vertically scaled infrastructure and single points of failure. The realization was a result of the database corruption, which was a result of using a vertically scaled relational database. Netflix migrated its customer data to a distributed NoSQL database, an open source database project named Apache Cassandra. This was the beginning of the move to become a "cloud native" company, running all of its software applications as highly distributed and resilient services in the cloud. Netflix settled on increasing the robustness of its online services by adding redundancy to its applications and databases in a scale-out infrastructure model.

As a part of Netflix's decision to move to the cloud, it would need to migrate its large application deployments to highly reliable distributed systems. It faced a major challenge: the teams at Netflix would have to re-architect their applications while moving away from an on-premise data center to a public cloud. In 2009, Netflix began its move to Amazon Web Services (AWS), and focused on three main goals: scalability, performance, and availability.

It was clear by the start of 2009 that demand was going to dramatically increase. In fact, Yury Izrailevsky, Vice President of Cloud and Platform Engineering at Netflix, said in a presentation at the AWS re:Invent conference in 2013 that it had increased by 100 times since 2009. "We would not be able to scale our services using an on-premise solution," said Izrailevsky.

Furthermore, he stated that the benefits of scalability in the cloud became more evident when looking at its rapid global expansion. "In order to give our European customers a better low-latency experience, we launched a second cloud region in Ireland. Spinning up a new data center in a different territory would take many months and millions of dollars. It would be a huge investment," he said.

As Netflix began its move to hosting its applications on Amazon Web Services, employees chronicled their learnings on Netflix's company blog. Many of Netflix's employees were advocating a move to a new kind of architecture that focused on horizontal scalability at all layers of the software stack.

John Ciancutti, who was then the Vice President of Personalization Technologies at Netflix, said on the company's blog in late 2010 that "cloud environments are ideal for horizontally scaling architectures. We don't have to guess months ahead what our hardware, storage, and networking needs are going to be. We can programmatically access more of these resources from shared pools within Amazon Web Services almost instantly."

What Ciancutti meant by being able to "programmatically access" resources was that developers and operators could programmatically access certain management APIs that are exposed by Amazon Web Services in order to give customers a controller for provisioning their virtualized computing infrastructure. RESTful APIs gave developers a way to build applications that manage and provision virtual infrastructure for their applications.

The layer cake in Figure 1-1 characterizes different cloud options characterized by different levels of abstraction.

Providing management services to control virtualized computing infrastructure is one of the primary concepts of cloud computing, called *Infrastructure as a Service*, commonly referred to as IaaS.

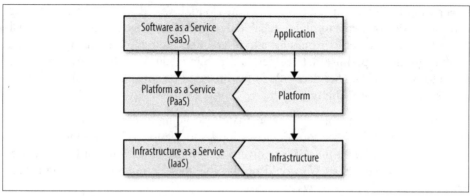

Figure 1-1. Cloud computing stack

Ciancutti admitted in the same blog post that Netflix was not very good at predicting customer growth or device engagement. This is a central theme behind cloud native companies. Cloud native is a mindset that admits to not being able to reliably predict when and where capacity will be needed.

In Yury Izrailevsky's 2013 re:Invent presentation, he said that "in the cloud, we can spin up capacity in just a few days as traffic eventually increases. We could go with a tiny footprint in the beginning and gradually spin it up as our traffic increases."

He went on to say, "As we become a global company, we have the benefit of relying on multiple Amazon Web Services regions throughout the world to give our customers a great interactive experience no matter where they are."

The economies of scale that benefited AWS international expansion also benefited Netflix. With AWS expanding availability zones to regions outside the United States, Netflix expanded its services globally using only the management APIs provided by AWS.

Izrailevsky quoted a general argument of cloud adoption by enterprise IT: "Sure, the cloud is great, but it's too expensive for us." His response to this argument was that "as a result of Netflix's move to the cloud, the cost of operations has decreased by 87%. We're paying one-eighth of what we used to pay in the data center."

Izrailevsky explained further why the cloud provided such large cost savings to Netflix: "It's really helpful to be able to grow without worrying about capacity buffers. We can scale to demand as we grow."

Microservices

We touch on microservices many times throughout this book. While this book is not exclusively about microservices, you often find that cloud native applications and microservices go hand in hand. One of the main ideas behind building microservices is the ability to have feature teams organize themselves and applications around specific business capabilities. This approach is not particularly novel by any means. Creating a system from small distributed components that work well together—and are split up in such a way as to minimize the resistance of delivering individual features into production—has been possible for decades. So, why now? Why is this kind of architecture just now becoming popular? Could it have something to do with the cloud?

Building software has always been hard. The difference between making sense and making do is often the result of someone else depriving you of your own poor choices. Technical decisions made yesterday will hamper your ability to make the right decisions for an architecture tomorrow. Now, it's true that we all want a clean slate—*tabula rasa*—and microservices give us a way to take poor decisions of yesterday and decompose them into new—and hopefully *better*—choices for tomorrow.

It's easy to comprehend a small thing—but much harder to comprehend the impact of its absence. If we scrutinize a well-designed monolithic application, we will see similar drives toward modularity, simplicity, and loose-coupling as we see in today's microservice architectures. One of the main differences, of course, is *history*. It isn't hard to understand how the layers of choices transformed a well-designed thing into a big horrific ball of mud. If one person made a poor choice in one small replaceable unit of an architecture, that choice can be more easily decomposed over time. But if the same person were to work on many separate modules of a well-designed monolith, the additional history may infect everyone else's ability to make desirable choices later on. So we end up having to compromise—we are *forced* into making just slightly better decisions on top of a smattering of choices that we never had a chance to make ourselves.

Software that is meant for change becomes a living thing—always transformed by history—and never immune to the shifting winds of survival. Because of this, we have to build with change in mind. We have to embrace change while resisting the urge to future-proof an architecture. After all, future-proofing is just a grand design dressed up as agile development. No matter how clever we are in a concerted up-front effort to design the perfect system, we cannot reliably predict how its function will change in the future—because very often it will not be up to us. The market tends to decide a product's fate. Because of this, we can only design with today in mind.

Microservices are not much more than an idea today. The patterns and practices of microservices are in a fluid state—still fluctuating while we patiently await a stable definition. Their embrace in a wider range of industry verticals is—for better or worse—still pending a final verdict.

There are two primary forces influencing the rapidity of architectural change: microservices and the cloud. The cloud has drastically driven down the cost and effort required to manage infrastructure. Today we are able to use self-service tools to provision infrastructure for our applications *on-demand*. From this, new, innovative tooling has begun to rapidly materialize—continually causing us to rethink and reshape our prior conventions. What was true yesterday about building software may not be true today—and in most cases, the truth is nebulous. We now find ourselves needing to make hard decisions on a foundation of mercurial assumptions: that our servers are physical. That our virtual machines are permanent. That our containers are stateless. Our assumptions surrounding the infrastructure layer are under a constant barrage of attack from an endless selection of new choices.

Splitting the Monolith

Netflix cites two major benefits of moving to a distributed systems architecture in the cloud from a monolith: agility and reliability.

Netflix's architecture before going cloud native comprised a single monolithic Java Virtual Machine (JVM) application. While there were multiple advantages of having one large application deployment, the major drawback was that development teams were slowed down, due to needing to coordinate their changes.

When building and operating software, increased centralization decreases the risk of a failure at an increased cost of needing to coordinate. Coordination takes time. The more centralized a software architecture is, the more time it will take to coordinate changes to any one piece of it.

Monoliths also tend not to be very reliable. When components share resources on the same virtual machine, a failure in one component can spread to others, causing downtime for users. The risk of making a breaking change in a monolith increases with the amount of effort by teams needing to coordinate their changes. The more changes that occur during a single release cycle, the greater the risk of a breaking change that will cause downtime. By splitting up a monolith into smaller, more singularly focused services, deployments can be made with smaller batch sizes on a team's independent release cycle.

Netflix not only needed to transform the way it builds and operates its software, it needed to transform the culture of its organization. Netflix moved to a new operational model called *DevOps*. In this new operational model, each team became a product group, moving away from the traditional project group structure. In a product group, teams were composed vertically, embedding operations and product management into each team. Product teams would have everything they needed to build and operate their software.

Netflix OSS

As Netflix transitioned to become a cloud native company, it also started to participate actively in open source. In late 2010, Kevin McEntee, then the Vice President of

Systems & Ecommerce Engineering, announced in a blog post the company's future role in open source.

McEntee stated that "the great thing about a good open source project that solves a shared challenge is that it develops its own momentum and it is sustained for a long time by a virtuous cycle of continuous improvement."

In the years that followed this announcement, Netflix open sourced more than 50 of its internal projects, each of which would become a part of the *Netflix OSS* brand.

Key employees at Netflix would later clarify the company's aspirations to open source many of its internal tools. In July 2012, Ruslan Meshenberg, Netflix's Director of Cloud Platform Engineering, published a post on the company's technology blog. The blog post, "Open Source at Netflix," explained why Netflix was taking such a bold move to open source so much of its internal tooling.

Meshenberg wrote in the blog post, on the reasoning behind its open source aspirations, that "Netflix was an early cloud adopter, moving all of our streaming services to run on top of AWS infrastructure. We paid the pioneer tax—by encountering and working through many issues, corner cases, and limitations."

The cultural motivations at Netflix to contribute back to the open source community and technology ecosystem are seen to be strongly tied to the principles behind the microeconomics concept known as *Economies of Scale*. "We've captured the patterns that work in our platform components and automation tools," Meshenberg continues. "We benefit from the scale effects of other AWS users adopting similar patterns, and will continue working with the community to develop the ecosystem."

In the advent of what has been referred to as the *era of the cloud*, we have seen that its pioneers are not technology companies such as IBM or Microsoft, but rather companies that were born on the back of the internet. Netflix and Amazon are both businesses that started in the late '90s as dot-com companies. Both companies started out by offering online services that aimed to compete with their *brick-and-mortar* counterparts.

Both Netflix and Amazon have in time surpassed the valuation of their *brick-and-mortar* counterparts. As Amazon entered the cloud computing market, it did so by turning its collective experience and internal tooling into a set of services. Netflix then did the same on the back of Amazon's services. Along the way, Netflix open sourced both its experiences and tooling, transforming into a cloud native company built on virtualized infrastructure services provided by AWS by Amazon. This is how the economies of scale are powering forward a revolution in the cloud computing industry.

In early 2015, on reports of Netflix's first quarterly earnings, the company was reported to be valued at $32.9 billion. As a result of this new valuation for Netflix, the company's value surpassed the value of the CBS network for the first time.

Cloud Native Java

Netflix has provided the software industry with a wealth of knowledge as a result of its move to become a cloud native company. This book will take Netflix's lessons and open source projects and apply them as a set of patterns with two central themes:

- Building resilient distributed systems using Spring and Netflix OSS
- Using continuous delivery to operate cloud native applications with Cloud Foundry

The first stop on our journey will be to understand a set of terms and concepts that we will use throughout this book to describe building and operating cloud native applications.

The Twelve Factors

The twelve-factor methodology is a popular set of application development principles compiled by the creators of the Heroku cloud platform. The *Twelve-Factor App* is a website that was originally created by Adam Wiggins, a co-founder of Heroku, as a manifesto that describes SaaS applications designed to take advantage of the common practices of modern cloud platforms.

On the website (*http://12factor.net*), the methodology starts out by describing a set of core foundational ideas for building applications.

Earlier in the chapter we talked about the promises that platforms make to users who are building applications. In Table 1-1, we have a set of ideas that explicitly state the value proposition of building applications that follow the twelve-factor methodology. These ideas break down further into a set of constraints—the 12 individual factors that distill these core ideas into a collection of opinions for how applications should be built.

Table 1-1. Core ideas of the twelve-factor application

Use **declarative** formats for setup automation, to minimize time and cost for new developers joining the project
Have a clean contract with the underlying operating system, offering **maximum portability** between execution environments
Are suitable for **deployment** on modern **cloud platforms**, obviating the need for servers and systems administration
Minimize divergence between development and production, enabling **continuous deployment** for maximum agility
And can **scale up** without significant changes to tooling, architecture, or development practices

The 12 factors listed in Table 1-2 describe constraints that help build applications that take advantage of the ideas in Table 1-1. The 12 factors are a basic set of constraints that can be used to build cloud native applications. Since the factors cover a wide range of concerns that are common practices in all modern cloud platforms, building twelve-factor apps is a common starting point in cloud native application development.

Table 1-2. The practices of a twelve-factor application

Codebase	One codebase tracked in revision control, many deploys
Dependencies	Explicitly declare and isolate dependencies
Config	Store config in the environment
Backing services	Treat backing services as attached resources
Build, release, run	Strictly separate build and run stages
Processes	Execute the app as one or more stateless processes
Port binding	Export services via port binding
Concurrency	Scale out via the process model
Disposability	Maximize robustness with fast startup and graceful shutdown
Dev/prod parity	Keep development, staging, and production as similar as possible
Logs	Treat logs as event streams
Admin processes	Run admin/management tasks as one-off processes

Outside of the twelve-factor website—which covers each of the 12 factors in detail—full books have been written that expand even more on each constraint. The twelve-factor methodology is now used in some application frameworks to help developers comply with some, or even all, of the 12 out of the box.

We'll be using the twelve-factor methodology throughout this book to describe how certain features of Spring projects were implemented to satisfy this style of application development. For this reason, it's important that we summarize each of the factors here.

Codebase

One codebase tracked in revision control, many deploys

Source code repositories for an application should contain a single application with a manifest to its application dependencies. There should be no need to recompile or package an application for different environments. The things that are unique to each environment should live external to the code, as shown in Figure 1-2.

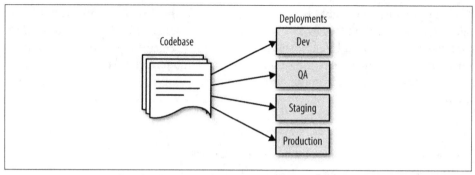

Figure 1-2. Source code is built once and deployed to each environment

Dependencies

Explicitly declare and isolate dependencies

Application dependencies should be explicitly declared, and any and all dependencies should be available from an artifact repository that can be downloaded using a dependency manager, such as Apache Maven.

Twelve-factor applications never rely on the existence of implicit systemwide packages required as a dependency to run the application. All dependencies of an application are declared explicitly in a manifest file that cleanly declares the detail of each reference.

Config

Store config in the environment

Application code should be strictly separated from configuration. The configuration of the application should be driven by the environment.

Application settings such as connection strings, credentials, or hostnames of dependent web services should be stored as environment variables, making them easy to change without deploying configuration files.

Any divergence in your application from environment to environment is considered an environment configuration, and should be stored in the environment and not with the application, as demonstrated in Figure 1-3.

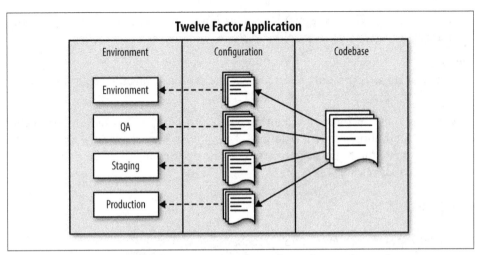

Figure 1-3. Externalizing environment-specific configuration in the environment

Backing Services

Treat backing services as attached resources

A backing service is any service that the twelve-factor application consumes as a part of its normal operation. Examples of backing services are databases, API-driven RESTful web services, an SMTP server, or an FTP server.

Backing services are considered to be *resources* of the application. These *resources* are attached to the application for the duration of operation. A deployment of a twelve-factor application should be able to swap out an embedded SQL database in a testing environment with an external MySQL database hosted in a staging environment without making changes to the application's code.

Build, Release, Run

Strictly separate build and run stages

The twelve-factor application strictly separates the build, release, and run stages.

Build stage
    The build stage takes the source code for an application and either compiles or bundles it into a package. The package that is created is referred to as a *build*.

Release stage
    The release stage takes a build and combines it with its config. The release that is created for the deploy is then ready to be operated in an execution environment. Each release should have a unique identifier, either using semantic versioning or

a timestamp. Each release should be added to a directory that can be used by the release management tool to rollback to a previous release.

Run stage

The run stage, commonly referred to as the *runtime,* runs the application in the execution environment for a selected release.

By separating each of these stages into separate processes, it becomes impossible to change an application's code at runtime. The only way to change the application's code is to initiate the build stage to create a new release, or to initiate a roll back to deploy a previous release.

Processes

Execute the app as one or more stateless processes

Twelve-factor applications are created to be stateless in a *share-nothing architecture.* The only persistence that an application may depend on is through a backing service. Examples of a backing service that provides persistence include a database or an object store. All resources to the application are attached as a backing service at runtime. A litmus test for whether or not an application is stateless is that the application's execution environment can be torn down and recreated without any loss of data.

Twelve-factor applications do not store state on a local filesystem in the execution environment.

Port Bindings

Export services via port binding

Twelve-factor applications are completely self-contained, which means that they do not require a web server to be injected into the execution environment at runtime in order to create a web-facing service. Each application will expose access to itself over an HTTP port that is bound to the application in the execution environment. During deployment, a routing layer will handle incoming requests from a public hostname by routing to the application's execution environment and the bound HTTP port.

 Josh Long, one of the coauthors of this book, is attributed with popularizing the phrase *"Make JAR not WAR"* in the Java community. Josh uses this phrase to explain how newer Spring applications are able to embed a Java application server, such as Tomcat, in a build's JAR file.

Concurrency

Scale out via the process model

Applications should be able to scale out processes or threads for parallel execution of work in an on-demand basis. JVM applications are able to handle in-process concurrency automatically using multiple threads.

Applications should distribute work concurrently, depending on the type of work that is used. Most application frameworks for the JVM today have this built in. Some scenarios that require data processing jobs that are executed as long-running tasks should utilize executors that are able to asynchronously dispatch concurrent work to an available pool of threads.

The twelve-factor application must also be able to scale out horizontally and handle requests load-balanced to multiple identical running instances of an application. By ensuring applications are designed to be stateless, it becomes possible to handle heavier workloads by scaling applications horizontally across multiple nodes.

Disposability

Maximize robustness with fast startup and graceful shutdown

The processes of a twelve-factor application are designed to be disposable. An application can be stopped at any time during process execution and gracefully handle the disposal of processes.

Processes of an application should minimize startup time as much as possible. Applications should start within seconds and begin to process incoming requests. Short startups reduce the time it takes to scale out application instances to respond to increased load.

If an application's processes take too long to start, there may be reduced availability during a high-volume traffic spike that is capable of overloading all available healthy application instances. By decreasing the startup time of applications to just seconds, newly scheduled instances are able to more quickly respond to unpredicted spikes in traffic without decreasing availability or performance.

Dev/Prod Parity

Keep development, staging, and production as similar as possible

The twelve-factor application should prevent divergence between development and production environments. There are three types of gaps to be mindful of.

Time gap
> Developers should expect development changes to be quickly deployed into production

Personnel gap
> Developers who make a code change are closely involved with its deployment into production, and closely monitor the behavior of an application after making changes

Tools gap
> Each environment should mirror technology and framework choices in order to limit unexpected behavior due to small inconsistencies

Logs

Treat logs as event streams

Twelve-factor apps write logs as an ordered event stream to stout. Applications should not attempt to manage the storage of their own logfiles. The collection and archival of log output for an application should instead be handled by the *execution environment*.

Admin Processes

Run admin/management tasks as one-off processes

It sometimes becomes the case that developers of an application need to run one-off administrative tasks. These kinds of tasks could include database migrations or running one-time scripts that have been checked in to the application's source code repository. They are considered to be admin processes. Admin processes should be run in the execution environment of an application, with scripts checked into the repository to maintain consistency between environments.

Summary

In this chapter we've looked at some of the motivations that have driven organizations to embrace certain constraints and architectural shifts. We've tried to familiarize you with some of the good ideas, in particular the twelve-factor manifesto, that have come before.

## CHAPTER 2

Bootcamp: Introducing Spring Boot and Cloud Foundry

In this chapter we will explore how to build cloud native applications using Spring Boot and Cloud Foundry.

What Is Spring Boot?

When we say that an application is *cloud native*, it means that it is designed to thrive in a cloud-based production environment. Spring Boot provides a way to create production-ready Spring applications with minimal setup time. The primary goals behind the creation of the Spring Boot project are central to the idea that users should be able to get up and running quickly with Spring.

Spring Boot also takes an opinionated view of the Spring platform and third-party libraries. An opinionated view means that Spring Boot lays out a set of familiar abstractions that are common to all Spring projects. This opinionated view provides the plumbing that all projects need, but without getting in the way of the developer. By doing this, Spring Boot makes it simple to swap components when project requirements change. Spring Boot builds upon the Spring ecosystem and third-party libraries, adding in opinions and establishing conventions to streamline the realization of production-ready applications.

Getting Started with the Spring Initializr

The *Spring Initializr* is an open source project (*https://github.com/spring-io/initializr*) and tool in the Spring ecosystem that helps you quickly generate new Spring Boot applications. Pivotal runs an instance of the Spring Initializr hosted on Pivotal Web

Services (*http://start.spring.io*). It generates Maven and Gradle projects with any specified dependencies, a skeletal entry point Java class, and a skeletal unit test.

In the world of monolithic applications, this cost may be prohibitive, but it's easy to amortize the cost of initialization across the lifetime of the project. When you begin migrating to a cloud native architecture, you'll find yourself needing to create more and more applications. Because of this, the friction of creating a new application in your architecture should be reduced to a minimum. The Spring Initializr helps reduce that up-front cost. It's both a web application that you can consume from your web browser and a REST API that will generate new projects for you.

For example, you can use the tool to generate a new Spring Boot project using a `curl` command:

```
curl http://start.spring.io
```

The results will look something like Figure 2-1.

Figure 2-1. Interacting with the Spring Initializr through the REST API

Alternatively, you can use the Spring Initializr from the browser (*http://start.spring.io*), as shown in Figure 2-2.

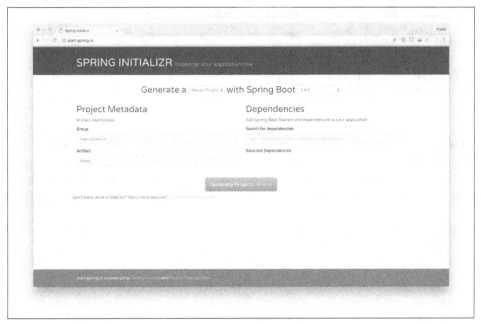

Figure 2-2. The Spring Initializr website

Now, let's suppose we would like to build a simple RESTful web service that talks to a SQL database (H2). We'll need to pull in the necessary libraries from the Spring ecosystem, which include Spring MVC, Spring Data JPA, and Spring Data REST.

To find these ingredients, you can begin typing the name of the *dependencies* in the search box or click "Switch to the full version" and then manually select the check-boxes for the desired dependencies. Most of these are called *Starter Project* dependencies.

A *starter* dependency is a type of opinionated add-on library that will automatically inject a set of basic features composed from other Spring ecosystem projects into your new Spring Boot application.

If we were to build a Spring Boot application from scratch, we would have to navigate a web of transitive dependencies. Because of this, we might encounter an issue if our application has dependencies sharing third-party libraries that have conflicting versions. Spring Boot handles conflicting transitive dependencies so that you only need to specify one version of the Spring Boot parent project, which then guarantees that any Spring Boot starter dependency on the classpath of your application will use compatible versions.

Table 2-1. Some example Spring Boot Starters for a typical Spring Boot application

Spring Project	Starter Projects	Maven `artifactId`
Spring Data JPA	JPA	`spring-boot-starter-data-jpa`
Spring Data REST	REST Repositories	`spring-boot-starter-data-rest`
Spring Framework (MVC)	Web	`spring-boot-starter-web`
Spring Security	Security	`spring-boot-starter-security`
H2 Embedded SQL DB	H2	`h2`

Let's do a quick exercise. Head to Spring Initializr and include starter dependencies for Web, H2, REST Repositories, and JPA. We'll leave everything else as default. Click Generate Project and an archive, demo.zip, will begin downloading. Decompress the archive and you will now have the source code of a skeletal project that is ready to import into an IDE of your choice.

Example 2-1. The contents of the generated Spring Boot application archive once decompressed

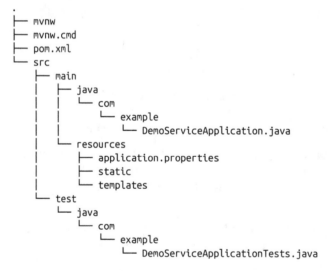

```
.
├── mvnw
├── mvnw.cmd
├── pom.xml
└── src
    ├── main
    │   ├── java
    │   │   └── com
    │   │       └── example
    │   │           └── DemoServiceApplication.java
    │   └── resources
    │       ├── application.properties
    │       ├── static
    │       └── templates
    └── test
        └── java
            └── com
                └── example
                    └── DemoServiceApplicationTests.java
```

In Example 2-1, we can see the directory structure of our generated application. The Spring Initializr provides a wrapper script—either the Gradle wrapper (gradlew) or a Maven wrapper (from the Maven wrapper project) mvnw—as a part of the contents of the generated project. You can use this wrapper to build and run the project. The wrapper downloads a configured version of the build tool on its first run. The version of Maven or Gradle is version controlled. This means that all subsequent users will have a reproducible build. There's no risk that someone will try to build your code with an incompatible version of Maven or Gradle. This also greatly simplifies continuous delivery: the build used for development is the exact same one used in the continuous integration environment.

The following command will run a clean installation of the Maven project, downloading and caching the dependencies specified in the pom.xml and installing the built .jar artifact into the local Maven repository (typically $HOME/.m2/repository/*):

```
$ ./mvnw clean install
```

To run the Spring Boot application from the command line, use the provided Spring Boot Maven plug-in, configured automatically in the generated pom.xml:

```
$ ./mvnw spring-boot:run
```

The web application should be up and running and available at http://localhost:8080. Don't worry, nothing particularly interesting has happened, *yet*.

Open the project's pom.xml file in a text editor of your choice: emacs, vi, TextMate, Sublime, Atom, Notepad.exe, etc., are all valid choices (Example 2-2).

Example 2-2. The demo-service project's pom.xml file dependencies section

```
<dependencies>

        ❶
        <dependency>
                <groupId>org.springframework.boot</groupId>
                <artifactId>spring-boot-starter-data-jpa</artifactId>
        </dependency>

        ❷
        <dependency>
                <groupId>org.springframework.boot</groupId>
                <artifactId>spring-boot-starter-data-rest</artifactId>
        </dependency>

        ❸
        <dependency>
                <groupId>org.springframework.boot</groupId>
                <artifactId>spring-boot-starter-web</artifactId>
        </dependency>

        ❹
        <dependency>
                <groupId>com.h2database</groupId>
                <artifactId>h2</artifactId>
                <scope>runtime</scope>
        </dependency>

        ❺
```

```
    <dependency>
            <groupId>org.springframework.boot</groupId>
            <artifactId>spring-boot-starter-test</artifactId>
            <scope>test</scope>
    </dependency>
</dependencies>
```

❶ `spring-boot-starter-data-jpa` brings in everything needed to persist Java objects using the Java ORM (Object Relational Mapping) specification and JPA (the Java Persistence API) and be productive out of the gate. This includes the JPA specification types, basic SQL Java database connectivity (JDBC) and JPA support for Spring, Hibernate as an implementation, Spring Data JPA, and Spring Data REST.

❷ `spring-boot-starter-data-rest` makes it trivial to export hypermedia-aware REST services from a Spring Data repository definition.

❸ `spring-boot-starter-web` brings in everything needed to build REST applications with Spring. It brings in JSON and XML marshalling support, file upload support, an embedded web container (the default is the latest version of Apache Tomcat), validation support, the Servlet API, and so much more. This is a redundant dependency, as `spring-boot-starter-data-rest` will automatically bring it in for us. It's highlighted here for clarity.

❹ `h2` is an in-memory, embedded SQL database. If Spring Boot detects an embedded database like H2, Derby, or HSQL on the classpath and it detects that you haven't otherwise configured a `javax.sql.DataSource` somewhere, it'll configure one for you. The embedded `DataSource` will spin up when the application spins up and it'll destroy itself (and all of its contents!) when the application shuts down.

❺ `spring-boot-starter-test` brings in all the default types needed to write effective mock and integration tests, including the Spring MVC test framework. It's assumed that testing support is needed, and this dependency is added by default.

The parent build specifies all the versions for these dependencies. In a typical Spring Boot project the only version explicitly specified is the one for Spring Boot itself. When one day a new version of Spring Boot is available, point your build to the new version and all the corresponding libraries and integrations get updated with it.

Next, open up the application's entry point class, `demo/src/main/java/com/example/DemoApplication.java`, in your favorite text editor and replace it with Example 2-3.

Example 2-3. A rudimentary Spring Boot application with a JPA entity Cat

```
package com.example;

import org.springframework.boot.SpringApplication;
import org.springframework.boot.autoconfigure.SpringBootApplication;
import org.springframework.data.jpa.repository.JpaRepository;
import org.springframework.data.rest.core.annotation.RepositoryRestResource;

import javax.persistence.Entity;
import javax.persistence.GeneratedValue;
import javax.persistence.Id;
```

❶
```
@SpringBootApplication
public class DemoApplication {

 public static void main(String[] args) {
   ❷
   SpringApplication.run(DemoApplication.class, args);
 }
}
```

❸
```
@Entity
class Cat {

 @Id
 @GeneratedValue
 private Long id;

 private String name;

 Cat() {
 }

 public Cat(String name) {
  this.name = name;
 }

 @Override
 public String toString() {
  return "Cat{" + "id=" + id + ", name='" + name + '\'' + '}';
 }

 public Long getId() {
  return id;
 }

 public String getName() {
  return name;
 }
```

```
}

❹
@RepositoryRestResource
interface CatRepository extends JpaRepository<Cat, Long> {
}
```

❶ Annotates a class as a Spring Boot application.

❷ Starts the Spring Boot application.

❸ A plain JPA entity to model a Cat entity.

❹ A Spring Data JPA repository (which handles all common create-read-update-and-delete operations) that has been exported as a REST API.

This code *should* work, but we can't be sure unless we have a test! If we have tests, we can establish a baseline working state for our software and then make measured improvements to that baseline quality. So, open up the test class, demo/src/test/java/com/example/DemoApplicationTests.java, and replace it with the code in Example 2-4.

Example 2-4. An integration test for our application

```
package com.example;

import org.junit.Before;
import org.junit.Test;
import org.junit.runner.RunWith;
import org.springframework.beans.factory.annotation.Autowired;

//@formatter:off
import org.springframework.boot.test.autoconfigure.web
  .servlet.AutoConfigureMockMvc;
//@formatter:on
import org.springframework.boot.test.context.SpringBootTest;
import org.springframework.http.MediaType;
import org.springframework.test.context.junit4.SpringRunner;
import org.springframework.test.web.servlet.MockMvc;

import java.util.stream.Stream;

import static org.junit.Assert.assertTrue;
//@formatter:off
import static org.springframework.test.web.servlet
  .request.MockMvcRequestBuilders.get;
import static org.springframework.test.web.servlet
  .result.MockMvcResultMatchers.content;
import static org.springframework.test.web.servlet
```

```
  .result.MockMvcResultMatchers.status;
//@formatter:on
```
❶

```
@RunWith(SpringRunner.class)
@SpringBootTest(webEnvironment = SpringBootTest.WebEnvironment.MOCK)
@AutoConfigureMockMvc
public class DemoApplicationTests {
```

❷
```
@Autowired
private MockMvc mvc;
```

❸
```
@Autowired
private CatRepository catRepository;
```

❹
```
@Before
public void before() throws Exception {
 Stream.of("Felix", "Garfield", "Whiskers").forEach(
  n -> catRepository.save(new Cat(n)));
}
```

❺
```
@Test
public void catsReflectedInRead() throws Exception {
 MediaType halJson = MediaType
  .parseMediaType("application/hal+json;charset=UTF-8");
 this.mvc
  .perform(get("/cats"))
  .andExpect(status().isOk())
  .andExpect(content().contentType(halJson))
  .andExpect(
   mvcResult -> {
    String contentAsString = mvcResult.getResponse().getContentAsString();
    assertTrue(contentAsString.split("totalElements")[1].split(":")[1].trim()
     .split(",")[0].equals("3"));
   });
 }
}
```

❶ This is a unit test that leverages the Spring framework test runner. We configure it to also interact nicely with the Spring Boot testing apparatus, standing up a mock web application.

❷ Inject a Spring MVC test MockMvc client with which we make calls to the REST endpoints.

❸ We can reference any other beans in our Spring application context, including `CatRepository`.

❹ Install some sample data in the database.

❺ Invoke the HTTP `GET` endpoint for the `/cats` resource.

 We'll learn more about testing in our discussion on testing in Chapter 4.

Start the application and manipulate the database through the HAL-encoded hypermedia REST API on `http://localhost:8080/cats`. If you run the test, it should be green!

Before we can get started building cloud native applications using Spring Boot, we'll need to get set up with a development environment.

Getting Started with the Spring Tool Suite

Thus far we've done everything using a text editor, but most developers today use an IDE. There are many fine choices out there, and Spring Boot works well with any of them. If you don't already have a Java IDE, you might consider the Spring Tool Suite (STS) (*http://spring.io/tools*). The Spring Tool Suite is an Eclipse-based IDE that packages up common ecosystem tooling to deliver a smoother Eclipse experience than what you'd get out of the box if you were to download the base Eclipse platform from Eclipse (*http://eclipse.org*). STS is freely available under the terms of the Eclipse Public License.

STS provides an in-IDE experience for the Spring Initializr. Indeed, the functionality in Spring Tool Suite, IntelliJ Ultimate edition, NetBeans, and the Spring Initializr web application itself all delegate to the Spring Initializr's REST API, so you get a common result no matter where you start.

You do *not need* to use any particular IDE to develop Spring or Spring Boot applications. The authors have built Spring applications in emacs, plain Eclipse, Apache Netbeans (with and without the excellent Spring Boot plug-in support that engineers from no less than Oracle have contributed), and IntelliJ IDEA Community edition and Ultimate edition with no problems. Spring Boot 1.x, in particular, needs Java 6 or better and support for editing plain `.properties` files, as well as support for working with Maven or Gradle-based builds. Any IDE from 2010 or later will do a good job here.

If you use Eclipse, the Spring Tool Suite has a lot of nice features that make working with Spring Boot-based projects even nicer:

- You can access all of the Spring guides in the STS IDE.
- You can generate new projects with the Spring Initializr in the IDE.
- If you attempt to access a type that doesn't exist on the classpath, but can be discovered within one of Spring Boot's `-starter` dependencies, then STS will automatically add that type for you.
- The *Boot Dashboard* makes it seamless to edit local Spring Boot applications and have them synchronized with a Cloud Foundry deployment. You can further debug and live-reload deployed Cloud Foundry applications, all within the IDE.
- STS makes editing Spring Boot `.properties` or `.yml` files effortless, offering auto-completion out of the box.
- The Spring Tool Suite is a stable, integrated edition of Eclipse released shortly after the mainline Eclipse release.

Installing Spring Tool Suite (STS)

Download and install the Spring Tool Suite (STS) (*http://www.spring.io*):

- Go to *https://spring.io/tools/sts*.
- Choose Download STS.
- Download, extract, and run STS.

After you have downloaded, extracted, and run the STS program, you will be prompted to choose a workspace location. Select your desired workspace location and click OK. If you plan to use the same workspace location each time you run STS, click on the option "Use this as the default and do not ask again." After you have provided a workspace location and clicked OK, the STS IDE will load for the first time (Figure 2-3).

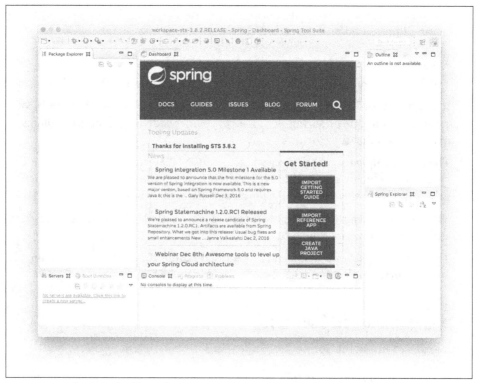

Figure 2-3. The STS dashboard

There are also packages available for numerous operating systems. For example, if you use Homebrew Cask on OS X or macOS Sierra, you can use the Pivotal tap (*https://github.com/pivotal/homebrew-tap*) and then say `brew cask install sts`.

Creating a New Project with the Spring Initializr

We could import the example that we just created from the Spring Initializr, directly, by going to File→Import→Maven and then pointing the import to `pom.xml` at the root of our existing `demo` project, but let's instead use STS to create our first Spring Boot application. We're going to create a simple "Hello World" web service using the Spring Boot starter project for web applications. To create a new Spring Boot application using a Spring Boot Starter project, choose File→New→Spring Starter Project from the menu, as shown in Figure 2-4.

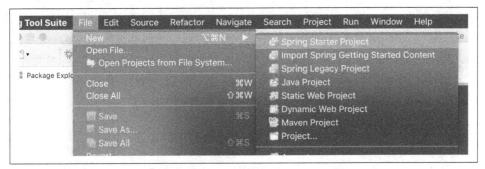

Figure 2-4. Create a new Spring Boot Starter Project

After choosing to create a new Spring Boot Starter Project, you will be presented with a dialog to configure your new Spring Boot application (Figure 2-5).

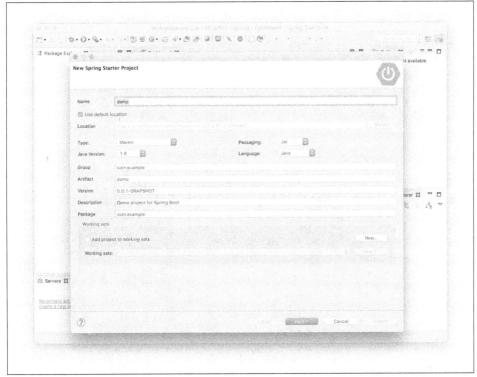

Figure 2-5. Configure your new Spring Boot Starter Project

You can configure your options, but for the purposes of this simple walkthrough, let's use the defaults and click Next. After clicking Next, you will see a set of Spring Boot Starter projects that you can choose for your new Spring Boot application. For our first application we're going to select Web (Figure 2-6).

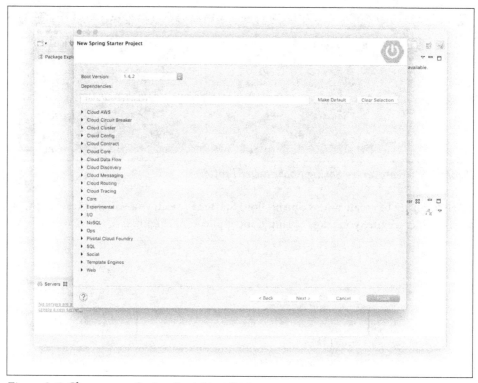

Figure 2-6. Choose your Spring Boot Start Project

Once you've made your selections, click Finish. After you click Finish, your Spring Boot application will be created and imported into the IDE workspace for you and be visible in the package explorer.

If you haven't already, expand the ***demo [boot]*** node in the Package Explorer and view the project contents, as shown in Figure 2-7.

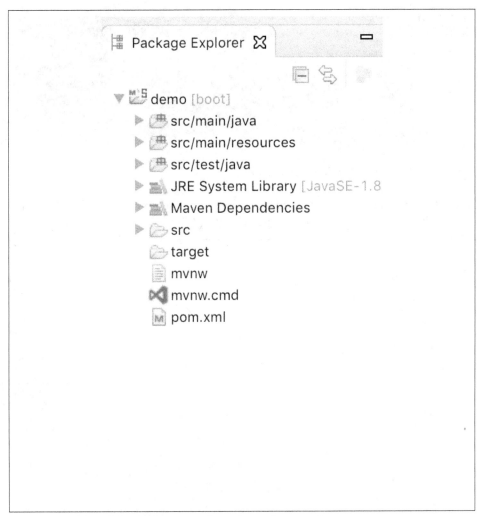

Figure 2-7. Expand the demo project from the package explorer

From the expanded project files, navigate to `src/main/java/com/example/DemoApplication.java`. Let's go ahead and run the application from the Run→Run menu (Figure 2-8).

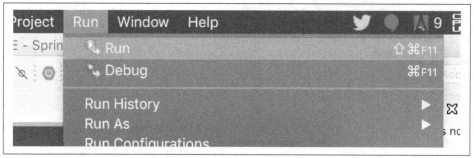

Figure 2-8. Run the Spring Boot application

After choosing the Run option from the menu, you'll be presented with a "Run As" dialog. Choose Spring Boot App and then click OK (Figure 2-9).

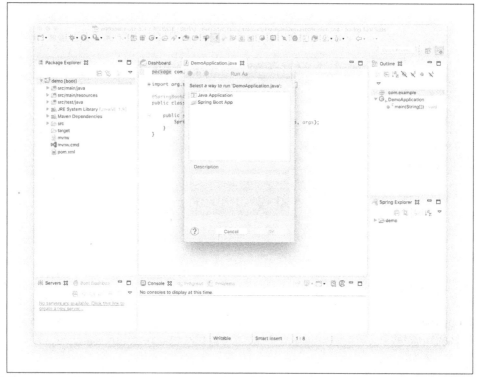

Figure 2-9. Choose Spring Boot App and launch the application

Your Spring Boot application will now start up (Figure 2-10). If you look at your STS console, you should see the iconic Spring Boot ASCII art and the version of Spring Boot as it starts up. The log output of the Spring Boot application can be seen here. You'll see that an embedded Tomcat server is being started up and launched on the default port of *8080*. You can access your Spring Boot web service from *http://local-host:8080*.

Figure 2-10. See the Spring Boot log output in the STS console

That's it! You've just created your first Spring Boot application using Spring Tool Suite.

The Spring Guides

The Spring guides (*https://spring.io/guides*) are a set of small, focused introductions to all manner of different topics in terms of Spring projects. There are many guides, most of which were written by experts on the Spring team, though some of them were contributed by ecosystem partners. Each Spring guide takes the same approach to providing a comprehensive yet consumable guide that you should be able to get through within 15–30 minutes. These guides are one of the most useful resources when you're getting started with Spring Boot.

As we can see in Figure 2-11, the Spring Guides website provides a collection of maintained examples that target a specific use case.

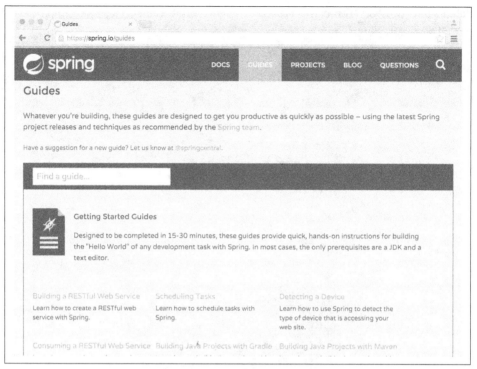

Figure 2-11. The Spring Guides website

In Figure 2-12, I've entered the search term *spring boot*, which will narrow down the list of guides to those that focus on Spring Boot.

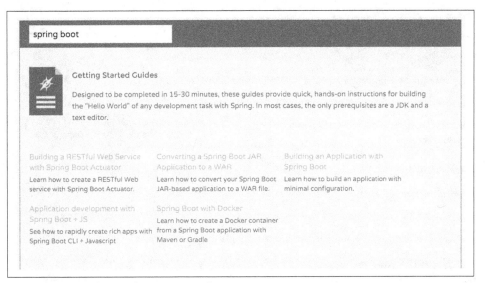

Figure 2-12. Exploring the Spring guides

As a part of each Spring guide, we'll find the following familiar features:

- Getting started
- Table of contents
- What you'll build
- What you'll need
- How to complete this guide
- Walkthrough
- Summary
- Get the code
- Link to GitHub repository

Let's now choose one of the basic Spring Boot guides, "Building an Application with Spring Boot" (*https://spring.io/guides/gs/spring-boot/*).

In Figure 2-13 we see the basic anatomy of a Spring guide. Each guide is structured in a familiar way to help you move through the content as effectively as possible. Each guide features a GitHub repository that contains three folders: complete, initial, and test. The complete folder contains the final working example so you can check your work. The initial folder contains a skeletal, almost empty filesystem that you can use to push past the boilerplate and focus on what's unique to the guide. The test folder has whatever's required to confirm that the complete project works.

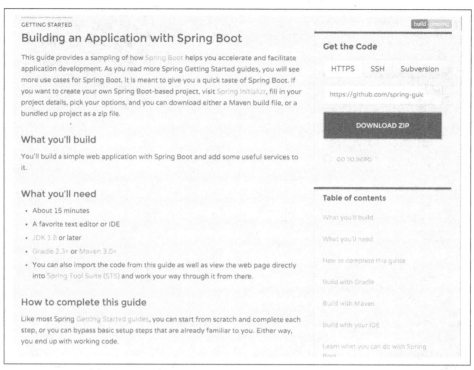

Figure 2-13. Building an Application with Spring Boot guide

 Throughout this book you'll find situations or scenarios that might require an expanded companion guide to help you get a better understanding of the content. It's recommended in this case that you take a look at the Spring guides and find a guide that best suits your needs.

Following the Guides in STS

If you're using the Spring Tool Suite, you can follow along with the guides from within the IDE. Choose File→New→Import Spring Getting Started Content (Figure 2-14).

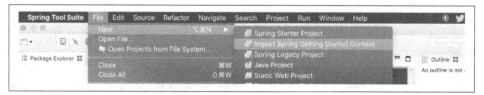

Figure 2-14. Import Spring Getting Started Content

You'll be given the same catalog of guides as you would at *spring.io/guides*, see Figure 2-15.

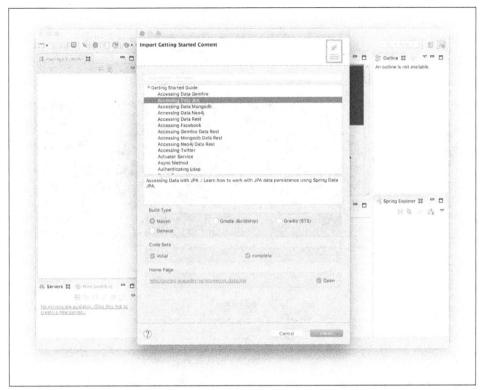

Figure 2-15. Choosing a guide from within the Import Spring Getting Started Content dialog

Select a guide and it'll be displayed within your IDE, and the associated code will be shown (Figure 2-16).

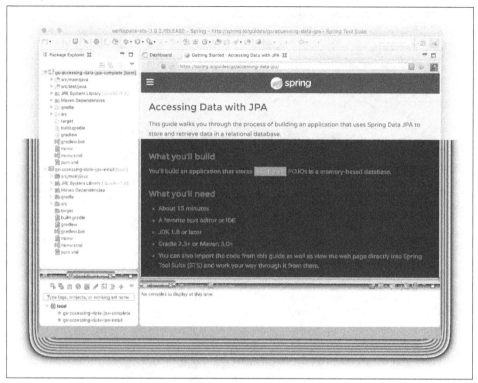

Figure 2-16. The IDE loads the guide and the relevant Git projects

Configuration

At the end of the day, a Spring application is a collection of objects. Spring manages them and their relationships for you, providing services to those objects as necessary. In order for Spring to support your objects—*beans*—it needs to be made aware of them. Spring provides a few different (complementary) ways to describe your beans.

Let's suppose we have a typical layered service, with a service object in turn talking to a `javax.sql.DataSource` to talk to an (in this case) embedded database, H2. We'll need to define a service. That service will need a datasource. We could instantiate that datasource in-place, where it's needed, but then we'd have to duplicate that logic whenever we wish to reuse the datasource in other objects. The resource acquisition and initialization is happening at the call site, which means that we can't reuse that logic elsewhere. We can see in Example 2-5 that the inline instantiation of the `Data Source` could pose a problem later.

Example 2-5. An application where the DataSource is initialized in the class, which means we can't really share the definition

```
package com.example.raai;

import com.example.Customer;
import org.springframework.core.io.ClassPathResource;
import org.springframework.jdbc.datasource.embedded.EmbeddedDatabaseBuilder;
import org.springframework.jdbc.datasource.embedded.EmbeddedDatabaseType;
import org.springframework.jdbc.datasource.init.DataSourceInitializer;
import org.springframework.jdbc.datasource.init.ResourceDatabasePopulator;
import org.springframework.util.Assert;

import javax.sql.DataSource;
import java.sql.Connection;
import java.sql.ResultSet;
import java.sql.SQLException;
import java.sql.Statement;
import java.util.ArrayList;
import java.util.Collection;
import java.util.List;

public class CustomerService {

 private final DataSource dataSource = new EmbeddedDatabaseBuilder()
  .setName("customers").setType(EmbeddedDatabaseType.H2).build();

 public static void main(String argsp[]) throws Throwable {
  CustomerService customerService = new CustomerService();

  ❶
  DataSource dataSource = customerService.dataSource;
  DataSourceInitializer init = new DataSourceInitializer();
  init.setDataSource(dataSource);
  ResourceDatabasePopulator populator = new ResourceDatabasePopulator();
  populator.setScripts(new ClassPathResource("schema.sql"),
   new ClassPathResource("data.sql"));
  init.setDatabasePopulator(populator);
  init.afterPropertiesSet();

  ❷
  int size = customerService.findAll().size();
  Assert.isTrue(size == 2);

 }

 public Collection<Customer> findAll() {
  List<Customer> customerList = new ArrayList<>();
  try {
   try (Connection c = dataSource.getConnection()) {
    Statement statement = c.createStatement();
    try (ResultSet rs = statement.executeQuery("select * from CUSTOMERS")) {
```

```
      while (rs.next()) {
        customerList.add(new Customer(rs.getLong("ID"), rs.getString("EMAIL")));
      }
     }
    }
   }
  catch (SQLException e) {
    throw new RuntimeException(e);
  }
  return customerList;
 }
}
```

❶ It's hard to stage the datasource, as the only reference to it is buried in a `private` `final` field in the `CustomerService` class itself. The only way to get access to that variable is by taking advantage of Java's *friend* access, where instances of a given object are able to see other instances, private variables.

❷ Here we use types from Spring itself, not JUnit, since the JUnit library is `test` scoped, to "exercise" the component. The Spring framework `Assert` class supports design-by-contract behavior, not unit testing!

As we can't plug in a mock datasource, and we can't stage the datasource any other way, we're forced to embed the *test* code in the component itself. This *won't* be easy to test in a proper fashion and it means we need `test`-time dependencies on the classpath for our main code.

We're using an embedded datasource, which would be the same in both development and production. In a realistic example, the configuration of environment-specific details—such as usernames and hostnames—would be parameterized; otherwise, any attempt to exercise the code might execute against a production datasource!

It would be cleaner to centralize the bean definition, outside of the call sites where it's used. How does our component code get access to that centralized reference? We could store it in static variables, but how do we test it, since we have static references littered throughout our code? How do we *mock* the reference out? We could store the references in some sort of shared context, like JNDI (Java Naming and Directory Interface), but we end up with the same problem: it's hard to test this arrangement without mocking out all of JNDI!

Instead of burying resource initialization and acquisition logic code in all of the consumers of those resources, we could create the objects and establish their wiring in one place: *in a single class*. This principle is called *Inversion of Control* (IoC).

The wiring of objects is separate from the components themselves. In teasing these things apart, we're able to build component code that is dependent on base-types and interfaces, not coupled to a particular implementation. This is called *dependency injection.* A component that is ignorant of how and where a particular dependency was created will not care if that dependency is a fake (*mock*) object during a unit test.

Instead, let's move the wiring of the objects—the configuration—into a separate class: a *configuration* class. Let's look at how this is supported with Spring's Java configuration in Example 2-6.

 What about XML? Spring debuted with support for XML-based configuration. XML configuration offers a lot of the same benefits of Java configuration: it's a centralized artifact separate from the components being wired. It's still supported, but it's not the best fit for a Spring Boot application that relies on Java configuration. In this book, we won't use XML-based configuration.

Example 2-6. A configuration class that extricates bean definitions from their call sites

```
package com.example.javaconfig;

import org.springframework.context.annotation.Bean;
import org.springframework.context.annotation.Configuration;
import org.springframework.jdbc.datasource.embedded.EmbeddedDatabaseBuilder;
import org.springframework.jdbc.datasource.embedded.EmbeddedDatabaseType;

import javax.sql.DataSource;

❶
@Configuration
public class ApplicationConfiguration {

  ❷
  @Bean(destroyMethod = "shutdown")
  DataSource dataSource() {
   return new EmbeddedDatabaseBuilder().setType(EmbeddedDatabaseType.H2)
     .setName("customers").build();
  }

  ❸
  @Bean
  CustomerService customerService(DataSource dataSource) {
   return new CustomerService(dataSource);
  }
}
```

❶ This class is a Spring @Configuration class, which tells Spring that it can expect to find definitions of objects and how they wire together in this class.

❷ We'll extract the definition of the DataSource into a bean definition. Any other Spring component can see, and work with, this single instance of the DataSource.

If 10 Spring components *depend* on the `DataSource`, then they will *all* have access to the same instance in memory, by default. This has to do with Spring's notion of scope. By default, a Spring bean is *singleton scoped*.

❸ Register the `CustomerService` instance with Spring and tell Spring to satisfy the `DataSource` by sifting through the other registered beans in the application context and finding the one whose type matches the bean provider parameter.

Revisit the `CustomerService` and remove the explicit `DataSource` creation logic (Example 2-7).

Example 2-7. A cleaner CustomerService where resource initialization and acquisition logic is externalized

```
package com.example.javaconfig;

import com.example.Customer;

import javax.sql.DataSource;
import java.sql.Connection;
import java.sql.ResultSet;
import java.sql.SQLException;
import java.sql.Statement;
import java.util.ArrayList;
import java.util.Collection;
import java.util.List;

public class CustomerService {

  private final DataSource dataSource;

  ❶
  public CustomerService(DataSource dataSource) {
   this.dataSource = dataSource;
  }

  public Collection<Customer> findAll() {
   List<Customer> customerList = new ArrayList<>();
   try {
    try (Connection c = dataSource.getConnection()) {
     Statement statement = c.createStatement();
     try (ResultSet rs = statement.executeQuery("select * from CUSTOMERS")) {
      while (rs.next()) {
       customerList.add(new Customer(rs.getLong("ID"), rs.getString("EMAIL")));
      }
     }
    }
   }
   catch (SQLException e) {
```

```
   throw new RuntimeException(e);
  }
  return customerList;
 }
}
```

❶ The definition of the `CustomerService` type is markedly simpler, since it now merely depends on a `DataSource`. We've limited its responsibilities, arguably, to things more in scope for this type: interacting with the `dataSource`, not defining the `dataSource` itself.

The configuration is explicit, but also a bit redundant. Spring could do some of the construction for us, if we let it! After all, why should *we* do all of the heavy lifting? We could use Spring's stereotype annotations to mark our own components and let Spring instantiate those for us based on convention.

Let's revisit the `ApplicationConfiguration` class and let Spring discover our stereo-typed components using *component scanning* (Example 2-8). We no longer need to explicitly describe how to construct a `CustomerService` bean, so we'll remove that definition too. The `CustomerService` type is exactly the same as before, except that it has the `@Component` annotation applied to it.

Example 2-8. Extract the DataSource configuration into a separate configuration class

```
package com.example.componentscan;

import org.springframework.context.annotation.Bean;
import org.springframework.context.annotation.ComponentScan;
import org.springframework.context.annotation.Configuration;
import org.springframework.jdbc.datasource.embedded.EmbeddedDatabaseBuilder;
import org.springframework.jdbc.datasource.embedded.EmbeddedDatabaseType;

import javax.sql.DataSource;

@Configuration
@ComponentScan
❶
public class ApplicationConfiguration {

 @Bean(destroyMethod = "shutdown")
 DataSource dataSource() {
  return new EmbeddedDatabaseBuilder().setType(EmbeddedDatabaseType.H2)
   .setName("customers").build();
 }

}
```

❶   This annotation tells Spring to discover other beans in the application context by scanning the current package (or below) and looking for all objects annotated with *stereotype* annotations like @Component. This annotation, and others that are themselves annotated with @Component, act as a kind of marker for Spring, similar to tags. Spring perceives them on components and creates a new instance of the object on which they're applied. It calls the no-argument constructor by default, or it will call a constructor with parameters so long as all the parameters themselves are satisfiable with references to other objects in the application context. Spring provides a lot of services as *opt-in* annotations expected on @Configu ration classes.

The code in our example uses a datasource directly, and we're forced to write a lot of low-level boilerplate JDBC code to get a simple result. Dependency injection is a powerful tool, but it's the least interesting aspect of Spring. Let's use one of Spring's most compelling features, the portable service abstractions, to simplify our interaction with the datasource. We'll swap out our manual and verbose JDBC-code and use Spring framework's JdbcTemplate instead (Example 2-9).

Example 2-9. Using the JdbcTemplate instead of low-level JDBC API calls

```
package com.example.psa;

import org.springframework.context.annotation.Bean;
import org.springframework.context.annotation.ComponentScan;
import org.springframework.context.annotation.Configuration;
import org.springframework.jdbc.core.JdbcTemplate;
import org.springframework.jdbc.datasource.embedded.EmbeddedDatabaseBuilder;
import org.springframework.jdbc.datasource.embedded.EmbeddedDatabaseType;

import javax.sql.DataSource;

@Configuration
@ComponentScan
public class ApplicationConfiguration {

  @Bean(destroyMethod = "shutdown")
  DataSource dataSource() {
   return new EmbeddedDatabaseBuilder().setType(EmbeddedDatabaseType.H2)
    .setName("customers").build();
  }

  ❶
  @Bean
  JdbcTemplate jdbcTemplate(DataSource dataSource) {
   return new JdbcTemplate(dataSource);
  }
```

```
}
```

❶ The JdbcTemplate is one of many implementations in the Spring ecosystem of the *template pattern*. It provides convenient utility methods that make working with JDBC a one-liner for common things. It handles resource initialization and acquisition, destruction, exception handling, and much more so that we can focus on the essence of the task at hand.

With the JdbcTemplate in place, our revised CustomerService is *much* cleaner (Example 2-10).

Example 2-10. A considerably simpler CustomerService

```
package com.example.psa;

import com.example.Customer;
import org.springframework.jdbc.core.JdbcTemplate;
import org.springframework.jdbc.core.RowMapper;
import org.springframework.stereotype.Component;

import java.util.Collection;

@Component
public class CustomerService {

 private final JdbcTemplate jdbcTemplate;

 public CustomerService(JdbcTemplate jdbcTemplate) {
  this.jdbcTemplate = jdbcTemplate;
 }

 public Collection<Customer> findAll() {
  ❶
  RowMapper<Customer> rowMapper = (rs, i) -> new Customer(rs.getLong("ID"),
   rs.getString("EMAIL"));
  ❷
  return this.jdbcTemplate.query("select * from CUSTOMERS ", rowMapper);
 }
}
```

❶ There are many overloaded variants of the query method, one of which expects a RowMapper implementation. It is a callback object that Spring will invoke for you on each returned result, allowing you to map objects returned from the database to the domain object of your system. The RowMapper interface also lends itself nicely to Java 8 lambdas!

❷ The query is a trivial one-liner. Much better!

As we control the wiring in a central place, in the bean configuration, we're able to *substitute* (or *inject*) implementations with different specializations or capabilities. If we wanted to, we could change all the injected implementations to support cross-cutting concerns without altering the consumers of the beans. Suppose we wanted to support logging the time it takes to invoke all methods. We could create a class that subclasses our existing `CustomerService` and then, in method overrides, insert logging functionality before and after we invoke the `super` implementation. The logging functionality is a cross-cutting concern, but in order to inject it into the behavior of our object hierarchy we'd have to override all methods.

Ideally, we wouldn't need to go through so many hoops to interpose trivial cross-cutting concerns over objects like this. Languages like Java that only support single-inheritance don't provide a clean way to address this use case for any arbitrary object. Spring supports an alternative: *aspect-oriented programming* (AOP). AOP is a larger topic than Spring, but Spring provides a very approachable subset of AOP for Spring objects. Spring's AOP support centers around the notion of an *aspect*, which codifies cross-cutting behavior. A *pointcut* describes the pattern that should be matched when applying an aspect. The pattern in a pointcut is part of a full-featured pointcut language that Spring supports. The pointcut language lets you describe method invocations for objects in a Spring application. Let's suppose we wanted to create an aspect that will match all method invocations, today and tomorrow, in our `CustomerService` example and interpose logging to capture timing.

Add `@EnableAspectJAutoProxy` to the `ApplicationConfiguration` `@Configuration` class to activate Spring's AOP functionality. Then, we need only extract our cross-cutting functionality into a separate type, an `@Aspect`-annotated object (Example 2-11).

Example 2-11. Extract the cross-cutting concern into a Spring AOP aspect

```
package com.example.aop;

import org.apache.commons.logging.Log;
import org.apache.commons.logging.LogFactory;
import org.aspectj.lang.ProceedingJoinPoint;
import org.aspectj.lang.annotation.Around;
import org.aspectj.lang.annotation.Aspect;
import org.springframework.stereotype.Component;

import java.time.LocalDateTime;

@Component
@Aspect
❶
public class LoggingAroundAspect {
```

```
private Log log = LogFactory.getLog(getClass());

❷
@Around("execution(* com.example.aop.CustomerService.*(..))")
public Object log(ProceedingJoinPoint joinPoint) throws Throwable {
 LocalDateTime start = LocalDateTime.now();

 Throwable toThrow = null;
 Object returnValue = null;

 ❸
 try {
  returnValue = joinPoint.proceed();
 }
 catch (Throwable t) {
  toThrow = t;
 }
 LocalDateTime stop = LocalDateTime.now();

 log.info("starting @ " + start.toString());
 log.info("finishing @ " + stop.toString() + " with duration "
  + stop.minusNanos(start.getNano()).getNano());

 ❹
 if (null != toThrow)
  throw toThrow;

 ❺
 return returnValue;
 }
}
```

❶   Mark this bean as an aspect.

❷   Declare that this method is to be given a chance to execute *around*—before and after—the execution of any method that matches the pointcut expression in the @Around annotation. There are numerous other annotations, but for now this one will give us a lot of power. For more, you might investigate Spring's support for AspectJ.

❸   When the method matching this pointcut is invoked, our aspect is invoked first, and passed a ProceedingJoinPoint which is a handle on the running method invocation. We can choose to interrogate the method execution, to proceed with it, to skip it, etc. This aspect logs before and after it proceeds with the method invocation.

❹   If an exception is thrown, it is cached and rethrown later.

❺ If a return value is recorded, it is returned as well (assuming no exception's been thrown).

We can use AOP directly, if we need to, but many of the really important cross-cutting concerns we're likely going to encounter in typical application development are already extracted out for us in Spring itself. An example is declarative transaction management. In our example, we have one method that is read-only. If we were to introduce another business service method—one that mutated the database multiple times in a single service call—then we'd need to ensure that those mutations all happened in a single *unit of work*; either every interaction with the stateful resource (the datasource) succeeds, or none of them do.

We don't want to leave the system in an inconsistent state. This is an ideal example of a cross-cutting concern: we might use AOP to begin a transactional block before every method invocation in a business service and commit (or roll back) that transaction upon the completion of the invocation. We *could* do that, but thankfully, Spring's declarative transaction support does this for us already; we don't need to write lower-level AOP-centric code to make it work. Add @EnableTransactionManagement to a configuration class and then delineate transactional boundaries on business services using the @Transactional annotation.

We have a service tier; a logical next step might be to build a web application. We could use Spring MVC to create a REST endpoint. To do that, we would need to configure Spring MVC itself, deploy it to a Servlet-compatible application server, and then configure the application server's interaction with Servlet API. It can be a lot of work before we can take that next step and realize a humble working web application and REST endpoint!

We've used straight JDBC here, but we could've elected to use an ORM layer. This would've invited even more complexity. None of it is too much, step-by-step, but taken together the cognitive load can be overwhelming.

This is where Spring Boot and its auto-configuration kick in.

In our first example in this chapter, we created an application with an interface, a JPA entity, a few annotations, and a public static void main entry-point class, and... that's it! Spring Boot started up, and presto! There was a working REST API running on http://localhost:8080/cats. The application supported manipulating JPA entities using the Spring Data JPA-based repository. It did a lot of things for which there was, seemingly, no explicit code—*magic*!

If you know much about Spring, then you'll no doubt recognize that we were using, among other things, the Spring framework and its robust support for JPA. Spring Data JPA is used to configure a declarative, interface-based repository. Spring MVC and Spring Data REST are used to serve an HTTP-based REST API, and even then

---

you might be wondering about where the web server itself came from. Each of these modules requires *some* configuration. Not much, usually, but certainly more than what we did there! They require, if nothing else, an annotation to *opt in* to certain default behavior.

Historically, Spring has opted to expose the configuration. It's a *configuration plane*— a chance to refine the behavior of the application. In Spring Boot, the priority is providing a sensible default and supporting easy overrides. It's a full-throated embrace of convention over configuration. Ultimately, Spring Boot's auto-configuration is the same sort of configuration that you could write by hand, with the same annotations and the same beans you might register, along with common sense defaults.

Spring supports the notion of a *service loader* to support registering custom contributions to the application without changing Spring itself. A service loader is a mapping of types to Java configuration class names that are then evaluated and made available to the Spring application later on. The registration of custom contributions happens in the `META-INF/spring.factories` file. Spring Boot looks in the `spring.factories` file for, among other things, all classes under the `org.springframework.boot.auto configure.EnableAutoConfiguration` entry. In the `spring-boot-autoconfigure.jar` that ships with the Spring Boot framework, there are *dozens* of different configuration classes here, and Spring Boot will try to evaluate them all! It'll try, but *fail*, to evaluate all of them, at least, thanks to various conditions—guards, if you like—that have been placed on the configuration classes and the `@Bean` definitions therein. This facility, to conditionally register Spring components, is from the Spring framework itself, on which Spring Boot is built. These conditions are wide-ranging: they test for the availability of beans of a given type, the presence of environment properties, the availability of certain types on the classpath, and more.

Let's review our `CustomerService` example. We want to build a Spring Boot version of the application that uses an embedded database and the Spring Framework `JdbcTemplate`, and then support building a web application. Spring Boot will do all of that for us. Revisit the `ApplicationConfiguration` (see Example 2-12) and turn it into a Spring Boot application accordingly.

Example 2-12. ApplicationConfiguration.java class

```
package com.example.boot;

import org.springframework.boot.autoconfigure.SpringBootApplication;

@SpringBootApplication
public class ApplicationConfiguration {
    ❶
}
```

❶ Look, Ma, no configuration! Spring Boot will contribute all the things we contributed ourselves, manually, and so much more.

Let's introduce a Spring MVC-based controller to expose a REST endpoint to respond to HTTP GET requests at /customers (Example 2-13).

Example 2-13. CustomerRestController.java class

```
package com.example.boot;

import com.example.Customer;
import org.springframework.web.bind.annotation.GetMapping;
import org.springframework.web.bind.annotation.RestController;

import java.util.Collection;

❶
@RestController
public class CustomerRestController {

  private final CustomerService customerService;

  public CustomerRestController(CustomerService customerService) {
    this.customerService = customerService;
  }

  ❷
  @GetMapping("/customers")
  public Collection<Customer> readAll() {
    return this.customerService.findAll();
  }
}
```

❶ @RestController is another stereotype annotation, like @Component. It tells Spring that this component is to serve as a REST controller.

❷ We can use Spring MVC annotations that map to the domain of what we're trying to do: in this case, to handle HTTP GET requests to a certain endpoint with @GetMapping.

You could create an entry point in the ApplicationConfiguration class (Example 2-14), then run the application and visit http://localhost:8080/custom ers in your browser. Cognitively, it's much easier to reason out what's happening in our business logic, *and* we've done more with less!

Example 2-14. Build a REST endpoint with Spring MVC

```
public static void main(String [] args){
  SpringApplication.run (ApplicationConfiguration.class, args);
}
```

We got more for less. We know that somewhere something else is doing the same configuration explicitly that we did earlier. Where is the JdbcTemplate being created? It's created in an auto-configuration class called JdbcTemplateAutoConfiguration, whose definition is shown in Example 2-15 (roughly).

Example 2-15. JdbcTemplateAutoConfiguration

```
@Configuration ❶
@ConditionalOnClass({ DataSource.class, JdbcTemplate.class }) ❷
@ConditionalOnSingleCandidate(DataSource.class) ❸
@AutoConfigureAfter(DataSourceAutoConfiguration.class) ❹
public class JdbcTemplateAutoConfiguration {

      private final DataSource dataSource;

      public JdbcTemplateAutoConfiguration(DataSource dataSource) {
            this.dataSource = dataSource;
      }

      @Bean
      @Primary
      @ConditionalOnMissingBean(JdbcOperations.class) ❺
      public JdbcTemplate jdbcTemplate() {
            return new JdbcTemplate(this.dataSource);
      }

      @Bean
      @Primary
      @ConditionalOnMissingBean(NamedParameterJdbcOperations.class) ❻
      public NamedParameterJdbcTemplate namedParameterJdbcTemplate() {
            return new NamedParameterJdbcTemplate(this.dataSource);
      }

}
```

❶ This is a normal @Configuration class.

❷ The configuration class should *only* be evaluated if the type DataSource.class and JdbcTemplate.class are somewhere on the classpath; otherwise, this would no doubt fail with an error like ClassNotFoundException.

❸ We only want this configuration class if, somewhere in the application context, a `DataSource` bean has been contributed.

❹ We know that `DataSourceAutoConfiguration` will contribute an embedded H2 datasource if we let it, so this annotation ensures that this configuration happens *after* that `DataSourceAutoConfiguration` has run. If a database is contributed, then this configuration class will evaluate.

❺ We want to contribute a `JdbcTemplate`, but only so long as the users (that's to say, so long as you and I) haven't already defined a bean of the same type in our own configuration classes.

❻ We want to contribute a `NamedParameterJdbcTemplate`, but only so long as one doesn't already exist.

Spring Boot's auto-configuration greatly reduces the actual code count and the cognitive load associated with that code. It frees us to focus on the essence of the business logic, leaving the tedium to the framework. If we want to exert control over some aspect of the stack, we're free to contribute beans of certain types, and those will be plugged in to the framework for us. Spring Boot is an implementation of the open-closed principal: it's open for extension but closed for modification.

You don't *need* to recompile Spring or Spring Boot in order to override parts of the machine. You may see your Spring Boot application exhibit some odd behavior that you want to override or customize. It's important to know how to customize the application and how to debug it. Specify the `--Ddebug=true` flag when the application starts up, and Spring Boot will print out the Debug Report, showing you all the conditions that have been evaluated and whether they're a positive or negative match. From there, it's easy to examine what's happening in the relevant auto-configuration class to ascertain its behavior.

Cloud Foundry

Spring Boot lets us focus on the essence of the application itself, but what good would all that newfound productivity be if we then lost it all struggling to move the application to production? Operationalizing an application is a daunting task, but one that must not be ignored. Our goal is to continuously deploy our application into a production-like environment, to validate in integration and acceptance tests that things will work when they're deployed to production. It's important to get to production as early and often as possible, for that is the only place where the customer, the party most invested in the outcome of a team's deliverable, can validate that it works.

If moving to production is arduous, a software team will inevitably come to fear the process and hesitate, increasing the delta between development and production pushes. This increases the backlog of work that hasn't been moved to production, which means that each push becomes more risky because there's more business value in each release. In order to de-risk the move to production, reduce the batch of work and increase the frequency of deployment. If there's a mistake in production, it should be as cheap as possible to fix it and deploy that fix.

The trick is to automate away everything that can be automated in the value chain, from product management to production, that doesn't add value to the process. Deployment is not a business differentiating activity; it adds no value to the process. It should be completely automated. You get velocity through automation.

Cloud Foundry is a cloud platform that wants to help. It's a Platform as a Service (PaaS). Cloud Foundry focuses not on hard disks, RAM, CPU, Linux installations, and security patches as an Infrastructure as a Service (IaaS) offering would, or on containers as you might get in a containers-as-a-service offering, but instead on applications and their services. Operators focus on applications and their services, nothing else. We'll see Cloud Foundry throughout this book, so for now let's focus on deploying the Spring Boot application we iteratively developed when looking at Spring's configuration support.

There are multiple implementations of Cloud Foundry, all based on the open source Cloud Foundry code. For this book we've run and deployed all applications on Pivotal Web Services (*http://run.pivotal.io*). Pivotal Web Services offers a subset of the functionality of Pivotal's on-premise Pivotal Cloud Foundry (*https://pivotal.io/plat form*) offering. It's hosted on Amazon Web Services, in the AWS East region. If you want to take your first steps with Cloud Foundry, PWS is an affordable and approachable option that serves projects large and small and is maintained by the operations team at Pivotal.

Go to the main page. You'll find a place to sign in to an existing account, or register a new one (Figure 2-17).

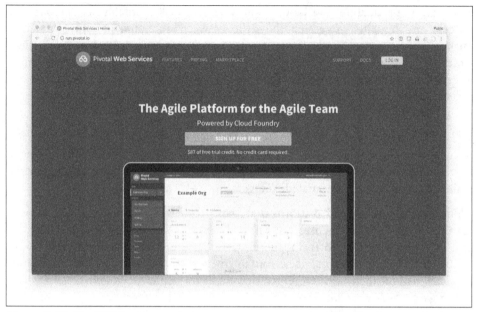

Figure 2-17. The PWS main page

Once logged in, you can interact with your account and get information about deployed applications (Figure 2-18).

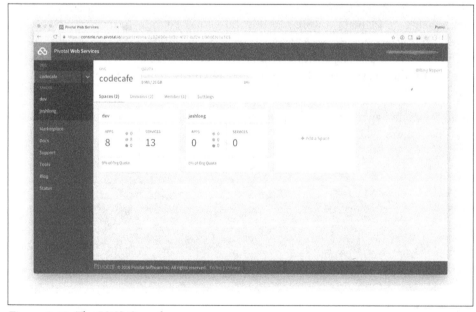

Figure 2-18. The PWS Console

Once you have an account, make sure you have the `cf` command-line interface (CLI) (*https://docs.cloudfoundry.org/cf-cli/install-go-cli.html*). You'll need to log in if you haven't before.

Target the appropriate Cloud Foundry instance using `cf target api.run.pivo tal.io`, and then log in using `cf login` (Example 2-16).

Example 2-16. Authenticating and targeting a Cloud Foundry organization and a space

```
→  cf login

API endpoint: https://api.run.pivotal.io

Email> email@gmail.com

Password>
Authenticating...
OK

Select an org (or press enter to skip):
1. marketing
2. sales
3. back-office

Org> 1
Targeted org back-office

Targeted space development

API endpoint:    https://api.run.pivotal.io (API version: 2.65.0)
User:            email@gmail.com
Org:             back-office    ❶
Space:           development ❷
```

❶ In Cloud Foundry, there might be many organizations to which a given user has access.

❷ Within that organization, there might be multiple environments (for example, `development`, `staging`, and `integration`).

Now that we have a valid account and are logged in, we can deploy our existing application in `target/configuration.jar`. We'll need to provision a database using the `cf create-service` command (Example 2-17).

Example 2-17. Create a MySQL database, bind it to our application, and then start the application

```
cf create-service p-mysql 100mb bootcamp-customers-mysql          ❶

cf push -p target/configuration.jar bootcamp-customers \
 --random-route --no-start                                        ❷

cf bind-service bootcamp-customers bootcamp-customers-mysql        ❸

cf start bootcamp-customers                                       ❹
```

❶ First we need to provision a MySQL database from the MySQL service (called p-mysql) at the 100mb plan. Here, we'll assign it a logical name, bootcamp-customers-mysql. Use cf marketplace to enumerate other services in a Cloud Foundry instance's service catalog.

❷ Then push the application's artifact, target/configuration.jar, to Cloud Foundry. We'll assign the application and a random route (a URL, in this case under the PWS cfapps.io domain), but we don't want to start it yet: it still needs a database!

❸ The database exists, but nobody can talk to it unless we bind it to an application. Ultimately, *binding* results in environment variables being exposed in the application, with the relevant connection information in the environmental variables.

❹ Now that the application is bound to a database, we can finally start it up!

When you push the application to Cloud Foundry, you're giving it an application binary, a .jar, not a virtual machine or a Linux container (though you *could* give it a Linux container). When Cloud Foundry receives the .jar, it will try to determine what the nature of the application is. Is it a Java application? A Ruby application? A .NET application? It'll eventually arrive at a Java application. It will pass the .jar to the Java buildpack. A *buildpack* is a directory full of scripts invoked according to a well-known life cycle. You can override the default buildpack used by specifying its URL, or you can let the default buildpack kick in. There are buildpacks for all manner of different languages and platforms, including Java, .NET, Node.js, Go, Python, Ruby, and a slew more. The Java buildpack will realize that the application is an executable main(String [] args) method, and that it is self-contained. It will pull down the latest OpenJDK version, and specify that our application is to run. All of this configuration is packaged into a Linux container, which Cloud Foundry's scheduler will then deploy across a cluster. Cloud Foundry can run hundreds of thousands of containers in a single environment.

In no time at all, the application will spin up and report a URL on the console at which the application has been exposed. Congratulations! Our application is now deployed to a Cloud Foundry instance.

In our application, we have one datasource bean, and so Cloud Foundry remapped it automatically to the single, bound MySQL service, overwriting the default embedded H2 datasource definition with one that points to a MySQL datasource.

There are a lot of aspects to the deployed application that we may want to describe on each deployment. In our first run, we used various `cf` incantations to configure the application, but that could get tedious quickly. Instead, let's capture our application's configuration in a Cloud Foundry manifest file, typically named `manifest.yml`. Here's a `manifest.yml` for our application that will work so long as we've already got a MySQL datasource provisioned with the same name as specified earlier (Example 2-18).

Example 2-18. A Cloud Foundry manifest

```
---
applications:
- name: bootcamp-customers                                        ❶
  buildpack: https://github.com/cloudfoundry/java-buildpack.git  ❷
  instances: 1
  random-route: true
  path: target/spring-configuration.jar                          ❸
  services:
    - bootcamp-customers-mysql                                   ❹
  env:
    DEBUG: "true"
    SPRING_PROFILES_ACTIVE: cloud                                ❺
```

❶ We provide a logical name for the application…

❷ …specify a buildpack…

❸ …specify which binary to use…

❹ …specify a dependency on provisioned Cloud Foundry services…

❺ …and specify environment variables to override properties to which Spring Boot will respond. `--Ddebug=true` (or `DEBUG: true`) enumerates the conditions in the auto-configuration, and `--Dspring.profiles.active=cloud` specifies which profiles, or logical groupings with arbitrary names, should be activated in a Spring application. This configuration says to start all Spring beans without any profile as well as those with the `cloud` profile.

Now, instead of writing all those cf incantations, just run `cf push -f manifest.yml`. Soon, your application will be up and running and ready for inspection.

Thus far we've seen that the Cloud Foundry experience is all about obtaining velocity through automation: the platform does as much of the undifferentiated heavy lifting as possible, letting you focus on the business logic that should matter. We've worked within the opinionated approach offered by Cloud Foundry: if your application needs something, you can declare as much in a cf incantation or in a `manifest.yml` and the platform will support you. It is surprising, therefore, that despite constraining inputs into the platform, Cloud Foundry is itself also easy to program. It provides a rich API that supports virtually everything you'd want to do. Taking things a step further, the Spring and Cloud Foundry teams have developed a Java Cloud Foundry client that supports all the major components in a Cloud Foundry implementation. The Cloud Foundry Java client *also* supports higher-level, more granular business operations that correspond to the things you might do using the cf CLI.

The Cloud Foundry Java client is built on the Pivotal Reactor 3.0 project. Reactor, in turn, underpins the reactive web runtime in Spring Framework 5. The Cloud Foundry Java client is *fast*, and as it's built on reactive principles—it's almost entirely non-blocking.

The Reactor project, in turn, is an implementation of the Reactive Streams initiative. The Reactive Streams initiative, according to the website (*http://www.reactive-streams.org*), "is an initiative to provide a standard for asynchronous stream processing with non-blocking back pressure." It provides a language and APIs to describe a potentially unlimited stream of *live* data that arrives asynchronously. The Reactor API makes it easy to write code that benefits from parallelization without writing coding to achieve parallelization. The goal is to avoid aggressive resource usage and isolate the blocking parts of cloud-based workloads in an efficient way. The Reactive Streams initiative defines *backpressure*; a subscriber can signal to the publisher that it does not wish to receive any more notifications. In essence, it's pushing back on the producer, throttling consumption until it can afford it.

The heart of this API is the `org.reactivestreams.Publisher` which may produce zero or more values, eventually. A `Subscriber` subscribes to notifications of new values from a `Publisher`. The Reactor project defines two useful specializations of the `Publisher`: `Mono` and `Flux`. A `Mono<T>` is a `Publisher<T>` that produces one value. A `Flux<T>` is a `Publisher<T>` that produces zero or more values.

Cardinality
Synchronous
Asynchronous
One

```
Cardinality

T

Future<T>

Many

Collection<T>

org.reactivestreams.Publisher<T>
```

We won't delve too deeply into reactive streams or the Reactor project, but know that it provides the foundations for the extraordinary efficiencies of the Cloud Foundry Java API. The Cloud Foundry Java API lends itself to parallelization of processing that is *very* difficult to achieve using the cf CLI. We've deployed the same application using the cf CLI, and a manifest.yml file; let's look at doing so in Java code. It's particularly handy to use the Cloud Foundry Java client in integration tests. In order to use the Cloud Foundry Java client, you'll need to configure some objects required to securely integrate with different subsystems in Cloud Foundry, including the log-aggregation subsystem, the Cloud Foundry REST APIs, and the Cloud Foundry authentication subsystem. We'll demonstrate the configuration of those components here, for posterity (Example 2-19), but it's very likely that you won't need to configure this functionality in a not-too-distant release of Spring Boot.

Example 2-19. Configure the Cloud Foundry Java client

```java
package com.example;

import org.cloudfoundry.client.CloudFoundryClient;
import org.cloudfoundry.operations.DefaultCloudFoundryOperations;
import org.cloudfoundry.reactor.ConnectionContext;
import org.cloudfoundry.reactor.DefaultConnectionContext;
import org.cloudfoundry.reactor.TokenProvider;
import org.cloudfoundry.reactor.client.ReactorCloudFoundryClient;
import org.cloudfoundry.reactor.doppler.ReactorDopplerClient;
import org.cloudfoundry.reactor.tokenprovider.PasswordGrantTokenProvider;
import org.cloudfoundry.reactor.uaa.ReactorUaaClient;
import org.springframework.beans.factory.annotation.Value;
import org.springframework.boot.SpringApplication;
import org.springframework.boot.autoconfigure.SpringBootApplication;
import org.springframework.context.annotation.Bean;

@SpringBootApplication
public class CloudFoundryClientExample {

 public static void main(String[] args) {
  SpringApplication.run(CloudFoundryClientExample.class, args);
 }

 ❶
```

```
@Bean
ReactorCloudFoundryClient cloudFoundryClient(
 ConnectionContext connectionContext, TokenProvider tokenProvider) {
 return ReactorCloudFoundryClient.builder()
  .connectionContext(connectionContext).tokenProvider(tokenProvider).build();
}
```

❷
```
@Bean
ReactorDopplerClient dopplerClient(ConnectionContext connectionContext,
 TokenProvider tokenProvider) {
 return ReactorDopplerClient.builder().connectionContext(connectionContext)
  .tokenProvider(tokenProvider).build();
}
```

❸
```
@Bean
ReactorUaaClient uaaClient(ConnectionContext connectionContext,
 TokenProvider tokenProvider) {
 return ReactorUaaClient.builder().connectionContext(connectionContext)
  .tokenProvider(tokenProvider).build();
}
```

❹
```
@Bean
DefaultCloudFoundryOperations cloudFoundryOperations(
 CloudFoundryClient cloudFoundryClient, ReactorDopplerClient dopplerClient,
 ReactorUaaClient uaaClient, @Value("${cf.org}") String organization,
 @Value("${cf.space}") String space) {
 return DefaultCloudFoundryOperations.builder()
  .cloudFoundryClient(cloudFoundryClient).dopplerClient(dopplerClient)
  .uaaClient(uaaClient).organization(organization).space(space).build();
}
```

❺
```
@Bean
DefaultConnectionContext connectionContext(@Value("${cf.api}") String apiHost) {
 if (apiHost.contains("://")) {
  apiHost = apiHost.split("://")[1];
 }
 return DefaultConnectionContext.builder().apiHost(apiHost).build();
}
```

❻
```
@Bean
PasswordGrantTokenProvider tokenProvider(@Value("${cf.user}") String username,
 @Value("${cf.password}") String password) {
 return PasswordGrantTokenProvider.builder().password(password)
  .username(username).build();
}
}
```

❶ The `ReactorCloudFoundryClient` is the client for the Cloud Foundry REST API.

❷ The `ReactorDopplerClient` is the client for Cloud Foundry's websocket-based log-aggregation subsystem, Doppler.

❸ The `ReactorUaaClient` is the client for UAA, the authorization and authentication subsystem in Cloud Foundry.

❹ The `DefaultCloudFoundryOperations` instance provides coarser-grained operations that compose the lower-level subsystem clients. Start here.

❺ The `ConnectionContext` describes the Cloud Foundry instance that we wish to target.

❻ The `PasswordGrantTokenProvider` describes our authentication.

It's trivial to get a simple proof-of-concept with this in place. Example 2-20 is a simple example that will enumerate all the deployed applications in a particular Cloud Foundry space and organization.

Example 2-20. List application instances

```java
package com.example;

import org.cloudfoundry.operations.CloudFoundryOperations;
import org.springframework.boot.CommandLineRunner;
import org.springframework.stereotype.Component;

@Component
class ApplicationListingCommandLineRunner implements CommandLineRunner {

  private final CloudFoundryOperations cf; ❶

  ApplicationListingCommandLineRunner(CloudFoundryOperations cf) {
   this.cf = cf;
  }

  @Override
  public void run(String... args) throws Exception {
   cf.applications().list().subscribe(System.out::println); ❷
  }
}
```

❶ Inject the configured `CloudFoundryOperations`...

❷ …and use it to enumerate all the deployed applications in this particular Cloud
Foundry space and organization.

For a more real-world example, let's deploy our `bootcamp-customers` application
using the Java client. Here's a simple integration test that provisions a MySQL service,
pushes the application to Cloud Foundry (but doesn't start it), binds environment
variables, binds the MySQL service, and then, *finally*, starts the application. First, let's
look at the skeletal code where we identify the deployable `.jar` and name our application and the service (Example 2-21). We'll delegate to two components, `Application`
`Deployer` and `ServicesDeployer`.

Example 2-21. The skeleton of an integration test that provisions an application

```
package bootcamp;

import org.cloudfoundry.operations.CloudFoundryOperations;
import org.junit.Test;
import org.junit.runner.RunWith;
import org.springframework.beans.factory.annotation.Autowired;
import org.springframework.beans.factory.annotation.Value;
import org.springframework.boot.autoconfigure.SpringBootApplication;
import org.springframework.boot.test.context.SpringBootTest;
import org.springframework.context.annotation.Bean;
import org.springframework.context.annotation.PropertySource;
import org.springframework.test.context.junit4.SpringJUnit4ClassRunner;

import java.io.File;
import java.time.Duration;
import java.util.HashMap;
import java.util.Map;
import java.util.concurrent.BrokenBarrierException;
import java.util.concurrent.CountDownLatch;
import java.util.concurrent.CyclicBarrier;

@RunWith(SpringJUnit4ClassRunner.class)
@SpringBootTest(classes = SpringConfigurationIT.Config.class)
public class SpringConfigurationIT {

 @Autowired
 private ApplicationDeployer applicationDeployer;

 @Autowired
 private ServicesDeployer servicesDeployer;

 @Test
 public void deploy() throws Throwable {

  File projectFolder = new File(new File("."), "../spring-configuration");
  File jar = new File(projectFolder, "target/spring-configuration.jar");
```

```
String applicationName = "bootcamp-customers";
String mysqlSvc = "bootcamp-customers-mysql";

Map<String, String> env = new HashMap<>();
env.put("SPRING_PROFILES_ACTIVE", "cloud");

Duration timeout = Duration.ofMinutes(5);
servicesDeployer.deployService(applicationName, mysqlSvc, "p-mysql", "100mb")
  ❶
  .then(
   applicationDeployer.deployApplication(jar, applicationName, env, timeout,
    mysqlSvc)) ❷
   .block(); ❸

}

@SpringBootApplication
public static class Config {

 @Bean
 ApplicationDeployer applications(CloudFoundryOperations cf) {
  return new ApplicationDeployer(cf);
 }

 @Bean
 ServicesDeployer services(CloudFoundryOperations cf) {
  return new ServicesDeployer(cf);
 }
 }

}
```

❶ First deploy the backing service (a MySQL instance)…

❷ …then the application, making sure to time out after five minutes…

❸ …and then blocking to prolong the test.

This example composes two Publisher instances, one describing the processing required to provision a service, and another describing the processing required to provision the application. The final call in the chain, .block(), triggers processing; it is a terminal method that activates the entire flow.

The ServicesDeployer takes the required parameters and provisions our MySQL instance (Example 2-22). It also unbinds and deletes the instance if it already exists.

Example 2-22. ServicesDeployer

```
package bootcamp;

import org.apache.commons.logging.Log;
import org.apache.commons.logging.LogFactory;
import org.cloudfoundry.operations.CloudFoundryOperations;
import org.cloudfoundry.operations.services.CreateServiceInstanceRequest;
import org.cloudfoundry.operations.services.DeleteServiceInstanceRequest;
import org.cloudfoundry.operations.services.ServiceInstanceSummary;
import org.cloudfoundry.operations.services.UnbindServiceInstanceRequest;
import org.reactivestreams.Publisher;
import reactor.core.publisher.Flux;
import reactor.core.publisher.Mono;

import java.util.function.Function;

class ServicesDeployer {

  private final Log log = LogFactory.getLog(getClass());

  private final CloudFoundryOperations cf;

  ServicesDeployer(CloudFoundryOperations cf) {
   this.cf = cf;
  }

  Mono<Void> deployService(String applicationName, String svcInstanceName,
   String svcTypeName, String planName) {

   return cf.services().listInstances().cache()❶
    .filter(si1 -> si1.getName().equalsIgnoreCase(svcInstanceName)) ❷
    .transform(unbindAndDelete(applicationName, svcInstanceName)) ❸
    .thenEmpty(createService(svcInstanceName, svcTypeName, planName)); ❹
  }

  private Function<Flux<ServiceInstanceSummary>, Publisher<Void>> unbindAndDelete(
   String applicationName, String svcInstanceName) {
   return siFlux -> Flux.concat(
    unbind(applicationName, svcInstanceName, siFlux),
    delete(svcInstanceName, siFlux));
  }

  private Flux<Void> unbind(String applicationName, String svcInstanceName,
   Flux<ServiceInstanceSummary> siFlux) {
   return siFlux.filter(si -> si.getApplications().contains(applicationName))
    .flatMap(
     si -> cf.services().unbind(
      UnbindServiceInstanceRequest.builder().applicationName(applicationName)
       .serviceInstanceName(svcInstanceName).build()));
  }
```

```
private Flux<Void> delete(String svcInstanceName,
 Flux<ServiceInstanceSummary> siFlux) {
 return siFlux.flatMap(si -> cf.services().deleteInstance(
  DeleteServiceInstanceRequest.builder().name(svcInstanceName).build()));
}

private Mono<Void> createService(String svcInstanceName, String svcTypeName,
 String planName) {
 return cf.services().createInstance(
  CreateServiceInstanceRequest.builder().serviceName(svcTypeName)
   .planName(planName).serviceInstanceName(svcInstanceName).build());
}
}
```

❶ List all application instances and cache them so that subsequent subscribers don't reevaluate the REST call.

❷ Filter all the service instances, keeping only the one that matches a particular name.

❸ Then unbind (if it is bound) and delete the service.

❹ Then, finally, create the service anew.

The ApplicationDeployer then provisions the application itself (Example 2-23). It binds to the service that we will have just provisioned using the ServicesDeployer.

Example 2-23. ApplicationDeployer

```
package bootcamp;

import org.cloudfoundry.operations.CloudFoundryOperations;
import org.cloudfoundry.operations.applications.PushApplicationRequest;
import org.cloudfoundry.operations.applications.
    SetEnvironmentVariableApplicationRequest;
import org.cloudfoundry.operations.applications.StartApplicationRequest;
import org.cloudfoundry.operations.services.BindServiceInstanceRequest;
import reactor.core.publisher.Flux;
import reactor.core.publisher.Mono;

import java.io.File;
import java.time.Duration;
import java.util.HashMap;
import java.util.Map;

class ApplicationDeployer {

 private final CloudFoundryOperations cf;
```

```
ApplicationDeployer(CloudFoundryOperations cf) {
  this.cf = cf;
}

Mono<Void> deployApplication(File jar, String applicationName,
  Map<String, String> envOg, Duration timeout, String... svcs) {
  return cf.applications().push(pushApp(jar, applicationName))❶
    .then(bindServices(applicationName, svcs)) ❷
    .then(setEnvironmentVariables(applicationName, new HashMap<>(envOg)))❸
    .then(startApplication(applicationName, timeout));❹

}

private PushApplicationRequest pushApp(File jar, String applicationName) {
  return PushApplicationRequest.builder().name(applicationName).noStart(true)
    .randomRoute(true)
    .buildpack("https://github.com/cloudfoundry/java-buildpack.git")
    .application(jar.toPath()).instances(1).build();
}

private Mono<Void> bindServices(String applicationName, String[] svcs) {
  return Flux
    .just(svcs)
    .flatMap(
    svc -> {
      BindServiceInstanceRequest request = BindServiceInstanceRequest.builder()
        .applicationName(applicationName).serviceInstanceName(svc).build();
      return cf.services().bind(request);
    }).then();
}

private Mono<Void> startApplication(String applicationName, Duration timeout) {
  return cf.applications().start(
    StartApplicationRequest.builder().name(applicationName)
      .stagingTimeout(timeout).startupTimeout(timeout).build());
}

private Mono<Void> setEnvironmentVariables(String applicationName,
  Map<String, String> env) {
  return Flux
    .fromIterable(env.entrySet())
    .flatMap(
    kv -> cf.applications().setEnvironmentVariable(
      SetEnvironmentVariableApplicationRequest.builder().name(applicationName)
        .variableName(kv.getKey()).variableValue(kv.getValue()).build())).then();
}
}
```

❶ First, we push the application binary (the path), specifying a buildpack, memory, and deployment properties like instance count. Importantly, we do *not* start the application yet. We'll do that *after* the environment variables and services are bound. This step is automatically handled for you when you use Cloud Foundry manifests.

❷ Bind the service instances to our application.

❸ Set environment variables for the application.

❹ And, finally, start the application.

Running the whole thing takes little time, and even less once you tune it by specifying that certain branches of the flow should be run on different threads. The Cloud Foundry Java client is very powerful, and one of the authors' favorite ways to describe complex systems. It's also very handy when the deployment requires more than a trivial amount of shell scripting.

Summary

In this chapter we looked ever so briefly at getting started with Spring Boot and supporting tools like the Spring Tool Suite, creating the Java configuration, and then moving that application to a cloud environment. We've automated the deployment of the code to a production environment, and it wouldn't be hard to stand up a continuous integration flow using Jenkins or Bamboo. In the next chapters, we'll look more heavily at all things Spring Boot and Cloud Foundry.

## CHAPTER 3

Twelve-Factor Application Style Configuration

In this chapter, we'll look at how to externalize application configuration.

The Confusing Conflation of "Configuration"

Let's establish some vocabulary. When we talk about *configuration* in Spring, we've *usually* talked about the inputs into the Spring framework's various `ApplicationCon text` (*http://bit.ly/2rjucwJ*) implementations that help the container understand how you want beans wired together. This might be an XML file to be fed into a `Class PathXmlApplicationContext` (*http://bit.ly/2rj2oZb*), or Java classes annotated a certain way to be fed into an `AnnotationConfigApplicationContext` (*http://bit.ly/ 2rjzd8j*). Indeed, when we talk about the latter, we refer to it as *Java configuration*.

In this chapter, however, we're going to look at configuration as it is defined in the Twelve-Factor application manifesto (*http://12factor.net/config*). In this instance, configuration refers to literal values that may change from one environment to another: things like passwords, ports and hostnames, or feature flags. This configuration defies magic constants embedded in the code. The manifesto provides a great litmus test for whether configuration has been done correctly: could the codebase of an application be open sourced at any moment without exposing and compromising important credentials? This sort of configuration refers only to the values that change from one environment to another; not, for example, to Spring bean wiring or Ruby route configuration.

Support in Spring Framework

Spring has supported twelve-factor–style configuration since the `PropertyPlacehol`
`derConfigurer` (*http://bit.ly/2riQBKw*) class was introduced. Once an instance is
defined, it replaces literals in the XML configuration with values that it resolved in
a `.properties` file. Spring's offered the `PropertyPlaceholderConfigurer` (*http://bit.ly/2rj5ixb*) since 2003. Spring 2.5 introduced XML namespace support, and with
it, XML namespace support for property placeholder resolution. This lets us substi-
tute bean definition literal values in the XML configuration for values assigned to
keys in an external property file (in this case, `simple.properties`, which may be on
the classpath or external to the application).

Twelve-factor–style configuration aims to eliminate the fragility of having *magic
strings*—values like database locators and credentials, ports, etc.—hardcoded in the
compiled application. If configuration is externalized, then it can be replaced without
requiring a rebuild of the code.

The PropertyPlaceholderConfigurer

Let's look at an example using the `PropertyPlaceholderConfigurer`, Spring XML
bean definitions, and an externalized `.properties` file. We simply want to print out
the value in the property file, which looks like Example 3-1.

Example 3-1. A property file: some.properties

```
configuration.projectName=Spring Framework
```

This is a Spring `ClassPathXmlApplicationContext`, so we use the Spring context
XML namespace and point it to our `some.properties` file. Then, in the bean definitions, use literals of the form `${configuration.projectName}` and Spring will
replace them at runtime with the values from our property file (Example 3-2).

Example 3-2. A Spring XML configuration file

```
<context:property-placeholder location="classpath:some.properties"/> ❶

<bean class="classic.Application">
    <property name="configurationProjectName" value="${configuration.projectName}"/>
</bean>
```

❶ A `classpath:` location refers to a file in the current compiled code unit
(`.jar`, `.war`, etc.). Spring supports many alternatives, including `file:` and `url:`,
that would let the file live external to the compiled unit.

Finally, here's a Java class to pull it all together (Example 3-3).

Example 3-3. A Java class that is to be configured with the property value

```
package classic;

import org.apache.commons.logging.LogFactory;
import org.springframework.context.support.ClassPathXmlApplicationContext;

public class Application {

 public static void main(String[] args) {
  new ClassPathXmlApplicationContext("classic.xml");
 }

 public void setConfigurationProjectName(String pn) {
  LogFactory.getLog(getClass()).info("the configuration project name is " + pn);
 }
}
```

The first examples used Spring's XML bean configuration format. Spring 3.0 and 3.1 improved things considerably for developers using Java configuration. These releases saw the introduction of the @Value annotation and the Environment abstraction.

The Environment Abstraction and @Value

The Environment (*http://bit.ly/2s3GiHf*) abstraction provides a bit of runtime indirection between the running application and the environment in which it is running, and lets the application ask questions ("what's the current platform's line.separa tor?") about the environment. The Environment acts as a map of keys and values. You can configure where those values are read from by configuring a Property Source on the Environment. By default, Spring loads up system environment keys and values, like line.separator. You can tell Spring to load up configuration keys from a file, specifically and in a fashion similar to what you may have done with earlier editions of Spring's property placeholder resolution, using the @PropertySource annotation.

The @Value annotation provides a way to inject environment values into constructors, setters, fields, etc. These values can be computed using the Spring Expression Language or using the property placeholder syntax, assuming one registers a PropertySourcesPlaceholderConfigurer (*http://bit.ly/2s3TQCz*), as we do in Example 3-4.

Example 3-4. Registering a PropertySourcesPlaceholderConfigurer

```
package env;
```

```
import org.apache.commons.logging.Log;
import org.apache.commons.logging.LogFactory;
import org.springframework.beans.factory.InitializingBean;
import org.springframework.beans.factory.annotation.Autowired;
import org.springframework.beans.factory.annotation.Value;
import org.springframework.context.annotation.AnnotationConfigApplicationContext;
import org.springframework.context.annotation.Bean;
import org.springframework.context.annotation.Configuration;
import org.springframework.context.annotation.PropertySource;
import org.springframework.context.support.PropertySourcesPlaceholderConfigurer;
import org.springframework.core.env.Environment;

import javax.annotation.PostConstruct;
```

❶
```
@Configuration
@PropertySource("some.properties")
public class Application {

  private final Log log = LogFactory.getLog(getClass());

  public static void main(String[] args) throws Throwable {
    new AnnotationConfigApplicationContext(Application.class);
  }
```

❷
```
  @Bean
  static PropertySourcesPlaceholderConfigurer pspc() {
    return new PropertySourcesPlaceholderConfigurer();
  }
```

❸
```
  @Value("${configuration.projectName}")
  private String fieldValue;
```

❹
```
  @Autowired
  Application(@Value("${configuration.projectName}") String pn) {
    log.info("Application constructor: " + pn);
  }
```

❺
```
  @Value("${configuration.projectName}")
  void setProjectName(String projectName) {
    log.info("setProjectName: " + projectName);
  }
```

❻
```
  @Autowired
  void setEnvironment(Environment env) {
    log.info("setEnvironment: " + env.getProperty("configuration.projectName"));
  }
```

❼
```
@Bean
InitializingBean both(Environment env,
 @Value("${configuration.projectName}") String projectName) {
 return () -> {
  log.info("@Bean with both dependencies (projectName): " + projectName);
  log.info("@Bean with both dependencies (env): "
   + env.getProperty("configuration.projectName"));
 };
}

@PostConstruct
void afterPropertiesSet() throws Throwable {
 log.info("fieldValue: " + this.fieldValue);
}
}
```

❶ The @PropertySource annotation is a shortcut, like property-placeholder, that configures a PropertySource from a .properties file.

❷ You need to register the PropertySourcesPlaceholderConfigurer as a static bean, because it is an implementation of BeanFactoryPostProcessor and must be invoked earlier in the Spring bean initialization life cycle. This nuance is invisible when you're using Spring's XML bean configuration.

❸ You can decorate fields with the @Value annotation (but don't! it frustrates testing)...

❹ ...or you can decorate constructor parameters with the @Value annotation...

❺ ...or you can use setters methods...

❻ ...or you can inject the Spring Environment object and resolve the key manually.

❼ You can use @Value annotatedparameters in Spring Java configuration @Bean provider method arguments, as well.

This example loads up the values from a file, simple.properties, and then has one value, configuration.projectName, made available in a variety of ways.

Profiles

The Environment also brings in *profiles* (*http://bit.ly/2s3RjbM*). It lets you ascribe labels (profiles) to groupings of beans. Use profiles to describe beans and bean graphs that change from one environment to another. You can activate one or more profiles at a time. Beans that do not have a profile assigned to them are always activated. Beans that have the profile default are activated only when there are no other active profiles. You can specify the profile attribute in bean definitions in XML, or alternatively, tag classes, configuration classes, individual beans, or @Bean-provider methods with @Profile.

Profiles let you describe sets of beans that need to be created differently in one environment versus another. You might, for example, use an embedded H2 javax.sql.DataSource in your local dev profile, but then switch to a javax.sql.DataSource for PostgreSQL that's resolved through a JNDI lookup or by reading the properties from an environment variable in Cloud Foundry (*http://cloud foundry.org*) when the prod profile is active. In both cases, your code works: you get a javax.sql.DataSource, but the decision about *which* specialized instance is used is decided by the active profile or profiles (Example 3-5).

Example 3-5. The example demonstrates that @Configuration classes can load different configuration files and contribute different beans based on the active profile

```
package profiles;

import org.apache.commons.logging.Log;
import org.apache.commons.logging.LogFactory;
import org.springframework.beans.factory.InitializingBean;
import org.springframework.beans.factory.annotation.Value;
import org.springframework.context.annotation.*;
import org.springframework.context.support.PropertySourcesPlaceholderConfigurer;
import org.springframework.core.env.Environment;
import org.springframework.util.StringUtils;

@Configuration
public class Application {

  private Log log = LogFactory.getLog(getClass());

  @Bean
  static PropertySourcesPlaceholderConfigurer pspc() {
   return new PropertySourcesPlaceholderConfigurer();
  }

  ❶
  @Configuration
  @Profile("prod")
  @PropertySource("some-prod.properties")
  public static class ProdConfiguration {

   @Bean
   InitializingBean init() {
    return () -> LogFactory.getLog(getClass()).info("prod InitializingBean");
```

```
  }
}

@Configuration
@Profile({ "default", "dev" })
❷
@PropertySource("some.properties")
public static class DefaultConfiguration {

  @Bean
  InitializingBean init() {
    return () -> LogFactory.getLog(getClass()).info("default InitializingBean");
  }
}

❸
@Bean
InitializingBean which(Environment e,
                       @Value("${configuration.projectName}") String projectName) {
  return () -> {
    log.info("activeProfiles: '"
          + StringUtils.arrayToCommaDelimitedString(e.getActiveProfiles()) + "'");
    log.info("configuration.projectName: " + projectName);
  };
}

public static void main(String[] args) {
  AnnotationConfigApplicationContext ac = new AnnotationConfigApplicationContext();
  ac.getEnvironment().setActiveProfiles("dev"); ❹
  ac.register(Application.class);
  ac.refresh();
}
}
```

❶ This configuration class and all the @Bean definitions therein will only be evaluated if the prod profile is active.

❷ This configuration class and all the @Bean definitions therein will only be evaluated if the dev profile *or* **no** profile—including dev—is active.

❸ This InitializingBean simply records the currently active profile and injects the value that was ultimately contributed by the property file.

❹ It's easy to programmatically activate a profile (or profiles).

Spring responds to a few other methods for activating profiles using the token spring_profiles_active or spring.profiles.active. You can set the profile using an environment variable (e.g., SPRING_PROFILES_ACTIVE), a JVM property (-

Dspring.profiles.active=..), a Servlet application initialization parameter, or programmatically.

Bootiful Configuration

Spring Boot (*http://spring.io/projects/spring-boot*) improves things considerably. Spring Boot will automatically load properties from a hierarchy of well-known places by default. The command-line arguments override property values contributed from JNDI, which override properties contributed from System.getProperties(), etc.

- Command-line arguments
- JNDI attributes from java:comp/env
- System.getProperties() properties
- OS environment variables
- External property files on filesystem: (config/)?application.(yml.proper ties)
- Internal property files in archive (config/)?application.(yml.properties)
- @PropertySource annotation on configuration classes
- Default properties from SpringApplication.getDefaultProperties()

If a profile is active (*http://bit.ly/2s3ytl0*), it will also automatically read in the configuration files based on the profile name, like *src/main/resources/application-foo.properties* where foo is the current profile.

If the SnakeYAML library (*https://bitbucket.org/asomov/snakeyaml*) is on the classpath, then it will also automatically load YAML files following basically the same convention.

 From the YAML specification's page (*http://yaml.org*), "YAML is a human friendly data serialization standard for all programming languages." YAML is a hierarchical representation of values. Where traditional *.properties* files specify hierarchy with a dot ("."), YAML files use a newline and an extra level of indenting. It can be refreshing to avoid having to specify common roots if you have extensive configuration trees.

Example 3-6 is an example *.yml* file.

Example 3-6. An application.yml property file. Data is hierarchical.

```
configuration:
  projectName : Spring Boot
management:
  security:
    enabled: false
```

Spring Boot also makes it much simpler to get the right result in common cases. It makes -D arguments to the java process and environment variables available as properties. It even normalizes them, so an environment variable $CONFIGURATION_PROJ ECTNAME or a -D argument of the form -Dconfiguration.projectname both become accessible with the key configuration.projectName in the same way that the spring_profiles_active token was earlier.

Configuration values are strings, and if you have enough configuration values it can be unwieldy trying to make sure those keys don't themselves become magic strings in the code. Spring Boot introduces a @ConfigurationProperties component type. Annotate a POJO—a Plain Old Java Object—with @ConfigurationProperties and specify a prefix, and Spring will attempt to map all properties that start with that prefix to the POJO's properties. In the example below, the value for configuration.proj ectName will be mapped to an instance of the POJO that all code can then inject and dereference to read the (type-safe) values. In this way, you only have the mapping from a (String) key in one place (Example 3-7).

Example 3-7. Properties are resolved automatically from src/main/resources/ application.yml

```
package boot;

import org.apache.commons.logging.Log;
import org.apache.commons.logging.LogFactory;
import org.springframework.beans.factory.annotation.Autowired;
import org.springframework.boot.SpringApplication;
import org.springframework.boot.autoconfigure.SpringBootApplication;
import org.springframework.boot.context.properties.ConfigurationProperties;
import org.springframework.boot.context.properties.EnableConfigurationProperties;
import org.springframework.stereotype.Component;

❶
@EnableConfigurationProperties
@SpringBootApplication
public class Application {

  private final Log log = LogFactory.getLog(getClass());

  public static void main(String[] args) {
    SpringApplication.run(Application.class);
```

```
    }

    @Autowired
    public Application(ConfigurationProjectProperties cp) {
     log.info("configurationProjectProperties.projectName = "
       + cp.getProjectName());
    }
    }

    ❷
    @Component
    @ConfigurationProperties("configuration")
    class ConfigurationProjectProperties {

     private String projectName; ❸

     public String getProjectName() {
      return projectName;
     }

     public void setProjectName(String projectName) {
      this.projectName = projectName;
     }
    }
```

❶ The @EnableConfigurationProperties annotation tells Spring to map proper-
    ties to POJOs annotated with @ConfigurationProperties.

❷ @ConfigurationProperties tells Spring that this bean is to be used as the root
    for all properties starting with configuration., with subsequent tokens mapped
    to properties on the object.

❸ The projectName field would ultimately have the value assigned to the property
    key configuration.projectName.

Spring Boot uses the @ConfigurationProperties mechanism extensively to let users
override bits of the system. You can see what property keys can be used to change
things, for example, by adding the org.springframework.boot:spring-boot-
starter-actuator dependency to a Spring Boot-based web application and then visiting http://127.0.0.1:8080/configprops.

> The Actuator endpoints are further discussed in Chapter 13. The
> endpoints are locked down, and require a username and password
> by default. You can disable security (if only to take a peek) by speci-
> fying management.security.enabled=false in your applica
> tion.properties file (or application.yml).

This will give you a list of supported configuration properties based on the types present on the classpath at runtime. As you add more Spring Boot types, you'll see more properties. This endpoint will *also* reflect the properties exported by your @ConfigurationProperties-annotated POJO.

Centralized, Journaled Configuration with the Spring Cloud Configuration Server

So far so good, but we'll need to do better. We're still missing answers for some common use cases:

- Changes to an application's configuration, as configured, would require restarts.
- There is no traceability: how do we determine what changes were introduced into production and, if necessary, roll back those changes?
- Configuration is decentralized; it's not immediately apparent where to go to change what.
- There is no out-of-the-box support for encryption and decryption for security.

The Spring Cloud Config Server

We could address the centralization of configuration by storing configuration in a single directory and pointing all applications to that directory. We could also version control the directory, using Git or Subversion. That would give us the support we desire for auditing and journaling. It still doesn't solve the last two requirements; we need something a bit more sophisticated. Let's look at the Spring Cloud Config Server (*http://cloud.spring.io/spring-cloud-config/*). Spring Cloud offers a configuration server and a client for the configuration server.

The Spring Cloud Config Server is a REST API to which our clients will connect to draw their configuration. It manages a version-controlled repository of configuration, too. It sits in between our clients and the repository of configuration and so is in an enviable position to interpose security on the communication from the clients to the service and on the communication from the service to the version-controlled repository of configuration. The Spring Cloud Config client contributes a new scope to client applications, the refresh scope, that allows us to reconfigure Spring components without restarting the application.

Technologies like the Spring Cloud Config Server are important, but they will add a cost to your operational overhead. Ideally, this competency should be managed by the platform, and automated. If you're using Cloud Foundry, there is a Config Server service, based on the Spring Cloud Config Server, in the service catalog.

Let's look at a simple example. First, we'll set up a Spring Cloud Config Server. Many Spring Boot applications may access a single configuration service. You have to get it running, somewhere, once. Then all other services need only know where to find the configuration service. The configuration service acts as a sort of proxy for configuration keys and values that it reads from a Git repository online or on a disk. Add `org.springframework.cloud : spring-cloud-config-server` to your Spring Boot application's build to bring in the Spring Cloud Config Server (Example 3-8).

Example 3-8. Use the @EnableConfigServer annotation to build a Config Server

```
package demo;

import org.springframework.boot.SpringApplication;
import org.springframework.boot.autoconfigure.SpringBootApplication;
import org.springframework.cloud.config.server.EnableConfigServer;

❶
@SpringBootApplication
@EnableConfigServer
public class Application {

 public static void main(String[] args) {
   SpringApplication.run(Application.class, args);
 }
}
```

❶ `@EnableConfigServer` installs the Spring Cloud Config Server.

Example 3-9 shows the configuration for the configuration service.

Example 3-9. The configuration server's configuration, src/main/resources/ application.yml

```
server.port=8888
spring.cloud.config.server.git.uri=\
  https://github.com/cloud-native-java/config-server-configuration-repository ❶
```

❶ Points to the working Git repository, either local or over the network (e.g., on GitHub (*http://github.com*)), that the Spring Cloud Config Server is to use.

This tells the Spring Cloud configuration service to look for configuration files for individual clients in the Git repository on GitHub. We specified a GitHub repository, but any valid Git URI would work. Indeed, it doesn't even have to be Git; you can use Subversion or even unmanaged directories (though we'd strongly discourage it). Here, we hardcoded the URI for the repository, but there's no reason it couldn't have come in from a `-D` argument, a `--` argument, or an environment variable.

Spring Cloud Config Clients

To play well in the Spring Cloud ecosystem, Spring Boot applications should provide a name. Set `spring.application.name` to a unique, useful, easily remembered name, something like `customer-service`. A Spring Cloud-based service looks for a file called `src/main/resources/bootstrap.(properties,yml)` that it expects to find to —you guessed it!—bootstrap the service. There, Spring Cloud will look for the name of the service (`spring.application.name`) and the location of the Spring Cloud Config Server from which it should draw its configuration. This file (`bootstrap.properties`) gets loaded earlier than other property files (including `application.yml` or `application.properties`). It makes sense: this file tells Spring where it's to find the rest of the application's configuration. If you have both an `application.properties` and a `bootstrap.properties`, `bootstrap.properties` will be loaded earlier.

The Config Server manages a directory full of `.properties` or `.yml` files. Spring Cloud serves configuration to connected clients by matching the client's `spring.application.name` to the configuration file in the directory. Thus, a configuration client that identifies itself as `foo-service` would see the configuration in `foo-service.yml` or `foo-service.properties`.

Run the Config Server and verify that your configuration service is working; point your browser to `http://localhost:8888/SERVICE/master` where `SERVICE` is the name you specify as `spring.application.name`. In our Git repository, there is a single file called `configuration-client.properties`. Use `configuration-client` as the value for `SERVICE`. We can see the JSON created for this configuration file in Figure 3-1.

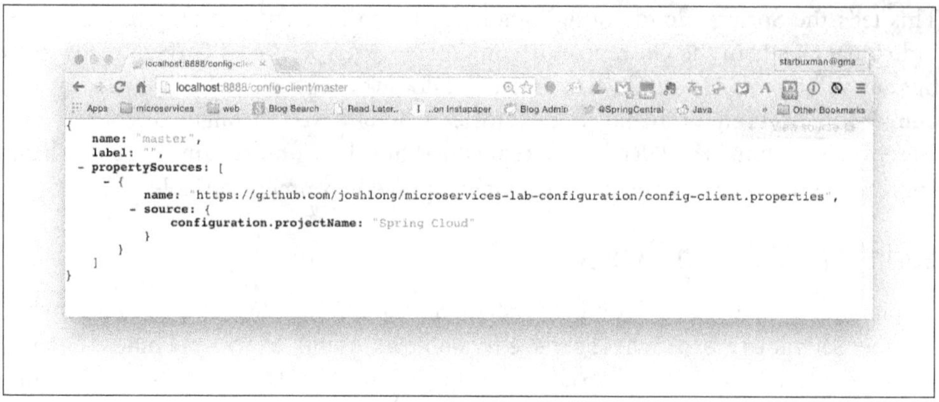

Figure 3-1. The output of the Spring Cloud Config Server confirming that it sees the configuration in our Git repository

Example 3-10 shows our configuration client's `bootstrap.yml`.

Example 3-10. bootstrap.yml example

```
spring:
  application:
    name: configuration-client
  cloud:
    config:
      uri: ${vcap.services.configuration-service.credentials.uri:http://localhost:↵
8888}
```

The Spring Cloud Config Server returns client-specific configuration by matching on the `spring.application.name`, but it can return global configuration—configuration that is visible to *every* client—from a file named `application.properties` or `application.yml` in the Spring Cloud Config Server's repository.

The configuration service returns JSON that contains all the configuration values in the `application.(properties,yml)` file as well as any service-specific configuration in `configuration-client.(yml,properties)`. It will *also* load any configuration for a given service *and* a specific profile, e.g., `configuration-client-dev.properties`, where `configuration-client` is the name of the client and `dev` is the name of a profile under which the client is running.

The values in the Spring Cloud Config Server are, from the perspective of any Spring Boot application, just another `PropertySource`, and resolvable in all the usual ways: through `@Value`-annotated class members as well as from the `Environment` abstraction.

Security

If your Git repository is secured, with HTTP BASIC, for example, then define `spring.cloud.config.server.git.username` and `spring.cloud.con fig.server.git.password` properties for the Spring Cloud Config Server to permit access to secured Git repositories.

You can protect the Spring Cloud Configuration Server itself with HTTP BASIC authentication as well. The easiest is to just include `org.springframework.boot : spring-boot-starter-security` and then define a `security.user.name` and a `security.user.password` property. The `spring-boot-starter-security` starter brings in Spring Security, so you could plug in a particular Spring Security `UserDe tailsService` implementation to override how authentication is handled.

The Spring Cloud Config Clients can encode the user and password in the `spring.cloud.config.uri` value—for example, `https://user:secret@host.com`.

Refreshable Configuration

Centralized configuration is a powerful thing, but changes to configuration aren't immediately visible to the beans that depend on it. Spring Cloud's *refresh* scope (and the convenient `@RefreshScope` annotation) offer a solution. Let's look at an example, `ProjectNameRestController`, in Example 3-11.

Example 3-11. A Config Server client application

```
package demo;

import org.springframework.beans.factory.annotation.Autowired;
import org.springframework.beans.factory.annotation.Value;
import org.springframework.cloud.context.config.annotation.RefreshScope;
import org.springframework.web.bind.annotation.RequestMapping;
import org.springframework.web.bind.annotation.RestController;

❶
@RestController
@RefreshScope
class ProjectNameRestController {

 private final String projectName;

 @Autowired
 public ProjectNameRestController(
  @Value("${configuration.projectName}") String pn) { ❷
  this.projectName = pn;
 }
```

```
@RequestMapping("/project-name")
String projectName() {
  return this.projectName;
 }
}
```

❶ The @RefreshScope makes this bean refreshable.

❷ Spring resolves the configuration value from the Config Server, which is just
   another PropertySource in the Environment.

The ProjectNameRestController is annotated with the @RefreshScope (*http://bit.ly/*
2s40VDm) annotation, a Spring Cloud-contributed scope that lets any bean recreate
itself (and re-read configuration values from the configuration service) in place. In
this case, the ProjectNameRestController will be recreated—its life cycle callbacks
honored, and @Value and @Autowired injects reestablished—whenever a *refresh* event
is triggered.

Fundamentally, all *refresh*-scoped beans will refresh themselves when they receive a
Spring ApplicationContext event of the type RefreshScopeRefreshedEvent. The
default implementation recreates any beans annotated with @RefreshScope, discard-
ing the entire bean and creating it anew. There's no reason your components can't also
respond to this event if you have a refreshable state that isn't otherwise tied to external values in the Spring Cloud Config server. Example 3-12 shows a simple component that simply increments a counter for every refresh event.

Example 3-12. A Config Server client application

```
package demo;

import org.apache.commons.logging.Log;
import org.apache.commons.logging.LogFactory;
import org.springframework.cloud.context.scope.refresh.RefreshScopeRefreshedEvent;
import org.springframework.context.event.EventListener;
import org.springframework.stereotype.Component;

import java.util.concurrent.atomic.AtomicLong;

@Component
public class RefreshCounter {

  private final Log log = LogFactory.getLog(getClass());

  private final AtomicLong counter = new AtomicLong(0); ❶

  ❷
  @EventListener
  public void refresh(RefreshScopeRefreshedEvent e) {
```

```
  this.log.info("The refresh count is now at: "
    + this.counter.incrementAndGet());
 }
}
```

❶ The component keeps an atomic counter…

❷ …that updates itself every time a RefreshScopeRefreshedEvent is observed.

There are various ways to trigger it. You can trigger the refresh by sending an empty
POST request to http://127.0.0.1:8080/refresh, which is a Spring Boot Actuator
endpoint that is exposed automatically. Example 3-13 shows how to do that using
curl.

*Example 3-13. Trigger a refresh event using the Spring Cloud Config Client on the /
refresh Actuator endpoint on a single instance*

```
curl -d{} http://127.0.0.1:8080/refresh
```

Alternatively, you can use the auto-configured Spring Boot Actuator JMX refresh
endpoint, as seen in Figure 3-2.

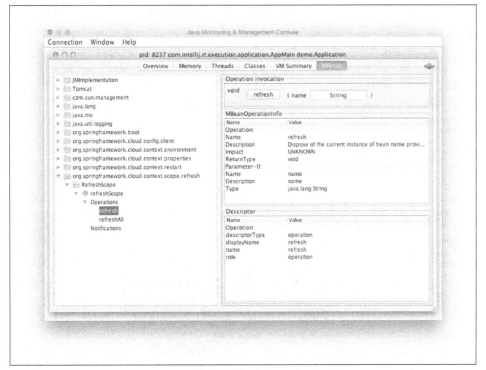

Figure 3-2. Using jconsole to activate the refresh (or refreshAll) Actuator endpoints

To see all this in action, make changes to the configuration file in Git, and at the very least git commit them. Then invoke the REST endpoint or the JMX endpoint on the node you want to see the configuration changed in, *not* the configuration server.

Both of those Spring Boot Actuator endpoints work on an ApplicationContext-by-ApplicationContext basis. If you have 10 running applications and want to see the updated configuration in all 10, then you'll need to call the Actuator on each instance. This is not very scalable!

The Spring Cloud Bus supports refreshing multiple ApplicationContext instances (e.g., many nodes) in one go. The Spring Cloud Bus (*http://cloud.spring.io/spring-cloud-bus/*) links all services through a Spring Cloud Stream–powered bus. Spring Cloud Stream supports different messaging technologies through its binder abstraction, implementations of which it provides for RabbitMQ, Apache Kafka, the Reactor Project, and more. You'll learn more about Spring Cloud Stream later in "Spring Cloud Stream" on page 344.

This is particularly powerful. You can tell one (or thousands!) of microservices to refresh themselves by sending a single message to a message bus. This prevents downtime and is friendlier than having to systematically restart individual services or nodes. Add the Spring Cloud Bus dependency for RabbitMQ (org.springframe work.cloud: spring-cloud-starter-bus-amqp) to the classpath.

Spring Boot's auto-configuration for RabbitMQ will attempt to connect to a local RabbitMQ instance by default. You can configure the specific host and port with properties contributed to the Spring Environment. It's convenient to keep all this configuration in a single place, in, say, the Spring Cloud Config Server. This way, *all* services that connect to the configuration service will *also* talk to the right RabbitMQ instance (Example 3-14).

Example 3-14. Specifying a RabbitMQ ConnectionFactory

```
spring:
  rabbitmq:
    host: my-rmq-host
    port: 5672
    username: user
    password: secret
```

These configuration values get fed to the Spring Boot AMQP auto-configuration and result in a ConnectionFactory instance. The Spring Cloud Bus client listens for messages, and on their receipt triggers a refresh event. If you have multiple Connection Factory instances in the Spring application context, you can *qualify* which instance, specifically, is to be used with the @BusConnectionFactory annotation. Qualify any other instance to be used for regular, non-bus-related processing, with Spring qualifier annotation, @Primary.

The Spring Cloud Bus exposes a *different* Actuator endpoint, /bus/refresh publish a message to the connected RabbitMQ broker that will trigger *all* cc nodes to refresh themselves. You can send the following message to *any* node spring-cloud-starter-bus-amqp auto-configuration, and it'll trigger a refres... *all* the connected nodes (Example 3-15).

Example 3-15. Trigger a refresh event with the Spring Cloud Event Bus

```
curl -d{} http://127.0.0.1:8080/bus/refresh
```

Summary

We've covered a *lot* here! Armed with all of this, it should be easy to package one artifact and then move that artifact from one environment to another without changes to the artifact itself.

## CHAPTER 4

Testing

A cloud native application is optimized for fast feedback at every tier, from components all the way to entire systems. Testing is the primary way to drive that feedback loop. Microservices come in systems. Spring Boot provides robust integration testing support: support to help capture the integration between components in a system.

As applications become increasingly distributed, the strategies for how we effectively write tests change considerably. The practice of *integration testing* focuses on writing and executing tests against a group of software modules that depend on one another. Integration testing is a standard practice in software development where developers who are working on separate modules or components are able to automate a set of test cases which exist to ensure that the expected functionality of integration remains true—*especially* when changes are made to code that affects an integration. It can often be the case that integration testing requires executing tests in a shared integration environment. In this scenario, applications may be subject to concurrently sharing external resources, such as a database or an application server.

Cloud native applications are designed to take advantage of the ephemeral nature of a cloud environment; we should focus on designing integration tests so that they can be executed in an ephemeral environment that is decoupled from other applications. In many cases, cloud native applications depend on backing services. Where necessary, these dependencies should be mocked so that integration tests can be executed in a decoupled build and test environment. When mocking an external dependency becomes untenable, any external backing service should be provisioned on-demand and torn down when testing has completed.

In this chapter we will focus on testing, generally, and on two primary integration testing topics. The first topic will be about how to design and create basic integration tests for Spring Boot applications. Here we will explore the tools and features of

Spring that are critical to how we create meaningful integration tests that are decoupled from external dependencies.

The second topic we will explore will be how to perform end-to-end integration testing in a microservice architecture. Here we will focus on the various forms of testing that execute over a collection of different services in a fully formed test environment that resembles production.

The Makeup of a Test

In this chapter, we'll assume you have a solid understanding of JUnit and Maven. We're going to be looking at integration testing, in particular. In our examples, all the tests will live in `src/test/{java,resources}`, though many organizations go so far as to set up a separate test-source tree for integration tests, so that it's clear what is meant to be run constantly, and quickly, and what is meant to be run less frequently— perhaps on every check-in or after major refactoring. Whatever your organizational approach, be sure that you automate running **all** the tests before promoting a binary closer to production.

Testing in Spring Boot

Testing in Spring Boot applications breaks down into two separate styles of testing: unit tests and integration tests. An integration test is any test that requires access to the Spring application context (the `ApplicationContext`) during test execution. Unit tests are written in such a way that a Spring application context is not required.

Add a test scoped dependency, `org.springframework.boot : spring-boot-starter-test`, to your `pom.xml` to enable testing support in your Spring Boot application. If you use the Spring Initializr (*http://start.spring.io*) to generate new projects (and you should!), this is done for you already.

In Example 4-1, we see a simple integration test inside a class `ApplicationTests`. The goal of the test named `contextLoads` is to assert that the `ApplicationContext` was successfully loaded and injected into the field named `applicationContext`. Simple, like the "hello world" of integration tests with Spring.

Example 4-1. Basic integration test loads the ApplicationContext

```
package demo;

import org.junit.Assert;
import org.junit.Test;
import org.junit.runner.RunWith;
import org.springframework.beans.factory.annotation.Autowired;
import org.springframework.boot.test.context.SpringBootTest;
```

```
import org.springframework.context.ApplicationContext;
import org.springframework.test.context.junit4.SpringRunner;

@SpringBootTest
@RunWith(SpringRunner.class)
public class ApplicationContextTests {

  @Autowired
  private ApplicationContext applicationContext;

  @Test
  public void contextLoads() throws Throwable {
   Assert.assertNotNull("the application context should have loaded.",
    this.applicationContext);
  }
}
```

There are two annotations on the `ApplicationTests` class, named `@RunWith` and `@SpringBootTest`. The `@RunWith` annotation is specific to the JUnit framework. The `@RunWith` annotation tells JUnit which test runner strategy to use. In this case, we want to run our test with the *Spring TestContext Framework*, a module in the Spring Framework that provides generic test support for Spring applications.

SpringRunner was introduced in Spring Boot 1.4. It is a more memorable and JUnit 5-ready alternative to the Spring Framework's `SpringJUnit4ClassRunner`, with which some of you may be more familiar.

The second annotation on the `ApplicationTests` class is `@SpringBootTest`. The `@SpringBootTest` annotation indicates that this class is a Spring Boot test class, and provides support to scan for a `ContextConfiguration` that tells the test class how to load the `ApplicationContext`. If no `ContextConfiguration` classes are specified as a parameter to the `@SpringBootTest` annotation, the default behavior is to load the `ApplicationContext` by scanning for a `@SpringBootConfiguration` annotation on a class in the package root.

As was explained earlier in Chapter 2, the `@SpringBootApplica` `tion` annotation is a *stereotype* definition that combines multiple lower-level annotations in a Spring Boot application. One of the lower-level nested annotations of `@SpringBootApplication` is the `@SpringBootConfiguration` annotation. This is how a `@Spring` `BootTest` class will find the application class that loads the correct `ApplicationContext`.

In Example 4-2, we see the folder structure of a basic Spring Boot application's source code. Notice that there are two source roots for the application, both with identical package structures. For the test methods inside the `ApplicationTests.java` file to be able to successfully scan and find the Spring Boot application class contained in `Application.java`—being annotated with `@SpringBootApplication`—the package structure should be identical in each of the source roots.

Example 4-2. The basic structure of a new Spring Boot project

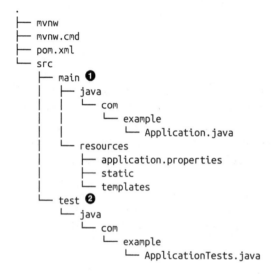

❶   The source root containing the application class

❷   The test source root containing the application's test classes

`Application.java` is a straightforward `main(String[] args)` method in a class with a `@SpringBootApplication` annotation.

Now that we have the basics covered on how the Spring Boot test starter dependency can be used to create an auto-configured JUnit test class, we can begin to design and create integration tests that target the interactions between various components that are loaded in an `ApplicationContext`.

Integration Testing

As was mentioned earlier, there are two styles of tests you'll want to create for your Spring Boot application: *unit tests* and *integration tests*. The main difference between the two styles of tests is that integration tests require a Spring context to test the integration between different components, and unit tests will test individual components

---

without any dependency on the Spring libraries. In this section we're going to focus strictly on writing integration tests in a Spring Boot application.

Spring Boot's auto-configuration can make it challenging to write integration tests and unit tests because it could be hard to isolate the things that change from one environment to another.

One of the important guidelines from the twelve-factor application methodology states that we should make sure to minimize the divergence between development and production. For most application frameworks other than Spring Boot, it would likely be important to follow this advice with strict reverence when building a cloud native application. For a cloud native Spring Boot application, the rules with regard to dev/prod parity can be bent somewhat, since auto-configuration allows us to switch external dependencies for mocked dependencies. Indeed, there is certainly a place for testing the end-to-end behavior of an application in an environment that exactly mirrors the backing services used in production—but more on that in Chapter 15.

Test Slices

Before Spring Boot 1.4 was released, integration tests were mostly written to be executed after loading the full Spring context of your application. In many ways this was a cumbersome side effect of auto-configuration, since not all integration tests will need access to a full `ApplicationContext`.

For example, what if I wanted to only test serialization and marshaling of Java objects to and from JSON? In this case there is little need to load auto-configuration for *Spring MVC* or *Spring Data JPA*. Do we really need a servlet container to be loaded if we're just testing JSON serialization? (No.) Spring Boot 1.4 or later support the notion of *test slices*–selective activation of slices of auto-configuration supporting discrete layers of the stack.

Test slices also provide the benefit of being able to cleanly swap out certain starter projects—for example, switching from *Spring Data JPA* to *Spring Data MongoDB*, without affecting integration tests unrelated to Spring Data. In addition to test slices, Spring Boot 1.4 includes more first-class support for writing integration test classes that allow developers to declaratively mock collaborating components in the Spring context using annotations.

Mocking in Tests

Mocking is usually talked about in the context of unit testing. In the simplest sense, *mock objects* allow us to isolate parts of the system under test by replacing collaborating components of a module with a simulated object that targets testing behavior in a controlled way. If one service module of an application requires access to an external backing service, perhaps taking the form of a call to another microservice, we can plug in a fake implementation of that backing service so that it becomes an invariant. The only variant is the component under test and its interaction with the mock.

Mocks in Spring Boot are a nuanced topic when talking about the differences between an integration test and a unit test. Mocks can be as useful in integration tests as they are in unit tests for a Spring Boot application. When writing integration tests in Spring Boot, it becomes possible to mock only selected components in the `Applica tionContext` of a test class. This helpful feature allows developers to test integrations between collaborating components while still being able to mock objects at the boundary of the application—the difference between a unit test and an integration test *still* being whether or not a Spring context is used at all. This distinction is important to remember and will aid communication between team members who are writing both unit tests and integration tests.

Spring Boot supports the `@MockBean` annotation. `@MockBean` instructs Spring to provide a mock of a bean in the application context, and to effectively *mute* the definition of the original, live bean in the application context. It creates a Mockito mock for a bean inside the `ApplicationContext`. In Example 4-3, we see the `AccountService Tests` class annotated with a `@RunWith(SpringRunner.class)` annotation—indicating that no `ApplicationContext` will be loaded during test execution. The component that is being tested in this class is the `AccountService` bean, which relies on an integration with an external microservice that is accessed through the `UserService` bean.

Example 4-3. Mocks the UserService and AccountRepository components using a @MockBean annotation

```
package demo.account;

import demo.user.User;
import demo.user.UserService;
import org.junit.Before;
import org.junit.Test;
import org.junit.runner.RunWith;
import org.springframework.boot.test.mock.mockito.MockBean;
import org.springframework.test.context.junit4.SpringRunner;

import java.util.Collections;
import java.util.List;

import static org.assertj.core.api.Assertions.assertThat;
import static org.mockito.BDDMockito.given;

@RunWith(SpringRunner.class)
public class AccountServiceTests {

    @MockBean
```

```
❶
private UserService userService;

@MockBean
private AccountRepository accountRepository;

private AccountService accountService;

@Before
public void before() {
  accountService = new AccountService(accountRepository, userService); ❷
}

@Test
public void getUserAccountsReturnsSingleAccount() throws Exception {
  given(this.accountRepository.findAccountsByUsername("user")).willReturn(
    Collections
      .singletonList(new Account("user", new AccountNumber("123456789")))); ❸

  given(this.userService.getAuthenticatedUser()).willReturn(
    new User(0L, "user", "John", "Doe")); ❹

  List<Account> actual = accountService.getUserAccounts(); ❺

  assertThat(actual).size().isEqualTo(1);
  assertThat(actual.get(0).getUsername()).isEqualTo("user");
  assertThat(actual.get(0).getAccountNumber()).isEqualTo(
    new AccountNumber("123456789"));
}
}
```

❶ Creates a Mockito mock for the UserService component.

❷ Creates a new instance of the AccountService with mocked components as parameters.

❸ Stubs the repository method call to findAccountsByUsername(String user name) with an Account list.

❹ Stubs the method call to getAuthenticatedUser() with a new instance of User.

❺ Calls the getUserAccounts() method of the AccountService while using the defined mocks.

In this example, we are mocking the behavior of collaborating components that will later need to be integration tested. In this unit test, we are able to test the functionality of the AccountService without making remote HTTP calls to a backing service inside the UserService bean. The same applies for the AccountRepository component. Normally this repository component would be defined as an auto-configured bean inside the ApplicationContext, which provides data management for an Account entity that is mapped to a table in a relational database. To reduce the complexity of testing just the functionality of the AccountService, we can create a mock for the AccountRepository component and describe the expected behavior of its test interaction. Now let's take a look at the contents of the AccountService, to understand better what it is doing.

The AccountService, the component that we are writing tests for, is defined in Example 4-4.

Example 4-4. The definition of the AccountService bean that depends on collaborating components

```
package demo.account;

import demo.user.UserService;
import org.springframework.beans.factory.annotation.Autowired;
import org.springframework.stereotype.Service;

import java.util.Collections;
import java.util.List;
import java.util.Optional;

@Service
public class AccountService {

  private final AccountRepository accountRepository;

  private final UserService userService; ❶

  @Autowired
  public AccountService(AccountRepository ar, UserService us) { ❷
    this.accountRepository = ar;
    this.userService = us;
  }

  public List<Account> getUserAccounts() {
    ❸
    return Optional.ofNullable(userService.getAuthenticatedUser())
      .map(u -> accountRepository.findAccountsByUsername(u.getUsername()))
      .orElse(Collections.emptyList());
  }
}
```

❶ The field for a UserService bean that will be injected through the constructor.

❷ Constructor-based injection will inject beans from the `ApplicationContext` for each parameter.

❸ The `getAuthenticatedUser()` method makes a remote HTTP call to a user microservice.

It's worth restating that the `AccountService` uses *constructor* injection. While we *could* have used field injection, we'd stymie our ability to understand what the component expects as preconditions in order to construct a valid object. *Always* use *constructor-based injection* instead of *field-based injection*. This is a good idea in general, but it takes on a whole new dimension when testing.

In `AccountService`, the Spring `ApplicationContext` provides a reference to the `AccountRepository`, if it is available. Create a new instance of `AccountService` and directly initialize the class with a mock object reference for the `AccountRepository` to override this behavior. Now our test class more closely resembles a unit test—which successfully isolates the functionality of the `AccountService` component from its collaborating dependencies.

Let's look at the `UserService` component. In its definition—shown in Example 4-5— the `UserService` class contains a single method that will make a remote HTTP call to a backing service's REST API in order to retrieve the authenticated `User`.

Example 4-5. The UserService bean makes remote HTTP calls to an external microservice

```
package demo.user;

import org.springframework.beans.factory.annotation.Autowired;
import org.springframework.beans.factory.annotation.Value;
import org.springframework.http.HttpHeaders;
import org.springframework.http.RequestEntity;
import org.springframework.stereotype.Service;
import org.springframework.web.client.RestTemplate;

import java.net.URI;

import static org.springframework.http.MediaType.APPLICATION_JSON_VALUE;
import static org.springframework.http.RequestEntity.get;

@Service
public class UserService {

  private final String serviceHost;

  private final RestTemplate restTemplate;
```

```
@Autowired
public UserService(RestTemplate restTemplate,
 @Value("${user-service.host:user-service}") String sh) {
 this.serviceHost = sh;
 this.restTemplate = restTemplate;
}

public User getAuthenticatedUser() {
 URI url = URI.create(String.format("http://%s/uaa/v1/me", serviceHost));
 RequestEntity<Void> request = get(url).header(HttpHeaders.CONTENT_TYPE,
  APPLICATION_JSON_VALUE).build();
 return restTemplate.exchange(request, User.class).getBody(); ❶
 }
}
```

❶ Makes a remote HTTP call to the specified URL and returns an instance of User.

In this fairly simple UserService component, we are using a RestTemplate to make a GET request to a remote dependency over HTTP. By creating a mock and stub for the getAuthenticatedUser method for the UserService defined in the AccountServi ceTests class, we further isolate the system under test by removing any dependency on an external service, as the remote resource may not be available in a build/test environment.

@MockBean is valuable for integration-testing a *Spring MVC* controller class that relies on multiple collaborating components that must integrate with remote services using HTTP—a common case for integration testing in microservices. Since we'll need a web environment for testing the *Spring MVC* controller, an ApplicationContext will be required. In this scenario we only want to create mocks for the services that make calls to remote applications. By mocking objects at the boundary of the web application, we can isolate test components from their remote web service dependencies. This allows us to integration-test the communication between modules of our application without going outside the boundaries of the JVM.

For integration tests that require a web environment, the @SpringBootTest annotation provides additional configurable parameters that refine how tests will run in a servlet environment.

Working with the Servlet Container in @SpringBootTest

As was mentioned earlier in the chapter, Spring Boot now provides multiple test annotations that help you target tests on specific slices of auto-configured classes.

Earlier in this chapter we saw an example of using @SpringBootTest to execute an integration test on a Spring Boot ApplicationContext. In a majority of cases, a Spring Boot application will need access to a servlet container—even if only to expose its health metrics from an HTTP endpoint. Traditionally, if a servlet container was required, we compiled a Spring MVC application as a `.war` artifact and deployed it to a running application server. Today, for Spring Boot applications, we recommend embedded `.jar` deployments.

The `@SpringBootTest` annotation should be used when you want to write integration tests on a fully configured `ApplicationContext` in a Spring Boot application. This annotation will also allow you to configure the servlet environment for your test context. `@SpringBootTest` supports a `webEnvironment` attribute to describe how Spring Boot should configure the embedded servlet container that your application uses at runtime. Table 4-1 summarizes some of the attributes for `@SpringBootTest`'s `webEnvironment` attribute.

Table 4-1. @SpringBootTest's webEnvironment attribute

Option	Description
MOCK	Loads a `WebApplicationContext` and provides a mock servlet environment.
DEFINED_PORT	Loads an `EmbeddedWebApplicationContext` and provides a real servlet environment on a defined port.
RANDOM_PORT	Loads an `EmbeddedWebApplicationContext` and provides a real servlet environment on a random port.
NONE	Loads an `ApplicationContext` using `SpringApplication` but does not provide any servlet environment (mock or otherwise).

Ultimately, the decision is about how long you want to delay feedback when running the tests. It's a trade-off between confidence in the result and speed of iteration.

In a majority of cases, a full-blown servlet environment may be overkill for your integration tests. The servlet container will need to be reloaded for every test class to run the tests contained within. While the time it takes to start a single servlet container will vary depending on the build/test environment, the total time it takes to execute each integration test may be unnecessarily long. In a world of continuous delivery and microservices, build time can easily become a limiting constraint.

Slices

Spring Boot provides multiple testing annotations that target a specific slice of your application.

@JsonTest

The `@JsonTest` annotation allows you to activate just the configuration to test JSON serialization and deserialization. Let's look at an example. We'll see the `UserTests` class that is annotated with `@JsonTest`. This class tests how the `User` object is serialized and deserialized (Example 4-6).

Example 4-6. Using @JsonTest to test JSON serialization/deserialization

```java
package demo.user;

import org.junit.Before;
import org.junit.Test;
import org.junit.runner.RunWith;
import org.springframework.beans.factory.annotation.Autowired;
import org.springframework.boot.test.autoconfigure.json.JsonTest;
import org.springframework.boot.test.json.JacksonTester;
import org.springframework.test.context.junit4.SpringRunner;

import static org.assertj.core.api.Assertions.assertThat;

@RunWith(SpringRunner.class)
@JsonTest
public class UserTests {

  private User user;

  @Autowired
  ❶
  private JacksonTester<User> json;

  @Before
  public void setUp() throws Exception {
    User user = new User("user", "Jack", "Frost", "jfrost@example.com");
    user.setId(0L);
    user.setCreatedAt(12345L);
    user.setLastModified(12346L);

    this.user = user;
  }

  @Test
  public void deserializeJson() throws Exception {
    String content = "{\"username\": \"user\", \"firstName\": \"Jack\", "
      + "\"lastName\": \"Frost\", \"email\": \"jfrost@example.com\"}";

    assertThat(this.json.parse(content)).isEqualTo(
      new User("user", "Jack", "Frost", "jfrost@example.com"));
    assertThat(this.json.parseObject(content).getUsername()).isEqualTo("user");
  }

  @Test
  public void serializeJson() throws Exception {
    ❷
    assertThat(this.json.write(user)).isEqualTo("user.json");
    assertThat(this.json.write(user)).isEqualToJson("user.json");
    assertThat(this.json.write(user)).hasJsonPathStringValue("@.username");

    ❸
```

```
    assertJsonPropertyEquals("@.username", "user");
    assertJsonPropertyEquals("@.firstName", "Jack");
    assertJsonPropertyEquals("@.lastName", "Frost");
    assertJsonPropertyEquals("@.email", "jfrost@example.com");
  }

  private void assertJsonPropertyEquals(String key, String value)
    throws java.io.IOException {
    assertThat(this.json.write(user)).extractingJsonPathStringValue(key)
      .isEqualTo(value);
  }
}
```

❶ AssertJ-based JSON tester backed by Jackson.

❷ Write the User object to JSON and compare to the user.json file.

❸ Asserts that the actual JSON result matches for an expected property value.

There are multiple options for asserting whether or not the actual result of the JSON serialization matches the expected result of the test method. The ability to map a JSON file on the classpath as a test resource goes a long way in cleaning up the body of test methods—especially when the expected JSON result has many properties. One way to perform a comparison is with clunky, hardcoded JSON strings in the test body, as in deserializeJson.

The serializeJson test, which takes the User object that was initialized in the setUp method and attempts to serialize it to JSON, demonstrates an alternative approach. In it we reference a user.json resource as a parameter to the isEqualTo method. Here we can specify a JSON file as a classpath resource in order to test that the Jackson JSON writer generates the expected result. The .json files live in a directory structure in src/main/resources that mirrors the package of the test class (Example 4-7).

Example 4-7. Structure of the test sources root containing the UserTests class

```
├─ ./src/test
│
├─ java
│   └─ demo
│       └─ user
│           ├─ UserControllerTest.java
│           ├─ UserRepositoryTest.java
│           └─ UserTests.java
└─ resources
    ├─ data-h2.sql
    └─ demo
        └─ user
            └─ user.json *
```

Let's look at the contents of user.json (Example 4-8).

Example 4-8. The contents of the user.json file in the test resources

```
{
  "username": "user",
  "firstName": "Jack",
  "lastName": "Frost",
  "email": "jfrost@example.com",
  "createdAt": 12345,
  "lastModified": 12346,
  "id": 0
}
```

@WebMvcTest

The @WebMvcTest annotation supports testing individual Spring MVC controllers in a Spring Boot application. This annotation auto-configures the necessary Spring MVC infrastructure needed to test interactions with controller methods (Example 4-9).

Example 4-9. Using @WebMvcTest to test a Spring MVC controller

```
package demo.account;

import org.junit.Test;
import org.junit.runner.RunWith;
import org.springframework.beans.factory.annotation.Autowired;
import org.springframework.boot.test.autoconfigure.web.servlet.WebMvcTest;
import org.springframework.boot.test.mock.mockito.MockBean;
import org.springframework.http.MediaType;
import org.springframework.test.context.junit4.SpringRunner;
import org.springframework.test.web.servlet.MockMvc;

import java.util.Collections;

import static org.mockito.BDDMockito.given;
import static org.springframework.test.web.servlet.request.MockMvcRequestBuilders↵
.get;
import static org.springframework.test.web.servlet.result.MockMvcResultMatchers↵
.content;
import static org.springframework.test.web.servlet.result.MockMvcResultMatchers↵
.status;

@RunWith(SpringRunner.class)
@WebMvcTest(AccountController.class)
public class AccountControllerTest {

  @Autowired
  private MockMvc mvc; ❶
```

```
@MockBean
private AccountService accountService; ❷

@Test
public void getUserAccountsShouldReturnAccounts() throws Exception {
  String content = "[{\"username\": \"user\", \"accountNumber\": \"123456789\"}]";

  ❸
  given(this.accountService.getUserAccounts()).willReturn(
    Collections.singletonList(new Account("user", "123456789")));

  ❹
  this.mvc.perform(get("/v1/accounts").accept(MediaType.APPLICATION_JSON))
    .andExpect(status().isOk()).andExpect(content().json(content));
  }
}
```

❶ Mock the MVC client for performing HTTP requests to Spring MVC controllers.

❷ Mocks the `AccountService` component that collaborates with the `AccountController`.

❸ Define the expected behavior of retrieving user accounts from the `accountService` bean.

❹ Finally, use the `MockMvc` client to assert for an expected HTTP result from the `AccountController`.

The `AccountControllerTest` demonstrates using the `MockMvc` client to execute faux requests to the Spring MVC controller under test. `MockMvc` is from the Spring MVC Test Framework. The test as configured stands up all the Spring MVC machinery—everything *except* an actual servlet container—and routes requests through from the client to the controller itself. The controller generates a response, which is sent back to the client. It's almost as if you were making calls to an actual service over the wire, except that, in this case, there's no HTTP service. Nothing ever spins up and starts serving requests on a `ServerSocket`.

@DataJpaTest

As of Spring Data 1.4, a new testing annotation is provided, named `@DataJpaTest`. This annotation is useful for Spring Boot applications that use the Spring Data JPA project. Embedded in-memory database support is provided for Spring Data JPA for testing. Later on, in our discussion of data access in Chapter 9, we will explore how to configure different Spring profiles for integration testing. We'll look at how to switch at runtime between MySQL and H2, an embedded in-memory relational database.

In Example 4-10, we see a test class named `AccountRepositoryTest` that is annotated with `@DataJpaTest`. Only the auto-configuration classes required for executing tests on Spring Data JPA repositories are activated under this slice. In the test method, we use the `TestEntityManager`, a convenience class from Spring Boot that supports a useful subset of a proper JPA `EntityManager` along with some extra utility methods that simplify commonly used idioms in tests. The `TestEntityManager` is a useful component used in the scope of JPA repository tests that allows you to interact with the underlying datastore to persist objects without needing to use a repository. We use it to persist a new instance of the `Account` entity that will represent the actual result that is expected to be returned from the `accountRepository`.

Example 4-10. Using @DataJpa to test a Spring Data JPA repository

```
package demo.account;

import demo.customer.CustomerRepository;
import org.junit.Test;
import org.junit.runner.RunWith;
import org.springframework.beans.factory.annotation.Autowired;
import org.springframework.boot.test.autoconfigure.orm.jpa.DataJpaTest;
import org.springframework.boot.test.autoconfigure.orm.jpa.TestEntityManager;
import org.springframework.test.context.junit4.SpringRunner;

import java.util.List;

import static org.assertj.core.api.Assertions.assertThat;

@RunWith(SpringRunner.class)
@DataJpaTest
public class AccountRepositoryTest {

  private static final AccountNumber ACCOUNT_NUMBER = new AccountNumber(
    "098765432");

  @Autowired
  private AccountRepository accountRepository;  ❶

  @Autowired
  private TestEntityManager entityManager;  ❷

  @Test
  public void findUserAccountsShouldReturnAccounts() throws Exception {
    this.entityManager.persist(new Account("jack", ACCOUNT_NUMBER));  ❸
    List<Account> account = this.accountRepository.findAccountsByUsername("jack");  ❹
    assertThat(account).size().isEqualTo(1);
    Account actual = account.get(0);
    assertThat(actual.getAccountNumber()).isEqualTo(ACCOUNT_NUMBER);
    assertThat(actual.getUsername()).isEqualTo("jack");
  }
```

```
@Test
public void findAccountShouldReturnAccount() throws Exception {
 this.entityManager.persist(new Account("jill", ACCOUNT_NUMBER));
 Account account = this.accountRepository
  .findAccountByAccountNumber(ACCOUNT_NUMBER);
 assertThat(account).isNotNull();
 assertThat(account.getAccountNumber()).isEqualTo(ACCOUNT_NUMBER);
}

@Test
public void findAccountShouldReturnNull() throws Exception {
 this.entityManager.persist(new Account("jack", ACCOUNT_NUMBER));
 Account account = this.accountRepository
  .findAccountByAccountNumber(new AccountNumber("000000000"));
 assertThat(account).isNull();
}
}
```

❶ Injects the `AccountRepository` from the `ApplicationContext`.

❷ Injects the `TestEntityManager` for managing persistence without using a repository.

❸ Persists a new `Account` entity to the in-memory database configured for the context.

❹ Finds the persisted `Account`.

@RestClientTest

The `@RestClientTest` annotation provides support to test Spring's `RestTemplate` and its interaction with REST services.

In Example 4-11, we see a unit test annotated with `@RestClientTest`. We specify that we will be targeting the `UserService` class and that we would like a `RestTemplate` to be registered as a part of the auto-configured test slice. In the test method `getAuthen ticatedUserShouldReturnUser()`, we use the `MockRestServiceServer` field (`server`) to mock the expected behavior of the intended HTTP request made by a `RestTemplate` inside the `UserService`. Notice how the expected JSON response is loaded from a classpath resource, from `user.json`.

Example 4-11. Using @RestClientTest to mock RestTemplate responses

```
package demo.user;

import org.junit.Test;
import org.junit.runner.RunWith;
```

```
import org.springframework.beans.factory.annotation.Autowired;
import org.springframework.beans.factory.annotation.Value;

//@formatter:off
import org.springframework.boot.test.autoconfigure.web.client.AutoConfigureWebClient;
import org.springframework.boot.test.autoconfigure.web.client.RestClientTest;
//@formatter:on

import org.springframework.core.io.ClassPathResource;
import org.springframework.http.MediaType;
import org.springframework.test.context.junit4.SpringRunner;
import org.springframework.test.web.client.MockRestServiceServer;

import static org.assertj.core.api.Assertions.assertThat;

//@formatter:off
import static org.springframework.test.web.client.match
        .MockRestRequestMatchers.requestTo;
import static org.springframework.test.web.client.response
        .MockRestResponseCreators.withSuccess;
//@formatter:on

❶
@RunWith(SpringRunner.class)
@RestClientTest({ UserService.class })
@AutoConfigureWebClient(registerRestTemplate = true)
public class UserServiceTests {

 @Value("${user-service.host:user-service}")
 private String serviceHost;

 @Autowired
 private UserService userService;

 @Autowired
 private MockRestServiceServer server;

 @Test
 public void getAuthenticatedUserShouldReturnUser() {
  this.server.expect(
   requestTo(String.format("http://%s/uaa/v1/me", serviceHost))).andRespond(
   withSuccess(new ClassPathResource("user.json", getClass()),
    MediaType.APPLICATION_JSON)); ❷

  User user = userService.getAuthenticatedUser();

  assertThat(user.getUsername()).isEqualTo("user");
  assertThat(user.getFirstName()).isEqualTo("John");
  assertThat(user.getLastName()).isEqualTo("Doe");
  assertThat(user.getCreatedAt()).isEqualTo(12345);
  assertThat(user.getLastModified()).isEqualTo(12346);
  assertThat(user.getId()).isEqualTo(0L);
```

```
    }
}
```

❶ Register a `RestTemplate` for the context of the auto-configured test slice.

❷ Mock the behavior of a `RestTemplate` request to the specified URL.

Any usage of `RestTemplate` that matches the stated expectation will instead return the contents of `user.json` after using `MockRestServiceServer` to mock the HTTP response from the remote service. The beauty of this is that we are able to target parts of the system under test by mocking the behavior of external services. This is a nifty feature that especially helps us test microservices that must coordinate with other services using HTTP. The question then becomes, how do we create integration tests that mock the actual behavior of a remote HTTP service instead of using `MockRest ServiceServer`? This is the subject of "Consumer-Driven Contract Testing" on page 114, which allows us to download stubs published by other services for the purpose of mocking service behavior for integration testing.

End-to-End Testing

End-to-end testing is an important part of ensuring that release components of a distributed application can be changed without breaking consumers. Further, a microservice architecture is a composition of many different services, with each application likely connected to multiple services in an ensemble of organized chaos that will require a sophisticated testing strategy. In this section, we will cover a few techniques for testing distributed cloud native applications.

End-to-end testing focuses on validating the functionality of an application's business features. As opposed to integration testing, end-to-end testing focuses on testing features from the user's perspective. For example, let's assume that a user of an application would like to register a new account. There is a sequence of actions that the user must perform to register a new account successfully. In most cases, the user interface of the application becomes the conduit for these activities, generating events that interact with backend APIs to accomplish the result of the workflow. If we take inventory of each event that is produced by the actions of a user who is registering a new account, we can translate the sequence of events into an end-to-end test.

There are multiple types of end-to-end tests, depending on what part of the system is under test. For backend developers who are building microservices, the end-to-end test for registering a new account will likely be a composite of API interactions between separate microservices, depending on the workflow. For end-to-end workflows that orchestrate a business feature that touches different microservices, managing state becomes an important consideration.

Testing Distributed Systems

We are usually referring to state when we talk about consistency in software. It is necessary to know exactly how state is shared and replicated across an architecture when developing applications in a distributed system. One of our favorite explanations of state goes all the way back to the birth of computing. Alan Turing first wrote about computing state in his seminal paper, "On computable numbers, with an application to the Entscheidungsproblem."[1] In the paper, Turing describes state using a thought experiment that theorizes how a machine can determine whether or not a number is computable. Turing's thought experiment introduces the concept of a *Turing Machine*—an imaginary mechanical device that is capable of computing numbers using a table of states.

The machine that Turing describes consists of an unbounded tape of squares containing symbols that span out in only two directions. The analogue that Turing uses to describe his machine is loosely based on that of a typewriter. The *machine* is allowed to scroll either left or right on the tape, scanning only one symbol at a time. The machine also has a table of states, mapping a symbol to a condition, which instructs the machine what to do next.

Let's look at an example. Let's assume Turing's machine is in an initial state of A. The machine's first scanned symbol from the tape is 0. The machine then looks up its instructions from the state table for its current state, which is still A. The instructions describe a condition: for a scanned symbol 0, write a 1. Before moving to the next position, the final instruction is a state change—from A to B. The state B will now contain a different set of instructions, depending on the scanned symbol at the next position. Now the machine may again scan a 0 from its new position, and because it is in state B, it will still write a 1—but this time the machine is instructed to move *left* on the tape instead of right.

Turing reduces to the essence what it means to program the behavior of his machine by switching between instructions that react and change based on inputs—outputting data in the process.

When we talk about state in modern applications, we are usually referring to a status field on a database record, represented as a column in a table. Let's take, for example, a user registering a new account on a website. The status of the user will transition from one state to another depending on the user's inputs. If the user has just finished registering for an account by submitting a form on a web page, the provided form fields will be processed and a record will be persisted to the database with the user registration details. One of the fields of this new user record is status, and can con-

---

1 "On computable numbers, with an application to the Entscheidungsproblem" (*http://bit.ly/2s6w8G0*), London Mathematical Society, 1937.

tain one of multiple values at any one time that describe the current state of a user. See Table 4-2 for some example records.

Table 4-2. User records containing a status field

first_name	last_name	email	status
Bob	Dylan	*bdylan@example.com*	PENDING
Taylor	Swift	*tswift@info.com*	CONFIRMED
Tracy	Chapman	*tchapman@test.com*	ARCHIVED
Bruno	Mars	*bmars@example.com*	INACTIVE

In Table 4-2, we see multiple rows of a database table containing user records. Each user in the table has a different value for the status column. For the user named *Bob Dylan*, we see the user's status is currently PENDING. Now, the behavior of the application will change from the user's perspective, depending on the value of the status column. For the PENDING status, before the user can sign in to the application, the user is required to confirm the listed email address. After a user confirms the email, the user's status will then transition to CONFIRMED, allowing the user to sign in and access other features of the application. If the user's status is set to ARCHIVED or INACTIVE, the user may be unable to sign in, depending on the requirements of the application. This workflow is often used in applications that implement a form of user authentication.

The problem that arrives with distributed systems development—and more specifically in microservices—is that workflows like the one described above won't be isolated within the boundaries of a single application. When we break up a monolithic application architecture into many separate services, network partitions will bisect workflows that would otherwise manage data within the context of a single transaction. So what does this mean for the developer?

The main problem with distributed applications is that state must be observed globally across separate machines, using information that is exchanged over a network to communicate state. For a single monolithic application that is connected to a single database, such as a relational database like MySQL, state can be consistently replicated across separate instances of the database—making it highly available. By storing a record containing state across multiple machines, we gain the benefit of being able to scale out and handle increased traffic.

The downside of distributing state is best summarized in the following question: how do we make sure that whenever we read a replicated record from a pool of machines, it is consistent with the state of a record stored on other machines in the pool?

The problem of distributing state and ensuring consistency is one of the hardest problems in computer science. Within the boundaries of a single machine and process, it can be quite simple to maintain the consistency of data—because whenever we read from memory, there is a single address referencing where that data is stored. If one thread locks the reference at the address with intention to change the state of a record, other threads will observe the lock before proceeding to modify the state of the record at that reference. When there is a single source of information for the state of a record, it can be globally accessed without the state of the record becoming inconsistent. This changes when state is replicated across the boundary of a single machine, where all replicas must be updated together and read together. If one of the replicas is different than the others, the state of the record is *inconsistent*, which can cause the behavior of the application to flip-flop between different states stored on different partitions.

When testing cloud native applications that are distributing state across separate microservices, it is essential to understand how to design end-to-end tests that test for data consistency. Eventual consistency is the best we can hope for when sharing state across the boundaries of separate microservices. We talk about designing for eventual consistency in our discussion of data integration solutions in Chapter 12. The key concern is to design testing conditions that make sure that state is always eventually consistent—maybe not consistent at the same exact time, but *always* eventually consistent without manual intervention. Do not share state between microservices where strong consistency is required. This is a simple rule of thumb for knowing when to avoid distributed transactions.

Another concern for microservice architectures is the manner in which we test integrations between different applications. For this kind of testing we may normally be required to execute end-to-end tests in an integration environment, where all applications and dependencies are bootstrapped for runtime execution, mirroring the deployment model of production. The cost in time associated with bootstrapping a complete end-to-end environment for integration testing a single microservice can be prohibitively expensive.

It can be greatly beneficial for a developer to be able to execute integration tests with many microservice dependencies as fast as possible, creating tighter feedback loops while also limiting resource contention in a shared build environment. One popular method for testing that helps to resolve some of these pains, and is quickly becoming a standard for testing microservices, is called *Consumer-Driven Contract Testing*.

Consumer-Driven Contract Testing

Consumer-Driven Contract Testing (CDC-T) was first introduced by Ian Robinson in 2006 as a practice of using published contracts to assert and maintain expectations between consumers and producers while preserving loose coupling between services. In the article that was originally published on Martin Fowler's website, Robinson describes service evolution in a service-oriented architecture (SOA) through the use of consumer-driven contracts.[2] In the years that followed, the practice and patterns of consumer-driven contracts introduced by Robinson were adapted to be used for testing the expectations between microservices.

The central premise of CDC-T is to allow producers and consumers in a microservice architecture to publish (and build off of) stubs in the form of a (consumer-driven) contract. The contract describes the call interface for a service. There is no sharing of libraries between microservices at runtime. Services may mutually share libraries during integration testing, in the case of a cyclical dependency between microservices. The producer first publishes stubs by defining a contract and integration test that uses the contract. Consumers are able to mock a producer by downloading the producer's versioned stubs from a shared location, like an artifact repository. Producers share stubs generated through a contract definition, but do not share types or client libraries. CDC-T strives to hide the implementation details of a producer's API.

Spring Cloud Contract

Spring Cloud Contract is an open source project in the Spring portfolio that provides framework components using a variant of consumer-driven contracts. Consumer-driven contracts are commonly used to integration-test distributed applications components like REST APIs and messaging exchanges between microservices. Spring Cloud Contract supports the ability to publish, simulate, and mock remote services using stubs.

For this example, we're going to create a consumer-driven contract that tests the integration between two microservices. We'll be testing two services: the *Account Microservice* and the *User Microservice*. The Account Microservice maintains a collection of accounts that belong to a user. For the users who own these accounts, the User Microservice will act as the repository for user records while also handling authentication.

These two microservices integrate simply. The Account Microservice retrieves the accounts of a user who is currently signed into a website. To do this, it contacts the User Microservice to get the name of the authenticated user from an HTTP request's session. The username that is returned from the User Microservice will be used to fetch accounts for the authenticated user on the Account Microservice. The relationship between the Account Microservice and the User Microservice is shown in Figure 4-1.

---

2 Ian Robinson, "Consumer-Driven Contracts: A Service Evolution Pattern" (*http://bit.ly/2s69I7x*), 2006.

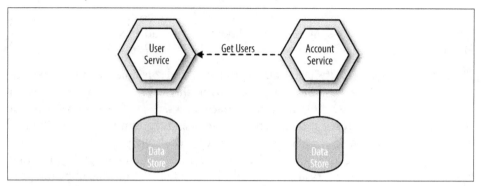

Figure 4-1. The Account Service is a consumer of the User Service

Now, let's explore the source code for the two Spring Boot projects, starting first with the User Microservice (Example 4-12).

Example 4-12. The Spring Boot application classes of the User Microservice

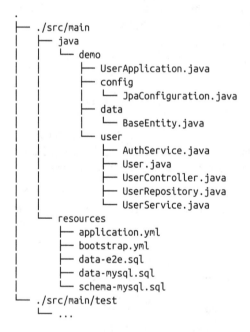

```
.
├── ./src/main
│   ├── java
│   │   └── demo
│   │       ├── UserApplication.java
│   │       ├── config
│   │       │   └── JpaConfiguration.java
│   │       ├── data
│   │       │   └── BaseEntity.java
│   │       └── user
│   │           ├── AuthService.java
│   │           ├── User.java
│   │           ├── UserController.java
│   │           ├── UserRepository.java
│   │           └── UserService.java
│   └── resources
│       ├── application.yml
│       ├── bootstrap.yml
│       ├── data-e2e.sql
│       ├── data-mysql.sql
│       └── schema-mysql.sql
└── ./src/main/test
    └── ...
```

In Example 4-12, we see the Spring Boot application source code for the User Micro-service. The directory structure here is focused on the application class files in the src/main/demo directory. This package contains the application code for the User Microservice. Since we already know how a basic Spring Boot application works, we're going to just explore the core functionality of this service that we will test using a consumer-driven contract.

The user package of the microservice contains the features we are interested in testing. Here we will find two service components containing the business logic of the application: AuthService and UserService. The UserService contains a method that is used to get the authenticated user of the session. The AuthService will be used to get the session information of the authenticated user. The UserService will then look up the user details from the UserRepository, using the ID returned by the AuthService as the lookup key.

In Example 4-13, we see a method called getUserByPrincipal that returns an instance of the User class. The User class is a domain entity that contains fields to describe an authenticated Principal. This method uses the name property of the Principal class to look up a User record from the UserRepository. For this example we are using a Spring Data JPA repository to talk to the database. (We explore Spring Data JPA in more detail in Chapter 9.)

Example 4-13. The UserService class retrieves the details of a user principal

```
package demo.user;

import org.springframework.beans.factory.annotation.Autowired;
import org.springframework.stereotype.Service;

import java.security.Principal;
import java.util.Optional;

@Service
public class UserService {

  private final UserRepository userRepository;

  @Autowired
  public UserService(UserRepository userRepository) {
    this.userRepository = userRepository;
  }

  public User getUserByPrincipal(Principal principal) {
    ❶
    return Optional.ofNullable(principal)
      .map(p -> userRepository.findUserByUsername(p.getName())).orElse(null);
  }
}
```

❶ Retrieves a User record using the name field of the Principal parameter.

This example is semi-realistic in the sense that it illustrates a common workflow in microservices that need to implement user-level security, but does not implement an authentication provider. The AuthService in this example contains only a dummy method that retrieves an empty implementation of java.security.Principal. In a real application, you would offload much of this to Spring Security instead.

Let's explore the UserController class, which defines a REST API that the Account Service will use to remotely fetch an authenticated user over HTTP.

In Example 4-14, we see the definition of the UserController class. This class defines a simple Spring MVC controller mapped to the /uaa/v1 endpoint. Here we have a single controller method called me. This method attempts to get a Principal for the session contained in the HTTP request context. The first step is to get the authenticated Principal from the AuthService. If the Principal is available and not null, then the controller method will call the UserService to fetch the User record from the database. Lastly, if the User or Principal could not be retrieved, the method returns a ResponseEntity with the HTTP status UNAUTHORIZED.

Example 4-14. The UserController class defines the application's REST controller

```
package demo.user;

import org.springframework.beans.factory.annotation.Autowired;
import org.springframework.http.HttpStatus;
import org.springframework.http.ResponseEntity;
import org.springframework.web.bind.annotation.RequestMapping;
import org.springframework.web.bind.annotation.RestController;

import java.security.Principal;
import java.util.Optional;

@RestController
@RequestMapping(path = "/uaa/v1")
public class UserController {

 private UserService userService;

 private AuthService authService;

 @Autowired
 public UserController(UserService userService, AuthService authService) {
  this.userService = userService;
  this.authService = authService;
 }

❶
```

```
@RequestMapping(path = "/me")
public ResponseEntity<User> me(Principal principal) throws Exception {
  return Optional.ofNullable(authService.getAuthenticatedUser(principal)) ❷
    .map(p -> ResponseEntity.ok().body(userService.getUserByPrincipal(p))) ❸
    .orElse(new ResponseEntity<User>(HttpStatus.UNAUTHORIZED)); ❹
 }
}
```

❶ Describes a @RequestMapping for a GET request to /uaa/v1/me.

❷ Get the authenticated user Principal from the AuthService.

❸ If the Principal is not null, look up the UserService.

❹ If the Principal is null, return an HTTP unauthorized error.

Next we're going to create a consumer-driven contract test for the UserController method that is mapped to the /uaa/v1/me endpoint. We will use *Spring Cloud Contract* to publish a specification for the User Microservice's REST API. This specification is published as a Maven artifact, which can be fetched by other microservices to mock a web server that emulates the tested behavior of the User Microservice. In this way, the User Microservice will only publish a specification that passes all the unit tests that were written for the UserController. By taking this approach, all consumers of the User Microservice will be able to integration-test against a mocked web server during test execution—as if it were the real thing!

Let's explore the test sources where we will define our consumer-driven contract for the User Microservice. The directory structure for our user tests is shown in Example 4-15.

Example 4-15. The test sources root of the User Microservice

```
.
├── ./src/main/test/java
│   └── demo
│       ├── UserServiceBase.java
│       └── user
│           ├── UserControllerTest.java
│           ├── UserRepositoryTest.java
│           └── UserTests.java
└── resources
    ├── contracts
    │   └── shouldReturnUser.groovy *
    ├── data-h2.sql
    └── demo
        └── user
            └── user.json
```

The testing strategies we use in this example for both the unit and integration tests are the same strategies we used in the examples earlier in this chapter. This time we're going to focus on how to create a Spring Cloud Contract stub definition for the User Microservice. The stub definition we create will define a consumer-driven test for fetching authenticated users.

Stub definitions in Spring Cloud Contract are used to describe the mocked (remote) service behavior of a consumer-driven test. These behaviors are called *expectations*, because they are the expectations set by a service producer about the behavior under test of the REST API methods that are exposed to consumers.

Each stub definition file will cover a single method of a `Controller` class. Since we only have one method in `UserController`, we will only create one stub definition file for the project, called `shouldReturnUser.groovy`. Stub definitions for Spring Cloud Contract are written using a Spring Cloud Contract Groovy-language DSL. By default, our stub definitions are located in the resource directory of the test sources root, which is typically found in `src/main/test/java/resources`. Let's look at this definition (Example 4-16).

Example 4-16. The stub definition in shouldReturnUser.groovy

```
package contracts

org.springframework.cloud.contract.spec.Contract.make {
    request {
        method 'GET'
        url '/uaa/v1/me'
        headers {
            header('Content-Type': consumer(regex('application/*json*')))
        }
    }
    response {
        status 200
        body([
                username    : value(producer(regex('[A-Za-z0-9]+'))),
                firstName   : value(producer(regex('[A-Za-z]+'))),
                lastName    : value(producer(regex('[A-Za-z]+'))),

//@formatter:off
                email       : value(producer(
                        regex('[A-Za-z0-9]+\\@[A-Za-z0-9]+\\.[A-Za-z]+'))),
//@formatter:on
                createdAt   : value(producer(regex('[0-9]+'))),
                lastModified: value(producer(regex('[0-9]+'))),
                id          : value(producer(regex('[0-9]+')))
        ])
        headers {
            header('Content-Type': value(
```

```
                    producer('application/json;charset=UTF-8'),
                    consumer('application/json;charset=UTF-8'))
            )
        }
    }
}
```

 If you're not familiar with Groovy DSL syntax, don't worry! The DSL for a stub definition in Spring Cloud Contract is simple and easy to pick up and learn. While we won't exhaustively cover the Groovy DSL here, you can find more details from the online documentation in the reference manual of the Spring Cloud Contract project.

Install the user-microservice artifacts in your local Maven repository or your Maven artifact repository. Our user-microservice is configured to publish not one, but *two* artifacts on every mvn install: the artifact itself, and the artifact containing the contract definition. This second artifact is what our consumer API, the account-microservice, will depend on. Example 4-17 shows the configuration for our Maven build.

Example 4-17. The configuration in the Maven build for the producer

```
<build>
  <plugins>
    <plugin>
      <groupId>org.springframework.boot</groupId>
      <artifactId>spring-boot-maven-plugin</artifactId>
      <executions>
        <execution>
        <goals>
          <goal>repackage</goal>
        </goals>
        </execution>
      </executions>
    </plugin>
    <plugin>
      <groupId>org.springframework.cloud</groupId>
      <artifactId>spring-cloud-contract-maven-plugin</artifactId>
      <version>${spring-cloud-contract.version}</version>
      <extensions>true</extensions>
      <configuration>
        <baseClassForTests>demo.UserServiceBase</baseClassForTests>
        <basePackageForTests>demo</basePackageForTests>
      </configuration>
    </plugin>
  </plugins>
</build>
```

Inspect your local Maven repository to confirm that both the artifact and the stub for the artifact have been deployed (Example 4-18).

Example 4-18. An example of the artifact files that should be installed to your local Maven repository

```
.
├── _remote.repositories
├── maven-metadata-local.xml
├── user-microservice-1.0.0-SNAPSHOT-stubs.jar
├── user-microservice-1.0.0-SNAPSHOT.jar
└── user-microservice-1.0.0-SNAPSHOT.pom

0 directories, 5 files
```

With the stubs deployed, it's trivial to use the stub runner in our consumer test to stand up a REST API that complies with the contract and that can integrate with our consumer. The API is real—it runs on an actual port and produces actual values, as defined by the specification. It's trivial and relatively cheap to run this test, as we're not dealing with an actual live-fire service connected to middleware and databases (Example 4-19).

Example 4-19. The Account Service unit tests the User Service's consumer-driven contract

```
package demo;

import demo.user.User;
import demo.user.UserService;
import org.junit.Test;
import org.junit.runner.RunWith;
import org.springframework.beans.factory.annotation.Autowired;
import org.springframework.boot.test.context.SpringBootTest;

//@formatter:off
import org.springframework.cloud.contract.stubrunner
        .spring.AutoConfigureStubRunner;
//@formatter:on
import org.springframework.test.context.junit4.SpringRunner;

import static org.assertj.core.api.Assertions.assertThat;
import static org.springframework.boot.test.context.SpringBootTest.*;

//@formatter:off
@RunWith(SpringRunner.class)
@SpringBootTest(webEnvironment = WebEnvironment.NONE)
@AutoConfigureStubRunner(
        ids = { "cnj:user-microservice:+:stubs:8081" },
        workOffline = true) ❶
```

```
//@formatter:on
public class ConsumerDrivenTests {

  @Autowired
  private UserService service; ❷

  @Test
  public void shouldReturnAuthenticatedUser() {
   User actual = service.getAuthenticatedUser();

    assertThat(actual).isNotNull();
    assertThat(actual.getUsername()).matches("[A-Za-z0-9]+");
    assertThat(actual.getFirstName()).matches("[A-Za-z]+");
    assertThat(actual.getLastName()).matches("[A-Za-z]+");
    assertThat(actual.getEmail()).matches(
      "[A-Za-z0-9]+\\@[A-Za-z0-9]+\\.[A-Za-z]+");
  }
}
```

❶   The @AutoConfigureStubRunner annotation specifies where to find the stub arti-
    fact (as Maven coordinates) and on what port the stub runner should run the
    mock service.

❷   Our unit test injects the *actual* UserService. Nothing mock about this service,
    only the replies it gets after it's made an HTTP call to the stubbed service!

Summary

As we explored in this chapter, microservice testing strategies can be quite different
than the garden variety unit and integration testing used in other kinds of web application architectures. Spring provides a powerful set of framework components and
projects for testing Spring Boot applications.

Spring has long provided solid support for integration-testing components within a
single application. Spring Boot extends that support, making it easier to compart-
mentalize configuration across layers of functionality. Spring Cloud extends this further, with Consumer-Driven Contract Testing (CDC-T). In this chapter we looked at
stubbing out a REST endpoint with Spring Cloud Contract, though it's worth men-
tioning that Spring Cloud Contract also supports messaging-based endpoints.

Testing is a key aspect of continuous delivery. In continuous delivery, software artifacts move through a pipeline, ultimately resulting in production-ready artifacts. As
software moves further in the continuous delivery pipeline, the tests become progressively more exhaustive and slow. Ideally, the unit tests and integration tests capture
80–90% of the use cases in a very short amount of time, confirming that—probably—
the code is in a condition to be pushed to production.

In this chapter we did *not* focus much on unit testing, or on other, more exhaustive but less-common sorts of tests that happen after integration tests. In Chapter 2, we looked at using the Cloud Foundry Java client to automate deployments to Cloud Foundry. In a cloud native system, *everything* is automated, including deployments. This is key to effective smoke tests and to obtaining consistency.

## CHAPTER 5

The Forklifted Application

So you've got that shiny new distributed runtime, infinite greenfield potential, and lots of existing applications; now what?

The Contract

Cloud Foundry aims to improve velocity by reducing or at least making consistent the operational concerns associated with deploying and managing applications. Cloud Foundry is an ideal place to run online web-based services and applications, service integrations, and back-office type processing.

Cloud Foundry (*http://cloudfoundry.org*) optimizes for the continuous delivery of web applications and services by making assumptions about the shape of the applications it runs. The *inputs* into Cloud Foundry are applications: Java (.jar or, if you insist, .war) binaries, Ruby on Rails applications, Node.js applications, etc. Cloud Foundry provides well-known operational benefits (log aggregation, routing, self-healing, dynamic scale-up and scale-down, security, etc.) to the applications it runs. There is an implied contract between the platform and the applications, and this contract allows the platform to keep promises to the applications it runs.

Some applications may never be able to meet that contract. Other applications might be able to, albeit with some soft-touch adjustments. In this chapter, we'll look at possible soft-touch refactorings to coerce legacy applications to run on Cloud Foundry.

The goal isn't, in this case, to build applications that are *native* to the cloud; it is to move existing workloads to the cloud to reduce an organization's operational surface area, to increase uniformity. Once an application is deployed on Cloud Foundry, it is at least as well off as it was before, and now there's one less *snowflake deployment*—a deployment that is needlessly different each time—to worry about. Less is more.

We distinguish this type of workload migration, called *application forklifting*, from building a *cloud native application*. Much of what we talk about on the Spring (*http://spring.io/blog*) and Pivotal (*http://pivotal.io/blog*) blogs these days is about building *cloud native applications*—applications that live and breathe in the cloud (they inhale and exhale as demand and capacity require) and that fully exploit the platform. That journey, while ideal and worth taking on, assuming the reward on investment is tangible, is a much longer, larger discussion and not the focus of this chapter. It *definitely* is the focus of all the *other* chapters in this book, though!

Application behavior is, broadly speaking, the sum of its environment and code. In this chapter, we'll look at strategies for moving a legacy Java application from some of the environments that legacy Java applications typically live in. We'll look at patterns typical of applications developed before the arrival of cloud computing, and the understanding of what patterns best serve applications running in the cloud. We'll look at some specific solutions and accompanying code.

Migrating Application Environments

There are some qualities that are common to all applications, and those qualities (like RAM and DNS routing) are configurable directly through the Cloud Foundry cf CLI tool, various dashboards, or in an application's manifest.yml file. If your application is a compliant application that just needs more RAM or a custom DNS route, then you'll have everything you need in the basic knobs and levers all applications can manipulate on Cloud Foundry.

The Out-of-the-Box Buildpacks

Things sometimes just aren't that simple, though. Your application may run in any number of snowflake environments, whereas Cloud Foundry makes very explicit assumptions about the environments its applications run in. These assumptions are encoded to some extent in the platform itself and in *buildpacks*, which were adopted from Heroku. Cloud Foundry and Heroku don't really care what kind of application they are running. They care about Linux containers, which are ultimately operating system processes. Buildpacks tell Cloud Foundry what to do given a Java .jar, a Rails application, a Java .war, a Node.js application, etc., and how to turn it into a container that the platform can treat like a process. A buildpack is a set of *callbacks*—shell scripts that respond to well-known calls—that the runtime will use to ultimately create a Linux container to be run. This process is called *staging*.

Cloud Foundry provides many out-of-the-box *system buildpacks* (*http://docs.pivotal.io/pivotalcf/buildpacks*). Those buildpacks can be customized or even completely replaced. If you want to run an application for which there is no existing buildpack provided out of the box (by the Cloud Foundry community (*http://bit.ly/2s6o0Fe*), Heroku (*https://www.heroku.com*), or Pivotal (*https://pivotal.io*)), then at least it's easy enough to develop and deploy your own (*http://docs.pivotal.io/pivotalcf/buildpacks/custom.html*). There are buildpacks for all manner of environments and applications out there, including one called *Sourcey* (*https://github.com/oetiker/sourcey-buildpack*) that simply compiles native code for you! (Admit it: you know of at least one legacy line-of-business application that requires a C compiler and an animal sacrifice *somewhere* in your organization, don't you?)

Custom(ized) Buildpacks

These buildpacks are meant to provide sensible defaults while remaining flexible. As an example, the default Java/JVM buildpack supports .war artifacts (*https://github.com/cloudfoundry/java-buildpack*) (which will run inside of an up-to-date version of Apache Tomcat), Spring Boot-style executable .jar artifacts, Play web framework applications, Grails applications, and much more. In addition, it supports plugging in numerous well-known Java agents like New Relic.

If the system buildpacks don't work for you and you want to use something different, you only need to tell Cloud Foundry where to find the code for the buildpack using the -b argument to cf push, as in Example 5-1.

Example 5-1. A (very) basic Java EE servlet

```
cf push -b https://github.com/a/custom-buildpack.git#my-branch  custom-app
```

Alternatively, you can specify the buildpack in the manifest.yml file that accompanies your application. As an example, suppose we have a Java EE application that has historically been deployed using IBM's WebSphere. IBM maintains a very capable WebSphere Liberty buildpack. To demonstrate this, let's say we want to deploy and run a basic Servlet (Example 5-2). (Let's ignore, for now, that we can run Servlet components in Spring Boot applications, as shown in "Using Servlet APIs in a Spring Boot Application" on page 576.)

Example 5-2. A (very) basic Java EE Servlet

```
package demo;

import javax.servlet.ServletException;
import javax.servlet.annotation.WebServlet;
import javax.servlet.http.HttpServlet;
import javax.servlet.http.HttpServletRequest;
import javax.servlet.http.HttpServletResponse;
import java.io.IOException;

@WebServlet("/hi")
public class DemoApplication extends HttpServlet {
```

```
protected void doGet(HttpServletRequest request, HttpServletResponse response)
  throws ServletException, IOException {

  response.setContentType("text/html");

  response.getWriter().print("<html><body><h3>Hello Cloud</h3></body></html>");
  }
}
```

To run this, we have specified the WebSphere Liberty buildpack in the application's manifest in Example 5-3.

Example 5-3. The manifest.yml for our WebSphere Liberty application

```
---
applications:
- name: wsl-demo
  memory: 1024M
  buildpack: https://github.com/cloudfoundry/ibm-websphere-liberty-buildpack.git
  instances: 1
  host: wsl-demo-${random-word}
  path: target/buildpacks.war
  env:
    SPRING_PROFILES_ACTIVE: cloud
    DEBUG: "true"
    debug: "true"
    IBM_JVM_LICENSE:  L-JWOD-9SYNCP
    IBM_LIBERTY_LICENSE: L-MCAO-9SYMVC
```

Some buildpacks lend themselves to customization. The Java buildpack (*https:// github.com/cloudfoundry/java-buildpack*)—which was originally developed by the folks at Heroku, and which the Spring and Cloud Foundry teams have since *radically* expanded upon—supports configuration through environment variables. The Java buildpack provides default configuration in the `config` directory for various aspects of the buildpack's behavior. You can override the behavior described in a given configuration file by providing an environment variable (prefixed with `JBP_CONFIG_`) of the same name as the configuration file, sans the `.yml` extension. Thus, borrowing an example from the excellent documentation (*https://github.com/cloudfoundry/java-buildpack/blob/master/README.md*), if we wanted to override the JRE version and the memory configuration (which lives in the `config/open_jdk_jre.yml` file in the buildpack), we might do what's shown in Example 5-4.

Example 5-4. Configuring the Java buildpack's JDK and JRE

```
cf set-env custom-app JBP_CONFIG_OPEN_JDK_JRE \
'[jre: {version: 1.7.0_+}, memory_calculator: {memory_heuristics: {heap: 85, ↵
stack: 10}}]'
```

Containerized Applications

Applications in the Java world that were developed for a J2EE/Java EE application server tend to be very *sticky* and hostile to migration outside of that application server. Java EE applications, for all their vaunted portability, use class loaders that behave inconsistently, offer different subsystems that themselves often require proprietary configuration files, and to fill in the many gaps, they often offer application server–specific APIs. If your application is completely intractable, and the various knobs and levers we've looked at so far don't give you enough control to migrate an application, there may still be hope!

 Before you reach for this last resort, be sure to look through the community buildpacks. There are buildpacks that stand up IBM's WebSphere (with contributions from IBM, since they have a PaaS based on Cloud Foundry!) and RedHat's WildFly, for example.

Cloud Foundry *also* supports running containerized (e.g., Docker) applications (*http://bit.ly/2s6DSrl*). This might be an alternative if you've already got an application containerized and just want to deploy and manage it with the same toolchain as all other applications. We don't recommend this approach, for a variety of reasons:

- The attack surface area for a Docker-based container running on Diego remains somewhat higher than that of a buildpack application, because Docker allows users to fully specify the contents of their root filesystems. A buildpack application runs on a trusted root filesystem.

- Building a container is extra work that imposes on developers and operations.

- It's harder to manage patches and updates for containerized operating systems, as they need to be rebuilt to see the changes. There's no easy way to centrally re-image and redeploy every single container if so required.

We've run the gamut from commonplace configuration to application- and runtime-specific buildpack overrides to opaque containerized applications. We start any attempts to forklift an application in this order, with simpler tweaks first. The goal is to do as little as possible and let Cloud Foundry do as much as possible.

Soft-Touch Refactoring to Get Your Application into the Cloud

In the last section we looked at things that you can do to move an application wholesale from its existing environment into a new one without modifying the code. We looked at techniques for moving simple applications that have fairly common requirements, all the way to very exotic requirements. We saw that there are ways to all but virtualize applications and move them to Cloud Foundry, but we didn't look at how to point applications to the backing services (databases, message queues, etc.) that they consume. We also ignored, for simplicity, that there are some classes of applications that could be made to work cleanly on Cloud Foundry with some minor, sometimes tedious, often easy changes.

It always pays off to have a comprehensive test suite in place to act as a harness against regressions when refactoring code. I understand that due to their very nature, some legacy applications won't have such a test suite in place. Proceed *carefully*, but quickly!

We'll look mostly at *soft-touch* adjustments that you could make to get your application working, hopefully with a minimum of risk. It should go without saying that, absent a test suite, more modular code will absorb changes more readily. It's a bitter irony then that the applications most in need of a comprehensive test suite are the ones that probably don't have it: large, monolithic, legacy applications. If you *do* have a test suite in place, you may not have smoke tests that validate connectivity and deployment of the application and its associated services. Such a suite of tests is necessarily harder to write but would be helpful precisely when undertaking something like forklifting a legacy application into a new environment.

Talking to Backing Services

A backing service is a service (databases, message queues, email services, etc.) that an application consumes. Cloud Foundry applications consume backing services by looking for their locators and credentials in an environment variable called VCAP_SERVICES. The simplicity of this approach is a feature: any language can pluck the environment variable out of the environment and parse the embedded JSON to extract things like service hosts, ports, and credentials.

Applications that depend on Cloud Foundry-managed backing services can tell Cloud Foundry to create that service on-demand. Service creation could also be called *provisioning*. Its exact meaning varies depending on context; for an email service it might mean provisioning a new email username and password. For a MongoDB backing service it might mean creating a new Mongo database and assigning access to that MongoDB instance. The backing service's life cycle is modeled by a Cloud Foundry service broker instance. Cloud Foundry service brokers are REST APIs that Cloud Foundry cooperates with to manage backing services. (We look at service brokers in more depth in Chapter 14.)

Once a broker is registered with Cloud Foundry, it is available through the cf market place command and can be provisioned on demand using the cf create-service command. Let's look at a hypothetical service creation example. The first parameter, mongo, is the name of the service. We're using something generic here, but it could as easily have been New Relic, or MongoHub, or ElephantSQL, or SendGrid, etc. The second parameter is the plan name—the level and quality of service expected from the service provider. Sometimes higher levels of service imply higher prices. The third parameter is the aforementioned logical name (Example 5-5).

Example 5-5. Creating a new backing service on Cloud Foundry

```
cf create-service mongo free my-mongo
```

It's not hard to create a service broker, but it might be more work than you need. If your application wants to talk to an existing, static service that isn't likely to move, and you just want to point your application to it, then you can use *user-provided services* (*http://bit.ly/2s6gPgp*). A user-provided service is a fancy way of saying "take this connection information and assign a logical name to it and make it something I can treat like any other managed backing service"—a JSON entry in VCAP_SERVICES.

A backing service created using the cf create-service command or as a user-provided service is invisible to any consuming applications until it is *bound* to an application; this adds the relevant connectivity information to that application's VCAP_SERVICES.

If Cloud Foundry supports the backing service that you need (like MySQL or MongoDB), and if your code has been written in such a way that it centralizes the initialization or acquisition of these backing services—ideally using something like dependency injection (which Spring makes dead simple!)—then switching is a matter of rewiring that isolated dependency. If your application has been written to support twelve-factor–style configuration where things like credentials, hosts, and ports are maintained in the environment or are at least external to the application build, then you may be able to readily point your application to its new services without even so much as a rebuild. For a deeper look at this topic, check out our discussion of twelve-factor app style service configuration in Chapter 3.

Often, it's just not this simple. Classic J2EE/Java EE applications often resolve services by looking them up in a well-known context: JNDI (Java Naming and Directory Interface). If your code was written to use dependency injection, then it'll be fairly simple to rewire the application to resolve its connection information from the Cloud Foundry environment. If not, then you'll need to rework your code, and ideally do so by introducing dependency injection to insulate your application from further code duplication. If you can point to one (and only one) place in the codebase that interacts with JNDI or Cloud Foundry, then you've done a good job. A well-organized codebase will deal with types, like javax.sql.DataSource and javax.jms.ConnectionFactory, and not JNDI lookups.

Achieving Service Parity with Spring

In this section, we'll look at some things that people tend to struggle with when moving applications to lighter-weight containers and, by extension, the cloud. This is by no means an exhaustive list.

Remote Procedure Calls

Cloud Foundry (and indeed the majority of clouds) are HTTP-first. It supports individually addressable nodes, and it even has support for nonroutable custom ports, but these features work against the grain and aren't supported in every environment. If you're doing RPC with RMI/EJB, for example, then you'll need to tunnel it through HTTP. Ignoring for now the wisdom of using RPC, it's easier if you do RPC through HTTP. There are many ways to do this, including XML-RPC, SOAP (bleargh!), and even Spring's HTTP Invoker service exporters (*http://bit.ly/2s6qYti*) and service clients, which funnel RMI payloads through HTTP. This last option is convenient because it supports rich APIs and Java types through Java serialization, but funnel the payloads over HTTP. It's *inconvenient*, because client and producer are now coupled and must agree upon types, but we digress. Example 5-6 demonstrates how to export a Spring bean, `SimpleMessageService`, through its interface using Spring's HTTP Invoker.

Example 5-6. Export a service using the HttpInvokerServiceExporter

```
package demo;

import org.springframework.boot.SpringApplication;
import org.springframework.boot.autoconfigure.SpringBootApplication;
import org.springframework.context.annotation.Bean;
import org.springframework.remoting.httpinvoker.HttpInvokerServiceExporter;

@SpringBootApplication
public class DemoApplication {

 public static void main(String[] args) throws Exception {
  SpringApplication.run(DemoApplication.class, args);
 }

 @Bean
 MessageService messageService() { ❶
  return new SimpleMessageService();
 }

 ❷
 @Bean(name = "/messageService")
 HttpInvokerServiceExporter httpMessageService() {
  HttpInvokerServiceExporter http = new HttpInvokerServiceExporter();
  http.setServiceInterface(MessageService.class);
```

```
  http.setService(this.messageService());
  return http;
 }
}
```

❶ The implementation itself needs to implement, at a minimum, the service interface specified in the `HttpInvokerServiceExporter`.

❷ The `HttpInvokerServiceExporter` maps the given bean to an HTTP endpoint (/
`messageService`) under the Spring `DispatcherServlet`.

The `Message` needs to implement `java.io.Serializable` to support serialization,
just as with straight RMI serialization. Spring provides mirror image components to
create clients for these remote services based on an agreed-upon service interface. In
Example 5-7, we'll use the `HttpInvokerProxyFactoryBean` to create a client-side
proxy to the remote service, bound to the same service contract. This shared contract,
by the way, is the quality of RPC that's so limiting: it couples the client to the types of
the service, and frustrates the service's ability to evolve without breaking the client.

> There are some new RPC frameworks, like gRPC, that support
> additive mutations to payloads. In these technologies, clients and
> services can interop so long as a common subset is agreed upon.

It's simple enough to build a client with the `HttpInvokerProxyFactoryBean` to talk to
this endpoint. This is the mirror image of the `HttpInvokerServiceExporter`.

*Example 5-7. Our test stands up an RPC client in DemoApplicationTests.java and then
calls it*

```
package demo;

import org.springframework.context.annotation.Bean;
import org.springframework.context.annotation.Configuration;
import org.springframework.remoting.httpinvoker.HttpInvokerProxyFactoryBean;

@Configuration
public class DemoApplicationClientConfiguration {

 @Bean
 HttpInvokerProxyFactoryBean client() {
  HttpInvokerProxyFactoryBean client = new HttpInvokerProxyFactoryBean();
  client.setServiceUrl("http://localhost:8080/messageService"); ❶
  client.setServiceInterface(MessageService.class); ❷
  return client;
```

```
    }
}
```

❶ The URL specified here is the string name specified on the service bean.

❷ Client-side code should inject the `messageService` type to be able to make calls to the downstream service.

HTTP sessions with Spring Session

Cloud Foundry (and most cloud environments in general) don't do well with multi-cast networking. HTTP session replication is commonly associated with multicast networking. In traditional application servers, session replication is a function of broadcast networking on a single cluster. Unfortunately, these traditional session replication schemes were not particularly performant, robust, or portable.

Spring Session (*http://spring.io/projects/spring-session*) can help. Spring Session is a drop-in replacement for the Servlet HTTP Session API that relies on an SPI to handle synchronization. Implementations of the SPI can talk to all manner of backends, including Redis, Apache Geode, and Hazelcast. These projects are focused, specifically, on making cluster and cross-cluster replication reliable. Additionally, they're readily supported on most cloud platforms. Redis, for example, is pre-deployed on most Cloud Foundry installations, and there's a very nice Hazelcast service broker (*https://docs.pivotal.io/partners/hazelcast/*).

 Technologies like Redis and Hazelcast are important, but they will add a cost to your operational overhead. Ideally, this competency should be managed by the platform, and automated. Given two options of roughly equal functionality, choose the one that is easiest to operationalize.

You just install Spring Session; you don't have to do anything else to your HTTP session code. The HTTP servlet specification provides for replacing the implementation in this manner, so this works consistently across servlet implementations. Spring Session in turn writes session state through the SPI. Redis is available as a backing service on Cloud Foundry. As multiple nodes spin up, they all talk to the same Redis cluster, and benefit from Redis's world-class state replication. In order to get Redis and Spring Session working, add `org.springframework.boot` : `spring-boot-starter-redis` and `org.springframework.session` : `spring-session` to your Spring Boot application.

The Servlet API requires that any objects written to the HTTP session that are intended for replication must support Java serialization. This constraint may be true for Spring Session implementations, too! On the other hand, it may *not* be, as some backends may not rely on Java serialization to do their work.

Spring Session gives you a few other features, for free:

- It supports working with an HTTP session from WebSockets.
- It supports easy "Sign Me Out of My Account" type features.
- It supports access to sessions that are not logically the same. That is, there's no reason two separate applications couldn't share the same session state.

For more, see "The Portable, Cloud-Ready HTTP Session" (*http://bit.ly/2s6CRzE*) on the Spring blog.

To see Example 5-8 at work, bring up Redis with the Redis CLI, then clear it using the FLUSHALL command.

Example 5-8. DemoApplication.java

```java
package demo;

import org.springframework.beans.factory.annotation.Autowired;
import org.springframework.beans.factory.annotation.Value;
import org.springframework.boot.SpringApplication;
import org.springframework.boot.autoconfigure.SpringBootApplication;
import org.springframework.web.bind.annotation.GetMapping;
import org.springframework.web.bind.annotation.RestController;

import javax.servlet.http.HttpSession;
import java.util.HashMap;
import java.util.Map;
import java.util.Optional;
import java.util.UUID;

@SpringBootApplication
public class DemoApplication {

 public static void main(String[] args) {
  SpringApplication.run(DemoApplication.class, args);
 }
}

@RestController
class SessionController {

 private final String ip;
```

```
@Autowired
public SessionController(@Value("${CF_INSTANCE_IP:127.0.0.1}") String ip) {
  this.ip = ip;
}

@GetMapping("/hi")
Map<String, String> uid(HttpSession session) {
  ❶
  UUID uid = Optional.ofNullable(UUID.class.cast(session.getAttribute("uid")))
    .orElse(UUID.randomUUID());
  session.setAttribute("uid", uid);

  Map<String, String> m = new HashMap<>();
  m.put("instance_ip", this.ip);
  m.put("uuid", uid.toString());
  return m;
}

}
```

❶ This example stores an attribute in the HTTP session if it's not already present. Subsequent calls to the /hi endpoint should return the same cached value in the HTTP session.

 Example 5-9 will delete *everything* in your Redis database!

Example 5-9. An empty Redis database

```
127.0.0.1:6379> flushall
OK

127.0.0.1:6379> keys *
(empty list or set)
```

Then, bring up the web application at http://localhost:8080/hi. Refresh it a few times and you'll see that the value in uuid is fixed after the first refresh, which triggers a new HTTP session that Spring Session will persist in Redis. Confirm as much by running the KEYS * command on the Redis instance again (Example 5-10).

Example 5-10. A Redis database with some session data

```
127.0.0.1:6379> keys *
(empty list or set)
```

```
127.0.0.1:6379> keys *
1) "spring:session:expirations:1490589000000"
2) "spring:session:sessions:expires:7c82002e-dd4d-4196-b9ae-1d93037192f4"
3) "spring:session:sessions:7c82002e-dd4d-4196-b9ae-1d93037192f4"
```

If you run FLUSHALL again it'll reset the database, and the next browser refresh will
yield a new uuid value.

The Java Message Service

We don't know of a good JMS solution for Cloud Foundry. It's invasive, but straightforward, to rework most JMS code to use the AMQP protocol, which RabbitMQ
speaks. If you're using Spring, then the primitives for dealing with JMS or RabbitMQ
(or indeed, Redis's publish-subscribe support) look and work similarly. RabbitMQ
and Redis are available on Cloud Foundry. An alternative approach that might work
is to use the RabbitMQ JMS client (*https://github.com/rabbitmq/rabbitmq-jms-client*).

Distributed transactions using the X/Open XA Protocol and JTA

If your application requires distributed transactions using the XA/Open protocol and
JTA, it's possible to configure standalone XA providers using Spring (*http://bit.ly/
2s6fg1Q*), and it's downright easy to do so using Spring Boot (*http://bit.ly/2s6mXFw*).
You don't need a Java EE-container hosted XA transaction manager. Example 5-11
defines a JMS message listener and a JPA-based service.

Example 5-11. Using JTA with Spring Boot's JTA auto-configuration

```
package demo;

import org.apache.commons.logging.Log;
import org.apache.commons.logging.LogFactory;
import org.springframework.beans.factory.annotation.Autowired;
import org.springframework.boot.SpringApplication;
import org.springframework.boot.autoconfigure.SpringBootApplication;
import org.springframework.data.jpa.repository.JpaRepository;
import org.springframework.jms.annotation.JmsListener;
import org.springframework.jms.core.JmsTemplate;
import org.springframework.stereotype.Component;
import org.springframework.stereotype.Service;

import javax.persistence.Entity;
import javax.persistence.GeneratedValue;
import javax.persistence.Id;
import javax.transaction.Transactional;

@SpringBootApplication
public class DemoApplication {

  public static void main(String[] args) throws Exception {
```

```java
  SpringApplication.run(DemoApplication.class, args) ;
 }
}

interface AccountRepository extends JpaRepository<Account, Long> {
}

@Entity
class Account {

 @Id
 @GeneratedValue
 private Long id;

 private String username;

 Account() {
 }

 public Account(String username) {
  this.username = username;
 }

 public String getUsername() {
  return this.username;
 }
}

@Component
class Messages {

 private Log log = LogFactory.getLog(getClass());

 @JmsListener(destination = "accounts")
 public void onMessage(String content) {
  log.info("----> " + content);
 }
}

@Service
@Transactional
class AccountService {

 @Autowired
 private JmsTemplate jmsTemplate;

 @Autowired
 private AccountRepository accountRepository;

 public void createAccountAndNotify(String username) {
  this.jmsTemplate.convertAndSend("accounts", username);
  this.accountRepository.save(new Account(username));
```

```
  if ("error".equals(username)) {
    throw new RuntimeException("Simulated error");
  }
 }
}
```

Spring Boot automatically enlists JDBC `XADataSource` and JMS `XAConnectionFac`
`tory` resources in a global transaction. A unit test demonstrates this by triggering a
rollback and then confirming that there are no side effects in either the JDBC `Data`
`Source` or the JMS `ConnectionFactory` (Example 5-12).

Example 5-12. Exercising JTA

```java
package demo;

import org.apache.commons.logging.Log;
import org.apache.commons.logging.LogFactory;
import org.junit.Test;
import org.junit.runner.RunWith;
import org.springframework.beans.factory.annotation.Autowired;
import org.springframework.boot.test.context.SpringBootTest;
import org.springframework.test.context.junit4.SpringRunner;

import static org.junit.Assert.assertEquals;

@RunWith(SpringRunner.class)
@SpringBootTest(classes = DemoApplication.class)
public class DemoApplicationTests {

 private Log log = LogFactory.getLog(getClass());

 @Autowired
 private AccountService service;

 @Autowired
 private AccountRepository repository;

 @Test
 public void contextLoads() {
  service.createAccountAndNotify("josh");
  log.info("count is " + repository.count());
  try {
   service.createAccountAndNotify("error");
  }
  catch (Exception ex) {
   log.error(ex.getMessage());
  }
  log.info("count is " + repository.count());
  assertEquals(repository.count(), 1);
 }
}
```

Spring Boot supports several properties that you can specify to configure where the underlying JTA implementations (Bitronix, Atomikos) store their transaction logs.

 Ideally, transaction logs should be stored someplace durable. Applications on Cloud Foundry do not have a guaranteed filesystem. If the application instance goes down, there is no guarantee that the contents of the filesystem will be available on other nodes or when the application instance is restarted (also, probably, on another node). You'll need to use something more permanent for absolute guarantees about recovery.

Cloud filesystems

Cloud Foundry doesn't provide a durable filesystem. You can use FUSE-based filesystems like SSHFS on Cloud Foundry. FUSE is a C/C++-level API for building filesystem implementations in userspace. There are all manner of FUSE-based filesystems that expose HTTP APIs, SSH connections, MongoDB filesystems, and much more as filesystems to UNIX-style operating systems. This lets you mount, in userspace, a remote filesystem using SSH, for example. Naturally, you're going to need a remote machine on which you have SSH access for this to work, but it's one valid option and it's particularly convenient in the case of JTA, which requires an actual honest-to-goodness java.io.File in order to keep promises about integrity of data. This is slower.

If you need to read and write bytes, and don't care if the I/O happens with a java.io.File or with an alternative, filesystem-like backing service, you might consider one of the many suitable alternatives, like a MongoDB GridFS-based solution (*http://bit.ly/2s6d8re*) or an Amazon Web services-based S3 solution. (We explore connecting to Amazon S3 in our discussion of creating service brokers in Chapter 14.) These backing services offer a filesystem-like API; you will read, write, and query bytes by a logical name. Spring Data MongoDB provides the very convenient GridFsTemplate that makes short work of reading and writing data.

Let's look at an example that persists file uploads to a MongoDB backend. When you run the application, open http://localhost:8080 to interact with the REST API.

 Technologies like MongoDB are important, but they will add a cost to your operational overhead. Ideally, this competency should be managed by the platform, and automated. If you're using Cloud Foundry, there is a MongoDB service in the service catalog.

Example 5-13. Using MongoDB's GridFS as a backing service for a REST API that reads and writes file data

```java
package demo;

import com.mongodb.gridfs.GridFSDBFile;
import org.springframework.beans.factory.annotation.Autowired;
import org.springframework.boot.SpringApplication;
import org.springframework.boot.autoconfigure.SpringBootApplication;
import org.springframework.data.mongodb.core.query.Query;
import org.springframework.data.mongodb.gridfs.GridFsCriteria;
import org.springframework.data.mongodb.gridfs.GridFsTemplate;
import org.springframework.http.HttpHeaders;
import org.springframework.http.HttpStatus;
import org.springframework.http.ResponseEntity;
import org.springframework.stereotype.Controller;
import org.springframework.web.bind.annotation.*;
import org.springframework.web.multipart.MultipartFile;

import java.io.ByteArrayOutputStream;
import java.util.List;
import java.util.Optional;
import java.util.stream.Collectors;

@SpringBootApplication
public class DemoApplication {

  public static void main(String[] args) {
    SpringApplication.run(DemoApplication.class, args);
  }
}

@Controller
@RequestMapping(value = "/files")
class FileController {

  @Autowired
  private GridFsTemplate gridFsTemplate;

  private static Query getFilenameQuery(String name) {
    return Query.query(GridFsCriteria.whereFilename().is(name));
  }

  ❶
  @RequestMapping(method = RequestMethod.POST)
  String createOrUpdate(@RequestParam MultipartFile file) throws Exception {
    String name = file.getOriginalFilename();
    maybeLoadFile(name).ifPresent(
      p -> gridFsTemplate.delete(getFilenameQuery(name)));
    gridFsTemplate.store(file.getInputStream(), name, file.getContentType())
      .save();
    return "redirect:/";
```

```
}

❷
@RequestMapping(method = RequestMethod.GET)
@ResponseBody
List<String> list() {
 return getFiles().stream().map(GridFSDBFile::getFilename)
  .collect(Collectors.toList());
}

❸
@RequestMapping(value = "/{name:.+}", method = RequestMethod.GET)
ResponseEntity<?> get(@PathVariable String name) throws Exception {
 Optional<GridFSDBFile> optionalCreated = maybeLoadFile(name);
 if (optionalCreated.isPresent()) {
  GridFSDBFile created = optionalCreated.get();
  try (ByteArrayOutputStream os = new ByteArrayOutputStream()) {
   created.writeTo(os);

   HttpHeaders headers = new HttpHeaders();
   headers.add(HttpHeaders.CONTENT_TYPE, created.getContentType());
   return new ResponseEntity<byte[]>(os.toByteArray(), headers, HttpStatus.OK);
  }
 }
 else {
  return ResponseEntity.notFound().build();
 }
}

private List<GridFSDBFile> getFiles() {
 return gridFsTemplate.find(null);
}

private Optional<GridFSDBFile> maybeLoadFile(String name) {
 GridFSDBFile file = gridFsTemplate.findOne(getFilenameQuery(name));
 return Optional.ofNullable(file);
}
}
```

❶ The /files endpoint accepts multipart file uploaded data and writes it to MongoDB's GridFS.

❷ The /files endpoint simply returns a listing of the files in GridFS.

❸ The /files/{name} endpoint reads the bytes from GridFS and sends them back
   to the client.

Alternatively, if your application's use of the filesystem is ephemeral—staging file
uploads or something—then you can use your Cloud Foundry application's tempo-

rary directory, but keep in mind that Cloud Foundry makes no guarantees about how long that data will survive.

HTTPS

Cloud Foundry terminates HTTPS requests at the highly available proxy that guards all applications. Any call that you route to your application will respond to HTTPS as well. If you're using on-premise Cloud Foundry, you can provide your own certificates centrally.

Email

Does your application use SMTP/POP3 or IMAP? If you are using email from within a Java application, you're likely using JavaMail. JavaMail is an API to support SMTP/POP3/IMAP–based email communication. There are many email providers-as-a-service. SendGrid (*http://bit.ly/2s6yNPK*), which is supported out of the box with Spring Boot, is a cloud-powered email provider with a simple API. Let's look at an example.

 Technologies like SendGrid are ideal because they're hosted and managed for you. You can even create a binding to their service using the service catalog on some flavors of Cloud Foundry, like Pivotal Web Services.

Example 5-14. Using Spring Boot's SendGrid support

```
package demo;

import com.sendgrid.SendGrid;
import org.springframework.beans.factory.annotation.Autowired;
import org.springframework.boot.SpringApplication;
import org.springframework.boot.autoconfigure.SpringBootApplication;
import org.springframework.web.bind.annotation.RequestMapping;
import org.springframework.web.bind.annotation.RequestParam;
import org.springframework.web.bind.annotation.RestController;

@SpringBootApplication
public class DemoApplication {

 public static void main(String[] args) {
  SpringApplication.run(DemoApplication.class, args);
 }
}

@RestController
class EmailRestController {

 @Autowired
```

```
  private SendGrid sendGrid;

 ❶
 @RequestMapping("/email")
 SendGrid.Response email(@RequestParam String message) throws Exception {
  SendGrid.Email email = new SendGrid.Email();
  email.setHtml("<hi>" + message + "</h1>");
  email.setText(message);
  email.setTo(new String[] { "user1@host.io" });
  email.setToName(new String[] { "Josh" });
  email.setFrom("user2@host.io");
  email.setFromName("Josh (sender)");
  email.setSubject("I just called.. to say.. I (message truncated)");
  return sendGrid.send(email);
 }

}
```

❶ This REST API takes a message as a request parameter and sends an email using
   the auto-configured SendGrid Java client. The auto-configuration expects a valid
   SendGrid username (`spring.sendgrid.username`) and password (`spring.send
   grid.password`). Remember that Spring Boot normalizes properties, and these
   values can be provided as environment variables: `SPRING_SENDGRID_USERNAME`,
   `SPRING_SENDGRID_PASSWORD`, etc.

Identity management

Identity management, authentication, and authorization is a very important capacity
in a distributed system. The ability to centrally describe users, roles, and permissions
is critical. Cloud Foundry ships with a powerful authentication and authorization ser‐
vice called UAA that you can talk to using Spring Security. Alternatively, you might
find that Stormpath (*https://stormpath.com*) is a worthy third-party hosted service
that can act as a façade in front of other identity providers, or be the identity provider
itself. There's even a very simple Spring Boot and Spring Security integration (*https://
github.com/stormpath/stormpath-sdk-java*)!

Technologies like Okta are important because they are fully hosted
and managed for you. They imply much less operational overhead
than something like Active Directory, which can be a full-time job
to administer!

In early 2017, Okta acquired Stormpath, committing to preserve
the experience for applications that build upon Stormpath, but
connecting them to an Okta backend.

Summary

Hopefully, you've found something in this chapter to help you forklift an intractable legacy application! If that's what you're attempting to do, then consider writing tests to automate verification of things you expect will be hostile. If you expect trouble migrating the database access, filesystem access, and email workers, then you might set up an endpoint that connects to a database, an endpoint that sends an email, and an endpoint that reads files in the way you'd like. As you make changes to the application to forklift, use a continuous integration technology to deploy the application and test those endpoints. Once all the endpoints work and you're sure that, by extension, everything else does, do a more exhaustive run and get the application certified. If you're worried about leaving those endpoints in, then feel free to remove them, but be sure to add a giant TODO or backlog item to add the Spring Boot Actuator at a later date. The Actuator provides an easily secured /health endpoint that will give you the same kind of feedback. While you're in the backlog, prioritize writing proper tests!

The goal of this chapter was to address common concerns typical of efforts to move existing legacy applications to the cloud. Usually that migration involves some combination of things we've addressed here. Once you've made the migration, have a strong cup of...water, or whatever! You've earned it. That's one less thing to manage and worry about. The platform will wear the pager for you now.

## PART II

Web Services

## CHAPTER 6

REST APIs

Amazon had a hard time scaling functionality in different teams as the organization became reliant on shared access to several databases across teams. This frustrated the ability of a given team to change functionality without impacting others in the organization. So, as Amazon.com CTO Werner Vogels explained in 2006 (*http://bit.ly/2s6wwEr*), all integration would be done in terms of APIs, not database calls.

This is an important first step in making the move to microservices: everything is an API. Representational State Transfer (REST) is far and away the most popular protocol supporting the web's millions of APIs.

REST was originally advanced by Dr. Roy Fielding as part of his doctoral dissertation (*http://bit.ly/2j4SIKI*) in 2000. Fielding helped define the HTTP specification and wanted to help illustrate how the web—an already proven, massively scalable, decentralized, failure-resistant fabric—could be used to build services. HTTP is an *existence proof* of the REST architecture's merits.

Where previous approaches to distributed services (like CORBA, EJB, RMI, and SOAP) focused more or less on exposing an object-oriented interface and methods as a remotely accessible service (RPC), REST instead focuses on the manipulation of remote *resources* or entities. Nouns, not verbs. Entities, not actions.

Leonard Richardson's Maturity Model

REST is all about exposing the mutations of business state with the verbs (GET, PUT, POST, DELETE, etc.) and idioms (HTTP headers, status codes, etc.) that HTTP already gives us to support service-to-service communication. The best REST APIs tend to exploit more of HTTP's capabilities. REST, for all of its benefits, is an architectural constraint on HTTP, not any sort of *standard*, and so we've seen a proliferation of APIs of varying degrees of compliance with RESTful principles. Leonard Richardson put forth his REST *maturity model* (*http://bit.ly/2s6elP9*) to help grade an API's compliance with REST's principles:

Level 0: The swamp of POX

(Naturally, it *would* be zero-indexed!) Describes APIs that use HTTP as a transport and nothing more. SOAP-based web services, for example, use HTTP, but they *could* as easily use JMS. They are, incidentally, HTTP-based. Such a service uses HTTP mainly as a tunnel through one URI. SOAP and XML-RPC are examples. They usually use only one HTTP verb (POST).

Level 1: Resources

Describes APIs that use multiple URIs to distinguish related nouns, but otherwise avoid the full features of HTTP.

Level 2: HTTP verbs

Describes APIs that leverage transport-native properties (like HTTP verbs and status codes) to enhance the service. If you do *everything* incorrectly with Spring MVC or JAX-RS or any other modern-day REST framework, you'll *still* probably end up with an API that's level 2 compliant! This is a *great* starting point.

Level 3: Hypermedia controls (HATEOAS, for Hypermedia as the Engine of Application State)

Describes APIs that require no *a priori* knowledge of a service in order to navigate it. Such a service promotes longevity through a uniform interface for interrogating a service's structure.

In this chapter, we'll look at how to use Spring to build REST services, starting at level 2. Later, we'll look at how to use hypermedia to promote uniform, self-describing services. REST APIs are meant to represent the HTTP contract between services in the system. API clients will use them, but humans must develop against them, so we will pay particular attention to developing approachable, correctly and consistently documented APIs as well.

 We're going to be using Spring MVC for this chapter. Spring works well with JAX-RS, too. If you are using the Spring Initializr (*http://start.spring.io*), select "Jersey (JAX-RS)" for a web application that supports JAX-RS. It's not too hard to get other implementations working with Spring, as well. For more on integrating other servlet-based frameworks, see the discussion on using traditional Java EE APIs (like servlets) from within a Spring Boot application in "Using Servlet APIs in a Spring Boot Application" on page 576.

REST is an important part of a cloud native application. While nothing about microservices stipulates or even requires REST, it is the most common approach to expose services.

HTTP lends itself to cloud native applications. HTTP is an ideal fit for service caching because it has no client-side state. Instead, each request is self-contained. This also implies that services can be horizontally scaled easily, so long as the state represented by the REST API can also scale horizontally. Caching reduces time-to-first-byte times. You can squeeze a lot of performance out of individual HTTP requests with caching and GZip compression, and with HTTP 2 on the horizon, this situation looks to improve considerably in the near term.

HTTP is content-type agnostic and includes support for content negotiation; one client may support only XML, another JSON or Google's Protocol Buffers. All may be served by the same services. This mechanism is extensible, too.

Simple REST APIs with Spring MVC

Add `org.springframework.boot : spring-boot-starter-web` to your build to bring in a servlet container and full configuration for Spring MVC. Spring MVC is a request/response-oriented HTTP framework. In Spring MVC, *controller* handler methods are mapped to HTTP requests and ultimately provide responses. Let's look at a REST API designed to manipulate `Customer` entities (Example 6-1).

Example 6-1. Our first @RestController, CustomerRestController

```
package demo;

import org.springframework.beans.factory.annotation.Autowired;
import org.springframework.http.HttpMethod;
import org.springframework.http.ResponseEntity;
import org.springframework.web.bind.annotation.*;
import org.springframework.web.servlet.mvc.method.annotation.MvcUriComponentsBuilder;
import org.springframework.web.servlet.support.ServletUriComponentsBuilder;

import java.net.URI;
import java.util.Collection;

@RestController
@RequestMapping("/v1/customers")
public class CustomerRestController {

 @Autowired
 private CustomerRepository customerRepository;

 ❶
 @RequestMapping(method = RequestMethod.OPTIONS)
 ResponseEntity<?> options() {

  //@formatter:off
  return ResponseEntity
   .ok()
```

```
        .allow(HttpMethod.GET, HttpMethod.POST,
            HttpMethod.HEAD, HttpMethod.OPTIONS,
            HttpMethod.PUT, HttpMethod.DELETE)
            .build();
    //@formatter:on
}

@GetMapping
ResponseEntity<Collection<Customer>> getCollection() {
  return ResponseEntity.ok(this.customerRepository.findAll());
}

❷
@GetMapping(value = "/{id}")
ResponseEntity<Customer> get(@PathVariable Long id) {
  return this.customerRepository.findById(id).map(ResponseEntity::ok)
    .orElseThrow(() -> new CustomerNotFoundException(id));
}

@PostMapping
ResponseEntity<Customer> post(@RequestBody Customer c) { ❸

  Customer customer = this.customerRepository.save(new Customer(c
    .getFirstName(), c.getLastName()));

  URI uri = MvcUriComponentsBuilder.fromController(getClass()).path("/{id}")
    .buildAndExpand(customer.getId()).toUri();
  return ResponseEntity.created(uri).body(customer);
}

❹
@DeleteMapping(value = "/{id}")
ResponseEntity<?> delete(@PathVariable Long id) {
  return this.customerRepository.findById(id).map(c -> {
    customerRepository.delete(c);
    return ResponseEntity.noContent().build();
  }).orElseThrow(() -> new CustomerNotFoundException(id));
}

❺
@RequestMapping(value = "/{id}", method = RequestMethod.HEAD)
ResponseEntity<?> head(@PathVariable Long id) {
  return this.customerRepository.findById(id)
    .map(exists -> ResponseEntity.noContent().build())
    .orElseThrow(() -> new CustomerNotFoundException(id));
}

❻
@PutMapping(value = "/{id}")
ResponseEntity<Customer> put(@PathVariable Long id, @RequestBody Customer c) {
  return this.customerRepository
    .findById(id)
```

```
.map(
 existing -> {
  Customer customer = this.customerRepository.save(new Customer(existing
   .getId(), c.getFirstName(), c.getLastName()));
  URI selfLink = URI.create(ServletUriComponentsBuilder.fromCurrentRequest()
   .toUriString());
  return ResponseEntity.created(selfLink).body(customer);
 }).orElseThrow(() -> new CustomerNotFoundException(id));

 }
}
```

❶ A handler method is designated with the @RequestMapping annotation. A class may contain a @RequestMapping annotation, in which case the method-level declarations override or add to the root, class-level mappings. The handler responds to the OPTIONS HTTP verb, which a client will issue when it wants to know what other HTTP verbs are supported for a given resource.

❷ This handler method returns individual records whose IDs are encoded as *path variables* in the @RequestMapping URI syntax: {id}.

❸ Data may be transferred from the client to the service, and the body of the data passed to the service as the handler's @RequestBody.

❹ The DELETE handler returns an HTTP 204 on success, or it throws an exception which ultimately results in a 404 on failure.

❺ The HEAD handler is meant only to confirm the existence of the resource, so it returns with a 204 on success, or it throws an exception which ultimately results in a 404 on failure, just as in the DELETE handler.

❻ The PUT handler is charged with updating an existing record. It uses @PathVariable parameters to specify which record to update. If the record does not exist, an exception that ultimately yields a 404 is thrown.

This is a basic Spring MVC REST controller. The @RequestMapping annotation maps handler methods to specifications of types of HTTP requests. The @RequestMapping annotation lets us further discriminate by headers in the request, by content-type sent and returned, by cookies, and more. The path specified is relative to the root of the application's context-path *unless* a controller-level @RequestMapping annotation specifies a path, in which case the handler-level path is relative to the path in the controller.

Spring MVC also supports HTTP method-specific annotations like
`@GetMapping`, `@PostMapping`, etc. These work just like `@RequestMap`
`ping`, though they imply the HTTP method. You can use them
interchangeably if your endpoint doesn't need to support more
than one HTTP method.

Content Negotiation

The handler methods return objects or, sometimes, the `ResponseEntity` envelope
with objects as a payload. When Spring MVC sees a return value, it uses a strategy
object, `HttpMessageConverter`, to convert the object into a representation suitable
for the client. The client specifies what kind of representation it expects using *content-
negotiation*. By default, Spring MVC looks at the incoming request's `Accept` header
for a media type, like `application/json`, `application/xml`, etc., that a configured
`HttpMessageConverter` is capable of creating, given the object and the desired media
type. This same process happens in reverse for data sent from the client *to* the service
and passed to the handler methods as `@RequestBody` parameters.

Content-negotiation is one of the most powerful features of HTTP: the same service
may serve clients that accept different protocols. Use media types to signal to the client the type of content being served. Normally, a media type *also* signals how the client is to process the content of the response. A client knows, for example, not to
bother trying to extract JSON strings out of a response with a media type of `image/`
`jpeg`.

Reading and Writing Binary Data

Thus far we've looked at JSON, but there's no reason REST resources couldn't serve
media like images or raw files. Let's look at how to read and write image data for a
profile endpoint, `/customers/{id}/photo` (Example 6-2).

Example 6-2. Reading and writing binary (image) data

```
package demo;

import org.apache.commons.logging.Log;
import org.apache.commons.logging.LogFactory;
import org.springframework.beans.factory.annotation.Autowired;
import org.springframework.beans.factory.annotation.Value;
import org.springframework.core.io.FileSystemResource;
import org.springframework.core.io.Resource;
import org.springframework.http.MediaType;
import org.springframework.http.ResponseEntity;
import org.springframework.util.Assert;
import org.springframework.util.FileCopyUtils;
```

```java
import org.springframework.web.bind.annotation.*;
import org.springframework.web.multipart.MultipartFile;

import java.io.*;
import java.net.URI;
import java.util.concurrent.Callable;

//@formatter:off
import static org.springframework.web.servlet
        .support.ServletUriComponentsBuilder.fromCurrentRequest;
//@formatter:on

@RestController
@RequestMapping(value = "/customers/{id}/photo")
public class CustomerProfilePhotoRestController {

 private File root;
 private final CustomerRepository customerRepository;
 private final Log log = LogFactory.getLog(getClass());

 @Autowired
 CustomerProfilePhotoRestController(
         @Value("${upload.dir:${user.home}/images}") String uploadDir,
         CustomerRepository customerRepository) {
  this.root = new File(uploadDir);
  this.customerRepository = customerRepository ;
  Assert.isTrue(this.root.exists() || this.root.mkdirs(),
   String.format("The path '%s' must exist.", this.root.getAbsolutePath()));
 }

 ❶
 @GetMapping
 ResponseEntity<Resource> read(@PathVariable Long id) {
  return this.customerRepository
   .findById(id)
   .map(
   customer -> {
    File file = fileFor(customer);

    Assert.isTrue(file.exists(),
     String.format("file-not-found %s", file.getAbsolutePath()));

    Resource fileSystemResource = new FileSystemResource(file);
    return ResponseEntity.ok().contentType(MediaType.IMAGE_JPEG)
     .body(fileSystemResource);
   }).orElseThrow(() -> new CustomerNotFoundException(id));
 }

 ❷
 @RequestMapping(method = { RequestMethod.POST, RequestMethod.PUT })
 Callable<ResponseEntity<?>> write(@PathVariable Long id,
  @RequestParam MultipartFile file) ❸
```

```
   throws Exception {
   log.info(String.format("upload-start /customers/%s/photo (%s bytes)", id,
    file.getSize())));
   return () -> this.customerRepository
    .findById(id)
    .map(
     customer -> {
      File fileForCustomer = fileFor(customer);
      try (InputStream in = file.getInputStream();
       OutputStream out = new FileOutputStream(fileForCustomer)) {
       FileCopyUtils.copy(in, out);
      }
      catch (IOException ex) {
       throw new RuntimeException(ex);
      }
      URI location = fromCurrentRequest().buildAndExpand(id).toUri(); ❹
      log.info(String.format("upload-finish /customers/%s/photo (%s)", id,
       location));
      return ResponseEntity.created(location).build();
     }).orElseThrow(() -> new CustomerNotFoundException(id));
   }

   private File fileFor(Customer person) {
    return new File(this.root, Long.toString(person.getId()));
   }
  }
```

❶ Spring MVC automatically returns the byte[] data—a file, URL resource,
InputStream, etc.—from the buffer underlying an org.springframe
work.core.io.Resource returned from a Spring MVC controller handler
method.

❷ File uploads may block and monopolize the Servlet container's threadpool.
Spring MVC *backgrounds* Callable<T> handler method returns values to a configured Executor thread pool and frees up the container's thread until the
response is ready.

❸ Spring MVC will automatically map multipart file upload data to an org.spring
framework.web.multipart.MultipartFile request parameter.

❹ It's good form when creating a resource to return an HTTP 201 (Created) status
code and return a Location header with the URI of the newly created resource.

Reading media is easy if the data can be represented with one of Spring's org.spring
framework.core.io.Resource implementations. There are many implementations
provided out of the box: FileSystemResource, GridFsResource (which is based on
MongoDB's Grid File System), ClassPathResource, GzipResource, VfsResource, Url

Resource, etc. Spring MVC automatically returns the byte[] data from the buffer underlying a `org.springframework.core.io.Resource` to the client.

Spring MVC applications run in a servlet container. The servlet container itself maintains a frontend thread pool that is used to respond to incoming HTTP requests; each time an incoming HTTP request arrives, a thread is dispatched to accept the request and produce a reply. It's important not to monopolize threads in the servlet container's thread pool. Spring MVC will move the flow of execution of the controller handler method to a separate thread pool—one provided by specifying a `TaskExecutor` bean—if a controller handler method returns a `java.util.concurrent.Callba ble<T>`, an `org.springframework.web.context.request.async.DeferredResult`, or a `org.springframework.web.context.request.async.WebAsyncTask`.

 Spring MVC also supports websockets and Server-Sent Events (SSE), both of which are asynchronous communication mechanisms, but they're also different beasts unto themselves and not what we're trying to achieve here.

A `Callable<T>` is simply a specialization of a `Runnable` that returns a result. Spring MVC invokes the `Callable` on the specified thread pool and, once the callable's produced a result, returns the result asynchronously as the reply to the original HTTP request.

A `WebAsyncTask` is basically the same thing; it wraps a `Callable<T>` but also provides fields to specify the `TaskExecutor` on which to run the `Callbale<T>`, and a timeout period after which a response will be committed.

A `DeferredResult` doesn't trigger execution elsewhere; instead, Spring MVC returns the servlet container thread to the pool and only triggers an async response when the `DeferredResult#setResult` method is called. `DeferredResult` instances may be cached and later updated in an out-of-band thread of execution. As an example, an endpoint might stash references to `DeferredResult` in a shared `ConcurrentHash Map<K,V>` mapped by a meaningful correlation ID that `@EventListener` or `@Rabbit Listener` annotated methods could later look up. Once obtained, those asynchronous threads could call `DeferredResult#setResult` and signal that the response should be returned to the client, finally.

Our example handles the write in a separate thread; it assumes that writing may be a slower operation than reading, which could benefit from caching. The example moves the upload, the write, to a separate thread by handling it in a `Callable<T>`. This is efficient from the perspective of the *service*, but irrelevant from the perspective of the *client*. The client will block, waiting for the reply, for as long as the `Calla ble<T>` is executing.

An alternative approach is to return *immediately*, returning an HTTP 202 `Accepted` status code and providing a `Location` header that either indicates where the newly created resource lives or at least where information about the status of its potentially long-lived creation exists.

Google Protocol Buffers

Content-negotiation lets us optimize, where possible, but provide fall-through support otherwise. A common example of this is Google Protocol Buffers. Google Protocol Buffers is an ideal choice for efficient, cross-platform communication. If the requesting client doesn't support Google Protocol Buffers, Spring can downgrade to JSON or XML thanks to content-negotiation. Smarter clients get smarter responses, but everybody can play.

Google Protocol Buffers is a highly efficient serialization format. Google Protocol Buffers messages carry no information to describe the *structure* of the message, only the data in the message. The *structure* is implied by the Google Protocol Buffer `.proto` schema definition. The schema can be used to generate a language-specific binding for interop; Google Protocol Buffers enjoys robust support across most of the languages and platforms you're likely to use. Services don't need to inspect incoming payloads for every request to understand and map their structure—it is done once when the schema is provided (Example 6-3).

Example 6-3. Google Protocol Buffers schema for a Customer message

```
package demo;

option java_package = "demo"; ❶

option java_outer_classname = "CustomerProtos"; ❷

message Customer { ❸
    optional int64 id = 1;
    required string firstName = 2;
    required string lastName = 3;
}


message Customers { ❹
    repeated Customer customer = 1;
}
```

❶ The language-specific package or module for the resulting types

❷ Google Protocol Buffer types can be nested inner classes if you specify the `java_outer_classname`; the resulting type will be `demo.CustomerProtos.Cus tomer`

❸ The schema for a single `Customer`

❹ The schema for a *collection* of `Customer`

Fields in the definition are assigned an integer offset to help the compiler understand what it is looking at in a stream of binary data. If a client knows about an older definition of a message, and a service replies with a more detailed message, the client will still be able to interoperate so long as the offsets are stable. This is ideal in a distributed system where clients and services may not always have the same *version* of a message. Independent deployability, the ability to deploy one service without a *flag day* deploy of others, is a very important feature of microservices. It lets teams iterate and evolve their services without constant synchronization overhead. Google Protocol Buffers supports this loose coupling.

The `protoc` compiler generates language-specific (Java, Python, C, .NET, PHP, Ruby, and a large number of other technologies besides) bindings to read and write messages described in a `.proto` schema. Let's script the generation of Java, Python, and Ruby bindings for our `Customer` Google Protocol Buffer definition. We can use these bindings to talk to our Google Protocol Buffers-powered REST endpoints (Example 6-4).

Example 6-4. A script to generate the required Java, Ruby, and Python clients

```
#!/usr/bin/env bash

SRC_DIR=`pwd`
DST_DIR=`pwd`/../src/main/

echo source:           ${SRC_DIR}
echo destination root: ${DST_DIR}

function ensure_implementations(){
    gem list | grep ruby-protocol-buffers || sudo gem install ruby-protocol-buffers
    go get -u github.com/golang/protobuf/{proto,protoc-gen-go}
}

function gen(){
    D=$1
    echo $D
    OUT=$DST_DIR/$D
    mkdir -p $OUT
    protoc -I=$SRC_DIR --${D}_out=$OUT $SRC_DIR/customer.proto
```

```
}

ensure_implementations

gen java
gen python
gen ruby
```

The resulting Java, Ruby, and Python clients are not very sophisticated, but they work. Example 6-5 shows the Python binding in action.

Example 6-5. A Python-language Google Protocol Buffer client; customer_pb2 is the client generated by protoc

```
#!/usr/bin/env python

import urllib

import customer_pb2

if __name__ == '__main__':
    customer = customer_pb2.Customer()
    customers_read = urllib.urlopen('http://localhost:8080/customers/1').read()
    customer.ParseFromString(customers_read)
    print customer
```

Example 6-6 shows the Ruby binding in action.

Example 6-6. A Ruby-language Google Protocol Buffer client; /customers.pb is the client generated by protoc

```
#!/usr/bin/ruby

require './customer.pb'
require 'net/http'
require 'uri'

uri = URI.parse('http://localhost:8080/customers/3')
body = Net::HTTP.get(uri)
puts Demo::Customer.parse(body)
```

Spring MVC ships with a custom HttpMessageConverter implementation that can read and write objects created using the generated Java bindings for our .proto definition. The protoc compiler will emit bindings for our Google Protobuf compiler that we can use when handling REST requests. Let's look at a REST API built to handle application/x-protobuf. Most of this service should seem familiar. Indeed, the main difference between this and what you've seen before, besides the URI path, is the additional tedium imposed by having to convert from a Customer to a Protobuffer-specific CustomerProtos.Customer DTO and back (Example 6-7).

Example 6-7. A REST service that leverages content-negotiation to serve content with the media type application/x-protobuf

```
package demo;

import org.springframework.beans.factory.annotation.Autowired;
import org.springframework.http.ResponseEntity;
import org.springframework.web.bind.annotation.*;

//@formatter:off
import org.springframework.web.servlet.mvc.method
        .annotation.MvcUriComponentsBuilder;
import static org.springframework.web.servlet.support
        .ServletUriComponentsBuilder.fromCurrentRequest;
//@formatter:on

import java.net.URI;
import java.util.Collection;
import java.util.List;
import java.util.stream.Collectors;


@RestController
@RequestMapping(value = "/v1/protos/customers")
public class CustomerProtobufRestController {

  private final CustomerRepository customerRepository;

  @Autowired
  public CustomerProtobufRestController(CustomerRepository customerRepository) {
    this.customerRepository = customerRepository;
  }

  @GetMapping(value = "/{id}")
  ResponseEntity<CustomerProtos.Customer> get(@PathVariable Long id) {
    return this.customerRepository.findById(id).map(this::fromEntityToProtobuf)
      .map(ResponseEntity::ok)
      .orElseThrow(() -> new CustomerNotFoundException(id));
  }

  @GetMapping
  ResponseEntity<CustomerProtos.Customers> getCollection() {
    List<Customer> all = this.customerRepository.findAll();
    CustomerProtos.Customers customers = this.fromCollectionToProtobuf(all);
    return ResponseEntity.ok(customers);
  }

  @PostMapping
```

```java
ResponseEntity<CustomerProtos.Customer> post(
 @RequestBody CustomerProtos.Customer c) {

  Customer customer = this.customerRepository.save(new Customer(c
   .getFirstName(), c.getLastName())));

  URI uri = MvcUriComponentsBuilder.fromController(getClass()).path("/{id}")
   .buildAndExpand(customer.getId()).toUri();
  return ResponseEntity.created(uri).body(this.fromEntityToProtobuf(customer));
 }

@PutMapping("/{id}")
ResponseEntity<CustomerProtos.Customer> put(@PathVariable Long id,
 @RequestBody CustomerProtos.Customer c) {

  return this.customerRepository
   .findById(id)
   .map(
    existing -> {

     Customer customer = this.customerRepository.save(new Customer(existing
      .getId(), c.getFirstName(), c.getLastName())));

     URI selfLink = URI.create(fromCurrentRequest().toUriString());

      return ResponseEntity.created(selfLink).body(
       fromEntityToProtobuf(customer));

    }).orElseThrow(() -> new CustomerNotFoundException(id));
 }

private CustomerProtos.Customers fromCollectionToProtobuf(
 Collection<Customer> c) {
 return CustomerProtos.Customers
  .newBuilder()
  .addAllCustomer(
   c.stream().map(this::fromEntityToProtobuf).collect(Collectors.toList()))
  .build();
}

private CustomerProtos.Customer fromEntityToProtobuf(Customer c) {
 return fromEntityToProtobuf(c.getId(), c.getFirstName(), c.getLastName());
}

private CustomerProtos.Customer fromEntityToProtobuf(Long id, String f,
 String l) {
 CustomerProtos.Customer.Builder builder = CustomerProtos.Customer
  .newBuilder();
 if (id != null && id > 0) {
  builder.setId(id);
 }
 return builder.setFirstName(f).setLastName(l).build();
```

```
        }
}
```

We need to register a custom `HttpMessageConverter` implementation to teach Spring MVC about the new content-type, as shown in Example 6-8.

Example 6-8. Register a custom HttpMessageConverter implementation to convert HTTP messages to application/x-protobuf and back

```
package demo;

import org.springframework.context.annotation.Bean;
import org.springframework.context.annotation.Configuration;
import org.springframework.http.converter.protobuf.ProtobufHttpMessageConverter;

@Configuration
class GoogleProtocolBuffersConfiguration {

 @Bean
 ProtobufHttpMessageConverter protobufHttpMessageConverter() {
  return new ProtobufHttpMessageConverter();
 }
}
```

The `RestTemplate` client supports the same content-negotiation mechanism as a Spring MVC service does; to *read* `application/x-protobuf` data, configure a `Proto bufHttpMessageConverter` on the `RestTemplate`.

Error Handling

Various handlers in our `CustomerRestController` operate on existing records and if that record is not found, throw an exception. These handlers could explicitly return a `ResponseEntity` with a 404 status, but this sort of error handling quickly becomes repetitive when duplicated across multiple handlers. Centralize error handling logic. Scale comes from consistency, which comes from automation. Spring MVC supports listening for, and responding to, error conditions in Spring MVC controllers with handler methods annotated with `@ExceptionHandler`. Normally, `@ExceptionHandler` handlers live in the same controller component as the handlers that may throw exceptions. These exception handlers aren't shared across multiple controllers, though. If you want to centralize exception handling logic, use a `@ControllerAdvice` component. A `@ControllerAdvice` is a special type of component that may introduce behavior (and respond to exceptions) for any number of controllers. They are a natural place to stick centralized `@ExceptionHandler` handlers.

Errors are an important part of an effective API. Errors should both uniquely and concisely indicate an error condition to automated clients *and* support humans, who must ultimately resolve or at least understand the implications of the error. It's paramount that errors be as helpful as possible. HTTP status codes are many things, but they are *not* particularly helpful. It is a common practice to send back an error code along with some sort of representation of the error and a human-readable error message. There is no official standard on the way errors should be encoded, beyond HTTP status codes, but a de-facto standard is the `application/vnd.error` content type (*https://github.com/blongden/vnd.error*); Spring HATEOAS supports this error representation. Add `org.springframework.boot : spring-boot-starter-hateoas` to the classpath. Spring HATEOAS provides `VndError` and `VndErrors` as envelope objects to represent an individual error or a collection of errors, respectively.

Let's look at Example 6-9, which shows a simple `@ControllerAdvice` that intercepts all exceptions thrown and properly handles them by sending back an HTTP status *and* a `VndError`.

Example 6-9. Centralized error handling with a @ControllerAdvice

```
package demo;

import org.springframework.hateoas.VndErrors;
import org.springframework.http.HttpHeaders;
import org.springframework.http.HttpStatus;
import org.springframework.http.MediaType;
import org.springframework.http.ResponseEntity;
import org.springframework.web.bind.annotation.ControllerAdvice;
import org.springframework.web.bind.annotation.ExceptionHandler;
import org.springframework.web.bind.annotation.RestController;

import java.util.Optional;

@ControllerAdvice(annotations = RestController.class)
public class CustomerControllerAdvice {

❶
  private final MediaType vndErrorMediaType = MediaType
    .parseMediaType("application/vnd.error");

❷
  @ExceptionHandler(CustomerNotFoundException.class)
  ResponseEntity<VndErrors> notFoundException(CustomerNotFoundException e) {
    return this.error(e, HttpStatus.NOT_FOUND, e.getCustomerId() + "");
  }

  @ExceptionHandler(IllegalArgumentException.class)
  ResponseEntity<VndErrors> assertionException(IllegalArgumentException ex) {
    return this.error(ex, HttpStatus.NOT_FOUND, ex.getLocalizedMessage());
  }

❸
```

```
private <E extends Exception> ResponseEntity<VndErrors> error(E error,
  HttpStatus httpStatus, String logref) {
  String msg = Optional.of(error.getMessage()).orElse(
    error.getClass().getSimpleName());
  HttpHeaders httpHeaders = new HttpHeaders();
  httpHeaders.setContentType(this.vndErrorMediaType);
  return new ResponseEntity<>(new VndErrors(logref, msg), httpHeaders,
    httpStatus);
 }
}
```

❶ There's no built-in media type for `application/vnd.error`, so we create our own.

❷ We have two handlers in this class, and they both respond to possible exceptions thrown in other components. This handler, specifically, responds to our `Custom erNotFoundException`, which in turn just extends `RuntimeException`.

❸ The `error` method builds up a `ResponseEntity` containing a `VndErrors` payload and conveys the media type and status code desired. Simple *and* useful.

Hypermedia

The API as built will work just fine—*if* a client knows which endpoint to call, when to call it, and with what HTTP method to make the call. The HTTP OPTIONS method helps with the last bit: understanding which HTTP method is available for a given resource. The rest of it, however, is implied, and, one hopes, well documented *somewhere*. The trouble with documentation is that few keep it up to date, and fewer still bother to read it. It ultimately drifts out of sync with the living specification of the service as defined in the code.

Dr. Fielding's thesis features heavily the *hypermedia tenet*. It refers to the idea that links (<link/> elements in HTML markup) in everyday resources provide information to the client—HTML browsers and their users—that ultimately leads to changes in application state. You may start your session at Amazon.com, enter a search, find a satisfying product to purchase, click to add it to the shopping cart, choose to check out, and then pay, all by way of navigations from one HTTP resource to another. Ultimately, you've changed system state. These links tell you where to go, and because they only appear when they're relevant (there's no refund link for products not yet paid for!), they imply *when* to go. These steps from one resource to another imply a *protocol*: a series of steps and interactions required to achieve an end, in software. This system works because we humans can parse the links, extract them from the user experience, and imply a sequence of steps based on visual cues from the site's design to understand their relevance.

Machine clients, on the other hand, aren't as clever as humans. Whereas humans click on links visually rendered using <a/> elements, automated clients traverse <link/> elements (even though humans can't *click* on them). These links have two important attributes: rel and href. There are many applications for this element, but the most common application in everyday use is loading stylesheet data, as shown in Example 6-10.

Example 6-10. Loading a document's stylesheet

```
<link rel="stylesheet" href="bootstrap.css">
```

These links provide metadata about the resource they're included in. The browser looks first at the rel attribute to understand what sort of resource is being linked. It optionally follows the href to load the linked resource. The client uses the rel attribute to make a determination about the *relevance* of the linked resource. The linked resource can live anywhere! The browser doesn't make any assumptions about the location *a priori*—it simply follows the href in the <link/> if one is available. The client is thus *decoupled* from the location of the resource.

The client (the browser) can still use the API, even if the locations of the resources in the API change. The client can determine which resource to follow by examining the rel attribute to understand the linked resource's *relevance*. The rel becomes the contract: as long as that stays stable, the client will never break.

Let's revisit the protocol for checking out from an Amazon.com-like API. Sure, the <link/> element is an XML element, but there's no reason the same approach—payloads accompanied by enriching links—couldn't work to our advantage in other encodings such as JSON. There's even a de facto standard encoding for describing these link elements in JSON. HAL, or *Hypertext Application Language* (*http://state less.co/hal_specification.html*), is a specialization of JSON with a content type of appli cation/hal+json. So instead of spending time building ad hoc structures to describe your REST resources, you can rely on HAL and implement HATEOAS (see Example 6-11).

> There are other competing standards for hypermedia representation. HAL just happens to be pretty popular, and useful.

Example 6-11. The earlier Customer REST resource described with HAL

```
{
  "id":1,
  "firstName":"Mark",
```

```
  "lastName":"Fisher",
  "_links": {
    "self": {"href":"http://localhost:8080/v2/customers/1"},
    "profile-photo": {"href":"http://localhost:8080/customers/1/photo/"}
  }
}
```

An API so described can be navigated with any HAL-compatible client. Spring Boot supports a *very* convenient HAL client called the *HAL Browser*. You can add it to any Spring Boot web application by adding the `org.springframework.boot : spring-boot-starter-actuator` and `org.springframework.data : spring-data-rest-hal-browser` dependencies. It registers a Spring Boot Actuator endpoint, so you'll need the Actuator as well (Figure 6-1).

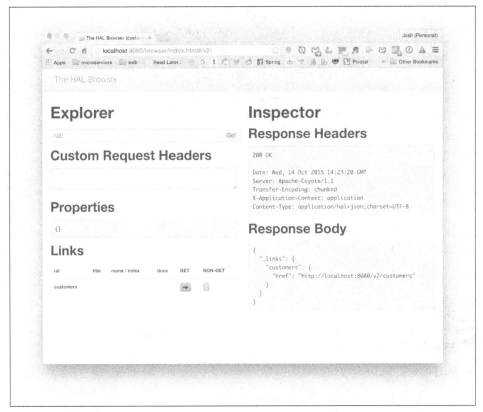

Figure 6-1. The default configured HAL browser Actuator endpoint

Spring HATEOAS (*http://spring.io/projects/spring-hateoas*) sits on top of Spring MVC and provides the necessary plumbing to consume and describe resources in terms of payloads and their related links. It depends on Spring MVC; instead of consuming and producing resources of type T, you consume and produce type `org.springframe`

work.hateoas.Resource<T> resources, for single objects, or org.springframe
work.hateoas.Resources<T>, for collections of objects.

In Spring HATEOAS, Resource is an envelope object that in turn contains a payload
and a set of related links. You're going to convert objects of type T to objects of type
Resource<T> or Resources<T> frequently. Codify the recipe for the conversion into
instances of Spring HATEOAS's org.springframework.hateoas.ResourceAssem
bler. Let's revisit our CustomerRestController, adding in hypermedia and Spring
HATEOAS (Example 6-12).

Example 6-12. A revised CustomerHypermediaRestController

```
package demo;

import org.springframework.beans.factory.annotation.Autowired;
import org.springframework.hateoas.Link;
import org.springframework.hateoas.Resource;
import org.springframework.hateoas.Resources;
import org.springframework.http.HttpMethod;
import org.springframework.http.ResponseEntity;
import org.springframework.web.bind.annotation.*;

//@formatter:off
import org.springframework.web.servlet.mvc.method
        .annotation.MvcUriComponentsBuilder;
import org.springframework.web.servlet.support
        .ServletUriComponentsBuilder;
//@formatter:on

import java.net.URI;
import java.util.Collections;
import java.util.List;
import java.util.stream.Collectors;

❶
@RestController
@RequestMapping(value = "/v2", produces = "application/hal+json")
public class CustomerHypermediaRestController {

  private final CustomerResourceAssembler customerResourceAssembler; ❷

  private final CustomerRepository customerRepository;

  @Autowired
  CustomerHypermediaRestController(CustomerResourceAssembler cra,
                                   CustomerRepository customerRepository) {
    this.customerRepository = customerRepository;
    this.customerResourceAssembler = cra;
  }
```

❸

```java
@GetMapping
ResponseEntity<Resources<Object>> root() {
 Resources<Object> objects = new Resources<>(Collections.emptyList());
 URI uri = MvcUriComponentsBuilder
  .fromMethodCall(MvcUriComponentsBuilder.on(getClass()).getCollection())
  .build().toUri();
 Link link = new Link(uri.toString(), "customers");
 objects.add(link);
 return ResponseEntity.ok(objects);
}
```

❹

```java
@GetMapping("/customers")
ResponseEntity<Resources<Resource<Customer>>> getCollection() {
 List<Resource<Customer>> collect = this.customerRepository.findAll().stream()
  .map(customerResourceAssembler::toResource)
  .collect(Collectors.<Resource<Customer>>toList());
 Resources<Resource<Customer>> resources = new Resources<>(collect);
 URI self = ServletUriComponentsBuilder.fromCurrentRequest().build().toUri();
 resources.add(new Link(self.toString(), "self"));
 return ResponseEntity.ok(resources);
}

@RequestMapping(value = "/customers", method = RequestMethod.OPTIONS)
ResponseEntity<?> options() {
 return ResponseEntity
  .ok()
  .allow(HttpMethod.GET, HttpMethod.POST, HttpMethod.HEAD, HttpMethod.OPTIONS,
   HttpMethod.PUT, HttpMethod.DELETE).build();
}

@GetMapping(value = "/customers/{id}")
ResponseEntity<Resource<Customer>> get(@PathVariable Long id) {
 return this.customerRepository.findById(id)
  .map(c -> ResponseEntity.ok(this.customerResourceAssembler.toResource(c)))
  .orElseThrow(() -> new CustomerNotFoundException(id));
}

@PostMapping(value = "/customers")
ResponseEntity<Resource<Customer>> post(@RequestBody Customer c) {
 Customer customer = this.customerRepository.save(new Customer(c
  .getFirstName(), c.getLastName()));
 URI uri = MvcUriComponentsBuilder.fromController(getClass())
  .path("/customers/{id}").buildAndExpand(customer.getId()).toUri();
 return ResponseEntity.created(uri).body(
  this.customerResourceAssembler.toResource(customer));
}

@DeleteMapping(value = "/customers/{id}")
ResponseEntity<?> delete(@PathVariable Long id) {
 return this.customerRepository.findById(id).map(c -> {
```

```
  customerRepository.delete(c);
  return ResponseEntity.noContent().build();
 }).orElseThrow(() -> new CustomerNotFoundException(id));
}

@RequestMapping(value = "/customers/{id}", method = RequestMethod.HEAD)
ResponseEntity<?> head(@PathVariable Long id) {
 return this.customerRepository.findById(id)
  .map(exists -> ResponseEntity.noContent().build())
  .orElseThrow(() -> new CustomerNotFoundException(id));
}

@PutMapping("/customers/{id}")
ResponseEntity<Resource<Customer>> put(@PathVariable Long id,
 @RequestBody Customer c) {
 Customer customer = this.customerRepository.save(new Customer(id, c
  .getFirstName(), c.getLastName()));
 Resource<Customer> customerResource = this.customerResourceAssembler
  .toResource(customer);
 URI selfLink = URI.create(ServletUriComponentsBuilder.fromCurrentRequest()
  .toUriString());
 return ResponseEntity.created(selfLink).body(customerResource);
 }
}
```

❶ Responses are sent not as plain ol' `application/json`, but as `application/hal +json`.

❷ We've injected a custom `ResourceAssembler` implementation to simplify conversion from T to `Resource<T>`.

❸ The root endpoint simply returns a collection of `Link` elements that act as a sort of menu: it should be possible to start at `/` and navigate without any *a priori* knowledge.

❹ The `GET` method on the `customers` collection is procedurally the same as before, but we've added a Spring HATEOAS `Link` to the resource. The `Link` is constructed using Spring MVC's handy `ServletUriComponentsBuilder`.

The rest of this class is basically as before. Most of the methods in the `CustomerHyper mediaRestController` lean on the injected `CustomerResourceAssembler` to do their work. The `CustomerResourceAssembler` is defined in Example 6-13.

Example 6-13. The CustomerResourceAssembler provides a default set of links for a given Customer entity

```
package demo;

import org.springframework.hateoas.Link;
import org.springframework.hateoas.Resource;
import org.springframework.hateoas.ResourceAssembler;
import org.springframework.stereotype.Component;
import org.springframework.web.servlet.mvc.method.annotation
        .MvcUriComponentsBuilder;

import java.net.URI;

@Component
class CustomerResourceAssembler implements
 ResourceAssembler<Customer, Resource<Customer>> {

 @Override
 public Resource<Customer> toResource(Customer customer) {

  Resource<Customer> customerResource = new Resource<>(customer);
  URI photoUri = MvcUriComponentsBuilder
   .fromMethodCall(
    MvcUriComponentsBuilder.on(CustomerProfilePhotoRestController.class).read(
     customer.getId())).buildAndExpand().toUri();

  URI selfUri = MvcUriComponentsBuilder
   .fromMethodCall(
    MvcUriComponentsBuilder.on(CustomerHypermediaRestController.class).get(
     customer.getId())).buildAndExpand().toUri();

  customerResource.add(new Link(selfUri.toString(), "self"));
  customerResource.add(new Link(photoUri.toString(), "profile-photo"));
  return customerResource;
 }
}
```

A `ResourceAssembler` is a natural place to conditionally include or exclude links based on an entity's state. Here, we check to see if a profile photo is present, and conditionally include the link for the profile photo. The links available describe the protocol of the client as it interacts with this system.

The hypermedia included in the results, along with the cues that HTTP (and the HTTP `OPTIONS` method) provide, make it easy to navigate through this API without any *a priori* documentation.

HAL hypermedia representation is but one of many popular options. 2009 saw the introduction of Web Application Description Language (*https://www.w3.org/Submis sion/wadl/*), which is a broad-scope approach to describing HTTP services. ALPS (*http://alps.io/spec/*) debuted more recently, and defines both possible state transitions *and* the attributes of the resources involved in those state transitions in a way that is media-type agnostic. Spring Data REST provides automatic support for ALPS.

Media Type and Schema

We've looked at using Spring HATEOAS to introduce hypermedia to a REST API. The goal is to give the client as much information as possible to be able to navigate the API without any prior knowledge. HTTP already dictates the possible verbs (PUT, POST, GET, DELETE, etc.) and hypermedia tells us where we can go for a given resource.

HTTP provides the notion of a content type. In theory, the content type provides enough information for any client to know what the content being served is and how to manipulate it. In practice, it's not sufficient. The content type of image/jpg tells us that we can decode the bytes being returned from a service by using a JPEG image reader. The content type application/json or application/hal+json tell us that the bytes being returned from a resource can be read in using a JSON reader, and that it may contain HAL-encoded links. These content types do *not* tell us whether a JSON document matches a certain structure. For this, you need a concept of a schema.

XML offers XML schema (*http://www.w3.org/XML/Schema*) to constrain the structure of an XML resource. A Google Protocol Buffer representation also has a schema. For JSON, things are less cut-and-dried, but there are many de facto alternatives like JSON Schema (*http://json-schema.org*). Schema provides a way to specify what the structure of a payload is.

API Versioning

The only thing we know for certain is that things will change; it's inevitable. Indeed, one of the biggest benefit of the cloud native architecture is that it encourages small batch changes—microservices—that can be evolved quickly and independently of others. Change is a *very* good problem to have; it implies evolution! We want to embrace change, but we don't want change to our APIs or imperil other parts of the system or third-party clients. We must find ways to evolve our services without unnecessarily breaking clients.

We could simply try to not break things. This is a bit like de-risking the process of release by refusing to release! But there is something to it. If you're only ever changing implementation details, then the visible surface area of an API shouldn't break. It's critical that you surface any potential breaks as early as possible. *Consumer-Driven Contract Testing* helps protect APIs from accidental breaks (for more on this, see our discussion in "Consumer-Driven Contract Testing" on page 114). Continuous integration provides a valuable feedback loop that can be used to continuously protect from accidental API breaks by testing as many clients as possible against the APIs under change.

Things will change, though. Clients and services should afford some flexibility to reduce sensitivity to changes. Martin Fowler talks about the idea of a *tolerant reader* (*https://martinfowler.com/bliki/TolerantReader.html*)—an API client that takes care to avoid oversensitivity to payload changes. A client might expect to find an order-id XML element or JSON element in a payload. JSON-Path or XPath queries let clients find elements and patterns in a structure while remaining indifferent to the order or depth of the pattern in the original structure.

Postel's law, also known as the *The Robustness Principle* (*https://en.wikipedia.org/wiki/ Robustness_principle*), says that service implementations should be conservative in what they produce, but liberal in what they accept from others. If a service only needs a subset of a given message payload to do its work, it should not protest if there is extra information in the message for which it may not immediately have any use.

It's easy to be more robust so long as changes are evolutionary and additive, not breaking. If an element that was expected in version 1 of a service should suddenly disappear in version 2, clients would most certainly break. A service should make explicit the assumptions about what clients will be able to work it. One approach is *semantic versioning*. A semantic version is one of the form MAJOR.MINOR.PATCH. The MAJOR version should change only when an API has breaking changes from its previous version. The MINOR version should change when an API has evolved, but existing clients should continue to work with it. A PATCH version change signals bug fixes to existing functionality.

Semantic versioning signals to clients what version of the API is available, but even if the clients are aware of the version, they may not be ready to move forward to the new version. If clients are forced to upgrade whenever a service is upgraded, it threatens one of the fundamental benefits of microservices: the ability to evolve independently. So it will sometimes be necessary to host multiple versions of an API. One approach might be to deploy and maintain two different codebases, side by side, but this can quickly become a maintenance nightmare. Instead, consider hosting the versioned APIs side by side in the same codebase. If possible, try to transform and forward requests to older endpoints to the newer endpoints, so that all requests are ultimately funneled to the same place. This reduces the testing burden.

A client will need to signal to the service which version of the API it intends to talk to. There are some common approaches in REST APIs: encode the version in the URL, encode it as an arbitrary (and proprietary) HTTP header, or encode it as part of the content type specified in the Accept header for the request (Example 6-14).

Example 6-14. The VersionedRestController demonstrates a few approaches to versioning REST APIs

```java
package demo;

import org.springframework.web.bind.annotation.*;

//@formatter:off
import static org.springframework.http
        .MediaType.APPLICATION_JSON_VALUE;
//@formatter:on

@RestController
@RequestMapping("/api")
public class VersionedRestController {

 //@formatter:off
 public static final String V1_MEDIA_TYPE_VALUE
        = "application/vnd.bootiful.demo-v1+json";

 public static final String V2_MEDIA_TYPE_VALUE
        = "application/vnd.bootiful.demo-v2+json";
 //@formatter:on

 private enum ApiVersion {
  v1, v2
 }

 public static class Greeting {

  private String how;

  private String version;

  public Greeting(String how, ApiVersion version) {
   this.how = how;
   this.version = version.toString();
  }

  public String getHow() {
   return how;
  }

  public String getVersion() {
   return version;
  }
 }

 ❶
 @GetMapping(value = "/{version}/hi", produces = APPLICATION_JSON_VALUE)
 Greeting greetWithPathVariable(@PathVariable ApiVersion version) {
  return greet(version, "path-variable");
```

```
}
```

❷

```
@GetMapping(value = "/hi", produces = APPLICATION_JSON_VALUE)
Greeting greetWithHeader(@RequestHeader("X-API-Version") ApiVersion version) {
  return this.greet(version, "header");
}
```

❸

```
@GetMapping(value = "/hi", produces = V1_MEDIA_TYPE_VALUE)
Greeting greetWithContentNegotiationV1() {
  return this.greet(ApiVersion.v1, "content-negotiation");
}
```

❹

```
@GetMapping(value = "/hi", produces = V2_MEDIA_TYPE_VALUE)
Greeting greetWithContentNegotiationV2() {
  return this.greet(ApiVersion.v2, "content-negotiation");
}

private Greeting greet(ApiVersion version, String how) {
  return new Greeting(how, version);
}
}
```

❶ This approach encodes version in the URL; Spring MVC will automatically map URL parameters into instances of the corresponding `ApiVersion` enum. Test it using `curl http://localhost:8080/api/V2/hi`.

❷ This approach automatically converts request headers into instances of the corresponding `ApiVersion` enum. Test it using `curl -H "X-API-Version:V1" http://localhost:8080/api/hi`.

❸ This controller handler handles requests for the `application/ vnd.bootiful.demo-v1+json` media-type. Test it using `curl -H "Accept:appli cation/vnd.bootiful.demo-v1+json" http://localhost:8080/api/hi`.

❹ This controller handler handles requests for the `application/ vnd.bootiful.demo-v2+json` media-type. Test it using `curl -H "Accept:appli cation/vnd.bootiful.demo-v2+json" http://localhost:8080/api/hi`.

Documenting REST APIs

The agile manifesto embraces working software over comprehensive documentation; that is, make it work, *then* document it. It's much better to have working software that explains itself correctly than to have documentation that may lie. Code is a living, breathing thing, and—as we imagine most have at some point experienced—documentation developed in parallel with code tends to drift out of sync with the realities of the code. The documentation serves as a map, but the code is the territory. If you find yourself lost, it's better to be familiar with the territory than the map!

Documentation is still a very natural, convenient thing, of course. Ever optimistic, we engineers have done a lot of work to colocate the documentation—information about an API—with the API itself. JavaDoc was the first large-scale example of this, though other languages have since introduced alternatives. JavaDoc is maintained by the developer, as it lives with the code. The hope is that developers will always see to it that the documentation reflects the realities of the code, because it lives with the code. Of course, we know this doesn't always happen! Sophisticated tools, beyond JavaDoc, can infer all manner of things about code.

Hypermedia provides many clues about a well-designed API's use. HTTP OPTION tells us what HTTP verbs are supported for a given resource. Hypermedia links tell us what relationships a resource has. Schema can tell us the structure of acceptable payloads for a given resource. There's no great way of documenting expected HTTP request parameters or headers, though, and there's no great way to explain motivation or intent. Documentation, at its best, describes motivation, not implementation. What remains missing is a way to complete the coverage of an API's use, as automatically as possible, and in such a way that the documentation is guaranteed to be in sync with the realities of the code it documents—the territory.

There are some options, like Swagger. Swagger requires intrusive changes to the code itself. Swagger relies upon strings embedded in the Java code in annotations on the API itself. It's fairly cumbersome to maintain human prose in, and it sometimes fails to adequately capture the intent of an API because it tries to automatically map language-specific constructs to the HTTP contract implied by those constructs.

Spring RESTDocs (*http://spring.io/projects/spring-restdocs*) takes a different approach; it's delivered as decorations for the Spring MVC *test* framework and as freeform prose expressed in Asciidoctor, a markup that's so natural we wrote this book in it!

Add Spring REST Docs as a `test` scoped dependency to the classpath: `org.springframework.restdocs` : `spring-restdocs-mockmvc`. Document your API by testing it. The interactions confirmed in the test are what we're trying to capture, after all. Let's look at Example 6-15.

Example 6-15. ApiDocumentation.java uses the Spring MVC test API to exercise an API

```
package demo;

import org.junit.Test;
import org.junit.runner.RunWith;
import org.springframework.beans.factory.annotation.Autowired;
import org.springframework.boot.test.autoconfigure.restdocs.AutoConfigureRestDocs;
```

```
import org.springframework.boot.test.autoconfigure.web.servlet.AutoConfigureMockMvc;
import org.springframework.boot.test.context.SpringBootTest;
import org.springframework.http.MediaType;
import org.springframework.test.context.junit4.SpringRunner;
import org.springframework.test.web.servlet.MockMvc;

import javax.servlet.RequestDispatcher;

import static org.hamcrest.Matchers.is;
import static org.hamcrest.Matchers.notNullValue;
import static org.springframework.restdocs.mockmvc.MockMvcRestDocumentation.document;
import static org.springframework.test.web.servlet.request.MockMvcRequestBuilders.
    get;
import static org.springframework.test.web.servlet.result.MockMvcResultHandlers.
    print;
import static org.springframework.test.web.servlet.result.MockMvcResultMatchers.
    jsonPath;
import static org.springframework.test.web.servlet.result.MockMvcResultMatchers.
    status;
//@formatter:off
❶
@AutoConfigureRestDocs(outputDir = "target/generated-snippets")
@RunWith(SpringRunner.class)
@SpringBootTest(classes = Application.class,
        webEnvironment = SpringBootTest.WebEnvironment.MOCK)
@AutoConfigureMockMvc
public class ApiDocumentation {
//@formatter:off

    ❷
    // @Rule public final RestDocumentation restDocumentation =
    //    new RestDocumentation(
    //    "target/generated-snippets");

    @Autowired
    private MockMvc mockMvc;

    @Test
    public void errorExample() throws Exception {
     this.mockMvc
       .perform(
        get("/error")
         .contentType(MediaType.APPLICATION_JSON)
         .requestAttr(RequestDispatcher.ERROR_STATUS_CODE, 400)
         .requestAttr(RequestDispatcher.ERROR_REQUEST_URI, "/customers")
         .requestAttr(RequestDispatcher.ERROR_MESSAGE,
           "The customer 'http://localhost:8443/v1/customers/123' does not exist"))
       .andDo(print()).andExpect(status().isBadRequest())
       .andExpect(jsonPath("error", is("Bad Request")))
       .andExpect(jsonPath("timestamp", is(notNullValue())))
       .andExpect(jsonPath("status", is(400)))
       .andExpect(jsonPath("path", is(notNullValue())))
```

```
  .andDo(document("error-example"));  ❸
}

@Test
public void indexExample() throws Exception {
  this.mockMvc.perform(get("/v1/customers")).andExpect(status().isOk())
    .andDo(document("index-example"));
}
}
```

❶ Test rules support cross-cutting concerns from the tests they're configured on. In this case, the `RestDocumentation` rule will emit Asciidoctor snippets to the `target/generated-snippets` directory when the tests are run.

❷ The `documentationConfiguration` static method simply registers the `RestDocumentation` object with the `MockMvc` object, which the tests use to exercise the API.

❸ · The string passed to the `document` method, `error-example`, defines the logical identifier for the automatically generated documentation for this test. In this case, the generated documentation will *also* live under a folder named `error-example`, in which we'll find `.adoc` files like `curl-request.adoc`, `http-request.adoc`, `http-response.adoc`, etc. Use these various generated snippets as includes in the creation of a larger Asciidoctor document.

Normally, the build's test plug-in finds classes ending in `Test` and runs them. We need to configure the test plug-in to include and run `*Documentation` classes, as well (Example 6-16).

Example 6-16. Including *Documentation.java in the Maven Surefire plug-in

```
<plugin>
  <groupId>org.apache.maven.plugins</groupId>
  <artifactId>maven-surefire-plugin</artifactId>
  <configuration>
    <includes>
      <include>**/*Documentation.java</include>
    </includes>
  </configuration>
</plugin>
```

The by-product of these tests will be automatically generated Asciidoctor snippets that are easily included in a larger Asciidoctor document (Example 6-17).

Example 6-17. The automatically generated Asciidoctor snippets after running the tests

```
.
├── customer-get-example
│   ├── curl-request.adoc
│   ├── http-request.adoc
│   ├── http-response.adoc
│   ├── links.adoc
│   └── response-fields.adoc
├── customer-update-example
│   ├── curl-request.adoc
│   ├── http-request.adoc
│   ├── http-response.adoc
│   └── request-fields.adoc
├── customers-create-example
│   ├── curl-request.adoc
│   ├── http-request.adoc
│   ├── http-response.adoc
│   ├── links.adoc
│   ├── request-fields.adoc
│   └── response-fields.adoc
├── customers-list-example
│   ├── curl-request.adoc
│   ├── http-request.adoc
│   ├── http-response.adoc
│   └── response-fields.adoc
├── error-example
│   ├── curl-request.adoc
│   ├── http-request.adoc
│   ├── http-response.adoc
│   └── response-fields.adoc
└── index-example
    ├── curl-request.adoc
    ├── http-request.adoc
    └── http-response.adoc

6 directories, 26 files
```

The approach varies from one tool to another, and the Spring RESTDocs project will have more detailed examples for your perusal, but it's easy enough to have Maven process AsciiDoctor documents using the `org.asciidoctor : asciidoctor-maven-plugin` plug-in, like in Example 6-18.

Example 6-18. The Asciidoctor Maven plug-in

```
<plugin>
  <groupId>org.asciidoctor</groupId>
  <artifactId>asciidoctor-maven-plugin</artifactId>
  <version>1.5.2</version>
  <executions>
    <execution>
```

```
          <id>generate-docs</id>
          <phase>prepare-package</phase>
          <goals>
            <goal>process-asciidoc</goal>
          </goals>
          <configuration>
             ❶
            <backend>html</backend>
            <doctype>book</doctype>
            <attributes>
              <snippets>${project.build.directory}/generated-snippets</snippets>   ❷
            </attributes>
          </configuration>
          </execution>
      </executions>
</plugin>
```

❶ As configured, the application will look in the `src/main/resources` directory for
    any valid `.adoc` files and then convert them to `.pdf` and `.html`.

❷ To simplify resolving the snippets and avoid repetition in the documentation
    itself, expose an attribute that resolves to the `generated-snippets` directory.

We won't reprint too much in the way of an Asciidoctor example here in the book—
you can follow along with the book's code—but you should understand that it's easy
to simply include those snippets whenever you want in an Asciidoctor document.
Here is how you would bring in the `response-fields.adoc` snippet: `include::{snip
pets}/error-example/response-fields.adoc[]`.

Once you've written your documentation and used the generated snippets as appropriate, it can be very convenient to serve the documentation as part of the served
resources for the application itself. Configure your build tool to copy the generated
output to Spring Boot's `src/main/resources/static` directory. Example 6-19 shows
how that looks with Maven.

*Example 6-19. Configuring the Maven resources plug-in to include the generated
documentation in Spring Boot's static directory so that it's available under http://local
host:8080/docs*

```
<plugin>
  <artifactId>maven-resources-plugin</artifactId>
  <executions>
    <execution>
      <id>copy-resources</id>
      <phase>prepare-package</phase>
      <goals>
        <goal>copy-resources</goal>
      </goals>
```

```
      <configuration>
      <outputDirectory>${project.build.outputDirectory}/static/docs</outputDirectory>
      <resources>
        <resource>
        <directory>${project.build.directory}/generated-docs</directory>
        </resource>
      </resources>
      </configuration>
    </execution>
  </executions>
</plugin>
```

The result is lean-and-mean, always up-to-date documentation that speaks for itself *and* turns the build green.

The Client Side

In this section, we'll look at various ways to work with a REST API, both interactively and programmatically.

REST Clients for Ad Hoc Exploration and Interaction

Spring Boot makes short work of standing up the HAL Browser in your own services to interact with HAL REST APIs. There are many competent, often free, tools that support interacting with REST APIs. Here are some of our favorites to have handy during development:

Firefox's Poster plug-in
This freely available Firefox plug-in is a handy utility that lives in the bottom right corner of the browser as a little yellow icon. Click it and you'll be presented with a dialog where you can describe and execute HTTP requests. It provides easy features for handling things like file uploads and content negotiation (see Figure 6-2).

Figure 6-2. The Firefox Poster plug-in provides a lot of bang for the buck

curl

The venerable curl command is a command-line utility that supports any manner of HTTP requests with convenient options for sending HTTP headers, custom request bodies, and more (Figure 6-3).

```
                         scripts — zsh — 75×12
                              zsh                              +
~/D/p/l/b/s/c/l/scripts git:master >>> cat upload_photo.sh     *
#!/bin/sh
set -e

uri=http://127.0.0.1:8080/people/$1/photo
resp=`curl -F "file=@$2" $uri`
echo $resp

~/D/p/l/b/s/c/l/scripts git:master >>>                         *
```

Figure 6-3. A script that uses curl

 The authors have become fans of HTTPie (*https://httpie.org*), too.

Google Chrome Advanced HTTP Client Extension

This extension lets you describe and execute HTTP requests *and* save their configuration for later reuse (Figure 6-4).

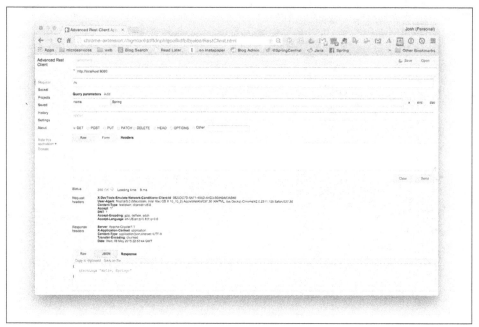

Figure 6-4. The Google Chrome Advanced HTTP Client

Advanced HTTP Client

This integrates nicely with the rest of the Google Chrome Developer Tools. You can open up the Developer Tools (which are in every Google Chrome installation) and inspect the *Network* tab. From there, it's easy to find the request that you crafted and triggered using the Advanced HTTP Client and then have it exported as a curl command (Figure 6-5).

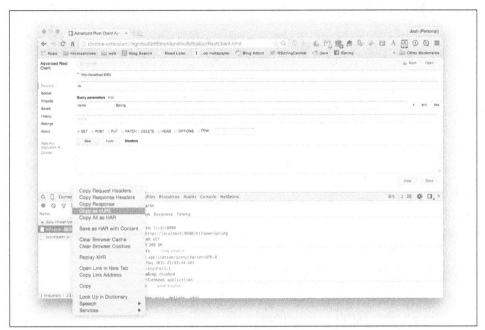

Figure 6-5. Using the Developer Tools in Google Chrome to get a curl invocation that replays the HTTP request—very handy!

PostMan

This handy Chrome extension provides saved HTTP queries, synchronization across devices, and collections, so that you can manage collections of related HTTP requests. This is becoming one of our go-to HTTP clients for serious work (Figure 6-6).

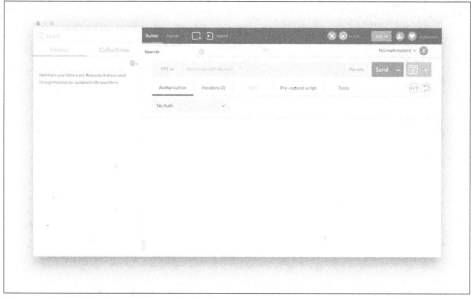

Figure 6-6. The PostMan HTTP Client

The RestTemplate

Spring's `RestTemplate` is a one-stop-shop HTTP client that supports common HTTP interactions with *template* methods; common HTTP interactions—`get`, `put`, `post`, etc.—become one-liners. The `RestTemplate` supports content negotiation using the same `HttpMessageConverter` strategy implementations as Spring MVC on the server side. It can both convert objects into a valid HTTP request body and convert HTTP responses into objects. It supports pluggable interceptors to centrally handle cross-cutting concerns like authentication with HTTP BASIC and OAuth, GZip compression, and service resolution.

Let's examine a REST API powered by Spring Data REST. Spring Data REST automatically creates a hypermedia API complete with HAL-style links for relationships based on specified Spring Data repositories. `Movie` entities have one or more `Actor` entities associated with them.

We'll need a `RestTemplate`. Spring Boot ships with a `RestTemplateBuilder` to make short work of configuring a `RestTemplate` instance (Example 6-20).

Example 6-20. Configure a RestTemplate

```
package actors;

import org.apache.commons.logging.Log;
```

```
import org.apache.commons.logging.LogFactory;
import org.springframework.boot.web.client.RestTemplateBuilder;
import org.springframework.context.annotation.Bean;
import org.springframework.context.annotation.Configuration;
import org.springframework.http.HttpRequest;
import org.springframework.http.client.ClientHttpRequestExecution;
import org.springframework.http.client.ClientHttpRequestInterceptor;
import org.springframework.web.client.RestTemplate;

@Configuration
public class RestTemplateConfiguration {

 @Bean
 RestTemplate restTemplate() {

  Log log = LogFactory.getLog(getClass());

  ClientHttpRequestInterceptor interceptor = (HttpRequest request, byte[] body,
   ClientHttpRequestExecution execution) -> {
   log.info(String.format("request to URI %s with HTTP verb '%s'",
    request.getURI(), request.getMethod().toString()));
   return execution.execute(request, body);
  };

  return new RestTemplateBuilder() ❶
   .additionalInterceptors(interceptor).build();
 }

}
```

❶ The `RestTemplateBuilder` provides a fluent DSL to configure interceptors, converters, and much more.

The `RestTemplate` is a general-purpose HTTP workhorse in the Spring framework. Let's put it to work in Example 6-21.

Example 6-21. Use the RestTemplate

```
package actors;

import com.fasterxml.jackson.databind.JsonNode;
import org.apache.commons.logging.Log;
import org.apache.commons.logging.LogFactory;
import org.junit.After;
import org.junit.Before;
import org.junit.Test;
import org.springframework.boot.builder.SpringApplicationBuilder;
import org.springframework.context.ConfigurableApplicationContext;
import org.springframework.core.ParameterizedTypeReference;
import org.springframework.hateoas.Resources;
import org.springframework.http.HttpMethod;
```

```java
import org.springframework.http.HttpStatus;
import org.springframework.http.MediaType;
import org.springframework.http.ResponseEntity;
import org.springframework.web.client.RestTemplate;

import java.net.URI;
import java.util.Collections;

import static org.junit.Assert.assertEquals;
import static org.junit.Assert.assertTrue;

public class RestTemplateTest {

    private Log log = LogFactory.getLog(getClass());

    private URI baseUri;

    private ConfigurableApplicationContext server;

    private RestTemplate restTemplate;

    private MovieRepository movieRepository;

    private URI moviesUri;

    @Before
    public void setUp() throws Exception {

        this.server = new SpringApplicationBuilder()
            .properties(Collections.singletonMap("server.port", "0"))
            .sources(DemoApplication.class).run();

        int port = this.server.getEnvironment().getProperty("local.server.port",
            Integer.class, 8080);

        this.restTemplate = this.server.getBean(RestTemplate.class);
        this.baseUri = URI.create("http://localhost:" + port + "/");
        this.moviesUri = URI.create(this.baseUri.toString() + "movies");
        this.movieRepository = this.server.getBean(MovieRepository.class);
    }

    @After
    public void tearDown() throws Exception {
        if (null != this.server) {
            this.server.close();
        }
    }

    @Test
    public void testRestTemplate() throws Exception {
        ❶
        ResponseEntity<Movie> postMovieResponseEntity = this.restTemplate
```

```
    .postForEntity(moviesUri, new Movie("Forest Gump"), Movie.class);
URI uriOfNewMovie = postMovieResponseEntity.getHeaders().getLocation();
log.info("the new movie lives at " + uriOfNewMovie);
```

❷

```
JsonNode mapForMovieRecord = this.restTemplate.getForObject(uriOfNewMovie,
  JsonNode.class);
log.info("\t..read as a Map.class: " + mapForMovieRecord);
assertEquals(mapForMovieRecord.get("title").asText(),
  postMovieResponseEntity.getBody().title);
```

❸

```
Movie movieReference = this.restTemplate.getForObject(uriOfNewMovie,
  Movie.class);
assertEquals(movieReference.title, postMovieResponseEntity.getBody().title);
log.info("\t..read as a Movie.class: " + movieReference);
```

❹

```
ResponseEntity<Movie> movieResponseEntity = this.restTemplate.getForEntity(
  uriOfNewMovie, Movie.class);
assertEquals(movieResponseEntity.getStatusCode(), HttpStatus.OK);
assertEquals(movieResponseEntity.getHeaders().getContentType(),
  MediaType.parseMediaType("application/json;charset=UTF-8"));
log.info("\t..read as a ResponseEntity<Movie>: " + movieResponseEntity);
```

❺

```
//@formatter:off
ParameterizedTypeReference<Resources<Movie>> movies =
        new ParameterizedTypeReference<Resources<Movie>>() {};
//@formatter:on
ResponseEntity<Resources<Movie>> moviesResponseEntity = this.restTemplate
  .exchange(this.moviesUri, HttpMethod.GET, null, movies);
Resources<Movie> movieResources = moviesResponseEntity.getBody();
movieResources.forEach(this.log::info);
assertEquals(movieResources.getContent().size(), this.movieRepository.count());
assertTrue(movieResources.getLinks().stream()
  .filter(m -> m.getRel().equals("self")).count() == 1);

  }
}
```

❶ The RestTemplate provides all the convenience methods you'd expect, supporting common HTTP verbs like POST.

❷ You can ask the RestTemplate to return responses converted to an appropriate
representation. Here, we're asking for a Jackson JsonNode return value. The Json
Node lets you interact with the JSON as you might an XML DOM node.

❸ The conversion applies to domain objects, where possible. Here, we've asked for the JSON to be mapped (also using Jackson) to a `Movie` entity.

❹ The `ResponseEntity<T>` return value is a wrapper for the response payload, converted as described before, and headers and status code information from the HTTP response.

❺ The REST API uses Spring HATEOAS's `Resources<T>` object to serve collections of `Resource<T>` instances, which in turn wrap payloads and provide links. In previous examples, we've signaled the return value by providing a `.class` literal, but Java provides no way to capture something like `Resources<Movie>.class` using class literals because the generic information is burned away at compile time, thanks to Java's type erasure. The only way to retain generic parameter information is to bake it into a type hierarchy through subclassing. This pattern, called the *type token* pattern, is supported with Spring's `ParameterizedTypeReference` type. `ParameterizedTypeReference` is an abstract type, and so must be subclassed. Here, what seems like an instance variable, `ptr`, is actually an anonymous subclass that can, at runtime, answer the question: "what's your generic parameter?" with "`Resources<Movie>`." The `RestTemplate` can use that to bind the returned JSON values correctly.

Our hypermedia API uses HAL, and HAL emits links to relevant resources. HAL-style links are ideal because one link follows another in a sort of chain. Resolving a specific resource is a matter of following the chain, *hopping* from one link to the next until you're finally at the relevant resource. This is straightforward, but fairly boilerplate code. If we start a resource retrieval at /, and need to get to /actors/search/by-movie?movie=Cars, then it's at *least* three hops:

- One to fetch the root resource / and find the `search` link
- Another to find the search link for the finder endpoint that queries by movie title, `by-movie`
- Another to actually run the search, passing in the `movie` request parameter `Cars`

Spring HATEOAS includes the handy `Traverson` client, which accepts a link *path* and follows the links for you, yielding the final result (Example 6-22).

 The Spring Java client is inspired by a JavaScript library of the same name (*https://github.com/basti1302/traverson*), so this capability is available to browser clients as well!

Example 6-22. Configure a Traverson client using a configured RestTemplate

```
package actors;

import
org.springframework.boot.context.embedded.EmbeddedServletContainer↵
InitializedEvent;
import org.springframework.context.annotation.Bean;
import org.springframework.context.annotation.Configuration;
import org.springframework.context.annotation.Lazy;
import org.springframework.context.event.EventListener;
import org.springframework.hateoas.MediaTypes;
import org.springframework.hateoas.client.Traverson;
import org.springframework.web.client.RestTemplate;

import java.net.URI;

@Configuration
public class TraversonConfiguration {

 private int port;

 private URI baseUri;

 //@formatter:off
 @EventListener
 public void embeddedPortAvailable(
    EmbeddedServletContainerInitializedEvent e) {
  this.port = e.getEmbeddedServletContainer().getPort();
  this.baseUri = URI.create("http://localhost:" + this.port + '/');
 }
 //@formatter:on

 ❶
 @Bean
 @Lazy
 Traverson traverson(RestTemplate restTemplate) {
  Traverson traverson = new Traverson(this.baseUri, MediaTypes.HAL_JSON);
  traverson.setRestOperations(restTemplate);
  return traverson;
 }
}
```

❶ Configure a `Traverson` client with the base URI, the `MediaType` instances that you want the client to handle, and the `RestTemplate` instance to delegate underlying HTTP calls to.

Use the `Traverson` client by describing a series of links as a path and then following that path (Example 6-23).

Example 6-23. Use the Traverson client with the RestTemplate

```
package actors;

import org.apache.commons.logging.Log;
import org.apache.commons.logging.LogFactory;
import org.junit.After;
import org.junit.Before;
import org.junit.Test;
import org.springframework.boot.builder.SpringApplicationBuilder;
import org.springframework.context.ConfigurableApplicationContext;
import org.springframework.core.ParameterizedTypeReference;
import org.springframework.hateoas.Resources;
import org.springframework.hateoas.client.Traverson;

import java.util.Collections;
import java.util.stream.Collectors;

import static org.junit.Assert.assertEquals;
import static org.junit.Assert.assertTrue;

public class TraversonTest {

 private Log log = LogFactory.getLog(getClass());

 private ConfigurableApplicationContext server;

 private Traverson traverson;

 @Before
 public void setUp() throws Exception {

  this.server = new SpringApplicationBuilder()
   .properties(Collections.singletonMap("server.port", "0"))
   .sources(DemoApplication.class).run();
  // this.server =
  // SpringApplication.run(DemoApplication.class);
  this.traverson = this.server.getBean(Traverson.class);
 }

 @After
 public void tearDown() throws Exception {
  if (null != this.server) {
   this.server.close();
  }
 }

 @Test
 public void testTraverson() throws Exception {

  String nameOfMovie = "Cars";
```

```
❶
Resources<Actor> actorResources = this.traverson
  .follow("actors", "search", "by-movie")
  .withTemplateParameters(Collections.singletonMap("movie", nameOfMovie))
  .toObject(new ParameterizedTypeReference<Resources<Actor>>() {
  });

  actorResources.forEach(this.log::info);
  assertTrue(actorResources.getContent().size() > 0);
  assertEquals(
    actorResources.getContent().stream()
     .filter(actor -> actor.fullName.equals("Owen Wilson"))
     .collect(Collectors.toList()).size(), 1);
 }
}
```

❶ The `Traverson#follow` method makes short work of traversing a *chain* of links, substituting appropriate parts of the URI parameters template as necessary. The `Traverson#follow` method also accepts a `ParameterizedTypeReference<T>` parameter, just as does the `RestTemplate`.

The `RestTemplate` is a central part to building REST services with Spring. In Spring Framework 5, there is a fully reactive client called the `WebClient` that offers a nice alternative to the `RestTemplate` for certain classes of interactions—particularly those with long-lived and input/output bound processing. The `RestTemplate` supports OAuth tokens in Spring Cloud Security and it supports service resolution in Spring Cloud, among other integrations.

Summary

In this chapter we've looked at how to effectively build REST APIs with Spring Boot. REST is one approach to building scalable services on the open, multiplatform, multi-language web. REST also mixes well with other concerns, like security, redundancy, and caching. We've talked about the principles of REST in terms of Spring, but they apply to any language and platform out there.

## CHAPTER 7

Routing

Cloud native systems are dynamic; services come and go as demand requires. Services must be able to discover and communicate with other services, even if one instance of a service disappears or new capacity is added to the system. We can't rely on fixed IP addresses; IP addresses couple clients to services. We need a bit of indirection to give us the desired flexibility to reroute dynamically.

We *could* use DNS, but DNS isn't necessarily a great fit in a cloud environment. DNS benefits from caching in the clients that use the DNS services. The caching means that clients may "resolve" stale IP addresses that no longer exist. You can invalidate those caches (quickly) with low time-to-live (TTL) values, but you'll then (necessarily) spend a lot of time re-resolving DNS records. In a cloud environment DNS requires extra time for resolution, because requests must leave the cloud and then reenter through the router. Many cloud providers support multihomed DNS resolution, with a private address and a public address. In this case, calls from one service to another within the cloud are fast and efficient and virtually free (in terms of provider-imposed costs for things like bandwidth), but it requires that your code base be aware of the complexity in the DNS scheme. It implies complexity of implementation that could also be pretty difficult to reproduce in a developer's local environment.

DNS is also a pretty simple protocol: it doesn't have the ability to answer basic questions about the state or the topology of the system. Suppose you have a REST client calling a service running on a node, mapped to DNS. If the instance is down, then our client will block. Hopefully we've all applied the suggestions in Michael Nygard's amazing book *Release It!* (Pragmatic Programmers), and specified aggressive client-side timeouts. Most people don't. (Pop quiz! What's the default timeout of Java's `java.net.URLConnection`? Are you *sure* you've configured appropriate client-side timeouts in all your code? *Positive?*)

Routing becomes particularly involved when you deal with DNS load balancing. A load balancer is yet another piece of operational infrastructure that you need to manage (or, more typically, that some other team manages) that has limitations. Your common load balancer will do fine for things like round-robin load balancing and most will even handle "sticky sessions," where requests from a client are pinned to a specific node based on common headers (like Java's JSESSIONID). Load balancers fall apart when you need to do anything more involved. What if you want to pin requests from a client to a specific node based on something besides a JSESSIONID, like an OAuth Access token, or a JSON Web Token (JWT)? Perhaps you're doing something stateful, like streaming video on a specific node—which you can't really load balance —but don't have a notion of an HTTP session.

All nodes in a DNS load balancing pool must also be routable (obviously). Sometimes we don't want our services to be routable via DNS! Security through obscurity is no security at all, of course, but we should always strive to keep our publicly exposed surface as minimal as possible. Indeed, even if we're OK with clients connecting directly to the node, we must ensure that nodes are correctly evicted from a load balancing ensemble if they're sick. Otherwise a client will be routed to a node that can't handle the request. Not all load balancers are smart enough to do that. Some will have the ability to query a service instance and ask it for its health, and based on the status code of the response, evict the node from the pool. (You might use Spring Boot's /health Actuator endpoint for this). Some platforms (like the JVM) have libraries that cache the first resolved IP from DNS, and reuse it on subsequent connections. This is a good idea in the large, but it can defeat DNS load balancing.

You can get around some of these limitations using a virtual load balancer, which acts as a sort of proxy, but virtual load balancers still don't solve the biggest problem. All centralized load balancers are ignorant of your system's state and its workloads. Even an ideal round-robin DNS load balancer will distribute the initial connections to different services, but not necessarily the workloads themselves. Not all requests are created equal. Some clients consume more resources than others, and may take longer to process. This can overwhelm some nodes and leave others idle if there's not an intelligent load balancing strategy in place.

In short, routing is (often) a programming discussion, and DNS isn't a great fit.

The DiscoveryClient Abstraction

There are alternative ways to get the effects of centralized load balancing. We want a logical mapping from a service's ID to the hosts and ports (the nodes) on which that service is available. A service registry is a good fit here. The main drawback with service registries is that they're invasive in your application code. Your code must be aware of, and work with, the registry. Some service registries, like Hashicorp Consul, can act as a DNS server for clients that can't adapt. A service registry, ultimately, is like a phone book for the cloud. It's a table of service instances and it provides an API. Some service registries are more sophisticated than others, but they all minimally support discovering which services are available and where those service instances live.

Not all service registries are created equal. They too are constrained by physics and the CAP theorem. The CAP states that it is impossible for a distributed system to provide more than two of three of the following properties: consistency, availability, and partitionability. Their job is to keep a consistent world view of the system. You need to evaluate for each potential service registry where the registry evaluates on the CAP theorem triangle. You also need to evaluate what features a given registry has, above and beyond its core function. Does it support security and encryption? Can it be used as a key/value store to centralize configuration, or should you use the Spring Cloud Config Server, as described in our discussion on configuration in Chapter 3?

Spring Cloud provides the DiscoveryClient abstraction to make it easy for clients to work with different types of service registries. The Spring Cloud DiscoveryClient abstraction makes it easy to plug in different implementations with ease. Spring Cloud plugs the DiscoveryClient abstraction into various parts of the stack, making its use almost transparent. As this is being written, there are production-worthy DiscoveryClient implementations for Cloud Foundry, Apache Zookeeper, Hashicorp Consul, and Netflix's Eureka, with at least one other nonproduction-worthy implementation available for ETCD. The abstraction is simple enough that you could adapt Spring Cloud to work with another service registry if you'd like to. Conceptually, the DiscoveryClient is read-only, as shown in Example 7-1.

Example 7-1. The DiscoveryClient abstraction

```
package org.springframework.cloud.client.discovery;

import java.util.List;
import org.springframework.cloud.client.ServiceInstance;

public interface DiscoveryClient {
    String description();

    ServiceInstance getLocalServiceInstance();

    List<ServiceInstance> getInstances(String var1);

    List<String> getServices();
}
```

Some service registries need the client to register themselves with the registry. The various DiscoveryClient abstraction implementations do this for you on application startup. The Cloud Foundry DiscoveryClient abstraction implementation does not require the client to register itself with the registry because Cloud Foundry already knows on which host and port a service lives; it *put* the service there in the first place!

There are many great choices for service registries. Because Spring provides an abstraction, we're not constrained in picking one. We can easily switch to another implementation later. In this chapter, we'll look at Netflix Eureka. Netflix Eureka has served Netflix well, at scale, for years. It's also easy enough to install and run for application development entirely using Spring Boot, which makes it doubly awesome!

 While Netflix Eureka *can* be configured to do virtually anything, you shouldn't undertake the work lightly. There's a lot of value in having proven recipes for security, scale, and redundancy, such as what you get when you use the Spring Cloud Services-based Netflix installation on Pivotal Cloud Foundry or Pivotal Web Services.

In order to set up a Eureka service registry, you'll need `org.springframework.cloud`: `spring-cloud-starter-eureka-server` in a Spring Boot project, and then you'll need to initialize it using `@EnableEurekaServer`, as shown in Example 7-2.

Example 7-2. Starting up a bare-bones Eureka service registry

```
package demo;

import org.springframework.boot.SpringApplication;
import org.springframework.boot.autoconfigure.SpringBootApplication;
import org.springframework.cloud.netflix.eureka.server.EnableEurekaServer;

❶
@EnableEurekaServer
@SpringBootApplication
public class EurekaServiceApplication {

 public static void main(String args[]) {
  SpringApplication.run(EurekaServiceApplication.class, args);
 }
}
```

❶ The `@EnableEurekaServer` annotation configures a bare-bones instance of the Eureka service registry.

This is *not* a production-worthy configuration! There are a lot of things we're conveniently hand-waving away in order to get things working and to demonstrate concepts. You're going to need to care for these things in a production environment. Netflix Eureka *can* handle your use cases, but that doesn't always mean that things like clustering (*https://github.com/spring-cloud/spring-cloud-netflix/ issues/203*) are easy! Hopefully, you're using a platform (like Cloud Foundry) that can automate the operational aspects of running something like this for you.

You'll need to configure the service registry. It's a common convention to start the service on port 8761, and we don't want the registry to try to register itself with other nodes (Example 7-3).

Example 7-3. Configuring a simple Eureka service registry

```
server.port=${PORT:8761}
❶
eureka.client.register-with-eureka=false
eureka.client.fetch-registry=false
❷
eureka.server.enable-self-preservation=false
```

❶ We don't want Eureka to try to register with itself.

❷ If a significant portion of the registered instances stop delivering heartbeats within a time span, Eureka assumes the issue is due to the network and does not de-register the services that are not responding. This is Eureka's self-preservation mode. Leaving this set to true is probably a good idea, but it also means that if you have a small set of instances (as you will, if you're trying these examples with a few nodes on a local machine) then you won't see the expected behavior when instances de-register.

Look at the snazzy new Eureka service registry in Figure 7-1! If you mouse over the Spring leaf, you'll see it's animated. We have *people* for that.

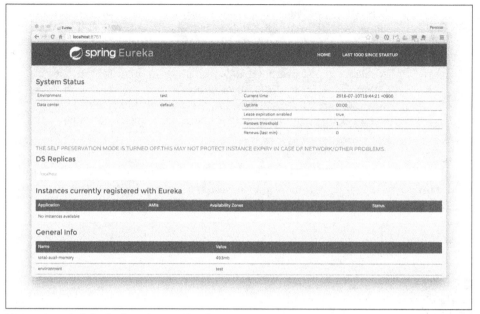

Figure 7-1. A default, bare-bones Eureka service registry

At this point, our registry is available. It is *not* highly available; in a production scenario this would be unacceptable. Indeed, Eureka will occasionally bark at us with a blood-red error message on the console, basically saying we need to configure replica nodes; otherwise we risk creating a very fragile deployment. Remember, Eureka will be the nervous system for our REST services: other services will talk to each other through Eureka.

But it's available. Let's stand up a client and a service and have them both register with the registry. We'll first build a trivial REST API, so that we have something to work with. This application uses `org.springframework.cloud : spring-cloud-starter-eureka` (which provides an implementation of Spring Cloud's `DiscoveryClient` for Netflix Eureka) and `org.springframework.boot : spring-boot-starter-web` (Example 7-4).

Example 7-4. A simple REST API that returns a greeting

```
package com.example;

import org.springframework.boot.SpringApplication;
import org.springframework.boot.autoconfigure.SpringBootApplication;
import org.springframework.cloud.client.discovery.EnableDiscoveryClient;
import org.springframework.util.StringUtils;
import org.springframework.web.bind.annotation.*;
```

```
import javax.servlet.http.HttpServletRequest;
import java.util.Collections;
import java.util.Map;
import java.util.Optional;

❶
@EnableDiscoveryClient
@SpringBootApplication
public class GreetingsServiceApplication {

  public static void main(String[] args) {
    SpringApplication.run(GreetingsServiceApplication.class, args);
  }
}

@RestController
class GreetingsRestController {

  ❷
  @RequestMapping(method = RequestMethod.GET, value = "/hi/{name}")
  Map<String, String> hi(
    @PathVariable String name,
    @RequestHeader(value = "X-CNJ-Name", required = false)
          Optional<String> cn) {
    String resolvedName =  cn.orElse(name);
    return Collections.singletonMap("greeting", "Hello, " + resolvedName + "!");
  }
}
```

❶ `@EnableDiscoveryClient` activates the Spring Cloud `DiscoveryClient` abstraction.

❷ This will respond a simple JSON structure with a `greeting` attribute.

Our service needs only to identify itself and configure how it will interact with Eureka. Spring Cloud will honor values it finds in `application.{yml,properties}`, just like Spring Boot, but it needs some values *earlier* in the life cycle of the application. It expects to find values like the address of the Spring Cloud Config Server in `boot strap.properties`, shown in Example 7-5.

Example 7-5. bootstrap.properties

```
spring.application.name=greetings-service  ❶

server.port=${PORT:0}  ❷

eureka.instance.instance-id=\  ❸
  ${spring.application.name}:${spring.application.instance_id:${random.value}}
```

❶ The application will be registered as `greetings-service`.

❷ And it will start on a random port.

❸ What distinct ID do we want for each registered service? Spring Cloud will give you a useful, node-specific default. We've overridden the default registered ID so that they're unique.

Start up a few instances of the `greetings-service` and then refresh the Eureka service registry and you'll see the newly registered instances. They're now advertising their presence and are available for consumption by other services (Figure 7-2).

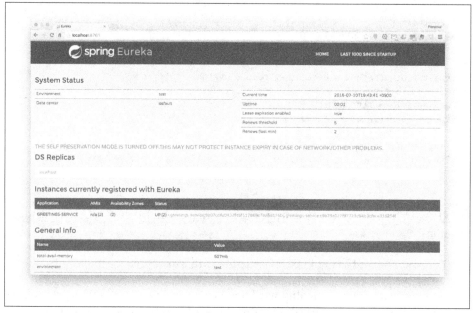

Figure 7-2. Eureka, now with registered instances!

Let's stand up a simple client—an *edge service*. We'll talk more about edge services in our discussion on edge services in Chapter 8, but for now suffice it to say that an edge service is the first port of call for requests coming into the system. The edge service will act as a client to the `greetings-service`, which it will resolve. It will interact with the `greetings-service` after resolving the service in the service registry.

Our new client also uses `spring-cloud-starter-eureka` and is annotated with `@Ena bleDiscoveryClient`. We can use the `DiscoveryClient` abstraction directly, if we'd like, to interrogate the registered service instances (Example 7-6).

Example 7-6. DiscoveryClientCLR.java

```java
package com.example;

import org.apache.commons.logging.Log;
import org.apache.commons.logging.LogFactory;
import org.springframework.beans.factory.annotation.Autowired;
import org.springframework.boot.CommandLineRunner;
import org.springframework.cloud.client.ServiceInstance;
import org.springframework.cloud.client.discovery.DiscoveryClient;
import org.springframework.stereotype.Component;

@Component
public class DiscoveryClientCLR implements CommandLineRunner {

  private final DiscoveryClient discoveryClient;

  private Log log = LogFactory.getLog(getClass());

  ❶
  @Autowired
  public DiscoveryClientCLR(DiscoveryClient discoveryClient) {
    this.discoveryClient = discoveryClient;
  }

  @Override
  public void run(String... args) throws Exception {

    ❷
    this.log.info("localServiceInstance");
    this.logServiceInstance(this.discoveryClient.getLocalServiceInstance());

    ❸
    String serviceId = "greetings-service";
    this.log.info(String.format("registered instances of '%s'", serviceId));
    this.discoveryClient.getInstances(serviceId)
      .forEach(this::logServiceInstance);
  }

  private void logServiceInstance(ServiceInstance si) {
    String msg = String.format("host = %s, port = %s, service ID = %s",
      si.getHost(), si.getPort(), si.getServiceId());
    log.info(msg);
  }
}
```

❶ Inject the Spring Cloud configured `DiscoveryClient` implementation.

❷ Get information on the current instance: that is, what information will be registered in Eureka for the current running application?

❸ Find and enumerate all the registered instances of the greetings-service.

The DiscoveryClient makes it easy to interact with the registry and enumerate all the registered instances. If there is more than one instance of the registered service, then it falls on us to select a specific version. We could randomly select from among the returned instances, which is effectively round-robin load balancing. We might want to do something else that takes advantage of awareness of the application and the instances, like weighted-response load balancing. Whatever the strategy, we need only describe it in code once, and then reuse it whenever we make a service call. This is the essence of client-side load balancing.

Netflix Ribbon is a client-side load balancing library. It supports different strategies for load balancing, including round-robin and weighted-response load balancing, but its real power lies in its extensibility. Let's look at the low-level example in Example 7-7.

Example 7-7. RibbonCLR.java

```java
package com.example;

import com.netflix.loadbalancer.*;
import org.apache.commons.logging.Log;
import org.apache.commons.logging.LogFactory;
import org.springframework.beans.factory.annotation.Autowired;
import org.springframework.boot.CommandLineRunner;
import org.springframework.cloud.client.discovery.DiscoveryClient;
import org.springframework.stereotype.Component;

import java.net.URI;
import java.util.List;
import java.util.stream.Collectors;
import java.util.stream.IntStream;

@Component
public class RibbonCLR implements CommandLineRunner {

  private final DiscoveryClient discoveryClient;

  private final Log log = LogFactory.getLog(getClass());

  @Autowired
  public RibbonCLR(DiscoveryClient discoveryClient) {
    this.discoveryClient = discoveryClient;
  }

  @Override
  public void run(String... args) throws Exception {

    String serviceId = "greetings-service";
```

❶
```
List<Server> servers = this.discoveryClient.getInstances(serviceId).stream()
 .map(si -> new Server(si.getHost(), si.getPort()))
 .collect(Collectors.toList());
```

❷
```
IRule roundRobinRule = new RoundRobinRule();

BaseLoadBalancer loadBalancer = LoadBalancerBuilder.newBuilder()
 .withRule(roundRobinRule).buildFixedServerListLoadBalancer(servers);

IntStream.range(0, 10).forEach(i -> {
❸
 Server server = loadBalancer.chooseServer();
 URI uri = URI.create("http://" + server.getHost() + ":" + server.getPort()
 + "/");
 log.info("resolved service " + uri.toString());
 });
 }
}
```

❶ Inject the Spring Cloud configured `DiscoveryClient` implementation.

❷ Get information on the current instance: that is, what information will be registered in Eureka for the current running application?

❸ Find and enumerate all the registered instances of the `greetings-service`.

This example worked, but it's tedious! Thankfully, Spring Cloud automatically integrates client-side load balancing at various levels of the framework automatically. A
particularly useful example is the auto-configuration for Spring's `RestTemplate`. The
`RestTemplate` supports interceptors to pre- and post-process HTTP requests as
they're made. We can use the Spring Cloud `@LoadBalanced` interceptor to signal to
Spring Cloud that we want it to configure a Ribbon-aware, load balancing interceptor
on the `RestTemplate` for us (Example 7-8).

Example 7-8. LoadBalancedRestTemplateConfiguration.java

```
package com.example;

import org.springframework.cloud.client.loadbalancer.LoadBalanced;
import org.springframework.context.annotation.Bean;
import org.springframework.context.annotation.Configuration;
import org.springframework.web.client.RestTemplate;

@Configuration
public class LoadBalancedRestTemplateConfiguration {
```

```
❶
@Bean
@LoadBalanced
RestTemplate restTemplate() {
 return new RestTemplate();
 }
}
```

❶ The @LoadBalanced annotation is a qualifier annotation. Spring uses these to disambiguate bean definitions and to flag certain beans for processing. Here, we're
flagging this particular RestTemplate instance as needing to have a load balancing interceptor configured.

This done, our work is much simpler! The load balancer will extract the URI for any
HTTP request and treat the host as a service ID to be resolved using a configured
DiscoveryClient (in this case, Netflix Eureka), and to be load balanced using Netflix
Ribbon (Example 7-9).

Example 7-9. LoadBalancedRestTemplateCLR.java

```
package com.example;

import com.fasterxml.jackson.databind.JsonNode;
import org.apache.commons.logging.Log;
import org.apache.commons.logging.LogFactory;
import org.springframework.beans.factory.annotation.Autowired;
import org.springframework.boot.CommandLineRunner;
import org.springframework.cloud.client.loadbalancer.LoadBalanced;
import org.springframework.http.ResponseEntity;
import org.springframework.stereotype.Component;
import org.springframework.web.client.RestTemplate;

import java.util.Collections;
import java.util.Map;

@Component
public class LoadBalancedRestTemplateCLR implements CommandLineRunner {

 private final RestTemplate restTemplate;

 private final Log log = LogFactory.getLog(getClass());

 ❶
 @Autowired
 public LoadBalancedRestTemplateCLR(@LoadBalanced RestTemplate restTemplate) {
  this.restTemplate = restTemplate;
 }

 @Override
```

```
public void run(String... strings) throws Exception {

  Map<String, String> variables = Collections.singletonMap("name",
    "Cloud Natives!");

  ❷
  ResponseEntity<JsonNode> response = this.restTemplate.getForEntity(
    "//greetings-service/hi/{name}", JsonNode.class, variables);
  JsonNode body = response.getBody();
  String greeting = body.get("greeting").asText();
  log.info("greeting: " + greeting);
  }
}
```

❶ We use the same @LoadBalanced qualifier annotation at both the bean producer
and injection site.

❷ We use the RestTemplate as we might otherwise, specifying for the host a service
ID (greetings-service) instead of a DNS address.

Cloud Foundry Route Services

Client-side load balancing gives us a lot of power over routing decisions and we have
an easier time, as developers, dictating routing logic in code. The routing is local to
our system of services, and if we need to change it, we can, without worrying about
impacting somebody else consuming the service. It's not realistic to expect that you
can demand all third-party clients use Netflix Ribbon and consume your API in the
same way, though. This becomes especially true when standing up edge services that
respond to client-side requests—requests from any number of different devices and
experiences. iOS clients, for example, aren't going to want to use Apache Zookeeper
and Netflix Ribbon to do their work. Here it can be useful to stand up an intermediary service that handles the request, handles routing, and then forwards the requests
to the downstream services. Such a component also has the benefit of being applica-
ble to services of all types, no matter the implementation language.

Cloud Foundry supports a special kind of component—a *route service*—that gives us
most of the benefits of client-side load balancing and having a centralized component
that enforces routing behavior. A route service is another extension plane in Cloud
Foundry, along with buildpacks, applications, and service brokers, that you can
develop and plug in to your platform. A route service is ultimately an HTTP service
that accepts all HTTP requests for a given host and domain, and then does whatever
it likes with them, including processing, transforming, or forwarding them.

Route services are meant to be generic proxies that are interposed in the request
chain for (theoretically) any kind of application, so some constraints apply. They
must support both HTTP *and* HTTPS. Cloud Foundry presently doesn't support

chaining route services for one request to another. Cloud Foundry treats route services as another type of user-provided service. They're a little different than the other types of user-provided services we've discussed in this book, in that the connection between a route service and an application is specified in terms of the hostname and domain of the applications, not the application name.

Let's look at an example. Since we need to accept and just pass through all incoming HTTP or HTTPS requests, we need to configure Spring's `RestTemplate` to trust everything and to ignore errors (Example 7-10).

Example 7-10. RouteServiceApplication.java

```java
package com.example;

import org.springframework.boot.SpringApplication;
import org.springframework.boot.autoconfigure.SpringBootApplication;
import org.springframework.context.annotation.Bean;
import org.springframework.http.client.ClientHttpResponse;
import org.springframework.http.client.SimpleClientHttpRequestFactory;
import org.springframework.web.client.DefaultResponseErrorHandler;
import org.springframework.web.client.RestTemplate;

import javax.net.ssl.HttpsURLConnection;
import javax.net.ssl.SSLContext;
import javax.net.ssl.TrustManager;
import javax.net.ssl.X509TrustManager;
import java.io.IOException;
import java.net.HttpURLConnection;
import java.net.Proxy;
import java.net.URL;
import java.security.KeyManagementException;
import java.security.NoSuchAlgorithmException;
import java.security.cert.CertificateException;
import java.security.cert.X509Certificate;

/**
 * @author Ben Hale
 */
@SpringBootApplication
public class RouteServiceApplication {

  public static void main(String[] args) {
    SpringApplication.run(RouteServiceApplication.class, args);
  }

  ❶
  @Bean
  RestTemplate restOperations() {
    RestTemplate restTemplate = new RestTemplate(
      new TrustEverythingClientHttpRequestFactory()); ❷
```

```java
restTemplate.setErrorHandler(new NoErrorsResponseErrorHandler()); ❸
return restTemplate;
}

private static class NoErrorsResponseErrorHandler extends
DefaultResponseErrorHandler {

@Override
public boolean hasError(ClientHttpResponse response) throws IOException {
  return false;
}
}

private static final class TrustEverythingClientHttpRequestFactory extends
SimpleClientHttpRequestFactory {

private static SSLContext getSslContext(TrustManager trustManager) {
  try {
    SSLContext sslContext = SSLContext.getInstance("SSL");
    sslContext.init(null, new TrustManager[] { trustManager }, null);
    return sslContext;
  }
  catch (KeyManagementException | NoSuchAlgorithmException e) {
    throw new RuntimeException(e);
  }
}

@Override
protected HttpURLConnection openConnection(URL url, Proxy proxy)
  throws IOException {
  HttpURLConnection connection = super.openConnection(url, proxy);
  if (connection instanceof HttpsURLConnection) {
    HttpsURLConnection httpsConnection = (HttpsURLConnection) connection;
    SSLContext sslContext = getSslContext(new TrustEverythingTrustManager());
    httpsConnection.setSSLSocketFactory(sslContext.getSocketFactory());
    httpsConnection.setHostnameVerifier((s, session) -> true);
  }
  return connection;
}
}

private static final class TrustEverythingTrustManager implements
X509TrustManager {

@Override
public void checkClientTrusted(X509Certificate[] x509Certificates, String s)
  throws CertificateException {
}

@Override
public void checkServerTrusted(X509Certificate[] x509Certificates, String s)
  throws CertificateException {
```

```
    }

    @Override
    public X509Certificate[] getAcceptedIssuers() {
     return new X509Certificate[0];
    }
   }
 }
```

❶ Configure a RestTemplate...

❷ That trusts everything...

❸ And ignores errors.

This route service logs all incoming requests before and after accepting them
(Example 7-11).

Example 7-11. Controller.java

```
package com.example;

import org.apache.commons.logging.Log;
import org.apache.commons.logging.LogFactory;
import org.slf4j.Logger;
import org.slf4j.LoggerFactory;
import org.springframework.beans.factory.annotation.Autowired;
import org.springframework.http.HttpHeaders;
import org.springframework.http.RequestEntity;
import org.springframework.http.ResponseEntity;
import org.springframework.web.bind.annotation.RequestMapping;
import org.springframework.web.bind.annotation.RestController;
import org.springframework.web.client.RestOperations;
import org.springframework.web.client.RestTemplate;

import java.net.URI;
import java.util.Arrays;
import java.util.Collections;

/**
 * @author Ben Hale
 */
@RestController
class Controller {

    ❶
    private static final String FORWARDED_URL = "X-CF-Forwarded-Url";

    private static final String PROXY_METADATA = "X-CF-Proxy-Metadata";
```

```
private static final String PROXY_SIGNATURE = "X-CF-Proxy-Signature";

private final Log logger = LogFactory.getLog(this.getClass());

private final RestOperations restOperations;

@Autowired
Controller(RestTemplate restOperations) {
  this.restOperations = restOperations;
}

❷
@RequestMapping(headers = { FORWARDED_URL, PROXY_METADATA, PROXY_SIGNATURE })
ResponseEntity<?> service(RequestEntity<byte[]> incoming) {

  this.logger.info("incoming request: " + incoming);

  HttpHeaders headers = new HttpHeaders();
  headers.putAll(incoming.getHeaders());
  headers.put("X-CNJ-Name", Collections.singletonList("Cloud Natives"));

  ❸
  URI uri = headers
    .remove(FORWARDED_URL)
    .stream()
    .findFirst()
    .map(URI::create)
    .orElseThrow(
      () -> new IllegalStateException(String.format("No %s header present",
        FORWARDED_URL)));

  ❹
  RequestEntity<?> outgoing = new RequestEntity<>(
    ((RequestEntity<?>) incoming).getBody(), headers, incoming.getMethod(), uri);

  this.logger.info("outgoing request: {}" + outgoing);

  return this.restOperations.exchange(outgoing, byte[].class);
  }
}
```

❶ Cloud Foundry passes along custom headers that provide context for an incoming request.

❷ We use the presence of these headers as a selector to determine if the route service should handle the request.

❸ In the request processing method, we determine the ultimate request by extracting the appropriate header…

❹ …and adapt the incoming request into an outgoing request to be executed using the RestTemplate.

This is a trivial example, but the possibilities are endless. We could preprocess requests and handle authentication, or perhaps adapt one type of authentication for another. We could insert logic to handle rate limiting, or we could forward requests in a certain way by relying on client-side load balancing. We could handle metering for requests going into the system. We could simply use this as a sort of generic service-level interstitial and enrich the request body with global state or request context (the user's clickstream information, perhaps?).

A lot of the things you may want to do here—metering, rate limiting, authentication, etc.—are generic concerns that you don't need necessarily to write code for. A lot of this functionality is well-addressed by API-gateway products like Apigee, that also distribute a Cloud Foundry route service that you can configure for your application. The Apigee API gateway is connected to your Apigee account, and all the policy you centrally configure there is automatically applied to your requests.

Using a route service is fairly straightforward, but not exactly the same as using any of the other types of route services. A route service is ultimately just a Cloud Foundry application that you've deployed. Suppose you've already deployed two applications to Cloud Foundry: route-service (the logging route service we just looked at), and a regular Spring Boot and Spring MVC application, downstream-service. Example 7-12 is an example of connecting an application (downstream-service) to a route service (route-service) for applications deployed on Pivotal Web Services where the domain is cfapps.io by default. (If you're using a deployed Cloud Foundry instance elsewhere, this won't be the case.)

Example 7-12. Connecting an application to a route service

```
cf create-user-provided-service route-service -r  https://my-route-service.cfapps.io
❶

cf bind-route-service cfapps.io route-service -hostname  my-downstream-service ❷
```

❶ Create a user-provided route service, pointing it to the URL for our deployed route-service.

❷ Bind that route service to any application whose route is http://my-downstream-service.cfapps.io.

Now visit the downstream-service in the browser a few times and then tail the logs for the route service (cf logs --recent route-service) to see the log output reflecting the requests.

Summary

For services deployed over HTTP (nothing says that they have to be, though!), routing is a critical concern which becomes even more important when the lifetime of a service is dynamic and when service topologies change. We want, for the purposes of homogeneous clients accessing the services from outside our system, to project that services are available in a fixed, well-known place but retain complete flexibility for intra-service communication. We can achieve these seemingly conflicting concerns with a little thoughtfulness and by leveraging some of the practices described in this chapter.

CHAPTER 8

Edge Services

Microservices don't exist in a vacuum. They ultimately serve clients. These clients are myriad: HTML5 clients, Android clients, iOS clients, PlayStations or XBoxes, Smart TVs, and indeed almost *anything* else these days has a MAC address (and, thanks to the magic of ARP, an IP address) and could act as a client to your service. *Anything.* The roads in Singapore capture sensor data to feed into a cloud-based brain that helps with traffic shaping. There are human beings walking around the planet with network-connected organs!

Clients have many different dimensions of capabilities that inform the types of payloads and services they can work with, or talk to:

- Some have limited memory capacity or processing power which affects how much content a client can manage.
- Some require specific content types or encodings.
- Some require different document models optimized for different clients—some hierarchical and some flat.
- Some clients' screen real estate may require data to be loaded incrementally instead of all at once.
- Document delivery may be more efficient streaming or chunked for certain clients.
- User interactions may change the responses required.
- They could influence the metadata fields, delivery method, interaction model, etc.

The cost of retrofitting every microservice in a system with a nontrivial number of microservices to accommodate each new client is prohibitive and would introduce a

215

complexity into the system that would quickly become overwhelming. Our goal should be to stay agile, to retain control over our destiny. Instead, handle these concerns in an intermediary service, called an *edge service*. Edge services are a sort of doorway for requests coming into the application. They are in an enviable position to handle client-specific concerns as well as cross-service concerns like security (authentication and authorization), rate limiting and metering, routing (for more on this, see the discussion on routing, filtering, API translation, client-adapter APIs, service-proxying, and so much more in Chapter 7).

The Greetings Service

In this chapter we'll look at addressing the concerns of edge services, but we'll do so in terms of a simple REST service called `greetings-service` and a Eureka service registry. Let's establish these services now. First, let's stand up a quick Netflix Eureka instance, the `service-registry` module. This is a typical Spring Boot application, as created on the Spring Initializr (*http://start.spring.io*). To it, we've added `org.spring framework.cloud : spring-cloud-starter-eureka-server` (Example 8-1).

Example 8-1. Set up a simple Netflix Eureka server in the service-registry module

```
package demo;

import org.springframework.boot.SpringApplication;
import org.springframework.boot.autoconfigure.SpringBootApplication;
import org.springframework.cloud.netflix.eureka.server.EnableEurekaServer;

❶
@EnableEurekaServer
@SpringBootApplication
public class EurekaServiceApplication {

  public static void main(String args[]) {
    SpringApplication.run(EurekaServiceApplication.class, args);
  }
}
```

❶ The `@EnableEurekaServer` annotation configures a bare-bones instance of the Eureka service registry.

The registry will need some minimal configuration, of course (Example 8-2).

Example 8-2. application.properties in the service-registry module

```
spring.application.name=eureka-service
❶
eureka.client.register-with-eureka=false
```

```
eureka.client.fetch-registry=false
```
❷
```
eureka.server.enable-self-preservation=false
```

❶ Tell Eureka not to register with itself.

❷ Ensure that Eureka doesn't bother to aggressively cache cluster information if it detects nodes are not responding within a certain threshold. This is a convenience during development, but you might disable it in production.

Run the `service-registry` and it'll spin up on port 8761. Then we'll need a simple REST API with which to work—a `greetings-service` that responds with a salutation. The service is fairly unremarkable except that it participates in service registration and discovery, advertising itself for other services to find (Example 8-3).

Example 8-3. `GreetingsServiceApplication.java` in the greetings-service module

```
package greetings;

import org.springframework.boot.SpringApplication;
import org.springframework.boot.autoconfigure.SpringBootApplication;
import org.springframework.cloud.client.discovery.EnableDiscoveryClient;
```

❶
```
@EnableDiscoveryClient
@SpringBootApplication
public class GreetingsServiceApplication {

 public static void main(String[] args) {
  SpringApplication.run(GreetingsServiceApplication.class, args);
 }
}
```

❶ Participate in service registration and discovery with the Spring Cloud `Discov eryClient` abstraction.

We will see many permutations of the same REST API in this chapter, so we've used Spring profiles to conditionally enable or disable them. The default `greetings-service`, the one that will run absent any other specified profile, looks like Example 8-4.

Example 8-4. `DefaultGreetingsRestController.java`

```
package greetings;

import org.springframework.context.annotation.Profile;
import org.springframework.web.bind.annotation.PathVariable;
```

```
import org.springframework.web.bind.annotation.RequestMapping;
import org.springframework.web.bind.annotation.RequestMethod;
import org.springframework.web.bind.annotation.RestController;

import java.util.Collections;
import java.util.Map;

@Profile({ "default", "insecure" })
@RestController
@RequestMapping(method = RequestMethod.GET, value = "/greet/{name}")
class DefaultGreetingsRestController {

 @RequestMapping
 Map<String, String> hi(@PathVariable String name) {
  return Collections.singletonMap("greeting", "Hello, " + name + "!");
 }
}
```

We'll revisit this example a few times in this chapter. Run it and it will register itself in Eureka as greetings-service, and spin up on port 8081 by default.

A Simple Edge Service

Let's stand up a simple client API—an *edge service*—called greetings-client, that will act as an intermediary between the outside world and our downstream services. This endpoint will act as a client to our downstream service, the greetings-service, that other clients (HTML5 clients, iOS clients, Android clients, etc.) will talk to. Let's look at different ways to create API adapters—something that returns a view of data, or a synthesis of data from other services into something new, specifically for a client.

The entry class for our new API adapter is simple enough: it uses Spring Cloud Dis coveryClient abstraction, as did greetings-service, so that other nodes may discover it with service registration and discovery. To start, it'll need a distinct port and a spring.application.name. Example 8-5 uses greetings-client for the application name.

Example 8-5. GreetingsClientApplication.java

```
package greetings;

import org.springframework.boot.SpringApplication;
import org.springframework.boot.autoconfigure.SpringBootApplication;
import org.springframework.cloud.client.discovery.EnableDiscoveryClient;

❶
@EnableDiscoveryClient
@SpringBootApplication
public class GreetingsClientApplication {
```

```
  public static void main(String[] args) {
    SpringApplication.run(GreetingsClientApplication.class, args);
  }
}
```

❶ Activate service registration and discovery.

Let's look at our first client endpoint. The endpoints use client-side load balancing (thanks to the Spring Cloud integration with Netflix Ribbon) so that we can issue requests to the downstream service with the `RestTemplate`. Each request is pre-processed by the interceptor that Spring Cloud contributes, using the `@LoadBalanced` qualifier annotation. The interceptor extracts the host from the URI, and works with the `DiscoveryClient` to discover all instances of the service in the registry. The discovered instances are passed to the Netflix Ribbon client-side load balancer, which then determines to which node the request should be routed.

The response from the eventual call to the REST service is JSON. Here we use Spring Framework's `ParameterizedTypeReference`, which is an implementation of the super type token pattern, to make short work of coercing the resulting JSON into a type we can work with. The `RestTemplate` uses the last parameter in the exchange invocation —an argument of type `Class<T>`, or `ParameterizedTypeReference<T>`—to determine what type is expected from the returned results. Here, we specify that we want the response JSON to be converted into a `Map<String, String>` (Example 8-6).

 The super type token pattern captures generic parameters in class literals to circumvent the limitations of *type erasure*—the fact that Java does not retain generic parameters on instance variables at runtime—in the Java language. It was originally espoused, to our knowledge, by Neal Gafter, who worked on the JDK team at Sun (*http://gafter.blogspot.com/2006/12/super-type-tokens.html*).

Example 8-6. RestTemplateGreetingsClientApiGateway.java

```
package greetings;

import org.springframework.beans.factory.annotation.Autowired;
import org.springframework.cloud.client.loadbalancer.LoadBalanced;
import org.springframework.context.annotation.Profile;
import org.springframework.core.ParameterizedTypeReference;
import org.springframework.http.HttpMethod;
import org.springframework.http.ResponseEntity;
import org.springframework.web.bind.annotation.*;
import org.springframework.web.client.RestTemplate;

import java.util.Map;
```

```
@Profile({ "default", "insecure" })
@RestController
@RequestMapping("/api")
class RestTemplateGreetingsClientApiGateway {

 private final RestTemplate restTemplate;

 @Autowired
 RestTemplateGreetingsClientApiGateway(
   @LoadBalanced RestTemplate restTemplate) { ❶
  this.restTemplate = restTemplate;
 }

 @GetMapping("/resttemplate/{name}")
 Map<String, String> restTemplate(@PathVariable String name) {

  //@formatter:off
  ParameterizedTypeReference<Map<String, String>> type =
      new ParameterizedTypeReference<Map<String, String>>() {};
  //@formatter:on

  ResponseEntity<Map<String, String>> responseEntity = this.restTemplate
   .exchange("http://greetings-service/greet/{name}", HttpMethod.GET, null,
    type, name);
  return responseEntity.getBody();
 }
}
```

❶ The @LoadBalanced annotation is a qualifier that connects the dependency consumer with the specific instance of the RestTemplate that Spring Cloud has configured with an interceptor to support client-side load balancing.

The RestTemplate makes it easy to call other services quickly and conveniently. Well,
conveniently if you only do it now and again; it can quickly become tedious if we
have to make more than a handful of REST calls. Our edge services will call a lot of
different services, so we'll need to simplify the work of building clients to work with
our services.

Netflix Feign

We want to simplify the work of calling downstream services. One option might be to
write an API client and then reuse that. It can be shared with other teams who can
use it to reduce their ramp-up time. This is sound strategy if you don't mind writing
the client in the first place and if you have a strategy to keep it consistent with the
service API (for more on how to ensure this consistency, see our discussion on
consumer-driven contract testing in Chapter 15), but there is always the risk that the
client ends up too smart—with business logic baked into the client that should be in
the service implementation itself. So we *could* build our own client, but that's an

uphill fight, and one that risks introducing more bugs and inconsistencies. Here, we might be tempted to use RPC technologies, and forego the benefits of using REST. We would discourage that, unless you have a particular use case that simply can't be met with REST. Instead, consider using something like Netflix Feign.

Netflix Feign is a library from Netflix that makes deriving service clients as simple as an interface definition and some conventions. It's well integrated with Spring Cloud. We can activate it by adding `@EnableFeignClients` to a configuration class (or the class annotated with `@SpringBootApplication`) and `org.springframework.cloud` : `spring-cloud-starter-feign` to the classpath. Here's a simple client built as an interface. Make sure you start the `greetings-client` with the `feign` Spring profile (Example 8-7).

Example 8-7. GreetingsClient.java

```
package greetings;

import org.springframework.cloud.netflix.feign.FeignClient;
import org.springframework.web.bind.annotation.PathVariable;
import org.springframework.web.bind.annotation.RequestMapping;
import org.springframework.web.bind.annotation.RequestMethod;

import java.util.Map;

❶
@FeignClient(serviceId = "greetings-service")
interface GreetingsClient {

    ❷
    @RequestMapping(method = RequestMethod.GET, value = "/greet/{name}")
    Map<String, String> greet(@PathVariable("name") String name); ❸
}
```

❶ The service ID is used in tandem with the `DiscoveryClient` abstraction and Netflix Ribbon to do client-side load balancing.

❷ We specify what endpoints should be called and how they should be called using Spring MVC request mapping annotations. You're no doubt used to seeing this on the *service* implementation, not the client!

❸ The return value is used to determine how to marshal the results. We don't need to use the super type token pattern anymore!

Then we can use the Feign client in our edge service (Example 8-8).

Example 8-8. FeignGreetingsClientApiGateway.java

```java
package greetings;

import org.springframework.beans.factory.annotation.Autowired;
import org.springframework.context.annotation.Profile;
import org.springframework.web.bind.annotation.*;

import java.util.Map;

❶
@Profile("feign")
@RestController
@RequestMapping("/api")
class FeignGreetingsClientApiGateway {

  private final GreetingsClient greetingsClient;

  @Autowired
  FeignGreetingsClientApiGateway(GreetingsClient greetingsClient) {
    this.greetingsClient = greetingsClient;
  }

  ❷
  @GetMapping("/feign/{name}")
  Map<String, String> feign(@PathVariable String name) {
    return this.greetingsClient.greet(name);
  }
}
```

❶   The edge service is running under the `feign` Spring profile.

❷   The call to the service becomes a method call, but one that instead still relies on REST. Our client is as simple and approachable as they come! Anybody who knows how to use Feign will figure out what's going on quickly with this technology.

API adapters can get fairly complex and fairly specific; these adapters are a natural place to put any client-specific handling that can't be described generically and applied to *all* requests. Eventually the problems of adapting APIs to clients start to look eerily like integration problems. For more on this, see our discussion of integration concerns in Chapter 10.

Thus far we've looked at using REST to call, and work with, data from other services. We've done so, and conveniently ignored the requirements for reliable service-to-service calls. For more on this, see our discussion of integration in Chapter 12.

Filtering and Proxying with Netflix Zuul

Thus far we've focused on client-specific integration with specific endpoints on downstream REST services. A lot of concerns are more generic and apply to all requests from clients from a given host to a service or group of services downstream. We can use a microproxy, Netflix Zuul (*https://github.com/Netflix/zuul*), to make short work of standing up filters that address concerns like rate limiting, proxying, and more.

 At the time of this writing there is a Spring Cloud incubator project called Spring Cloud Gateway that aims to provide a more seamless alternative to Zuul based on the Spring Framework 5 reactive runtime. The code is not yet Generally Available (GA) or stable, so we will focus on Netflix's very capable, genre-defining Zuul project for two reasons: it works well, and it's ubiquitous: familiarity with it will serve you if you later elect to use Spring Cloud Gateway.

Zuul's architect, Mikey Cohen, gave a nice talk at SpringOne Platform 2016 that introduces some of Zuul's applications (*http://www.slideshare.net/MikeyCohen1/zuul-netflix-springone-platform*). It's used to serve most of the frontends for Netflix.com and more than *1,000 device types*. It is the adapter layer that handles hundreds of permutations of protocols and device versions. In Netflix's environment-particular deployment, it is fronted by more than 50 AWS Elastic Load Balancers and handles tens of *billions* of requests per day across 3 AWS regions. It's deployed in over 20 production Zuul clusters fronting more than 10 origin systems for Netflix.com. Zuul is, in short, a workhorse component.

Zuul filters are deeply rooted in production. They contain dynamic routing logic, handle load balancing and service protection, and provide tools to debug and analyze problem pathways. A Zuul gateway can be a quality assurance tool in that it provides a single place to observe the flow of data through a system.

Zuul filters can be used to create a top-level context for requests into a system, handling concerns like geolocation, cookie propagation, and token decryption. They can address cross-cutting concerns like authentication. They can be used in request or response normalization, handling device-specific weirdness like chunked encoding requirements, header truncations, URL encoding fixes, etc. They are an ideal place to do targeted routing, perhaps in order to isolate specific (albeit faulty) requests. They can be used to handle traffic shaping, do global routing world wide, handle dead-node and zone-failover logic, and detect and prevent attacks.

All of these possibilities are distinctly generic: they apply to all manner of services. Zuul is *not* the right place to put business logic specific to a particular service. Keep business logic out of the edge tier.

Zuul filters are not the same as a traditional servlet `Filter`. It's assumed that you're filtering the results of *proxied* requests and not, particularly, the requests to the edge service itself.

Zuul filters are an ideal place to address routing from the client to downstream services. If your services are registered in a service registry for which there is a Spring Cloud `DiscoveryClient` implementation configured, then it's a simple matter of adding an `@EnableZuulProxy` to your application code (along with `org.springframe work.cloud : spring-cloud-starter-zuul` to the classpath); then Spring Cloud, working with the `DiscoveryClient`, will set up routes that proxy downstream services for you. You can interrogate those routes using the `RouteLocator`, as we do in Example 8-9.

Example 8-9. ZuulConfiguration.java

```
package greetings;

import org.apache.commons.logging.Log;
import org.apache.commons.logging.LogFactory;
import org.springframework.boot.CommandLineRunner;
import org.springframework.cloud.netflix.zuul.EnableZuulProxy;
import org.springframework.cloud.netflix.zuul.filters.RouteLocator;
import org.springframework.context.annotation.Bean;
import org.springframework.context.annotation.Configuration;

@Configuration
@EnableZuulProxy
class ZuulConfiguration {

  @Bean
  CommandLineRunner commandLineRunner(RouteLocator routeLocator) { ❶
   Log log = LogFactory.getLog(getClass());
   return args -> routeLocator.getRoutes().forEach(
    r -> log.info(String.format("%s (%s) %s", r.getId(), r.getLocation(),
     r.getFullPath())));
  }

}
```

❶ The `RouteLocator` is an abstraction that has a few interesting implementations. Spring Cloud configures an implementation that is aware of the `Discovery Client` if it's been so configured.

Zuul has set up convenient routes for us based on the service IDs, so assuming we've already stood up the `service-registry` and the `greetings-service`, we should see reflected in the output of the previous example that there's a service, `greetings-service`, available for consumption through the proxy. The `greetings-client` is supposed to start at `http://localhost:8082`, so you could invoke the `greetings-service` at `http://localhost:8082/greetings-service/greet/World` where the context-path, `greetings-service`, is drawn from the service ID in the registry. You can also set up arbitrary routes. Example 8-10 shows the configuration required to do that.

Example 8-10. application.properties

```
zuul.routes.hi.path = /lets/**  ❶
```

```
zuul.routes.hi.serviceId = greetings-service  ❷
```

❶ The path on the edge service that should be mapped to...

❷ ...a service (or, alternatively, a full URL specified *instead* of `serviceId` as the `.location`).

In this configuration, we map the requests to the `greetings-service`—everything from / and below, to `/lets/*` on the edge service. Start the application and try it out at `http://localhost:8082/lets/greet/World`. These routes are an ideal thing to keep in the Spring Cloud Config Server, where they can be updated later without restarting the edge service; you can force Zuul to dynamically reload them.

One way to achieve this is to simply invoke the Spring Cloud `refresh` endpoint, which we looked at in our discussion of twelve-factor configuration in Chapter 3. Change the configuration in the Spring Cloud Config Server, commit the changes (to Subversion or Git), and then send an empty HTTP POST (e.g., `curl -d{} http://localhost:8082/refresh`) to the `refresh` endpoint or to the Spring Cloud event bus (`/bus/refresh`). This will result in the publication of a `RefreshScopeRefreshedE vent`, which components in the Zuul machinery will respond to by reconfiguring themselves.

Alternatively, you can use the `/routes` Actuator endpoint, as seen in Figure 8-1, that Zuul automatically configures for you. That endpoint will return the configured routes if you send an HTTP GET, and will trigger a refresh of the configuration if you send an HTTP POST. This is an alternative to using the `refresh` endpoint because it applies *only* to the Zuul routes, and not to any other (potentially heavier-weight) infrastructure that may be caught in a refresh event.

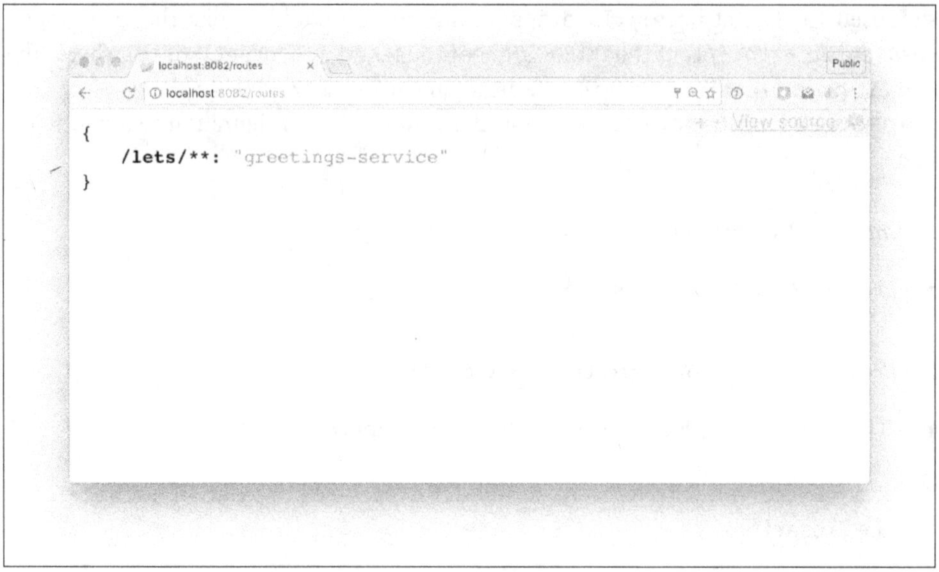

Figure 8-1. The Zuul routes from the routes endpoint

Zuul will also invalidate and reconfigure existing routes based on `HeartbeatEvent` events being published from the `DiscoveryClient`. Thus, Zuul will remove the route from its configuration if a node should de-register from Eureka (or any other service registry supported through the `DiscoveryClient`).

Naturally, if you have some sort of internal state that depends on these routes, you can listen directly for these events and respond in whatever way is appropriate for your application (Example 8-11).

Example 8-11. RoutesListener.java

```
package greetings;

import org.apache.commons.logging.Log;
import org.apache.commons.logging.LogFactory;
import org.springframework.beans.factory.annotation.Autowired;
import org.springframework.cloud.client.discovery.DiscoveryClient;
import org.springframework.cloud.client.discovery.event.HeartbeatEvent;
import org.springframework.cloud.netflix.zuul.RoutesRefreshedEvent;
import org.springframework.cloud.netflix.zuul.filters.RouteLocator;
import org.springframework.context.event.EventListener;
import org.springframework.stereotype.Component;

@Component
class RoutesListener {

 private final RouteLocator routeLocator;
```

```
private final DiscoveryClient discoveryClient;

private Log log = LogFactory.getLog(getClass());

@Autowired
public RoutesListener(DiscoveryClient dc, RouteLocator rl) {
  this.routeLocator = rl;
  this.discoveryClient = dc;
}

❶
@EventListener(HeartbeatEvent.class)
public void onHeartbeatEvent(HeartbeatEvent event) {
  this.log.info("onHeartbeatEvent()");
  this.discoveryClient.getServices().stream().map(x -> " " + x)
    .forEach(this.log::info);
}

❷
@EventListener(RoutesRefreshedEvent.class)
public void onRoutesRefreshedEvent(RoutesRefreshedEvent event) {
  this.log.info("onRoutesRefreshedEvent()");
  this.routeLocator.getRoutes().stream().map(x -> " " + x)
    .forEach(this.log::info);
}
}
```

❶ Listen to events being published by the `DiscoveryClient` machinery.

❷ Listen to events being published by the Zuul routing machinery, specifically.

Zuul, at its core, is a proxy. You can write `ZuulFilter` implementations that are integrated into the proxy life cycle itself, *or* write regular `javax.servlet.Filter` implementations that Filter requests made into the Zuul Servlet. Let's look at a simple `Filter` that exposes access control headers to allow cross-origin request scripting so that other JavaScript clients can call this service from another origin. In a simple application, it would make sense to serve up the JavaScript and HTML5 assets from the same application that exposes the Zuul proxy. In a more mature application, the (static) client code would probably live in a content delivery network (CDN). This is where we run into a problem: calls from the JavaScript code to the edge service containing the proxy would run afoul of cross-origin request forgery protections, since JavaScript code lives in a sandbox, and is unable to make requests outside of its origin domain.

The only way to get around this is to expose the `Access-Control-Allow-Headers`, `Access-Control-Allow-Methods`, `Access-Control-Allow-Origin`, and (optionally) the `Access-Control-Max-Age` headers on an edge service, explicitly permitting requests from the HTML5 client to the edge service. We **could** route requests from the HTML5 client directly to each of our services in the service registry, but then we'd need to change every single downstream microservice, adding in these access control headers. If we wanted to see that reflected in the downstream service, we'd have to ask every team involved to update their code. It could take ages, and in the meantime we'd lose the autonomy we sought in moving to microservices in the first place. Instead, let's configure a filter at the edge service that does this for us.

The simplest option would be a filter that allows *all* requests by specifying *. There are some limitations, though. If our CORS request includes cookies, we must *also* specify `withCredentials: true` in our JavaScript code, and our service must *also* return `Access-Control-Allow-Credentials: true`. Even then, our request would be wide open to all clients! One option is to keep a dynamic white list on the edge service, filtering clients against those registered registered in the registry. The `Discovery Client` gives us what we need to support this.

 If our static assets live in a CDN, then the CDN's origin (IP or hostname) would need to appear in the registry. We can achieve this explicitly using the service registry's API. Alternatively, if we're using Netflix Eureka, we could use a sidecar process like Netflix's Prana (*https://github.com/Netflix/Prana*) to do the registration for us.

Let's look at a trivial `javax.servlet.Filter` to dynamically white-list requests into the edge service (Example 8-12).

Example 8-12. CorsFilter.java—you'll need to start the application with the cors Spring profile activated

```
package greetings;

import org.apache.commons.logging.Log;
import org.apache.commons.logging.LogFactory;
import org.springframework.beans.factory.annotation.Autowired;
import org.springframework.cloud.client.ServiceInstance;
import org.springframework.cloud.client.discovery.DiscoveryClient;
import org.springframework.cloud.client.discovery.event.HeartbeatEvent;
import org.springframework.context.annotation.Profile;
import org.springframework.context.event.EventListener;
import org.springframework.core.Ordered;
import org.springframework.core.annotation.Order;
import org.springframework.http.HttpHeaders;
import org.springframework.stereotype.Component;
import org.springframework.util.StringUtils;

import javax.servlet.*;
```

```java
import javax.servlet.http.HttpServletRequest;
import javax.servlet.http.HttpServletResponse;
import java.io.IOException;
import java.net.URI;
import java.util.Collections;
import java.util.List;
import java.util.Map;
import java.util.concurrent.ConcurrentHashMap;
import java.util.stream.Collectors;

@Profile("cors")
@Component
@Order(Ordered.HIGHEST_PRECEDENCE + 10)
class CorsFilter implements Filter {

  private final Log log = LogFactory.getLog(getClass());

  private final Map<String, List<ServiceInstance>> catalog = new ConcurrentHashMap<>();

  private final DiscoveryClient discoveryClient;

  ❶
  @Autowired
  public CorsFilter(DiscoveryClient discoveryClient) {
   this.discoveryClient = discoveryClient;
   this.refreshCatalog();
  }

  ❷
  @Override
  public void doFilter(ServletRequest req, ServletResponse res, FilterChain chain)
   throws IOException, ServletException {
   HttpServletResponse response = HttpServletResponse.class.cast(res);
   HttpServletRequest request = HttpServletRequest.class.cast(req);
   String originHeaderValue = originFor(request);
   boolean clientAllowed = isClientAllowed(originHeaderValue);

   if (clientAllowed) {
    response.setHeader(HttpHeaders.ACCESS_CONTROL_ALLOW_ORIGIN,
     originHeaderValue);
   }

   chain.doFilter(req, res);
  }

  ❸
  private boolean isClientAllowed(String origin) {
   if (StringUtils.hasText(origin)) {
    URI originUri = URI.create(origin);
    int port = originUri.getPort();
    String match = originUri.getHost() + ':' + (port <= 0 ? 80 : port);
```

```
  this.catalog.forEach((k, v) -> {
    String collect = v
      .stream()
      .map(
      si -> si.getHost() + ':' + si.getPort() + '(' + si.getServiceId() + ')')
      .collect(Collectors.joining());
  });

  boolean svcMatch = this.catalog
    .keySet()
    .stream()
    .anyMatch(
    serviceId -> this.catalog.get(serviceId).stream()
      .map(si -> si.getHost() + ':' + si.getPort())
      .anyMatch(hp -> hp.equalsIgnoreCase(match)));
  return svcMatch;
 }
 return false;
}

➍
@EventListener(HeartbeatEvent.class)
public void onHeartbeatEvent(HeartbeatEvent e) {
 this.refreshCatalog();
}

private void refreshCatalog() {
 discoveryClient.getServices().forEach(
  svc -> this.catalog.put(svc, this.discoveryClient.getInstances(svc)));
}

@Override
public void init(FilterConfig filterConfig) throws ServletException {
}

@Override
public void destroy() {
}

private String originFor(HttpServletRequest request) {
 return StringUtils.hasText(request.getHeader(HttpHeaders.ORIGIN)) ? request
  .getHeader(HttpHeaders.ORIGIN) : request.getHeader(HttpHeaders.REFERER);
 }
}
```

➊ We'll use the Spring Cloud `DiscoveryClient` to interrogate the service topology.

➋ The `doFilter` method for a standard Servlet `Filter` is as you'd expect…

➌ …it sets the access control headers if the client is determined to be within a known set of services.

❹ Proactively invalidate the local cache, and then cache the set of registered services whenever the `DiscoveryClient` receives a heartbeat event.

Once that's done, we need a static HTML5 application to try things out. This application, in the `html5-client` module, leverages service registration and discovery through the Spring Cloud `DiscoveryClient` abstraction. It exposes an endpoint, `/greetings-client-uri`, which in turn returns a valid URI for an instance of the `greetings-client` edge service that our JavaScript code can use to craft an HTTP Ajax call to the edge service running on another node (Example 8-13).

Example 8-13. Html5Client.java

```
package client;

import org.springframework.beans.factory.annotation.Autowired;
import org.springframework.boot.SpringApplication;
import org.springframework.boot.autoconfigure.SpringBootApplication;
import org.springframework.cloud.client.discovery.EnableDiscoveryClient;
import org.springframework.cloud.client.loadbalancer.LoadBalancerClient;
import org.springframework.http.MediaType;
import org.springframework.web.bind.annotation.GetMapping;
import org.springframework.web.bind.annotation.RequestMapping;
import org.springframework.web.bind.annotation.RequestMethod;
import org.springframework.web.bind.annotation.RestController;

import java.util.Collections;
import java.util.Map;
import java.util.Optional;

@RestController
@EnableDiscoveryClient
@SpringBootApplication
public class Html5Client {

  private final LoadBalancerClient loadBalancerClient;

  @Autowired
  Html5Client(LoadBalancerClient loadBalancerClient) {
    this.loadBalancerClient = loadBalancerClient;
  }

  public static void main(String[] args) {
    SpringApplication.run(Html5Client.class, args);
  }

❶
  //@formatter:off
  @GetMapping(value = "/greetings-client-uri",
          produces = MediaType.APPLICATION_JSON_VALUE)
```

```
//@formatter:on
Map<String, String> greetingsClientURI() throws Exception {
  return Optional
    .ofNullable(this.loadBalancerClient.choose("greetings-client"))
    .map(si -> Collections.singletonMap("uri", si.getUri().toString()))
    .orElse(null);
 }
}
```

❶ This endpoint returns a single instance of the downstream `greetings-client` endpoint, whose endpoints we can access thanks to the edge services `Access-Control-*` headers. Here, we're using the `LoadBalancerClient` to return an instance using whatever load balancer strategy we have configured. By default, the client-side load balancer will use Netflix's Ribbon, which in turn will use round-robin load balancing.

The JavaScript code itself is nothing all that exciting—a jQuery application (anybody remember jQuery?)—that uses the resolved URI from the `html5-client` application to call the the edge service (the `greetings-client`), which in turn invokes the `greetings-service`. The application updates the local page's DOM to reflect the response.

 The HTML5 application brings in jQuery using the WebJars project (*http://www.webjars.org*). WebJars lets us manage JavaScript dependencies in our Maven build. In order to get jQuery, we needed only to add two dependencies to our build: `org.webjars : jquery : 2.1.1`, which brings in the library itself, and `org.web jars : webjars-locator`, which Spring Boot and other JVM-based web frameworks can use to map from ambiguous JavaScript imports where the version of the library is purposefully unclear (`<script src="/webjars/jquery/jquery.min.js"></script>`) to concrete versions of the library imported with WebJars on the classpath.

Example 8-14 shows the code.

Example 8-14. The code uses jQuery (It's almost retro-novel?)

```
<!doctype html>
<html lang="en">
<head>
    <meta charset="utf-8"/>
    <meta http-equiv="X-UA-Compatible" content="IE=edge"/>
    <title>Demo</title>
    <meta name="description" content=""/>
    <meta name="viewport" content="width=device-width"/>
```

```
    <base href="/"/>
</head>
<body>

<div id="message"></div>

<script src="/webjars/jquery/jquery.min.js"></script>
<script>

    ❶
    var greetingsClientUrl = location.protocol + "//" + window.location.host
        + "/greetings-client-uri";
    $.ajax({url: greetingsClientUrl}).done(function (data) {
        var nameToGreet = window.prompt("who would you like to greet?");
        var greetingsServiceUrl = data['uri'] + "/lets/greet/" + nameToGreet;
        console.log('greetingsServiceUrl: ' + greetingsServiceUrl);
        ❷
        $.ajax({url: greetingsServiceUrl}).done(function (greeting) {
            $("#message").html(greeting['greeting']);
        });
    });
</script>
</body>
</html>
```

❶ Load from the current host information on where to find the greetings-client.

❷ Make a call to the cross-origin service using the resolved URI.

To see everything working, launch (in this order; otherwise you'll have to wait for everything to connect by the service registry) the following services: service-registry, greetings-service, edge-service (with the cors profile), and html5-client. Open up Eureka (http://localhost:8761) to find the IP under which the html5-client instance is now available. Grab that IP and paste it into the browser, with the port 8083, as seen in Figure 8-2.

 It's important that you use the correct host and port to access the HTML 5 client: otherwise, the CorsFilter won't permit the request, since it checks incoming requests for hosts and ports registered in the service registry. (It's probably not going to work with, or use, localhost, for example.)

Figure 8-2. A CORS request from our HTML5 client

Not bad! A simple servlet `Filter` can do a lot of cool things for us. The Servlet API has no specific knowledge of which proxied downstream service we're calling, though. If we want the possibility to have that awareness, we need to write a Zuul filter.

A Custom Zuul Filter

The `CorsFilter` is a standard `Filter`, and it works for all requests made into the edge service, including all requests made into Zuul (and the Zuul Servlet, which Spring Boot automatically wires up for you). That said, Zuul has a specialized pipeline for filtering requests that are specifically being routed through the Zuul proxy. There are four default types of Zuul filters, though of course you can add custom types if the need should arise:

- *pre* filters are executed before the request is routed
- *routing* filters can handle the actual routing of the request
- *post* filters are executed after the request has been routed
- *error* filters execute if an error occurs in the course of handling the request

Spring Cloud registers several useful Zuul filters out of the box, assuming the relevant auto-configuration conditions are met:

- `AuthenticationHeaderFilter` (**pre**)—a filter that looks for requests that are being proxied and removes the `authorization` header before it's sent downstream.

- `OAuth2TokenRelayFilter` (**pre**)—a filter that propagates an OAuth access token if it's available in the incoming request.

- `ServletDetectionFilter` (**pre**)—detects whether an HTTP servlet request has already been run through the Zuul filter pipeline.

- `Servlet30WrapperFilter` (**pre**)—wraps an incoming HTTP request with a Servlet 3.0 decorator.

- `FormBodyWrapperFilter` (**pre**)—wraps an incoming HTTP request with a decorator containing metadata about the multipart file upload.

- `DebugFilter` (**pre**)—contributes parameters to support debugging if the request contains an Archaius property.

- `SendResponseFilter` (**post**)—commits a response to the output (if the upstream filters have contributed one).

- `SendErrorFilter` (**post**)—if the reply contains an error, this filter forwards it to a configurable endpoint.

- `SendForwardFilter` (**post**)—if the reply contains a forward, this filter sends the requisite forward.

- `SimpleHostRoutingFilter` (**route**)—a filter that takes the incoming request and decides, based on the URL, which node to route the proxied request to.

- `RibbonRoutingFilter` (**route**)—a filter that takes the incoming request and decides, based on the URL, to which node to route the proxied request. It does this using configurable routing and client-side load balancing powered by Netflix Ribbon.

Let's suppose we wanted to add another generic, cross-cutting concern. A simple example might be a rate limiter. A rate helps systems guarantee SLAs by staggering requests to downstream services that exceed a certain rate. The token bucket algorithm (*https://en.wikipedia.org/wiki/Token_bucket*) is based on an analogy of a fixed-capacity bucket into which tokens, normally representing a unit of bytes or a single packet of predetermined size, are added at a fixed rate. An alternative algorithm, the leaky bucket algorithm (*https://en.wikipedia.org/wiki/Leaky_bucket*), is based on an analogy of how a bucket with a leak will overflow if either the average rate at which water is poured in exceeds the rate at which the bucket leaks, or if more water than the capacity of the bucket is poured in all at once.

A simple rate limiter is easy enough to implement using a Zuul filter. This implementation uses the Guava `RateLimiter` class. It is fairly naive, in that it limits requests across *all* proxied services and service instances, not per service instance, and not even for a particular service. We must first configure the Guava `RateLimiter` in Example 8-15.

Example 8-15. The Guava RateLimiter is configured to permit a request only once every 10 seconds; this is a nonsensically low value so as to be illustrative of what's happening

```
package greetings;

import com.google.common.util.concurrent.RateLimiter;
import org.springframework.context.annotation.Bean;
import org.springframework.context.annotation.Configuration;
import org.springframework.context.annotation.Profile;

@Profile("throttled")
@Configuration
class ThrottlingConfiguration {

  @Bean ❶
  RateLimiter rateLimiter() {
    return RateLimiter.create(1.0D / 10.0D);
  }
}
```

❶ Specify how many requests are permitted per second. Here, we specify that .10 requests are permitted per second. Or, put another way, one request is permitted every 10 seconds.

With this in place, we can easily design a `ZuulFilter` that limits incoming requests (Example 8-16).

Example 8-16. A rate-limiting ZuulFilter

```
package greetings;

import com.google.common.util.concurrent.RateLimiter;
import com.netflix.zuul.ZuulFilter;
import com.netflix.zuul.context.RequestContext;
import com.netflix.zuul.exception.ZuulException;
import org.springframework.beans.factory.annotation.Autowired;
import org.springframework.context.annotation.Profile;
import org.springframework.core.Ordered;
import org.springframework.http.HttpStatus;
import org.springframework.http.MediaType;
import org.springframework.stereotype.Component;
import org.springframework.util.ReflectionUtils;

import javax.servlet.http.HttpServletResponse;
```

```java
@Profile("throttled")
@Component
class ThrottlingZuulFilter extends ZuulFilter {

  private final HttpStatus tooManyRequests = HttpStatus.TOO_MANY_REQUESTS;

  private final RateLimiter rateLimiter;

  @Autowired
  public ThrottlingZuulFilter(RateLimiter rateLimiter) {
    this.rateLimiter = rateLimiter;
  }

  ❶
  @Override
  public String filterType() {
    return "pre";
  }

  ❷
  @Override
  public int filterOrder() {
    return Ordered.HIGHEST_PRECEDENCE;
  }

  ❸
  @Override
  public boolean shouldFilter() {
    return true;
  }

  ❹
  @Override
  public Object run() {
    try {
      RequestContext currentContext = RequestContext.getCurrentContext();
      HttpServletResponse response = currentContext.getResponse();

      if (!rateLimiter.tryAcquire()) {

        ❺
        response.setContentType(MediaType.TEXT_PLAIN_VALUE);
        response.setStatus(this.tooManyRequests.value());
        response.getWriter().append(this.tooManyRequests.getReasonPhrase());

        ❻
        currentContext.setSendZuulResponse(false);

        throw new ZuulException(this.tooManyRequests.getReasonPhrase(),
          this.tooManyRequests.value(), this.tooManyRequests.getReasonPhrase());
      }
    }
```

```
  catch (Exception e) {
   ReflectionUtils.rethrowRuntimeException(e);
  }
  return null;
 }
}
```

❶ This particular filter is a pre filter that gets run before a proxied request is made.

❷ The filter should run as early on as possible…

❸ …and it should always run. You might disable the filter based on some attribute of the request or dimension of configuration, though.

❹ The run() method is the centerpeice to a ZuulFilter. In here, you do the work of filtering a given request.

❺ The filter attempts to acquire a permit from the Guava RateLimiter and if it fails, sends back an HTTP status code 429 - Too Many Requests, along with an error message.

❻ Explicitly abort proxying the request. If we fail to do this the request will be proxied automatically.

Run the greetings-client edge service with the profile throttled. If you visit the greetings-client edge service at, let's say, http://localhost:8082/lets/greet/ Eva, you'll get a valid JSON response for every 10 seconds of time; otherwise you'll get a response that says Too Many Requests.

Security on the Edge

Edge services represent the first line of defense against possibly malicious requests from the outside. Edge services are a logical place to handle cross-cutting concerns like security. Security is tedious, and as it needs to be addressed for every service, it can end up being duplicative. Security is a place where the force multipliers of a plat-form (like Cloud Foundry) and the convention-over-configuration approach sup-ported by Spring Boot can really help. As requests come into a system, we'll authenticate them at the edge, and then propagate the authentication context to downstream services.

Authentication simply means that we want to identify the actor making a particular request. Could we get away with using usernames and passwords? Or x509 certifi-cates? If we are simply trying to answer the question, "Who is making this request?" then those and similar alternatives might seem to be enough—*if* done correctly. But getting it right is *hard* (*http://bit.ly/2vnx3DD*). Ideally, you should tune the hash to take a minimum amount of time to validate (perhaps .5 seconds). This means that the minimum amount of time to validate the username and password is .5 seconds (plus all the real work). Passwords make it hard to control who has access to a system, because if one leaks, then all uses of it are rendered invalid. People share passwords across systems, too. Usually, *who is making the request* is not the only question you're trying to answer, even if you are ensuring that passwords are sufficiently random and stored securely (you're probably not).

In today's world, not all clients are created equal. Knowing the client on which the user is making a request is almost as important as knowing who is making the request. We need to be able to reason about both dimensions when standing up services for a diverse world of clients. An API provider may trust some clients more than others, and need to limit access accordingly.

As an example, think about all the places you use Facebook. Facebook offers numerous clients: on the iPad, as a web page, as an Android application, etc. It's very common to find a "Sign in with Facebook" button option on many websites. The button dumps you on Facebook.com where you'll be prompted to log in if you're not already logged in, and then it'll prompt you to approve certain permissions for the requesting website. Once you've confirmed access, Facebook will redirect you back to the original website, which will now have what it needs to access your Facebook profile information and fill out its own profile with your information, effectively signing you in. In this example, you never enter your Facebook password in the third-party web application. The third-party website has only limited permission to act on your behalf, reading certain information and perhaps doing certain things. If ever you decide you want to end your profile with that third-party website you need only log in to Facebook and revoke permissions for that website. Importantly, you don't have to change your password. The password is still valid, and all your other connected clients are still valid. The distinction here is that *your* account—but only as accessed through that third-party website (a client)—is no longer valid.

Compare that with the experience you'd enjoy when using Facebook's official iPhone application. The iOS application was developed by the engineers at Facebook. There is less worry that they're going to abuse your trust and do malicious things on your behalf with your Facebook.com profile information and account, naturally. In this instance, Facebook.app, as it runs on your iOS device, is more than happy to let you enter a username and password on the device. It doesn't need to redirect you to Facebook.com in the browser—nor should it. Facebook.com *already* has your password, and they're more than happy to secure the iPhone application's login screen.

Two different Facebook.com clients—one more trusted than the other—and one profile. Each client had different permissions. The official Facebook.com iPhone application basically has full control over your account, where the third-party website might only be able to read your email and full name.

OAuth

Enter OAuth. OAuth is a standard that has three incarnations: 1.0, 1.0.a, and 2.0. OAuth 2.0 is the most relevant and recommended edition, so we'll focus on OAuth 2.0. *OAuth* (which is short for "open authorization") is a standard for token-based authorization on the internet. Tokens reduce the window of time when usernames and passwords are exposed. Tokens decouple clients from passwords, ensuring that an errant client never has the ability to lock you out of your own account. Tokens may represent a client acting on behalf of a particular user, or they may represent a token without a particular user context.

OAuth is an *authorization* protocol ("what permissions does the user have?"), rather than an *authentication* protocol ("who is this user?"), so you still have to handle the authentication somewhere and then transfer control to OAuth. OAuth provides to clients a "secure delegated access" to services on behalf of the owner of the data being accessed on the service. Once authenticated, clients use tokens to authorize requests. Tokens are client-specific.

Some terminology when thinking about OAuth:

- **Client**: An application that's making protected requests. Often, but not always, the client is making the requests on behalf of an end user (the resource owner). This could be an iPhone or Android application, an HTML5 browser-client… even a watch! Clients don't have to have a user context, though. A client might represent a back-office analytics job, for example, that needs limited permissions. In the Facebook.com example, this might be your native iOS application or your desktop web browser.

- **Resource owner**: Usually this refers to the end user ("Juergen," "Michelle," "Dave," "Margarette," etc.) who can grant a client permission to access their information. In the Facebook.com example, this might be you or me.

- **Resource server**: The server hosting the protected resource, capable of accepting and responding to protected requests containing access tokens. This refers to the secured API that the client is trying to talk to. In the Facebook.com example, this would refer to the Facebook APIs supporting access to all things—your profile, your Friend graph, etc.

- **Authorization server**: The server issuing access tokens to the client after successfully authenticating the resource owner and obtaining authorization. In Facebook.com, this is the service that you're redirected to in order to authenticate and that provides tokens. For all intents and purposes, for Facebook.com, the authorization server and the resource server are the same thing, but they don't *need* to be.

The first step in OAuth is to obtain authorization, basically to get past the point of authentication. There are four well-known grant types, or flows, to achieve this.

Service-Side Applications

In the "Sign in with Facebook" flow described above, the client is redirected from the third-party website to the Facebook.com login screen. In your browser, you'll see the comforting Secure padlock icon in the address bar, indicating you're on a certified location running over HTTPS. You can take comfort knowing that you *are* on Face-book.com. Then you enter your username and password and submit the form, and you'll be prompted to confer certain authorities to the requesting client. If you click Allow, Facebook.com will redirect to the requesting client with an authorization code. The client, on the server side, will call the Facebook.com authorization server and present the authorization code, which it'll exchange for an access token. The requesting client now has an access token, and it will store that access token in a database and use it to make calls to the Facebook.com resource server on your behalf.

In this scenario, the access token never leaks to client-side JavaScript code running in the browser. The only thing that's visible to the client (or to the user driving the client) is the authorization code. This indirection protects against man-in-the-middle attacks where somebody could otherwise intercept an access token and use that to make calls on your behalf.

This whole flow is called the *authorization code grant*. It is useful when you want to prevent the access token from leaking to someplace where it could be readily intercepted.

HTML5 and JavaScript Single-Page Applications

Single-page applications (SPAs) run entirely in the browser after loading the source code from a web page. An SPA can't keep any secrets, of course, because its source code is visible by clicking View Source. In this flow a user clicks a Sign In button and is prompted to approve access, just as before. If the user clicks Allow, the service redirects the user back to the single-page application site with an access token in the URL fragment (the part after the # part of a URL, e.g., `http://some-third-party-service.com/an_oauth_callback#token=12345..`). JavaScript applications are able to read this part of the URL, and changing the fragment in a URL doesn't force the browser to make a new request. This is called the *implicit grant*. In this case, the flow is optimized *specifically* to leak the access token to the client code because there is no service-side component.

Applications Without Users

In all of the examples we've looked at thus far, we've talked about a client acting on behalf of a user to access that user's protected resources. It is possible for a client, without a particular user, to request an access token using only the client credentials. This might be useful for applications that need to access protected information, but don't have a particular user context like batch applications or analytics or anything that's noninteractive. Such a client would be authenticated, and could have its permissions limited. This is called the *client credentials grant*.

Trusted Clients

OAuth 2 supports a password grant that would be useful if you were developing the client for a service that trusted the client. Imagine you were developing the Facebook.app experience for Facebook.com: in this case, the user experience of having to redirect to Facebook.com inside of Facebook.app and then *Approve* that Facebook.app has permissions to read and manipulate your Facebook.com data would seem a little redundant (Facebook.com *already* has your username and password!). In this instance, the trusted client—developed by engineers who work at Facebook itself —would simply transmit the user's username and password. There's no real risk of Facebook.app suddenly obtaining your username and password as, of course, they already had it! Indeed, if you can't trust Facebook.app to not act maliciously with your Facebook.com data, then you may want to reconsider using Facebook altogether! In this flow, the user transmits a username and password directly to the authorization server in exchange for an access token. This is called the *resource owner password credentials* grant.

It is beyond the scope of this book to fully explore OAuth. We recommend the excellent (and concise!) book on the topic, *Getting Started with OAuth 2.0* by Ryan Boyd (O'Reilly).

We'll set up an OAuth authorization server and protect our clients with OAuth, but first, let's review some Spring Security basics.

Spring Security

Remember that we said that OAuth is an authentication delegating protocol—it needs something to answer the question, "Is this person who he or she claims to be?" We will use Spring Security to answer that question. Spring Security has integrations with virtually every conceivable type of identity provider out there, and if it doesn't, it's trivial to write your own integration.

Authentication is all about *who* is making the request. Is it dsyer or jhoeller? In Spring Security, implementations of the `AuthenticationManager` interface handle authentication, broadly (Example 8-17).

Example 8-17. org.springframework.security.authentication.Authentication Manager

```
public interface AuthenticationManager {

        Authentication authenticate(Authentication authentication)
                        throws AuthenticationException;
}
```

AuthenticationManager instances return an Authentication instance with the authenticated property set to true if the requesting authentication is valid. They throw an AuthenticationException if the request is invalid, or null if they can't decide. At this level, there is no assumption about the nature of the identity provider against which authentication requests are authenticated. There are no assumptions about the nature of the requests themselves—they could be HTTP requests, local method invocations, RPC service invocations, asynchronous messages, etc. There are no assumptions about the nature of the authentication attempt itself; the request may contain tokens, usernames and passwords, certificates, etc. The AuthenticationMan ager is purposely imprecise.

ProviderManager is a common implementation of AuthenticationManager that in turn delegates to a chain of AuthenticationProvider implementation instances. The AuthenticationProvider instances work almost identically to the Authentication Manager, except that they can *also* confirm that they can handle a given Class<?> of Authentication. This makes it easier to selectively handle authentication requests efficiently. The ProviderManager arrangement means that a single Authentication Manager can handle different types of authentications through delegation.

ProviderManager objects may themselves have a parent AuthenticationManager implementation which acts as a fallback; if no AuthenticationProvider implementa- tion is able to authenticate the request, it falls to the parent AuthenticationManager to handle the authentication request. It's possible to have a global AuthenticationMan ager and then nested ProviderManager instances that are logically specific to a group of protected resources. There are ProviderManager instances that interface with serv- ices like LDAP, or a backend javax.sql.DataSource-based database, for authentica- tion queries. The latter case—talking to a data store to retrieve information about a user given a username—is common enough that there is a specific type of Authenti cationProvider, DaoAuthenticationProvider, that in turn delegates to an imple- mentation of the UserDetailsService interface (Example 8-18).

Example 8-18. org.springframework.security.core.userdetails.UserDetails Service

```
public interface UserDetailsService {

  UserDetails loadUserByUsername(String username)
    throws UsernameNotFoundException; ❶
}
```

❶ Return a `UserDetails` implementation or throw an exception. You should never return `null`.

The contract is simple: return an implementation of a `UserDetails` object given a username. The `UserDetails` is supposed to encapsulate answers to questions Spring Security will need to authenticate a user by username and password. What is the user's username? What is the user's password? Is the account for this user still active and not locked or expired? What authorities does the user have? An *authority*, particularly, is represented by the `GrantedAuthority` type, that in turn holds a string. The meaning of the string changes from one system to another. It might correspond to your system's notion of authorities, scopes, permissions, roles, or something else entirely. However you use a `GrantedAuthority`, it's meant to support *authorization*, not authentication.

Authorization is all about ascertaining the permissions a requester has—what a user is allowed and not allowed to do. The core interface here is `AccessDecisionManager`. An `AccessDecisionManager` makes an access control decision for a given combination of an authentication object, a collection of configuration attributes (`ConfigAttribute` instances), and for the passed-in `object` context. The `ConfigAttribute` collection contains generic parameters of the request that might even be Spring Expression Language statements. The `object` parameter is a context against which the access decision should be made. It could be *anything* that the user may want to access: a method invocation, a protected HTTP endpoint, a `Message<T>`, etc. The configuration attributes and the context, taken together, provide everything required for an `AccessDecisionManager` to perform authorization (Example 8-19).

Example 8-19. org.springframework.security.access.AccessDecisionManager

```
public interface AccessDecisionManager {

  void decide(Authentication authentication, Object context,
    Collection<ConfigAttribute> configAttributes)
      throws AccessDeniedException, InsufficientAuthenticationException; ❶

  boolean supports(ConfigAttribute attribute);
```

```
  boolean supports(Class<?> clazz);
}
```

❶   An exception is thrown if the request cannot be authorized.

The AccessDecisionManager, in turn, delegates to DecisionVoter instances, very much like the AuthenticationManager delegates to AuthenticationProvider instances (Example 8-20).

Example 8-20. org.springframework.security.access.AccessDecisionVoter

```
public interface AccessDecisionVoter<S> {

  int ACCESS_GRANTED = 1;
  int ACCESS_ABSTAIN = 0;
  int ACCESS_DENIED = -1;

  boolean supports(ConfigAttribute attribute);

  boolean supports(Class<?> clazz);

  int vote(Authentication authentication,
    S object,
    Collection<ConfigAttribute> attributes);
}
```

All right! You may want to reread the last few paragraphs dissecting the hierarchies of Spring Security a few times. If you don't internalize all of it, you'll still be fine! What you really need to take away from all of this is that Spring Security handles both *authentication* and *authorization* with two discrete and logical type hierarchies. In both hierarchies there is a root interface that has an implementation that in turn delegates to a chain of instances that look similar to the root interface. This means that both support the chain of responsibility pattern.

All of this is very low-level. You won't need to know, let alone install and configure, most of these types in a Spring Boot-based application today. Even lower-level Spring Security applications have defaults for most of these types, even without Spring Boot. Regardless, it's useful to have as a backdrop when you learn about web application security. In the web tier, Spring Security is installed as a single javax.servlet.Filter (from the perspective of the web container) that in turn delegates to other *virtual* chains of Filter instances (of which Spring Security alone is aware). Each protected web endpoint can have its own chain of filters. The order of these virtual filters matters—the more specific rules should come before the more generic, fall-through filters. The chain that responds to requests for /api/** ought to come *before* the chain for /**, for example. Later, when we secure parts of our edge service, we'll look at restricting access to parts of the web application and specifying how to handle unauthenticated requests as well as sign-in and sign-out for requests that access protected resources.

With all of this as the backdrop, let's revisit our OAuth implementation. We need to answer the question, *who is making the request?* We can configure and plug in any `AuthenticationManager` we want to handle the chore, but for our purposes let's suppose we have a database of usernames and passwords. We can plug in an implementation of `UserDetailsService` that uses JPA (or whatever other technology you want) to authenticate usernames and passwords. We'll create a JPA entity, `Account`, that we want to consult whenever an authentication requests arrives (Example 8-21).

 As in many other chapters, we'll use the compile-time annotation processor Project Lombok (*https://projectlombok.org*) to simplify synthesis of acessors, mutators, constructors and so on.

Example 8-21. Account

```
package auth.accounts;

import lombok.AllArgsConstructor;
import lombok.Data;
import lombok.NoArgsConstructor;

import javax.persistence.Entity;
import javax.persistence.GeneratedValue;
import javax.persistence.Id;

@Data
@AllArgsConstructor
@NoArgsConstructor
@Entity
public class Account {

  @Id
  @GeneratedValue
  private Long id;

  private String username, password; ❶

  private boolean active; ❷

  public Account(String username, String password, boolean active) {
    this.username = username;
    this.password = password;
    this.active = active;
  }
```

}

❶ The username and password are expected.

❷ When we implement our `UserDetailsService`, we'll need to answer four varia-
tions of the question, *is the account active?*

We'll need a Spring Data repository to make short work of interacting with `Account`
records in the database (Example 8-22).

Example 8-22. AccountRepository

```
package auth.accounts;

import org.springframework.data.jpa.repository.JpaRepository;

import java.util.Optional;

public interface AccountRepository extends JpaRepository<Account, Long> {
❶
 Optional<Account> findByUsername(String username);
}
```

❶ When we implement the `UserDetailsService` instance, we'll need to be able to
respond to a query given a `username`, so let the Spring Data repository figure it
out for us.

Finally, we'll contribute a `UserDetailsService` implementation. Spring Security will
automatically plug it in for us if it detects an implementation in the Spring `Applica
tionContext`. This implementation maps the `Optional<Account>` from our reposi-
tory to a concrete implementation of `UserDetails` (called a `User` in Spring Security),
and assigns some static `GrantedAuthority` instances.

 In a more sophisticated example, you might dynamically determine
the `GrantedAuthority` instances based on whatever criteria you
specify, or if nothing else, by reading the criteria from the database.

*Example 8-23. AccountConfiguration.java—in this class we contribute a
UserDetailsService instance that knows about our Account types*

```
package auth.accounts;
```

```
import org.springframework.context.annotation.Bean;
import org.springframework.context.annotation.Configuration;
import org.springframework.security.core.authority.AuthorityUtils;
import org.springframework.security.core.userdetails.User;
import org.springframework.security.core.userdetails.UserDetailsService;
import org.springframework.security.core.userdetails.UsernameNotFoundException;

@Configuration
public class AccountConfiguration {

  @Bean
  UserDetailsService userDetailsService(AccountRepository accountRepository) {
  ❶
    return username -> accountRepository
     .findByUsername(username)
     .map(
      account -> {
       boolean active = account.isActive();
       return new User(account.getUsername(), account.getPassword(), active,
        active, active, active, AuthorityUtils.createAuthorityList("ROLE_ADMIN",
          "ROLE_USER"));
      })
     .orElseThrow(
      () -> new UsernameNotFoundException(String.format("username %s not found!",
       username)));
  }
}
```

❶ The contract for a `UserDetailsService` implementation is simple: given a `String username`, return a `UserDetails` implementation *or* throw a `Username NotFoundException`. In no case, however, should you return `null`.

With all of this done, we've just configured all we need to be able to work with Spring Security. Our goal is to then use this configuration to validate tokens from incoming users—but this configuration is most of what we'd need to also authenticate using HTTP BASIC, or from a sign-in form in an HTML page somewhere. This is foundational Spring Security, and you would've written similar code even 10 or more years ago, before the era of the cloud natives.

Spring Cloud Security

Spring Cloud Security makes it easy to integrate security into our microservices. It can talk to any OAuth-compliant authorization server and declaratively protect resource servers. We'll lock down our own REST APIs, but first let's stand up an OAuth authorization server using Spring Security OAuth.

A Spring Security OAuth Authorization Server

We'll set up a new microservice, one that's going to handle authorization duties in a module called auth-service. This module has org.springframework.cloud : spring-cloud-starter-config, org.springframework.cloud : spring-cloud-starter-eureka, org.springframework.cloud : spring-cloud-starter-oauth2, org.springframework.boot : spring-boot-starter-data-jpa, org.springframework.boot : spring-boot-starter-web, and org.springframework.boot : spring-boot-starter-actuator on the classpath. This authorization server works with the service registry (our Netflix Eureka instance) and so participates in service registration and discovery using the @EnableDiscoveryClient annotation.

> Technologies like the Spring Cloud Security Authorization Server play an important in an architecture. In this section, we'll look at creating a simple stripped-down version of our own, but it's important to understand that this isn't business-differentiating functionality. Ideally, this should be somebody else's competency. Third-party OAuth-capable identity providers like Okta or Cloud Foundry can provide the User Account Authentication (UAA) Server, which is *based on* the Spring Cloud Security Authorization Server we're looking at here. Security is hard; reuse expertise wherever possible!

OAuth needs to know how to authenticate the users, which we handled by integrating a UserDetailsService, and it needs to know about the clients that may connect and what authorities those clients have. These clients must be described up front. Just as we modeled users with an Account entity, we'll use a Client entity and adapt it to the clients expected by Spring Security OAuth (Example 8-24).

Example 8-24. Client.java

```
package auth.clients;

import lombok.AllArgsConstructor;
import lombok.Data;
import lombok.NoArgsConstructor;
import org.springframework.util.StringUtils;

import javax.persistence.Entity;
import javax.persistence.GeneratedValue;
import javax.persistence.Id;

@Data
@AllArgsConstructor
@NoArgsConstructor
@Entity
```

```
public class Client {

  @Id
  @GeneratedValue
  private Long id;

  private String clientId;

  private String secret;

  private String scopes = StringUtils
    .arrayToCommaDelimitedString(new String[] { "openid" });

  private String authorizedGrantTypes = StringUtils
    .arrayToCommaDelimitedString(new String[] { "authorization_code",
      "refresh_token", "password" });

  private String authorities = StringUtils
    .arrayToCommaDelimitedString(new String[] { "ROLE_USER", "ROLE_ADMIN" });

  private String autoApproveScopes = StringUtils
    .arrayToCommaDelimitedString(new String[] { ".*" });

  public Client(String clientId, String clientSecret) {
    this.clientId = clientId;
    this.secret = clientSecret;
  }
}
```

Later, we'll need to be able to find a client by its `clientId`, so we'll need a Spring Data
JPA repository for that, along with a custom finder method (Example 8-25).

Example 8-25. ClientRepository.java

```
package auth.clients;

import org.springframework.data.jpa.repository.JpaRepository;

import java.util.Optional;

public interface ClientRepository extends JpaRepository<Client, Long> {

  Optional<Client> findByClientId(String clientId); ❶
}
```

❶ Find a client by its `clientId`.

Many popular services offer the ability to register ad hoc clients that can then use
their APIs. Facebook and Twitter, for example, let you register third-party clients on
their developer portals. You could easily create your own using the Spring Data

repository we've just established. Indeed, if you annotated your Spring Data repository to use Spring Data REST, you could even allow programmatic, REST-based registration of clients. At any rate, it wouldn't be hard to expose a self-service form to allow teams in your organization to register their own clients and expected grant types. For our purposes, it'll suffice to hardcode the client details.

Spring Security OAuth requires a bit of configuration as well. It needs to know how it will authenticate users, so we must point it to a valid `AuthenticationManager` instance (the one established automatically when we installed our custom `UserDetailsService` will do just fine) and we must point it to the `ClientDetailsService`, both of which we do in the `AuthorizationServerConfiguration`.

We must adapt our `Client` instances to the `ClientDetails` interface, as we did the `Account` entities to the `UserDetailsService` interface. In Example 8-26, we'll use a specific type of `ClientDetails`, `BaseClientDetails`, to do the job.

Example 8-26. ClientConfiguration.java

```java
package auth.clients;

import org.springframework.beans.factory.annotation.Autowired;
import org.springframework.cloud.client.discovery.DiscoveryClient;
import org.springframework.cloud.client.discovery.event.HeartbeatEvent;
import org.springframework.cloud.client.loadbalancer.LoadBalancerClient;
import org.springframework.context.annotation.Bean;
import org.springframework.context.annotation.Configuration;
import org.springframework.context.event.EventListener;
import org.springframework.security.oauth2.provider.ClientDetailsService;
import org.springframework.security.oauth2.provider.ClientRegistrationException;
import org.springframework.security.oauth2.provider.client.BaseClientDetails;

import java.util.Collections;
import java.util.List;
import java.util.Optional;
import java.util.Set;
import java.util.concurrent.ConcurrentSkipListSet;
import java.util.stream.Collectors;

@Configuration
public class ClientConfiguration {

    private final LoadBalancerClient loadBalancerClient;

    @Autowired
    public ClientConfiguration(LoadBalancerClient client) {
        this.loadBalancerClient = client;
    }

    @Bean
```

```
ClientDetailsService clientDetailsService(ClientRepository clientRepository) {
 return clientId -> clientRepository
  .findByClientId(clientId)
  .map(
   client -> {

    BaseClientDetails details = new BaseClientDetails(client.getClientId(),
     null, client.getScopes(), client.getAuthorizedGrantTypes(), client
      .getAuthorities());
    details.setClientSecret(client.getSecret());

    ❶
    // details.setAutoApproveScopes
    //     (Arrays.asList(client.getAutoApproveScopes().split(",")));

    ❷
    String greetingsClientRedirectUri = Optional
     .ofNullable(this.loadBalancerClient.choose("greetings-client"))
     .map(si -> "http://" + si.getHost() + ':' + si.getPort() + '/')
     .orElseThrow(
      () -> new ClientRegistrationException(
       "couldn't find and bind a greetings-client IP"));

    details.setRegisteredRedirectUri(Collections
     .singleton(greetingsClientRedirectUri));
    return details;
   })
   .orElseThrow(
    () -> new ClientRegistrationException(String.format(
     "no client %s registered", clientId)));
 }
}
```

❶ Think about the Facebook.com use case. When a client requests a token, they're prompted to both log in *and* explicitly confer all requested scopes. We could instead configure it so that all requested scopes are conferred just by authenticating, if we set `autoApproveScopes` to the names of whatever scopes are being requested.

❷ The client should specify a URI to which the authorization service should redirect after the user has approved the requested scopes. We can automatically determine, and load balance, that URI using the service registry and the `LoadBalancerClient`, in this particular case, since the registry and all clients are using the same service registry. In this example, we've hardcoded the URI based upon what we know this client will need, though there's no reason it couldn't also be kept on the client JPA record itself.

The `AuthorizationServerConfiguration` extends `AuthorizationServerConfigurerAdapter`, which in turn implements `AuthorizationServerConfigurer`. `Authoriza` tionServerConfigurer is a callback interface that Spring Security OAuth will call at the right phase in the initialization life cycle, allowing us an opportunity to configure various parts of the service's behavior. Override the configure(ClientDetailsServiceConfigurer clients) method to configure the clients and override the configure(AuthorizationServerEndpointsConfigurer endpoints) method to connect Spring Security OAuth with the AuthenticationManager configured earlier. This is where Spring Security OAuth, which handles authorization, delegates authentication to Spring Security (Example 8-27).

Example 8-27. AuthorizationServerConfiguration.java

```
package auth;

import org.springframework.beans.factory.annotation.Autowired;
import org.springframework.context.annotation.Configuration;
import org.springframework.security.authentication.AuthenticationManager;

//@formatter:off
import org.springframework.security.oauth2
        .config.annotation.configurers.ClientDetailsServiceConfigurer;
import org.springframework.security.oauth2
        .config.annotation.web.configuration.AuthorizationServerConfigurerAdapter;
import org.springframework.security.oauth2
        .config.annotation.web.configuration.EnableAuthorizationServer;
import org.springframework.security.oauth2
        .config.annotation.web.configurers.AuthorizationServerEndpointsConfigurer;
import org.springframework.security.oauth2
        .provider.ClientDetailsService;
//@formatter:on

@Configuration
@EnableAuthorizationServer
class AuthorizationServerConfiguration extends
 AuthorizationServerConfigurerAdapter {

 private final AuthenticationManager authenticationManager;

 private final ClientDetailsService clientDetailsService;

 @Autowired
 public AuthorizationServerConfiguration(
  AuthenticationManager authenticationManager,
  ClientDetailsService clientDetailsService) {
  this.authenticationManager = authenticationManager;
  this.clientDetailsService = clientDetailsService;
 }

 @Override
 public void configure(ClientDetailsServiceConfigurer clients) throws Exception {
```

```
❶
  clients.withClientDetails(this.clientDetailsService);
}

@Override
public void configure(AuthorizationServerEndpointsConfigurer endpoints)
  throws Exception {
  ❷
  endpoints.authenticationManager(this.authenticationManager);
}
}
```

❶ Configure the OAuth clients.

❷ Connect Spring Security OAuth with Spring Security by way of its `Authentica tionManager` instance.

Securing the Greetings Resource Server

We've come this far, but where does the rubber hit the road? Suppose we have a REST API that we want to protect: we want to reject requests that don't have a valid access token in them. We can protect a resource server by annotating it with `@EnableResour ceServer`. So configured, Spring Security OAuth will reject requests that don't have a valid access token. If a request *does* have a valid access token, it'll need some way to turn that access token into a Spring Security `Authentication`. An access token is meaningless in and of itself. It needs to be translated, to be related to an authenticated user in the system. We can point the protected resource server to a user info endpoint where Spring Security OAuth will exchange the token for details about the user: on the `greetings-service` resource server, specify `security.oauth2.resource.userIn foUri=http://auth-service/uaa/user`.

This URL isn't using a proper hostname; instead it uses a service ID to be resolved in the service registry. We've extracted a service-registry-aware and, optionally, OAuth-aware `RestTemplate` into a shared auto-configuration class in a separate module, called `security-autoconfiguration`. The library contains just an auto-configuration class, `TokenRelayAutoConfiguration`, which configures a client-side load-balancer-aware `RestTemplate` for us. Example 8-28 shows the configuration.

Example 8-28. TokenRelayAutoConfiguration.java

```
package relay;

import feign.RequestInterceptor;

//@formatter:on
import org.springframework.boot.autoconfigure
```

```
        .condition.ConditionalOnBean;
import org.springframework.boot.autoconfigure
        .condition.ConditionalOnClass;
import org.springframework.boot.autoconfigure
        .condition.ConditionalOnWebApplication;
import org.springframework.boot.autoconfigure
        .security.oauth2.resource.UserInfoRestTemplateFactory;
//@formatter:off

import org.springframework.cloud.client.loadbalancer.LoadBalanced;
import org.springframework.context.annotation.Bean;
import org.springframework.context.annotation.Configuration;
import org.springframework.context.annotation.Lazy;
import org.springframework.context.annotation.Profile;
import org.springframework.http.HttpHeaders;

//@formatter:on
import org.springframework.security
        .oauth2.client.OAuth2ClientContext;
import org.springframework.security
        .oauth2.client.OAuth2RestTemplate;
import org.springframework.security
        .oauth2.client.filter.OAuth2ClientContextFilter;
import org.springframework.security
        .oauth2.config.annotation.web.configuration.EnableResourceServer;
import org.springframework.web.client.RestTemplate;
//@formatter:off

@Configuration
@ConditionalOnWebApplication
@ConditionalOnClass(EnableResourceServer.class)
public class TokenRelayAutoConfiguration {

 public static final String SECURE_PROFILE = "secure";

 @Configuration
 @Profile("!" + SECURE_PROFILE)
 public static class RestTemplateConfiguration {

  ❶
  @Bean
  @LoadBalanced
  RestTemplate simpleRestTemplate() {
   return new RestTemplate();
  }
 }

 @Configuration
 @Profile(SECURE_PROFILE)
 public static class SecureRestTemplateConfiguration {

  ❷
```

```
  @Bean
  @Lazy
  @LoadBalanced
  OAuth2RestTemplate anOAuth2RestTemplate( UserInfoRestTemplateFactory factory) {
    return factory.getUserInfoRestTemplate();
  }
}

@Configuration
@Profile(SECURE_PROFILE)
@ConditionalOnClass(RequestInterceptor.class)
@ConditionalOnBean(OAuth2ClientContextFilter.class)
public static class FeignAutoConfiguration {

  ❸
  @Bean
  RequestInterceptor requestInterceptor(OAuth2ClientContext clientContext ) {
  return requestTemplate -> requestTemplate.header(HttpHeaders.AUTHORIZATION,
    clientContext.getAccessToken().getTokenType() + ' '
      + clientContext.getAccessToken().getValue());
  }
 }
}
```

❶ Install a plain load-balanced RestTemplate in the non-secure profile.

❷ Install a load-balanced RestTemplate that will also propagate an OAuth token (if it's present) in the secure profile.

❸ Propagate OAuth access tokens across Feign invocations. We'll look at this later.

Finally, we must define that user information endpoint, /uaa/user. When a request is made against one of our protected REST services, a filter configured by Spring Cloud Security sees the access token in the incoming request and then translates that token into information about the client and user behind the request. The token is opaque— it doesn't contain any information itself, and it must be exchanged for actionable information. The body of this information, of course, tends to change from one authorization server to another. On Facebook it might consist of information about the Facebook user and his or her friend graph. On GitHub it might contain information about the GitHub user and his or her commits. Many of these endpoints expose at least a JSON attribute called name.

If we configure our authorization server to also be a resource server by adding @Ena bleResourceServer, Spring Security OAuth will automatically provide a java.security.Principal for any Spring MVC handler method handling a request containing an access token. Spring Security OAuth will also convert a java.security.Principal into a JSON structure that our resource server can use.

Let's change the authorization server and create an endpoint to exchange tokens for a `Principal` (Example 8-29).

Example 8-29. PrincipalRestController.java

```java
package auth;

import org.springframework.web.bind.annotation.RequestMapping;
import org.springframework.web.bind.annotation.RestController;

import java.security.Principal;

@RestController
class PrincipalRestController {

    ❶
    @RequestMapping("/user")
    Principal principal(Principal p) {
      return p;
    }

}
```

❶ When a request bearing a token comes in, return the hydrated `Principal` to the requester.

Our authorization server will start with a context-path of /uaa and it will start on port 9191 (Example 8-30).

Example 8-30. bootstrap.properties

```properties
spring.application.name=auth-service
❶
server.context-path=/uaa
security.sessions=if_required
logging.level.org.springframework.security=DEBUG
spring.jpa.hibernate.ddl-auto=create
spring.jpa.generate-ddl=true
```

❶ `spring.application.name` identifies the application to the service registry.

With all of this in place, we should be able to generate an access token. Our test shows us how to craft the request to the authorization server to generate a valid access token using the password grant. In the password grant, we exchange the username and password for an access token. This is the simplest way to prove that our OAuth authorization server is working.

Example 8-31 shows how to test that everything is working with the `curl` command.

Example 8-31. Obtaining an access token using the password grant type using curl

```
curl \
  -X POST \
  -H"authorization: Basic aHRtbDU6cGFzc3dvcmQ=" \
  -F"password=spring" \
  -F"client_secret=password" \
  -F"client_id=html5" \
  -F"username=jlong" \
  -F"grant_type=password" \
  -F"scope=openid" \
  http://localhost:9191/uaa/oauth/token
```

When we run that `curl` invocation and pipe the results to the JSON pretty printer (`json_pp`), we get the following response (Example 8-32).

Example 8-32. The JSON response returned from the OAuth2 authorization server

```
{
   "scope" : "openid",
   "expires_in" : 40222,
   "token_type" : "bearer",
   "refresh_token" : "12164df0-12a6-43d9-b631-8418aec28612",
   "access_token" : "6815d559-784c-496a-b50e-b8c91eb17ffd"
}
```

The `access_token` is the critical ingredient. With it, we can attempt to call a secured resource server. Let's lock down our resource server and communicate with it using our newly minted access token.

If we're able to generate a valid access token given a valid client ID, client secret, username, and password, then we have everything we need to build a JavaScript client that accesses data from the edge service, which in turn talks to the `greetings-service`. The first step is to confirm that we have locked down the edge service (the `greetings-service`). Add the configuration shown in Example 8-33 to the edge service codebase. It will only work if the edge service is started with the `secure` profile active.

Example 8-33. OAuthResourceConfiguration.java

```
package greetings;

import org.springframework.context.annotation.Configuration;
import org.springframework.context.annotation.Profile;
//@formatter:off
import org.springframework.security.oauth2.config.annotation
        .web.configuration.EnableOAuth2Client;
import org.springframework.security.oauth2.config.annotation
```

```
          .web.configuration.EnableResourceServer;
//@formatter:on

@Configuration
❶
@Profile("secure")
❷
@EnableResourceServer
❸
@EnableOAuth2Client
class OAuthResourceConfiguration {
}
```

❶ The configuration is active only if the service is launched with the secure profile.

❷ @EnableResourceServer will reject requests it sees that aren't authenticated.

❸ @EnableOAuth2Client also perpetuates whatever token is seen in the request, allowing the node to act as a client to another secured node.

You can inject the authenticated java.security.Principal into your Spring MVC controller methods. Here is our earlier greetings endpoint rewritten to customize the results of the output using the authenticated principal (Example 8-34). It only exists when the greetings-service is run under the secure Spring profile. Restart the greetings-service if it's not already running, adding in that profile.

Example 8-34. SecureGreetingsRestController.java

```
package greetings;

import org.springframework.context.annotation.Profile;
import org.springframework.web.bind.annotation.PathVariable;
import org.springframework.web.bind.annotation.RequestMapping;
import org.springframework.web.bind.annotation.RequestMethod;
import org.springframework.web.bind.annotation.RestController;

import java.security.Principal;
import java.util.Collections;
import java.util.Map;

@Profile("secure")
@RestController
@RequestMapping(method = RequestMethod.GET, value = "/greet/{name}")
public class SecureGreetingsRestController {

 @RequestMapping
 Map<String, String> hi(@PathVariable String name, Principal p) {
  return Collections.singletonMap("greeting",
   "Hello, " + name + " from " + p.getName() + "!");
```

```
    }
}
```

You can take the access token that we've just generated and submit a request to the greetings-service (Example 8-35).

Example 8-35. curl the secured result

```
curl -H"authorization: bearer ..."
{"greeting":"Hello, Tammie from jlong!"}
```

After you've made the request and seen that it works, try making the request again, but this time tamper with the token value—you might remove a letter or change some characters—and confirm it rejects the request. After that, try making the same request again without specifying the authorization header (remove the -H option and argument) to confirm it rejects the request.

So far we've proven we can lock down access to a particular REST API and permit requests with a valid access token. Where does the access token originate, though? You're not expecting visitors to the website to whip out curl to obtain an access token, right? We need to provide a flow for a user to establish a token.

Build an OAuth-Secured Single-Page Application

Let's return to our edge service. We've thus far stood up an authorization server and secured our greetings-service REST API, rejecting requests that didn't have a valid access token in them using the @EnableResourceServer annotation. In order to demonstrate the security in action, we made a request to the authorization server to get an access token in exchange for a username and password, using the password grant. Our users, of course, aren't going to send HTTP requests using curl on the command line to an authorization server to log in to our website. We need to connect the sign-in flow and client-side UI to Spring Security OAuth. When a user visits a web page with client-side JavaScript, they'll be redirected to the auth-service and prompted to sign in and optionally approve of certain requests. Once confirmed, the edge service will have an access token that it can propagate in all requests to all downstream services which, if they're secured like the greetings-service is, can use the token to identify who is making the request and on what client the request is being made. This is called *single sign-on* in Spring Cloud Security.

Let's look at a simple client-side application, written using Angular.js, that displays some state from a protected, secured REST API. We'll authenticate using an implicit grant that then redirects to the authorization server to prompt for a username and password and to approve of the requested scopes, then we'll return to the client UI. In this example we'll see how Spring Cloud Security makes this whole process seamless.

We've already got an edge service that has some endpoints we want to be secured, but we're also going to add an index.html and some JavaScript to the src/main/resour ces/static directory. Those resources need to be visible to all. We need to protect only the REST APIs under /api/* (those we established earlier that are driven by the RestTemplate or Netflix Feign). We'll provide a ResourceServerConfigurerAdapter to require a valid access token by adding @EnableResourceServer and then configur-ing the application (Example 8-36).

Example 8-36. SecureResourceConfiguration.java

```
package greetings;

import org.springframework.context.annotation.Configuration;
import org.springframework.context.annotation.Profile;
//@formatter:off
import org.springframework.security.config.annotation.web.builders.HttpSecurity;
import org.springframework.security.oauth2.config.annotation.web
        .configuration.EnableResourceServer;
import org.springframework.security.oauth2.config.annotation.web
        .configuration.ResourceServerConfigurerAdapter;
//@formatter:on

❶
@Profile("secure")
@Configuration
@EnableResourceServer
class SecureResourceConfiguration extends ResourceServerConfigurerAdapter {

  @Override
  public void configure(HttpSecurity http) throws Exception {
    http.antMatcher("/api/**").authorizeRequests() ❷
      .anyRequest().authenticated();
  }
}
```

❶   This configuration will only work so long as the **secure** profile is active.

❷   Only requests to /api/* should be secure. Everything else is insecure.

We need to configure the single sign-in and sign-out functionality for the client. Our application will expose a /login endpoint, some JavaScript assets, and a home page, /index.html, which will be loaded if someone goes to /. In the edge service, we're not merely rejecting requests that don't have a valid access token; we're going to initiate the acquisition of an access token by redirecting to a sign-in screen. We can install an authentication filter and an authentication entry point to set up the local endpoints (like /login) that will trigger the authentication dance between the edge service and the authentication server with the @EnableOAuth2Sso annotation. Let's look at the SSO configuration, and specify what endpoints should trigger the SSO flow using a `WebSecurityConfigurerAdapter` (Example 8-37).

Example 8-37. SsoConfiguration.java

```java
package greetings;

import org.springframework.context.annotation.Configuration;
import org.springframework.context.annotation.Profile;

//@formatter:off
import org.springframework.boot.autoconfigure
        .security.oauth2.client.EnableOAuth2Sso;
import org.springframework.security.config.annotation
        .web.builders.HttpSecurity;
import org.springframework.security.config.annotation
        .web.configuration.WebSecurityConfigurerAdapter;
//@formatter:on

import org.springframework.security.web.csrf.CookieCsrfTokenRepository;

❶
@Profile("sso")
@Configuration
❷
@EnableOAuth2Sso
class SsoConfiguration extends WebSecurityConfigurerAdapter {

  @Override
  protected void configure(HttpSecurity http) throws Exception {
   // @formatter:off
        http.antMatcher("/**").authorizeRequests() ❸
                .antMatchers( "/", "/app.js", "/login**", "/webjars/**
                ").permitAll().anyRequest()
                .authenticated().and().logout().logoutSuccessUrl("/").permitAll()
                    .and().csrf()
                .csrfTokenRepository(CookieCsrfTokenRepository.withHttpOnlyFalse());
     // @formatter:on
  }
}
```

❶ This configuration will only work if the `sso` profile is active.

❷ `@EnableOAuth2Sso` registers all the necessary machinery to trigger the SSO flow.

❸ We want to protect all resources *except* the following particular resources.

Our edge service is an OAuth client. It will obtain a user context by forcing the user to log in, but it needs to identify itself as a particular client. We can specify what client it is, in particular, in the configuration (Example 8-38).

Example 8-38. bootstrap-sso.properties

```
security.oauth2.client.client-id=html5    ❶
security.oauth2.client.client-secret=password


security.oauth2.client.access-token-uri=http://localhost:9191/uaa/oauth/token  ❷
security.oauth2.client.user-authorization-uri=\
  http://localhost:9191/uaa/oauth/authorize

security.basic.enabled=false
```

❶ Identify the client ID and secret that we will use to obtain a user context.

❷ Point our edge service to the OAuth authorization server.

That's all we need to do to get the SSO flow working on the server side, on the edge service. Let's write an Angular.js client-side controller that attempts to read secure information and prompts us to authenticate if we're not already authenticated. Example 8-39 shows the HTML template for the Angular.js application and its (only) controller, home.

Example 8-39. index.html

```html
<!doctype html>
<html lang="en">
<head>
    <meta charset="utf-8"/>
    <meta http-equiv="X-UA-Compatible" content="IE=edge"/>
    <title>Edge Service</title>
    <meta name="description" content=""/>
    <meta name="viewport" content="width=device-width"/>
    <base href="/"/>
    <script type="text/javascript"
            src="/webjars/jquery/jquery.min.js"></script>
    <script type="text/javascript"
            src="/webjars/bootstrap/js/bootstrap.min.js"></script>
    <script type="text/javascript"
            src="/webjars/angularjs/angular.min.js"></script>
</head>

<body ng-app="app" ng-controller="home as home">

<div class="container" ng-show="!home.authenticated">
```

```
    <a href="/login">Login </a>
</div>

<div class="container" ng-show="home.authenticated">

    ❶
    Logged in as:
    <b><span ng-bind="home.user"></span></b> <br/>

    Token:
    <b><span ng-bind="home.token"></span> </b><br/>

    Greeting from Zuul Route: <b>
    <span ng-bind="home.greetingFromZuulRoute"></span></b> <br/>

    Greeting from Edge Service (Feign):
    <b><span ng-bind="home.greetingFromEdgeService"></span></b><br/>
</div>

❷
<script type="text/javascript" src="app.js"></script>
</body>
</html>
```

❶ We'll display authentication information, and we'll display protected data by contacting a secured REST endpoint on the same node.

❷ The JavaScript logic lives in another file, app.js.

The template, in turn, lays out a panel that prints information acquired and bound in the JavaScript logic. The crux of the JavaScript application is that it will call a secured endpoint on the local node, /user. If the request has an access token, it'll succeed; and if it lacks one, it'll initialize the authentication flow.

The /user endpoint just dumps information about the authenticated user, identical to what we did earlier on the auth-service with the /uaa/user endpoint. The edge-service is annotated with @EnableResourceServer, so the /user endpoint returns that principal for consumption in the JavaScript application. Example 8-40 shows the code for the /user endpoint in the edge service (though you would be forgiven for thinking it's the code from the auth-service!).

Example 8-40. PrincipalRestController

```
package greetings;

import org.springframework.context.annotation.Profile;
import org.springframework.web.bind.annotation.RequestMapping;
import org.springframework.web.bind.annotation.RestController;
```

```
import java.security.Principal;

@Profile("secure")
@RestController
class PrincipalRestController {

  @RequestMapping("/user")
  public Principal user(Principal principal) {
   return principal;
  }
}
```

Let's look at our Angular.js (JavaScript) application logic (Example 8-41).

Example 8-41. app.js

```
var app = angular.module("app", []);
```

❶
```
app.factory('oauth', function () {
    return {details: null, name: null, token: null};
});

app.run(['$http', '$rootScope', 'oauth', function ($http, $rootScope, oauth) {

    $http.get("/user").success(function (data) {

        oauth.details = data.userAuthentication.details;
        oauth.name = oauth.details.name;
        oauth.token = data.details.tokenValue;
```

❷
```
        $http.defaults.headers.common['Authorization'] = 'bearer ' + oauth.token;
```

❸
```
        $rootScope.$broadcast('auth-event', oauth.token);
    });
}]);

app.controller("home", function ($http, $rootScope, oauth) {

    var self = this;

    self.authenticated = false;
```

❹
```
    $rootScope.$on('auth-event', function (evt, ctx) {
        self.user = oauth.details.name;
        self.token = oauth.token;
        self.authenticated = true;
```

```
        var name = window.prompt('who would you like to greet?');

    ❺
    $http.get('/greetings-service/greet/' + name)
        .success(function (greetingData) {
            self.greetingFromZuulRoute = greetingData.greeting;
        })
        .error(function (e) {
            console.log('oops!' + JSON.stringify(e));
        });

    ❻
    $http.get('/lets/greet/' + name)
        .success(function (greetingData) {
            self.greetingFromEdgeService = greetingData.greeting;
        })
        .error(function (e) {
            console.log('oops!' + JSON.stringify(e));
        });
    });
});
```

❶ For this application to work, we'll need a singleton object in which to store authentication details.

❷ The code in `app.run` is invoked as the application is loaded, making it an ideal place to do any sort of initialization. Call the secured `/user` endpoint to read authentication information. An unauthenticated request will result in a redirect to the `auth-service`, where we'll be required to sign in and accept the grant for permission. The `authorization-service` will redirect back to this page, and this call will succeed allowing us to set up a default value for the `Authorization` header for all Ajax calls made through Angular.js's `$http` client.

❸ The publication of an event to any and all components that are interested in the news that our authentication information has been obtained.

❹ In this Angular.js application, we have one controller, `home`, that binds four fields to the markup in our template, presented in `index.html`.

❺ In order to be sure everythng's working as expected, the Angular.js client invokes endpoints in our edge service through the Zuul proxy and through...

❻ ...the Feign-powered API.

If you run the `service-registry`, `auth-service`, `greetings-service` (with `secure` profile), and `edge-service` (with the `secure` and `sso` profiles), you should be able to visit the edge service and be redirected to the `auth-service`. Let's look at what that sequence looks like:

1. Visit the edge service on 8082 and immediately be redirected to the auth-service (Figure 8-3).

Figure 8-3. Visit the edge service

2. Here you may have to approve the requested scopes (Figure 8-4).

Figure 8-4. Approve requested scopes

3. Then you will be redirected back to the application, where you'll be able to try again (Figure 8-5). It'll work, as the edge-service will have a valid access token, so it'll prompt you to provide a name to send to the edge-service endpoints (which in turn will call the greetings-service).

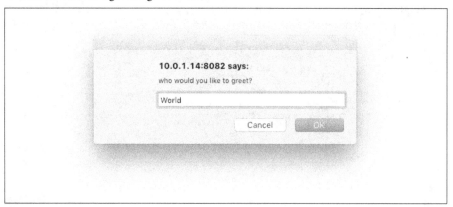

Figure 8-5. The Zuul routes

4. And of course, then it will print out the results, culminating a request that originated on the edge-service, went to the auth-service, then went to the edge-service, which in turn called the greetings-service (Figure 8-6).

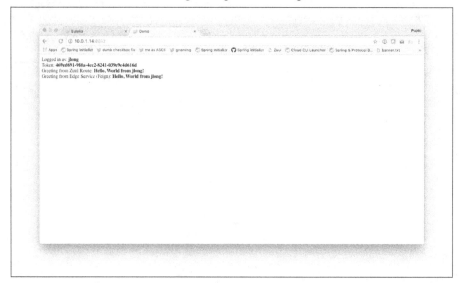

Figure 8-6. Results

Spring Cloud Security's SSO support simultaneously protects resources that live at the `edge-service` and establishes the machinery needed to configure an OAuthRestTem plate that can make secure calls to downstream services (in this case, to the greetings-service). The edge-service is both a protected resource and the client to a protected resource. The edge-service, like the greetings-service, has on the classpath the edge-security-autoconfiguration module we described earlier.

Summary

In this chapter we've looked at a lot of the orthogonal concerns required to build effective edge services. While much of what we discussed in this chapter could be accorded its own chapter and dedicated discussion, we've limited the discussion to the role these concerns play in integrating rich clients (HTML5 clients, iOS clients, Android clients, etc.) into a microservices-based system.

We looked at how to effectively and quickly build clients to simplify some of the work of communication with downstream services using the RestTemplate as well as Netflix's Feign. We looked at how to integrate client-side load balancing.

We developed an OAuth auth-service that delegates authentication to a JPA-backed AuthenticationProvider. We could, alternatively, delegate authentication to another OAuth-compatible authentication service altogether. Your authorization server could act as a façade for one or more other, downstream, authorization services like Facebook or GitHub. In this chapter's code, there's an example, social-auth-service, that does just that. It's a bit more involved, but it should make for an interesting example if you want to pursue that route.

Edge services are very similar to a lot of other techniques and patterns, at least conceptually: SOFEA (service-oriented front end applications), BFFs (backends-for-frontends), and API gateways all have overlapping responsibilities. Whatever you call it, these services should be thin on business logic, and serve the goal of integrating more clients with more services without forsaking forward velocity.

## PART III

Data Integration

## CHAPTER 9

Managing Data

This chapter will address some of the concerns of managing data when building a scalable cloud native application. We will review some familiar methods for modeling the data of a domain. We'll take a look at how Spring Data projects expose repositories for managing data. We will also look at a few examples of microservices that manage exclusive data access to a data source using the Spring Data projects.

Modeling Data

Well-constructed data models help us effectively communicate the desires of a business's domain in our software applications. Domain models, like the one in Figure 9-1, can be constructed to express the most important aspects of a business's domain. One of the most successful techniques for domain modeling was first presented by Eric Evans in his seminal book, *Domain-Driven Design: Tackling Complexity in the Heart of Software* (Addison-Wesley).

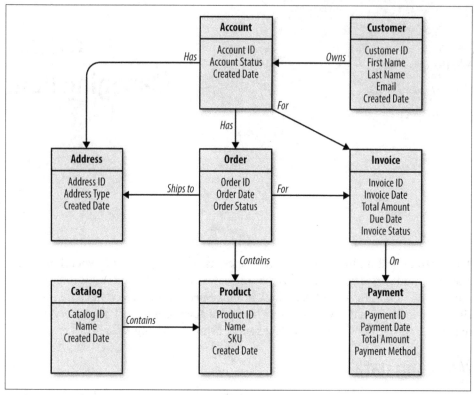

Figure 9-1. A domain model expressing the relationships between domain classes

Evans popularized the concepts of domain-driven design by advancing the idea that both the domain experts in the business and the software engineers in the IT organization should be able to effectively communicate using unambiguous terms that describe objects and modules in a software application.

The problem that domain-driven design purported to solve was *complexity*. Evans subtitled his book *"Tackling Complexity in the Heart of Software"*; what he meant by this was that technologists should focus on making software easier to create and maintain by untangling the complexity in the underlying model of the business. This complexity exists in the tangle of business processes and functions that companies create to serve customers; domain models map out this complexity and provide technologists a language to write better software for the business.

Consider the following example. If an engineer names a *Customer* as a *User* inside a software module, the engineers are then forced to use ambiguous terms that may mean something entirely different to the business's domain experts. Here is a user story for customer account management:

> As a customer, I want to be able to create users that are able to manage a set of accounts.

This user story was written by a domain expert. The story describes an account management use case and clearly distinguishes between a *customer* and a *user*, but does not disambiguate whether or not a *user* can also be a *customer*.

Without a domain model that distinguishes this difference, an engineer may decide that the simplest solution in code would be to have a single domain class named User. Later on in a separate release the business may then clarify that a Customer is not the same thing as a User. This clarification would later turn out to be a costly design decision with stark consequences for new feature development, causing the software engineers to miss their original release date.

Most data stores focus on being the best kind of data store that they can be, while minimally investing in usability. It is our opinion that anything that makes it simpler for the business and technologists to talk about the same things, concretely, is worth pursuing. Your data store is not a place to store bytes; it is a repository for the entities and relationships that describe your business domain. Our goal is always to maximize the returns on our investments (of both time and money) in a particular technology while minimizing code required to work with a particular data store that little advances our business objectives. This is where Spring, and Spring Data in particular, strives to help.

Relational Database Management Systems (RDBMS)

The relational database model has been the staple of transactional data storage solutions for many decades. As technology continues to evolve to cloud native architectures, the market is starting to demand other types of data models that have the same transactional guarantees as RDBMS. SQL databases have become a sort of jack-of-all-trades, but master of none. A SQL database today doesn't offer the strongest transactional requirements, compared to all persistence technologies. It is, ironically, not the best way to talk about relationships in a graph. A SQL database supports binary data, but not particularly well or efficiently. Many databases have geospatial support, but not necessarily the most compelling such support. SQL databases can handle a large number of read transactions, but often only after the schema designer has denormalized the model and made concessions regarding consistency to achieve higher availability. In short, while the RDBMS isn't going anywhere, there may be specialized alternatives worth investigating. If you are using an RDBMS, JPA, which sits on top of JPA implementations like Hibernate, can be a good fit if you're mapping records to and from an RDBMS schema. JPA (and object-relational mappers—ORMs—in general) let developers focus more on the domain model and less on the nuances of the RDBMS itself. You sacrifice (some) control for ease of evolution.

NoSQL

NoSQL databases provide a variety of data models with specialized traits that are optimized to address the needs of particular use cases. This is advantageous in microservices, since we can decompose the bounded contexts of a domain model to use a specialized trait of a NoSQL database. Access to the data is done in terms of the microservice API, so clients are unconcerned about what technology is used.

Polyglot Persistence is a term popularized by Martin Fowler to describe an architecture that uses multiple types of database models. Applications that standardize on a single relational database can slowly be decomposed to use microservices that manage their own NoSQL database, depending on the use case of that facet of the application. This is especially useful for greenfield—brand new—projects where the business is demanding more complex solutions, delivered rapidly. Since NoSQL databases provide trait-specific data models that are optimized for a use case, there is less need to bend a relational database model to solve a certain problem.

Spring Data

Spring Data (*http://projects.spring.io/spring-data*) is an open source umbrella project that provides a familiar abstraction for interacting with a data store while preserving the special traits of its database model. There are more than a dozen (official) Spring Data projects that cover a range of popular databases, including RDBMS and NoSQL data models. There are Spring Data modules supporting JDBC, JPA, MongoDB, Neo4J, Redis, Elasticsearch, Solr, Gemfire, Cassandra, and Couchbase, among others.

 JPA, and Spring Data JPA by extension, covers all of the popular RDBMS vendors, including Oracle, MySQL, PostgreSQL, SQL Server, H2, HSQL, Derby, and many more.

Structure of a Spring Data Application

When getting started with Spring Data, it's helpful to understand the patterns that are used to design a data access layer. Let's start by understanding what basic ingredients are used to interact with a data store.

Domain Class

The first ingredient is an entity class that represents an object in your domain model. A *domain class* is a basic class that functions as a model for your domain data. These domain classes consist of a set of private fields, and expose their contents using public getters and setters, depending on the design of your domain model (Example 9-1).

Example 9-1. A basic domain class representing a User model

```
public class User { ❶

    private Long id;
    private String firstName; ❷
    private String lastName;
    private String email;
```

❶ The name of the class represents a concept—a noun or an entity—in a domain model.

❷ Private fields are mapped to data object properties in a native data store

> Domain classes represent entities that map to data objects (such as tables) in an application's data store.

Repositories

The primary method for accessing data in a Spring Data application is a *repository*. Eric Evans introduced the idea of a repository in his book, *Domain-Driven Design*. The Spring framework has long supported a stereotype annotation, `@Repository`, which—besides marking a class as a `@Component`—signals to Spring that the bean may throw persistence-technology-specific exceptions, and that those exceptions should be normalized to the hierarchy that Spring provides. In this way, consumers need only worry about one type of exception for things like constraint violations.

Spring Data takes the support even further. Spring Data can provide implementations of user-provided interface definitions whose data management methods' signatures are defined in compliance with Spring Data conventions. You can define your own interface definition methods, or instead extend any of a handful of convenient provided interface definitions. The most basic but still useful implementation of these interfaces is `CrudRepository`.

> *CRUD* is an acronym for *CREATE, READ, UPDATE,* and *DELETE.* These four verbs describe the basic management capabilities for data in any kind of persistent storage technology. Not coincidentally, the HTTP protocol uses slightly different verbs to manage resources as network transactions, which are *POST, GET, PATCH,* and *DELETE.*

The CrudRepository supports common CRUD operations given two pieces of information: the domain class's type and its ID type. We could use the CrudRepository interface if we wanted to create a repository for a User domain class (Example 9-2).

Example 9-2. A Spring Data repository for a User domain class

```
public interface UserRepository extends CrudRepository<User, Long> {
}
```

We won't need to implement the UserRepository interface. Spring Data will provide a bean that implements the contract, and which we can inject into any other Spring beans as needed.

Organizing Java Packages for Domain Data

The style in which we organize our packages is a more important consideration when building microservices. We recommend that you organize your classes and packages in the way you feel most comfortable with, but we will propose a pattern we've found suitable for building microservices using Spring Data and Spring Boot.

First we need to determine what the bounded contexts are in our domain model. Let's consider the domain model in Figure 9-2 for this exercise.

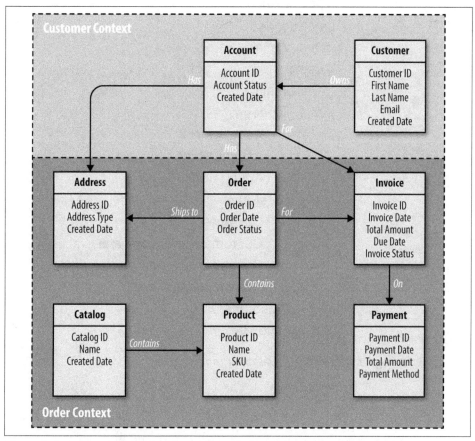

Figure 9-2. A domain model with two bounded contexts

The diagram represents a domain model that has a clear boundary between the Cus
tomer context and the Order context. Let's assume we would like to create two microservices to cover each of these bounded contexts. We will need to organize our
packages so that later we can easily migrate domain classes and repositories for a
domain concept. To best prepare ourselves for this refactoring exercise, we can group
domain classes and repositories that manage a single domain class into a single package. In Figures 9-3 and 9-4, we look at how code is structured in this domain.

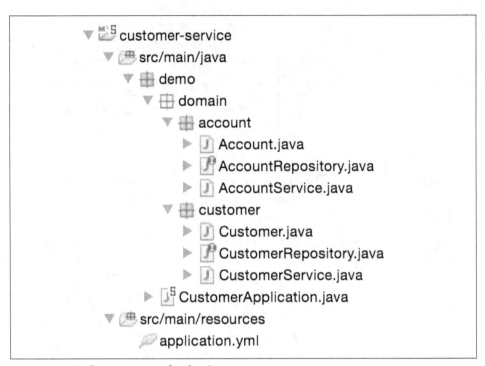

Figure 9-3. Package structure for the Customer context

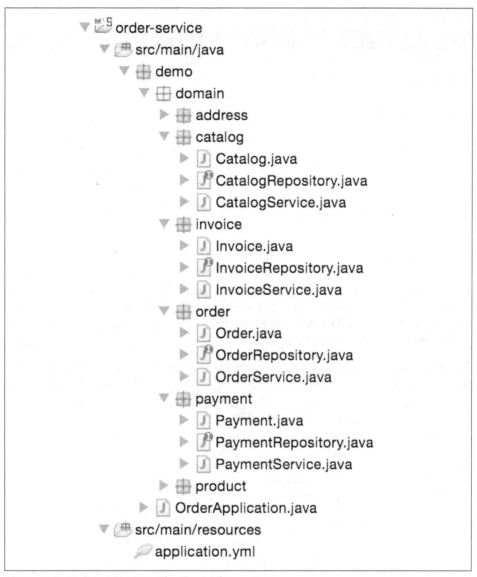

Figure 9-4. Package structure for the Order context

Supported repositories

Spring Data projects support multiple kinds of repositories that extend the Reposi
tory interface. Table 9-1 shows just a few.

Table 9-1. Common Spring Data Repositories

Repository Type	Spring Data Project	Purpose
Repository	Spring Data Commons	Provides the core abstraction for Spring Data repositories
CrudRepository	Spring Data Commons	Extends Repository and adds utility for basic CRUD operations
PagingAndSortingRepository	Spring Data Commons	Extends CrudRepository and adds utility for paging and sorting records
JpaRepository	Spring Data JPA	Extends PagingAndSortingRepository and adds utility for JPA and RDBMS database models
MongoRepository	Spring Data MongoDB	Extends PagingAndSortingRepository and adds utility for managing MongoDB documents
CouchbaseRepository	Spring Data Couchbase	Extends CrudRepository and adds utility for managing Couchbase documents

Each repository interface that ships with Spring Data provides an abstraction for a specific utility that may be needed for your Spring Data application. The table above describes some of the many repository interfaces in the Spring Data ecosystem of projects. Both the CrudRepository and PagingAndSortingRepository interfaces are members of the Spring Data Commons library, providing abstractions that are used by the vendor-specific Spring Data projects.

The MongoRepository interface is the primary repository abstraction used in the Spring Data MongoDB project, specifically. This repository extends the PagingAndSortingRepository interface, providing basic data management capabilities to interact with paged database records (Figure 9-5).

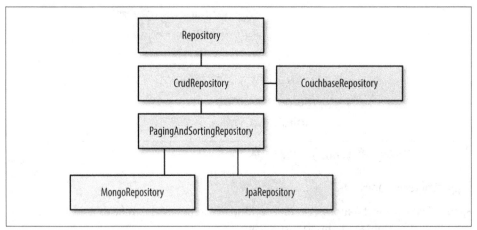

Figure 9-5. The three base repositories in Spring Data Commons provide basic data access to vendor-specific data stores

Getting Started with RDBMS Data Access on JDBC

Spring Boot uses auto-configuration to bootstrap dependencies of your application using a set of default settings. We'll need to configure at least a SQL DataSource, JDBC, and JPA. Spring Boot will configure a connection to a local data store if it finds one of a handful of well-known DataSource drivers on the classpath. In our example, we'll use MySQL; add mysql : mysql-connector-java to your classpath. It'll configure JPA if we add the spring-boot-starter-data-jpa starter to the classpath, as well. The JPA starter automatically takes the auto-configured javax.sql.DataSource pointing to MySQL and uses it as the data source for our JPA configuration.

You can customize the DataSource through some convenient JDBC and JPA properties. Ideally, sensitive information for things like data sources would live external to the application code itself. For more on configuration, see our discussion of configuration in Chapter 3. It's not unreasonable to keep less sensitive, development-time-only defaults in the configuration in the codebase itself, under a development-specific profile. Example 9-3 shows an example.

Example 9-3. Sample application.yml

```
spring:
  profiles:
    active: development
---
spring:
  profiles: development
  jpa:
    database: MYSQL
  datasource: ❶
    url: jdbc:mysql://localhost/test
    username: dbuser
    password: dbpass
```

❶ The spring.datasource property block is where you configure RDBMS-specific connection details.

 By default, Spring Boot auto-configures a connection pool for our JDBC DataSource. The connection pool is based on Apache Tomcat DBCP, by default, but you can configure Commons DBCP or Hikari CP by adding the right library to the classpath.

Spring's JDBC Support

The JdbcTemplate is one of the classic data access mechanisms in the Spring Framework. The JdbcTemplate provides management functions over SQL-based relational databases that support the JDBC specification. This section is going to walk through how to use JdbcTemplate.

 The JdbcTemplate may well be the most pervasive and well-known implementation of the template design pattern, owing to its visibility since the early days of Spring. The Spring Data project includes numerous other template implementations supporting other data stores.

Now we can execute SQL queries to the MySQL database that we've configured as a data source using application.yml for the development profile. Let's create a User table and interact with those records using the JdbcTemplate (Example 9-4).

Example 9-4. Work with our data source using raw SQL and the JdbcTemplate

```
package demo;

import org.slf4j.Logger;
import org.slf4j.LoggerFactory;
import org.springframework.beans.factory.annotation.Autowired;
import org.springframework.boot.CommandLineRunner;
import org.springframework.jdbc.core.JdbcTemplate;
import org.springframework.jdbc.core.RowMapper;
import org.springframework.stereotype.Component;

import java.util.List;
import java.util.stream.Collectors;
import java.util.stream.Stream;

@Component
class JdbcCommandLineRunner implements CommandLineRunner {

  private final Logger log = LoggerFactory.getLogger(getClass());

  private final JdbcTemplate jdbcTemplate;

  @Autowired
  JdbcCommandLineRunner(JdbcTemplate jdbcTemplate) {
    this.jdbcTemplate = jdbcTemplate;
  }

  @Override
  public void run(String... strings) throws Exception {
    ❶
```

```
jdbcTemplate.execute("DROP TABLE user IF EXISTS");
jdbcTemplate
 .execute("CREATE TABLE user( id serial, first_name " +
    " VARCHAR(255), last_name VARCHAR(255), email VARCHAR(255))");

❷
List<Object[]> userRecords = Stream
 .of("Michael Hunger michael.hunger@jexp.de",
   "Bridget Kromhout bridget@outlook.com", "Kenny Bastani kbastani@yahoo.com",
   "Josh Long jlong@hotmail.com").map(name -> name.split(" "))
 .collect(Collectors.toList());

jdbcTemplate
 .batchUpdate(
   "INSERT INTO user(first_name, last_name, email) VALUES (?,?,?)",
   userRecords);

❸
RowMapper<User> userRowMapper = (rs, rowNum) -> new User(rs.getLong("id"),
 rs.getString("first_name"), rs.getString("last_name"), rs.getString("email"));

List<User> users = jdbcTemplate.query(
 "SELECT id, first_name, last_name, email FROM user WHERE first_name = ?",
 userRowMapper, "Michael");

users.forEach(user -> log.info(user.toString()));
 }
}
```

❶ Create the schema.

❷ Conjure up a few sample records and write them to the database using the convenient batchUpdate functionality in the JdbcTemplate.

❸ Visit every record by *mapping* them to objects and then logging the results of
   those objects.

This code is hopefully concise enough to grasp in one go. If you have ever used the
straight JDBC API then you know that a majority of the code has to do with creating
DataSources, Connections, and Statements; cursing through result sets; managing
transactions; dealing with exceptions that'll likely never arise; and rolling back if anything should go wrong. The JdbcTemplate does away with all that and lets us focus
on the essence of the problem at hand. When we run a query, it automatically creates
a statement, runs the query, visits each record, and gives our provided RowMapper<T>
implementation a callback to transform the result.

Run the example and you'll see the result, *Michael Hunger*, reflected on the console
(Example 9-5).

Example 9-5. Interact with the data source using raw SQL and the JdbcTemplate

```
User(id=1, firstName=Michael, lastName=Hunger, email=michael.hunger@jexp.de)
```

The example was necessarily trivial, and designed to highlight one of the core concepts in Spring, a template object. We'll see this sort of support throughout Spring Data. To keep things simple, we ran SQL statements to create the schema and table in the Java code. There is a cleaner alternative, however. By convention, Spring will evaluate two files for us on application startup: `src/main/resources/schema.sql` and `src/main/resources/data.sql`. Put any schema DDL (data definition language), such as the statements to create our user and table, in `schema.sql`. We could have put our sample records for *Bridget*, *Michael*, etc., into the `data.sql` file. Then, our code would need only the last few lines to do with the querying and mapping of records from the data source.

Spring Data Examples

Earlier we explored some of the basic concepts of Spring Data: domain classes and repositories. Now we'll dive deeper into example projects that use different technologies. We will cover example data services for the following Spring Data projects.

- Spring Data JPA (MySQL)
- Spring Data MongoDB
- Spring Data Neo4j
- Spring Data Redis

Keep in mind that we will also be using Project Lombok (*https://projectlombok.org/*), the compile-time annotation processor, to reduce the amount of boilerplate code in our codebase. `@Data` tells Lombok to generate accessors and mutators, a `toString` method, and an `equals/hashCode` method. `@NoArgsConstructor` tells Lombok to generate a constructor with no arguments. `@AllArgsConstructor` tells Lombok to generate a constructor that takes every field in the class. We're free to generate our own constructors, or override any of the accessors/mutators, even in the presence of these annotations.

The example domain we will use for these sets of data examples will be an online storefront. We will use a domain model that describes an enterprise resource planning (ERP) application. Each one of our services will extend itself to a particular bounded context of the domain.

The online storefront application we will use for our example projects will be for the fictitious company *Monolithic Ltd.*, which is a clothing brand that is looking to move its application development for its online store to the cloud.

Monolithic Ltd. has been having trouble enabling development teams to deploy new features in its existing online store. Inspired by its move to more modern methods of software development, the startup company has decided to rebrand its offering to *Cloud Native Clothing*.

Let's take a look at the domain model that *Cloud Native Clothing* will be using to construct its new online store (Figure 9-6).

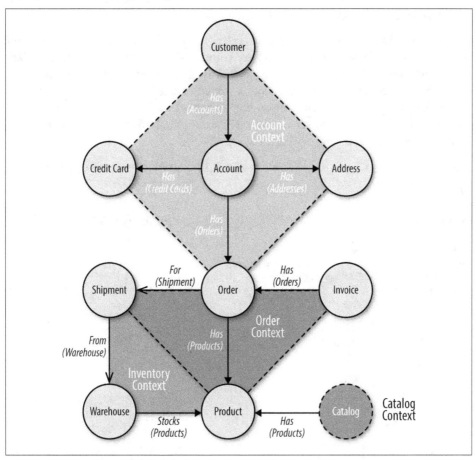

Figure 9-6. Cloud Native Clothing's Domain Model

We can see from the *Cloud Native Clothing* domain model that we have several bounded contexts. Each bounded context in the diagram is labeled as a context. According to the principles set forth in DDD, bounded contexts are a way to modularize a part of a business's domain into separate unified models. Each bounded context can have a set of unrelated concepts while making explicit the connection between shared concepts. We've decided to create a model that can articulate the concepts of a business domain while also articulating how the application is well-constructed, using Spring Data repositories.

Each domain class in the diagram is represented as a circle. Each circle also represents a Spring Data repository. Repositories, in the context of the diagram, are required for any domain class that will need to expose query capabilities within a bounded context; hence when using this type of model we'll always consider a circle to be both a *domain class* and a *repository*. The interrelationships between repositories indicate some level of connectedness in each domain class.

Concepts that are connected by a *directed relationship* indicate an *explicit relationship* between domain classes. Concepts that are connected by dotted lines indicate inferred connectedness through a *repository join*. A dotted line would indicate that there should be a repository query that acts as a joined bridge between domain concepts. The bridge should only be valid within the context of a shared concept of a domain class that exists between two repositories. For example, *Account* bridges the connection between *Order* and *Address* (Figure 9-7).

In SQL this concept is simply referred to as a JOIN query between tables, as shown in Example 9-6.

Example 9-6. Lookup orders for an address by joining on the account table

```
SELECT o.* FROM orders o
INNER JOIN account ac ON o.accountId = ac.Id
INNER JOIN address ad ON ad.accountId = ac.Id
WHERE ad.id = 0
```

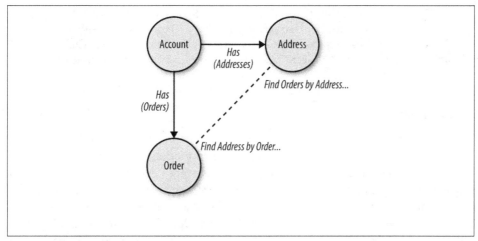

Figure 9-7. Inferred relationships can be looked up through a shared domain class

We will use these bounded contexts to create three separate data services that use a specific Spring Data project (Table 9-2).

Table 9-2. Microservices for our Cloud Native Clothing application

Service	Datasource	Spring Data Project
Account Service	MySQL	Spring Data JPA
Order Service	MongoDB	Spring Data MongoDB
Inventory Service	Neo4j	Spring Data Neo4j

Spring Data JPA

The Spring Data JPA project offers data management support for RDBMS and SQL. It's worth noting that the Spring Data JPA project is the only Spring Data project that provides repository abstractions for RDBMS, but there is a community-supported, third-party project called Spring Data JBDC (*https://github.com/nurkiewicz/spring-data-jdbc-repository*) which does a pretty good job supporting JDBC directly.

JPA stands for `Java Persistence API`, which was first described and introduced as a part of JSR 220 of the JCP (Java Community Process). JPA provides the abstraction and implementations for vendor-specific ORM technologies, such as Hibernate and DataNucleus. This is a powerful facet of the Spring Data project that allows you to use virtually any RDBMS technology that provides a driver that supports the JPA specification.

You don't have to use JPA to support SQL ORM in a Spring Boot application. There are very capable Spring Boot integrations for the third-party projects MyBatis and JOOQ, among others. Check them out! We cover JPA because it's very common, not because it's the sole option.

Account Service

We will use Spring Data JPA for our Account Service. The Account Service covers the account context of *Cloud Native Clothing's* domain model. Spring Data JPA is somewhat of a special project in the Spring Data ecosystem. *Spring Data JPA* provides a single library that plays nicely with multiple (JDBC-capable) data sources, where the other Spring Data projects work with one kind of data source. One knock-on benefit of this is that we can use an embedded data source for testing and switch to a more full-featured database elsewhere. We'll take advantage of Spring's *profiles* to achieve a clean separation.

In this section we're going to walk through the main concerns of setting up a Spring Data JPA application for the `Account Service` of *Cloud Native Clothing*.

Using profiles for different data sources

We've added three dependencies to our Maven build to enable our JPA domain:

- `org.springframework.boot : spring-boot-starter-data-jpa`
- `com.h2database : h2`
- `mysql : mysql-connector-java`

Now that we have the skeleton for our Spring Data JPA project with MySQL and H2 database drivers on the classpath, we need to configure our application to use the two databases in the correct context. The MySQL database runs externally from our application; we will connect to it remotely while running the application. We only want to use the embedded H2 database when running our integration tests. Spring provides a way to configure your application to run with a separate set of configurations depending on what the active profile is at runtime. In the `application.yml` file, you can create a `development` profile and a `test` profile (Example 9-7).

Example 9-7. Configure your application for development and test

```
spring:
  profiles:
    active: development  ❶
---
spring:
  profiles: development  ❷
```

```
  jpa:
    show_sql: false
    database: MYSQL
    generate-ddl: true
  datasource:
    url: jdbc:mysql://192.168.99.100:3306/dev
    username: root
    password: dbpass
---
spring:
  profiles: test ❸
  jpa:
    show_sql: false
    database: H2
  datasource:
    url: jdbc:h2:mem:testdb;DB_CLOSE_ON_EXIT=FALSE
```

❶   This is the active profile by default when running the application.

❷   This is the configuration for the development profile.

❸   This is the configuration for the test profile.

Now that we have two separate profiles defined for development and test configurations, we need to configure our integration tests to use the test profile. Since we've set the active profile in the application properties to default to development, our integration tests will try to use the development profile, and we don't want that. To solve this we need to override the active profile when in the context of our integration tests only.

With this setup, we need only specify @ActiveProfiles in our Spring integration tests, pointing to the test profile. When we run our integration tests for the Account Service, we will use the H2 embedded in-memory database. By using an embedded database we can run tests in any build environment and not worry about having to connect to an external dependency.

Describing the Account Service's domain with JPA

We'll create JPA entities for our Account Service's domain classes. A JPA class is an annotated domain class that will be mapped to a table in our relational database (either MySQL or H2 in this case).

There are four bounded contexts in the domain model for our *Cloud Native Clothing*. In the *Account Context* we can see that there are five repositories: *Account, Address, Order, CreditCard,* and *Customer* (Figure 9-8).

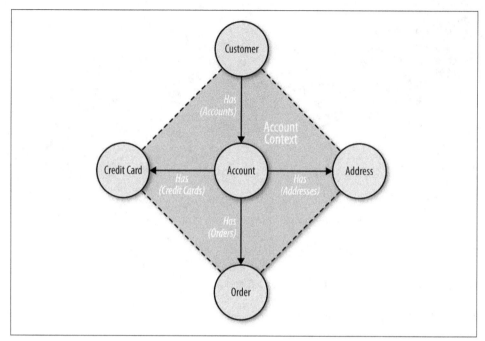

Figure 9-8. Account Context for the Account Service

The next step to create our *Account Service* is to construct our domain classes. Each Spring Data project has a slightly different process to create a domain class. For Spring Data JPA we have a few tools in our toolbox that we can use to annotate parts of our domain classes to match the domain model in the *Account Context*.

Now let's create each of our domain classes for the `Account Service` as JPA entity classes using the JPA annotations described in the last table. We need to create domain classes for each of the concepts in the *Account Context*, which includes the following objects (shown in Figure 9-9).

- `Account`
- `Customer`
- `CreditCard`
- `Address`

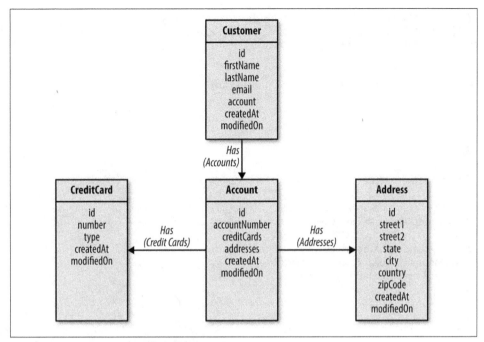

Figure 9-9. Entity relationship diagram for Account Context

We will create a domain class with the properties listed in the diagram above. Each domain class will have annotated properties for relationships to the Account class.

Let's look at some of the types in our domain, and how they're mapped with JPA annotations in Examples 9-8 through 9-11 and in Figure 9-9.

Example 9-8. The Account domain class as a JPA entity

```
package demo.account;

import demo.address.Address;
import demo.creditcard.CreditCard;
import demo.customer.Customer;
import demo.data.BaseEntity;
import lombok.AllArgsConstructor;
import lombok.Data;
import lombok.NoArgsConstructor;

import javax.persistence.*;
import java.util.HashSet;
import java.util.Set;

@Entity
@Data
```

```
@NoArgsConstructor
@AllArgsConstructor
public class Account extends BaseEntity {

  @Id
  @GeneratedValue(strategy = GenerationType.AUTO)
  private Long id; ❶

  private String accountNumber;

  ❷
  @OneToMany(cascade = CascadeType.ALL, fetch = FetchType.EAGER)
  private Set<CreditCard> creditCards = new HashSet<>();

  @OneToMany(cascade = CascadeType.ALL, fetch = FetchType.EAGER)
  private Set<Address> addresses = new HashSet<>();

  public Account(String accountNumber, Set<Address> addresses) {
    this.accountNumber = accountNumber;
    this.addresses.addAll(addresses);
  }

  public Account(String accountNumber) {
    this.accountNumber = accountNumber;
  }
}
```

❶ The @GeneratedValue will increment a unique ID for the @Id field. Here, we've (redundantly and explicitly) specified that the primary key should use an auto-incrementing value.

❷ The @OneToMany annotation describes an FK relationship to a JPA entity.

Example 9-9. The Customer domain class as a JPA entity

```
package demo.customer;

import demo.account.Account;
import demo.data.BaseEntity;
import lombok.AllArgsConstructor;
import lombok.Data;
import lombok.NoArgsConstructor;

import javax.persistence.*;

@Entity
@Data
@NoArgsConstructor
@AllArgsConstructor
public class Customer extends BaseEntity {
```

```
@Id
@GeneratedValue(strategy = GenerationType.AUTO)
private Long id;

private String firstName;

private String lastName;

private String email;

@OneToOne(cascade = CascadeType.ALL)
private Account account;

public Customer(String firstName, String lastName, String email,
  Account account) {
  this.firstName = firstName;
  this.lastName = lastName;
  this.email = email;
  this.account = account;
 }
}
```

Example 9-10. The Address domain class as a JPA entity

```
package demo.address;

import demo.data.BaseEntity;
import lombok.AllArgsConstructor;
import lombok.Data;
import lombok.NoArgsConstructor;

import javax.persistence.*;

@Entity
@Data
@NoArgsConstructor
@AllArgsConstructor
public class Address extends BaseEntity {

  @Id
  @GeneratedValue(strategy = GenerationType.AUTO)
  private Long id;

  private String street1;

  private String street2;

  private String state;

  private String city;
```

```
  private String country;

  private Integer zipCode;

  @Enumerated(EnumType.STRING)
  private AddressType addressType;

  public Address(String street1, String street2, String state, String city,
    String country, AddressType addressType, Integer zipCode) {
    this.street1 = street1;
    this.street2 = street2;
    this.state = state;
    this.city = city;
    this.country = country;
    this.addressType = addressType;
    this.zipCode = zipCode;
  }

}
```

Example 9-11. The CreditCard domain class as a JPA entity

```
package demo.creditcard;

import demo.data.BaseEntity;
import lombok.AllArgsConstructor;
import lombok.Data;
import lombok.NoArgsConstructor;
import lombok.ToString;

import javax.persistence.*;

@Data
@NoArgsConstructor
@AllArgsConstructor
@Entity
public class CreditCard extends BaseEntity {

  @Id
  @GeneratedValue(strategy = GenerationType.AUTO)
  private Long id;

  private String number;

  @Enumerated(EnumType.STRING)
  private CreditCardType type;

  public CreditCard(String number, CreditCardType type) {
    this.number = number;
    this.type = type;
  }
}
```

Notice that we have provided some parameters to the @OneToMany annotations in various classes (Example 9-12).

Example 9-12. We can customize the mapping in the @OneToMany annotation

```
@OneToMany(cascade = CascadeType.ALL, fetch = FetchType.EAGER)
private Set<Address> address = new HashSet<>();
```

- `CascadeType.ALL` indicates that committing a transaction cascades to all referenced JPA entities.
- `FetchType.EAGER` indicates that relationships will automatically be populated.

The @OneToMany annotation describes a foreign key relationship between tables managed by JPA entity classes. In the case of Account's relationship with Address, we have a cardinality of 1..* or *one-to-many*.

Auditing with JPA

We can also apply auditing for JPA classes to record the creation date of a record as well as the time the record was last modified. This is the responsibility of the BaseEntity class which each of our JPA entities will inherit. Let's take a look at what the BaseEntity class looks like (Example 9-13).

Example 9-13. The BaseEntity class provides JPA auditing

```
package demo.data;

import lombok.Data;
import org.springframework.data.annotation.CreatedDate;
import org.springframework.data.annotation.LastModifiedDate;
import org.springframework.data.jpa.domain.support.AuditingEntityListener;

import javax.persistence.EntityListeners;
import javax.persistence.MappedSuperclass;

@Data
@MappedSuperclass
❶
@EntityListeners(AuditingEntityListener.class)
❷
public class BaseEntity {

@CreatedDate
private Long createdAt; ❸

@LastModifiedDate
private Long lastModified; ❹
```

}

❶ This annotation designates a super class that JPA entities inherit from.

❷ This designates an auditing callback listener that will observe the life cycle of JPA operations.

❸ This annotation will save a timestamp when a record is created.

❹ This annotation will apply an updated timestamp when a record is updated.

There is one last step to enable JPA auditing for our Spring Boot application. We need to apply the `@EnableJpaAuditing` annotation to our application's configuration class.

Now that we have a handle on how to create JPA entity classes with mapped super classes, we can do the same for our other domain classes in the *Account Context*. Let's now create our repositories so that we can manage our data for the *Account Service*.

The `Account` and `Customer` entities are our aggregate entities—all other entities live and die when `Account` and `Customer` entities live and die. So we'll create repositories to manage them (Examples 9-14 and 9-15).

Example 9-14. AccountRepository definition

```
package demo.account;

import org.springframework.data.repository.PagingAndSortingRepository;

public interface AccountRepository extends
 PagingAndSortingRepository<Account, Long> {

}
```

Example 9-15. CustomerRepository definition

```
package demo.customer;

import org.springframework.data.repository.PagingAndSortingRepository;

import java.util.Optional;

public interface CustomerRepository extends
 PagingAndSortingRepository<Customer, Long> {

❶
 Optional<Customer> findByEmailContaining(String email);
}
```

❶ In this repository we define, by convention, a custom finder method that returns an `Optional<Customer>` containing either a `Customer` or nothing. Behind the scenes, this finder method gets turned into a query using JPA-QL. We can override the precise query with the `@Query` annotation.

Integration Tests

With our entities in place, we can confirm that everything works as expected (Example 9-16).

Example 9-16. AccountApplicationTests definition

```
package service;

import com.mysql.jdbc.AssertionFailedException;
import demo.AccountApplication;
import demo.account.Account;
import demo.address.Address;
import demo.address.AddressType;
import demo.creditcard.CreditCard;
import demo.creditcard.CreditCardType;
import demo.customer.Customer;
import demo.customer.CustomerRepository;
import org.junit.Assert;
import org.junit.Test;
import org.junit.runner.RunWith;
import org.springframework.beans.factory.annotation.Autowired;
import org.springframework.boot.test.context.SpringBootTest;
import org.springframework.test.context.ActiveProfiles;
import org.springframework.test.context.junit4.SpringRunner;

import java.util.Collection;
import java.util.Optional;

import static demo.creditcard.CreditCardType.VISA;

@RunWith(SpringRunner.class)
@SpringBootTest(classes = AccountApplication.class)
@ActiveProfiles(profiles = "test")
public class AccountApplicationTests {

  @Autowired
  private CustomerRepository customerRepository;

  @Test
  public void customerTest() {
    Account account = new Account("12345");
    Customer customer = new Customer("Jane", "Doe", "jane.doe@gmail.com", account);
    CreditCard creditCard = new CreditCard("1234567890", VISA);
```

```
customer.getAccount().getCreditCards().add(creditCard);

String street1 = "1600 Pennsylvania Ave NW";
Address address = new Address(street1, null, "DC", "Washington",
  "United States", AddressType.SHIPPING, 20500);
customer.getAccount().getAddresses().add(address);

customer = customerRepository.save(customer);
Customer persistedResult = customerRepository.findOne(customer.getId());
Assert.assertNotNull(persistedResult.getAccount());      ❶
Assert.assertNotNull(persistedResult.getCreatedAt());
Assert.assertNotNull(persistedResult.getLastModified());  ❷

Assert.assertTrue(persistedResult.getAccount().getAddresses().stream()
  .anyMatch(add -> add.getStreet1().equalsIgnoreCase(street1)));  ❸

customerRepository.findByEmailContaining(customer.getEmail())  ❹
  .orElseThrow(
    () -> new AssertionFailedException(new RuntimeException(
      "there's supposed to be a matching record!")));
  }
}
```

❶   We've successfully persisted a record and a one-to-one relationship.

❷   We've successfully persisted a record and the auditing mechanism has worked.

❸   We've successfully persisted a record and an association.

❹   Here, we rely upon our custom finder method to look for all Customer entities with a particular email.

Spring Data MongoDB

The *Spring Data MongoDB* project provides repository-based data management for MongoDB.

MongoDB is a NoSQL database that is well known for its ease of use and simplified data model. MongoDB is categorized as a *document-oriented* database, which means that records are stored as hierarchical JSON-*like* documents. It's easy to connect to a MongoDB instance if you add org.springframework.boot : spring-boot-starter-data-mongodb to the classpath of your application. There are properties, like spring.data.mongodb.host, spring.data.mongodb.port, and spring.data.mongodb.database, that you can specify to connect to a particular instance. Otherwise, Spring Boot will configure a connection to the local instance.

Order Service

We are going to use *Spring Data MongoDB* for our Order Service, which will function as the backend service for the order context in *Cloud Native Clothing's* domain model. Similar to the last section, we're going to walk through setting up a *Spring Data MongoDB* application. Much of what we learned creating the `Account Service` will be re-applied here.

 Not all Spring Data projects support running `datasource` as an embedded in-memory database, such as with *Spring Data JPA* and H2 or HSQLDB. Since MongoDB is written in C++, it cannot be embedded as a process inside a JVM application. For this section you'll need to download and install MongoDB (*http://www.mongodb.org/*).

Create a new project using the Spring Initializr and ensure that you've selected `org.springframework.boot : spring-boot-starter-data-mongodb` from the dependencies.

For the `Order Service` we are going to refer back to *Cloud Native Clothing's* domain model for the *Order Context* (Figure 9-10).

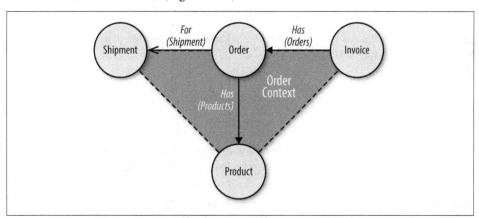

Figure 9-10. Order Context for the Order Service

In the *Order Context* we can see that we have four domain classes: *Invoice*, *Order*, *Product*, and *Shipment*. In order to understand how we can construct our domain classes, let's take a look at the primary use cases for the `Order Service`, shown in Table 9-3.

Table 9-3. Primary use cases for the Order Service

Behavior	Domain Classes
An *order* is *placed* for a set of *products* and their quantities.	Order, Product
A *shipment* is *delivered* to an *address* for an *order*.	Shipment, Address, Order
An *invoice* is *generated* for a set of *orders* of an *account*.	Invoice, Order, Account

This table presents a simpler set of primary use cases than we would normally see in an enterprise application. These three use cases describe the most salient behaviors of the Order Service. Notice that domain classes interact with each other. In domain-driven design it is important to break down use cases into statements that describe behaviors of an actor's interactions with domain objects.

Document classes with MongoDB

We saw earlier in the chapter that each domain class in our Account Service was annotated using a JPA annotation called @Entity. For other Spring Data projects the pattern used for domain class annotations remains the same. Each Spring Data project's semantics for annotations are specific to the traits of the model of the database. For Spring Data MongoDB we can use a @Document annotation on a class to indicate that it is a representation of a document in MongoDB.

The first document class we will create is an Invoice. From our primary use cases we have one statement that we can use to describe how we should construct the Invoice domain class:

- An *invoice* is *generated* for a set of *orders* of an *account*.

The goal here is to create a model class that supports this use case's behavior without being too restrictive. When we create a new invoice in the Order Service, we should require that the invoice can be looked up by the account number. This account number will refer back to an Account's domain class that is managed by the Account Service. We will also provide a field for a set of orders rather than just a single order for each invoice. We also will require that a billing address is provided for the Invoice; this address describes where the invoice should be sent (Examples 9-17 and 9-18).

> The reason we use a document database for the order service is that it is an aggregate store. This is useful because line items in an order should not be modified after the order has been submitted by the user. The product for each line item should represent the state of the product at the time of the order.

Example 9-17. The Invoice domain class as a MongoDB document

```
package demo.invoice;

import demo.address.Address;
import demo.address.AddressType;
import demo.data.BaseEntity;
import demo.order.Order;
import lombok.AllArgsConstructor;
import lombok.Data;
import lombok.NoArgsConstructor;
import org.springframework.data.annotation.Id;
import org.springframework.data.mongodb.core.mapping.Document;

import java.util.ArrayList;
import java.util.List;

@Data
@AllArgsConstructor
@NoArgsConstructor
@Document
public class Invoice extends BaseEntity {

  @Id
  private String invoiceId;

  private String customerId;

  private List<Order> orders = new ArrayList<Order>();

  private Address billingAddress;

  private InvoiceStatus invoiceStatus;

  public Invoice(String customerId, Address billingAddress) {
    this.customerId = customerId;
    this.billingAddress = billingAddress;
    this.billingAddress.setAddressType(AddressType.BILLING);
    this.invoiceStatus = InvoiceStatus.CREATED;
  }

  public void addOrder(Order order) {
    order.setAccountNumber(this.customerId);
    orders.add(order);
  }
}
```

Example 9-18. A status enum for the state of an Invoice

```
package demo.invoice;

public enum InvoiceStatus {
```

```
 CREATED, SENT, PAID
}
```

We will need a Spring Data MongoDB repository to simplify management of instances of our document (Example 9-19).

Example 9-19. An InvoiceRepository, complete with a custom finder method

```
package demo.invoice;

import demo.address.Address;
import org.springframework.data.repository.PagingAndSortingRepository;

public interface InvoiceRepository extends
 PagingAndSortingRepository<Invoice, String> {

 Invoice findByBillingAddress(Address address);
}
```

We can see from our `Invoice` domain class that we are referencing a set of `Order` classes. Let's also refer back to the primary use cases that provide us with more detail about an `Order`:

- An *order* is *placed* for a set of *products* and their quantities.
- A *shipment* is *delivered* to an *address* for an *order*.

These two statements describe several domain class interactions. To fulfill the requirements of the first statement, we will use a new object class called `LineItem` to describe a `Product` and its quantity ordered. Each `LineItem` will refer to a remote reference to a `Product` that is stored in the `Inventory Service`, which we will create later in the chapter. The second use case statement describes the creation of a `Ship ment` that is delivered to an `Address` for an `Order`. To fulfill this statement's requirements, we will require that an account number and shipping address is provided in the constructor of the `Order` class. Finally, we will provide a status object that describes the state of an `Order` object as it is moved from an initial state to a final state (Examples 9-20 and 9-21).

Example 9-20. The Order domain class

```
package demo.order;

import demo.address.Address;
import demo.address.AddressType;
import demo.data.BaseEntity;
import lombok.AllArgsConstructor;
import lombok.Data;
```

```
import lombok.NoArgsConstructor;
import org.springframework.data.annotation.Id;
import org.springframework.data.mongodb.core.mapping.Document;

import java.util.ArrayList;
import java.util.List;

@Data
@NoArgsConstructor
@AllArgsConstructor
@Document
public class Order extends BaseEntity {

  @Id
  private String orderId;

  private String accountNumber;

  private OrderStatus orderStatus;

  private List<LineItem> lineItems = new ArrayList<>();

  private Address shippingAddress;

  public Order(String accountNumber, Address shippingAddress) {
    this.accountNumber = accountNumber;
    this.shippingAddress = shippingAddress;
    this.shippingAddress.setAddressType(AddressType.SHIPPING);
    this.orderStatus = OrderStatus.PENDING;
  }

  public void addLineItem(LineItem lineItem) {
    this.lineItems.add(lineItem);
  }
}
```

Example 9-21. A status enum for the state of an Order

```
package demo.order;

public enum OrderStatus {
  PENDING, CONFIRMED, SHIPPED, DELIVERED
}
```

Now we will create a LineItem class that describes a reference to a Product in the catalog and the state of that product at the time the order was placed (Example 9-22).

Example 9-22. The LineItem class

```
package demo.order;
```

```
import lombok.AllArgsConstructor;
import lombok.Data;
import lombok.NoArgsConstructor;

@Data
@NoArgsConstructor
@AllArgsConstructor
public class LineItem {

 private String name, productId;

 private Integer quantity;

 private Double price, tax;

}
```

Auditing with MongoDB

We can support auditing with MongoDB entities. We'll first need a base entity from which other entities can inherit common fields used for auditing, as depicted in the following listing (Example 9-23).

Example 9-23. The auditing abstract base class

```
package demo.data;

import lombok.Data;
import org.joda.time.DateTime;

@Data
public class BaseEntity {

 private DateTime lastModified, createdAt;
}
```

Then, we will need to configure an `AbstractMongoEventListener`—as demonstrated in Example 9-24—to contribute these values on entity life cycle changes.

Example 9-24. A listener can be used to audit MongoDB transactions

```
package demo.data;

import org.joda.time.DateTime;
import org.springframework.data.mongodb.core.mapping.event.AbstractMongoEventListener;
import org.springframework.data.mongodb.core.mapping.event.BeforeSaveEvent;
import org.springframework.stereotype.Component;

@Component
class BeforeSaveListener extends AbstractMongoEventListener<BaseEntity> {
```

```
@Override
public void onBeforeSave(BeforeSaveEvent<BaseEntity> event) {

  DateTime timestamp = new DateTime();

  if (event.getSource().getCreatedAt() == null)
    event.getSource().setCreatedAt(timestamp);

  event.getSource().setLastModified(timestamp);

  super.onBeforeSave(event);
  }
}
```

Integration Tests

Now that we have created the data layer for our Order Service, let's walk through creating an integration test (Example 9-25). We are going to perform the following steps in our test:

- Create a new Order
- Add a LineItem to the new Order
- Save the Order using OrderRepository

Example 9-25. An integration test for our MongoDB components

```
package orders;

import demo.OrderApplication;
import demo.address.Address;
import demo.invoice.Invoice;
import demo.invoice.InvoiceRepository;
import demo.order.LineItem;
import demo.order.Order;
import demo.order.OrderRepository;
import org.junit.After;
import org.junit.Assert;
import org.junit.Before;
import org.junit.Test;
import org.junit.runner.RunWith;
import org.springframework.beans.factory.annotation.Autowired;
import org.springframework.boot.test.context.SpringBootTest;
import org.springframework.test.context.junit4.SpringRunner;

@RunWith(SpringRunner.class)
@SpringBootTest(classes = OrderApplication.class)
public class OrderApplicationTest {
```

```
@Autowired
private OrderRepository orderRepository;

@Autowired
private InvoiceRepository invoiceRepository;

@Before
@After
public void reset() {
 orderRepository.deleteAll();
 invoiceRepository.deleteAll();
}

@Test
public void orderTest() {

 Address shippingAddress = new Address("1600 Pennsylvania Ave NW", null, "DC",
  "Washington", "United States", 20500);
 Order order = new Order("12345", shippingAddress);
 order.addLineItem(new LineItem("Best. Cloud. Ever. (T-Shirt, Men's Large)",
  "SKU-24642", 1, 21.99, .06));
 order.addLineItem(new LineItem("Like a BOSH (T-Shirt, Women's Medium)",
  "SKU-34563", 3, 14.99, .06));
 order.addLineItem(new LineItem(
  "We're gonna need a bigger VM (T-Shirt, Women's Small)", "SKU-12464", 4,
  13.99, .06));
 order.addLineItem(new LineItem("cf push awesome (Hoodie, Men's Medium)",
  "SKU-64233", 2, 21.99, .06));
 order = orderRepository.save(order);
 ❶
 Assert.assertNotNull(order.getOrderId());
 Assert.assertEquals(order.getLineItems().size(), 4);

 ❷

 Assert.assertEquals(order.getLastModified(), order.getCreatedAt());
 order = orderRepository.save(order);
 Assert.assertNotEquals(order.getLastModified(), order.getCreatedAt());

 ❸

 Address billingAddress = new Address("875 Howard St", null, "CA",
  "San Francisco", "United States", 94103);
 String accountNumber = "918273465";

 Invoice invoice = new Invoice(accountNumber, billingAddress);
 invoice.addOrder(order);
 invoice = invoiceRepository.save(invoice);
 Assert.assertEquals(invoice.getOrders().size(), 1);

 ❹

 Assert.assertEquals(invoiceRepository.findByBillingAddress(billingAddress),
  invoice);
```

```
  }
}
```

❶ First, we confirm that we've written data to the persistence store…

❷ …then we confirm that auditing is working…

❸ …then we confirm that nested associations work.

❹ Here we use a custom finder method that Spring Data MongoDB turns into a BSON-query against the MongoDB `Invoice` document.

Spring Data Neo4j

The *Spring Data Neo4j* project provides repository-based data management for Neo4j, a popular NoSQL graph database. A *graph database* represents database objects as a connected graph of nodes and relationships. Nodes and relationships can contain both simple value types and complex value types. A graph database is based on the principles of graph theory. The mathematics behind graph theory make it possible for a graph database to trivially traverse millions of relationships per second and to model large interconnected datasets. At first blush this might seem the same value proposition for a *Relational* database, but it's not: try modeling the Facebook friend graph in an RDBMS and then doing a leftouter join! In a graph the relationship between nodes is as important as the nodes themselves. A relationship may feature a direction, unidirectional or bidirectional; a person "is the employee of" another.

This connected model is useful when combined with Cypher, Neo4j's declarative query language that is similar to SQL. The Cypher query language provides the ability to query and manage data using patterns, as opposed to SQL, which uses a strict schema that must be defined prior to querying your data. Further, Neo4j provides the ability to define graph traversals, eliminating SQL joins that make complex queries hard to read and write.

In this section we will use Spring Data Neo4j to create an `Inventory Service` for *Cloud Native Clothing's* online store's backend. Here's what we want to achieve:

- Provide an overview of *Cloud Native Clothing's* requirements for inventory management
- Review how Neo4j manages database objects as a connected graph
- Design a graph data model for inventory management
- Implement Spring Data domain classes as Neo4j nodes
- Create repositories to manage domain classes for Neo4j nodes

Inventory Service

We're going to break down the construction of our Inventory Service into two parts: design and implementation. We'll need to work through how we're going to construct a graph data model that describes our inventory context for *Cloud Native Clothing's* online store.

Let's consider the example of our *Cloud Native Clothing* online store. A clothing store might have a seasonal catalog, which it can use to change the set of products on its website at the start of each quarter. Not all products in the catalog will necessarily be different. There might be some products in the store that are sold year-round. Because of this, catalogs could have a hierarchy: for example, a base catalog for products offered year-round, and a seasonal catalog that changes product lines each quarter.

We'll also need to connect products to the inventory over a collection of warehouses that are located around the world. Each of these warehouses may have a product from our catalog. We can track our global inventory of products and use this information to create shipments that are closest to the delivery location. This is a complex undertaking, to say the least. To solve this problem we need to tackle the complexity of a connected model without spending so much time on its design.

Neo4j provides us the flexibility to model our data in an intuitive way, and we can map that data to a Spring Data application using the abstractions we have already learned in previous sections in this chapter.

The inventory context described in Figure 9-11 shows a simplified view of what we will need to construct for our application. To fit this application to the requirements we talked about earlier, with functions such as shipping and inventory management, we'll need to design a graph model that we can use to construct our domain classes and repositories. Let's begin by doing an overview of how Neo4j's property graph data model can be used to manage connected data using Spring Data Neo4j.

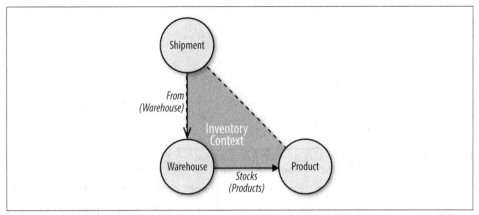

Figure 9-11. Context for the Inventory Service

Configuring Neo4j

Spring Boot provides auto-configuration for the Spring Data Neo4j project. We can use a set of features that take advantage of the specialized traits of a graph database. In order to build a Neo4J application, we'll need `org.springframework.boot : spring-boot-starter-data-neo4j` in our Maven build. You can point your application to a particular Neo4J instance using any of the many properties, `spring.data.neo4j.uri`, `spring.data.neo4j.username`, `spring.data.neo4j.password`, etc. Now that our Spring Boot project is configured to use Spring Data Neo4j, we can build out an application using the familiar abstractions we've used in previous examples to manage connected data in a Neo4j database.

Graph data modeling with Neo4j

Graph data modeling is much more intuitive than modeling domain data for a RDBMS. In this section we're going to go over how Neo4j's property graph data model can be used to create a diagram of nodes and relationships that we will use to construct our Spring Data repositories and domain classes. Let's start by reviewing how Neo4j manages data objects as entities in a graph model.

Neo4j has two native data entities, a *node* and a *relationship*. Nodes are used to store a map of key/value properties. Relationships also allow you to store a map of properties. Simple value types, such as a *color* or *gender*, can be stored as a property on a node. Complex value types, such as an *address*, should be represented as a separate node. The relationship is used to connect nodes together, such as connecting an *address* node to a *shipment* node.

In Figure 9-12 we see a shipment node connected to two address nodes. The relationship type, *HAS_ADDRESS*, can be connected to multiple addresses.

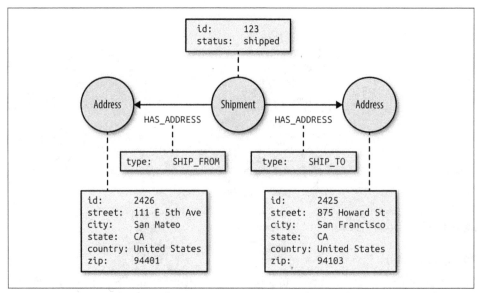

Figure 9-12. Properties on relationships are used to qualify complex value types of a node

Using Cypher, we can express a query to get each address for a thishipment:

```
MATCH (shipment:Shipment)-[r:HAS_ADDRESS]->(address)
WHERE shipment.id = 123
RETURN address
```

In this query we are first matching all shipment nodes, described by (`shipment:Ship ment`). Nodes and relationships in Cypher use ASCII art to describe graph entities as patterns. A node is encapsulated by parentheses, with a colon symbol separating the variable that Cypher should store the results in, such as (`shipment`), and a label that describes which group a node belongs to, such as (`:Shipment`), indicating a node has a *Shipment* label.

If we were to use the query above on the graph data described in Figure 9-12, we would get back the following results:

```
Detailed Query Results

Query Results

+--------------------------------------------------------------------------------------+
| address                                                                              |
+--------------------------------------------------------------------------------------+
| Node[7]{street:"875 Howard St",country:"United States",id:2425,city:"San Francisco",zip:"94103",state:"CA"} |
| Node[6]{street:"111 E 5th Ave",country:"United States",id:2426,city:"San Mateo",zip:"94401",state:"CA"}     |
+--------------------------------------------------------------------------------------+
2 rows
54 ms
```

Here we see that we've retrieved both addresses for a specific shipment with the ID 123. What if we wanted to only query the address of the warehouse that a shipment was shipped from? We could modify the Cypher query to the following:

```
MATCH (shipment:Shipment)-[r:HAS_ADDRESS { type: "SHIP_FROM" }]->(address)
WHERE shipment.id = 123
RETURN address
```

Now we'll get back only one of the two addresses, as shown in the results below:

```
Detailed Query Results

Query Results

+--------------------------------------------------------------------------------------------------+
| address                                                                                          |
+--------------------------------------------------------------------------------------------------+
| Node[6]{street:"111 E 5th Ave",country:"United States",id:2426,city:"San Mateo",zip:"94401",state:"CA"} |
+--------------------------------------------------------------------------------------------------+
1 row
71 ms
```

By modifying the first Cypher query to include a property type on the *HAS_ADDRESS* relationship, ()-[r:HAS_ADDRESS { type: "SHIP_FROM" }]->(), which should equal *SHIP_FROM*, we are able to get back the address information of where a shipment was shipped from.

Now that we know how Neo4j models data as graphs, we can create a graph model describing the nodes and relationships of our inventory microservice.

In Figure 9-13 we see each node with its label and the relationships between the nodes, which provides us with a rough sketch of how to construct our domain classes and repositories using Spring Data Neo4j in a Spring Boot application.

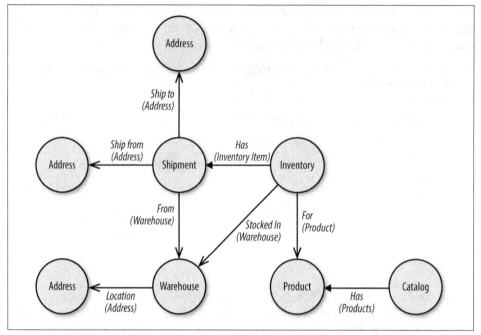

Figure 9-13. Graph model for the inventory bounded context

In Spring Data Neo4j, labels in our Neo4j graph model, such as the ones we have on our nodes in Figure 9-13, will become our Spring Data repositories. We will have repositories for each of the following node labels, shown in our graph data model:

- Address
- Shipment
- Inventory
- Product
- Catalog
- Warehouse

We'll need to create domain classes, in their own respective packages, for each of the node labels described in Figure 9-13. The first class is an entity to model an Address, as seen in Example 9-26.

Example 9-26. The Address domain class as a Neo4j label

```
package demo.address;

import lombok.AllArgsConstructor;
```

```
import lombok.Data;
import lombok.NoArgsConstructor;
import org.neo4j.ogm.annotation.GraphId;
import org.neo4j.ogm.annotation.NodeEntity;

@Data
@NoArgsConstructor
@AllArgsConstructor
@NodeEntity
public class Address {

  @GraphId
  private Long id;

  private String street1, street2, state, city, country;

  private Integer zipCode;

  public Address(String street1, String street2, String state, String city,
    String country, Integer zipCode) {
    this.street1 = street1;
    this.street2 = street2;
    this.state = state;
    this.city = city;
    this.country = country;
    this.zipCode = zipCode;
  }
}
```

The Product, shown in Example 9-27, models something available for sale, its unit price, and its product ID (you might see it called a *SKU* in some parts of the world).

Example 9-27. The Product domain class as a Neo4j label

```
package demo.product;

import demo.catalog.Catalog;
import lombok.AllArgsConstructor;
import lombok.Data;
import lombok.NoArgsConstructor;
import org.neo4j.ogm.annotation.GraphId;
import org.neo4j.ogm.annotation.NodeEntity;
import org.neo4j.ogm.annotation.Relationship;

import java.util.HashSet;
import java.util.Set;

@Data
@NoArgsConstructor
@AllArgsConstructor
@NodeEntity
```

```
public class Product {

  @GraphId
  private Long id;

  private String name, productId;

  private Double unitPrice;

  public Product(String name, String productId, Double unitPrice) {
    this.name = name;
    this.productId = productId;
    this.unitPrice = unitPrice;
  }

}
```

A Warehouse, shown in Example 9-28, models the logical name for a structure holding physical goods, and the location of that structure.

Example 9-28. The Warehouse domain class as a Neo4j label

```
package demo.warehouse;

import demo.address.Address;
import lombok.AllArgsConstructor;
import lombok.Data;
import lombok.NoArgsConstructor;
import org.neo4j.ogm.annotation.GraphId;
import org.neo4j.ogm.annotation.NodeEntity;
import org.neo4j.ogm.annotation.Relationship;

@NoArgsConstructor
@AllArgsConstructor
@Data
@NodeEntity
public class Warehouse {

  @GraphId
  private Long id;

  private String name;

  @Relationship(type = "HAS_ADDRESS")
  private Address address;

  public Warehouse(String n, Address a) {
    this.name = n;
    this.address = a;
  }
```

```java
 public Warehouse(String name) {
  this.name = name;
 }
}
```

The Inventory, shown in Example 9-29, describes how much of a given product a given warehouse has in stock (or *inventory*).

Example 9-29. The Inventory domain class as a Neo4j label

```java
package demo.inventory;

import demo.product.Product;
import demo.warehouse.Warehouse;
import lombok.AllArgsConstructor;
import lombok.Data;
import lombok.NoArgsConstructor;
import org.neo4j.ogm.annotation.GraphId;
import org.neo4j.ogm.annotation.NodeEntity;
import org.neo4j.ogm.annotation.Relationship;

@Data
@NoArgsConstructor
@AllArgsConstructor
@NodeEntity
public class Inventory {

 @GraphId
 private Long id;

 private String inventoryNumber;

 @Relationship(type = "PRODUCT_TYPE", direction = "OUTGOING")
 private Product product;

 @Relationship(type = "STOCKED_IN", direction = "OUTGOING")
 private Warehouse warehouse;

 private InventoryStatus status;

 public Inventory(String inventoryNumber, Product product, Warehouse warehouse,
  InventoryStatus status) {
  this.inventoryNumber = inventoryNumber;
  this.product = product;
  this.warehouse = warehouse;
  this.status = status;
 }

}
```

The Shipment entity, shown in Example 9-30, models information from a set of inventories to a shipping Address.

Example 9-30. The Shipment domain class as a Neo4j label

```
package demo.shipment;

import demo.address.Address;
import demo.inventory.Inventory;
import demo.warehouse.Warehouse;
import lombok.AllArgsConstructor;
import lombok.Data;
import lombok.NoArgsConstructor;
import org.neo4j.ogm.annotation.GraphId;
import org.neo4j.ogm.annotation.NodeEntity;
import org.neo4j.ogm.annotation.Relationship;

import java.util.HashSet;
import java.util.Set;

@Data
@NoArgsConstructor
@AllArgsConstructor
@NodeEntity
public class Shipment {

  @GraphId
  private Long id;

  @Relationship(type = "CONTAINS_PRODUCT")
  private Set<Inventory> inventories = new HashSet<>();

  @Relationship(type = "SHIP_TO")
  private Address deliveryAddress;

  @Relationship(type = "SHIP_FROM")
  private Warehouse fromWarehouse;

  private ShipmentStatus shipmentStatus;

  public Shipment(Set<Inventory> inventories, Address deliveryAddress,
    Warehouse fromWarehouse, ShipmentStatus shipmentStatus) {
    this.inventories = inventories;
    this.deliveryAddress = deliveryAddress;
    this.fromWarehouse = fromWarehouse;
    this.shipmentStatus = shipmentStatus;
  }
}
```

A Catalog, shown in Example 9-31, is an enumeration of Product instances available grouped under some (possibly arbitrary) group name.

Example 9-31. The Catalog domain class as a Neo4j label

```java
package demo.catalog;

import demo.product.Product;
import lombok.AllArgsConstructor;
import lombok.Data;
import lombok.NoArgsConstructor;
import org.neo4j.ogm.annotation.GraphId;
import org.neo4j.ogm.annotation.NodeEntity;
import org.neo4j.ogm.annotation.Relationship;

import java.util.Collection;
import java.util.HashSet;
import java.util.Set;
import java.util.stream.Collector;

@Data
@NoArgsConstructor
@AllArgsConstructor
@NodeEntity
public class Catalog {

 @GraphId
 private Long id;

 @Relationship(type = "HAS_PRODUCT", direction = Relationship.OUTGOING)
 private Set<Product> products = new HashSet<>();

 private String name;

 public Catalog(String n, Collection<Product> p) {
  this.name = n;
  this.products.addAll(p);
 }

 public Catalog(String name) {
  this.name = name;
 }

}
```

Spring Data Neo4j uses the same abstractions for repositories that we've used in previous examples in this chapter. We'll again use the PagingAndSortingRepository abstraction in our inventory service to indicate that we would like Spring Data to provide repositories with built-in paging and sorting features, as shown in Example 9-32.

Example 9-32. Paging and sorting repository for the Address label in Neo4j

```
package demo.address;

import org.springframework.data.neo4j.repository.GraphRepository;

public interface AddressRepository extends GraphRepository<Address> {
}
```

In each package, containing a domain class from our graph model, we'll create a repository so we can manage our domain data. For example, the snippet from Example 9-32 is a repository definition that would be located in the *address* package of the project. This AddressRepository will allow us to manage data for our nodes in Neo4j with the label Address.

Our package structure for the Inventory Service project should now look like the packages in Figure 9-14.

Figure 9-14. Package structure of the inventory service

Integration Tests

Now that we have created the data layer for our Inventory Service, let's walk through creating a simple end-to-end integration test. In our test, we will take the following steps, shown in Example 9-33:

- Create a warehouse
- Create a list of products
- Create a catalog
- Create shipment addresses
- Create inventory for products
- Create a shipment of product inventory

Example 9-33. An integration test for our Neo4j graph

```
package demo;

import demo.address.Address;
import demo.address.AddressRepository;
import demo.catalog.Catalog;
import demo.catalog.CatalogRepository;
import demo.inventory.Inventory;
import demo.inventory.InventoryRepository;
import demo.product.Product;
import demo.product.ProductRepository;
import demo.shipment.Shipment;
import demo.shipment.ShipmentRepository;
import demo.shipment.ShipmentStatus;
import demo.warehouse.Warehouse;
import demo.warehouse.WarehouseRepository;
import org.apache.commons.lang3.exception.ExceptionUtils;
import org.junit.Assert;
import org.junit.Before;
import org.junit.Test;
import org.junit.runner.RunWith;
import org.neo4j.ogm.session.Session;
import org.springframework.beans.factory.annotation.Autowired;
import org.springframework.boot.test.context.SpringBootTest;
import org.springframework.test.context.junit4.SpringRunner;

import java.util.*;
import java.util.stream.Collectors;
import java.util.stream.Stream;

import static demo.inventory.InventoryStatus.*;

@RunWith(SpringRunner.class)
@SpringBootTest(classes = InventoryApplication.class)
public class InventoryApplicationTests {

    @Autowired
    private ProductRepository products;
```

```java
@Autowired
private ShipmentRepository shipments;

@Autowired
private WarehouseRepository warehouses;

@Autowired
private AddressRepository addresses;

@Autowired
private CatalogRepository catalogs;

@Autowired
private InventoryRepository inventories;

@Autowired
private Session session;

@Before
public void setup() {
 try {
  this.session.query("MATCH (n) OPTIONAL MATCH (n)-[r]-() DELETE n, r;",
   Collections.emptyMap()).queryResults();
 }
 catch (Exception e) {
  Assert.fail("can't connect to Neo4j! " + ExceptionUtils.getMessage(e));
 }
}

@Test
public void inventoryTest() {

 ❶
 List<Product> products = Stream
  .of(
   new Product("Best. Cloud. Ever. (T-Shirt, Men's Large)", "SKU-24642", 21.99),
   new Product("Like a BOSH (T-Shirt, Women's Medium)", "SKU-34563", 14.99),
   new Product("We're gonna need a bigger VM (T-Shirt, Women's Small)",
    "SKU-12464", 13.99),
   new Product("cf push awesome (Hoodie, Men's Medium)", "SKU-64233", 21.99))
  .map(p -> this.products.save(p)).collect(Collectors.toList());

 Product sample = products.get(0);
 Assert.assertEquals(this.products.findOne(sample.getId()).getUnitPrice(),
  sample.getUnitPrice());

 ❷
 this.catalogs.save(new Catalog("Spring Catalog", products));

 ❸
 Address warehouseAddress = this.addresses.save(new Address("875 Howard St",
  null, "CA", "San Francisco", "United States", 94103));
```

```
Address shipToAddress = this.addresses.save(new Address(
  "1600 Amphitheatre Parkway", null, "CA", "Mountain View", "United States",
  94043));

❹
Warehouse warehouse = this.warehouses.save(new Warehouse("Pivotal SF",
  warehouseAddress));
Set<Inventory> inventories = products
  .stream()
  .map(
    p -> this.inventories.save(new Inventory(UUID.randomUUID().toString(), p,
      warehouse, IN_STOCK))).collect(Collectors.toSet());
Shipment shipment = shipments.save(new Shipment(inventories, shipToAddress,
  warehouse, ShipmentStatus.SHIPPED));
Assert.assertEquals(shipment.getInventories().size(), inventories.size());
 }
}
```

❶ Persist some products…

❷ …create a catalog…

❸ …create some shipping addresses…

❹ …and create a shipment.

Spring Data Redis

The Spring Data Redis project provides Spring integration for the Redis key-value store. Redis is an open source NoSQL database and is one of the most popular key-value stores in use today. While Redis is categorized as a key-value store, it can be best explained as an in-memory *data structure store*. Redis differs from most other data stores because it is able to store different kinds of complex data structures as values. What makes Redis most interesting is that it provides different sets of operations for each kind of data structure that it supports.

The data structures that Redis supports are:

- Strings
- Lists
- Sets
- Hashes
- Sorted sets
- Bitmaps and HyperLogLogs

The benefit of using a distributed data store—one designed for operations on complex data structures—is that multiple processes, applications, and servers are able to concurrently operate on values with the same key. Typically, to do this from multiple applications requires some form of deserialization into a language's supported data structures (for instance, a list or set), before operating on its value.

Redis solves this problem by providing programmatic access to perform operations on its supported data structures as an API. This means that operations on its data structures can be applied atomically with a greater degree of transactional granularity than using serialization.

Redis is also often used for interprocess communication and messaging. In addition to specialized support for operating on data structures, Redis can be a message broker, supporting publish/subscribe messaging.

Caching

The most popular use case for Redis is caching. Spring Data Redis implements Spring framework's CacheManager abstraction, which makes it an excellent choice for centralized caching of records in a microservice architecture. In this section we're going to explore a Spring Boot application that uses *Spring Data Redis* to manage a cache of user records.

As we can see in Figure 9-15, the *User Service* (colored in green) is a Spring Boot application and will have the responsibility of managing resources for the User domain class. We can also see that there is a *User Web* application, colored in blue. This Spring Boot application will be a consumer of the *User Service* and take the role of a web application that depends on the *User* resource that is managed by the *User Service*.

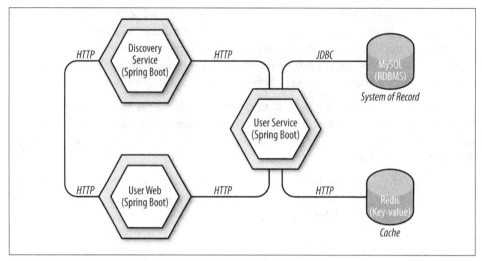

Figure 9-15. A service architecture diagram for the User Service and User Web applications

The *User Service* provides a REST API to allow consumers to remotely manage *User* resources over HTTP. The *User Web* application will assume the role of a frontend application that hosts a single-page application for managing users. This Spring Boot application will host static HTML/CSS and JavaScript and consume a REST API that is exposed from the *User Service*.

> In Figure 9-15, the color blue indicates a service that is stateless, with no dependency on an attached database. The color green is a service that has one or more connections to a database provider and is exclusively managing persistence of a set of resources, in this case the *User* resource.

When adding a caching layer to our Spring Boot applications, we have to consider many different scenarios of how our data will be used. Caching is an important part of any microservice architecture, since there will be a great deal of demand for interaction with resources for each service that has a REST API. We can see from Figure 9-15 that we have two data stores: one that is a MySQL database and one that is a Redis server. Records will be stored and persisted to disk from the *User Service* to its attached MySQL database. When a record is requested from another service, the response will become cached by replicating the record to the Redis server, where it will be available in-memory and served to consumers for a prescribed expiration before being cached again.

The goal of caching is to increase performance and to offload database hits and connection pool utilization from our primary data store by using a secondary high-availability store. Consider the scenario where we have a limited number of database connections to our MySQL database. If we exceed the number of connections that our database will allow, the database could go down or not be available until connections are recycled and released back to the pool. To solve this problem, we can use a secondary store that stores records in-memory so that a majority of traffic will be served from the in-memory cache of records, saving database connections and hits to our primary data store. This is essential in a microservice architecture, where resources must be both efficiently served to consumers as well as durably persisted to disk.

Spring Boot will auto-configure a `RedisTemplate` for us, deferring to configuration values (`spring.redis.host`, `spring.redis.port`, etc.) specified in the `Environment`, if we have `org.springframework.boot : spring-boot-starter-data-redis` on the classpath. It'll go one step further and configure a Spring Cache `CacheManager` for us if we add `@EnableCaching` to a `@Configuration` class.

 Make sure to scrutinize the TTL expiration time that you're configuring for resources in a microservice architecture. When you have many Spring Boot applications in your architecture, there will be some cases where records are rarely updated but requested frequently. In this case, you'll want to make sure to lengthen your expiration time for these types of objects. For resources that change often and are requested frequently, you'll want to set a lower expiration time, especially if those records are being modified without cache eviction.

For our example we have a fairly typical Spring Data JPA-based service in dire need of caching. We can use the Spring Data Redis-backed cache abstraction to selectively cache, or *memoize*, specific calls.

In Example 9-34, we'll take a look at the `UserService` class, which implements the logic for each of the REST API methods for the `User` resource from the `UserControl ler`. This class will also contain our caching annotations for managing the insertion, retrieval, and eviction of replicated `User` records from MySQL into Redis.

Example 9-34. `UserService` manages User records with annotation-driven cache operations

```
package demo;

import org.springframework.beans.factory.annotation.Autowired;
import org.springframework.cache.annotation.CacheEvict;
import org.springframework.cache.annotation.CachePut;
import org.springframework.cache.annotation.Cacheable;
import org.springframework.stereotype.Service;
```

```
@Service
public class UserService {

 private final UserRepository userRepository;

 @Autowired
 public UserService(UserRepository userRepository) {
  this.userRepository = userRepository;
 }

 @CacheEvict(value = "user", key = "#user.getId()")
 ❶
 public User createUser(User user) {

  User result = null;

  if (!userRepository.exists(user.getId())) {
   result = this.userRepository.save(user);
  }

  return result;
 }

 @Cacheable(value = "user")
 ❷
 public User getUser(String id) {
  return this.userRepository.findOne(id);
 }

 @CachePut(value = "user", key = "#id")
 ❸
 public User updateUser(String id, User user) {

  User result = null;

  if (userRepository.exists(user.getId())) {
   result = this.userRepository.save(user);
  }

  return result;
 }

 @CacheEvict(value = "user", key = "#id")
 ❹
 public boolean deleteUser(String id) {

  boolean deleted = false;

  if (userRepository.exists(id)) {
   this.userRepository.delete(id);
   deleted = true;
  }
```

```
  return deleted;
 }
}
```

❶ Evicts the User record with the supplied ID from the Redis cache.

❷ Gets a cached record from Redis or puts a User record from MySQL into the Redis cache.

❸ Evicts a User record and replaces it with the newly updated User record.

❹ Evicts the User record with the supplied ID from the Redis cache.

In Example 9-34, we have our UserService class, which is responsible for performing cache operations as well as managing database records for the User entity class in MySQL. This service is using annotation-driven caching to manage the life cycle of a replicated record in Redis. The four CRUD operations in this class are fairly simple. The primary key from the User record is being used as the generated key for the cache manager provided for Redis. The caching annotations are using Spring Expression Language (SpEL) to access the key from the parameters of the methods.

 When sharing a Redis server as a shared cache for different services, it's important to remember that the generation of the key will not include a namespace that includes the service name. This means that if you have an identifier that is the same for different domain concepts that are resources managed by different services, there will be a collision that will cause one sensitive resource to be substituted for another. In this case, you might have a service that returns an Account record when the request was for a User record. Always be careful when sharing caches. Make sure to generate keys that use a unique namespace for the service that owns a cached record.

Redis can serve as the caching backbone for any number of services. In this example, we looked at caching, but you can also use Redis as a backend for HTTP Sessions, a topic we explore further in Chapter 5, when we discuss forklifting legacy applications to a cloud environment by reworking their use of HTTP sessions to use Spring Session in "HTTP sessions with Spring Session" on page 134.

Summary

In this chapter we explored how to create Spring Boot applications that take advantage of various Spring Data projects. We created a full backend for *Cloud Native Clothing's* online store, using different Spring Data Projects for each application:

- Account Service (JPA—MySQL)
- Order Service (MongoDB)
- Inventory Service (Neo4j)

We also looked at how we might cache results from a service based on any one of these data sources using Spring Data Redis.

## CHAPTER 10

Messaging

Messaging supports connecting publishing application events to services across processes and networks. Messaging has a lot of applications, many of which Martin Fowler captures in this blog post, *What do you mean by "Event-Driven"? (https://martinfowler.com/articles/201701-event-driven.html)*:

- **Event notifications**: One system sends event messages to notify other systems of a change in the domain. There is no expectation that the recipient of the message produce a reply. The source system doesn't expect it, and doesn't use it. The event notification is immutable, which means that the contents of the event message should not include data that has been modified after the event was generated.

- **Event-carried state transfer**: These are events where a message does not contain any data that requires the receiver to call back to the source system. These forms of event messages will include everything the recipient will need to process an event.

- **Event sourcing**: Event sourcing is a practice that includes storing a log of domain events that have caused the state of the system to change over time. In this scenario, events can be replayed from any point in time to recreate the current state of the system.

Message brokers like Apache Kafka, RabbitMQ, ActiveMQ, or MQSeries act as the repository and hub for messages. Producers and consumers connect to a message broker, not to each other. Traditional brokers are fairly static, but offerings like RabbitMQ and Apache Kafka can scale as needed. Messaging systems decouple producer from consumer. A producer or a consumer does not need to share the same location, exist in the same place or process, or even be available at the same time. These qualities are even *more* important in a cloud environment, where services are fluid and ephemeral. Cloud platforms support elasticity—they can grow and shrink as demand requires. Messaging systems are an ideal way to throttle load when systems are down and to load-balance when scale requires.

 Technologies like RabbitMQ and Apache Kafka are important, but they will add a cost to your operational overhead. Ideally, this competency should be managed by the platform and automated. If you're using Cloud Foundry, there are, for example, RabbitMQ services in the service catalog.

Event-Driven Architectures with Spring Integration

We've looked thus far at processing that we initiate, on our schedule. But the world doesn't run on our schedule: we are surrounded by events that drive everything we do. The logical windowing of data is valuable, but some data just can't be treated in terms of windows. Some data is continuous and connected to events in the real world. In this section we'll look at how to work with data driven by events.

When we think of events, most of us probably think of messaging technologies, like JMS, RabbitMQ, Apache Kafka, Tibco Rendezvous, or IBM MQSeries. These technologies let us connect different autonomous clients through messages sent to centralized middleware, in much the same way that email lets humans connect to each other. The message broker stores delivered messages until such time as the client can consume and respond to it (in much the same way as an email inbox does).

Most of these technologies have an API and a usable client that we can use. Spring has always had good low-level support for messaging technologies; you'll find sophisticated low-level support for the JMS API, AMQP (and brokers like RabbitMQ), Redis, and Apache Geode.

There are many types of events in the world, of course. Receiving an email is one example. Receiving a tweet is another. A new file in a directory? That's an event too. An XMPP-powered chat message? Also an event. Your MQTT-powered microwave sending a status update? That's also an event.

It's all a bit overwhelming! If you're looking at the landscape of different event sources out there, then you're (hopefully) seeing a lot of opportunity *and* complexity. Some of the complexity comes from the act of integration itself. How do you build a system that depends on events from these various systems? You might address integration in terms of point-to-point connections between the various event sources...but this will result eventually in *spaghetti architecture*. It's a mathematically poor idea, too, as every integration point needs a connection with every other one. It's a binomial coefficient: n(n-1) / 2. Thus, for 6 services you'd need 15 different point-to-point connections!

Instead, let's take a more structured approach to integration with Spring Integration. At the heart of Spring Integration are the Spring framework MessageChannel and Mes sage<T> types. A Message<T> object has a payload and a set of headers that provide metadata about the message payload itself. A MessageChannel is like a java.util.Queue; Message<T> objects flow through MessageChannel instances.

Spring Integration supports the integration of services and data across multiple, otherwise incompatible, systems. Conceptually, composing an integration flow is similar to composing a pipes-and-filters flow on a UNIX OS with stdin and stdout:

Example 10-1. An example of using the pipes-and-filters model to connect otherwise singly focused command-line utilities

```
cat input.txt |  grep ERROR | wc -l > output.txt
```

Here, we take data from a source (the file input.txt), pipe it to the grep command to filter the results and keep only the lines that contain the token ERROR. Then we pipe it to the wc utility to count how many lines there are. Then, the final count is written to an output file, output.txt. These components—cat, grep, and wc—know nothing of each other. They were not designed with each other in mind. Instead, they know only how to read from stdin and write to stdout. This normalization of data makes it very easy to compose complex solutions from simple atoms. In the example, the cat command turns the file data into data that any process aware of stdin can read. It *adapts* the inbound data into the normalized format: lines of strings on stdout. At the end, the redirect (>) operator turns the normalized data, lines of strings, into data on the filesystem. It *adapts* it. The pipe (|) character is used to signal that the output of one component should flow to the input of another.

A Spring Integration flow works the same way: data is normalized into Message<T> instances. Each Message<T> has a payload and headers—metadata about the payload in a Map<K,V>—that are the input and output of different messaging components. These messaging components are typically provided by Spring Integration, but it's easy to write and use your own. There are all manner of messaging components supporting all of the Enterprise Application Integration patterns (*http://www.enterprisein tegrationpatterns.com/*) (filters, routers, transformers, adapters, gateways, etc.). The Spring framework MessageChannel is a named conduit through which Message<T> flows between messaging components. They're pipes, and by default, they work sort of like a java.util.Queue. Data in, data out.

Messaging Endpoints

These MessageChannel objects are connected through messaging endpoints: Java objects that do different things with the messages. Spring Integration will do the right thing when you give it a Message<T>, or just a T for the various components. Spring Integration provides a component model that you might use, or a Java DSL. Each messaging endpoint in a Spring Integraton flow may produce an output value which is then sent to whatever is downstream, or `null`, which terminates processing.

Inbound gateways take incoming requests from external systems, process them as `Message<T>`, and send a reply. Outbound gateways take `Message<T>`, forward them to an external system, and await the response from that system. They support request and reply interactions.

An *inbound adapter* is a component that takes messages from the outside world and turns them into a Spring `Message<T>`. An *outbound adapter* does the same thing, in reverse; it takes a Spring `Message<T>` and delivers it as the message type expected by the downstream system. Spring Integration ships with a set of different adapters for technologies and protocols, including MQTT, Twitter, email, (S)FTP(S), XMPP, TCP/UDP, etc.

There are two types of inbound adapters: either a *polling adapter* or an *event-driven adapter*. The inbound polling adapter is configured to automatically pull at a certain interval or at a rate defined by an upstream message source.

A *gateway* is a component that handles both requests and replies. For example, an *inbound* gateway would take a message from the outside world, deliver it to Spring Integration, and then deliver a reply message back to the outside world; a typical HTTP flow might look like this. An *outbound* gateway would take a Spring integration message and deliver it to the outside world, then take the reply and deliver it back in the Spring integration. You might see this when using the RabbitMQ broker if you've specified a reply destination.

A *filter* is a component that applies some sort of condition to determine whether an incoming message should proceed. Think of a filter like an `if (...)` test in Java.

A *router* takes an incoming message and applies a test (any test you want) to determine where to send that message downstream. Think of a router as a switch statement for messages.

A *transformer* takes a message and does something with it, optionally enriching or changing it, and then it sends the message out.

A *splitter* takes a message and then, based on some property of the message, divides it into multiple smaller messages that are then forwarded downstream. For example, you might have an incoming message for an order and then forward a message for each line item in that order to some sort of fulfillment flow.

An *aggregator* takes multiple messages, correlated through some unique property, and synthesizes a message that is sent downstream.

The integration flow is aware of the system, but the involved components used in the integration don't need to be. This makes it easy to compose complex solutions from small, otherwise siloed services. The act of building a Spring Integration flow is rewarding in and of itself. It forces a logical decomposition of services; they must be able to communicate in terms of messages that contain payloads. The schema of the payload is the contract. This property is very useful in a distributed system.

From Simple Components, Complex Systems

Spring Integration supports *event-driven architectures* because it can help detect and then respond to events in the external world. For example, you can use Spring Integration to poll a filesystem every 10 seconds and publish a `Message<T>` whenever a new file appears. You can use Spring Integration to act as a listener to messages delivered to an Apache Kafka topic. The adapter handles responding to the external event, which frees you from worrying too much about originating the message and lets you focus on handling the message once it arrives. It's the integration equivalent of dependency injection.

Dependency injection leaves component code free of worries about resource initialization and acquisition, and leaves it free to focus on writing code with those dependencies. Where did the `javax.sql.DataSource` field come from? Who cares! Spring wired it in. It may have gotten it from a mock in a test, from JNDI in a classic application server, or from a configured Spring Boot bean. Component code remains ignorant of those details. You can explain dependency injection with the "Hollywood Principle": "Don't call me, I'll call you!"

Dependent objects are provided to an object, instead of the object having to initialize or look up the resource. This same principle applies to Spring Integration: code is written in such a way that it's ignorant of where messages are coming from. It simplifies development considerably.

So let's start a simple example that responds to new files appearing in a directory, logs the observed file, and then dynamically routes the payload to one of two possible flows based on a simple test, using a router.

We'll use the Spring Integration Java DSL, which works very nicely with lambdas in Java 8. Each `IntegrationFlow` chains components together implicitly. We can make this chaining explicit by providing connecting `MessageChannel` references, as shown in Example 10-2.

Example 10-2. An example of using the pipes-and-filters model to connect otherwise singularly focused command-line utilities

```
package eda;

import org.apache.commons.logging.Log;
import org.apache.commons.logging.LogFactory;
import org.springframework.beans.factory.annotation.Value;
```

```
import org.springframework.context.annotation.Bean;
import org.springframework.context.annotation.Configuration;
import org.springframework.integration.dsl.IntegrationFlow;
import org.springframework.integration.dsl.IntegrationFlows;
import org.springframework.integration.dsl.channel.MessageChannels;
import org.springframework.integration.dsl.file.Files;
import org.springframework.messaging.MessageChannel;

import java.io.File;

@Configuration
public class IntegrationConfiguration {

  private final Log log = LogFactory.getLog(getClass());

  @Bean
  IntegrationFlow etlFlow(
   @Value("${input-directory:${HOME}/Desktop/in}") File dir) {

   return IntegrationFlows
    ❶
     .from(Files.inboundAdapter(dir).autoCreateDirectory(true),
      consumer -> consumer.poller(spec -> spec.fixedRate(1000)))
      ❷
     .handle(File.class, (file, headers) -> {
      log.info("we noticed a new file, " + file);
      return file;
     })
      ❸
     .routeToRecipients(
      spec -> spec.recipient(csv(), msg -> hasExt(msg.getPayload(), ".csv"))
       .recipient(txt(), msg -> hasExt(msg.getPayload(), ".txt"))).get();
  }

  private boolean hasExt(Object f, String ext) {
   File file = File.class.cast(f);
   return file.getName().toLowerCase().endsWith(ext.toLowerCase());
  }

   ❹
  @Bean
  MessageChannel txt() {
   return MessageChannels.direct().get();
  }

   ❺
  @Bean
  MessageChannel csv() {
   return MessageChannels.direct().get();
  }

   ❻
```

```
@Bean
IntegrationFlow txtFlow() {
  return IntegrationFlows.from(txt()).handle(File.class, (f, h) -> {
    log.info("file is .txt!");
    return null;
  }).get();
}

❼
@Bean
IntegrationFlow csvFlow() {
  return IntegrationFlows.from(csv()).handle(File.class, (f, h) -> {
    log.info("file is .csv!");
    return null;
  }).get();
 }
}
```

❶ Configure a Spring Integration inbound File adapter. We also want to configure
    how the adapter consumes incoming messages and at what millisecond rate the
    poller that sweeps the directory should scan.

❷ This method announces that we've received a file, and then forwards the payload
    onward.

❸ Route the request to one of two possible integration flows, derived from the
    extension of the file, through well-known MessageChannel instances.

❹ The channel through which all files with the .txt extension will travel.

❺ The channel through which all files with the .csv extension will travel.

❻ The IntegrationFlow to handle files with .txt.

❼ The IntegrationFlow to handle files with .csv.

The channel is a logical decoupling; it doesn't matter what's on either end of the channel, so long as we have a pointer to it. Today the consumer that comes from a channel
might be a simple logging MessageHandler<T>, as in this example, but tomorrow it
might be a component that writes a message to Apache Kafka. We can also begin a
flow from the moment it arrives in a channel. How, exactly, it arrives in the channel is
irrelevant. We could accept requests from a REST API, or adapt messages coming in
from Apache Kafka, or monitor a directory. It doesn't matter so long as we somehow
adapt the incoming message into a java.io.File and submit it to the right channel.

Let's suppose we have a batch process that works on files. Traditionally, such a job
would run at a fixed time, on a scheduler like cron, perhaps. This introduces idle time

between runs, and that idle period delays the results we're looking for. We can use Spring Integration to kick off a batch job whenever a new `java.io.File` appears, instead. Spring Integration provides an inbound file adapter. We'll listen for messages coming from the inbound file adapter and then transform them into a message whose payload is a `JobLaunchRequest`. The `JobLaunchRequest` describes which `Job` to launch, and it describes the `JobParameters` for that job. Finally, the `JobLaunchRequest` is forwarded to a `JobLaunchingGateway`, which then produces as its output a `JobExecution` object that we inspect to decide where to route execution. If a job completes normally, we'll move the input file to a directory of completed jobs. Otherwise, we'll move the file to an error directory.

We'll have one main flow that forwards execution to one of two branches of execution, represented by two channels: `invalid` and `completed` (Example 10-3).

Example 10-3. The two MessageChannel instances

```
package edabatch;

import org.springframework.context.annotation.Bean;
import org.springframework.context.annotation.Configuration;
import org.springframework.integration.dsl.channel.MessageChannels;
import org.springframework.messaging.MessageChannel;

@Configuration
class BatchChannels {

  @Bean
  MessageChannel invalid() {
   return MessageChannels.direct().get();
  }

  @Bean
  MessageChannel completed() {
   return MessageChannels.direct().get();
  }

}
```

The main flow, called `etlFlow`, monitors a directory (`directory`) at a fixed rate and turns each event into a `JobLaunchRequest` (Example 10-4).

Example 10-4. The two EtlFlowConfiguration instances

```
package edabatch;

import org.springframework.batch.core.*;
import org.springframework.batch.core.launch.JobLauncher;
import org.springframework.batch.integration.launch.JobLaunchRequest;
```

```java
import org.springframework.batch.integration.launch.JobLaunchingGateway;
import org.springframework.beans.factory.annotation.Value;
import org.springframework.context.annotation.Bean;
import org.springframework.context.annotation.Configuration;
import org.springframework.integration.dsl.IntegrationFlow;
import org.springframework.integration.dsl.IntegrationFlows;
import org.springframework.integration.dsl.file.Files;
import org.springframework.integration.support.MessageBuilder;
import org.springframework.messaging.Message;

import java.io.File;

import static org.springframework.integration.file.FileHeaders.ORIGINAL_FILE;

@Configuration
class EtlFlowConfiguration {

    ❶
    @Bean
    IntegrationFlow etlFlow(
      @Value("${input-directory:${HOME}/Desktop/in}") File directory,
      BatchChannels c, JobLauncher launcher, Job job) {

      return IntegrationFlows
        .from(Files.inboundAdapter(directory).autoCreateDirectory(true),
          cs -> cs.poller(p -> p.fixedRate(1000)))
        .handle(
        File.class,
        (file, headers) -> {

          String absolutePath = file.getAbsolutePath();
               ❷
          JobParameters params = new JobParametersBuilder().addString("file",
            absolutePath).toJobParameters();

          return MessageBuilder.withPayload(new JobLaunchRequest(job, params))
            .setHeader(ORIGINAL_FILE, absolutePath)
            .copyHeadersIfAbsent(headers).build();
        })
           ❸
        .handle(new JobLaunchingGateway(launcher))
           ❹
        .routeToRecipients(
          spec -> spec.recipient(c.invalid(), this::notFinished).recipient(
          c.completed(), this::finished)).get();
    }

    private boolean finished(Message<?> msg) {
      Object payload = msg.getPayload();
      return JobExecution.class.cast(payload).getExitStatus()
        .equals(ExitStatus.COMPLETED);
    }
```

```
private boolean notFinished(Message<?> msg) {
 return !this.finished(msg);
 }

}
```

❶ This EtlFlowConfiguration starts off the same as in the previous example.

❷ Set up some JobParameters for our Spring Batch job using the JobParameters Builder.

❸ Forward the job and associated parameters to a JobLaunchingGateway.

❹ Test to see if the job exited normally by examining the JobExecution.

The last component in the Spring Integration flow is a router that examines the Exit Status from the Job and determines which directory the input file should be moved to. If the file was completed successfully, it will be routed to the completed channel. If there was an error or if the job terminated early for some reason, it will be routed to the invalid channel.

The FinishedFileFlowConfiguration configuration listens for incoming messages on the completed channel, moves its incoming payload (a java.io.File) to a comple ted directory, and then queries the table to which the data was written (Example 10-5).

Example 10-5. The FinishedFileFlowConfiguration instances

```
package edabatch;

import org.apache.commons.logging.Log;
import org.apache.commons.logging.LogFactory;
import org.springframework.batch.core.JobExecution;
import org.springframework.beans.factory.annotation.Value;
import org.springframework.context.annotation.Bean;
import org.springframework.context.annotation.Configuration;
import org.springframework.integration.dsl.IntegrationFlow;
import org.springframework.integration.dsl.IntegrationFlows;
import org.springframework.integration.file.FileHeaders;
import org.springframework.jdbc.core.JdbcTemplate;

import java.io.File;
import java.util.List;

import static edabatch.Utils.mv;

@Configuration
```

```
class FinishedFileFlowConfiguration {

 private Log log = LogFactory.getLog(getClass());

 @Bean
 IntegrationFlow finishedJobsFlow(BatchChannels channels,
  @Value("${completed-directory:${HOME}/Desktop/completed}") File finished,
  JdbcTemplate jdbcTemplate) {
  return IntegrationFlows
    .from(channels.completed())
    .handle(JobExecution.class,
      (je, headers) -> {
       String ogFileName = String.class.cast(headers
         .get(FileHeaders.ORIGINAL_FILE));
       File file = new File(ogFileName);
       mv(file, finished);
       List<Contact> contacts = jdbcTemplate.query(
         "select * from CONTACT",
         (rs, i) -> new Contact(
           rs.getBoolean("valid_email"),
           rs.getString("full_name"),
           rs.getString("email"),
           rs.getLong("id")));
       contacts.forEach(log::info);
       return null;
      }).get();
 }

}
```

The InvalidFileFlowConfiguration configuration listens for incoming messages on
the invalid channel, moves its incoming payload (a java.io.File) to an errors
directory, and then terminates the flow (Example 10-6).

Example 10-6. The InvalidFileFlowConfiguration instances

```
package edabatch;

import org.springframework.batch.core.JobExecution;
import org.springframework.beans.factory.annotation.Value;
import org.springframework.context.annotation.Bean;
import org.springframework.context.annotation.Configuration;
import org.springframework.integration.dsl.IntegrationFlow;
import org.springframework.integration.dsl.IntegrationFlows;
import org.springframework.integration.file.FileHeaders;

import java.io.File;

import static edabatch.Utils.mv;

@Configuration
```

```
class InvalidFileFlowConfiguration {

@Bean
IntegrationFlow invalidFileFlow(BatchChannels channels,
 @Value("${error-directory:${HOME}/Desktop/errors}") File errors) {
 return IntegrationFlows
   .from(channels.invalid())
   .handle(JobExecution.class,
     (je, headers) -> {
      String ogFileName = String.class.cast(headers
        .get(FileHeaders.ORIGINAL_FILE));
      File file = new File(ogFileName);
      mv(file, errors);
      return null;
     }).get();
 }

}
```

The `MessageChannel` definitions serve to decouple different integration flows. We're able to reuse common functionality and compose higher-order systems using only a channel as a connection. The `MessageChannel` is the interface.

Message Brokers, Bridges, the Competing Consumer Pattern, and Event Sourcing

The last example was fairly straightforward. It's a simple flow that works in terms of messages (events). We're able to begin processing as soon as possible without overwhelming the system. As our integration is built in terms of channels, and every component could consume or produce messages with a channel, it would be trivial to introduce a message broker in between the inbound file adapter and the node that actually launches the Spring Batch job. This would help us scale out the work across a cluster, like one powered by Cloud Foundry.

That said, you're not likely going to be integrating filesystems in a cloud native architecture. You will, however, probably have other, nontransactional event sources (message producers) and sinks (message consumers) with which you'll want to integrate.

We could use the saga pattern and design compensating transactions for every service with which we integrate and any possible failure conditions, but we might be able to get away with something simpler if we use a message broker. Message brokers are conceptually very simple: as messages are delivered to the broker, they're stored and delivered to connected consumers. If there are no connected consumers, the broker will store the messages and redeliver them upon connection of a consumer.

Message brokers typically offer two types of destinations (think of them as mailboxes): **publish-subscribe** and **point-to-point**.

Publish-Subscribe Destination

A *publish-subscribe* destination delivers one message to all connected consumers. It's a bit like broadcasting a message over a megaphone to a full room.

Publish-subscribe messaging supports event collaboration, wherein multiple systems keep their own view or perspective of the state of the world. As new events arrive from different components in the system, with updates to the state of domain objects, each system will react by updating its perspective view of the application's state.

Suppose you had a catalog of products. As new entries were added to the *ProductSer-vice*, it might publish an event describing the delta. The *SearchEngine* service might consume the messages and then update an index on a locally bound ElasticSearch service instance. The *InventoryService* might update data contained in a locally bound RDBMS service instance. The *RecommendationService* might decide to update data in a locally bound Neo4j service instance. These systems no longer need to *ask* the *Pro-ductService* for anything.

If you record every domain event in an ordered log, you have the ability to do tempo-ral queries by recreating the state of the system at any previous point in time. If any service should fail, its local state may be recreated entirely from the log. This practice is called *Event Sourcing*, and it's a very powerful tool when building distributed sys-tems.

Point-to-Point Destination

A *point-to-point* destination delivers one message to one consumer, even if there are multiple connected consumers. This is a bit like telling one person in a group a secret. If you connect multiple consumers and they all work as fast as they can to drain mes-sages from the point-to-point destination, you get something that resembles load bal-ancing: the work gets divided by the number of connected consumers. This approach, called the *competing consumers* pattern, simplifies load balancing work across multi-ple consumers. It's an ideal way to leverage the elasticity of a cloud computing envi-ronment like Cloud Foundry, where horizontal capacity is elastic and (virtually) infinite.

Message brokers also have their own, resource-local notion of a transaction. A pro-ducer may deliver a message and then, if necessary, withdraw it, effectively rolling the message back. A consumer may accept delivery of a message, attempt to do some-thing with it, and then acknowledge the delivery—or, if something should go wrong, return the message to the broker, effectively rolling back the delivery. *Eventually* both sides will agree upon the state. This is different than a distributed transaction in that the message broker introduces the variable of time, or temporal decoupling. In doing so, it simplifies the integration between services. This property makes it easier to rea-son about state in a distributed system. You can ensure that two otherwise nontransactional resources will *eventually* agree upon state. In this way, a message broker *bridges* the two otherwise nontransactional resources.

A message broker complicates the architecture by adding another moving part to the system. Message brokers have well-known recipes for disaster recovery, backups, and scale out. An organization will need to know how to do this, and then it can reuse that across all services. The alternative is that *every* service be forced to reinvent or, less desirably, go without these qualities. If you're using a platform like Cloud Foundry, which already manages the message broker for you, then using a message broker should be a *very* easy decision.

Logically, message brokers make a lot of sense as a way to connect different services. Spring Integration provides ample support here, with adapters that produce and consume messages from a diverse set of brokers.

Spring Cloud Stream

While Spring Integration is on solid footing to solve the problems of service-to-service communication with message brokers, it might seem a bit too clumsy for microservices. We want to support messaging with the same ease as we think about REST-based interactions with Spring. We're not going to connect our services using Twitter or email. More likely, we'll use RabbitMQ or Apache Kafka or similar message brokers with known interaction modes. We could explicitly configure inbound and outbound RabbitMQ or Apache Kafka adapters, of course. Instead, let's move up the stack a little bit, to simplify our work and remove the cognitive dissonance of configuring inbound and outbound adapters every time we want to work with another service.

Spring integration does a great job of decoupling components in terms of `Message Channel` objects. A `MessageChannel` is a nice level of indirection. From the perspective of our application logic, a channel represents a logical conduit to some downstream service that will route through a message broker.

In this section, we'll look at Spring Cloud Stream. Spring Cloud Stream sits atop Spring Integration, with the channel at the heart of the interaction model. It implies conventions and supports easy externalization of configuration. In exchange, it makes the common case of connecting services with a message broker much cleaner and more concise.

Let's have a look at a simple example. We'll build a producer and a consumer. The producer will expose a REST API endpoint that, when invoked, publishes a message into two channels: one for *broadcast*, or publish-subscribe-style messaging, and the other for *point-to-point* messaging. We'll then stand up a consumer to accept these incoming messages.

Spring Cloud Stream makes it easy to define channels that are then connected to messaging technologies. We can use *binder* implementations to—by convention—connect to a broker. In this example, we'll use RabbitMQ, a popular message broker that speaks the AMQP specification. The binder for Spring Cloud Stream's RabbitMQ support is `org.springframework.cloud:spring-cloud-starter-stream-rabbit`.

There are clients and bindings in dozens of languages, and this makes RabbitMQ (and the AMQP specification in general) a fine fit for integration across different languages and platforms. Spring Cloud Stream builds on Spring Integration (which provides the necessary inbound and outbound adapters), and Spring Integration in turn builds on Spring AMQP (which provides the low-level `AmqpOperations`, `RabbitTemplate`, a RabbitMQ `ConnectionFactory` implementation, etc.). Spring Boot auto-configures a `ConnectionFactory` based on defaults or properties. On a local machine with an unadulterated RabbitMQ instance, this application will work out of the box.

A Stream Producer

The centerpiece of Spring Cloud Stream is a *binding*. A binding defines logical references to other services through `MessageChannel` instances that we'll leave to Spring Cloud Stream to connect for us. From the perspective of our business logic, these downstream or upstream messaging-based services are unknowns on the other side of `MessageChannel` objects. We don't need to worry about how the connection is made, for the moment. Let's define two channels: one for broadcasting a greeting to all consumers and another for sending a greeting point-to-point, once, to whichever consumer happens to receive it first (Example 10-7).

Example 10-7. A simple MessageChannel-centric greetings producer

```
package stream.producer;

import org.springframework.cloud.stream.annotation.Output;
import org.springframework.messaging.MessageChannel;

public interface ProducerChannels {

❶
String DIRECT = "directGreetings";

String BROADCAST = "broadcastGreetings";

@Output(DIRECT)
❷
MessageChannel directGreetings();

@Output(BROADCAST)
MessageChannel broadcastGreetings();
}
```

❶ By default, the name of the stream (which we'll work with in other parts of the system) is based on the `MessageChannel` method itself. It is useful to provide a String constant in the interface so we can reference without any magic strings.

❷ Spring Cloud Stream provides two annotations: `@Output` and `@Input`. An `@Output` put annotation tells Spring Cloud Stream that messages put into the channel will be sent out (usually, and ultimately, through an outbound channel adapter in Spring Integration).

We need to give Spring Cloud Stream an idea of what to do with data sent into these channels, which we can do with some well-placed properties in the environment. Example 10-8 shows what our producer's `application.properties` looks like.

Example 10-8. A simple MessageChannel-centric greetings producer

```
spring.cloud.stream.bindings.broadcastGreetings.destination=greetings-pub-sub  ❶
spring.cloud.stream.bindings.directGreetings.destination=greetings-p2p

spring.rabbitmq.addresses=localhost  ❷
```

❶ In these two lines, the sections just after `spring.cloud.stream.bindings.` and just before `.destination` have to match the name of the Java `MessageChannel`. This is the application's local perspective on the service it's calling. The bit after the = sign is the agreed-upon rendezvous point for the producer and the consumer. Both sides need to specify the exact name here. This is the name of the destination in whatever broker we've configured.

❷ We're using Spring Boot's auto-configuration to create a RabbitMQ `Connection Factory`, which Spring Cloud Stream will depend on.

In Example 10-9, we'll look at a simple producer that stands up a REST API that then publishes messages to be observed in the consumer.

Example 10-9. A simple MessageChannel-centric greetings producer

```
package stream.producer.channels;

import org.springframework.beans.factory.annotation.Autowired;
import org.springframework.boot.SpringApplication;
import org.springframework.boot.autoconfigure.SpringBootApplication;
import org.springframework.cloud.stream.annotation.EnableBinding;
import org.springframework.http.ResponseEntity;
import org.springframework.messaging.MessageChannel;
import org.springframework.messaging.support.MessageBuilder;
import org.springframework.web.bind.annotation.PathVariable;
```

```
import org.springframework.web.bind.annotation.RequestMapping;
import org.springframework.web.bind.annotation.RestController;
import stream.producer.ProducerChannels;

@SpringBootApplication
@EnableBinding(ProducerChannels.class)
❶
public class StreamProducer {

 public static void main(String args[]) {
  SpringApplication.run(StreamProducer.class, args);
 }
}

@RestController
class GreetingProducer {

 private final MessageChannel broadcast, direct;

 ❷
 @Autowired
 GreetingProducer(ProducerChannels channels) {
  this.broadcast = channels.broadcastGreetings();
  this.direct = channels.directGreetings();
 }

 @RequestMapping("/hi/{name}")
 ResponseEntity<String> hi(@PathVariable String name) {
  String message = "Hello, " + name + "!";

  ❸
  this.direct.send(MessageBuilder.withPayload("Direct: " + message).build());

  this.broadcast.send(MessageBuilder.withPayload("Broadcast: " + message)
   .build());
  return ResponseEntity.ok(message);
 }
}
```

❶ The @EnableBinding annotation activates Spring Cloud Stream.

❷ We inject the hydrated ProducerChannels and then dereference the required channels in the constructor so that we can send messages whenever somebody makes an HTTP request at /hi/{name}.

❸ This is a regular Spring framework channel, so it's simple enough to use the Mes sageBuilder API to create a Message<T>.

Style matters, of course, so while we've reduced the cost of working with our downstream services to an interface, a few lines of property declarations and a few lines of messaging-centric channel manipulation, we *could* do better if we used Spring Integration's messaging gateway support. A messaging gateway, as a design pattern, is meant to hide the client from the messaging logic behind a service. From the client perspective, a gateway may seem like a regular object. This can be very convenient. You might define an interface and synchronous service today and then extract it out as a messaging gateway based implementation tomorrow, and nobody would be the wiser. Let's revisit our producer and, instead of sending messages directly with Spring Integration, let's send messages using a messaging gateway (Example 10-10).

Example 10-10. A messaging gateway producer implementation

```
package stream.producer.gateway;

import org.springframework.beans.factory.annotation.Autowired;
import org.springframework.boot.SpringApplication;
import org.springframework.boot.autoconfigure.SpringBootApplication;
import org.springframework.cloud.stream.annotation.EnableBinding;
import org.springframework.http.ResponseEntity;
import org.springframework.integration.annotation.Gateway;
import org.springframework.integration.annotation.IntegrationComponentScan;
import org.springframework.integration.annotation.MessagingGateway;
import org.springframework.web.bind.annotation.PathVariable;
import org.springframework.web.bind.annotation.RequestMapping;
import org.springframework.web.bind.annotation.RequestMethod;
import org.springframework.web.bind.annotation.RestController;
import stream.producer.ProducerChannels;


@SpringBootApplication
@EnableBinding(ProducerChannels.class)
❶
@IntegrationComponentScan
❷
public class StreamProducer {

  public static void main(String args[]) {
    SpringApplication.run(StreamProducer.class, args);
  }
}

❸
@MessagingGateway
interface GreetingGateway {

 @Gateway(requestChannel = ProducerChannels.BROADCAST)
 void broadcastGreet(String msg);

 @Gateway(requestChannel = ProducerChannels.DIRECT)
 void directGreet(String msg);
}
```

```
@RestController
class GreetingProducer {

  private final GreetingGateway gateway;

  ❹
  @Autowired
  GreetingProducer(GreetingGateway gateway) {
   this.gateway = gateway;
  }

  @RequestMapping(method = RequestMethod.GET, value = "/hi/{name}")
  ResponseEntity<?> hi(@PathVariable String name) {
   String message = "Hello, " + name + "!";
   this.gateway.directGreet("Direct: " + message);
   this.gateway.broadcastGreet("Broadcast: " + message);
   return ResponseEntity.ok(message);
  }
}
```

❶ The @EnableBinding annotation activates Spring Cloud Stream, as before.

❷ Many Spring frameworks register stereotype annotations for custom components, but Spring Integration can also turn interface definitions into beans, so we
need a custom annotation to activate Spring Integration's component scanning to
find our declarative, interface-based messaging gateway.

❸ The @MessagingGateway is one of the many messaging endpoints supported by
Spring Integration (as an alternative to the Java DSL, which we've used thus far).
Each method in the gateway is annotated with @Gateway, where we specify which
message channel the arguments to the method should go on. In this case, it'll be
as though we sent the message onto a channel and called .send(Mes
sage<String>) with the argument as a payload.

❹ The GreetingGateway is just a regular bean, as far as the rest of our business
logic is concerned.

A Stream Consumer

On the other side, we want to accept delivery of messages and log them out. We'll
create channels using an interface. It's worth reiterating: these channel names *do not*
have to line up with the names on the producer side—only the names of the destinations in the brokers do (Example 10-11).

Example 10-11. The channels for incoming greetings

```
package stream.consumer;

import org.springframework.cloud.stream.annotation.Input;
import org.springframework.messaging.SubscribableChannel;

public interface ConsumerChannels {

 String DIRECTED = "directed";

 String BROADCASTS = "broadcasts";

 ❶
 @Input(DIRECTED)
 SubscribableChannel directed();

 @Input(BROADCASTS)
 SubscribableChannel broadcasts();

}
```

❶ The only thing worth noting here is that these channels are annotated with `@Input` (naturally!) and that they return a `MessageChannel` subtype that supports *subscribing* to incoming messages, `SubscribableChannel`.

Remember, all bindings in Spring Cloud Stream are publish-subscribe by default. We can achieve the effect of exclusivity and a direct connection with a consumer group. For example: given, say, 10 instances of a consumer in a group named foo, only 1 instance would see a message delivered to it. In a distributed system, we can't be assured that a service will always be running, so we'll take advantage of *durable subscriptions* to ensure that messages are redelivered as soon as a consumer reconnects to the broker (Example 10-12).

Example 10-12. The application.properties for our consumer

```
spring.cloud.stream.bindings.broadcasts.destination=greetings-pub-sub  ❶

spring.cloud.stream.bindings.directed.destination=greetings-p2p  ❷
spring.cloud.stream.bindings.directed.group=greetings-p2p-group
spring.cloud.stream.bindings.directed.durableSubscription=true
server.port=0
spring.rabbitmq.addresses=localhost
```

❶ This should look fairly familiar, given what we just covered in the producer.

❷ Here we configure a destination, as before, but we *also* give our directed consumer an exclusive consumer group. Only one node among all the active consumers in the group `greetings-p2p-group` will see an incoming message. We ensure that the broker will store and redeliver failed messages as soon as a consumer is reconnected by specifying that the binding has a `durableSubscription`.

Finally, in Example 10-13, let's look at the Spring Integration Java DSL-based consumer. This should look very familiar.

Example 10-13. A consumer driven by the Spring Integration Java DSL

```
package stream.consumer.integration;

import org.apache.commons.logging.Log;
import org.apache.commons.logging.LogFactory;
import org.springframework.boot.SpringApplication;
import org.springframework.boot.autoconfigure.SpringBootApplication;
import org.springframework.cloud.stream.annotation.EnableBinding;
import org.springframework.context.annotation.Bean;
import org.springframework.integration.dsl.IntegrationFlow;
import org.springframework.integration.dsl.IntegrationFlows;
import org.springframework.messaging.SubscribableChannel;
import stream.consumer.ConsumerChannels;

@SpringBootApplication
@EnableBinding(ConsumerChannels.class)
❶
public class StreamConsumer {

 public static void main(String args[]) {
  SpringApplication.run(StreamConsumer.class, args);
 }

❷
 private IntegrationFlow incomingMessageFlow(SubscribableChannel incoming,
  String prefix) {

  Log log = LogFactory.getLog(getClass());

  return IntegrationFlows
   .from(incoming)
   .transform(String.class, String::toUpperCase)
   .handle(
   String.class,
   (greeting, headers) -> {
    log.info("greeting received in IntegrationFlow (" + prefix + "): "
     + greeting);
    return null;
   }).get();
 }

 @Bean
```

```
IntegrationFlow direct(ConsumerChannels channels) {
  return incomingMessageFlow(channels.directed(), "directed");
}

@Bean
IntegrationFlow broadcast(ConsumerChannels channels) {
  return incomingMessageFlow(channels.broadcasts(), "broadcast");
}
}
```

❶ As before, we see @EnableBinding activates the consumer channels.

❷ This @Configuration class defines two IntegrationFlow flows that do basically
   the same thing: take the incoming message, transform it by capitalizing it, and
   then log it. One flow listens for the broadcasted greetings and the other for the
   direct, point-to-point greetings. We stop processing by returning null in the final
   component in the chain.

Try it out: run one instance of one of the producer nodes (whichever one) and run
three instances of the consumer. Visit http://localhost:8080/hi/World and
observe in the consumers' logs that all three have the message sent to the broadcast
channel; one (although there's no telling which, so check all of the consoles) will have
the message sent to the direct channel. Raise the stakes by killing all of the consumer
nodes, then visiting http://localhost:8080/hi/Again. All the consumers are down,
but we specified that the point-to-point connection is durable, so as soon as you
restart one of the consumers you'll see the direct message arrive and be logged to the
console.

Summary

Messaging provides a communications channel for complex distributed interactions.
We'll see in later chapters that you can connect batch processing solutions, workflow
engines, and services in terms of a messaging substrate.

## CHAPTER 11

Batch Processes and Tasks

The cloud gives us unprecedented scale. It costs virtually nothing to spin up new application instances to accommodate demand, and once the dust has settled, it's easy to scale down. This means that, as long as the work at hand lends itself to parallelization, we improve our efficiency with scale. Many problems are *embarrassingly parallel*; they require no coordination between nodes. Others may require some coordination. Both of these types of workloads are ideal for a cloud computing environment, while others are inherently serial. For work that is not particularly parallelized, a cloud computing environment is ideal for horizontally scaling computation to multiple nodes. In this chapter, we will look at a few different ways, both old and new, to ingest and process data using microservices.

Batch Workloads

Batch processing has a long history. *Batch processing* refers to the idea that a program processes *batches* of input data at the same time. Historically, batch processing is a more efficient way of utilizing computing resources. The approach amortizes the cost of a set of machines by prioritizing windows of interactive work—when operators are using the machines—and noninteractive work in the evening hours, when the machine would otherwise be idle. Today, in the era of the cloud, with virtually infinite and ephemeral computing capacity, efficient machine utilization isn't a particularly compelling reason to adapt batch processing.

Batch processing is also attractive when working with large data sets. Sequential data —SQL data, .csv files, etc., in particular—lends itself to being processed in batches. Expensive resources, like files, SQL table cursors, and transactions may be preserved over a chunk of data, allowing processing to continue more quickly.

Batch processing supports the logical notion of a *window*—an upper and lower bound that delimits one set of data from another. Perhaps the window is temporal: all records from the last 60 minutes, or all logs from the last 24 hours. Perhaps the window is logical: the first 1,000 records, or all the records with a certain property.

If the dataset being processed is too large to fit into memory, then it's possible to process it in smaller chunks. A chunk is an efficient (albeit resource-centric) division of a batch of data. Suppose you want to visit every record in a product sales database that spans over 20 million rows. Without paging, executing SELECT * FROM PRODUCT_SALES may cause the entire dataset to be loaded into memory, which could quickly overwhelm the system. Paging through this large dataset is far more efficient, loading only a thousand (or ten thousand!) records at a time. Process chunks either sequentially or in parallel, moving forward until eventually visiting all records of a large query—without having to load everything into memory at the same time.

Batch provides processing efficiencies, if your system is able to tolerate stale data. Many systems fit into this category: for example, a weekly sales report won't need to calculate last week's sales until the end of the week.

Spring Batch

Spring Batch is a framework that's designed to support processing large volumes of records. Spring Batch includes logging/tracing, transaction management, job processing statistics, job restart, skip, and resource management. It has become an industry standard for batch processing on the JVM.

At the heart of Spring Batch is the notion of a job—which in turn might have multiple steps. Each step would then provide a context to an optional ItemReader, ItemProcessor, and ItemWriter (Figure 11-1).

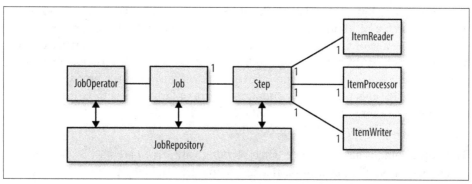

Figure 11-1. The domain of a Spring Batch job

Batch jobs have multiple steps. A step is meant to do some sort of preparation, or staging, of data before it's sent off to the next step. You may guide the flow of data from one step to another with routing logic: conditions, concurrence, and basic loop-ing. Steps might also define generic business functionality in a *tasklet*. In this case, you're using Spring Batch to orchestrate the *sequence* of an execution. Steps may extend `ItemReader`, `ItemProcessor`, and `ItemWriter` implementations for more defined processing.

An `ItemReader` takes input from the outside world (`.csv` or XML documents, SQL databases, directories, etc.) and adapts it into something that we can work with logi-cally in a job: an *item*. The item can be anything. An item could be a record from a database or a paragraph from a text file, a record from a `.csv` file, or a stanza of an XML document. Spring Batch provides useful, out-of-the-box `ItemReader` imple-mentations; `ItemReader` implementations read one item at a time, but accumulate the resulting items in a buffer that matches a specified *chunk* size.

If an `ItemProcessor` is specified, then it will be given each item from the `ItemReader`. An `ItemProcessor` is meant to handle processing and transformation: data goes in, data goes out. An `ItemProcessor` is an ideal place for any staging or validation—or general-purpose business logic not specifically concerned with input and output.

If an `ItemWriter` is specified, then it will be given the *accumulated* (not individual) items from the `ItemProcessor` (if so configured) or the `ItemReader`. The `ItemWriter` writes the accumulated chunk of items to a resource like a database or a file. The `Item Writer` writes as many as it can, up to the specified chunk size, per write.

This is what we mean when we talk about *batch* processing. Writing batches of items is more efficient for most types of I/O. It becomes more efficient to write batches of lines in a buffer, and much more efficient to batch the writes to a database.

Our First Batch Job

Let's look first at a high-level `Job` and the flow of the configured `Step` instances (Example 11-1).

Example 11-1. A trivial Job with three Step instances

```
package processing;

import org.springframework.batch.core.Job;
import org.springframework.batch.core.Step;
import org.springframework.batch.core.configuration.annotation.JobBuilderFactory;
import org.springframework.batch.core.configuration.annotation.StepBuilderFactory;
import org.springframework.batch.core.launch.support.RunIdIncrementer;
import org.springframework.context.annotation.Bean;
import org.springframework.context.annotation.Configuration;
import org.springframework.web.client.HttpStatusCodeException;
import processing.email.InvalidEmailException;
```

```
import java.util.Map;

@Configuration
class BatchConfiguration {

  ❶
  @Bean
  Job etl(JobBuilderFactory jbf, StepBuilderFactory sbf,
    Step1Configuration step1, ❷
    Step2Configuration step2, Step3Configuration step3) throws Exception {

    Step setup = sbf.get("clean-contact-table").tasklet(step1.tasklet(null)) ❸
      .build();

    Step s2 = sbf.get("file-db").<Person, Person>chunk(1000)
      ❹
      .faultTolerant()
      ❺
      .skip(InvalidEmailException.class).retry(HttpStatusCodeException.class)
      .retryLimit(2).reader(step2.fileReader(null)) ❻
      .processor(step2.emailValidatingProcessor(null)) ❼
      .writer(step2.jdbcWriter(null)) ❽
      .build();

    ❾
    Step s3 = sbf.get("db-file")
      .<Map<Integer, Integer>, Map<Integer, Integer>>chunk(100)
      .reader(step3.jdbcReader(null)).writer(step3.fileWriter(null)).build();

    return jbf.get("etl").incrementer(new RunIdIncrementer()) ❿
      .start(setup) ⓫
      .next(s2).next(s3).build(); ⓬
  }
}
```

❶ Define a Spring Batch Job using the `JobBuilderFactory` and `StepBuilderFac` tory.

❷ We also need beans for each step, so those have been defined in configuration classes and injected to be easily dereferenced.

❸ The first `Step` will use a `Tasklet`—a sort of free-form callback in which you can do anything. You describe when it's executed relative to the rest of the job by including it in a `Step`.

❹ We want to write 10 records at a time to the configured `ItemWriter`.

❺ We want to handle possible failures, so we configure the job's skip policy (on what exceptions an individual record should be skipped) and retry policy (on what exceptions should the step be retried for a given item and how many times). Spring Batch gives you a lot of knobs and levers here so that you don't have to abort the whole job just because of a single record with malformed data.

❻ Here we dereference the FlatFileItemReader from Step1Configuration. The ItemReader reads data from a .csv file and turns it into a Person POJO. The @Bean definition expects parameters, but Spring will provide those. It's fine to call the method with null arguments, as the bean will have already been created (with the container-provided parameters) and the return value of the method will be the cached, pre-created instance.

❼ The ItemProcessor is an ideal place to insert a call to a web service to validate that the email on the Person record is valid.

❽ Dereference an ItemWriter to write to a JDBC DataSource.

❾ This step runs a query against the just-persisted data from the first step, calculates how frequently records have a given age, and then writes those calculations to an output .csv.

❿ A Spring Batch Job is parameterized. These parameters contribute to the *identity* of the job. This identity is maintained in the metadata tables for your database. In this example, the metadata tables are being persisted in MySQL. If we attempt to start the same Job with the same parameters twice, it'll refuse to run, as it's already *seen* the job before, and recorded as much in the metadata tables. Here, we configure a RunIdIncrementer that derives a new key by incrementing an existing one (called the run.id parameter) if it already exists.

⓫ Now we string together the flow of the steps in the job, starting with the setup step, and continuing to the s1 step and the s3 step.

⓬ Finally, build the Job.

Let's say we run the job and something goes wrong: a read fails and the job aborts. Spring Batch will run through the configured retry and skip policies and attempt to carry on. If the job should fail, its progress will be recorded in the metadata tables, and an operator can then decide to intervene and possibly restart (as opposed to start another, duplicate instance) the job. The job will need to resume where it left off. This is possible, as some ItemReader implementations read stateful resources whose progress can be recorded, like a file.

This job is not particularly performant. As configured, it will read from the Item Reader in a single thread, serially. We could configure a TaskExecutor implementation for the Job, and Spring Batch will read concurrently, effectively dividing the read time by however many threads the configured TaskExecutor supports.

 You can retry failed jobs with recorded offsets *or* you can parallelize the reads with a TaskExecutor, but *not* both! This is because the offset is stored in a thread local and so would end up corrupting the values observed in other threads.

Spring Batch is stateful; it keeps metadata tables for all of the jobs running in a database. The database records, among other things, how far along the job is, what its exit code is, whether it skipped certain rows (and whether that aborted the job or it was just skipped). Operators (or autonomous agents) may use this information to decide whether to rerun the job or to intervene manually.

It's dead simple to get everything running. When the Spring Boot auto-configuration for Spring Batch kicks in, it looks for a DataSource and attempts to create the appropriate metadata tables based on schema on the classpath, automatically (Example 11-2).

Example 11-2. The Spring Batch metadata tables in MySQL

```
mysql> show tables;
+------------------------------+
| Tables_in_batch              |
+------------------------------+
| BATCH_JOB_EXECUTION          |
| BATCH_JOB_EXECUTION_CONTEXT  |
| BATCH_JOB_EXECUTION_PARAMS   |
| BATCH_JOB_EXECUTION_SEQ      |
| BATCH_JOB_INSTANCE           |
| BATCH_JOB_SEQ                |
| BATCH_STEP_EXECUTION         |
| BATCH_STEP_EXECUTION_CONTEXT |
| BATCH_STEP_EXECUTION_SEQ     |
+------------------------------+
9 rows in set (0.00 sec)
```

In the example, we configure two levels of fault tolerance: a certain step could be retried two times before it's considered an error. We use a third-party web service, which may or may not be available. You can simulate the service's availability by turning off your machine's internet connection. You'll observe that it'll fail to connect, throw an HttpStatusCodeException subclass, and then be retried. We also want to skip records that aren't validated, so we've configured a skip policy that, whenever an exception is thrown that can be assigned to the InvalidEmailException type, skips the processing on that row.

Let's inspect the configuration for the individual steps. First, the setup step (Example 11-3).

Example 11-3. Configure the first Step, which has only a Tasklet

```
package processing;

import org.apache.commons.logging.Log;
import org.apache.commons.logging.LogFactory;
import org.springframework.batch.core.step.tasklet.Tasklet;
import org.springframework.batch.repeat.RepeatStatus;
import org.springframework.context.annotation.Bean;
import org.springframework.context.annotation.Configuration;
import org.springframework.jdbc.core.JdbcTemplate;

@Configuration
class Step1Configuration {

 @Bean
 Tasklet tasklet(JdbcTemplate jdbcTemplate) {

  Log log = LogFactory.getLog(getClass());

  return (contribution, chunkContext) -> { ❶
   log.info("starting the ETL job.");
   jdbcTemplate.update("delete from PEOPLE");
   return RepeatStatus.FINISHED;
  };
 }
}
```

❶ The Tasklet is a general-purpose callback in which you can do anything. In this case, we stage the PEOPLE table by deleting any data.

The Tasklet stages the table for the second step, which reads data from an input file, validates the email, and then writes the results our freshly cleared database table. This step ingests data from a .csv file with three columns: a person's name, age, and email (Example 11-4).

Example 11-4. The contents of a .csv file to ingest

```
tam mie,30,tammie@email.com
srinivas,35,srinivas@email.com
lois,53,lois@email.com
bob,26,bob@email.com
jane,18,jane@email.com
```

```
jennifer,20,jennifer@email.com
luan,34,luan@email.com
toby,24,toby@email.com
toby,24,toby@email.com
...
```

This step demonstrates configuring a typical `ItemReader`, `ItemProcessor`, and `Item Writer` (Example 11-5).

Example 11-5. Read records from a .csv file and load them into a database table

```
package processing;

import org.springframework.batch.core.configuration.annotation.StepScope;
import org.springframework.batch.item.ItemProcessor;
import org.springframework.batch.item.database.JdbcBatchItemWriter;
import org.springframework.batch.item.database.builder.JdbcBatchItemWriterBuilder;
import org.springframework.batch.item.file.FlatFileItemReader;
import org.springframework.batch.item.file.builder.FlatFileItemReaderBuilder;
import org.springframework.beans.factory.annotation.Value;
import org.springframework.context.annotation.Bean;
import org.springframework.context.annotation.Configuration;
import org.springframework.core.io.Resource;
import processing.email.EmailValidationService;
import processing.email.InvalidEmailException;

import javax.sql.DataSource;

@Configuration
class Step2Configuration {

  @Bean
  @StepScope
  ❶
  FlatFileItemReader<Person> fileReader(
    @Value("file://#{jobParameters['input']}") Resource in) ❷
    throws Exception {

    ❸
    return new FlatFileItemReaderBuilder<Person>().name("file-reader")
      .resource(in).targetType(Person.class).delimited().delimiter(",")
      .names(new String[] { "firstName", "age", "email" }).build();
  }

  @Bean
  ItemProcessor<Person, Person> emailValidatingProcessor(
    EmailValidationService emailValidator) { ❹
    return item -> {
      String email = item.getEmail();
      if (!emailValidator.isEmailValid(email)) {
        throw new InvalidEmailException(email);
```

```
    }
    return item;
  };
}

@Bean
JdbcBatchItemWriter<Person> jdbcWriter(DataSource ds) { ❺
  return new JdbcBatchItemWriterBuilder<Person>()
    .dataSource(ds)
    .sql(
    "insert into PEOPLE( AGE, FIRST_NAME, EMAIL)"
    + " values (:age, :firstName, :email)").beanMapped().build();
  }
}
```

❶ Beans annotated with @StepScope are not singletons; they're created anew each time an instance of the job is run.

❷ The @Value uses the Spring Expression Language to obtain the input job parameter from the Spring Batch jobParameters context. This is a common practice in batch jobs: you might run the job today pointing to a file reflecting today's date, and run the same job tomorrow with a different file for a different date.

❸ Spring Batch's Java configuration DSL provides convenient builder APIs to configure common ItemReader and ItemWriter implementations. Here, we configure an ItemReader that reads a comma-separated line from the in file and maps the columns to names that in turn map to the fields on our Person POJO. The fields are then overlaid on an instance of the Person POJO, and that Person is returned from the ItemReader to be accumulated.

❹ The custom ItemProcessor simply delegates to our EmailValidationService implementation, which in turn calls a REST API.

❺ The JdbcBatchItemWriter takes the results of the ItemProcessor<Person,Person> and writes it to the underlying SQL datastore using a SQL statement that we provide. The named parameters for the SQL statement correspond to the Java-Bean properties on the Person POJO instance being produced from the ItemProcessor.

The ingest is now complete. In the final step we'll analyze the results, identifying how common a given age is among the records ingested (Example 11-6).

Example 11-6. Analyze the data and report the results to an output file

```
package processing;
```

```
import org.springframework.batch.core.configuration.annotation.StepScope;
import org.springframework.batch.item.database.JdbcCursorItemReader;
import org.springframework.batch.item.database.builder.JdbcCursorItemReaderBuilder;
import org.springframework.batch.item.file.FlatFileItemWriter;
import org.springframework.batch.item.file.builder.FlatFileItemWriterBuilder;
import org.springframework.batch.item.file.transform.DelimitedLineAggregator;
import org.springframework.beans.factory.annotation.Value;
import org.springframework.context.annotation.Bean;
import org.springframework.context.annotation.Configuration;
import org.springframework.core.io.Resource;

import javax.sql.DataSource;
import java.util.Collections;
import java.util.Map;

@Configuration
class Step3Configuration {

  ❶
  @Bean
  JdbcCursorItemReader<Map<Integer, Integer>> jdbcReader(DataSource dataSource) {
    return new JdbcCursorItemReaderBuilder<Map<Integer, Integer>>()
      .dataSource(dataSource)
      .name("jdbc-reader")
      .sql("select COUNT(age) c, age a from PEOPLE group by age")
      .rowMapper(
        (rs, i) -> Collections.singletonMap(rs.getInt("a"), rs.getInt("c")))
      .build();
  }

  ❷
  @Bean
  @StepScope
  FlatFileItemWriter<Map<Integer, Integer>> fileWriter(
    @Value("file://#{jobParameters['output']}") Resource out) {
    //@formatter:off
    DelimitedLineAggregator<Map<Integer, Integer>> aggregator =
      new DelimitedLineAggregator<Map<Integer, Integer>>() {
      {
        setDelimiter(",");
        setFieldExtractor(ageAndCount -> {
          Map.Entry<Integer, Integer> next = ageAndCount.entrySet().iterator()
            .next();
          return new Object[] { next.getKey(), next.getValue() };
        });
      }
    };
    //@formatter:on

    return new FlatFileItemWriterBuilder<Map<Integer, Integer>>()
      .name("file-writer").resource(out).lineAggregator(aggregator).build();
```

```
    }
}
```

❶ The `JdbcCursorItemReader` executes a query and then visits every result in the result set. Using the same `RowMapper<T>` used by Spring Framework's `JdbcTem plate`, it maps each row into an object that we want for the processor and/or writer: a single key `Map<Integer,Integer>` that reflects an age, and a count of how frequent that age is in the result set.

❷ The writer is stateful, and needs to be recreated on every run of the `Job`, because each job writes the results to a differently named file. The `FlatFileItemWriter` needs a `LineAggregator` instance to figure out how to turn the incoming POJO (our `Map<Integer,Integer>`) and turn it into columns to be written to an output .csv file.

Now all that's needed is to run it! Spring Boot's auto-configuration will run the job for us, on startup, by default. This job requires parameters (`input` and `output`), though, so we've disabled the default behavior and explicitly launched the job in a `CommandLi neRunner` instance (Example 11-7).

Example 11-7. The entry point into our batch application

```
package processing;

import org.springframework.batch.core.Job;
import org.springframework.batch.core.JobParametersBuilder;
import org.springframework.batch.core.configuration.annotation.EnableBatchProcessing;
import org.springframework.batch.core.launch.JobLauncher;
import org.springframework.beans.factory.annotation.Value;
import org.springframework.boot.CommandLineRunner;
import org.springframework.boot.SpringApplication;
import org.springframework.boot.autoconfigure.SpringBootApplication;
import org.springframework.context.annotation.Bean;
import org.springframework.jdbc.core.JdbcTemplate;
import org.springframework.web.client.RestTemplate;

import javax.sql.DataSource;
import java.io.File;

@EnableBatchProcessing
@SpringBootApplication
public class BatchApplication {

 public static void main(String[] args) {
  SpringApplication.run(BatchApplication.class, args);
 }

 @Bean
```

```
RestTemplate restTemplate() {
  return new RestTemplate();
}

@Bean
JdbcTemplate jdbcTemplate(DataSource dataSource) {
  return new JdbcTemplate(dataSource);
}

❶
@Bean
CommandLineRunner run(JobLauncher launcher, Job job,
  @Value("${user.home}") String home) {
  return args -> launcher.run(job,
    new JobParametersBuilder().addString("input", path(home, "in.csv"))
     .addString("output", path(home, "out.csv")).toJobParameters());
}

private String path(String home, String fileName) {
  return new File(home, fileName).getAbsolutePath();
}
}
```

❶ The `CommandLineRunner` runs when the application starts up. In it, we just hard-code some path references pointing to the local filesystem and pass those in as `JobParameter` instances.

The `Job` will run synchronously by default. The `JobLauncher#run` method returns a `JobExecution` that you can use to interrogate the status of the job once it completes. If the configured `JobLauncher` has a `TaskExecutor`, you can run the job asynchronously.

Spring Batch is designed to safely handle large amounts of data, though so far we've only looked at a single node. Later, we'll look at how to partition the processing of a Spring Batch `Job` with *"Remote Partitioning a Spring Batch Job with Messaging" on page 366.*

Spring Cloud Task is a generic abstraction designed to manage (and make observable) processes that run to completion and then terminate. We'll look at it later, but suffice it to say that it works with any Spring Boot-based service that defines an implementation of `CommandLineRunner` or `ApplicationRunner`, both of which are simple callback interfaces that, when perceived on a Spring bean, are given a callback with the application's `String [] args` array from the `main(String args[])` method. Spring Boot automatically configures a `CommandLineRunner` that runs any existing Spring Batch `Job` instances in the Spring application context. So our Spring Batch jobs are *already* prime candidates to be run and managed as jobs with Spring Cloud Task! We'll look at this more when we discuss *"Task Management" on page 375.*

Scheduling

One question that often comes up here is, "How do I schedule these jobs?" If your jobs are fat-`.jar`-based deployables that draw their configuration from ambient configuration sources like command-line parameters or environment variables, then it might be enough to just use good ol' `cron` if you only have a single node.

If you want finer-grained control over the way your jobs are scheduled, you could just use the `ScheduledExecutorService` in the JDK, or even move up the abstraction a bit and leverage Spring's `@Scheduled` annotation, which in turn delegates to a `java.util.concurrent.Executor` instance. The main flaw with this approach is that there's no bookkeeping done on whether a job has been run or not; there's no built-in notion of a cluster. What happens if the node running a job should die? Will it get replaced and restarted on another node? What if the node that died should somehow be restored? How do you avoid the classic split-brain problem, where two nodes, each operating under the assumption that it is the leader, end up running concurrently?

There are commercial schedulers like BMC, Flux Scheduler, or Autosys. These tools are powerful enough to schedule workloads, no matter what the job type, across a cluster; they work, although perhaps not as readily as you'd hope in a cloud environment. If you want more control over the scheduling and life cycle of your jobs, you might check out Spring's integration with the the Quartz Enterprise Job scheduler (*http://www.quartz-scheduler.org/*). Quartz runs well in a cluster and should have what you need to get the job done. It's also open source and easy enough to get working in a cloud environment.

Another approach here might be to use *leadership election* to manage the promotion and demotion of leader nodes in a cluster. The leader node would need to be stateful, or risk running the same work twice. Spring Integration has an abstraction to support uses cases around leadership election and distributed locks, with implementations delegating to Apache Zookeeper, Hazelcast, and others. It makes it easy to transactionally rotate one node out of leadership and another one in. It provides implementations that work with Apache Zookeeper, Hazelcast, and Redis. Such a leader node would farm work to other nodes in a cluster, on a schedule. The communication between nodes could be something as simple as messaging. We'll explore messaging a little later in this chapter.

There are many answers here, but it's worth underscoring that it's not a particularly interesting question, as many workloads today are event-driven, not schedule-driven.

Remote Partitioning a Spring Batch Job with Messaging

Earlier, we saw that the `TaskExecutor` makes it easy to parallelize the reads in a Spring Batch `Job`. Spring Batch also supports parallelizing the writes through two mechanisms, *remote partitioning* and *remote chunking*.

Functionally, both remote partitioning and remote chunking forward control of a single step to another node in a cluster, typically connected through a messaging substrate (connected through Spring Framework `MessageChannel` instances).

Remote partitioning publishes a message to another node containing the range of records (e.g., 0–100, 101–200, etc.) to be read. There, the actual `ItemReader`, `ItemPro cessor`, and/or `ItemWriter` are run. This approach requires that the worker node have full access to all the resources of the leader node. If the worker node is to read a range of records from a file, for example, then it would need access to that file. The statuses returned from the configured worker nodes are aggregated by the leader node. So, if your job is I/O-bound in the `ItemReader` and `ItemWriter`, prefer remote partitioning.

Remote chunking is similar to remote partitioning, except that data is read on the leader node and sent over the wire to the leader node for processing. The results of the processing are then sent *back* to the leader node to be written. So if your job is CPU-bound in an `ItemProcessor`, prefer remote chunking.

Both remote chunking and remote partitioning lend themselves to the elasticity of a platform like Cloud Foundry. You can spin up as many nodes as you want to handle processing, let the job run, then spin down.

 Spring Batch lead Michael Minella does a good job explaining all this in detail in a 2012 talk for the Chicago Java Users Group (*https://www.youtube.com/watch?v=CYTj5YT7CZU*).

Batch processing is almost always I/O-bound, so we find more applications for remote partitioning than remote chunking (though your mileage may vary). Let's look at an example. In order for remote partitioning to work, both the leader and the worker node need access to the Spring Batch `JobRepository`, which owns the state behind different instances of Spring Batch instances. The `JobRepository`, in turn, needs a few other components. So any remote partitioning application will have code that lives only on the worker nodes, code that lives only on the leader node, and code that lives in both. Thankfully, Spring provides a natural mechanism for enforcing this division within a single code base: *profiles*! Profiles let us tag certain objects and conditionally, at runtime, toggle those objects on or off (Example 11-8).

Example 11-8. We've defined a set of profiles for this application

```
package partition;

public class Profiles {

  public static final String WORKER_PROFILE = "worker"; ❶

  public static final String LEADER_PROFILE = "!" + WORKER_PROFILE; ❷
}
```

❶ The profile for the worker nodes.

❷ The profile that is active, as long as the `worker` profile is *not* active.

In a remote partitioning application, there are one or more worker nodes and a leader node. The leader node coordinates with the worker nodes using messaging. Specifically, it communicates with worker nodes over `MessageChannel` instances, which may be Spring Cloud Stream-powered `MessageChannel` instances connected to message brokers like RabbitMQ or Apache Kafka.

Let's look at a simple Spring Batch `Job` that reads all the records in one table (our `PEOPLE` table) and copies them to another empty table called `NEW_PEOPLE`. This is a simple example with one step, so we aren't distracted by the job's domain and can focus on the components required to achieve the solution.

The entry point into the application activates Spring Batch and Spring Integration, and configures a `JdbcTemplate` and a default poller to be used for Spring Integration components that periodically poll a downstream component (Example 11-9).

Example 11-9. The entry point into the application

```
package partition;

import org.springframework.batch.core.configuration.annotation.EnableBatchProcessing;
import org.springframework.boot.SpringApplication;
import org.springframework.boot.autoconfigure.SpringBootApplication;
import org.springframework.context.annotation.Bean;
import org.springframework.integration.annotation.IntegrationComponentScan;
import org.springframework.integration.dsl.core.Pollers;
import org.springframework.integration.scheduling.PollerMetadata;
import org.springframework.jdbc.core.JdbcTemplate;

import javax.sql.DataSource;
import java.util.concurrent.TimeUnit;

@EnableBatchProcessing
❶
@IntegrationComponentScan
```

```
@SpringBootApplication
public class PartitionApplication {

  public static void main(String args[]) {
    SpringApplication.run(PartitionApplication.class, args);
  }

  ❷
  @Bean(name = PollerMetadata.DEFAULT_POLLER)
  PollerMetadata defaultPoller() {
    return Pollers.fixedRate(10, TimeUnit.SECONDS).get();
  }

  @Bean
  JdbcTemplate jdbcTemplate(DataSource dataSource) {
    return new JdbcTemplate(dataSource);
  }
}
```

❶ Activate Spring Batch and Spring Integration.

❷ Specify a default, global poller for `MessageChannel` implementations that require polling.

The application has a single Spring Batch `Job` with two steps. The first step is a `Task let` step that stages the database by emptying it (truncate in MySQL) (Example 11-10). The second step is a partitioned step whose configuration we'll look at in Example 11-11.

Example 11-10. The partitioned Step configuration

```
package partition;

import org.springframework.batch.core.Job;
import org.springframework.batch.core.configuration.annotation.JobBuilderFactory;
import org.springframework.batch.core.launch.support.RunIdIncrementer;
import org.springframework.context.annotation.Bean;
import org.springframework.context.annotation.Configuration;
import org.springframework.context.annotation.Profile;

@Configuration
@Profile(Profiles.LEADER_PROFILE)
❶
class JobConfiguration {

  @Bean
  Job job(JobBuilderFactory jbf, LeaderStepConfiguration lsc) {
    return jbf.get("job").incrementer(new RunIdIncrementer())
      .start(lsc.stagingStep(null, null)) ❷
      .next(lsc.partitionStep(null, null, null, null)) ❸
```

```
    .build();
  }
}
```

❶ The Job only exists in the leader node profile.

❷ The Tasklet resets the NEW_PEOPLE table.

❸ The partitioned Step farms the work out to other nodes.

The partitioned Step doesn't do any work on the leader node. Instead, it acts as a sort of proxy node, dispatching work to worker nodes. The partitioned Step needs to know how many worker nodes (the grid size) will be available. In Example 11-10, we've provided a hardcoded value through a property for the grid size, but the size of the worker node pool could be dynamically resolved by looking up the service instances dynamically using the Spring Cloud DiscoveryClient abstraction, for instance, or by interrogating the underlying platform's API (e.g., the Cloud Foundry API Client (*https://docs.cloudfoundry.org/buildpacks/java/java-client.html*)) and asking it for the size.

Example 11-11. The configuration for the partitioned Step

```
package partition;

import org.springframework.batch.core.Step;
import org.springframework.batch.core.configuration.annotation.StepBuilderFactory;
import org.springframework.batch.core.explore.JobExplorer;
import org.springframework.batch.core.partition.PartitionHandler;
import org.springframework.batch.core.partition.support.Partitioner;
import org.springframework.batch.integration.partition.MessageChannelPartitionHandler;
import org.springframework.batch.repeat.RepeatStatus;
import org.springframework.beans.factory.annotation.Value;
import org.springframework.context.annotation.Bean;
import org.springframework.context.annotation.Configuration;
import org.springframework.integration.core.MessagingTemplate;
import org.springframework.jdbc.core.JdbcOperations;
import org.springframework.jdbc.core.JdbcTemplate;

@Configuration
class LeaderStepConfiguration {

❶
  @Bean
  Step stagingStep(StepBuilderFactory sbf, JdbcTemplate jdbc) {
    return sbf.get("staging").tasklet((contribution, chunkContext) -> {
      jdbc.execute("truncate NEW_PEOPLE");
      return RepeatStatus.FINISHED;
    }).build();
```

```
}

❷
@Bean
Step partitionStep(StepBuilderFactory sbf, Partitioner p, PartitionHandler ph,
  WorkerStepConfiguration wsc) {
  Step workerStep = wsc.workerStep(null);
  return sbf.get("partitionStep").partitioner(workerStep.getName(), p)
    .partitionHandler(ph).build();
}

❸
@Bean
MessageChannelPartitionHandler partitionHandler(
  @Value("${partition.grid-size:4}") int gridSize,
  MessagingTemplate messagingTemplate, JobExplorer jobExplorer) {
  //@formatter:off
  MessageChannelPartitionHandler ph =
      new MessageChannelPartitionHandler();
  //@formatter:on
  ph.setMessagingOperations(messagingTemplate);
  ph.setJobExplorer(jobExplorer);
  ph.setStepName("workerStep");
  ph.setGridSize(gridSize);
  return ph;
}

❹
@Bean
MessagingTemplate messagingTemplate(LeaderChannels channels) {
  return new MessagingTemplate(channels.leaderRequestsChannel());
}

❺
@Bean
Partitioner partitioner(JdbcOperations jdbcTemplate,
  @Value("${partition.table:PEOPLE}") String table,
  @Value("${partition.column:ID}") String column) {
  return new IdRangePartitioner(jdbcTemplate, table, column);
}
}
```

❶ The first Step in the Job on the leader node resets the database.

❷ The next step, the partition step, needs to know which worker step to invoke on
the remote nodes, a Partitioner and a PartitionHandler.

❸ The PartitionHandler is responsible for taking the original StepExecution on
the leader node and dividing it into a collection of StepExecution instances that
it will farm out to worker nodes. The PartitionHandler wants to know how

many worker nodes there will be so that it can divide the work accordingly. This particular `PartitionHandler` implementation coordinates with worker nodes using `MessageChannel` instances...

❹ ...and so requires a `MessagingOperations` implementation to send and/or receive messages conveniently.

❺ The `Partitioner` is responsible for partitioning the workload. In this case, the partitioning is done with some basic division of the IDs of the records in the origin table, `PEOPLE`. In all the code we'll look at in this example, this is possibly the most tedious, and it is typically specific to your business domain and application.

The worker nodes pick up the work from the broker and route the requests to a `StepExecutionRequestHandler`, which then uses a `StepLocator` to resolve the actual step in the worker application context to run (Example 11-12).

Example 11-12. The configuration for the partitioned step

```
package partition;

import org.springframework.batch.core.explore.JobExplorer;
import org.springframework.batch.core.step.StepLocator;
import org.springframework.batch.integration.partition.BeanFactoryStepLocator;
import org.springframework.batch.integration.partition.StepExecutionRequest;
import org.springframework.batch.integration.partition.StepExecutionRequestHandler;
import org.springframework.context.annotation.Bean;
import org.springframework.context.annotation.Configuration;
import org.springframework.context.annotation.Profile;
import org.springframework.integration.dsl.IntegrationFlow;
import org.springframework.integration.dsl.IntegrationFlows;
import org.springframework.integration.dsl.support.GenericHandler;
import org.springframework.messaging.MessageChannel;

@Configuration
@Profile(Profiles.WORKER_PROFILE)
❶
class WorkerConfiguration {

 ❷
 @Bean
 StepLocator stepLocator() {
  return new BeanFactoryStepLocator();
 }

 ❸
 @Bean
 StepExecutionRequestHandler stepExecutionRequestHandler(JobExplorer explorer,
  StepLocator stepLocator) {
```

```
StepExecutionRequestHandler handler = new StepExecutionRequestHandler();
handler.setStepLocator(stepLocator);
handler.setJobExplorer(explorer);
return handler;
}

❹
@Bean
IntegrationFlow stepExecutionRequestHandlerFlow(WorkerChannels channels,
 StepExecutionRequestHandler handler) {

 MessageChannel channel = channels.workerRequestsChannels();
 //@formatter:off
 GenericHandler<StepExecutionRequest> h =
         (payload, headers) -> handler.handle(payload);
 //@formatter:on
 return IntegrationFlows.from(channel)
  .handle(StepExecutionRequest.class, h)
  .channel(channels.workerRepliesChannels()).get();
 }
}
```

❶ These objects should be present only in the worker node and under the worker profile.

❷ The StepLocator is responsible for locating a Step implementation by name. In this case, it'll resolve the Step by sifting through the beans in the containing Bean Factory implementation.

❸ The StepExecutionRequestHandler is the counterpart on the worker node to the PartitionHandler on the leader: it accepts incoming requests and turns them into executions of a given Step, the results of which are then sent in reply.

❹ The StepExecutionRequestHandler is unaware of the MessageChannel instances on which incoming StepExecutionRequests will arrive, so we use Spring Integration to trigger the StepExecutionRequestHandler bean's #handle(StepExecutionRequest) method in response to messages, and to ensure that the return value is sent out as a messsage on a reply channel.

Finally, in Example 11-13, the actual step is activated, along with information on which data to read. It is important that the reader have access to the same state (in this case, a JDBC DataSource) as the leader node.

Example 11-13. The configuration for the partitioned step

```
package partition;
```

```
import org.springframework.batch.core.Step;
import org.springframework.batch.core.configuration.annotation.StepBuilderFactory;
import org.springframework.batch.core.configuration.annotation.StepScope;
import org.springframework.batch.item.database.JdbcBatchItemWriter;
import org.springframework.batch.item.database.JdbcPagingItemReader;
import org.springframework.batch.item.database.Order;
import org.springframework.batch.item.database.builder.JdbcBatchItemWriterBuilder;
import org.springframework.batch.item.database.support.MySqlPagingQueryProvider;
import org.springframework.beans.factory.annotation.Value;
import org.springframework.context.annotation.Bean;
import org.springframework.context.annotation.Configuration;

import javax.sql.DataSource;
import java.util.Collections;

@Configuration
class WorkerStepConfiguration {

➊
@Value("${partition.chunk-size}")
private int chunk;

➋
@Bean
@StepScope
JdbcPagingItemReader<Person> reader(DataSource dataSource,
 @Value("#{stepExecutionContext['minValue']}") Long min,
 @Value("#{stepExecutionContext['maxValue']}") Long max) {

 MySqlPagingQueryProvider queryProvider = new MySqlPagingQueryProvider();
 queryProvider
   .setSelectClause("id as id, email as email, age as age, first_name as firstName");
 queryProvider.setFromClause("from PEOPLE");
 queryProvider.setWhereClause("where id >= " + min + " and id <= " + max);
 queryProvider.setSortKeys(Collections.singletonMap("id", Order.ASCENDING));

 JdbcPagingItemReader<Person> reader = new JdbcPagingItemReader<>();
 reader.setDataSource(dataSource);
 reader.setFetchSize(this.chunk);
 reader.setQueryProvider(queryProvider);
 reader.setRowMapper((rs, i) -> new Person(rs.getInt("id"), rs.getInt("age"),
   rs.getString("firstName"), rs.getString("email")));
 return reader;
}

➌
@Bean
JdbcBatchItemWriter<Person> writer(DataSource ds) {
 return new JdbcBatchItemWriterBuilder<Person>()
   .beanMapped()
   .dataSource(ds)
   .sql(
```

```
   "INSERT INTO NEW_PEOPLE(age,first_name,email) VALUES(:age, :firstName, :email )")
   .build();
}

❹
@Bean
Step workerStep(StepBuilderFactory sbf) {
 return sbf.get("workerStep").<Person, Person>chunk(this.chunk)
  .reader(reader(null, null, null)).writer(writer(null)).build();
 }
}
```

❶ This is a Spring Batch job, at the end of the day, so the JdbcPagingItemReader implementation still cares about chunking through the records.

❷ Note that we're using a JdbcPagingItemReader and not an implementation like JdbcCursorItemReader, as we don't have the ability to share a JDBC result cursor across all the worker nodes. Ultimately, both implementations let us divide a large JDBC ResultSet into smaller pieces, and it's useful to know when and where to apply which. The ItemReader will receive in the ExecutionContext sent from the PartitionHandler a map of keys and values that provide useful information, including, in this case, the bounds of the rows to be read. As these values are unique for every execution of the Step, the ItemReader has been given the @StepScope.

❸ The JdbcBatchItemWriter writes the fields of the Person POJO to the database by mapping the POJO properties to the named parameters in the SQL statement.

❹ Finally, we build the worker Step. This should be very familiar at this point.

Finally, the application components are connected with MessageChannel implementations. Three of those definitions—leaderRequests, workerRequests, and workerReplies—are defined using Spring Cloud Stream and in this example, RabbitMQ. One last MessageChannel—leaderRepliesAggregatedChannel—is used only to connect two components in-memory. We'll leave you to peruse the source code—LeaderChannels, WorkerChannels, and application.properties—to see those definitions; they're redundant, given our earlier discussion of Spring Cloud Stream.

You'll need the PEOPLE table setup, as well as a duplicate version of this identically configured table called NEW_PEOPLE. Launch a few instances of the worker nodes using the worker profile. Then launch the leader node by not specifying a specific profile. Once those are all running, you can launch an instance of the job. This example does *not* run the Job on application launch, but you can trigger a run through a REST endpoint that's included in the source code: curl -d{} http://localhost:8080/migrate.

Task Management

Spring Boot knows what to do with our `Job`; when the application starts up, Spring Boot runs all `CommandLineRunner` instances, including the one provided by Spring Boot's Spring Batch auto-configuration. From the outside looking in, however, there is no logical way to know how to *run* this job. We don't know, necessarily, that it describes a workload that will terminate and produce an exit status. We don't have common infrastructure that captures the start and end time for a task. There's no infrastructure to support us if an exception occurs. Spring Batch surfaces these concepts, but how do we deal with things that aren't Spring Batch `Job` instances, like `CommandLineRunner` or `ApplicationRunner` instances? Spring Cloud Task helps us here. Spring Cloud Task provides a way of identifying, executing, and interrogating... well...*tasks*!

A *task* is something that starts and has an expected terminal state. Tasks are ideal abstractions for any ephemeral process or workload that may require an atypically long amount of time (longer than an ideal transaction in the main request and response flow of a service; this might imply seconds, hours, or even days!). Tasks describe workloads that run once (in response to an event) or on a schedule. Common examples include:

- Somebody requests that the system generated and send *Reset Password* email
- A Spring Batch `Job` that runs whenever a new file arrives in a directory
- An application that periodically garbage-collects stray files, or audits inconsistent data or message queue logs
- Dynamic document (or report) generation
- Media transcoding

A key aspect of a task is that it provides a uniform interface for parameterization. Spring Cloud Task tasks accept parameters and Spring Boot configuration properties. If you specify parameters, Spring Cloud Task will perpetuate them as `CommandLine Runner` or `ApplicationRunner` arguments, or as Spring Batch `JobParameter` instances. Tasks may be configured using Spring Boot configuration properties. Indeed, as we'll see later, Spring Cloud Data Flow is even smart enough to let you interrogate the list of known properties for a given task and render a form for task-specific properties.

 If you want your task to benefit from the smart integration with the Spring Cloud Data Flow, you'll need to include the Spring Boot configuration processor (`org.springframework.boot : spring-boot-configuration-processor`) and define a `@Configuration Properties` component.

Let's look at a simple example (Example 11-14). Start a new Spring Boot project with nothing in it, and then add org.springframework.cloud : spring-cloud-task-starter.

Example 11-14. A self-contained Spring Boot application that contributes a CommandLineRunner which Spring Cloud Task will run for us

```
package task;

import org.apache.commons.logging.Log;
import org.apache.commons.logging.LogFactory;
import org.springframework.boot.CommandLineRunner;
import org.springframework.boot.SpringApplication;
import org.springframework.boot.autoconfigure.SpringBootApplication;
import org.springframework.cloud.task.configuration.EnableTask;
import org.springframework.cloud.task.repository.TaskExplorer;
import org.springframework.context.annotation.Bean;
import org.springframework.data.domain.PageRequest;

import java.util.stream.Stream;

❶
@EnableTask
@SpringBootApplication
public class HelloTask {

 private Log log = LogFactory.getLog(getClass());

 public static void main(String args[]) {
  SpringApplication.run(HelloTask.class, args);
 }

 @Bean
 CommandLineRunner runAndExplore(TaskExplorer taskExplorer) {
  return args -> {
   Stream.of(args).forEach(log::info);

   ❷
   taskExplorer.findAll(new PageRequest(0, 1)).forEach(
    taskExecution -> log.info(taskExecution.toString()));
  };
 }
}
```

❶   Activate Spring Cloud Task.

❷   Inject the Spring Cloud Task TaskExplorer to inspect the current running task's execution.

When you run the example, the `CommandLineRunner` runs just as we'd expect it would in a non-Task-based application. Helpfully, though, we can inject the `TaskExplorer` to dynamically interrogate the runtime about the status of the running task (or indeed, any tasks). The `TaskExplorer` knows about the `CommandLineRunner`, `Applica tionRunner`, and Spring Batch `Job` instances in our application context. You gain support for Spring Batch `Job` workloads with Spring Cloud Task's Batch integration (`org.springframework.cloud:spring-cloud-task-batch`).

We'll revisit Spring Cloud Task in our later discussion of Spring Cloud Data Flow.

Process-Centric Integration with Workflow

While Spring Batch gives us rudimentary workflow capabilities, its purpose is to support processing of large datasets, not to weave together autonomous agents and human agents in a comprehensive workflow. *Workflow* is the practice of explicitly modeling the progression of work through a system of autonomous (and human!) agents. Workflow systems define a state machine and constructs for modeling the progression of that state toward a goal. Workflow systems are designed to be both a technical artifact and a description of a higher-level business process.

Workflow overlaps a lot with the ideas of business process management and business process modeling (both, confusingly, abbreviated as BPM). BPM refers to the technical capability to describe and run a workflow process, but also to the management discipline of automating business. Analysts use BPM to identify business processes, which they model and execute with a workflow engine like Activiti (*https://www.activiti.org*).

Workflow systems support ease of modeling processes. Typically, workflow systems provide design-time tools that facilitate visual modeling. The main goal of this is to arrive at an artifact that minimally specifies the process for both business and technologists. A process model is not directly executable code, but a series of steps. It is up to developers to provide appropriate behavior for the various states. Workflow systems typically provide a way to store and query the state of various processes. Like Spring Batch, workflow systems provide a built-in mechanism to design compensatory behavior in the case of failures.

From a design perspective, workflow systems help keep your services and entities stateless and free of what would otherwise be irrelevant process state. We've seen many systems where an entity's progression through fleeting, one-time processes was represented as Booleans (`is_enrolled`, `is_fulfilled`, etc.) on the entity and in the databases themselves. These flags muddy the design of the entity for very little gain.

Workflow systems map roles to sequences of steps. These roles correspond more or less to swimlanes in UML. A workflow engine, like a swimlane, may describe *human* task lists as well as autonomous activities.

Is workflow for everybody? Decidedly not. We've seen that workflow is most useful for organizations that have complex processes, or are constrained by regulation and policy and need a way to interrogate process state. It's optimal for collaborative processes where humans and services drive toward a larger business requirement; examples include loan approval, legal compliance, insurance reviews, document revision, and document publishing.

Workflow simplifies design to free your business logic from the strata of state required to support auditing and reporting of processes. We look at it in this section because, like batch processing, it provides a meaningful way to address failure in a complex, multiagent, and multinode process. It is possible to model a saga execution coordinator on top of a workflow engine, although a workflow engine is not itself a saga execution coordinator. We get a lot of the implied benefits, though, if we use it correctly. We'll see later that workflows also lend themselves to horizontal scale on a cloud environment through messaging infrastructure.

Let's walk through a simple exercise. Suppose you have a signup process for a new user. The business cares about the progression of new signups as a metric. Conceptually, the signup process is a simple affair: the user submits a new signup request through a form, which then must be validated and if there are errors, fixed. Once the form is correct and accepted, a confirmation email must be sent. The user has to click on the confirmation email and trigger a well-known endpoint, confirming the email is addressable. The user may do this in a minute or in two weeks...or a year! The long-lived transaction is still valid. We could make the process even more sophisticated and specify timeouts and escalations within the definition of our workflow. For now, however, this is an interesting enough example that involves both autonomous and human work toward the goal of enrolling a new customer (Figure 11-2).

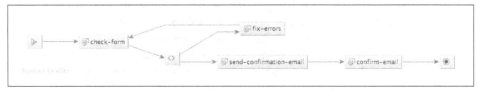

Figure 11-2. A sign-up process modeled using BPMN 2.0 as viewed from IntelliJ IDEA's yFiles-powered BPMN 2.0 preview

Alfresco's Activiti project (*http://activiti.org*) is a *business process engine*. It supports process definitions in an XML standard called BPMN 2.0 that enjoys robust support across multiple vendors' tooling and IDEs. The business process designer defines BPMN business processes using tools (from, say, WebMethods, Activiti, or IBM), and can then run the defined process in Activiti (or, in theory, in any other tool). Activiti also provides a modeling environment, is easy to deploy standalone or use in a cloud-based service, and is Apache 2 licensed. Conveniently for us, Activiti also offers a convenient Spring Boot auto-configuration.

 As this book was being developed, the main developers on the Activiti project forked the project into a new Apache 2 licensed, completely backward-compatible effort called Flowable (*http://www.flowable.org/*). You should definitely watch that space if you like Activiti.

In Activiti, a `Process` defines an archetypical process definition. A `ProcessInstance` is a single execution of a given process. A `ProcessInstance` is uniquely defined by its process variables, which parameterize the process's execution. Think of them as command-line arguments, like `JobParameter` parameters for a Spring Batch `Job`.

The Activiti engine, like Spring Batch, keeps its execution state in a relational database. If you're using the Spring Boot auto-configuration, it'll automatically install the relevant tables for you—provided you have a `DataSource` in your application context somewhere. Example 11-15 shows the relevant tables.

Example 11-15. The Activiti metadata tables in MySQL

```
mysql> show tables;
+-----------------------------+
| Tables_in_activiti          |
+-----------------------------+
| ACT_EVT_LOG                 |
| ACT_GE_BYTEARRAY            |
| ACT_GE_PROPERTY            |
| ACT_HI_ACTINST             |
| ACT_HI_ATTACHMENT          |
| ACT_HI_COMMENT             |
| ACT_HI_DETAIL              |
| ACT_HI_IDENTITYLINK        |
| ACT_HI_PROCINST            |
| ACT_HI_TASKINST            |
| ACT_HI_VARINST             |
| ACT_ID_GROUP               |
| ACT_ID_INFO                |
| ACT_ID_MEMBERSHIP          |
| ACT_ID_USER                |
| ACT_PROCDEF_INFO           |
| ACT_RE_DEPLOYMENT          |
| ACT_RE_MODEL               |
| ACT_RE_PROCDEF             |
| ACT_RU_EVENT_SUBSCR        |
```

```
| ACT_RU_EXECUTION             |
| ACT_RU_IDENTITYLINK          |
| ACT_RU_JOB                   |
| ACT_RU_TASK                  |
| ACT_RU_VARIABLE              |
+------------------------------+
24 rows in set (0.00 sec)
```

The Spring Boot auto-configuration expects any BPMN 2.0 documents to be in the
src/main/resources/processes directory of an application, by default. In
Example 11-16, we'll take a look at the definition of a BPMN 2.0 signup process.

Example 11-16. The signup.bpmn20.xml business process definition

```xml
<?xml version="1.0" encoding="UTF-8"?>
<definitions
        xmlns:xsi="http://www.w3.org/2001/XMLSchema-instance"
        xmlns:activiti="http://activiti.org/bpmn"
        xmlns="http://www.omg.org/spec/BPMN/20100524/MODEL"
        typeLanguage="http://www.w3.org/2001/XMLSchema"
        expressionLanguage="http://www.w3.org/1999/XPath"
        targetNamespace="http://www.activiti.org/bpmn2.0">


    <process name="signup" id="signup">
        ❶
        <startEvent id="start"/>

        ❷
        <sequenceFlow sourceRef="start" targetRef="check-form"/>

        ❸
        <serviceTask id="check-form" name="check-form"
            activiti:expression="#{checkForm.execute(execution)}"/>

        <sequenceFlow sourceRef="check-form"
          targetRef="form-completed-decision-gateway"/>

        ❹
        <exclusiveGateway id="form-completed-decision-gateway"/>

        <sequenceFlow name="formOK" id="formOK"
                      sourceRef="form-completed-decision-gateway"
                      targetRef="send-confirmation-email">
            <conditionExpression xsi:type="tFormalExpression">${formOK == true}
            </conditionExpression>
        </sequenceFlow>

        <sequenceFlow id="formNotOK" name="formNotOK"
                      sourceRef="form-completed-decision-gateway"
                      targetRef="fix-errors">
```

```
            <conditionExpression xsi:type="tFormalExpression">${formOK == false}
            </conditionExpression>
        </sequenceFlow>

        ❺
        <userTask name="fix-errors" id="fix-errors">
            <humanPerformer>
                <resourceAssignmentExpression>
                    <formalExpression>customer</formalExpression>
                </resourceAssignmentExpression>
            </humanPerformer>
        </userTask>

        <sequenceFlow sourceRef="fix-errors" targetRef="check-form"/>

        ❻
        <serviceTask id="send-confirmation-email" name="send-confirmation-email"
            activiti:expression="#{sendConfirmationEmail.execute(execution)}"/>

        <sequenceFlow sourceRef="send-confirmation-email"
          targetRef="confirm-email"/>

        ❼
        <userTask name="confirm-email" id="confirm-email">
            <humanPerformer>
                <resourceAssignmentExpression>
                    <formalExpression>customer</formalExpression>
                </resourceAssignmentExpression>
            </humanPerformer>
        </userTask>

        <sequenceFlow sourceRef="confirm-email" targetRef="end"/>

        <endEvent id="end"/>
    </process>
</definitions>
```

❶ The first state is the startEvent. All processes have a defined start and end.

❷ The sequenceFlow elements serve as guidance to the engine about where to go next. They're logical, and are represented as lines in the workflow model itself.

❸ A serviceTask is a state in the process. Our BPMN 2.0 definition uses the Activiti-specific activiti:expression attribute to delegate handling to method, execute(ActivityExecution) on a Spring bean (called checkForm). Spring Boot's auto-configuration activates this behavior.

❹ After the form is submitted and checked, the checkForm method contributes a Boolean *process variable* called formOK, whose value is used to drive a decision downstream. A process variable is context that's visible to participants in a given process. Process variables can be whatever you'd like, though we tend to keep them as trivial as possible to be used later to act as claim checks for real resources elsewhere. This process expects one input process variable, customerId.

❺ If the form is invalid, work flows to the fix-errors user task. The task is contributed to a worklist and assigned to a human. This task list is supported through a Task API in Activiti. It's trivial to query the tasklist and start and complete tasks. The task list is meant to model work that a human being must perform. When the process reaches this state, it pauses, waiting to be explicitly completed by a human at some later state. Work flows from the fix-errors task back to the checkForm state. If the form is now fixed (valid), work proceeds to the next state.

❻ If the form is valid, then work flows to the send-confirmation-email service task. This simply delegates to another Spring bean to do its work, perhaps using SendGrid.

❼ The email should contain a link that, when clicked, triggers an HTTP endpoint that then completes the outstanding task and moves the process to completion.

This process is trivial, but it provides a clean representation of the moving pieces in the system. We can see that we will need *something* to take the inputs from the user, resulting in a customer record in the database and a valid customerId that we can use to retrieve that record in downstream components. The customer record may be in an invalid state (the email might be invalid), and may need to be revisited by the user. Once things are in working order, state moves to the step where we send a confirmation email that, once received and confirmed, transitions the process to the terminal state.

Let's look at a simple REST API that drives this process along. For brevity, we've not extrapolated out an iPhone client or an HTML5 client, but it's certainly a natural next step. The REST API is kept as simple as possible for illustration. A *very* logical next step might be to use hypermedia to drive the client's interactions with the REST API from one state transition to another (Example 11-17). For more on this possibility, check out the REST chapter and the discussion of hypermedia and HATEOAS in "Hypermedia" on page 165.

Example 11-17. The SignupRestController that drives the process

```
package com.example;

import org.activiti.engine.RuntimeService;
import org.activiti.engine.TaskService;
import org.activiti.engine.task.TaskInfo;
```

```
import org.apache.commons.logging.Log;
import org.apache.commons.logging.LogFactory;
import org.springframework.beans.factory.annotation.Autowired;
import org.springframework.http.ResponseEntity;
import org.springframework.util.Assert;
import org.springframework.web.bind.annotation.*;

import java.util.Collections;
import java.util.List;
import java.util.stream.Collectors;

@RestController
@RequestMapping("/customers")
class SignupRestController {

  public static final String CUSTOMER_ID_PV_KEY = "customerId";

  private final RuntimeService runtimeService;

  private final TaskService taskService;

  private final CustomerRepository customerRepository;

  private Log log = LogFactory.getLog(getClass());

  ❶
  @Autowired
  public SignupRestController(RuntimeService runtimeService,
   TaskService taskService, CustomerRepository repository) {
   this.runtimeService = runtimeService;
   this.taskService = taskService;
   this.customerRepository = repository;
  }

  ❷
  @PostMapping
  public ResponseEntity<?> startProcess(@RequestBody Customer customer) {
   Assert.notNull(customer);
   Customer save = this.customerRepository.save(new Customer(customer
    .getFirstName(), customer.getLastName(), customer.getEmail()));

   String processInstanceId = this.runtimeService.startProcessInstanceByKey(
    "signup",
    Collections.singletonMap(CUSTOMER_ID_PV_KEY, Long.toString(save.getId())))
    .getId();
   this.log.info("started sign-up. the processInstance ID is "
    + processInstanceId);

   return ResponseEntity.ok(save.getId());
  }

  ❸
```

```
@GetMapping("/{customerId}/signup/errors")
public List<String> readErrors(@PathVariable String customerId) {
 // @formatter:off
 return this.taskService
   .createTaskQuery()
    .active()
    .taskName("fix-errors")
    .includeProcessVariables()
    .processVariableValueEquals(CUSTOMER_ID_PV_KEY, customerId)
   .list()
    .stream()
    .map(TaskInfo::getId)
   .collect(Collectors.toList());
 // @formatter:on
}
```

❹

```
@PostMapping("/{customerId}/signup/errors/{taskId}")
public void fixErrors(@PathVariable String customerId,
 @PathVariable String taskId, @RequestBody Customer fixedCustomer) {

 Customer customer = this.customerRepository.findOne(Long
   .parseLong(customerId));
 customer.setEmail(fixedCustomer.getEmail());
 customer.setFirstName(fixedCustomer.getFirstName());
 customer.setLastName(fixedCustomer.getLastName());
 this.customerRepository.save(customer);

 this.taskService.createTaskQuery().active().taskId(taskId)
   .includeProcessVariables()
   .processVariableValueEquals(CUSTOMER_ID_PV_KEY, customerId).list()
   .forEach(t -> {
   log.info("fixing customer# " + customerId + " for taskId " + taskId);
   taskService.complete(t.getId(), Collections.singletonMap("formOK", true));
   });
}
```

❺

```
@PostMapping("/{customerId}/signup/confirmation")
public void confirm(@PathVariable String customerId) {
 this.taskService.createTaskQuery().active().taskName("confirm-email")
   .includeProcessVariables()
   .processVariableValueEquals(CUSTOMER_ID_PV_KEY, customerId).list()
   .forEach(t -> {
   log.info(t.toString());
   taskService.complete(t.getId());
   });
 this.log.info("confirmed email receipt for " + customerId);
 }
}
```

❶ The controller will work with a simple Spring Data JPA repository as well as two services that are auto-configured by the Activiti Spring Boot support. The Runti meService lets us interrogate the process engine about running processes. The TaskService lets us interrogate the process engine about running human tasks and tasklists.

❷ The first endpoint accepts a new customer record and persists it. The newly minted customer is fed as an input process variable into a new process, where the customer's customerId is specified as a process variable. Here, the process flows to the check-form serviceTask, which will nominally check that the input email is valid; if it is, then a confirmation email is sent. Otherwise, the customer will need to address any errors in the input data.

❸ If there are any errors, we want the user's UI experience to arrest forward progress, so the process queues up a user task. This endpoint queries for any outstanding tasks for this particular user and then returns a collection of outstanding task IDs. Ideally, this might also return validation information that can drive the UX for the human using some sort of interactive experience to enroll.

❹ Once the errors are addressed client-side, the updated entity is persisted in the database and the outstanding task is marked as complete. At this point the process flows to the send-confirmation-email state, which will send an email that includes a link the user will have to click to confirm the enrollment.

❺ The final step, then, is a REST endpoint that queries any outstanding email confirmation tasks for the given customer.

We start this process with a potentially invalid entity, the customer, whose state we need to ensure is correct before we can proceed. We model this process to support iteration on the entity, backtracking to the appropriate step so long as there is an invalid state.

Let's complete our tour by examining the beans that power the process's two service Task elements; check-form and send-confirmation-email.

Both the CheckForm and SendConfirmationEmail beans are uninteresting; they're simple Spring beans. CheckForm implements a trivial validation that ensures the first name and last name are not null, and then uses the Mashape email validation REST API (introduced in the discussion on Spring Batch) to validate that the email is in a valid form. The CheckForm bean validates the state of a given Customer record and then contributes a process variable to the running ProcessInstance, a Boolean called formOK, which then drives a decision to continue with the process or force the user to try again (Example 11-18).

Example 11-18. The CheckForm bean that validates the customer's state

```java
package com.example;

import com.example.email.EmailValidationService;
import org.activiti.engine.RuntimeService;
import org.activiti.engine.impl.pvm.delegate.ActivityExecution;
import org.springframework.beans.factory.annotation.Autowired;
import org.springframework.stereotype.Service;

import java.util.Collections;
import java.util.Map;

import static org.apache.commons.lang3.StringUtils.isEmpty;

@Service
class CheckForm {

  private final RuntimeService runtimeService;  ❶

  private final CustomerRepository customerRepository;

  private final EmailValidationService emailValidationService;

  @Autowired
  public CheckForm(EmailValidationService emailValidationService,
   RuntimeService runtimeService, CustomerRepository customerRepository) {
    this.runtimeService = runtimeService;
    this.customerRepository = customerRepository;
    this.emailValidationService = emailValidationService;
  }

  ❷
  public void execute(ActivityExecution e) throws Exception {
    Long customerId = Long.parseLong(e.getVariable("customerId", String.class));
    Map<String, Object> vars = Collections.singletonMap("formOK",
     validated(this.customerRepository.findOne(customerId)));
    this.runtimeService.setVariables(e.getId(), vars);  ❸
  }

  private boolean validated(Customer customer) {
    return !isEmpty(customer.getFirstName()) && !isEmpty(customer.getLastName())
     && this.emailValidationService.isEmailValid(customer.getEmail());
  }

}
```

❶   Inject the Activiti RuntimeService.

---

❷ The `ActivityExecution` is a context object. You can use it to access process variables, the process engine itself, and other interesting services.

❸ Then use it to articulate the outcome of the test.

The `SendConfirmationEmail` has the same basic form.

So far, we've looked at workflow in the context of a single node. We've ignored one of the most promising aspects of the cloud: scale! Modeling a workflow helps us identify embarrassingly parallel processing opportunities. Every state in the process expects inputs (in the form of process variables and preconditions) and provides outputs (in the form of side effects and process variables). The workflow manages the process state.

Our business logic is executed at the right time, depending on state. Thus far everything we've done has happened either in the same node or on whatever node the client is using to interact with the system to satisfy the user-assigned tasklists. If the automatic processing takes any nontrivial amount of time, it's safer to move that work to another node—any node! This is the cloud, after all. We have the capacity; it's just a matter of using it.

In a BPMN process, the `serviceTask` element is a wait state: the engine will pause there (and dispose of any held resources) until it is explicitly *signaled*. Anything out of band could signal the process: a message from an Apache Kafka broker arrives, an email, a button click, or the conclusion of a long-running process. We can take advantage of this behavior and move potentially long-running processing to another node, and then, on completion, signal that the process should be resumed. The workflow engine keeps track of the state of all run and running processes, so it's possible to query for any orphaned processes and act accordingly. Workflow gives us the ability to naturally break apart involved business processes, decompose them into isolated steps, and distribute them across a cluster; *and* it provides the tools to be able to recover should something go wrong in the distribution of work.

Let's look in Example 11-19 at how to farm execution out to worker nodes in Spring Cloud Stream's `MessageChannel` definitions. As we did in the remote-partitioning Spring Batch job, we'll think of the solution in terms of the leader node and worker nodes. The *leader node* is simply the node that originates the processing. The leader node features an HTTP endpoint (`http://localhost:8080/start`) to initiate processing. The process is necessarily trivial, so we can focus on the distribution.

Example 11-19. An asynchronous business process, async.bpmn20.xml

```
<?xml version="1.0" encoding="UTF-8"?>
<definitions xmlns:activiti="http://activiti.org/bpmn"
             id="definitions"
```

```
        xmlns="http://www.omg.org/spec/BPMN/20100524/MODEL"
        typeLanguage="http://www.w3.org/2001/XMLSchema"
        expressionLanguage="http://www.w3.org/1999/XPath"
        targetNamespace="http://www.activiti.org/bpmn2.0">

    <process id="asyncProcess">

        <startEvent id="start"/>

        <sequenceFlow id="f1" sourceRef="start" targetRef="spring-gateway"/>

        ❶
        <serviceTask id="spring-gateway"
          activiti:delegateExpression="#{gateway}"/>

        <sequenceFlow id="f2" sourceRef="spring-gateway"
          targetRef="confirm-movement"/>

        ❷
        <scriptTask id="confirm-movement" scriptFormat="groovy">
            <script>
                println 'Moving on..'
            </script>
        </scriptTask>

        <sequenceFlow id="f3" sourceRef="confirm-movement" targetRef="end"/>

        <endEvent id="end"/>

    </process>

</definitions>
```

❶ As soon as the process begins, it enters a serviceTask state. Here we use an Activiti delegate, a Spring bean called gateway, to process this state. The process will
stop in that handler until it is signaled.

❷ Once signaled, the process will continue to the scriptTask, and we'll see Moving
on! recorded on the console.

The gateway bean is the key. It is an implementation of the Activiti ReceiveTaskActi
vityBehavior that writes a message to a Spring Cloud Stream-powered leaderRe
quests MessageChannel. The executionId is the payload for the message, and is
required to later signal the request. We must take care to perpetuate it in either the
message headers or the payload (as we do in this example). When a reply message is
received on another Spring Cloud Stream-powered MessageChannel, the replies
Flow calls RuntimeService#signal(executionId), which in turn resumes the execution of the process (Example 11-20).

Example 11-20. The LeaderConfiguration defines how requests are sent out to, and what happens when the replies come back from, the worker nodes

```
package com.example;

import org.activiti.engine.ProcessEngine;
import org.activiti.engine.impl.bpmn.behavior.ReceiveTaskActivityBehavior;
import org.activiti.engine.impl.pvm.delegate.ActivityBehavior;
import org.activiti.engine.impl.pvm.delegate.ActivityExecution;
import org.springframework.context.annotation.Bean;
import org.springframework.context.annotation.Configuration;
import org.springframework.context.annotation.Profile;
import org.springframework.integration.dsl.IntegrationFlow;
import org.springframework.integration.dsl.IntegrationFlows;
import org.springframework.integration.support.MessageBuilder;
import org.springframework.messaging.Message;

@Configuration
@Profile(Profiles.LEADER)
class LeaderConfiguration {

  ❶
  @Bean
  ActivityBehavior gateway(LeaderChannels channels) {
   return new ReceiveTaskActivityBehavior() {

    @Override
    public void execute(ActivityExecution execution) throws Exception {

     Message<?> executionMessage = MessageBuilder.withPayload(execution.getId())
       .build();

     channels.leaderRequests().send(executionMessage);
    }
   };
  }

  ❷
  @Bean
  IntegrationFlow repliesFlow(LeaderChannels channels, ProcessEngine engine) {
   return IntegrationFlows.from(channels.leaderReplies())
    .handle(String.class, (executionId, map) -> {
    engine.getRuntimeService().signal(executionId);
    return null;
   }).get();
  }
}
```

❶ As soon as the process begins, it enters a serviceTask state. Here we use an Activiti delegate, a Spring bean called gateway, to process this state. The process will stop in that handler until it is signaled.

❷ Once signaled, the process will continue to the scriptTask and we'll see Moving on! recorded on the console.

The worker node works only with MessageChannel instances: there is no awareness (beyond the String executionId header) of Activiti or of the workflow engine. The worker nodes are free to do whatever they want; perhaps they launch a Spring Batch Job or a Spring Cloud Task. Workflow is ideal for any long-running processes, so whatever you want to do could be done here: video transcoding, document generation, image analysis, etc. (Example 11-21).

Example 11-21. The WorkerConfiguration defines how requests are sent out to, and what happens when the replies come back from, the worker nodes

```
package com.example;

import org.apache.commons.logging.Log;
import org.apache.commons.logging.LogFactory;
import org.springframework.context.annotation.Bean;
import org.springframework.context.annotation.Configuration;
import org.springframework.context.annotation.Profile;
import org.springframework.integration.dsl.IntegrationFlow;
import org.springframework.integration.dsl.IntegrationFlows;
import org.springframework.integration.dsl.support.GenericHandler;

@Configuration
@Profile(Profiles.WORKER)
class WorkerConfiguration {

 @Bean
 IntegrationFlow requestsFlow(WorkerChannels channels) {

  Log log = LogFactory.getLog(getClass());

  ❶
  return IntegrationFlows.from(channels.workerRequests())
   .handle((GenericHandler<String>) (executionId, headers) -> {
    ❷
    headers.entrySet().forEach(e -> log.info(e.getKey() + '=' + e.getValue()));
    log.info("sending executionId (" + executionId + ") to workerReplies.");
    return executionId;
   }).channel(channels.workerReplies()) ❸
   .get();
 }
}
```

❶ Whenever a new message arrives...

❷ ...enumerate the headers and do whatever other business logic we want, ensuring we perpetuate the `executionId` payload...

❸ ...which gets sent on the `workerReplies` channel, back to the leader node.

Distribution with Messaging

Though this chapter has talked a lot about long-running processes (Spring Batch, Spring Cloud Task, and workflow), *messaging* is what makes these topics worthy of discussion in a book about going cloud native! These old-guard disciplines become very useful tools when we can leverage the opportunity for scale that the cloud presents us.

Summary

We've only begun to scratch the surface of the possibilities in data processing. Naturally, each of these technologies speaks to a large array of different technologies themselves. We might, for example, use Apache Spark or Apache Hadoop in conjunction with Spring Cloud Data Flow. They also compose well. It's trivial to scale out processing of a Spring Batch `job` across a cluster using Spring Cloud Stream as the messaging fabric.

## CHAPTER 12

Data Integration

Microservices are optimized for teams, easily evolving independent parts of the system. Each team works on its own deliverable, or feature, independently of the rest of the organization—a separate codebase, a separate release cycle, and possibly separate technologies! A side effect of this isolation is that services are distributed. Service boundaries are explicit, and data access happens through the service boundary. This implies process distribution and network partitions. In Chapter 9, we looked at how to model bounded contexts and interact with popular data sources like MongoDB or Redis. It's trivial to stand up individual services that manage their own data source; the question is: how do these nodes communicate? How do they agree upon state?

In this chapter, we'll look at a few different ways, old and new, to take data from different microservices and integrate them. One of the key concerns we'll try to address is integrity of the data in the face of distribution. The distributed systems literature is vast and comprehensive. There are seminal papers, such as "Managing Update Conflicts in Bayou, a Weakly Connected Replicated Storage System," (*http://bit.ly/2vjbzaN*) which breaks down the problem of consistency in a distributed database architecture. There is also Eric Brewer's "CAP Theorem," (*http://dl.acm.org/citation.cfm?id=343502*) which states that any distributed system can have at most two of three desirable properties:

- Consistency (C), which is equivalent to having a single, up-to-date copy of the data
- High availability (A) of that data (for updates)
- Tolerance to network partitions (P)

In practice, CAP only prohibits perfect availability *and* consistency in the presence of partitions. It is rare, however, to need perfect availability *and* consistency. Instead, we'll look at patterns that allow us to build systems that arrive—eventually—in a consistent state, and we'll look at ways to integrate failure management patterns, or compensatory actions, in the case of failures. This chapter is not meant to highlight and address every possible failure mode! There are a good many ways a system can fail, as Kyle Kingsbury's epic distributed systems class indicates (*https://github.com/aphyr/distsys-class*)!

The nature of the data sets we work with has evolved to match the nature of our applications and the economics that inform their architecture, from traditional workday-oriented, offline, batch, and finite workloads to international, 24/7, always on, and infinite event- and stream-based workloads. Whatever technologies we choose to use must support these disparate types of workloads.

Distributed Transactions

At first blush, it might seem like distributed transactions can help guarantee consistency between services. Distributed transactions are supported in Java through the JTA API. JTA is an implementation of the X/Open XA architecture. In a two-phase commit transaction, there's a *coordinator* that enlists resources in a transaction. Each resource is then told to prepare to commit. The resources respond that they're ready to proceed and then, finally, are asked to commit, all at the same time. If every resource replies that they've committed, then the transaction is a success. If not, the resources are asked to roll back.

Distributed transactions are a poor fit in a cloud native world. The coordinator is a single point of failure—a very chatty single point of failure, requiring a lot of communication between each node before a transaction can be effectively handled. This communication can needlessly overwhelm networks. Distributed transactions also require that all participating resources be aware of the transaction coordinator, which isn't likely in a system full of REST APIs that don't speak the X/Open protocol. Sometimes this approach is required, though we don't recommend it. If you want to learn how to lift and shift existing JTA-based applications, see the discussion on distributed transactions with JTA in "JTA and XA Transaction Management" on page 585.

Isolating Failures and Graceful Degradation

The goal, ultimately, is to obtain the correct results from possibly distributed services. Services fail, but we can compensate for this by retrying a request a few times until such time as the service is available. Put another way: be persistent! We can retry a request, or indeed any potentially volatile unity of work, with the Spring Retry library. Spring Retry was extracted from Spring Batch (we talk about Spring Batch and other technologies designed to support long-running processing in "Batch Workloads" on page 353) and is now usable independently of Spring Batch. You can use Spring Retry to try to set up middleware connections like datasources or message queues—a particularly useful pattern when standing up infrastructure in a possibly nondeterministic order where, for example, the database starts serving requests *after* the service that depends on it has started. You can use Spring Retry to call downstream services that may or may not be available.

Let's look at a simple REST client that calls another service. If the call succeeds, we'll return the service response; however, if the call fails, it'll throw an exception, which Spring Retry will route to a handler method annotated with the @Recover method. The recovery method returns the same response as the recoverable method. In our example, it'll return the string OHAI. It'll do this for as many attempts as you permit it. By default, it'll call three times. It'll back off for increasingly longer periods before it exhausts its retries, finally failing (Example 12-1). Use the @EnableRetry annotation on a configuration class to activate Spring Retry.

Example 12-1. Spring Retry helps us retry, with increasing backoff periods between attempts, to invoke potentially flaky downstream services

```
package demo;

import org.apache.commons.logging.Log;
import org.apache.commons.logging.LogFactory;
import org.springframework.beans.factory.annotation.Autowired;
import org.springframework.beans.factory.annotation.Value;
import org.springframework.core.ParameterizedTypeReference;
import org.springframework.http.HttpMethod;
import org.springframework.retry.annotation.Backoff;
import org.springframework.retry.annotation.Recover;
import org.springframework.retry.annotation.Retryable;
import org.springframework.stereotype.Component;
import org.springframework.web.client.RestTemplate;

import java.util.Date;
import java.util.Map;

@Component
public class RetryableGreetingClient implements GreetingClient {

  private final RestTemplate restTemplate;

  private final String serviceUri;

  private Log log = LogFactory.getLog(getClass());

  @Autowired
  public RetryableGreetingClient(RestTemplate restTemplate,
   @Value("${greeting-service.uri}") String domain) {
   this.restTemplate = restTemplate;
   this.serviceUri = domain;
  }
```

❶
```
@Retryable(include = Exception.class, maxAttempts = 4,
    backoff = @Backoff(multiplier = 5))
@Override
public String greet(String name) {
 long time = System.currentTimeMillis();

 Date now = new Date(time);

 this.log.info("attempting to call the greeting-service " + time + "/"
  + now.toString());

 ParameterizedTypeReference<Map<String, String>> ptr =
  new ParameterizedTypeReference<Map<String, String>>() {
  };

 return this.restTemplate
  .exchange(this.serviceUri + "/hi/" + name, HttpMethod.GET, null, ptr, name)
  .getBody().get("greeting");
}
```

❷
```
@Recover
public String recoverForGreeting(Exception e) {
 return "OHAI";
}

}
```

❶ This is the method that may fail, and if it does it'll throw an exception. If we
wanted to retry and recover on a specific type of failure, we could specify a specific type of Exception.

❷ You may specify as many recovery methods as you like, typed by the Exception
that they recover from.

Spring Retry might be just what you need for quick and easy recovery and smart
backoff heuristics. Sometimes, however, services may need more time to recover, and
the deluge of requests and retries can negatively impact their ability to come online.
We can use a *circuit breaker* to statefully gate requests based on whether previous
requests have succeeded, or to fall back to a recovery method, as we did with Spring
Retry.

A circuit breaker achieves some of the same things as Spring Retry. It's a component
that invokes a fallback mechanism on an exceptional case. It's no mere try-catch handler, though. It keeps a state machine. If a circuit breaker observes enough successive
failures, it'll route requests to the fallback pathway directly, foregoing attempts to call

the known-to-fail pathway. This is different than Spring Retry, in that Spring Retry doesn't divert requests proactively.

Presently, Spring supports two circuit breakers. The Spring Retry project also provides a circuit breaker, which we could use, and we can use the Spring Cloud integration for the Netflix Hystrix circuit breaker. Let's look at Netflix Hystrix.

When should you use Hystrix over Spring Retry? Hystrix, at the moment, enjoys better observability support. There's an accompanying Hystrix dashboard that takes as its input a server-sent event stream that it can use to visualize the flow of requests through a circuit breaker. The Spring integration for Hystrix, provided by a community library called Javanica, can be a little off-putting, as it requires a String to name method that should be used, where Spring Retry's approach relies upon exceptions and typed exception handlers. Hystrix has the ability to bulkhead requests using individual threadpools, where Spring Retry does not, currently. A thread-isolated Hystrix circuit breaker can more easily *walk away* from a failed call if a request to a service dependency should run too long. This requires far more resources, of course, since each client has its own threadpool. Hystrix also supports semaphore-based isolation, which is more or less the effect you get using Spring Retry. If you're OK with semaphore-based isolation, have limited computational resources, want a cleaner API (and one more keeping with continuity), use Spring Retry. If you absolutely *must* have thread-based isolation or want to visualize circuit breakers, use Hystrix.

Let's look at a client that's calling a potentially shaky service, in Example 12-2.

Example 12-2. This circuit breaker gives our downstream service time to breathe

```
package demo;

import com.netflix.hystrix.contrib.javanica.annotation.HystrixCommand;
import org.apache.commons.logging.Log;
import org.apache.commons.logging.LogFactory;
import org.springframework.beans.factory.annotation.Autowired;
import org.springframework.beans.factory.annotation.Value;
import org.springframework.core.ParameterizedTypeReference;
import org.springframework.http.HttpMethod;
import org.springframework.stereotype.Component;
import org.springframework.web.client.RestTemplate;

import java.util.Date;
import java.util.Map;

@Component
public class CircuitBreakerGreetingClient implements GreetingClient {

  private final RestTemplate restTemplate;

  private final String serviceUri;
```

```
private Log log = LogFactory.getLog(getClass());

@Autowired
public CircuitBreakerGreetingClient(RestTemplate restTemplate,
 @Value("${greeting-service.uri}") String uri) {
 this.restTemplate = restTemplate;
 this.serviceUri = uri;
}

❶
@HystrixCommand(fallbackMethod = "fallback")
public String greet(String name) {
 long time = System.currentTimeMillis();
 Date now = new Date(time);
 this.log.info("attempting to call " + "the greeting-service " + time + "/"
  + now.toString());

 //@formatter:off
 ParameterizedTypeReference<Map<String, String>> ptr =
  new ParameterizedTypeReference<Map<String, String>>() {
  };
 //@formatter:on
 return this.restTemplate
  .exchange(this.serviceUri + "/hi/" + name, HttpMethod.GET, null, ptr, name)
  .getBody().get("greeting");
}

public String fallback(String name) {
 return "OHAI";
}

}
```

❶ This is the method that may fail, and if it does, it'll throw an exception.

The circuit breaker can be either open or closed. If it's closed, then the circuit breaker will attempt to invoke the happy path, and then, on exception, call the fallback. If the circuit is open, the circuit breaker will route requests directly to the recovery method. Eventually, however, the circuit will close again and attempt to reintroduce traffic. If it fails again, it'll go back to open. The circuit breaker also emits a server-sent event stream that we can monitor using the Hystix Dashboard and Spring Cloud Turbine. For more on that, consult the discussion on observable applications in Chapter 13.

If you're using a platform like Cloud Foundry, then there's no reason a downstream service need be down for long. Cloud Foundry has a heartbeat mechanism that will automatically restart a downed service, and it can even be made to scale a service up automatically as demand spikes. Retries and circuit breakers make it easy for the client experience to degrade gracefully in the inevitable case of a service failure. Netflix and other high performing organizations will build in graceful degradation. As an example, you might imagine calls to a hypothetical search engine service failing. It would impact the user experience if the client were shown a stacktrace.

In these examples, our recovery method was an up-front concern; we *had* to think about the failure case and dealing with the compensatory transaction required, should there be a failure. This is a virtue. Assuming that errors will happen and then confronting the possibility up-front promotes more robust systems. We've looked at how to build resilience in the case of a service failure for which we have no other immediate recourse; this sort of thing works well if we care about immediate side effects.

Now let's look at architectures that use messaging as a way of guaranteeing that *eventually* services will converge upon a consistent state, even if a service is down at the moment. An architecture built using messaging embraces the fact that failures will happen, and architects accordingly, whereas the circuit breaker attempts to react and compensate for the ineluctable eventuality of a failure across partitions. To paraphrase Gregor Hohpe, coauthor of the authoritative treatment of messaging and application integration, *Enterprise Integration Patterns* (Addison-Wesley): messaging is a more honest architecture. It acknowledges that decoupled services may sometimes be down. We learned about basic messaging support in the Spring ecosystem in our discussion of messaging in Chapter 10. Please refer to that for a bit of background. The following sections imply messaging.

The Saga Pattern

In a sufficiently distributed system, where work spans multiple nodes, it's a fact of life: some requests will fail and yield inconsistent outcomes. The saga pattern was originally designed to handle long-lived transactions *on the same node*. A traditional long-lived transaction is a bottleneck in a distributed system, as resources must be maintained for the duration of the transaction. These resources are then unavailable to the system. This effectively gates the systemwide throughput of a system.

Hector Garcia-Molina introduced the saga pattern in 1987. A saga is a long-lived transaction that can be written as a sequence of subtransactions. It's a collection of subtransactions; we can call them *requests* in a distributed system. The transactions need to be interleavable; they can't depend on one another and must be reorderable. Each transaction must also define a compensatory transaction that undoes the transaction's effect, returning the system to a semantically consistent state. These compensatory transactions are developer-defined. This requires a bit of forethought in designing a system to ensure that the system is always in a semantically consistent state. The saga pattern trades off consistency for availability; the side effects of each subtraction are visible to the rest of the system before the whole saga has completed.

A saga is based on the idea of a saga execution coordinator (SEC). A saga execution coordinator is the keeper of the *saga log*. The saga log is a log that keeps track of ongoing transactions and durably records progress. A saga execution coordinator keeps no state of its own in the process, however. Should there be a failure, it's then trivial to spin up a new saga execution coordinator to replace it. The SEC keeps track of which transactions in a saga are in flight and how far they've progressed. If a saga transaction fails, the SEC must start the compensatory transaction. If the compensatory transaction fails, the SEC will retry it (there are those retries again!). This has a few implications for our architecture. Saga transactions should be designed for *at-most-once* semantics. Compensatory saga transactions should be designed for *at-least-once* semantics; they should be idempotent and leave no observable side effects if executed multiple times. There are a lot of good resources on this particular pattern, but we heartily recommend Caitie McCaffrey's GOTO 2015 talk on the Saga pattern (*https://www.youtube.com/watch?v=xDuwrtwYHu8*) as a good introduction. It's not too hard to build a working SEC on top of the primitives a workflow system like Activiti provides. (For more on Activiti and workflow, see "Process-Centric Integration with Workflow" on page 377).

CQRS (Command Query Responsibility Segregation)

Each microservice in a system is intended to be a *bounded context*—it's internally consistent. Entities within the bounded context mean one thing, and only one thing, and only within a particular bounded context. With each bounded context having its own database, there are a number of different ways to leverage common data. Services manage writes to their own database, but they may need read-only access to data in other systems.

Suppose you are building an ecommerce engine. There might be a service to manage fulfillment, another to manage the online shopping cart, another to manage shipping, another for customer service, another for the product catalog service, and another still for the product search engine, etc. While all these services serve the ultimate goals of moving products to customers, they do not all share the same domain model. The domain model for shipping service may involve all sorts of details related to parcels and delivery vehicles that would encumber the domain for the shopping cart service.

In such a system, the product catalog would manage the updates to all information related to products. Other systems, like the product search engine, might manage a search index that stores things like product reviewer comments and the product descriptions in an Elasticsearch cluster. It would *not* manage information like the price, the warehouses where a particular product might be located, and the like.

A microservice may contain one or more *aggregates*. An aggregate is a root object and its children that are manipulated atomically: an order and its line items, a customer support inquiry and its followups, a passenger and the associated luggage, a patient and the associated medical history, etc.

How do we ensure that writes to a microservice (writes that transactionally update an aggregate) are visible to other services without sharing databases and violating the encapsulation we hope to achieve in moving to microservices in the first place? Should the writer of the data be required to update all other services that depend in some way on that data? (Wouldn't that only slow down the write path?) Additionally, how do we support optimal reads of shared data in different services? After all, a hypothetical product search engine would be best served by a full text search engine, not an RDBMS; there is no *one true representation* of the data!

CQRS (Command Query Responsibility Segregation), a pattern we first heard coined by Greg Young, provides a solution: separate the writes from the reads. *Command* messages drive updates to aggregates in a service. If you want to ask questions of the system, you send a *query*. A query is supported through views (or *query models*). A *query* returns results, but does not have any observable side effects.

Any time a command updates the domain model and is persisted, an event (a message) triggers all observing query models to update their own representations. If a query model is ultimately the sum of all the events that it has processed, it stands that you could rebuild a view model by replaying the events from the very beginning. Indeed, if you've persisted every event in an event store, then you could rebuild the entire system state! This is called *event sourcing*. You do not need to use event sourcing with CQRS, but one serves the other. It's not hard to get a first-cut event store. Some use Apache Kafka as an event store, and others use SQL databases. There are even purpose-built event stores like Greg Young's Event Store (*https://getevent store.com*) and Chris Richardson's Eventuate (*http://eventuate.io/*), both fine candidates for your consideration.

Let's walk through a simple REST API to manage *complaint* tickets. Irate customers want to file complaints.

Writes are written to the command service (perhaps by a client talking to a REST API), which then publishes commands on a command bus. A command might represent the lodging of a new complaint, the addition of a comment to a complaint, or the addition of a customer support representative on a complaint. A command handler is invoked to handle the command, and must first and foremost validate the incoming command. If everything is all right, it publishes one or more domain events.

Event handlers respond to a new domain event in many useful ways. The primary result of a domain event is some sort of mutation of an aggregate's state. One domain event can also spawn more events that can be sent to other microservices. This is why many developers of microservices are attracted to CQRS—as a way to publish and subscribe to domain events originating from applications outside of a bounded context. This approach provides us with a mechanism to ensure referential integrity of domain data. Messages to other microservices can be used to handle domain events that allow maintenance of pesky foreign key relationships relating domain data from other records in the distributed system. A query service then responds to queries for the processed state, returning it unchanged from the query model data store.

The default case is for the domain (command) model and the query model to exist in a single application, in the same process. When CQRS combines with microservices, things get a bit complex, to say the least. Let's take a look at a "simple" microservice implementing CQRS.

Is a CQRS system a distributed monolith? When most people think of a single microservice today, they think of an independent service component. In most cases, a microservice is built as an application that focuses on doing one thing well. Most importantly, the service can be upgraded and deployed independently of other services. A conventional CQRS system has multiple components, and that leaves some wondering, "Is this a distributed monolith?" A distributed monolith happens when a feature is delivered that requires a coordinated deployment of multiple separate components at the same time. Microservices are all about empowering small independent teams to continuously deliver features as a part of a larger ecosystem of other microservices. Since the separated components of CQRS can still be independently deployed, we can say that each unit of deployment still satisfies the minimum requirements for independently delivering features into production. One feature of a microservice should require at most one deployable unit.

We could get most of the way to a CQRS architecture using straight Spring Cloud Stream and Spring Data, but we'd have to fill in some gaps, like event sourcing and command routing, ourselves. Instead, we'll use the Axon Framework (*http://axonfra mework.org*). Axon is a framework developed by Allard Buijze (*https://twitter.com/ allardbz*) and his team at Trifork. Axon has a lot of good things going for it: it's been around for seven years (and counting!), and it's always worked nicely with Spring. It even provides a handy Spring Boot auto-configuration, offered as the recommended approach. Axon has been evolving to rapidly incorporate more and more of the Spring Cloud ecosystem, as well.

The Axon project draws its name from the axon terminal. In the nervous system, an axon (one of the components of a neuron) transports electrical signals. These neurons are interconnected in very complex arrangements. The axon terminal is responsible for transmitting these signals from one neuron to another.

Let's look at an example Axon application.

The Complaints API

Let's implement our hypothetical `complaint` service. We'll also build another micro-service that supports reporting statistics for the complaints. The main complaint service will support creating and closing a complaint, as well as adding comments to a complaint. We will want to ensure that a comment can't be added to a complaint that is no longer open. For these operations—adding a complaint, closing it, and adding comments—all writes are communicated using *commands*. A command is a message —an object—that has parameters that our command handlers will use to carry out their work. A command message has little or no behavior—just data.

In this example, as elsewhere in the book, we'll make prolific use of the Lombok project. Lombok is a framework to support compile-time annotation processing. It defines several useful compile-time annotations like `@Data` (which adds getters and setters for fields in an object and provides a useful `toString` and `equals` method), and `@AllArgsConstructor` or `@NoArgsConstructor`, which generate constructors for all the fields in the class and a constructor that accepts no parameters, respectively.

The entry point into the complaints API is a REST API. HTTP requests are handled in Spring MVC handler methods, which then dispatch commands on the command bus (Example 12-3).

Example 12-3. The complaints API

```
package complaints;

import org.axonframework.commandhandling.gateway.CommandGateway;
import org.springframework.beans.factory.annotation.Autowired;
import org.springframework.http.HttpStatus;
import org.springframework.http.MediaType;
import org.springframework.http.ResponseEntity;
import org.springframework.web.bind.annotation.*;
import org.springframework.web.util.UriComponents;
import org.springframework.web.util.UriComponentsBuilder;

import java.net.URI;
import java.util.*;
import java.util.concurrent.CompletableFuture;

import static org.springframework.http.MediaType.APPLICATION_JSON_VALUE;

//@formatter:off
```

```
@RestController
@RequestMapping(value = "/complaints",
  consumes = APPLICATION_JSON_VALUE,
  produces = APPLICATION_JSON_VALUE)
class ComplaintsRestController {
//@formatter:on

  private final CommandGateway cg;

  @Autowired
  ComplaintsRestController(CommandGateway cg) {
    this.cg = cg;
  }

  ❶
  @PostMapping
  CompletableFuture<ResponseEntity<?>> createComplaint(
    @RequestBody Map<String, String> body) {

    String id = UUID.randomUUID().toString();
    FileComplaintCommand complaint = new FileComplaintCommand(id,
      body.get("company"), body.get("description"));

    return this.cg.send(complaint).thenApply(
      complaintId -> {
        URI uri = uri("/complaints/{id}",
          Collections.singletonMap("id", complaint.getId()));
        return ResponseEntity.created(uri).build();
      });
  }

  ❷
  @PostMapping("/{complaintId}/comments")
  @ResponseStatus(HttpStatus.NOT_FOUND)
  CompletableFuture<ResponseEntity<?>> addComment(
    @PathVariable String complaintId, @RequestBody Map<String, Object> body) {

    Long when = Long.class.cast(body.getOrDefault("when",
      System.currentTimeMillis()));

    AddCommentCommand command = new AddCommentCommand(complaintId, UUID
      .randomUUID().toString(), String.class.cast(body.get("comment")),
      String.class.cast(body.get("user")), new Date(when));

    return this.cg.send(command).thenApply(commentId -> {

      Map<String, String> parms = new HashMap<>();
      parms.put("complaintId", complaintId);
      parms.put("commentId", command.getCommentId());

      URI uri = uri("/complaints/{complaintId}/comments/{commentId}", parms);
```

```
    return ResponseEntity.created(uri).build();
  });
}

@DeleteMapping("/{complaintId}")
CompletableFuture<ResponseEntity<?>> closeComplaint(
 @PathVariable String complaintId) {
 CloseComplaintCommand csc = new CloseComplaintCommand(complaintId);
 return this.cg.send(csc).thenApply(none -> ResponseEntity.notFound().build());
}

private static URI uri(String uri, Map<String, String> template) {
 UriComponents uriComponents = UriComponentsBuilder.newInstance().path(uri)
   .build().expand(template);
 return uriComponents.toUri();
 }
}
```

❶ The writes (as HTTP POST requests) go through the /complaints endpoint,
   which in turn uses the CommandGateway to send the command to the CommandBus.
   The result of a #send on the CommandGateway is a CompletableFuture<T>. Spring
   MVC knows how to work with a CompletableFuture<T>—it'll return a response
   to the client only when the result of the CompletableFuture has materialized. In
   the meantime, it'll unblock the HTTP request processing thread, moving the
   work to a background thread.

❷ In order to add a comment to a given complaint, the AddCommentCommand must
   carry the identifier of the parent complaint in the command. This is used in the
   aggregate to tie the command to the right instance of the aggregate.

The *command gateway* asynchronously dispatches the commands to the appropriate
command handlers based on type. Ultimately, the command gateway delegates to a
command router, which resolves where the command handlers should be invoked. By
default it's in the same node, but there are alternative strategies to load-balance those
calls. One implementation supports JGroups, and another supports the Spring Cloud
DiscoveryClient abstraction for service location.

A *command handler*, in Axon parlance, is just a method in a bean annotated with
@CommandHandler. Any Spring bean can define command handlers. Our API supports three operations, so there are three commands, at least: creating a complaint
(FileComplaintCommand), adding a comment (AddCommentCommand), and closing a
complaint (CloseComplaintCommand). See Example 12-4.

Example 12-4. The FileComplaintCommand command signals that a new complaint should be created

```
package complaints;

import lombok.AllArgsConstructor;
import lombok.Data;
import lombok.NoArgsConstructor;
import org.axonframework.commandhandling.TargetAggregateIdentifier;

@Data
@AllArgsConstructor
@NoArgsConstructor
public class FileComplaintCommand {

  @TargetAggregateIdentifier
  private String id; ❶

  private String company, description; ❷

}
```

❶ We'll revisit the significance of `@TargetAggregateIdentifier` shortly…

❷ …otherwise, this is a plain ol' Java object—a POJO. We need to know the complaint itself, and the company against whom we'd like to lodge the complaint.

Example 12-5. The AddCommentCommand command signals that a comment should be added to an existing complaint

```
package complaints;

import lombok.AllArgsConstructor;
import lombok.Data;
import lombok.NoArgsConstructor;
import org.axonframework.commandhandling.TargetAggregateIdentifier;

import java.util.Date;

@Data
@NoArgsConstructor
@AllArgsConstructor
public class AddCommentCommand {

  @TargetAggregateIdentifier
  private String complaintId; ❶

  private String commentId, comment, user;
```

```
  private Date when;
}
```

❶ Even though, ultimately, in our query model, this will result in the contribution of one or more objects in a child relationship, it's still something that is managed in terms of the owning complaint whose ID we include here.

Example 12-6. The CloseComplaintCommand command signals that a complaint should be closed

```
package complaints;

import lombok.AllArgsConstructor;
import lombok.Data;
import lombok.NoArgsConstructor;
import org.axonframework.commandhandling.TargetAggregateIdentifier;

❶
@Data
@AllArgsConstructor
@NoArgsConstructor
public class CloseComplaintCommand {

 @TargetAggregateIdentifier
 private String complaintId;
}
```

❶ The only thing we need to know is on which entity to act.

A command handler's job is to validate the command object payload, inspect that the command is valid, and then manipulate the domain model's state. A command handler *could* load up a JdbcTemplate or a Spring Data repository and perform the write there, on the spot. But then it would need to publish an event so that interested observers may update their query models accordingly. Here, a command handler could dispatch events on the Axon event bus to any and all interested listeners. Any component may also express interest in events by specifying *event handlers*. We recommend that, instead of performing the write in the command handler, the command handlers publish an event and then perform the writes in an event handler. In this way we train our brain to think of updates to our own domain as the same as updates to a third-party API.

Some coordination may be required between commands. How would we know in the command handler for the AddCommentCommand that a complaint is still open when we try to create a child comment if we can't load and inspect the parent complaint? We need that information, somehow. A normal Spring component won't do; a nominal Spring component should be a stateless singleton. Each call to an event handler on a regular Spring component is routed to a stateless singleton bean which should have no recollection of previous transactions related to the complaint.

Enter Axon aggregates. An *aggregate* is a stateful component whose identity is the result of the mutations applied after processing domain events. Axon uses an Axon repository implementation to load aggregates. Some repositories store the aggregate itself (e.g., using JPA), while others use the past events to reconstruct current state (this is called event sourcing). The distinction is a choice we can make based on the requirements of our system. Our aggregate is an event-sourcing aggregate: it will replay events to recreate the latest state of any given aggregate. Let's look at an example, then we'll dissect what's happening (Example 12-7).

Example 12-7. The ComplaintAggregate aggregate contains both command handlers and event sourcing handlers

```
package complaints.command;

import complaints.*;
import org.axonframework.commandhandling.CommandHandler;
import org.axonframework.commandhandling.model.AggregateIdentifier;
import org.axonframework.eventsourcing.EventSourcingHandler;
import org.axonframework.spring.stereotype.Aggregate;
import org.springframework.util.Assert;

import static org.axonframework.commandhandling.model.AggregateLifecycle.apply;

❶
@Aggregate
public class ComplaintAggregate {

  ❷
  @AggregateIdentifier
  private String complaintId;

  private boolean closed;

  public ComplaintAggregate() {
  }

  ❸
  @CommandHandler
  public ComplaintAggregate(FileComplaintCommand c) {
    Assert.hasLength(c.getCompany());
    Assert.hasLength(c.getDescription());
    apply(new ComplaintFiledEvent(c.getId(), c.getCompany(), c.getDescription()));
  }

  ❹
  @CommandHandler
  public void resolveComplaint(CloseComplaintCommand ccc) {
```

```
  if (!this.closed) {
   apply(new ComplaintClosedEvent(this.complaintId));
  }
}


❺
@CommandHandler
public void addComment(AddCommentCommand c) {
 Assert.hasLength(c.getComment());
 Assert.hasLength(c.getCommentId());
 Assert.hasLength(c.getComplaintId());
 Assert.hasLength(c.getUser());
 Assert.notNull(c.getWhen());
 Assert.isTrue(!this.closed);
 apply(new CommentAddedEvent(c.getComplaintId(), c.getCommentId(),
   c.getComment(), c.getUser(), c.getWhen()));
}


❻
@EventSourcingHandler
protected void on(ComplaintFiledEvent cfe) {
 this.complaintId = cfe.getId();
 this.closed = false;
}


❼
@EventSourcingHandler
protected void on(ComplaintClosedEvent cce) {
 this.closed = true;
}

}
```

❶ The @Aggregate stereotype annotation signals that this object is a bean whose life cycle Spring manages.

❷ When a command is dispatched on the CommandGateway, its @TargetAggregate Identifier attribute links it to this aggregate by a value in its @AggregateIdentifier-annotated field.

❸ A new instance of the aggregate will be created when a FileComplaintCommand is dispatched. If validation is successful, then a ComplaintFiledEvent is dispatched. The ComplaintFiledEvent gets written to the event store and then dispatched to any event handlers and event-sourcing handlers (like on(ComplaintFiledEvent cce)) in this aggregate and in other components.

❹ The complaint will be closed when a CloseComplaintCommand is dispatched. If validation is successful, then a ComplaintClosedEvent is dispatched. The Com `plaintClosedEvent` gets written to the event store and then dispatched to any event handlers and event-sourcing handlers (like `on(ComplaintClosedEvent cce)`) in this aggregate and in other components.

❺ A new comment will be added to the complaint when a `AddCommentCommand` is dispatched. If validation is successful, then a `CommentAddedEvent` is dispatched.

❻ This first event-sourcing handler initializes an aggregate, providing it a aggregate identifier and (redundantly) initializing the `closed` Boolean to `false`.

❼ The second event-sourcing handler sets the `closed` Boolean to `true` on receipt of a `ComplaintClosedEvent`.

Thus, Axon supports two types of event listeners. If an event is to be processed outside of an aggregate, then use `@EventListener` when specifying an event handler. If an aggregate, specifically, handles an event and that event contributes to the durable identity of an aggregate, then use an `@EventSourcingHandler` when specifying an event handler.

When a command handler publishes an event destined to manipulate a specific instance of an aggregate, Axon needs a way to route that event to the right instance of an aggregate. Events may provide an identifier (annotated with `@TargetAggregate Identifier`) that links it to a particular instance of an aggregate. If a command handler exists in an aggregate, then Axon will load the right instance of that aggregate from the repository and process the command on that instance of the aggregate.

 Why embrace event sourcing? In our sample domain, one serving the use case of customer service, it is valuable to keep a history of the complaint's mutations. We want to be able to replay the events that led to an aggregate's ultimate state. If you prefer that the Axon repository instead just load the aggregate from the database, add `@Entity` to the aggregate and drop the `@AggregateIdentifier`, replacing it with JPA's `@Id`. You would also drop the `@EventSourcingHandler`-annotated methods.

Here is the `ComplaintAggregate` along with its command handlers and event handlers. When the `FileComplaintCommand` is published, it's used to create a new instance of this aggregate. When the `AddCommentCommand` is published, it triggers an event that has a target `@AggregateIdentifier` that Axon uses to route handling back to this aggregate instance. Axon will rehydrate the aggregate by loading the events from the event store and calling the appropriate event-sourcing handlers, which should, when replayed in order, result in an aggregate that reflects the latest state of that aggregate.

You may have noticed that the events are mirror images of the commands, turning the imperative verb into the past participle: e.g., `FileComplaintCommand` results in a `ComplaintFiledEvent`. This is typical, but there's no reason that a command couldn't result in the creation of multiple events, which in turn launch more commands. The event-sourcing handlers on this aggregate are persisted in the event store automatically when you call the `AggregateLifecycle#apply` method within the command handler. When Axon tries to reconstruct the aggregate, it will know to call the same event-sourcing handlers in the same order to arrive at the latest known and valid state for the aggregate.

Let's look at the events. As with the commands, these are merely parcels of data with very little intrinsic state (Examples 12-8 through 12-10).

Example 12-8. The ComplaintFiledEvent is dispatched when a complaint is filed

```
package complaints;

import lombok.AllArgsConstructor;
import lombok.Data;

@Data
@AllArgsConstructor
public class ComplaintFiledEvent {

  private final String id;

  private final String company;

  private final String complaint;
}
```

Example 12-9. The CommentAddedEvent is dispatched when a comment is added to a parent complaint

```
package complaints;

import lombok.AllArgsConstructor;
import lombok.Data;

@Data
@AllArgsConstructor
public class ComplaintClosedEvent {

  private String complaintId;

}
```

Example 12-10. The ComplaintClosedEvent is dispatched when a complaint is closed

```
package complaints;

import lombok.AllArgsConstructor;
import lombok.Data;

@Data
@AllArgsConstructor
public class ComplaintClosedEvent {

 private String complaintId;

}
```

The events tie updates to the command model to updates in the query model or models. In the query (or *view model*), components listen for events and update the query model accordingly. In this case, the query model is *also* driven by a Spring Data JPA-powered repository, though it could be handled using MongoDB, HBase, Neo4J, a file on a filesystem, or anything else. The view model consists of two JPA entities, Com plaintQueryObject and CommentQueryObject. The ComplaintQueryObject owns a collection of CommentQueryObject instances. The ComplaintEventProcessor translates events into operations on the query model, updating or persisting JPA entities as needed (Example 12-11).

Example 12-11. The ComplaintEventProcessor

```
package complaints.query;

import complaints.CommentAddedEvent;
import complaints.ComplaintClosedEvent;
import complaints.ComplaintFiledEvent;
import org.axonframework.eventhandling.EventHandler;
import org.springframework.beans.factory.annotation.Autowired;
import org.springframework.stereotype.Component;

import java.util.Collections;

@Component
public class ComplaintEventProcessor {

 private final ComplaintQueryObjectRepository complaints;

 private final CommentQueryObjectRepository comments;

 ❶
 @Autowired
 ComplaintEventProcessor(ComplaintQueryObjectRepository complaints,
  CommentQueryObjectRepository comments) {
```

```
  this.complaints = complaints;
  this.comments = comments;
 }

 @EventHandler
 public void on(ComplaintFiledEvent cfe) {
  ComplaintQueryObject complaint = new ComplaintQueryObject(cfe.getId(),
   cfe.getComplaint(), cfe.getCompany(), Collections.emptySet(), false);
  this.complaints.save(complaint);
 }

 @EventHandler
 public void on(CommentAddedEvent cae) {
  ComplaintQueryObject complaint = this.complaints
   .findOne(cae.getComplaintId());
  CommentQueryObject comment = new CommentQueryObject(complaint,
   cae.getCommentId(), cae.getComment(), cae.getUser(), cae.getWhen());
  this.comments.save(comment);
 }

 @EventHandler
 public void on(ComplaintClosedEvent cce) {
  ComplaintQueryObject complaintQueryObject = this.complaints.findOne(cce
   .getComplaintId());
  complaintQueryObject.setClosed(true);
  this.complaints.save(complaintQueryObject);
 }
}
```

❶ This event processor uses two Spring Data JPA-based repository implementations.

We've already taken care to write our updates in a way that is essentially asynchronous and independent from the processing of the commands. The event handlers update the complaint domain model asynchronously and independently of the commands that dispatch the events. We can *also* publish these events to other nodes in the system using messaging.

Axon features out-of-the-box distribution of events over AMQP, a protocol supported by brokers like RabbitMQ. We need to configure our application to talk to a RabbitMQ instance. Add the Spring Boot RabbitMQ starter, `spring-boot-starter-amqp`, and configure a RabbitMQ `ConnectionFactory` (you can rely on the defaults or specify properties in your `Environment`), and Axon will broadcast events accordingly. Let's look at the configuration required to publish events from our complaints API. First, we need to configure the name of the destination that we want to use in our `application.properties` in Example 12-12.

Example 12-12. application.properties

```
axon.amqp.exchange=complaints
logging.level.org.axonframework=DEBUG
```

That, of course, refers to an exchange (`complaints`) in RabbitMQ that may or may not exist, so we need to configure the AMQP components, as well. AMQP makes the creation and administration of broker-side components like queues and exchanges a part of the protocol, so all RabbitMQ clients can configure them as we do in Example 12-13.

Example 12-13. The AmqpConfiguration

```java
package complaints;

import org.springframework.amqp.core.*;
import org.springframework.beans.factory.annotation.Autowired;
import org.springframework.context.annotation.Bean;
import org.springframework.context.annotation.Configuration;

@Configuration
class AmqpConfiguration {

  private static final String COMPLAINTS = "complaints";

  ❶
  @Bean
  Exchange exchange() {
   return ExchangeBuilder.fanoutExchange(COMPLAINTS).build();
  }

  ❷
  @Bean
  Queue queue() {
   return QueueBuilder.durable(COMPLAINTS).build();
  }

  ❸
  @Bean
  Binding binding() {
   return BindingBuilder.bind(queue()) //
    .to(exchange()).with("*").noargs();
  }

  ❹
  @Autowired
  public void configure(AmqpAdmin admin) {
   admin.declareExchange(exchange());
   admin.declareQueue(queue());
   admin.declareBinding(binding());
```

```
    }
}
```

❶ The messages arrive at the exchange...

❷ ...which then forwards them to a queue.

❸ We link these two together using a binding...

❹ ...and make sure that RabbitMQ declares them accordingly.

The Complaint Statistics API

With this infrastructure in place, it's trivial to connect other nodes to these events so that they can update their respective query models. The `demo-complaints-stats` module is a REST API that responds to the `ComplaintFiledEvent` event to update a tally of companies to complaints received. We must tell Axon to drain events from RabbitMQ and dispatch them to the appropriate event handlers. Axon exposes a concept called an *event processor*, as events may come from different sources. We specify that this processor, based on AMQP, is called `complaints` in our configuration (Example 12-14).

Example 12-14. application.properties

```
axon.eventhandling.processors.statistics.source=statistics
server.port=8081
```

Finally, we must set up an AMQP message listener container in order to process incoming messages. We must tie the incoming messages to the AMQP-based processor using a property in the configuration in Example 12-15.

Example 12-15. ComplaintsStatsApplication

```
package complaints;

import com.rabbitmq.client.Channel;
import org.axonframework.amqp.eventhandling.spring.SpringAMQPMessageSource;
import org.axonframework.serialization.Serializer;
import org.springframework.amqp.core.Message;
import org.springframework.amqp.rabbit.annotation.RabbitListener;
import org.springframework.boot.SpringApplication;
import org.springframework.boot.autoconfigure.SpringBootApplication;
import org.springframework.context.annotation.Bean;

@SpringBootApplication
public class ComplaintsStatsApplication {
```

```
public static void main(String[] args) {
 SpringApplication.run(ComplaintsStatsApplication.class, args);
}

❶
@Bean
SpringAMQPMessageSource statistics(Serializer serializer) {
 return new SpringAMQPMessageSource(serializer) {

  @Override
  @RabbitListener(queues = "complaints")
  public void onMessage(Message message, Channel channel) throws Exception {
   super.onMessage(message, channel);
  }
 };
 }
}
```

❶ Configure how inbound events should be consumed and dispatched.

The main listener in this trivial REST API is in the REST API itself. It keeps a (concurrency-friendly!) map of counts of complaints observed for each company (Example 12-16).

Example 12-16. The StatisticsRestController

```
package complaints;

import org.axonframework.config.ProcessingGroup;
import org.axonframework.eventhandling.EventHandler;
import org.springframework.web.bind.annotation.GetMapping;
import org.springframework.web.bind.annotation.RestController;

import java.util.concurrent.ConcurrentHashMap;
import java.util.concurrent.ConcurrentMap;
import java.util.concurrent.atomic.AtomicLong;

❶
@ProcessingGroup("statistics")
@RestController
class StatisticsRestController {
 //@formatter:off
 private final ConcurrentMap<String, AtomicLong> statistics =
  new ConcurrentHashMap<>();
 //@formatter:on

 ❷
 @EventHandler
 public void on(ComplaintFiledEvent event) {
  statistics.computeIfAbsent(event.getCompany(), k -> new AtomicLong())
```

```
  .incrementAndGet();
}
```

❸
```
@GetMapping
public ConcurrentMap<String, AtomicLong> showStatistics() {
 return statistics;
}
}
```

❶ We want only event messages from the `statistics` processor group.

❷ As an event arrives, we update the in-memory Map…

❸ …and then expose it under the REST endpoint. Issue an HTTP GET to `http://localhost:8081/` by default.

And with that, we've stood up two services, one of which relies upon, but isn't coupled to, another service. It wouldn't be hard to introduce more services into the mix. Components don't need to know, or care, about how other services manage their state.

So far we've only begun to scratch the surface of what you can do with Axon and CQRS. Axon 3 is a *huge* overhaul that fully embraces Spring Boot. Axon integrates numerous corners of the Spring ecosystem already. We hope to see easy integration with Spring `MessageChannel` instances, instead of specific coupling to RabbitMQ, in a future revision. Axon makes it easy to get going with CQRS in a clean, consistent fashion. You can start with a command and query model in the same node, and then spread out across multiple nodes by using messaging. You can start without support for event sourcing, and then integrate it if the use case arises. Axon also provides support for aggregates that participate in *sagas*, which we looked at in "The Saga Pattern" on page 399, though this will have to remain a topic for another day.

Spring Cloud Data Flow

In Chapter 10, we looked at how the right abstractions—Spring Integration and Spring Cloud Stream—let us work with other systems in terms of the `MessageChan nel`. Spring Cloud Stream leaves as a matter of convention and external configuration the connections through message brokers required to do so. As far as our services are concerned, data comes in from a channel and leaves through a channel. Channels are the pipes in a pipes-and-filters architecture, connecting different components to each other. The "interface" for these components is uniform: a `Message<T>`. This is very similar to the way `stdin` and `stdout` on the command line work: data-in and data-out. The transport is well understood in that all the components agree to interoperate on what kind of payloads to produce or consume. In a UNIX shell environment, it's easy to compose arbitrarily complex solutions out of singly focused command-line utilities, piping data through `stdin` and `stdout`. We can do the same thing with our Spring Cloud-based messaging microservices. Spring Cloud Stream raises the abstraction level so that we can focus on the business logic and ignore the details of conveyance from one service to another. We can create higher order systems and orchestrate our messaging microservices with Spring Cloud Data Flow.

Spring Cloud Data Flow supports easy creation of staged event-driven architectures (SEDA), an ideal pattern in a cloud where services need to be robust enough to absorb extra load and scale horizontally.

 What is SEDA? *SEDA* refers to a software architecture that decomposes event-driven applications into a set of stages connected by queues. It avoids the high overhead associated with thread-based concurrency models, and decouples event and thread scheduling from application logic. Services can stay available by throttling incoming load on each event queue. This prevents resources from being overcommitted when demand exceeds service capacity. See our discussion on messaging in Chapter 10 for more.

At the heart of Spring Cloud Data Flow are the concepts of streams and tasks.

A *stream* represents a logical stringing together of different Spring Cloud Stream-based modules—applications. Spring Cloud Data Flow ultimately deploys and launches different applications and overrides their default Spring Cloud Stream binding destinations so that data flows from one node to another in the way we describe. Complex event processing, sensor analytics, log analytics, online trading, and so many other event-centric scenarios are easy to model in the world of streams.

A *task*, on the other hand, is any process whose execution status we want to inspect but that we also expect to, ultimately if not immediately, terminate.

Strictly speaking, Spring Cloud Data Flow doesn't *deploy* your applications; it delegates that work to a Spring Cloud Deployer implementation. Where most data analytics platforms (like Apache Flink or Apache Spark or Apache Hadoop) define their own clustering runtimes, the Spring Cloud Data Flow team went to great lengths to ensure that Spring Cloud Data Flow could leverage existing and quite capable runtimes. The Spring Cloud Deployer (*https://github.com/spring-cloud/spring-cloud-deployer*) project defines an abstraction to manage tasks or streams locally or on runtimes and platforms like Cloud Foundry (*http://cloudfoundry.org*), Apache YARN, Mesos, or Kubernetes. There are community-contributed and maintained implementations for Hashicorp Nomad (*http://bit.ly/2s9VzpU*) and RedHat Openshift (*http://bit.ly/2salrSV*) as well. It provides two key interfaces: `AppDeployer` and `TaskLauncher`. The `AppDeployer` concerns itself with the life cycle of deployment, and `TaskLauncher` concerns itself with the life cycle of an execution. `AppDeployer` supports deploying, undeploying, and asking for the status of (potentially indeterminately long-lived) applications. `TaskLauncher` supports starting, cancelling, and cleaning up instances of so-deployed applications.

 In this example, we'll look at the *local* Spring Cloud Data Flow implementation, which needs only compiled `.jar` artifacts deployed into the local Maven repository to work.

To find a Data Flow implementation for your distribution fabric, check out the Spring Cloud Data Flow project page (*http://cloud.spring.io/spring-cloud-dataflow/*). There you'll find implementations for numerous technologies, incuding the *Local Server*, which we'll use in our examples here. The integration tests for the code in this chapter deploy to, and use, the Spring Cloud Data Flow Cloud Foundry Server implementation to achieve true horizontal scalability.

Streams

Streams are further subdivided into three types of components: *sources* (where messages are produced), *processors* (in which an incoming message is processed and then sent out) and *sinks* (where an incoming message is consumed). In Spring Cloud Data Flow, each of these components are manifest at runtime as a distinct, running Spring Cloud Stream-powered application instance. A source and a sink correspond more or less to the notion of a Spring Integration inbound adapter and outbound adapter, respectively, while a processor corresponds more or less to the notion of a Spring Integration transformer. All streams are made up of combinations of these three components. Spring Cloud Data Flow automatically composes and combines these application instances with Spring Cloud Stream-powered bindings, connecting one running application to another in another process or another node altogether.

By default, the Spring Cloud Data Flow server is a blank canvas. It needs registered applications—the building blocks of more complex solutions—to compose into custom stream and task definitions. Before you start writing and registering custom applications, try to use some of the many prebuilt applications provided by the Spring Cloud Stream App Starters project (*https://github.com/spring-cloud/spring-cloud-stream-app-starters*). You can register applications manually, one at a time, or in bulk with an application properties file. Spring Cloud Data Flow will launch these applications on any of the various Spring Cloud Deployer implementations, and it will connect them using any of the various Spring Cloud Stream binders. This implies multiple dimensions of configuration are required: should the application description refer to a Maven artifact or a Docker repository artifact? Should the application description refer to an application compiled against the Spring Cloud Stream RabbitMQ binder or the Spring Cloud Stream Apache Kafka binding? Happily, there are definitions on the Spring Cloud Stream App Starters home page (*http://cloud.spring.io/spring-cloud-stream-app-starters/*).

You can catalog all the custom applications in your system and register them with the Spring Cloud Data Flow server, as well. Here is a simple application property file for several modules (Example 12-17). Each line specifies the type of component (a source, a sink, a processor, etc.), a logical name for the application, and a URL that is resolvable using an `org.springframework.core.io.Resource` implementation on the classpath. Spring Cloud Data Flow provides new implementations supporting Maven repository lookup and Docker registry lookup, among others.

Example 12-17. A custom application definition property file

```
source.account-web=maven://org.cnj:account-web:0.0.1-SNAPSHOT
sink.account-worker=maven://org.cnj:account-worker:0.0.1-SNAPSHOT
source.order-web=maven://org.cnj:order-web:0.0.1-SNAPSHOT
sink.order-worker=maven://org.cnj:order-worker:0.0.1-SNAPSHOT
source.payment-web=maven://org.cnj:payment-web:0.0.1-SNAPSHOT
sink.payment-worker=maven://org.cnj:payment-worker:0.0.1-SNAPSHOT
source.warehouse-web=maven://org.cnj:warehouse-web:0.0.1-SNAPSHOT
sink.warehouse-worker=maven://org.cnj:warehouse-worker:0.0.1-SNAPSHOT
```

If none meet your requirements, it's easy to build a custom application.

Suppose we want to plug a custom application into a stream definition. Use the Spring Initializr (*http://start.spring.io*), select the binder you wish to use (RabbitMQ or Apache Kafka), and then fill in the code with a trivial processor that takes its input String message, adds { before and } after the body of the message, and then forwards the message on (Example 12-18).

Example 12-18. A trivial Spring Cloud Data Flow processor

```
package stream;

import org.springframework.boot.SpringApplication;
import org.springframework.boot.autoconfigure.SpringBootApplication;
import org.springframework.cloud.stream.annotation.EnableBinding;
import org.springframework.cloud.stream.messaging.Processor;
import org.springframework.integration.annotation.MessageEndpoint;
import org.springframework.integration.annotation.ServiceActivator;
import org.springframework.integration.support.MessageBuilder;
import org.springframework.messaging.Message;

@MessageEndpoint
❶
@EnableBinding(Processor.class)
❷
```

```
@SpringBootApplication
public class ProcessorStreamExample {

  public static void main(String[] args) {
   SpringApplication.run(ProcessorStreamExample.class, args);
  }

  @ServiceActivator(inputChannel = Processor.INPUT, outputChannel = Processor.OUTPUT)
  public Message<String> process(Message<String> in) {
   return MessageBuilder.withPayload("{" + in.getPayload() + "}") ❸
    .copyHeadersIfAbsent(in.getHeaders()).build();
  }
}
```

❶ This is a Spring Integration messaging component that...

❷ ...depends on the default Spring Cloud Stream `Processor` binding, which provides a well-known `input` and a well-known `output` `MessageChannel` definition.

❸ The processor wraps its payload with curly brackets.

We've installed this processor application into our local Maven repository with a
group ID of `cnj`, an artifact ID of `stream-example`, and a version of `1.0.0-SNAPSHOT`.
If we register this processor as an application in an application definition file under,
say, the name `brackets`, we can use it in larger solutions. It becomes another building
block. Using a mix of custom and prebuilt applications, we can assemble more
sophisticated solutions using the Spring Cloud Data Flow stream DSL. Suppose we
wanted to connect the output of the `time` source (which produces a `Message` every
second) to our newly imported `brackets` processor, and then connect the output of
the `brackets` processor to a component that logs its inputs, `log`. Such a stream is
easily realized with the Spring Cloud Data Flow stream DSL, as evidenced by
Example 12-19 and the figure that follows.

Example 12-19. A trivial stream definition

```
time | brackets | log
```

This definition would result in three distinct operating system processes being spun
up, possibly on different nodes, depending on the Spring Cloud Deployer implementation in use. The processes are bound to each other dynamically through a Spring

Cloud Stream binder (RabbitMQ, Apache Kafka, etc.). Suppose we wanted to log both the product of the first stream and the product of the time source. We can use a *tap* in Spring Cloud Data Flow to route the product of one component (a source or a processor) to another component, *in addition to* any connection already established. Let's see how that is done in Example 12-20 and the image that follows.

Example 12-20. Tap the results of the time source

```
BRACKETED_STREAM=time | brackets | log ❶
:BRACKETED_STREAM.time > log ❷
```

❶ Assign the definition to a variable name…

❷ …then dereference the component whose output we wish to tap in terms of the variable name.

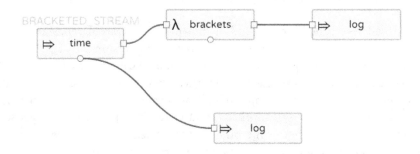

Streams are ideal for potentially infinite amounts of processing. As the components are connected through queues, they can be easily scaled up and down using whatever mechanisms are available to you in the distribution fabric of your Spring Cloud Deployer implementation. On Cloud Foundry, it's as trivial as saying cf scale - i .., where .. is the logical name assigned to the application instance for a component in the Spring Cloud Data Flow stream definition. The queues absorb extra load, ensuring that even if you don't have enough capacity, the overall system will remain stable. Streams are an ideal way to describe staged event-driven architectures (SEDAs).

Tasks

Spring Cloud Data Flow can also manage the life cycle and deployment of Spring Batch-based tasks. Use the Spring Initializr to generate a Spring Cloud application. Add org.springframework.cloud: spring-cloud-task-core, org.springframe work.cloud : spring-cloud-task-batch, and org.springframework.boot : spring-boot-starter-batch to the project's classpath to activate Spring Batch, Spring Cloud Task, and the Spring Cloud Task bridge (Example 12-21).

Example 12-21. A simple Spring Batch Job defined in a Spring Cloud Task example

```
package task;

import org.apache.commons.logging.Log;
import org.apache.commons.logging.LogFactory;
import org.springframework.batch.core.Job;
import org.springframework.batch.core.Step;
import org.springframework.batch.core.configuration.annotation.EnableBatchProcessing;
import org.springframework.batch.core.configuration.annotation.JobBuilderFactory;
import org.springframework.batch.core.configuration.annotation.StepBuilderFactory;
import org.springframework.batch.repeat.RepeatStatus;
import org.springframework.boot.SpringApplication;
import org.springframework.boot.autoconfigure.SpringBootApplication;
import org.springframework.cloud.task.configuration.EnableTask;
import org.springframework.context.annotation.Bean;

@EnableTask
❶
@EnableBatchProcessing
@SpringBootApplication
public class BatchTaskExample {

 private Log log = LogFactory.getLog(getClass());

 public static void main(String[] args) {
  SpringApplication.run(BatchTaskExample.class, args);
 }

 @Bean
 Step tasklet(StepBuilderFactory sbf, BatchTaskProperties btp) {
  return sbf.get("tasklet").tasklet((contribution, chunkContext) -> {
   log.info("input = " + btp.getInput());
   return RepeatStatus.FINISHED;
  }).build();
 }

 @Bean
 Job hello(JobBuilderFactory jbf) {
  Step step = this.tasklet(null, null);
  return jbf.get("batch-task").start(step).build();
 }
}
```

❶ Activate Spring Cloud Task abstraction.

Install this task application in your local Maven repository with a group ID of cnj, an artifact ID of task-example, and a version of 1.0.0-SNAPSHOT for use later.

The REST API

The heart of Spring Cloud Data Flow is a server that provides a REST API to manage streams and tasks. The server persists its state in a relational database; it uses an embedded H2 instance by default, though you can provide your own data source definition. You drive this API through the Spring Cloud Data Flow DataFlowTemplate, through a web application that comes bundled along with the Data Flow server, or through an interactive shell.

While it is possible to stand up Spring Cloud Data Flow as a Spring Boot module, we recommend you just spin up the turnkey prebuilt .jar application implementations for each Spring Cloud Deployer type distributed and described on the project's page (*http://cloud.spring.io/spring-cloud-dataflow/*). It boils down to downloading the current version and then running the .jar with the java command.

 When you run the Cloud Foundry version, it's the same basic process, except that you'll also specify a number of properties (or environment variables) that help the Cloud Foundry client used in the deployer authenticate and interact with your Cloud Foundry target.

Launch the server and it'll spin up on port 9393, ready to use.

Meet the Data Flow Clients

With the server up, there are a few things we will commonly want to do:

- Register existing task and stream applications (those in the Maven repository, or in a Docker repository)
- Define streams and tasks
- Launch streams and tasks
- Interrogate the status of the running streams and tasks

So we will need a Spring Cloud Data Flow client! Which client you use depends entirely on what you're trying to achieve. If you're an operator or a developer, you'll probably want to get started using the dashboard. It provides a guided experience, surfacing all the useful functions of Spring Cloud Data Flow as functions of the user interface. If you want to know what's possible and want a place to experiment and get fast, visual feedback, start with the dashboard. Operators will eventually prefer the shell; it provides a scriptable way to describe higher-level operations. If, as a developer, you need to automate certain aspects of Spring Cloud Data Flow, or integrate some of its behavior in a larger application, then you'll appreciate the `DataFlowTem plate`.

The Dashboard

The dashboard web application is installed at `http://localhost:9393/dashboard`. The dashboard makes it easy to visually describe complex Spring Cloud Data Flow application definitions and to manage them. The dashboard includes a visual modeling tool called Spring Flo that supports building stream definitions interactively.

If you want to register applications, you can do so one at a time or in bulk under the *Apps* tab (Figure 12-1).

Figure 12-1. The main screen for the Spring Cloud Data Flow dashboard, the Apps tab

You can point Spring Cloud Data Flow to any valid `org.springframe work.core.io.Resource`-resolvable URI for a definition of an application. Earlier, we installed a `processor` and a `task` application into our Maven repository. To install the processor, assign it a name, select *Processor* as the application type, and enter the URI: `maven://cnj:stream-example:1.0.0-SNAPSHOT`. Figure 12-2 captures the UI as we do this.

Figure 12-2. Registering a custom processor in the dashboard

You could alternatively bulk-register multiple applications, either by referencing an application definition file or by pasting the contents of one directly into the input form field. Figure 12-3 captures the UI as we do this.

Figure 12-3. Bulk registration of application definitions

You can also choose to bulk-register some of the convenient prepackaged and pre-written applications provided by the Spring Cloud Data Flow team with your choice of binding and packaging. Figure 12-4 captures the UI as we do this.

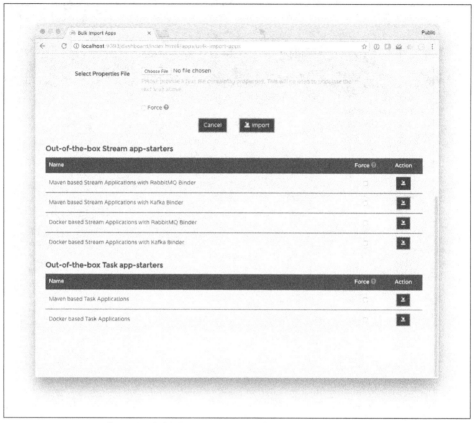

Figure 12-4. Using the out-of-the-box Stream application starters

Now you can define custom stream definitions using the registered applications. Figure 12-5 captures the UI as we do this.

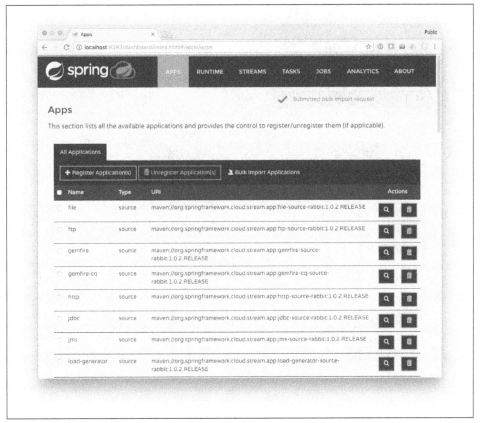

Figure 12-5. The Streams tab

The easiest (and our preferred) way to design a new stream is to use the Spring Flo visual designer. The designer round-trips between the visual model (which you can manipulate with your mouse) and the text in the form. The visual modeling tool is really handy: drag an item from the palette on the left (a `source`, a `sink`, or a `processor`) and connect the components using their *ports* (the little square icons on the right or left of the square shapes). Figure 12-6 captures the UI as we do this.

Figure 12-6. Design your stream

From there, it's dead simple to deploy the stream definition. You'll need to give it a logical name. Figure 12-7 captures the UI as we do this.

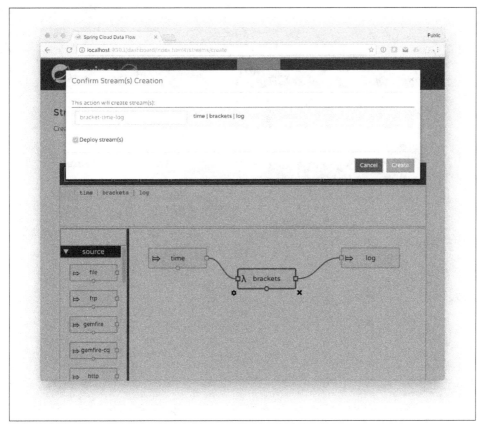

Figure 12-7. Give it a name

You'll be able to see the deployed streams in the Streams tab. Click the arrow to expand the visual representation. You'll also have an at-a-glance perspective on whether the stream has been deployed successfully. If you're using the local deployer, check the logs of the Spring Cloud Data Flow server for information on where to find the logs for the deployed applications. Figure 12-8 captures the UI as we do this.

Figure 12-8. Stream definitions

The same basic workflow applies to registering tasks, except that you don't need to deploy a task. You define a task once (based on a registered task application) and launch one or many instances of it. Click the Create Definition icon next to the relevant task. Figure 12-9 captures the UI as we do this.

Figure 12-9. The simple-job task

Then define the things that will be true from one run to another for that task. You may want your tasks to always have a certain Actuator setting, or to reflect a particular Spring profile. Specify these sorts of things here. Figure 12-10 captures the UI as we do this.

Figure 12-10. Specify a particular Spring profile

You can launch an instance of a task definition whenever you want. Figure 12-11 captures the UI as we do this.

Figure 12-11. Review the task definitions

When you launch an instance of the task, you'll be asked to specify execution-specific arguments (which are passed to the `CommandLineRunner` and `ApplicationRunner` as arguments, and to a Spring Batch `Job` as job parameters). Figure 12-12 captures the UI as we do this.

Figure 12-12. Specify the instance arguments and properties

And then finally, Launch the task! Figure 12-13 captures the UI as we do this.

Figure 12-13. Review the tasks and their status

The Spring Cloud Data Flow shell

If you want to move up a bit higher, there's a Spring Shell (*http://bit.ly/2vHRPQM*)-powered interactive shell. Download the shell executable by following the documentation at the Spring Cloud Data Flow page (*http://bit.ly/2vI40Nx*). Once the shell is on your local machine, launch it with `java -jar spring-cloud-dataflow-server-local-....RELEASE.jar`, replacing `....` with the relevant version of the shell that you have downloaded.

Run the shell (Example 12-22).

Example 12-22. An empty shell

```
  ___                           ___  __   __        __
 / __| _ _  _ _ (_)_ _  __ _  / __| |  \  / _|       _|
 \__ \| '_|| '_|| | ' \/ _` | | (__  | |) || _|     |_ |
 |___/|_|  |_|  |_|_||_\__, |  \___| |__/ |_|        |_|
```

```
|___/| ._/|_|  |_|_| |_|\_, |  \___|_|\__/ \_,_|\_,_|
__ |_|  _        _|_/                 _____
| _\ __| |_ __ _ |  _| |  ___      _  \ \ \ \ \
| | |/_.`| _/_.`| | |_ | |/_\ \ /\ / /  \ \ \ \ \ \
| |_| |(_| | || (_| | | _| | |(_)\ V  V /   / / / / / /
|___/ \_,_|\_,_| |_|  |_|\__/ \_/\_/   /_/_/_/_/_/
```

1.1.2.RELEASE

```
Welcome to the Spring Cloud Data Flow shell. For assistance hit TAB or type "help".
dataflow:>app list
No registered apps.
You can register new apps with the 'app register' and 'app import' commands.
```

Run app list to see what applications are installed (Example 12-23).

Example 12-23. We're not going to get far this way

```
dataflow:>app list
No registered apps.
You can register new apps with the 'app register' and 'app import' commands.
```

Nothing! We won't get far like this. Let's import some RabbitMQ-bound and Maven-packaged applications (Example 12-24).

Example 12-24. Importing the RabbitMQ-bound applications

```
dataflow:>app import --uri http://bit.ly/stream-applications-rabbit-maven
```

Not bad! Let's create a simple stream using two default apps: time, which produces a new message on a timer, and log, which logs incoming messages to stdout (Example 12-25).

Example 12-25. Setting up a Spring Cloud Data Flow pipeline

```
dataflow:>stream create --name ticktock --definition "time | log" ❶
Created new stream 'ticktock'

dataflow:>stream deploy --name ticktock ❷
Deployed stream 'ticktock'
```

❶ This defines a stream that takes produced times and then pipes them to the logs.

❷ The stream needs to be deployed. This will invoke the underlying deployer, which in turn launches the module. In the local case, it basically does java -

---

`jar ..` on the resolved `.jar` for the module. On Cloud Foundry, it'll start up new app instances for each application.

Both `time` and `log` are full Spring Cloud Stream applications. They expose well-known channels: `output` for the source `time`, `input` for the sink `log`), and Spring Cloud Data Flow stitches them together, arranging for messages that leave the `log` application's `output` channel to be routed to the `time` application's `input` channel. In the console of the Data Flow server, you'll observe output confirming that the involved applications have been launched and are running (Example 12-26).

Example 12-26. The logs confirming that the applications have been launched and pointing us to the various logs

```
...
.. : FrameworkServlet 'dispatcherServlet': initialization completed in 11 ms
.. : deploying app ticktock.log instance 0
   Logs will be in /var/folders/cr/grkckb753fld3lbmt386jp740000gn/T/spring-.log
.. o.s.c.d.spi.local.LocalAppDeployer : deploying app ticktock.time instance 0
   Logs will be in /var/folders/cr/grkckb753fld3lbmt386jp740000gn/T/spring-.time
...
```

The `stdout` logs for the `log` application should reflect a never-ending stream of new timestamps.

Let's throw our custom bracket processor into the mix. First, we need to register it (Example 12-27).

Example 12-27. Using the shell to register and deploy a stream

```
dataflow:>app register --name brackets --type processor \ ❶
    --uri maven://cnj:stream-example:jar:1.0.0-SNAPSHOT
Successfully registered application 'processor:brackets'


dataflow:>stream create --name bracketedticktock --definition "time | brackets | log"
Created new stream 'bracketedticktock' ❷


dataflow:>stream list ❸
```

Stream Name	Stream Definition	Status
bracketedticktock	time | brackets | log	undeployed

```
dataflow:>stream deploy --name bracketedticktock ❹
Deployed stream 'bracketedticktock'
```

❶ We must first register the application so that Spring Cloud Data Flow is aware of it.

❷ Create a stream that stitches the time, the log, and the newly registered bracket component together.

❸ Confirm that the stream's been registered.

❹ Deploy the stream.

Now, let's kick off a simple task and see what that looks like, using the timestamp task (Example 12-28).

Example 12-28. Launching the timestamp task

```
dataflow:>task create --name whattimeisit --definition timestamp  ❶
Created new task 'whattimeisit'
```

```
dataflow:>task list  ❷
```

Task Name	Task Definition	Task Status
whattimeisit	timestamp	unknown

```
dataflow:>task launch --name whattimeisit  ❸
Launched task 'whattimeisit'
```

```
dataflow:>task list  ❹
```

Task Name	Task Definition	Task Status
whattimeisit	timestamp	complete

❶ Create a task that launches the trivial Spring Cloud Task called timestamp and prints out the value.

❷ Enumerate the existing tasks.

❸ Launch the task and give it a logical name by which to refer to it later.

❹ List the tasks. In this case the task is complete, and we see that reflected.

Inspect the logs and you should see the time printed. Now let's kick off a Spring Batch-based task (Example 12-29).

Example 12-29. Using the shell to register and launch our custom Spring Batch-based task

```
dataflow:>app register --name args --type task \   ❶
 --uri maven://cnj:task-example:jar:1.0.0-SNAPSHOT
Successfully registered application 'task:args'


dataflow:>task create --definition "args --p1=1 --p2=2" --name args   ❷
Created new task 'args'


dataflow:>task launch --name args   ❸
Launched task 'args'


dataflow:>task list   ❹
```

Task Name	Task Definition	Task Status
args	args	complete

❶ We must first register the application so that Spring Cloud Data Flow is aware of it.

❷ Create a (potentially) parameterized instance of the application.

❸ Launch an instance of the task.

❹ Note the task's exit status.

The Spring Cloud Data Flow shell is powerful because it supports both interactive sessions with the server *and* scriptability. If you want complete control, however, you'll need to look at the DataFlowTemplate.

The DataFlowTemplate

We could use the RestTemplate and work with Spring Cloud Data Flow's APIs for managing applications, streams, tasks, users, and more. The APIs are handily laid out as hypermedia links when you visit http://localhost:9393. We could also visit the Spring Boot Actuator endpoints exposed under http://localhost:9393/management/ by default. We could get there, with some effort, after sorting out authentication, handling the hypermedia relationship traversals, and more. If, instead, you use the JVM (which we hope is a given, at this point in this particular book), then you could use the `DataFlowTemplate`, a convenient client interface for all the interesting functionality in the Spring Cloud Data Flow server. Add the library to the classpath: `org.springframework.cloud : spring-cloud-dataflow-rest-client`. It is convenient to install everything we need initialized in the Spring Cloud Data Flow server implementation on application startup with the `DataFlowTemplate`. This initialization can include application definitions, the streams and tasks that use them, and the deployment of those streams and tasks. Here's a trivial component that listens for the `ApplicationReadyEvent` application context event (which Spring Boot publishes after the application is all but running in an application's initialization) and talks to the freshly installed server (Example 12-30).

Example 12-30. A Data Flow Initializer

```
package dataflow;

import org.springframework.beans.factory.annotation.Autowired;
import org.springframework.beans.factory.annotation.Value;
import org.springframework.boot.context.event.ApplicationReadyEvent;
import org.springframework.cloud.dataflow.rest.client.DataFlowTemplate;
import org.springframework.cloud.dataflow.rest.client.TaskOperations;
import org.springframework.context.event.EventListener;
import org.springframework.stereotype.Component;
import org.springframework.web.client.RestTemplate;

import java.net.URI;
import java.net.URL;
import java.util.*;
import java.util.stream.Stream;

@Component
class DataFlowInitializer {

  private final URI baseUri;

  @Autowired
  public DataFlowInitializer(@Value("${server.port}") int port) {
    this.baseUri = URI.create("http://localhost:" + port);
  }

  @EventListener(ApplicationReadyEvent.class)
  public void deployOnStart(ApplicationReadyEvent e) throws Exception {

    ❶
    DataFlowTemplate df = new DataFlowTemplate(baseUri, new RestTemplate());

    ❷
    Stream
      .of("http://bit.ly/stream-applications-rabbit-maven",
```

```
new URL(baseUri.toURL(), "app.properties").toString()).parallel()
.forEach(u -> df.appRegistryOperations().importFromResource(u, true));

❸
TaskOperations taskOperations = df.taskOperations();
Stream.of("batch-task", "simple-task").forEach(tn -> {
 String name = "my-" + tn;
 taskOperations.create(name, tn);
 Map<String, String> properties = Collections.singletonMap(
  "simple-batch-task.input", System.getenv("HOME") + "Desktop/in.csv");
 List<String> arguments = Arrays.asList("input=in", "output=out");
 taskOperations.launch(name, properties, arguments);
});

❹
Map<String, String> streams = new HashMap<>();
streams.put("bracket-time", "time | brackets | log");
streams
 .entrySet()
 .parallelStream()
 .forEach(
  stream -> df.streamOperations().createStream(stream.getKey(),
   stream.getValue(), true));
 }
}
```

❶ Define the `DataFlowTemplate` as long after the initialization of the Data Flow server as possible (when the `ApplicationReadyEvent` Spring ApplicationContext event is published), because the `DataFlowTemplate` makes REST calls to the Data Flow server in its constructor; ensure that the REST API is usable before we call it.

❷ Preregister application definitions referencing both the standard set of application definitions and a few of our own custom task and stream definitions.

❸ Register and launch instances of two tasks, `batch-task` and `simple-task`.

❹ This defines (and deploys) a stream definition called `bracket-time`.

Spring Cloud Data Flow lets developers build higher-order systems from smaller, singly focused components. It is optimized for scalable processing and integration of applications and data. Fundamentally, Spring Cloud Data Flow is batch and messaging for a cloud native world.

Summary

We've only begun to scratch the surface of the possibilities in data processing. Naturally, each of these technologies in turn speaks to a large array of different technologies. We might, for example, use Apache Spark or Hadoop in conjunction with Spring Cloud Data Flow. We could use Activiti or Spring Statemachine with Spring Cloud Task. They also compose well. It's trivial to scale out processing of a Spring Batch job across a cluster using Spring Cloud Stream as the messaging fabric, for example. We've looked at techniques and technologies designed to support correct results resilience in processing, first through retries and recovery methods, then through messaging-centric patterns like the Saga pattern, Command Query Responsibility Segregation (CQRS), and staged event-driven architectures (SEDA).

## PART IV

Production

CHAPTER 13

The Observable System

There are two key technical aspects to building a production-worthy system:

- *We must build a system that scales sufficiently, and that can handle the business requirements.* In most of this book, we have focused on this aspect. We've looked at patterns that support safely introducing distribution into a system, which in turn supports easier distribution of work. We've largely waved away discussions of capacity planning, because our main goals have been to avoid introducing single points of failure, *not* to handle Google scale. A sufficiently decomposed system may still falter at much greater scale, but you can address those issues when you come to them.

  When you meet these requirements, be clear about what you mean by *scalability*. There are many different ways to characterize scalability in a system, but unless you are sure of where your system is, you won't be able to get it where you want it to go. You can use these measurements to feed into a model of your system's scalability. One very useful model is defined in the Universal Scalability Law (*http://bit.ly/2sa2QpX*), which Baron Schwartz describes in his book *Practical Scalability Analysis with the Universal Scalability Law* (*http://bit.ly/2s9U23m*). Coda Hale created a useful modeling library, usl4j (*https://github.com/codahale/usl4j*), that—given observations (measurements) about any two dimensions of Little's law (*https://en.wikipedia.org/wiki/Little%27s_law*)—gives you a model for predicting any dimension from any other dimension. Such a model supports scaling to meet particular requirements. Here, a cloud platform like Cloud Foundry can make life easier as it supports easy horizontal scaling. We'll look at how to measure a system in this chapter. These measurements feed into scalability models.

- *We must build a system that does the right thing when things don't work as expected.* An application must support ease of remediation.

Both of these requirements demand that we have visibility into the system—that we be able to measure the system. Beyond the technical requirements, visibility supports the business, as well. If we're to truly iterate in an agile fashion, then software must be shippable and *releasable*, if not *released*, to the customer after every iteration. The "customer" may be a client, a nonprofit, an open source project, or yourself. The "customer" describes whatever draws value from the software. The sooner that software is released to the customer, the sooner it releases value. Released software derisks continued development by capturing business value. Released and *working* software derisks continued development by capturing business value.

How do we know if it's working? Software is silent. It runs just as quietly when it's working as when it's dead. There are no telltale sounds or smells that signal its malfunction. When we build software, we need to build in a definition of *working*. This helps us set expectations for normal operating behavior—a *baseline*. A baseline serves as a basis for measured improvements in behavior.

In this chapter, we'll look at the *nonfunctional* or *cross-functional* capabilities that all applications need if we're to have a hope of operationalizing them. The majority of this chapter relates to *observability*—a measure for how well internal states of a system can be inferred by knowledge of its external outputs.

The rub is that these capabilities are not business differentiators; they're *not* what your organization went into business to address! Yet, they're critical to the continued and safe operation and evolution of an application. Michael Nygard, in his epic tome *Release It!* (Pragmatic), details these sorts of capabilities and concerns in dizzying detail. The punchline is that code-complete is *not* the same as production-ready. Software can not be released if it is not production-ready. Done must mean done.

You Build It, You Run It

The developer's instinct historically has been to ignore these sort of nonfunctional requirements. After all, if they don't contribute to the feature set and the customers aren't charmed by their presence, why focus on these things at all? Certainly, they shouldn't be a subject of concern at project inception! Developers didn't want to be bothered with code changes to support these requirements when they had business-differentiating functionality to add and an ever-growing backlog. It wasn't *their* problem if the software failed in the dead of night; the help desk would handle it! No help desk or operations team wants to be saddled with a black-box piece of software (into which they have absolutely no visibility) that's malfunctioning at 4 a.m., so they cared deeply about observability and did what they could, save change the code itself, to support it. The result was that developers would write software and chuck it over an imaginary wall to operations, and operations would instrument what they could without changing the code.

If ever developers and operations did become aware of each other, it was usually a point of contention over some perceived loss of autonomy that developers felt because of the way the application had been operationalized. Developers wanted to release code, and operations wanted to ensure the stability of the production system. Such a dynamic is not ideal. It results in a disconnect between the business outcome and the stability of the systems. Today, of course, we talk about *DevOps*; the idea that both operations and developers are charged with ensuring the stability of the system *and* with business outcomes. They are two sides of the same coin, working toward shared goals. Many high-performing organizations have adopted a simple mantra as a way of reducing the go-between time between developers and operations: "you build it, you run it." Teams are now charged with the maintenance of their code in production.

You will be a *lot* more interested in building robust systems with no failure points that support observability and remediation if you know you might be awakened at 4 a.m. to support them!

Murder Mystery Microservices

The need to support observability becomes even more critical in the cloud, when building distributed systems. With Microservices, every outage is more like a murder mystery (*http://bit.ly/2sa2XBT*). *Increment Magazine* (which is a fascinating new foray into the world of on-call operations) looked at "What happens when the pager goes off?" (*http://bit.ly/2s9XZVP*). They describe the fairly standardized, high-level framework that a large swath of high-performing organizations across the industry follow in response to an incident. Broadly, here are the basic steps:

Triage
> Somewhere in the system, something is wrong. In this stage, the job is to identify where it *might* be malfunctioning, to assess the impact and severity of the incident and to classify it.

Coordinate
> In this phase, work needs to begin toward mitigation. This work may be done by another team (the developers) or the same team that triaged the incident. Typically, groups of people communicate through established channels (chat, Slack, Skype, Google Hangouts, etc.). Work underway must be documented and shared. Many organizations create war rooms and set up conference calls.

Mitigate
> At this stage, the goal is to reduce the impact of the incident and to restore system stability, *not* to resolve the root cause and *not* to fix the root of the problem. As an example, if a system has failed because of a deployment, the mitigation step would be to roll back the change, *not* try to fix the underlying problem.

Resolve

Mitigation may only stop the incident in its tracks, preventing it from further impacting other users, but not fix the root cause. In the Resolve stage, developers do root-cause analysis and resolution. Existing users may still be affected, requiring resolution. Time is of the essence here, but teams must be careful to observe normal quality-guarding practices like testing any hotfixes. Many organizations measure both mean time to mitigation (MTTM) and mean time to resolution (MTTR).

Follow-up

In this stage, an organization attempts to internalize lessons from the incident by doing blameless postmortems, making and assigning follow-up tasks, and holding incident review meetings. The incident is considered over only once all the follow-up tasks are done.

At every step, it is *incredibly* important to have support in the organization for communication between people and for visibility into the system itself.

Twelve-Factor Operations

An operationalized application is one that is *built* for production. Such an application will, as we'll see in this chapter, work with a diverse ecosystem of tools (centralized log processing, health and process managers, job schedulers, distributed tracing systems, and so on) beyond the business-differentiating functionality that is the essence of the application.

We will, by building our application with key tenets from the twelve-factor manifesto in mind, and by working with the conventions of Spring Boot and Spring Cloud, benefit from this infrastructure if it is available. Make no mistake, however, that *something* needs to supply that infrastructure. Deploying into production blind, with no supporting infrastructure, is not an option. If the twelve-factor manifesto describes a set of good, clean, cloud-hygiene principles for building production-ready applications, then *something* needs to satisfy the other side of the contract and support what Andrew Clay Shafer (*https://twitter.com/littleidea*) refers to as *twelve-factor operations*. Something needs to run apps and services as stateless processes, provide a well-known application life cycle, make it easy to externalize configuration, support log management, provide backing services, make it easy to scale applications horizontally, provide declarative port binding, etc. Cloud Foundry, naturally, does a very good job supporting the operational requirements.

In this chapter we'll look at how to surface node-by-node information and how to centralize that information to support the single-pane-of-glass experience required for quick comprehension of a system's behavior. It is critical that we capture the behavior of the *system*, not just the applications in the system.

The map is not the terrain. Just as looking at a map of Manhattan has far less fidelity than actually walking through Manhattan, a system has emergent behavior that cannot be captured in an architecture diagram of the system. It can only be captured through effective, systemwide monitoring.

The New Deal

The requirements to successfully deploy applications into production have not changed drastically. What *has* changed is how divorced developers can afford to be from operational concerns, if the organization is to prosper, and how apathetic operations can be to application requirements that may risk system stability. The handoff between developers and operations used to be an opaque deliverable, something like a Servlet container-compatible `.war`. The application deployed in this black box benefited from some container-provided services, like a built-in start and stop script and a central log spout. Operators needed to further customize such a container in order for any of those container promises to be meaningful. Operators would then need to ensure a whole world of supporting infrastructure was in place so that the application would enjoy stability in production:

Process scheduling and management
> What component will start the application and gracefully shut it down? How do we ensure that it isn't running twice on the same host?

Application health and remediation
> How do operators know if the application is running well? What happens if the application process dies? What happens if the host itself dies?

Log management
> How do operators see the logs spooling from application instances? How are collection and analysis handled?

Application visibility and transparency
> How do operators capture application state, or quantify application state as metrics, and analyze and visualize them?

Route management
> Is the application exposed to the internet? Load-balanced? Do the routes update correctly when the application is restarted on another host?

Distributed tracing
> Who is accessing the system? Which services are involved in processing a transaction, and what is the latency of those requests? What does the average call graph look like?

Application performance management
> How do operators diagnose and address complex application performance problems?

—"A Bad System Will Beat a Good Person Every Time", by W. Edwards Deming

Deming said that in the context of people, not about distributed systems or the systems that run it, but we think it equally applies there. If the system we use to manage our software makes doing the right thing difficult, then people won't do it.

It is critical that supporting observability and these best practices be as friction-free as possible so that it is a no-brainer to introduce it consistently across services and projects. Organizations large and small know the dreaded corporate Wiki page ("The 500 Easy Steps to Production"), full of boilerplate and manual work to be done before a service may be deployed. Here, Cloud Foundry and Spring Boot stand strong. Cloud Foundry provides support for the twelve-factor operations requirements, and Spring Boot (and its auto-configuration, which we talked about in our discussion of Spring Boot basics in Chapter 2) codifies the application and customization of the principles of the twelve-factor application. They reduce the cognitive overhead of doing the right thing to almost nil. We need only get it right once, and reuse from there. Undifferentiated heavy lifting is the enemy of velocity.

This infrastructure is hard to get right and expensive to develop. It is also, very importantly, not business-differentiating functionality. We believe that opinionated platforms, like Heroku or distributions of the open source Cloud Foundry, provide the best mix of supporting infrastructure and ease of use. These platforms make certain assumptions about the applications—that they are transactional, online web applications written in compliance with the tenets of the twelve-factor manifesto. These assumptions make it easy for the platform to meet certain requirements; they reduce the surface area for variability in a codebase. These assumptions support automation and increase velocity.

Observability

Observability is a tricky thing. If you have a monolithic application, things are in some ways easier. If something goes wrong with the system, there can be no question at least of *where* the error occurred: *the error is coming from inside the building*! Things become markedly more complicated in a distributed system as interactions between components make failure isolation critical. You wouldn't drive a single passenger car without instrumentation, gauges, and windows supporting visibility; how could you hope to operate air traffic control for hundreds of airplanes without visibility?

Improved visibility supports business's continued investment and changing priorities for a system. Operations uses *good* visibility to at least connect eyes to potential system problems (*alerting*) and to aid in response to incidents. In some cases, they can also use good observability to make automatic or at least push-button-simple the response to incidents.

Ideally, operational and business visibility can be correlated and used to drive a *single-pane-of-glass* experience—a dashboard. In this chapter, we'll look at how to collect and understand *historical* and *present* status and how to support forward-looking *predictions*. Predictions, in particular, are driven by models based on historical data.

Historical data is data stored *somewhere* for a period of time. Historical data may drive long-term business insight, where fresher, more recent data may support operational telemetry, error analysis, and debugging.

Your system is a complex machine with lots of moving parts. It is difficult to know which information to collect and which to ignore, so err on the side of caution and collect as much as possible.

Push Versus Pull Observability and Resolution

Some monitoring and observability tools take a *pull-based* approach, where centralized infrastructure pulls data from services at an interval, and some monitoring infrastructure expects events about the status of different nodes to *push* that information to it. Many of the tools that we'll look at in this chapter can work in one fashion or the other—or sometimes both. It's up to you to decide upon which approach you'd like.

For a lot of organizations, the discussion is one of resolution. How often do you update monitoring infrastructure? In a dynamic environment, things may come and go as they need to. Indeed, the life span of a service might be only seconds or minutes when we talk about ad hoc tasks. If a system employs pull-based monitoring, the interval between pulls may be longer than the entire span of a running application! The monitoring infrastructure is effectively blind to entire running components, and could possibly miss out on major peaks and valleys in the data. This is one strong reason to embrace push-based monitoring for these kinds of components.

Here, we benefit considerably from Spring's flexibility: it often provides events that we can use to trigger monitoring events. As you read this chapter, ask yourself whether a given approach is pull- or push-based, and ask how you could conceivably turn something pull- to push-based if needed.

Capturing an Application's Present Status with Spring Boot Actuator

The present status of an application is the kind of information you would project onto a dashboard, perhaps then visualized on a giant screen in the office where people can see it. You may or may not keep all of this information for later use. Present-state status is like the speedometer in a car: it should tell you as concisely and quickly as possible whether there's trouble or not.

If you had to distill your system's state into a visualization (red to indicate danger, green to indicate that everything is all right, or yellow to indicate that something is perhaps amiss but within tolerable ranges), what information would you choose? That's present-state information.

Present status might include information like memory, thread pools, database connections, and total requests processed. It might include statistics like requests per second (for all parts of the system that have requests, including HTTP endpoints and message queues), 95% percentiles for response times, errors encountered, and the state of circuit breakers.

The *Spring Boot Actuator* framework provides out-of-the-box support for surfacing information about the application through endpoints. Endpoints collect information and sometimes interact with other subsystems. These endpoints may be viewed a number of different ways (using REST or JMX, for example). We'll focus on REST endpoints. Endpoints are pluggable, and various Spring Boot-based subsystems often contribute additional endpoints where appropriate. To use Spring Boot Actuator, add `org.springframework.boot : spring-boot-starter-actuator` to your project's build. Add `org.springframework.boot : spring-boot-starter-web` to have the custom endpoints exposed as REST endpoints.

> From the Spring Boot documentation (*https://docs.spring.io/spring-boot/docs/current/reference/htmlsingle/*): "an actuator is a manufacturing term, referring to a mechanical device for moving or controlling something. Actuators can generate a large amount of motion from a small change."

Table 13-1 lists a few of the Actuator endpoints.

Table 13-1. A few of the Actuator endpoints

Endpoint	Usage
/info	Exposes information about the current service.
/metrics	Exposes quantifiable values about the service.
/beans	Exposes a graph of all the objects that Spring Boot has created for you.
/configprops	Exposes information about all the properties available to configure the current Spring Boot application.
/mappings	Exposes all the HTTP endpoints that Spring Boot is aware of in this application as well as any other metadata (such as specified content-types or HTTP verbs in the Spring MVC mapping).
/health	A description of the state of components in the system: *UP*, *DOWN*, etc. Also returns HTTP status codes.

Endpoint	Usage
/loggers	Shows and modifies the loggers in the application.
/auditevents	Shows all the `AuditEvent` instances that have been recorded by the `AuditEventReposi tory`. These are events that connect authenticated `Principal` entities to events in the system. You can capture and emit custom events, as well.
/cloudfoundryap plication	Exposes information from a Cloud Foundry-based management UI to be augmented with Spring Boot Actuator information. An application status page might include the full Spring Boot /health output, in addition to "running" or "stopped." This information is secured and requires a valid token from Cloud Foundry's UAA authentication and authorization service. If your application is not running on Cloud Foundry, you can disable this endpoint with `manage ment.cloudfoundry.enabled=false`.
/env	Returns all of the known environment properties, such as those in the operating system's environment variables or the results of `System.getProperties()`.

Let's look at some of these endpoints in a bit more depth.

Metrics

Everybody generalizes from too few data points. At least I do.
—Parand Darugar (*https://twitter.com/parand/status/854793437043761152*)

Metrics are numbers. In the Spring Boot Actuator framework, there are three kinds of metrics: public metrics (which we'll look at shortly), gauges, and counters. A *gauge* records a single value, all at once, and requires no tabulation. A *counter* records a delta (an increment or decrement); it is a value that is reached over time, with tabulation. Metrics are numbers and so are easy to store, graph, and query. There are some metrics that operations, and operations alone, will care about: host-specific information like RAM use, disk space, and requests per second. Everybody in the organization will care about semantic metrics: how many orders were made in the last hour, how many orders were placed, how many new account sign-ups have occurred, which products were sold and how many, etc. By default, Spring Boot exposes these metrics at /metrics (Example 13-1).

Example 13-1. Metrics from an application's /metrics endpoint

```
{
    "classes" : 9731,
    "heap.committed" : 570368,
    "nonheap.used" : 72430,
    "systemload.average" : 3.328125,
    "gauge.response.customers.id" : 7,
    "gc.ps_marksweep.count" : 2,
    "nonheap" : 0,
    "counter.status.200.customers" : 1,  ❶
    "counter.status.200.customers.id" : 2,
    "mem.free" : 390762,
```

```
    "heap.used" : 179605,
    "classes.unloaded" : 0,
    "gauge.response.star-star.favicon.ico" : 4,
    "instance.uptime" : 47231,
    "counter.status.200.star-star.favicon.ico" : 2,
    "threads.peak" : 21,
    "nonheap.init" : 2496,
    "threads.totalStarted" : 27,
    "mem" : 642797,
    "httpsessions.max" : -1,
    "counter.customers.read.found" : 2,
    "gc.ps_marksweep.time" : 96,
    "uptime" : 52379,
    "threads" : 21,
    "customers.count" : 6,
    "gc.ps_scavenge.count" : 6,
    "heap.init" : 262144,
    "httpsessions.active" : 0,
    "nonheap.committed" : 74112,
    "gc.ps_scavenge.time" : 87,
    "counter.status.200.admin.metrics" : 2,
    "datasource.primary.usage" : 0,
    "processors" : 8, ❷
    "gauge.response.customers" : 9,
    "heap" : 3728384,
    "gauge.response.admin.metrics" : 4,
    "threads.daemon" : 19,
    "datasource.primary.active" : 0,
    "classes.loaded" : 9731
}
```

❶   The metrics include counts of requests, their paths, and their HTTP status codes
    already. Here, 200 is the HTTP status code.

❷   The Spring Boot Actuator *also* captures other salient information about the sys-
    tem, like how many processors are available.

The metrics *already* record a lot of useful information for us: they record all requests
made (and the corresponding HTTP status code), and information about the environment (like the JVM's threads, loaded classes, and information about any configured DataSource instances). Spring Boot conditionally registers metrics based on the
subsystems in play.

You can contribute your own metrics using the org.springframe
work.boot.actuate.metrics.CounterService to record deltas ("one more request
has been made") or the org.springframework.boot.actuate.metrics.GaugeSer
vice to capture absolute values ("there are 140 users connected to the chat room").
See Example 13-2.

Example 13-2. Collecting customer metrics with the CounterService

```
package demo.metrics;

import org.springframework.beans.factory.annotation.Autowired;
import org.springframework.boot.actuate.metrics.CounterService;
import org.springframework.http.ResponseEntity;
import org.springframework.web.bind.annotation.*;
import org.springframework.web.servlet.support.ServletUriComponentsBuilder;

import java.net.URI;

@RestController
@RequestMapping("/customers")
public class CustomerRestController {

  private final CounterService counterService; ❶

  private final CustomerRepository customerRepository;

  @Autowired
  CustomerRestController(CustomerRepository repository,
   CounterService counterService) {
   this.customerRepository = repository;
   this.counterService = counterService;
  }

  @RequestMapping(method = RequestMethod.GET, value = "/{id}")
  ResponseEntity<?> get(@PathVariable Long id) {
   return this.customerRepository.findById(id).map(customer -> {
    String metricName = metricPrefix("customers.read.found");
    this.counterService.increment(metricName); ❷
    return ResponseEntity.ok(customer);
   }).orElseGet(() -> {
    String metricName = metricPrefix("customers.read.not-found");
    this.counterService.increment(metricName); ❸
    return ResponseEntity.class.cast(ResponseEntity.notFound().build());
   });
  }

  @RequestMapping(method = RequestMethod.POST)
  ResponseEntity<?> add(@RequestBody Customer newCustomer) {
   this.customerRepository.save(newCustomer);
   ServletUriComponentsBuilder url = ServletUriComponentsBuilder
    .fromCurrentRequest();
   URI location = url.path("/{id}").buildAndExpand(newCustomer.getId()).toUri();
   return ResponseEntity.created(location).build();
  }

  @RequestMapping(method = RequestMethod.DELETE)
  ResponseEntity<?> delete(@PathVariable Long id) {
   this.customerRepository.delete(id);
```

```
    return ResponseEntity.notFound().build();
  }

  @RequestMapping(method = RequestMethod.GET)
  ResponseEntity<?> get() {
   return ResponseEntity.ok(this.customerRepository.findAll());
  }

  ❹
  protected String metricPrefix(String k) {
   return k;
  }

}
```

❶ The `CounterService` is auto-configured for you. If you're using Java 8, you'll get a better performing implementation than on an earlier Java version.

❷ Record how many requests resulted in a successful match…

❸ …and how many were a miss.

❹ We'll override this method in the next example to change the key used for the metric.

The `CounterService` and `GaugeService` capture metrics as they're updated, in transaction. In order for us to capture metrics, we need to update code to emit the correct metrics when an event worth observing happens. It's not always easy to insert instrumentation into the request path of our business components; perhaps it would be easier to capture those metrics retroactively. The Spring Boot Actuator `org.springframework.boot.actuate.endpoint.PublicMetrics` interface supports centralizing metrics collection. Spring Boot provides implementations of this interface internally to surface information about the JVM environment, Apache Tomcat, the configured `DataSource`, etc. In Example 13-3, we will look at an example that captures information about customers in our application.

Example 13-3. A custom PublicMetrics implementation exposing how many customers exist in the system

```
package demo.metrics;

import org.springframework.beans.factory.annotation.Autowired;
import org.springframework.boot.actuate.endpoint.PublicMetrics;
import org.springframework.boot.actuate.metrics.Metric;
import org.springframework.stereotype.Component;

import java.util.Collection;
```

```java
import java.util.HashSet;
import java.util.Set;

@Component
class CustomerPublicMetrics implements PublicMetrics {

  private final CustomerRepository customerRepository;

  @Autowired
  public CustomerPublicMetrics(CustomerRepository customerRepository) {
    this.customerRepository = customerRepository;
  }

  @Override
  public Collection<Metric<?>> metrics() {

    Set<Metric<?>> metrics = new HashSet<>();

    long count = this.customerRepository.count();

    ❶
    Metric<Number> customersCountMetric = new Metric<>("customers.count", count);
    metrics.add(customersCountMetric);
    return metrics;
  }
}
```

❶ This metric reports the aggregate count of Customer records in the database.

So far we've looked at metrics as fixed-point-in-time quantities. They represent a value as of the moment you review it. These are useful, but they don't have context. For some values, a fixed point-in-time value is pointless. Absent history—the perspective of time—it's hard to know whether a value represents an improvement or a regression. Given the axis of time, we can take a value and derive statistics: averages, medians, means, percentiles, etc.

The Spring Boot Actuator seamlessly integrates with the Dropwizard Metrics library. Coda Hale (*http://twitter.com/coda*) developed the Dropwizard Metrics library while at Yammer to capture gauges, counters, and a handful of other types of metrics. Add `io.dropwizard.metrics:metrics-core` to your classpath to get started.

The Dropwizard Metrics library includes support for meters. A *meter* measures the rate of events over time (e.g., "orders per second"). If the Dropwizard Metrics library is on the classpath, and you prefix any metric captured through the CounterService or GaugeService with meter., the Spring Boot Actuator framework will delegate to the Dropwizard Metrics Meter implementation to calculate and persist this metric.

From the Dropwizard Metrics documentation (*https://dropwizard.github.io/metrics/ 3.1.0/manual/core/*): "Meters measure the rate of the events in a few different ways.

The mean rate is the average rate of events. It's generally useful for trivia, but as it represents the total rate for your application's entire lifetime (e.g., the total number of requests handled, divided by the number of seconds the process has been running), it doesn't offer a sense of recency. Luckily, meters also record three different exponentially-weighted moving average rates: the 1-, 5-, and 15-minute moving averages."

The `Meter` doesn't need to retain *all* values it records as it uses an exponentially weighted moving average; it retains a set of samples of values, over time. This makes it memory-efficient even over great periods of time. Let's revise our example to use a `Meter` and then review the effect on the recorded metrics. We'll simply extend the `CustomerRestController` that we looked at in Example 13-3, overriding the `metric Prefix` method to prefix all `CounterService` metrics with `meter.`, instead (see Examples 13-4 and 13-5).

Example 13-4. Collecting metered metrics with the CounterService and the Dropwizard Metrics library

```
package demo.metrics;

import org.springframework.beans.factory.annotation.Autowired;
import org.springframework.boot.actuate.metrics.CounterService;
import org.springframework.web.bind.annotation.RequestMapping;
import org.springframework.web.bind.annotation.RestController;

@RestController
@RequestMapping("/metered/customers")
public class MeterCustomerRestController extends CustomerRestController {

  @Autowired
  MeterCustomerRestController(CustomerRepository repository,
   CounterService counterService) {
   super(repository, counterService);
  }

  @Override
  protected String metricPrefix(String k) {
   return "meter." + k; ❶
  }
}
```

❶ Prefix all recorded metrics with `meter.`

Example 13-5. Metrics powered by the Dropwizard Meter

```
{
    "meter.customers.read.fifteenMinuteRate" : 0.102683423806518,
    "meter.customers.read.meanRate" : 0.00164167411117908,
```

```
"meter.customers.read.fiveMinuteRate" : 0.0270670566473226,
"meter.customers.read.oneMinuteRate" : 9.07998595249702e-06
...
}
```

A counter and gauge capture a single value. A meter captures the number of values over a time period. A meter does *not* tell us anything about the frequencies of values in a data set. A *histogram* is a statistical distribution of values in a stream of data: it shows how many times a certain value occurs. It lets you answer questions like "What percent of orders have more than one item in the cart?" The Dropwizard Metrics His togram measures the minimum, maximum, mean, and median, as well as percentiles: 75th, 90th, 95th, 98th, 99th, and 99.9th percentiles.

If you've taken a basic statistics class, you know that we need all data points in order to derive these values with perfect accuracy. This can be an *overwhelming* amount of data, even over a small period of time. Suppose your application saw 1,000 logical transactions a second and that there were 10 requests, or actions, per request. Over a day, that's 864,000,000 values (24×60×60×1000×10)! If we're using Java, that's eight bytes per long, and more than *six gigabytes* of data per day! Many applications won't have this much traffic, but many applications will. Either way, it's not hard to scale it up and down and see that it's *eventually* going to be a problem for you.

The Dropwizard Metrics library uses *reservoir sampling* to keep a statistically representative sample of measurements as they happen. As time progresses, the Dropwizard Histogram creates samples of older values and uses those samples to derive new samples going forward. The result isn't perfect (it's lossy), but it's efficient. The Spring Boot Actuator framework will automatically convert any value submitted using the GaugeService with a metric key prefix of histogram. into a Dropwizard Histogram if the Dropwizard Metrics library is on the classpath.

Let's look at Example 13-6, which captures histograms for file uploads.

Example 13-6. Collecting a distribution of file upload sizes using the Dropwizard Metrics histogram implementation

```
package demo.metrics;

import org.apache.commons.logging.Log;
import org.apache.commons.logging.LogFactory;
import org.springframework.beans.factory.annotation.Autowired;
import org.springframework.boot.actuate.metrics.GaugeService;
import org.springframework.web.bind.annotation.RequestMapping;
import org.springframework.web.bind.annotation.RequestMethod;
import org.springframework.web.bind.annotation.RequestParam;
import org.springframework.web.bind.annotation.RestController;
import org.springframework.web.multipart.MultipartFile;
```

```
@RestController
@RequestMapping("/histogram/uploads")
public class HistogramFileUploadRestController {

 private final GaugeService gaugeService;

 private Log log = LogFactory.getLog(getClass());

 @Autowired
 HistogramFileUploadRestController(GaugeService gaugeService) {
  this.gaugeService = gaugeService;
 }

 @RequestMapping(method = RequestMethod.POST)
 void upload(@RequestParam MultipartFile file) {
  long size = file.getSize();
  this.log.info(String.format("received %s with file size %s",
   file.getOriginalFilename(), size));
  this.gaugeService.submit("histogram.file-uploads.size", size); ❶
 }
}
```

❶ Prefix all recorded metrics with `histogram.` to have them converted into Dropwizard `Histogram` instances behind the scenes.

Example 13-6 maintains a histogram for file upload sizes. We used `curl` to upload
three different files of varying size, randomly (see Table 13-2).

Table 13-2. The sample files and their sizes

File Size	Filename	Frequency
8.0K	${HOME}/Desktop/1.png	2
32K	${HOME}/Desktop/2.png	5
40K	${HOME}/Desktop/3.png	3

The `/metrics` confirm what the data table tells us (Example 13-7).

Example 13-7. Metrics powered by the Dropwizard histogram

```
{
    ...
    "histogram.file-uploads.size.snapshot.98thPercentile" : 38803,
    "histogram.file-uploads.size.snapshot.999thPercentile" : 38803,
    "histogram.file-uploads.size.snapshot.median" : 29929,
    "histogram.file-uploads.size.snapshot.mean" : 27154.1998413605,
    "histogram.file-uploads.size.snapshot.75thPercentile" : 38803,
    "histogram.file-uploads.size.snapshot.min" : 6347,
    "histogram.file-uploads.size.snapshot.max" : 38803,
    "histogram.file-uploads.size.count" : 10,
```

```
    "histogram.file-uploads.size.snapshot.95thPercentile" : 38803,
    "histogram.file-uploads.size.snapshot.99thPercentile" : 38803,
    "histogram.file-uploads.size.snapshot.stdDev" : 11639.4103925448,
    ...
}
```

The Dropwizard Metrics library also supports timers. A *timer* measures the rate that a particular piece of code is called and the distribution of its duration. It answers the question: how long does it *usually* take for a given type of request to be run, and what are atypical durations? The Spring Boot Actuator framework will automatically convert any metric starting with `timer.` that's submitted using the `GaugeService` into a `Timer`.

You can time requests using a variety of mechanisms. Spring itself ships with the venerable `StopWatch` class, which is perfect for our purposes (Example 13-8).

Example 13-8. Capturing timings using the Spring StopWatch

```java
package demo.metrics;

import org.springframework.beans.factory.annotation.Autowired;
import org.springframework.boot.actuate.metrics.GaugeService;
import org.springframework.http.ResponseEntity;
import org.springframework.util.StopWatch;
import org.springframework.web.bind.annotation.RequestMapping;
import org.springframework.web.bind.annotation.RequestMethod;
import org.springframework.web.bind.annotation.RestController;

@RestController
public class TimedRestController {

 private final GaugeService gaugeService;

 @Autowired
 public TimedRestController(GaugeService gaugeService) {
  this.gaugeService = gaugeService;
 }

 @RequestMapping(method = RequestMethod.GET, value = "/timer/hello")
 ResponseEntity<?> hello() throws Exception {
  StopWatch sw = new StopWatch(); ❶
  sw.start();
  try {
   Thread.sleep((long) (Math.random() * 60) * 1000);
   return ResponseEntity.ok("Hi, " + System.currentTimeMillis());
  }
  finally {
   sw.stop();
   this.gaugeService.submit("timer.hello", sw.getLastTaskTimeMillis());
  }
```

```
    }

}
```

❶ This is the Spring framework `StopWatch`, which we use here to count how long a
   request took.

The timer gives us all that a histogram does and then some, specifically for durations
(Example 13-9).

Example 13-9. The results of the Timer in the metrics output

```
{
    ...
    "timer.hello.snapshot.stdDev" : 11804,
    "counter.status.200.timer.hello" : 7,
    "timer.hello.snapshot.75thPercentile" : 35004,
    "timer.hello.meanRate" : 0.0561559793104086,
    "timer.hello.snapshot.mean" : 27639,
    "timer.hello.snapshot.min" : 2007,
    "timer.hello.snapshot.max" : 42003,
    "timer.hello.snapshot.median" : 35004,
    "timer.hello.snapshot.98thPercentile" : 42003,
    "timer.hello.fifteenMinuteRate" : 0.182311662062598,
    "timer.hello.snapshot.99thPercentile" : 42003,
    "timer.hello.snapshot.999thPercentile" : 42003,
    "timer.hello.oneMinuteRate" : 0.0741487724647533,
    "timer.hello.fiveMinuteRate" : 0.153231174431025,
    "timer.hello.count" : 7,
    "gauge.response.timer.hello" : 28008,
    "timer.hello.snapshot.95thPercentile" : 42003
    ...
}
```

The Dropwizard Metrics library enriches the Spring Boot metrics subsystem. It gives
us access to a bevy of statistics that we wouldn't have otherwise had.

Joined-up views of metrics

Thus far our examples have all run on a single node or host; one instance, one host. It
will become critical to centralize the metrics from across all services and instances as
we scale out. We can use a time series database (TSDB) to centrally collect and store
metrics. A *time series database* is a database that's optimized for the collection, analysis and, sometimes, visualization of metrics over time. There are many popular time
series databases, like Ganglia (*http://ganglia.info*), Graphite (*https://github.com/
graphite-project/*), OpenTSDB (*http://opentsdb.net*), InfluxDB (*https://influ
xdata.com*), and Prometheus (*https://prometheus.io*). A time series database stores
values for a given key over a period of time. Usually, they work in tandem with some-

thing that supports graphing of the data in the time series database. There are many fine technologies for graphing time series data, the most popular of which seems to be Grafana (*http://grafana.org/*). Alternative visualization technologies abound. Many companies have open sourced their visualization tools, such as: Vimeo's Graph Explorer (*https://github.com/vimeo/graph-explorer*), TicketMaster's Metrilyx (*https://tech.ticketmaster.com/2014/08/14/announcing-metrilyx/*), and Square's Cubism.js (*http://square.github.io/cubism/*).

Spring Boot supports writing metrics to a time series database using implementations of the `MetricsWriter` interface. Out of the box, Spring Boot can publish metrics to a Redis instance, JMX (possibly more useful for development), out over a Spring framework `MessageChannel`, or to any service that speaks the StatsD protocol (*https://github.com/etsy/statsd/wiki*). StatsD was a proxy originally written in Node.js by folks at Etsy to act as a proxy for Graphite/Carbon, but the protocol itself has become so popular that many clients and services now speak the protocol, and StatsD itself supports multiple backend implementations besides Graphite, including InfluxDB (*https://influxdata.com*), OpenTSDB (*http://opentsdb.net*), and Ganglia (*http://ganglia.info*). To take advantage of the various `MetricWriter` implementations, simply define a bean of the appropriate type and annotate it with `@ExportMetricWriter`. Dropwizard also supports publishing metrics to downstream systems through its `*Reporter` implementations, if StatsD doesn't suit your use case or you want more control.

Metric data dimensions

The data you create in a time series database is still data, even if the dimensions of that data would seem to be very limited: a metric has a key and a value, at least. Therein lies the rub; there's very little in the way of *schema*. Different time series databases provide improvements and offer other dimensions of data. Some offer the notion of *labels* or *tags*. The only dimension common to all time series databases, however, is a key. Most implementations we've seen use hierarchical keys (e.g., `a.b.c.`). Many time series databases support glob queries (e.g., `a.b.*`), which will return all metrics that match the prefix `a.b`. Each path component in a key should have a clear, well-defined purpose, and volatile path components should be kept as deep into the hierarchy as possible. Design your keys and metrics to support what will certainly be a growing number of metrics. Think carefully about what you capture in your metrics, be it through hierarchical keys or other dimensions like labels and tags.

How will you encode requests across different products in the same time series database? Capture the component name, e.g., `order-service`.

How will you encode different types of activities or processes? HTTP requests, messaging-based back-office requests, back-office batch jobs, or something else?

```
order-service.tasks.fulfillment.validate-shipping  or  order-service.req
uests.new-order?
```

Consider how you will encode the information so that it could ultimately be correlated to product management-facing systems like HP's Vertica (*https://www.vertica.com/*) or Facebook's Scuba? While we'd like to claim that *all* operational telemetry directly translates into business metrics, it's just not true. It can be useful, though, to have a way of capturing this information and connecting it. You can do this up front in the metrics' keys themselves, or perhaps using labels and tags.

How will you correlate requests to A/B tests (or experiments) where a sample of the population runs through a code path for a given feature that behaves differently than the majority of requests. This helps to gauge whether a feature works, and is well-received. The implication here is that you may have the same metric in two different code paths, one a different, *experimental* alternative to the other. Many organizations have a system for experiments, and surface experiment numbers that should be incorporated into the metrics.

As always, schema is a subjective matter, and new time series databases differentiate on the richness of the data collected *and* the scale! Some time series databases are lossy, while others scale horizontally, almost infinitely. You should choose your time series database just like any other database, carefully considering the opportunities for schema design. On the one hand, it should be friction-free for developers to capture metrics. On the other hand, some forethought can go a long way later.

Shipping metrics from a Spring Boot application

You can readily find hosted versions of many of these time series databases. One is Hosted Graphite (*https://www.hostedgraphite.com/*), which is easy to integrate with. It preconfigures Graphite, Graphite Composer, and Grafana. Grafana and Graphite Composer both let you build graphs based on collected metrics. You can, of course, run your own Graphite instance, but keep in mind the goal is, as always, to get to production as quickly as possible, so we tend to prefer cloud-based services (Software as a Service, or SaaS); we don't like to run software unless we can sell it. There are a few worthy options for connecting to Graphite available to the Spring Boot developer. You can use Spring Boot's `StatsdMetricWriter`, which speaks the StatsD protocol and works with many of the aforementioned backends. You can also use one of the myriad native Dropwizard Metrics reporter implementations if, for example, you'd prefer to use a native protocol besides StatsD. We'll do that here to communicate natively with Graphite, as demonstrated in Example 13-10.

Example 13-10. Configuring a Dropwizard Metrics GraphiteReporter instance

```
package demo.metrics;
```

```
import com.codahale.metrics.MetricRegistry;
import com.codahale.metrics.graphite.Graphite;
import com.codahale.metrics.graphite.GraphiteReporter;
import org.springframework.beans.factory.annotation.Value;
import org.springframework.context.annotation.Bean;
import org.springframework.context.annotation.Configuration;

import javax.annotation.PostConstruct;
import java.util.concurrent.TimeUnit;

@Configuration
class ActuatorConfiguration {

  ActuatorConfiguration() {
    java.security.Security.setProperty("networkaddress.cache.ttl", "60"); ❶
  }

  @Bean
  GraphiteReporter graphiteWriter(
    @Value("${hostedGraphite.apiKey}") String apiKey,
    @Value("${hostedGraphite.url}") String host,
    @Value("${hostedGraphite.port}") int port, MetricRegistry registry) {

    GraphiteReporter reporter = GraphiteReporter.forRegistry(registry)
      .prefixedWith(apiKey) ❷
      .build(new Graphite(host, port));
    reporter.start(1, TimeUnit.SECONDS);
    return reporter;
  }

}
```

❶ Prevent DNS caching, because HostedGraphite.com nodes may move and be mapped to a new DNS route.

❷ HostedGraphite.com's service (*http://HostedGraphite.com*) establishes authentication using an API key and expects that you transmit it as part of the prefix field. This is, admittedly, a bit of an ugly hack, but there is otherwise no obvious place to put the authentication information!

Drive traffic to the CustomerRestController or MeterCustomerRestController, and you'll see the traffic reflected in graphs that you can create on HostedGraphite.com in either the Grafana interface or the Graphite composer interface, depicted in Figures 13-1 and 13-2.

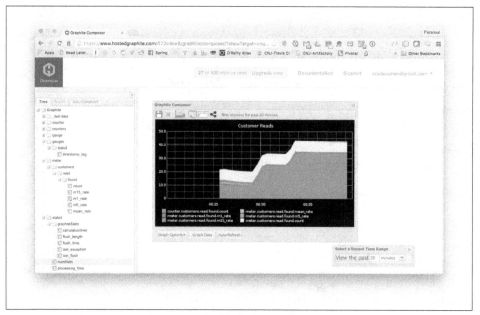

Figure 13-1. The Graphite Composer dashboard

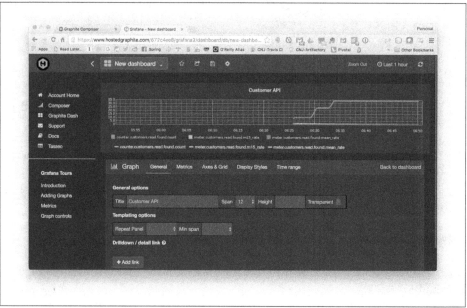

Figure 13-2. The Grafana dashboard

Identifying Your Service with the /info Endpoint

Ideally, you're developing your code in a continuous delivery pipeline. In a continuous delivery pipeline, *every* commit *could* result in a push to production. Ideally, this happens many times a day. If something goes wrong, the first thing people will want to know is which version of the code is running. Give your service the ability to identify itself using the /info endpoint.

The /info endpoint is intentionally left blank. The /info endpoint is a natural place to put information about the service itself. What's the service name? Which git com mit triggered the build that ultimately resulted in the push to production? What is the service version?

You can contribute custom properties by prefixing properties with info. in the environment through the normal channels (application.properties, application.yml, etc.). You can also surface information about the state of the git source code repository when the project was built by adding in the pl.project13.maven : git-commit-id-plugin Maven plug-in. This plug-in is preconfigured for Maven users in the Spring Boot parent Maven build. It generates a file, git.properties, containing the git.branch and git.commit properties. The /info endpoint will know to look for it if it's available (Example 13-11).

Example 13-11. The Git branch, and commit id and time exposed from /info

```
{
  git: {
    branch: "master",
    commit: {
      id: "407359e",
      time: "2016-03-23T00:47:09+0100"
    }
  }
  ...
}
```

It's very simple to add custom properties, as well. Any environment property prefixed with info. will be added to the output of this endpoint. Spring Boot's default Maven plug-in configuration, for example, is already set up to handle Maven resource filtering. You can take advantage of Maven resource filtering to emit custom properties captured at build time, like the Maven project.artifactId and project.version (Example 13-12).

Example 13-12. Capturing custom build-time information like the project's artifactId and version with the /info endpoint by contributing properties during the build with Maven resource filtering

```
info.project.version=@project.version@
info.project.artifactId=@project.artifactId@
```

Once that's done, bring up your /info endpoint and identify what's happening (Example 13-13).

Example 13-13. Capturing custom build-time information like the project's artifactId and version with the /info endpoint

```
{
  ...
  project: {
    artifactId: "actuator",
    version: "1.0.0-SNAPSHOT"
  }
}
```

Health Checks

An application needs a way of volunteering its health to infrastructure. A good health check should provide an aggregate status that sums up the reported statuses for individual components in play. Health checks are often used by load balancers to determine the viability of a node. Load balancers may evict nodes based on the HTTP status code returned. The org.springframework.boot.actuate.endpoint.Health Endpoint collects all org.springframework.boot.actuate.health.HealthIndica tor implementations in the application context and exposes them. Example 13-14 shows the output of the default /health endpoint in our sample application.

Example 13-14. The output of the default /health endpoint for our sample application

```
{
  status: "UP",
  diskSpace: {
    status: "UP",
    total: 999334871040,
    free: 735556071424,
    threshold: 10485760
  },
  redis: {
    status: "UP",
    version: "3.0.7"
  },
  db: {
```

```
        status: "UP",
        database: "H2",
        hello: 1
    }
}
```

Spring Boot automatically registers common `HealthIndicator` implementations based on various auto-configurations for JavaMail, MongoDB, Cassandra, JDBC, SOLR, Redis, ElasticSearch, the filesystem, and more. These health indicators are all the things your service works with that may fail, independently of your service. In the example above we see that Redis, the filesystem, and our JDBC `DataSource` are all automatically accounted for.

Let's contribute a custom `HealthIndicator`. The contract for a `HealthIndicator` is simple: when asked, return a `Health` instance with the appropriate status. Other components in the system need to be able to influence the returned `Health` object. You *could* directly inject the relevant `HealthIndicator` and manipulate its state in every component that might affect that state, but this couples a *lot* of application code to a secondary concern, the health status. An alternative approach is to use Spring's `ApplicationContext` event bus to publish events within components and manipulate the `HealthIndicator` based on acknowledged events.

In the following code blocks, we'll establish an emotional health indicator (Example 13-15) that is happy (`UP`) or sad (`DOWN`) when it receives a `SadEvent` (Example 13-16) or a `HappyEvent` (Example 13-17), accordingly.

Example 13-15. An emotional HealthIndicator

```
package demo.health;

import org.springframework.boot.actuate.health.AbstractHealthIndicator;
import org.springframework.boot.actuate.health.Health;
import org.springframework.context.event.EventListener;
import org.springframework.stereotype.Component;

import java.util.Date;
import java.util.Optional;

@Component
class EmotionalHealthIndicator extends AbstractHealthIndicator {

    private EmotionalEvent event;

    private Date when;

    ❶
    @EventListener
    public void onHealthEvent(EmotionalEvent event) {
```

```
  this.event = event;
  this.when = new Date();
}

❷
@Override
protected void doHealthCheck(Health.Builder builder) throws Exception {
//@formatter:off
  Optional
    .ofNullable(this.event)
    .ifPresent(
    evt -> {
      Class<? extends EmotionalEvent> eventClass = this.event.getClass();
      Health.Builder healthBuilder = eventClass
            .isAssignableFrom(SadEvent.class) ? builder
      .down() : builder.up();
      String eventTimeAsString = this.when.toInstant().toString();
      healthBuilder.withDetail("class", eventClass).withDetail("when",
        eventTimeAsString);
    });
//@formatter:off
  }

}
```

❶ We'll connect this listener method to `ApplicationContext` events using the `@EventListener` annotation.

❷ The `doHealthCheck` method uses the `Health.Builder` to toggle the state of the health indicator based on the last known, recorded `EmotionalEvent`.

Example 13-16. The SadEvent

```
package demo.health;

public class SadEvent extends EmotionalEvent {
}
```

Example 13-17. The HappyEvent

```
package demo.health;

public class HappyEvent extends EmotionalEvent {
}
```

Now, any component in the `ApplicationContext` needs only publish an appropriate event to trigger an according status change (Example 13-18).

Example 13-18. The emotional REST endpoint

```
package demo.health;

import org.springframework.beans.factory.annotation.Autowired;
import org.springframework.context.ApplicationEventPublisher;
import org.springframework.web.bind.annotation.RequestMapping;
import org.springframework.web.bind.annotation.RestController;

@RestController
class EmotionalRestController {

  private final ApplicationEventPublisher publisher; ❶

  @Autowired
  EmotionalRestController(ApplicationEventPublisher publisher) {
   this.publisher = publisher;
  }

  @RequestMapping("/event/happy")
  void eventHappy() {
   this.publisher.publishEvent(new HappyEvent()); ❷
  }

  @RequestMapping("/event/sad")
  void eventSad() {
   this.publisher.publishEvent(new SadEvent());
  }
}
```

❶ Spring automatically exposes an implementation of the `ApplicationEventPub`
    `lisher` interface for use in component code. Indeed, the `ApplicationContext`
    Spring is using to run your application probably already *is* an `ApplicationEvent`
    `Publisher`.

❷ From there it's trivial to dispatch an event between components.

Events make it easier to support operational information without slowing down the
request path of business logic unconcerned with, for example, a health endpoint.

Audit Events

Events are a great way to capture almost anything in a system. Spring Boots supports
using events to support auditing, which ties events in the application to the authenticated users that triggered them, through audit events. Let's look at a REST endpoint
that also has Spring Security (`org.springframework.boot : spring-boot-starter-`
`security`) on the classpath. In order to get a trivial demo working, we've configured a
custom `UserDetailsService` implementation (Example 13-19).

Example 13-19. A few hardcoded users

```
package com.example;

import org.springframework.security.core.authority.AuthorityUtils;
import org.springframework.security.core.userdetails.User;
import org.springframework.security.core.userdetails.UserDetails;
import org.springframework.security.core.userdetails.UserDetailsService;
import org.springframework.security.core.userdetails.UsernameNotFoundException;
import org.springframework.stereotype.Service;

import java.util.Arrays;
import java.util.Optional;
import java.util.Set;
import java.util.concurrent.ConcurrentSkipListSet;

@Service
class SimpleUserDetailsService implements UserDetailsService {

  private final Set<String> users = new ConcurrentSkipListSet<>();

  SimpleUserDetailsService() {
    ❶
    this.users.addAll(Arrays.asList("pwebb", "dsyer", "mbhave", "snicoll",
      "awilkinson"));
  }

  @Override
  public UserDetails loadUserByUsername(String s)
    throws UsernameNotFoundException {
    ❷
    return Optional
      .ofNullable(this.users.contains(s) ? s : null)
      .map(x -> new User(x, "pw", AuthorityUtils.createAuthorityList("ROLE_USER")))
      .orElseThrow(() -> new UsernameNotFoundException("couldn't find " + s + "!"));
  }
}
```

❶ We hardcode a list of users (dsyer, pwebb, etc.) and...

❷ ...passwords (pw, for every user—don't try this at home!) with a fixed role (ROLE_USER).

The Spring Boot auto-configuration locks down the HTTP endpoints using HTTP BASIC authentication, by default. Spring Security will generate events related to authentication and authorization: whether someone has authenticated (or tried, unsuccessfully), whether someone has signed out, etc. You can also create your own audit events. Let's look at a trivial HTTP endpoint example that relies upon the fact that Spring Security will make available the currently authenticated java.security.Principal for injection into Spring MVC handler methods (Example 13-20).

Example 13-20. A trivial (but secure) HTTP endpoint

```java
package com.example;

import org.springframework.beans.factory.annotation.Autowired;
import org.springframework.boot.actuate.audit.AuditEvent;
import org.springframework.boot.actuate.audit.AuditEventRepository;
import org.springframework.boot.actuate.audit.listener.AuditApplicationEvent;
import org.springframework.context.ApplicationEventPublisher;
import org.springframework.web.bind.annotation.GetMapping;
import org.springframework.web.bind.annotation.RestController;

import java.security.Principal;
import java.util.Collections;

@RestController
class GreetingsRestController {

  public static final String GREETING_EVENT = "greeting_event".toUpperCase();

  private final ApplicationEventPublisher appEventPublisher;

  @Autowired
  GreetingsRestController(ApplicationEventPublisher appEventPublisher) {
    this.appEventPublisher = appEventPublisher;
  }

  @GetMapping("/hi")
  String greet(Principal p) { ❶
    String msg = "hello, " + p.getName() + "!";

    AuditEvent auditEvent = new AuditEvent(p.getName(), ❷
      GREETING_EVENT, ❸
      Collections.singletonMap("greeting", msg)); ❹

    this.appEventPublisher.publishEvent( ❺
      new AuditApplicationEvent(auditEvent));

    return msg;
  }

}
```

❶ Inject the currently authenticated Principal and...

❷ ...use it to create an AuditEvent, dereferencing the authenticated Principal name...

❸ …along with an event name (it's arbitrary, use something meaningful to your system) and…

❹ …any extra metadata you'd like included in the log.

❺ Finally, use the Spring application context event mechanism to dispatch the `AuditEvent` with a wrapper, `AuditApplicationEvent`.

You can call the secure endpoint, authenticating using HTTP BASIC. We're using the friendy `httpie` client, but you're free to use whatever you want (Example 13-21).

Example 13-21. The output of the /auditevents Actuator HTTP endpoint

```
{
    "events" : [
        {
            "timestamp" : "2017-04-26T14:01:10+0000",
            "principal" : "dsyer",
            "type" : "AUTHENTICATION_SUCCESS",
            "data" : {
                "details" : {
                    "sessionId" : null,
                    "remoteAddress" : "127.0.0.1"
                }
            }
        },
        {
            "timestamp" : "2017-04-26T14:01:10+0000",
            "data" : {
                "greeting" : "hello, dsyer!"
            },
            "type" : "GREETING_EVENT",
            "principal" : "dsyer"
        }
    ]
}
```

The audit events mechanism makes it trivial to capture information about users in the system. Spring Boot has a component called `AuditListener` that listens for events and records them using an `AuditEventRepository` implementation (Example 13-22). By default, this implementation is in-memory, though it would be trivial to implement it using some sort of persistent backing store. Contribute your own implementation and Spring Boot will honor that instead.

You can also listen (and react) to audit events in your own code using the same event listener mechanisms as you would any other Spring events.

Example 13-22. A simple AuditApplicationEvent listener

```java
package com.example;

import org.apache.commons.logging.Log;
import org.apache.commons.logging.LogFactory;
import org.springframework.boot.actuate.audit.AuditEvent;
import org.springframework.boot.actuate.audit.listener.AbstractAuditListener;
import org.springframework.boot.actuate.audit.listener.AuditApplicationEvent;
import org.springframework.context.ApplicationListener;
import org.springframework.context.event.EventListener;
import org.springframework.stereotype.Component;

@Component
class SimpleAuditEventListener {

  private Log log = LogFactory.getLog(getClass());

  @EventListener(AuditApplicationEvent.class)
  public void onAuditEvent(AuditApplicationEvent event) {
    this.log.info("audit-event: " + event.toString());
  }
}
```

Application Logging

Here we are, the future! We have self-driving cars and houses that talk to us. We can spin up a thousand servers in the blink of an eye! And yet, the venerable logfile remains one of the best ways we have to understand a given node or system's behavior. Logs reflect a process's rhythm, its activity. Logging requires intrusive statements be added to the code, but the resulting logfiles themselves are one of the most decoupled tools out there. There are entire ecosystems, tools, languages, and big-data platforms that have developed entirely around usefully mining data from logs.

You undertake two decisions when logging:

Log output
    Where do you want the log output to appear? In a file? On the console? In a SyslogD service?

Log levels
    What granularity of output do you want? Do you want every little hiccup to be printed out, or just the things that may threaten the world?

Specifying Log Output

Logs appear by default on the console in a Spring Boot application. You can optionally configure writing out to a file or some other log appender, but the console is a particularly sensible default.

If you're doing development, you'll want to see the logs as they arrive, and if you're running your application in a cloud environment, then you shouldn't need to worry about where the logs get routed to. This is one of the tenets of the twelve-factor manifesto (*http://12factor.net/logs*):

> A twelve-factor app never concerns itself with routing or storage of its output stream. It should not attempt to write to or manage logfiles. Instead, each running process writes its event stream, unbuffered, to stdout. During local development, the developer will view this stream in the foreground of their terminal to observe the app's behavior.

Log collectors or log multiplexers, like Cloud Foundry's Loggregator (*https://github.com/cloudfoundry/loggregator*) or Logstash, take the resulting logs from disparate processes and unify them into a single stream, possibly forwarding that stream onward to someplace where it may be analyzed. Log data should be as structured as possible—use consistent delimiters, define groups, and support something like a log *schema*—to support analysis. Logs should be treated as event streams; they tell a story about the behavior of the system. Log information might be the *output* of one process and the *input* to another downstream analytical process. One very popular log multiplexer, Logstash, provides numerous plug-ins that let you pipeline logs from multiple input sources and connect those logs to a central analytics system like Elasticsearch, a full-text search engine powered by Lucene.

Another log multiplexer, Loggregator, will aggregate and forward logs to your console, using `cf logs $YOUR_APP_NAME`, or to any SyslogD protocol-compliant service, including on-premise or hosted services like ElasticSearch (via Logstash), Papertrail (*https://papertrailapp.com*), Splunk (*http://www.splunk.com*), Splunk Storm, Sumo-Logic or, of course, SyslogD itself (*http://bit.ly/2sabkxc*). Configure a log drain as you would any user-provided service, specifying `-l` to signal that it's to be a log drain, as shown in Example 13-23.

Example 13-23. Create a user-provided service

```
cf cups my-logs -l syslog://logs.papertrailapp.com:PORT
```

Then, it's just a service that's available for any application to bind to, as shown in Example 13-24.

Example 13-24. Binding the service to an application

```
cf bind-service my-app my-logs && cf restart my-app
```

Loggregator also publishes log messages on the websocket protocol, so it's very simple to programmatically *listen* to logs coming off any Cloud Foundry applications. We're using Java, and so benefit from the Cloud Foundry Java client's easy integration with this websocket feed.

Pivotal Cloud Foundry also offers *correlated logging* (as depicted in Figure 13-3)—it'll show you metrics about requests on a timeline, and then show you the logs for interesting periods of time on the timelines.

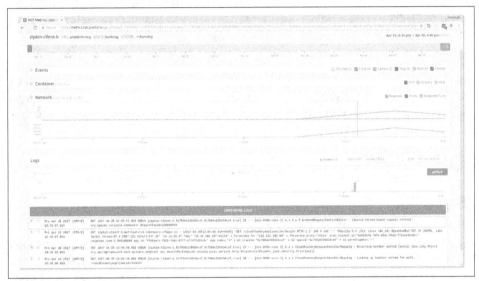

Figure 13-3. Correlated logging on Pivotal's AppsManager

Specifying Log Levels

Logs have become such a natural extension of an application's state that it can be dizzying and difficult to even begin to choose which logging technology to use. If you're using Spring Boot, you're probably fine just using the defaults. Spring Boot uses Commons Logging for all internal logging, but leaves the underlying log implementation open. Default configurations are provided for the JDK's logging support, Log4J, Log4J2, and Logback. In each case loggers are preconfigured to use console output, with optional file output also available.

By default, Spring Boot will use Logback, which in turn can capture and forward logs produced from other logging technologies like Apache Commons Logging, Log4j, Log4J2, etc. What does this mean? It means that all the likely log producing dependencies on the classpath will work just fine out of the box, and arrive on the console in a well-known configured format that includes the date and time, log level, process ID, the thread name, the logger name, and the actual log message. It'll even include color codes if you're viewing the logs on a console!

You can use Spring Boot to manage log levels generically by specifying the levels in the Spring environment (as a property in `application.properties` or your Spring Cloud Config Server instance). Spring understands, and will appropriately map to the underlying logging provider, the following log levels: ERROR, WARN, INFO, DEBUG, or TRACE. You can also specify OFF to mute all output. Log levels are ordered by priority; it's less important that somebody see statements in DEBUG intended to aid development than it is that they see potentially stability-threatening messages logged to ERROR. If you set a log level to ERROR, then nothing from that package except messages logged to ERROR will be visible. If you set the log level to TRACE, then *all* log messages from that package will be visible. A level shows all output from that level and every level below it. Let's look at an example.

Log levels are hierarchical: if you set package a to WARN, then package a.b will *also* be set to WARN. There is a distinction between the configured log levels and the effective log levels. Example 13-25 shows the configuration to change the log level to ERROR for all code in the demo package.

Example 13-25. Specifying an arbitrary log level in the Spring environment

```
logging.level.demo=error
```

If you run this application, you'll see that even though we have emitted the same message multiple times at different log levels, only one message is emitted on the console. Try it out by making an HTTP GET to `http://localhost:8080/log`, then change the log level to TRACE and restart the application. You'll see the same message logged multiple times, and in different colors if your terminal supports it, in Example 13-26.

Example 13-26. A Java application that logs three messages at different log levels

```
package demo;

import org.apache.commons.logging.Log;
import org.apache.commons.logging.LogFactory;
import org.springframework.boot.CommandLineRunner;
import org.springframework.boot.SpringApplication;
import org.springframework.boot.autoconfigure.SpringBootApplication;
import org.springframework.web.bind.annotation.GetMapping;
import org.springframework.web.bind.annotation.PostMapping;
import org.springframework.web.bind.annotation.RequestParam;
import org.springframework.web.bind.annotation.RestController;

import javax.annotation.PostConstruct;
import java.util.Optional;

@SpringBootApplication
@RestController
```

```
public class LoggingApplication {

 private Log log = LogFactory.getLog(getClass());

 public static void main(String args[]) {
  SpringApplication.run(LoggingApplication.class, args);
 }

 LoggingApplication() {
  triggerLog(Optional.empty());
 }

 @GetMapping("/log")
 public void triggerLog(@RequestParam Optional<String> name) {
  String greeting = "Hello, " + name.orElse("World") + "!";
  this.log.warn("WARN: " + greeting); ❶
  this.log.info("INFO: " + greeting);
  this.log.debug("DEBUG: " + greeting);
  this.log.error("ERROR: " + greeting);
 }
}
```

❶ None, one, or all of these log messages will appear, depending on the log level you specify.

Thus far we've restarted the process to see the log levels updated, but we can also interrogate and *dynamically*, while the process is running, reconfigure log levels using the Spring Boot Actuator /loggers endpoint. If we use an HTTP GET, the endpoint shows us all the configured log levels in our application (Example 13-27).

Example 13-27. Enumerate all the log levels

```
{
    "loggers" : {
        ... ❶
        "org.springframework.boot.actuate.endpoint" : {
            "effectiveLevel" : "INFO",
            "configuredLevel" : null
        },
        "demo" : {
            "effectiveLevel" : "ERROR",
            "configuredLevel" : "ERROR"
        }
    },
    "levels" : [
        "OFF",
        "ERROR",
        "WARN",
        "INFO",
        "DEBUG",
```

```
      "TRACE"
    ]
}
```

❶ This excerpts only a handful of lines from *thousands* more lines of configuration!

You can get details for a specific logger using /loggers/{logger}, where {logger} is the name of your package or log hierarchy name. In our example, we could call /loggers/demo to confirm the configuration for this particular level. You can call /loggers/ROOT to find the root log level that informs all otherwise unspecified and more specific log levels.

You can also *update* configured log levels using an HTTP POST to the relevant loggers endpoint.

Example 13-28 updates the configured level for the demo package.

Example 13-28. Update a log level

```
curl -i -X POST -H 'Content-Type: application/json' \
  -d '{"configuredLevel": "TRACE"}' \
  http://localhost:8080/loggers/demo
```

This is useful enough, but it only applies to a single instance. If you're running on the cloud and have a few instances running at the same time, it's more useful to ratchet up or down log levels for the deployed application. If you are using Pivotal Web Services or Pivotal Cloud Foundry, this is simple. In Figures 13-4 and 13-5, we'll peruse an application's logs with the Pivotal AppsManager dashboard, and then we'll reconfigure the log levels for a Spring Boot application.

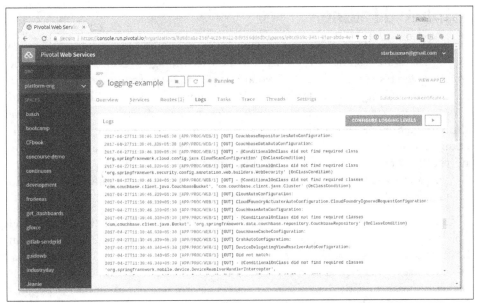

Figure 13-4. Perusing an application's logs from the AppsManager dashboard

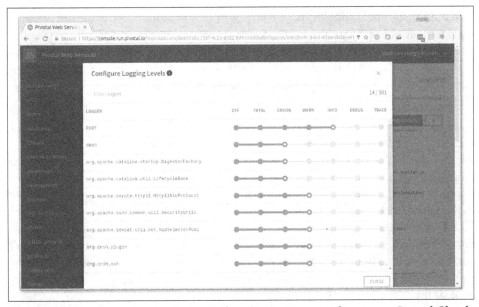

Figure 13-5. Reconfiguring the log levels for a Spring Boot Application on Pivotal Cloud Foundry or Pivotal Web Services

Distributed Tracing

There are many options to support understanding your application and performance profile. There are agent-based instrumentation technologies, things like New Relic (which integrates seamlessly with Pivotal Cloud Foundry (*https://newrelic.com/part ner/pivotal*)) and App Dynamics (which also integrates seamlessly with Pivotal Cloud Foundry (*https://docs.pivotal.io/partners/appdynamics/index.html*)), which use Java agents and automatic instrumentation to give you a low-level perspective of an application's performance behavior. These tools are worth investigation, as they can give you runtime perspective visibility into an application's performance. APM tools can give you a cross-language and technology dashboard of an application's end-to-end behavior from HTTP request down to low-level data source access.

Advances in technology and cloud computing have made it easier to stand up and deploy services with ease. Cloud computing enables us to automate away the pain (from days or weeks—gasp!—to minutes) associated with standing up new services. This increase in velocity in turn enables us to be more agile, to think about smaller batches of independently deployable services. The proliferation of new services complicates reasoning about systemwide and request-specific performance characteristics.

When all of an application's functionality lives in a *monolith*—what we call applications written as one, large, unbroken deployable like a .war or .ear—it's much easier to reason about where things have gone wrong. Is there a memory leak? It's in the monolith. Is a component not handling requests correctly? It's in the monolith. Messages getting dropped? Also probably in the monolith. Distribution changes everything.

Systems behave differently under load and at scale. The specification of a system's behavior often diverges from the actual behavior of the system, and the actual behavior may itself vary in different contexts. It is important to contextualize requests as they transit through a system. It's also important to be able to talk about the nature of a specific request and to be able to understand that specific request's behavior relative to the general behavior of similar requests in the past minute, hour, day, or whatever other useful interval provides a statistically significant sampling. Context helps us establish whether a request was abnormal and whether it merits attention. You can't trace bugs in a system until you've established a baseline for what *normal* is. How long is *long*? For some systems it might be microseconds; for others it might be seconds or minutes.

In this section, we'll look at how Spring Cloud Sleuth, which supports distributed tracing, can help us establish this context and help us better understand a system's actual behavior (its *emergent* behavior), not just its specified behavior.

Finding Clues with Spring Cloud Sleuth

Tracing is simple, in theory. As a request flows from one component in a system to another, through ingress and egress points, *tracers* add logic—instrumentation—where possible to perpetuate a unique *trace ID* that's generated when the first request is made. As a request arrives at a component along its journey, a new *span ID* is assigned for that component and added to the trace. A trace represents the whole journey of a request, and a span is each individual hop, or request, along the way. Spans may contain *tags*, or metadata, that can be used to later contextualize the request and perhaps correlate a request to a specific transaction. Spans typically contain common tags like start timestamps and stop timestamps, though it's easy to associate semantically relevant tags like a business entity ID with a span.

Let's suppose we had two services, `service-a` and `service-b`. If an HTTP request arrived at `service-a`, and it in turn sent a message to Apache Kafka to `service-b`, then we would have one trace ID, but two spans. Each span would have request-specific tags. The first span might have details of the HTTP request. The second span might have details of the message sent to the Apache Kafka broker.

Spring Cloud Sleuth (*http://cloud.spring.io/spring-cloud-sleuth/*) (`org.springframe work.cloud:spring-cloud-starter-sleuth`) automatically instruments common communication channels:

- Requests over messaging technologies like Apache Kafka (*http://bit.ly/2s9PsBY*) or RabbitMQ (or any other messaging system for which there is a Spring Cloud Stream (*http://cloud.spring.io/spring-cloud-stream/*) binder)
- HTTP headers received at Spring MVC controllers
- Requests that pass through a Netflix Zuul microproxy
- Requests made with the `RestTemplate`, etc.
- Requests made through the Netflix Feign REST client
- …and indeed most other types of requests and replies that a typical Spring-ecosystem application might encounter

Spring Cloud Sleuth sets up useful log formatting for you that logs the trace ID and the span ID. Assuming you're running Spring Cloud Sleuth-enabled code in a microservice whose `spring.application.name` is `my-service-id`, you will see something like Example 13-29 in the logs for your microservice.

Example 13-29. Logs coming off a Spring Cloud Sleuth-instrumented application

```
2016-02-11 17:12:45.404 INFO [my-service-id,73b62c0f90d11e06,73b6etydf90d11e06,false]
  85184 --- [nio-8080-exec-1] com.example.MySimpleComponentMakingARequest    : ...
```

In that example, `my-service-id` is the `spring.application.name`, `73b62c0f90d11e06` is the trace ID, and `73b6etydf90d11e06` is the span ID. This information is very useful, and you can use whatever log analytics tools you have at your disposal to mine it; you can see the flow of a request through different services if you have all the logs, and the trace information, in a single place available for query and analysis.

Spring Cloud Sleuth instrumentation usually consists of two components: an object that does the *tracing* of some subsystem, and the specific `SpanInjector<T>` instance for that subsystem. The tracer is usually some sort of interceptor, listener, filter, etc., that you can insert into the request flow for the component under trace. You can create and contribute your own tracing if for some reason the component you need isn't already accounted for out of the box.

How Much Data Is Enough?

Which requests should be traced? Ideally, you'll want enough data to see trends reflective of live, operational traffic. You don't want to overwhelm your logging and analysis infrastructure, though. Some organizations may only keep requests for every thousand requests, or every ten, or every million! By default, the threshold is 10%, or .1, though you may override it by configuring a sampling percentage (Example 13-30).

Example 13-30. Changing the sampling threshold percentage

```
spring.sleuth.sampler.percentage = 0.2
```

Alternatively, you may register your own `Sampler` bean definition and make the decision about which requests should be sampled. You can make more intelligent choices about which things to trace, for example, by ignoring successful requests, perhaps checking whether some component is in an error state, or really anything else. Example 13-31 shows the `Sampler` definition.

Example 13-31. The Spring Cloud Sampler interface

```
package org.springframework.cloud.sleuth;

import org.springframework.cloud.sleuth.Span;

public interface Sampler {
    boolean isSampled(Span s);
}
```

The `Span` given as an argument represents the span for the current in-flight request in the larger trace. You can do interesting and request-specific types of sampling if you'd like. You might decide to only sample requests that have a 500 HTTP status code, for example.

Make sure to set realistic expectations for your application and infrastructure. It may well be that the usage patterns for your applications require something more sensitive or less sensitive to detect trends and patterns. This is meant to be online telemetry; most organizations don't warehouse this data more than a few days or, at the upper bound, a week.

OpenZipkin: A Picture Is Worth a Thousand Traces

Data collection is a start, but the goal is to *understand* the data, not just collect it. In order to appreciate the big picture, we need to get beyond individual events. We'll use the OpenZipkin project (*https://github.com/openzipkin*). OpenZipkin is the open source version of Zipkin (Figure 13-6), a project that originated at Twitter in 2010, and is based on the Google Dapper papers (*http://research.google.com/pubs/pub36356.html*).

Figure 13-6. OpenZipkin is the open source version of Zipkin

 Previously, the open source version of Zipkin evolved at a different pace than the version used internally at Twitter. OpenZipkin represents the synchronization of those efforts: OpenZipkin (*https://github.com/openzipkin*) *is* Zipkin and when we refer to Zipkin in this post, we're referring to the version reflected in OpenZipkin.

Zipkin provides a REST API that clients talk to directly. This REST API is written with Spring MVC and Spring Boot. Zipkin even supports a Spring Boot-based implementation of this REST API. Using that is as simple as using Zipkin's `@EnableZipkin Server` directly. The Zipkin Server delegates writes to the persistence tier via a `SpanStore`. Presently, there is support for using MySQL or an in-memory `SpanStore` out of the box.

As an alternative to talking to the Zipkin REST API directly, we can *also* publish messages to the Zipkin server over a Spring Cloud Stream binder like RabbitMQ or Apache Kafka, which is what you see in Example 13-32. Create a new Spring Boot application, add `org.springframework.cloud : spring-cloud-sleuth-zipkin-stream` to the classpath, and then add `@EnableZipkinStreamServer` to a Spring Boot application to accept and adapt incoming Spring Cloud Stream-based Sleuth `Span` instances into Zipkin's `Span` type. It will then persist them, using a configured `Span Store`. You may use whatever Spring Cloud Stream binding you like, but in this case we'll use Spring Cloud Stream RabbitMQ (`org.springframework.cloud : spring-cloud-starter-stream-rabbitmq`).

Example 13-32. The Zipkin server code

```
package demo;

import org.springframework.boot.SpringApplication;
import org.springframework.boot.autoconfigure.SpringBootApplication;
import org.springframework.cloud.sleuth.zipkin.stream.EnableZipkinStreamServer;

❶
@EnableZipkinStreamServer
@SpringBootApplication
public class ZipkinApplication {

  public static void main(String[] args) {
    SpringApplication.run(ZipkinApplication.class, args);
  }
}
```

❶   This tells the Zipkin server to listen for incoming spans

Add the Zipkin UI (`io.zipkin : zipkin-ui`) to the classpath of the Zipkin Stream server to visualize requests. Bring up the UI (also at `http://localhost:9411`, where the stream server lives) and you find all the recent traces, if there are any. If there aren't, let's create some.

With the server up and running, we can stand up a couple of clients and make some requests. Let's look at two trivial services, imaginatively named `zipkin-client-a` and `zipkin-client-b`. Both services have the required binder (`org.springframework.cloud : spring-cloud-starter-stream-rabbit`) and the Spring Cloud Sleuth Stream client (`org.springframework.cloud : spring-cloud-sleuth-stream`) on the classpath.

The client, `zipkin-client-a`, is configured to run on port 8082. There is a property, `message-service`, to tell the client where to find its service. You could as easily use service registration and discovery here, though. The client makes a request of the downstream service using a `RestTemplate` bean defined in the main class. It's important that the client—in this case the `RestTemplate`—be a Spring bean. The Spring Cloud Sleuth configuration needs to know where to find the bean if it's to be able to configure a Sleuth-aware interceptor for all requests that flow through it (Example 13-33).

Example 13-33. The message client

```
package demo;

import org.springframework.beans.factory.annotation.Autowired;
import org.springframework.beans.factory.annotation.Value;
import org.springframework.core.ParameterizedTypeReference;
import org.springframework.http.HttpMethod;
import org.springframework.web.bind.annotation.RequestMapping;
import org.springframework.web.bind.annotation.RestController;
import org.springframework.web.client.RestTemplate;

import java.util.Map;

@RestController
class MessageClientRestController {

@Autowired
private RestTemplate restTemplate;

@Value("${message-service}")
private String host;

@RequestMapping("/")
Map<String, String> message() {

  //@formatter:off
  ParameterizedTypeReference<Map<String, String>> ptr =
        new ParameterizedTypeReference<Map<String, String>>() { };
  //@formatter:on

  return this.restTemplate.exchange(this.host, HttpMethod.GET, null, ptr)
    .getBody();
 }
}
```

The service, `zipkin-client-b`, is configured to run on port 8081. It takes all the trace headers from the inbound request and includes them in its replies, along with a message (Example 13-34).

Example 13-34. The message service

```
package demo;

import org.springframework.web.bind.annotation.RequestMapping;
import org.springframework.web.bind.annotation.RestController;

import javax.servlet.http.HttpServletRequest;
import java.util.Collections;
import java.util.HashMap;
import java.util.List;
import java.util.Map;
import java.util.stream.Collectors;

@RestController
class MessageServiceRestController {

 @RequestMapping("/")
 Map<String, String> message(HttpServletRequest httpRequest) {

  List<String> traceHeaders = Collections.list(httpRequest.getHeaderNames())
    .stream().filter(h -> h.toLowerCase().startsWith("x-"))
    .collect(Collectors.toList()); ❶

  Map<String, String> response = new HashMap<>();
  response.put("message", "Hi, @ " + System.currentTimeMillis());
  traceHeaders.forEach(h -> response.put(h, httpRequest.getHeader(h)));
  return response;
 }
}
```

❶ Collect all headers contributed by Spring Cloud Sleuth (those starting with x-)
from the outgoing request from zipkin-client-a and include them in the generated JSON response, along with a unique message.

Make a few requests at http://localhost:8082. You'll get replies similar to what we
see in Example 13-35.

Example 13-35. A sample reply coming from the traced request

```
{
    "x-b3-parentspanid" : "9aa83c71878b6cd4",
    "x-b3-sampled" : "1",
    "message" : "Hi, 1493358280026",
    "x-b3-traceid" : "9aa83c71878b6cd4",
    "x-span-name" : "http:",
    "x-b3-spanid" : "668b8e088a35f1db"
}
```

Now you can inspect the requests in the Zipkin server, at `http://localhost:9411`. You can sort by most recent, longest, etc., for finer-grained control over which results you see. In Figure 13-7, we see the results when searching for traces in the Zipkin server.

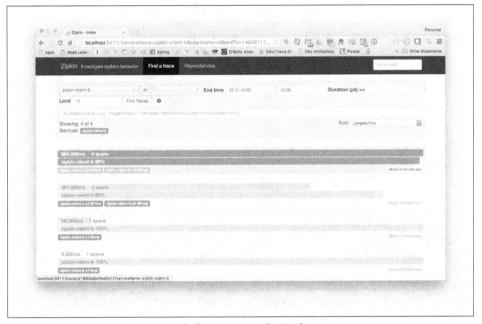

Figure 13-7. The results of a search for traces on the Zipkin main page

You can inspect the trace's details, as shown in Figure 13-8.

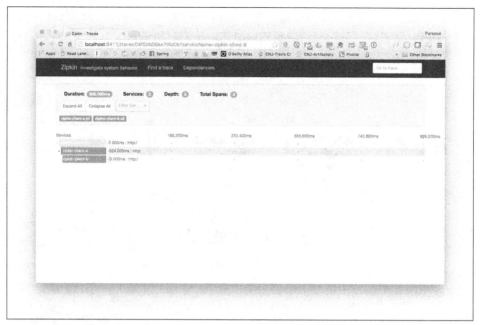

Figure 13-8. Details page showing the individual spans for a single trace

Each individual span also carries with it information (*tags*) about the particular request it's associated with. You can view this detail by clicking on an individual span, as shown in Figure 13-9.

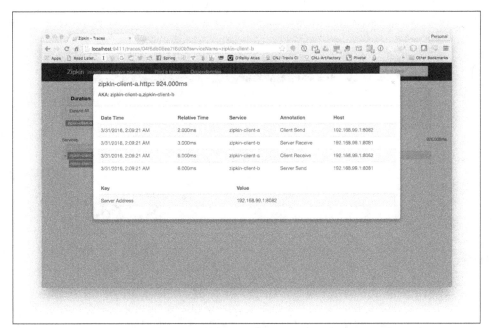

Figure 13-9. Details panel showing relevant information and associated tags for a given span

Zipkin is an enviable position: it knows how services interact with each other. It knows the topology of your system. It'll even generate a handy visualization of that topology if you click on the Dependencies tab, as depicted in Figure 13-10.

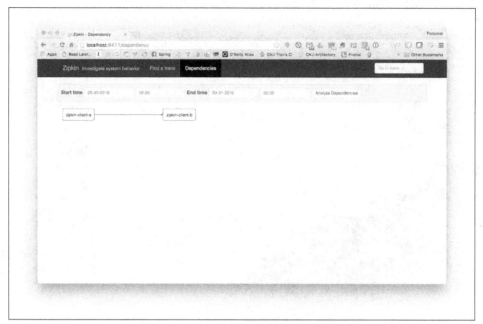

Figure 13-10. Visualization of the topology of your services

Each element in the visualization can give you further information still, including which components use it and how many (traced) calls have been made. You can see this in Figure 13-11.

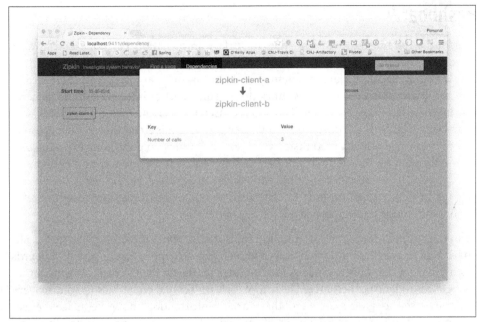

Figure 13-11. Details for each service in the dependencies visualization

If you move your application into a cloud platform, like Cloud Foundry, the routing infrastructure should be smart enough to *also* originate or perpetuate trace headers. Cloud Foundry does: as requests enter the system at the cloud router, headers are added or perpetuated to your running application (like your Spring application).

Tracing Other Platforms and Technologies

For Spring-based workloads, distributed tracing couldn't be easier. However, tracing, by its very nature, is a cross-cutting concern for all services, no matter which technology stack they're implemented in. The OpenTracing initiative (*https://github.com/opentracing*) is an effort to standardize the vocabulary and concepts of modern tracing for multiple languages and platforms. The OpenTracing API has support from multiple *very* large organizations and has as its lead one of the original authors on the original Google Dapper paper. The effort defines language bindings; there are already implementations for JavaScript, Python, Go, etc. The Spring team will keep Spring Cloud Sleuth conceptually compatible with this effort and will track it. It is expected, but not implied, that the bindings will as often as not have Zipkin as their backend.

> The OpenTracing effort is relatively nascent, so you may find that it's easier to just use an OpenZipkin client binding for another langugage, instead of the OpenTracing-based implementation.

Dashboards

Thus far we've mostly looked at ways to surface information per node and how to customize that information. But that's only useful insofar as we can connect it to a bigger picture about the larger system. The Actuator, for example, publishes information about any given node, but assumes there's some sort of infrastructure to soak up this information and consolidate it, similar to the way Google manages services with their Borg Monitoring ("Borgmon") approach. Borgmon is a centralized management and monitoring solution used inside Google, but it relies on each node exposing service information. Borgmon-aware services publish information over HTTP endpoints, even if the services they monitor aren't themselves HTTP. We'll see several options in this chapter on how to centralize and visualize the system itself, beyond the node-by-node endpoints provided by Actuator.

In this section we'll look at a few handy tools that support the ever-important dashboard experience that both operations and business will appreciate. These dashboards often build on the tools we've looked at so far, presenting the relevant information in a single, at-a-glance experience. These tools rely on service registration and discovery to discover services in a system and then surface information about them. See the section on routing in Chapter 7 for details on working with a service registry like Netflix's Eureka. In this section, we rely on a Netflix Eureka registry being available so that our dashboards can discover and monitor the deployed services in our system. We might alternatively use Hashicorp Consul or Apache Zookeeper, or any other registry for which there's a Spring Cloud `DiscoveryClient` abstraction implementation available.

Monitoring Downstream Services with the Hystrix Dashboard

We can't add instrumention to other teams' code. We can't insist that they build their applications using best-of-breed technologies like Cloud Foundry and Spring Cloud. We can't make other teams, and other organizations, do anything, usually. The best we can do is protect ourselves from potential failures in downstream code. One way to do this is to wrap potentially shaky service-to-service calls with a circuit breaker.

Spring Cloud supports easy integration with the Netflix Hystrix circuit breaker. We looked at it in "Isolating Failures and Graceful Degradation" on page 394. As a recap, let's look at a trivial example that randomly inserts failure when issuing calls to either `http://google.com` or `http://yahoo.com` (Example 13-36).

Example 13-36. Use the Hystrix circuit breaker (assuming that you've specified @EnableCircuitBreaker somewhere)

```
package com.example;
```

```java
import com.netflix.hystrix.contrib.javanica.annotation.HystrixCommand;
import org.springframework.beans.factory.annotation.Autowired;
import org.springframework.http.ResponseEntity;
import org.springframework.web.bind.annotation.RequestMapping;
import org.springframework.web.bind.annotation.RequestMethod;
import org.springframework.web.bind.annotation.RestController;
import org.springframework.web.client.RestTemplate;

import java.net.URI;
import java.util.Random;

@RestController
class ShakyRestController {

 @Autowired
 private RestTemplate restTemplate;

 ❶
 public ResponseEntity<String> fallback() {
  return ResponseEntity.ok("ONOES");
 }

 ❷
 @HystrixCommand(fallbackMethod = "fallback")
 @RequestMapping(method = RequestMethod.GET, value = "/google")
 public ResponseEntity<String> google() {
  return this.proxy(URI.create("http://www.google.com/"));
 }

 @HystrixCommand(fallbackMethod = "fallback")
 @RequestMapping(method = RequestMethod.GET, value = "/yahoo")
 public ResponseEntity<String> yahoo() {
  return this.proxy(URI.create("http://www.yahoo.com"));
 }

 private ResponseEntity<String> proxy(URI url) {

  if (new Random().nextInt(100) > 50) {
   throw new RuntimeException("tripping circuit breaker!");
  }

  ResponseEntity<String> responseEntity = this.restTemplate.getForEntity(url,
   String.class);

  return ResponseEntity.ok()
   .contentType(responseEntity.getHeaders().getContentType())
   .body(responseEntity.getBody());
 }

}
```

❶ Provide a fallback behavior that gets called when a circuit throws an exception. In this case we return a silly `String`.

❷ We decorate our various REST calls with a circuit breaker so that downstream service calls that may fail are safely handled.

Each node that uses the Hystrix circuit breaker also emits a server-sent event (SSE) heartbeat stream for every node that contains a circuit breaker. The SSE stream is accessible from `http://localhost:8000/hystrix.stream`, assuming the default configuration and that the above code was listening on port 8000. That stream is constantly updated. It contains information about the flow of traffic through the circuit, including how many requests were made, whether the circuit is open (in which case requests are failing and being diverted to the *fallback* handler) or closed (and thus requests that are attempted succeed in reaching the downstream service), and statistics about the traffic itself. While we cannot instrument other people's services, we *can* monitor the flow of requests through our circuit breakers as a sort of virtual monitor for downstream services. If the circuit breaker is open, and requests aren't going through, then it probably indicates that the downstream service is down.

We *can* monitor the circuit breakers. The circuit breaker stream is not much to look at directly, but you can take that stream and give it to another component, the Hystrix Dashboard, which visualizes the flow of requests through the circuits on a specific node.

Create a new Spring Boot application and add `org.springframework.cloud : spring-cloud-starter-hystrix-dashboard` to the classpath. Add `@EnableHystrix Dashboard` to a `@Configuration` class and then start the application. The Hystrix Dashboard UI is available at `/hystrix.html`.

Not bad! But this is still just one node. It is untenable at scale, where you have more than one instance of the same service, or multiple services besides. A single-node-aware Hystrix Dashboard will not be very useful; you'd have to plug in every `/hystrix.stream` address one at a time. We can use Spring Cloud Turbine to multiplex all the streams from all the nodes into one stream. We can then plug the resulting aggregate stream into our Hystrix Dashboard. Spring Cloud Turbine can aggregate services using service registration and discovery (via the Spring Cloud `Dis coveryClient` service registry abstraction) or through messaging brokers like RabbitMQ and Apache Kafka exposed (via the Spring Cloud Stream messaging abstraction).

Add `org.springframework.boot : spring-boot-starter-web`, `org.springframe work.cloud : spring-cloud-starter-stream-rabbit`, and `org.springframe work.cloud : spring-cloud-starter-turbine-stream` to a new Spring Boot application (Example 13-37).

Example 13-37. Use Spring Cloud Turbine to aggregate the the server-sent event heartbeat streams from multiple circuit breakers, across multiple nodes, into one stream

```
package com.example;

import org.springframework.boot.SpringApplication;
import org.springframework.boot.autoconfigure.SpringBootApplication;
import org.springframework.cloud.netflix.turbine.stream.EnableTurbineStream;

❶
@EnableTurbineStream
@SpringBootApplication
public class TurbineApplication {

 public static void main(String[] args) {
   SpringApplication.run(TurbineApplication.class, args);
 }
}
```

❶   Stand up the Spring Cloud Stream-based Turbine aggregation stream.

When the Spring Cloud Turbine service starts, it will serve a stream at `http://local host:8989/hystrix.stream`, where 8989 is the default port. You can override the port by specifying `turbine.stream.port`. We specified 8010 for the book's example.

All clients that have circuit breakers in them will need to be updated a bit to support the involvement of Spring Cloud Turbine. Add a Spring Cloud Stream binding (we're using `spring-cloud-starter-stream-rabbit`), and then add `org.springframe work.cloud : spring-cloud-netflix-hystrix-stream`. This last dependency adapts circuit breaker status updates to messages sent over your particular Spring Cloud Stream binder choice. As part of this, Spring Cloud Turbine will need information about the local node and the cluster. The easiest way to give it that information is to use service registration and discovery. Add a `DiscoveryClient` abstraction implementation (we're using `org.springframework.cloud : spring-cloud-starter-eureka`) to the classpath, as well.

 This will of course require that Netflix's Eureka service registry be running somewhere as well. For more details, see our discussion of service registration and discovery in Chapter 7. We'll use a service registry a fair amount as we look at ways to observe systems, not just individual nodes. You may as well get one running and keep it running if you're following along from here.

Restart your client and then revisit the circuit breaker dashboard. Plug in the hys trix.stream endpoint from the Spring Cloud Turbine (`http://localhost:8010/`

`hystrix.stream`, if you're using our code). Figure 13-12 shows the results of viewing the Hystrix stream.

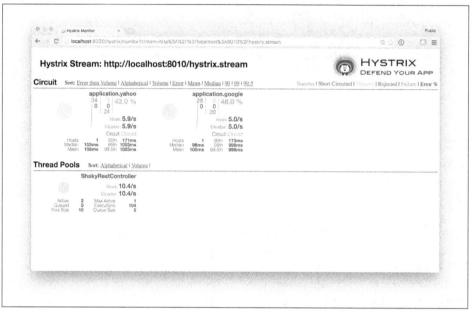

Figure 13-12. The Hystrix Dashboard

 Technologies like the Hystrix Dashboard are important, but they will add a cost to your operational overhead. Ideally, this competency should be managed by the platform, and automated. If you're using Cloud Foundry, there is a Hystrix Dashboard backing service in the service catalog that is already wired to use Spring Cloud Turbine, ready to use.

Codecentric's Spring Boot Admin

Spring Boot Admin (*https://github.com/codecentric/spring-boot-admin*) is a project from the folks at Codecentric. It provides an aggregated view of services and supports dropping down into a Spring Boot-based service's Actuator-exposed endpoints (logs, JMX environment, request logs, etc.)

To use it, you'll need to stand up a service registry (we're using the pre-described Netflix Eureka instance). Set up a new Spring Boot application and add the following dependencies to the classpath: `de.codecentric : spring-boot-admin-server` and `de.codecentric : spring-boot-admin-server-ui`. The version itself will vary, of course, so check out the Git repository and your favorite Maven repository. In this example, we're using `1.5.0` (Example 13-38).

Example 13-38. Standing up an instance of the Spring Boot Admin

```
package com.example;

import de.codecentric.boot.admin.config.EnableAdminServer;
import org.springframework.boot.SpringApplication;
import org.springframework.boot.autoconfigure.SpringBootApplication;
import org.springframework.cloud.client.discovery.EnableDiscoveryClient;

@EnableDiscoveryClient
@EnableAdminServer
@SpringBootApplication
public class SpringBootAdminApplication {

  public static void main(String[] args) {
    SpringApplication.run(SpringBootAdminApplication.class, args);
  }
}
```

We'll connect the clients to the server with Spring Cloud's `DiscoveryClient` support. Add `org.springframework.cloud : spring-cloud-starter-eureka` and the `@Enable DiscoveryClient` annotation to both the Spring Boot Admin service and all the clients. We avoid the need for our clients to be explicitly aware of the Spring Boot Admin with service registration and discovery. You may alternatively use the Spring Boot Admin client dependency, `de.codecentric : spring-boot-admin-starter-client`. If you use the Spring Boot Admin client dependency, then you'll need to specify a `spring.boot.admin.url` property, pointing the clients to the Spring Boot Admin server instance.

Your client will need the Spring Boot Actuator, as well. In Spring Boot 1.5 or greater, the Actuator endpoints are locked down and require authentication. The simplest way to get around that is to disable authentication (`management.security.enabled = false`) for the management endpoints themselves; otherwise some functionality in the Spring Boot Admin will not work.

Start your client and then visit the Spring Boot Admin (shown in Figure 13-13).

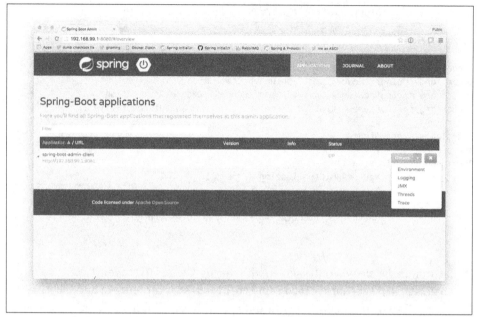

Figure 13-13. The central screen for the Spring Boot Admin that lists registered services

In our example, we run it on port **8080**, as shown in Figures 13-14 and 13-15.

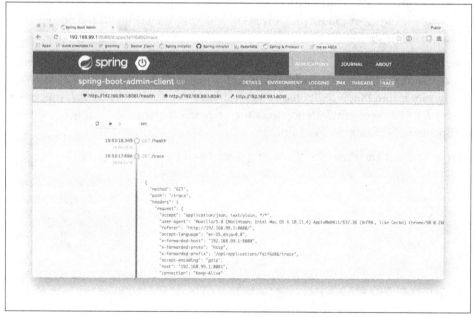

Figure 13-14. The Spring Boot Admin enumeration of requests (/trace)

Figure 13-15. The Spring Boot Admin details screen

The Spring Boot Admin gives yet another way to see the aggregation of services in a system and drill down into their state.

Ordina Microservices Dashboard

Ordina's JWorks division created another dashboard that provides a very handy *visual* enumeration of the registered services in a system. It also discovers services through Spring Cloud's DiscoveryClient support, so you'll need the aforementioned service registry stood up and an implementation on the client classpath (Example 13-39).

Example 13-39. Standing up an instance of the Microservices Dashboard

```
package com.example;

import be.ordina.msdashboard.EnableMicroservicesDashboardServer;
import org.springframework.boot.SpringApplication;
import org.springframework.boot.autoconfigure.SpringBootApplication;
import org.springframework.cloud.client.discovery.EnableDiscoveryClient;

@SpringBootApplication
@EnableDiscoveryClient
@EnableMicroservicesDashboardServer
public class MicroservicesDashboardServerApplication {

  public static void main(String[] args) {
```

```
SpringApplication.run(MicroservicesDashboardServerApplication.class, args);
 }
}
```

The Microservices Dashboard (Figure 13-16) provides a visualization of how services are connected together. It features four different lanes meant to reflect layers of components in a system:

- UI components are just that: user interface components, like Angular directives, for example.

- Resources might be information drawn from the Spring Boot Actuator /mappings endpoint with the default spring mappings excluded or hypermedia links exposed on an index resource through an index controller.

- Microservices are services discovered (Spring Boot or not) using Spring Cloud's DiscoveryClient abstraction.

- Backends are any HealthIndicators found on the discovered microservices—components that services depend upon that may fail.

Figure 13-16. The Microservices Dashboard enumerating the discovered services and providing information on interesting components in those services

The Microservices Dashboard supports drilling down by node states, name, types, and groups. You can add *virtual* nodes—nodes that aren't automatically discovered but about which you'd like to make the Microservices Dashboard aware. If nothing else, they could be placeholders for things that should be there, eventually, for planning purposes.

Pivotal Cloud Foundry's AppsManager

The two dashboards we just looked at rely on Spring Boot's Actuator to surface information about the Java process. Ultimately, though, you're going to run code on a platform, and in that platform there will be other moving parts, like the container (which in turn has its own health to be monitored) that runs the the application process itself, backing services, and so on. If you're using something like Cloud Foundry, there is no reason you couldn't run .NET applications or Python applications or whatever other technologies you'd like, and they too will have their own status. Arguably, the optimal dashboard would centralize visibility into all applications in a system. If more detailed diagnostics, such as those in the Spring Boot Actuator, are available, then that resolution of detail should be visible, too. The Pivotal Cloud Foundry AppsManager gets this just right. We have touched on it already in this chapter, so we'll only present an overview of the AppsManager.

We can review all the applications for a given user who belongs to a particular organization and a particular space—this is shown in Figure 13-17.

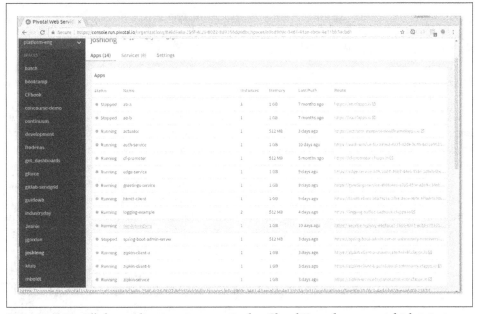

Figure 13-17. All the applications in a particular Cloud Foundry space, which is in turn part of an organization

We can review the details of an individual application as well, as shown in Figure 13-18.

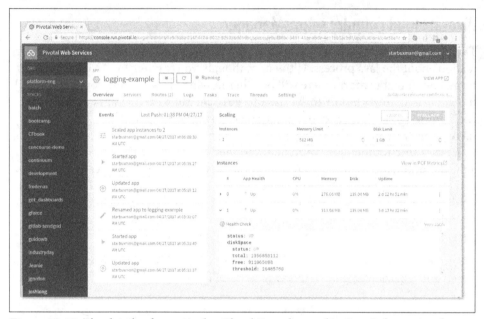

Figure 13-18. The details of a particular Cloud Foundry application. Information from the Spring Boot Actuator is visible as well.

Remediation

Thus far we've focused on surfacing information about the state of the system, on improving visibility. What do we do with this knowledge? In a static, pre-cloud environment, improved visibility can be used to trigger alerting, which then (hopefully) results in a pager going off or somebody getting an email. By the time alerting has happened, it's probably too late and somebody's already had a bad experience on the system. Cloud computing (which supports manipulation with APIs) changes this dynamic: we can solve software problems *with* software. If, for example, the system needs more capacity, we don't need to file an ITIL ticket; just make an API request. We can support *automatic remediation*.

Distributed computing changes the way we should think about application instance availability. In a sufficiently distributed system, having a single instance that is available 100% of the time becomes near impossible. Instead, the focus must be on building a system where service is somehow restored; we must optimize time to remediation. If time to remediation is zero seconds, then we are *effectively* 100% highly available, but this change in approach has profound implications in how we architect our system. We can only achieve this effect if we can program the platform itself.

The platform can even do basic remediation for you, automatically. Most cloud platforms provide health monitoring. If you ask Cloud Foundry to stand up 10 instances of an application, it'll ensure that there are at least 10 instances. Even if an instance should die, Cloud Foundry will restart it.

Most cloud platforms, including Pivotal Web Services and Pivotal Cloud Foundry, support *autoscaling*. An autoscaler monitors container-level information like RAM and CPU and, if necessary, adds capacity by launching new application instances. On Pivotal Web Services, you need only create a service instance of the type `app-autoscaler` and then bind it to the application. You'll need to configure it in the management panel on the Pivotal Web Services Console.

Example 13-40. Creating an autoscaler service on Pivotal Web Services

```
cf marketplace
Getting services from marketplace in org platform-eng / space joshlong as ..
OK

service        plans        description
..
app-autoscaler  bronze, gold  Scales bound applications in response to load (beta)
..
```

There is still room for yet more advanced remediation. There are some inspiring examples out there, like Netflix's Winston (*http://bit.ly/2vncwz6*), LinkedIn's Nurse (*http://bit.ly/2vnaMFX*), Facebook's FBAR (*http://bit.ly/2vnp89p*), and the open source StackStorm (*https://stackstorm.com*). These tools make it easy to define pipelines composed of atoms of functionality that, when combined, solve a problem for you. These tools work in terms of well-known input events, triggered by monitoring agents or sensors or other indicators deployed in the system. In a traditional architecture these events would trigger alerting, which is useful, but for some classifications of problems it's also possible to trigger automatic remediation flows.

We encourage you to investigate some of these approaches. Most of them are rooted in environments that don't have the benefits of the layers of guarantees made by a platform like Cloud Foundry, though. In our case, we don't need to solve problems like restarting services or load balancing. We also don't need to worry about alerting for low-level things like heartbeat detection; the platform will manage that for us.

There are still some gaps in our visibility, though—things that we alone know to look for because we know the specifics of our architecture. It's not hard to find the components in our architecture that tell a story about our system's capacity. These components expose information that we can monitor, or react to. Spring Integration makes it simple to process events from different event sources and to string together components over messaging technologies like RabbitMQ or Apache Kafka. Spring Cloud Data Flow builds upon Spring Integration, providing a Bash shell-like DSL that lets you compose arbitrary streams of processing and then orchestrate them on a distributed processing fabric like YARN or Cloud Foundry. See our discussion of Spring Integration (Chapter 10) and Spring Cloud Data Flow (Chapter 12) for more. Spring Cloud Data Flow is an ideal toolbox to assemble processing pipelines that respond to insight coming from our own custom event sources.

There are a lot of things you might look at as prompts for action. We are in an enviable position—all the knobs and levers we need to turn or pull to solve many classes of problems have APIs. We can use software to fix faltering software. Let's suppose we have a consumer that takes a nontrivial amount of time to respond to messages. We can look at the throughput of a queue in your message broker to decide that we should add more consumers to help more efficiently drain the queue and keep within a service-level agreement (SLA).

In the source code for this chapter there are a few handy Spring Cloud Data Flow *sources* (a component that produces events as messages) and *sinks* (a component that does something in response to events). The `rabbit-queue-metrics` source monitors a given RabbitMQ queue and publishes information about it: the queue depth (how many messages haven't been processed), the consumer count (how many clients are listening for messages on the other end), and the queue name itself. The `cloudfoundry-autoscaler` sink responds to incoming messages (which should be a number) and adds or reduces instances for a given application until that number falls within a prescribed range. The range and relevance of the number is for you to ascribe. It's trivial, once you've registered the custom sources and sinks, to connect these two things by taking the output of the source, extracting the queue size from the information, and then sending it to the autoscaler sink.

Example 13-41. Using Spring Cloud Data Flow to automatically scale applications based on queue depth

```
rabbit-queue-metrics
  --rabbitmq.metrics.queueName=remediation-demo.remediation-demo↵
-group |
 transform --expression=headers['queue-size'] |
 cloudfoundry-autoscaler --applicationName=remediation-rabbitmq-consumer
   --instance↵
CountMaximum=10  --thresholdMaximum=5
```

There are a lot of input variables that go into understanding how to support and fix a broken system. If you capture and distill those events, and connect them to automatic handlers, you have the basis for an automated incident response system for certain simple classes of problems. Spring Cloud Data Flow is purpose-built for this sort of ad hoc event-monitoring and response-based approach. In the source code for this chapter we've also included a Spring Cloud Data Flow *source* component to monitor Cloud Foundry application metrics like RAM and hard disk usage. You could build a similar remediation flow based on an application's other metrics.

Summary

We've only begun to look at the possibilities in this chapter; if you're feeling overwhelmed, *good*! This subject is of a *critical* importance in a cloud native system, and failure to architect with observability in mind only tempts disaster. These are often called "day two problems"—things you won't realize you need until after you get to production. It is dramatically less painful on "day two" if you think about these things on "day one." Spring Boot, Spring Cloud, and Cloud Foundry are purpose-built to quickly and easily integrate and support these requirements with a minimum of ceremony.

You'll note that, while a lot of what we talked about in this chapter was introduced in terms of open source clients, some of the backing services we mentioned are hosted SaaS offerings, and they typically cost. This is a *feature*; as explained earlier, our goal is to never run software we can't sell. It's better to let the platform, and third parties for whom these concerns are core competencies, satisfy these nonfunctional requirements instead.

Consider extracting all these production-centric requirements into a separate Spring Boot auto-configuration on which microservices in your organization build. You can even create your own starter dependencies and meta-annotations. This way, you need only configure how you handle logs, metrics, tracing, etc., once, and then simply add the appropriate auto-configuration to the classpath. If you are using a platform like Cloud Foundry, it is trivial to stand up the relevant backing services to support your application. Taken together, an application framework like Spring Boot (which supports twelve-factor applications) and a platform like Cloud Foundry (which supports twelve-factor operations) help you get to production, safely and quickly.

## CHAPTER 14

Service Brokers

A backing service is a service (databases, message queues, email services, etc.) that an application consumes at runtime, over the network. Cloud Foundry applications consume backing services by looking for their locators and credentials in an environment variable called VCAP_SERVICES. The simplicity of this approach is a feature: any language can pluck the environment variable out of the environment and parse the embedded JSON to extract things like service hosts, ports, and credentials. The code of an application should make no distinction as to whether the backing service is local, or provided and managed by the platform. This decoupling makes it easy for an application to migrate from one environment to another: simply redefine the environment variable with environment-appropriate values and restart the application.

In Cloud Foundry, applications talk to *all* services through this indirection. Cloud Foundry manages a set of backing services and a set of applications. An operator must specify which applications can see the connection information for a particular backing service. This is called a service binding. A single application may be bound to many backing services, and many applications may be bound to a single backing service. There are two ways to contribute services to be bound to applications in Cloud Foundry: service brokers and user-defined services. Ultimately, they both end up as entries in the VCAP_SERVICES environment variable.

An operator may create *user-defined* services if they want an application to talk to middleware or some other resource running off-platform. This is particularly valuable for connections to legacy resources running in an organization, like Ye Olde Sybase Instance or mainframes, or indeed, other REST APIs that are just applications running on the platform somewhere.

It makes sense to use service broker services, as opposed to user-defined services, if a resource is commonly used and supports multitenancy. The service brokers are themselves applications that are responsible for dynamically provisioning instances of middleware and providing the connection information to the platform which then binds it to application. A service broker is a recipe that the platform uses to conjure up a new service instance, on-demand. A service broker must also handle the life cycle of the service in question, creating it and destroying it when asked. The platform talks to a service broker through a uniform REST API that all service brokers must support.

The Life of a Backing Service

The Cloud Foundry *services marketplace* is a *catalog* of service offerings that are exposed to users of the platform. An operator may provision any service from the services catalog in a consistent fashion. Applications and their services are provisioned uniformly by the platform.

The command cf create-service (or cf cs) is used to create a new service instance.

Example 14-1. Creating a new service using the CF CLI

```
NAME:
    create-service - Create a service instance

USAGE:
    cf create-service SERVICE PLAN SERVICE_INSTANCE [-c PARAMETERS_AS_JSON] [-t TAGS]
```

In Example 14-1, we can see the input parameters needed to create a new service instance. The first parameter is the name of the *service* offering from the marketplace catalog. The cf marketplace command retrieves a list of services that have available plans for a given user account.

Run this command on Pivotal's hosted Cloud Foundry instance (called *Pivotal Web Services*), and you'll find that there is a rediscloud service in the marketplace with a variety of plans. The rediscloud service in the marketplace allows us to create a service instance that will provide a Redis database deployment to which we can bind our applications. Take a deeper look at each of the service plans for this Redis offering using the command cf marketplace -s rediscloud (Example 14-2).

Example 14-2. A list of service plans for a Redis deployment

```
$ cf marketplace -s rediscloud

Getting service plan information for service rediscloud for user...
OK

service plan   description        free or paid
100mb          Basic              paid
```

```
250mb          Mini                 paid
500mb          Small                paid
1gb            Standard             paid
2-5gb          Medium               paid
5gb            Large                paid
10gb           X-Large              paid
50gb           XX-Large             paid
30mb           Lifetime Free Tier   free
```

We see that there are different paid tiers of resources and a 30mb plan that is provided as a free tier. Let's create a new service instance of Redis that uses this free tier plan of 30mb (Example 14-3).

Example 14-3. Create a new Redis service instance

```
cf create-service rediscloud 30mb my-redis
```

Now that we have created a new service instance (my-redis), we are able to bind an existing application to it. Let's assume here that we have an application named user-api, which houses a Spring Boot application that uses Redis for caching users stored in a MySQL database. We can automatically connect to the Redis service instance after binding it to our Spring Boot application. The command to bind to a service instance is cf bind-service (Example 14-4).

Example 14-4. Binding a service instance to an app

```
NAME:
   bind-service - Bind a service instance to an app

USAGE:
   cf bind-service APP_NAME SERVICE_INSTANCE [-c PARAMETERS_AS_JSON]
```

Since we know that the application name we want to bind to is user-api and the service instance name is my-redis, we can now bind our user application to our newly created Redis database instance (Example 14-5).

Example 14-5. Bind my-redis service instance to the user-api app

```
cf bind-service user-api my-redis
```

When binding an application to a service instance in Cloud Foundry, a service broker will provide a set of environment variables that describe the service instance to the application. We can see the result of this for our my-redis binding by looking at the user-api environment variables using the cf env user-api command (Example 14-6).

Example 14-6. Display the environment variables for user-api application

```
$ cf env user-api

Getting env variables for app user-api in org user-org...
OK

System-Provided:
{
 "VCAP_SERVICES": {  ❶
  "rediscloud": [
   {
    "credentials": {  ❷
     "hostname": "pub-redis-9809.us-east-1-3.7.ec2.redislabs.com",
     "password": "not-a-real-password",
     "port": "17709"
    },
    "label": "rediscloud",
    "name": "my-redis",  ❸
    "plan": "30mb",  ❹
    "tags": [
     "Data Stores",
     "Data Store",
     "Caching",
     "Messaging and Queuing",
     "key-value",
     "caching",
     "redis"
    ]
   }
  ]
 }
}
```

❶ VCAP_SERVICES describe all service instance bindings for an app.

❷ The credentials are provided for the bound service instance.

❸ The name of a service instance we created as my-redis from rediscloud.

❹ The plan we chose when creating the my-redis free tier instance.

So far, we've provisioned a new service instance using the rediscloud service broker and bound it to our application, consistent with the idea of a backing service as defined in the twelve-factor manifesto (*https://12factor.net/backing-services*). We explored how to create service instances and bindings using the service catalog in Cloud Foundry's marketplace. We also saw how service brokers inject connection details into an application deployment using the system-provided VCAP_SERVICES environment variable.

The View from the Platform

Let's now explore the mechanics behind the Cloud Foundry platform that will allow us to develop our own custom service brokers using Spring Boot. Cloud Foundry is composed of a number of web service modules that communicate over HTTP, resembling some of the distributed system architectures that we've talked about in this book. The composition of these services is exposed as one seamless REST API, the *Cloud Controller API*. The Cloud Controller API is the primary interface for clients to trigger the orchestration of an underlying cloud provider's virtual infrastructure. It is the primary contract that describes the functions of the Cloud Foundry platform.

The Cloud Controller also maintains a database for many of the domain resources that are used when interacting with Cloud Foundry, such as org(anization)s, spaces, user roles, service definitions, service instances, apps, and more. Since the Cloud Controller is the owner of both service definitions and service instances, it is this very module of Cloud Foundry that allows for the life cycle management of external service brokers, which can take the form of databases and other middleware services.

The *service broker API* is a REST API that describes the expectations of the Cloud Controller for third-party service broker applications. Typically, service brokers are not a part of a Cloud Foundry release. Brokers are only added after a Cloud Foundry release has been provisioned. They are attached as backing services that must be registered with the Cloud Controller API.

A service broker describes a catalog of services that it can provide. These show up in the Cloud Foundry marketplace, which you can see using `cf marketplace`. The catalog describes one or more services and their plans. A service's plan relates to different service levels, often associated with different costs. An operator may decide to create a new service instance by specifying the name of the service and the associated plan. You use `cf create-service` to do this. A created service might represent a virtual machine that's been spun up, or a resource that's been initialized. Operators may (optionally) bind a service instance to their application with `cf bind-service`. Here, the service broker must furnish credentials that an application might use to connect to the provisioned service. A service broker must also handle deleting service instances and service instance bindings.

Table 14-1 shows the REST endpoints expected from a service broker.

Table 14-1. Service broker routes

Description	Route	Method
Read the catalog describing the plans available in the service broker	/v2/catalog	GET
Delete a binding between a service broker and an application	/v2/service_instances/{instanceId}/ service_bindings/{bindingId}	DELETE

Description	Route	Method
Create a new service instance binding between an application and a service	/v2/service_instances/{instanceId}/ service_bindings/{bindingId}	PUT
Retrieve the status of the last operation performed by the service broker	/v2/service_instances/{instanceId}/ last_operation	GET
Retrieve a service instance	/v2/service_instances/{instanceId}	GET
Create a new service instance	/v2/service_instances/{instanceId}	PUT
Delete a service instance	/v2/service_instances/{instanceId}	DELETE
Update a service instance	/v2/service_instances/{instanceId}	PATCH

Implementing a Service Broker with Spring Cloud Cloud Foundry Service Broker

In this section, we'll be taking the lessons learned throughout this book to create a service broker with Spring Boot. Creating service brokers is an essential part of extending and customizing the Cloud Foundry platform. There are open source examples in a variety of different languages and platforms that demonstrate how to create a service broker; we will use the Spring Cloud Cloud Foundry Service Broker (*http://cloud.spring.io/spring-cloud-cloudfoundry-service-broker/*) project to make short work of the nonessential requirements of building a service broker: managing the life cycle of service instances and service instance bindings.

A Simple Amazon S3 Service Broker

Amazon Web Services (AWS) provides a rich ecosystem of services that our applications can leverage, even if we're not running on that platform. Amazon S3 is very useful for persisting data. A core tenet of cloud native applications is that application instances are stateless; we can't trust that the virtual machine instance we're running our application on will always be the one it will run on, and we can't be sure that the filesystem for our instance will always be there. S3 provides a way to attach some data storage, as a backing service, to our applications. Amazon S3 is not a filesystem as your operating system might understand it, so it won't work as a direct replacement for the JDK's java.io.File. It has its own API. It serves the same goals, so making it easy to interface with Amazon S3 will prove useful in forklifting existing applications to the cloud. A service broker is a great way to integrate legacy (but sometimes necessary) services like FTP, filesystems, and email—or indeed, any multitenant-capable service in your organization that doesn't already have support on the platform.

Implementing a service broker consists of two tasks: provisioning the resources represented by the service, and implementing the service broker REST API. The Spring Cloud Cloud Foundry Service Broker project will provide the REST API if we satisfy three key components:

- An instance of a `Catalog` bean, which describes to the cloud controller the available services provided by this service broker.

- An implementation of `ServiceInstanceService` to manage creating and destroying service instances.

- An implementation of `ServiceInstanceBindingService` to manage creating and destroying service instance bindings.

The Service Catalog

The first step for implementing a service broker is to create a *service catalog* that describes what your broker will do. The catalog will also provide a collection of service plans that can be used to describe different aspects of how a backing service will be created and operated. Let's take, for example, a database that is provided as a service through a service broker. Our Amazon S3 broker will only provide a single plan, which is an S3 bucket with logically (though probably not *financially!*) unlimited file storage (Example 14-7).

Example 14-7. The interface contract for a broker's service catalog

```
package cnj;

import org.springframework.beans.factory.annotation.Autowired;
import org.springframework.beans.factory.annotation.Value;
import org.springframework.cloud.servicebroker.model.Catalog;
import org.springframework.cloud.servicebroker.model.Plan;
import org.springframework.cloud.servicebroker.model.ServiceDefinition;
import org.springframework.context.annotation.Bean;
import org.springframework.context.annotation.Configuration;

import java.util.Collections;
import java.util.List;
import java.util.Map;

@Configuration
class CatalogConfiguration {

  private final String spacePrefix;

  @Autowired
  CatalogConfiguration( ❶
   @Value("${vcap.application.space_id:${USER:}}") String spaceId) {
   this.spacePrefix = spaceId + '-';
  }

  @Bean
  Catalog catalog() {
```

```java
  Plan basic = buildBasicPlan();  ❷
  ServiceDefinition definition = buildS3ServiceDefinition(basic);  ❸
  return new Catalog(Collections.singletonList(definition));
}

private ServiceDefinition buildS3ServiceDefinition(Plan basic) {
  String description = "Provides AWS S3 access";
  String id = this.spacePrefix + "1489291412183";
  String name = "s3-service-broker";
  boolean bindable = true;
  List<Plan> plans = Collections.singletonList(basic);
  return new ServiceDefinition(id, name, description, bindable, plans);
}

private Plan buildBasicPlan() {
  String planName = "basic";
  String planDescription = "Amazon S3 bucket with unlimited storage";
  boolean free = true;
  boolean bindable = true;
  String planId = this.spacePrefix + "249722552510577";
  Map<String, Object> metadata = Collections.singletonMap("costs",
   Collections.singletonMap("free", true));
  return new Plan(planId, planName, planDescription, metadata, free, bindable);
 }
}
```

❶ A service broker service and plan must have a unique ID that is global to the entirety of the CloudFoundry instance to which you're deploying. So here, we do some gymnastics to inject the Cloud Foundry space (or at least the username) as a prefix for the otherwise stable, static IDs. The values are random, and were generated ahead of time. So assuming you deploy the service broker only once per space (which is a fair assumption), the service catalog should be unique. If you want to update the service broker, it's useful to use stable service IDs. Otherwise, just use a UUID.

❷ Create a simple plan instance (which is free).

❸ Then register the plan as part of our one service definition. There's no reason a single service broker can't host *multiple* service definitions (one for each interesting service in the Amazon Web Services catalog, for example!).

The catalog's configuration is hardcoded into the application for brevity, though there's no reason it couldn't be maintained in external configuration, perhaps in conjunction with the Spring Cloud Config Server.

Managing Service Instances

The Spring Cloud Cloud Foundry Service Broker expects an implementation of the interface `ServiceInstanceService` (Example 14-8).

Example 14-8. The definition of a ServiceInstanceService

```
public interface ServiceInstanceService {
  CreateServiceInstanceResponse createServiceInstance(
    CreateServiceInstanceRequest r);
  UpdateServiceInstanceResponse updateServiceInstance(
    UpdateServiceInstanceRequest r);
  DeleteServiceInstanceResponse deleteServiceInstance(
    DeleteServiceInstanceRequest r);
  GetLastServiceOperationResponse getLastOperation(
    GetLastServiceOperationRequest r);
}
```

Most of these methods should be pretty straightforward, with the exception of the `GetLastServiceOperationRequest`. This method is used to return the status of an *asynchronous* operation. By default, service brokers are synchronous: a call to a REST endpoint returns when the work is done. This isn't always the case: imagine a service broker that provisions a Hadoop cluster or a Spark cluster, or a service broker trying to dismantle such a cluster in a delete call. This work may necessarily take far longer than any reasonable timeout set on the service broker would permit. In our case, we can return that the service call always returned successfully; the calls to Amazon Web Services aren't expensive.

Our implementation of the `ServiceInstanceService` will respond to these requests and persist the relevant information in a SQL database (MySQL, specifically) so that we can correlate requests against an actual service instance to resources managed by this service broker (Example 14-9).

Example 14-9. The definition of a ServiceInstance

```
package cnj;

import lombok.Data;
import lombok.EqualsAndHashCode;
import lombok.NoArgsConstructor;
import lombok.ToString;
import org.springframework.cloud.servicebroker.model.CreateServiceInstanceRequest;
import org.springframework.cloud.servicebroker.model.DeleteServiceInstanceRequest;
import org.springframework.cloud.servicebroker.model.UpdateServiceInstanceRequest;

import javax.persistence.Entity;
import javax.persistence.Id;
```

```
@Entity
❶
@Data
❷
@NoArgsConstructor
@ToString
@EqualsAndHashCode
class ServiceInstance {

 @Id
 private String id;

 private String serviceDefinitionId;

 private String planId;

 private String organizationGuid;

 private String spaceGuid;

 private String dashboardUrl;

 private String username, accessKeyId, secretAccessKey;

 ❸
 public ServiceInstance(CreateServiceInstanceRequest request) {
  this.serviceDefinitionId = request.getServiceDefinitionId();
  this.planId = request.getPlanId();
  this.organizationGuid = request.getOrganizationGuid();
  this.spaceGuid = request.getSpaceGuid();
  this.id = request.getServiceInstanceId();
 }

 public ServiceInstance(DeleteServiceInstanceRequest request) {
  this.id = request.getServiceInstanceId();
  this.planId = request.getPlanId();
  this.serviceDefinitionId = request.getServiceDefinitionId();
 }

 public ServiceInstance(UpdateServiceInstanceRequest request) {
  this.id = request.getServiceInstanceId();
  this.planId = request.getPlanId();
 }
}
```

❶   The ServiceInstance is a JPA entity...

❷   ...that uses the Lombok project's @Data constructor to eliminate a lot of tedious code generation for getters and setters, a no-argument constructor, a toString method, and an equals/hashCode pair...

---

❸ …with various copy constructors supporting creation, deletion, and update requests.

We'll need to persist their details in a SQL database (in this project, MySQL). A Spring Data JPA repository makes it trivial to be able to move on (Example 14-10).

Example 14-10. The definition of a ServiceInstanceRepository

```
package cnj;

import org.springframework.data.jpa.repository.JpaRepository;

interface ServiceInstanceRepository extends
 JpaRepository<ServiceInstance, String> {
}
```

When creating a new service instance, we'll need to integrate with Amazon Web Services using their provided Java SDK to manage the creation of both the IAM user and the S3 bucket. This is the the meat of our broker. The bulk of this logic lives in a custom service implementation in the code base called the S3Service. We won't reprint its code here; see the book's source code, as it's a lot of tedious logic built with the Amazon Web Services Java SDK. The only thing worth understanding is that the Amazon Web Services Java SDK requires authorization, which we configure thusly (Example 14-11).

Example 14-11. Configuration class containing bean definitions for an authenticated AmazonS3 client

```
package cnj.s3;

import com.amazonaws.auth.BasicAWSCredentials;
import com.amazonaws.services.identitymanagement.AmazonIdentityManagementClient;
import com.amazonaws.services.s3.AmazonS3Client;
import org.springframework.beans.factory.annotation.Value;
import org.springframework.context.annotation.Bean;
import org.springframework.context.annotation.Configuration;

@Configuration
class S3Configuration {

 @Bean
 AmazonS3Client amazonS3Client(BasicAWSCredentials credentials) {
  return new AmazonS3Client(credentials);
 }

 @Bean
 AmazonIdentityManagementClient identityManagementClient(
  BasicAWSCredentials awsCredentials) {
```

```
    return new AmazonIdentityManagementClient(awsCredentials);
}


❶
@Bean
BasicAWSCredentials awsCredentials(
 @Value("${aws.access-key-id}") String awsAccessKeyId,
 @Value("${aws.secret-access-key}") String awsSecretAccessKey) {
 return new BasicAWSCredentials(awsAccessKeyId, awsSecretAccessKey);
}


@Bean
S3Service s3Service(AmazonIdentityManagementClient awsId, AmazonS3Client s3) {
 return new S3Service(awsId, s3);
 }
}
```

❶ In order for this to work, you'll need to configure an Amazon Web Services access token and Amazon Web Services access secret. In our continuous integration environments, this is provided as an environment variable.

With our S3Service in place, the ServiceInstanceService implementation goes quickly. In the case of S3, there really isn't anything to *provision*—Amazon Web Services already has S3 warmed up and running and ready to use. So instead, the bulk of the service instance has to do with creating an S3 user whose identity we persist. Later, when we bind an application to the provisioned S3 instance, we will recall the persisted information and provide it to the cloud controller to expose in the environment of the running application. This means that all bound applications will have the same credentials. This may or may not be what you want, but it's a sensible behavior if you trust the parties developing the applications (Example 14-12).

Example 14-12. The definition of a DefaultServiceInstanceService

```
package cnj;

import cnj.s3.S3Service;
import cnj.s3.S3User;
import org.apache.commons.logging.Log;
import org.apache.commons.logging.LogFactory;
import org.springframework.beans.factory.annotation.Autowired;
import org.springframework.cloud.servicebroker.exception.ServiceBrokerException;
import org.springframework.cloud.servicebroker.model.*;
import org.springframework.cloud.servicebroker.service.ServiceInstanceService;
import org.springframework.stereotype.Service;

@Service
class DefaultServiceInstanceService implements ServiceInstanceService {

 private final S3Service s3Service;
```

```
private final ServiceInstanceRepository instanceRepository;

private Log log = LogFactory.getLog(getClass());

@Autowired
DefaultServiceInstanceService(S3Service s3Service,
 ServiceInstanceRepository instanceRepository) {
 this.s3Service = s3Service;
 this.instanceRepository = instanceRepository;
}

@Override
public CreateServiceInstanceResponse createServiceInstance(
 CreateServiceInstanceRequest request) {
 if (!this.exists(request.getServiceInstanceId())) {
  ServiceInstance si = new ServiceInstance(request);
  S3User user = s3Service.createS3UserAndBucket(si.getId());   ❶
  si.setSecretAccessKey(user.getAccessKeySecret());
  si.setUsername(user.getUsername());
  si.setAccessKeyId(user.getAccessKeyId());
  this.instanceRepository.save(si);
 }
 else {
  this.error("could not create serviceInstance "
   + request.getServiceInstanceId());
 }
 return new CreateServiceInstanceResponse();
}

@Override
public DeleteServiceInstanceResponse deleteServiceInstance(
 DeleteServiceInstanceRequest request) {
 String sid = request.getServiceInstanceId();
 if (this.exists(sid)) {
  ServiceInstance si = this.instanceRepository.findOne(sid);
  ❷
  boolean deleteSucceeded = this.s3Service.deleteBucket(si.getId(),
   si.getAccessKeyId(), si.getUsername());
  if (!deleteSucceeded) {
   log.error("could not delete the S3 bucket for service instance " + sid);
  }
  this.instanceRepository.delete(si.getId());
 }
 else {
  this.error("could not delete the S3 service instance " + sid);
 }
 return new DeleteServiceInstanceResponse();
}

❸
@Override
```

```
public UpdateServiceInstanceResponse updateServiceInstance(
 UpdateServiceInstanceRequest request) {
 String sid = request.getServiceInstanceId();
 if (this.exists(sid)) {
  ServiceInstance instance = this.instanceRepository.findOne(sid);
  this.instanceRepository.delete(instance);
  this.instanceRepository.save(new ServiceInstance(request));
 }
 else {
  this.error("could not update serviceInstance " + sid);
 }
 return new UpdateServiceInstanceResponse();
}

@Override
public GetLastServiceOperationResponse getLastOperation(
 GetLastServiceOperationRequest request) {
 return new GetLastServiceOperationResponse()
  .withOperationState(OperationState.SUCCEEDED);
}

private void error(String msg) {
 throw new ServiceBrokerException(msg);
}

private boolean exists(String serviceInstanceId) {
 return instanceRepository.exists(serviceInstanceId);
 }
}
```

❶ Most of this method is bookkeeping, save for this line, where we interact with the
     Amazon Web Services API by way of our S3Service to create an S3 bucket and
     an S3User that has access to that bucket.

❷ The delete operation undoes the creation, deleting the user and the bucket.

❸ The update operation does nothing to the actually provisioned S3 bucket or user,
     but merely updates the persisted metadata about the service instance itself.

The functional result of a backing service is that all necessary information on how to
consume it are injected into the application's container as environment variables. This
process is what we refer to in Cloud Foundry as *binding to a service instance*. The
result of binding to a service instance is that the connection information about how
to consume the service is injected into an application's container. When the application is staged in a container and then started, it will be able to locate the environment
variables for the service instance's connection information. It will then use these
details to locate and connect to the running instance of the service. Let's look at how
we bind our service instance to a backing application.

Service Bindings

It can often be confusing to determine the dividing line between offering a function as a service through the platform or implementing it in each application. There is a good rule of thumb for determining when to delegate function in your application to a backing service through the platform.

If you need to implement the same functionality in all of your applications, that functionality should instead be provided *as a service* through the platform.

The goal of cloud native application development is to reduce the amount of time spent on any development that isn't central to the business logic of your applications. The platform is more than an operational tool for running applications in the cloud; it's a machine that strips away the code that turns an application into legacy, and instead provides it as a replaceable service. For example, many applications in an architecture may need the ability to store files. By providing a service broker that can provide applications with a connection to an Amazon S3 bucket, each application will not need to spend time worrying about implementing custom code to make storing files possible. The only thing the application's developers will need to do is bind to a service instance and start storing and retrieving files.

In the Spring Cloud Cloud Foundry Service Broker, this functionality is provided by implementations of the `ServiceInstanceBindingService` (Example 14-13).

Example 14-13. The definition of the ServiceInstanceBindingService

```
public interface ServiceInstanceBindingService {

  CreateServiceInstanceBindingResponse createServiceInstanceBinding(
      CreateServiceInstanceBindingRequest r);

  void deleteServiceInstanceBinding(DeleteServiceInstanceBindingRequest r);
}
```

As with the `ServiceInstanceBindingService`, we'll need to record information about the binding of the application. We do this using another JPA entity, `ServiceIn stanceBinding` (Example 14-14):

Example 14-14. The definition of the ServiceInstanceBinding

```
package cnj;

import lombok.Data;
import lombok.NoArgsConstructor;

import javax.persistence.Entity;
import javax.persistence.Id;
```

```
@Entity
@Data
@NoArgsConstructor
public class ServiceInstanceBinding {

  @Id
  private String id;

  private String serviceInstanceId, syslogDrainUrl, appGuid;

  public ServiceInstanceBinding(String id, String serviceInstanceId,
    String syslogDrainUrl, String appGuid) {
    this.id = id;
    this.serviceInstanceId = serviceInstanceId;
    this.syslogDrainUrl = syslogDrainUrl;
    this.appGuid = appGuid;
  }
}
```

We'll persist the `ServiceInstanceBinding` with another Spring Data JPA repository, `ServiceInstanceBindingRepository` (Example 14-15).

Example 14-15. Definition of a ServiceInstanceBindingRepository for managing service instance entities

```
package cnj;

import org.springframework.data.jpa.repository.JpaRepository;

public interface ServiceInstanceBindingRepository extends
  JpaRepository<ServiceInstanceBinding, String> {

}
```

In our implementation of the `ServiceInstanceBindingService`, we'll use these two repositories to do the bulk of the work. The `DefaultServiceInstanceBindingSer vice` needs to only recall persisted S3 credentials from the database and bring them to the client (Example 14-16).

Example 14-16. The definition of the DefaultServiceInstanceBindingService

```
package cnj;

import org.springframework.beans.factory.annotation.Autowired;

//@formatter:off
import org.springframework.cloud.servicebroker.exception.
        ServiceInstanceBindingDoesNotExistException;
```

```
import org.springframework.cloud.servicebroker.exception.
        ServiceInstanceBindingExistsException;
import org.springframework.cloud.servicebroker.model
        .CreateServiceInstanceAppBindingResponse;
import org.springframework.cloud.servicebroker.model
        .CreateServiceInstanceBindingRequest;
import org.springframework.cloud.servicebroker.model
        .CreateServiceInstanceBindingResponse;
import org.springframework.cloud.servicebroker.model
        .DeleteServiceInstanceBindingRequest;
import org.springframework.cloud.servicebroker.service
        .ServiceInstanceBindingService;
//@formatter:on

import org.springframework.stereotype.Service;

import java.util.HashMap;
import java.util.Map;

@Service
class DefaultServiceInstanceBindingService implements
 ServiceInstanceBindingService {

 private final ServiceInstanceBindingRepository bindingRepository;

 private final ServiceInstanceRepository instanceRepository;

 @Autowired
 DefaultServiceInstanceBindingService(ServiceInstanceBindingRepository sibr,
  ServiceInstanceRepository sir) {
  this.bindingRepository = sibr;
  this.instanceRepository = sir;
 }

 @Override
 public CreateServiceInstanceBindingResponse createServiceInstanceBinding(
  CreateServiceInstanceBindingRequest request) {
  String bindingId = request.getBindingId();
  {
   ServiceInstanceBinding binding;
   if ((binding = this.bindingRepository.findOne(bindingId)) != null) {
    throw new ServiceInstanceBindingExistsException(
     binding.getServiceInstanceId(), binding.getId());
   }
  }

  ❶
  ServiceInstance serviceInstance = this.instanceRepository.findOne(request
   .getServiceInstanceId());

  String username = serviceInstance.getUsername();
  String secretAccessKey = serviceInstance.getSecretAccessKey();
```

```
String accessKeyId = serviceInstance.getAccessKeyId();

❷
Map<String, Object> credentials = new HashMap<>();
credentials.put("bucket", username);
credentials.put("accessKeyId", accessKeyId);
credentials.put("accessKeySecret", secretAccessKey);

Map<String, Object> resource = request.getBindResource();
String appGuid = String.class.cast(resource.getOrDefault("app_guid",
  request.getAppGuid()));

❸
ServiceInstanceBinding binding = new ServiceInstanceBinding(bindingId,
  request.getServiceInstanceId(), null, appGuid);

this.bindingRepository.save(binding);

❹
return new CreateServiceInstanceAppBindingResponse()
  .withCredentials(credentials);
}

@Override
public void deleteServiceInstanceBinding(
 DeleteServiceInstanceBindingRequest request) {
 String bindingId = request.getBindingId();
 if (this.bindingRepository.findOne(bindingId) == null) {
  throw new ServiceInstanceBindingDoesNotExistException(bindingId);
 }
 this.bindingRepository.delete(bindingId);
 }
}
```

❶ This method looks up the existing service instance (created in the ServiceInstan
    ceService implementation)…

❷ …and returns a Map<K,V> containing information that will be useful to the
    bound application. The contents of this map are completely arbitrary—you can
    put whatever you want in it. It will be turned into a JSON structure that the con-
    suming application will read in.

❸ Once we're ready, record the derived binding information in the database…

❹ …and return a CreateServiceInstanceAppBindingResponse containing the cre-
    dentials.

It's important to remember that once we've created a ServiceIn stanceBinding on the broker, the Cloud Controller will become the system of record for the binding, which makes the credentials an immutable object that can only be changed by recreating the binding.

Securing the Service Broker

The Cloud Controller will expect that the S3 service broker's API is secured with HTTP basic authentication. Every request made from the Cloud Controller to the S3 broker will contain an Authentication header that encodes the username and password that the broker must validate.

The Spring Boot application for the S3 broker uses Spring Security to implement HTTP basic authentication. Feel free to override this configuration at length, but for our purposes we've used the convenient Spring Boot auto-configuration properties security.user.name and security.user.password to hardcode the username and password as admin. These can, of course, be overridden with environment variables, e.g., SECURITY_USER_PASSWORD and SECURITY_USER_NAME.

This example uses an AuthenticationManager backed by an in-memory representation of the users. This is the default behavior of an almost-all-but-default Spring Boot application with spring-boot-starter-security on the classpath. In a more sophisticated service broker example, you may want to create an administration tool that allows operators of the platform to manage the broker's settings stored, perhaps, in a database.

 Security is a major consideration when creating service brokers that extend the platform. It's important that access to the broker's APIs are restricted to communication with the Cloud Controller only. Since the Cloud Controller only supports HTTP basic authentication, if the broker were to have its APIs accessible through a public host or route, it would be a major security vulnerability that could expose the internals of the underlying infrastructure the platform manages.

And with that, we're done! The application, as designed, is a working service broker. We need only deploy it and tell the Cloud Controller about it.

Deployment

Now that we've created our Amazon S3 service broker, we can begin testing that it works by deploying it to a distribution of Cloud Foundry. The service broker can be configured to run on any distribution of Cloud Foundry.

Releasing with BOSH

There are multiple options for deploying custom Cloud Foundry service brokers. A popular option for releasing service brokers is to use a tool named BOSH (*BOSH outer shell*). BOSH is a release engineering tool for managing deployments. It can use a variety of different *Cloud Provider Interfaces* (CPIs) to communicate with an Infrastructure as a Service (IaaS) platform like Amazon Web Services, Google Compute Engine, OpenStack, vSphere, and Microsoft Azure. A CPI is an executable component of the BOSH architecture that is used as a translation layer to communicate with APIs exposed by an IaaS provider. The CPI takes the proprietary APIs of an IaaS and translates its comparable functions to a common domain language that is used in BOSH to describe complex deployments. BOSH manages the virtual resources on an IaaS platform, and ensures that the actual system state manages the described state. In this way, BOSH is different than configuration management tools like Puppet or Chef that support converged infrastructure. These tools try to take existing nodes and modify them to accord with prescribed state. BOSH supports immutable infrastructure—it recreates the world from scratch, every single time, from the virtual machine images on up.

At the heart of BOSH is the idea of a release. A release needs to contain source files, configuration files, installation scripts, etc. In short, it contains everything required to reproducibly release a given component. An Apache Zookeeper release might contain the source code for Apache Zookeeper, its configuration defaults, and initialization scripts.

Not all releases are the same. It might make sense, for example, to have two Zookeeper nodes in an integration testing environment, but dozens in a production environment. Deployment manifests parameterize BOSH releases; they describe how many nodes are required, configuration properties that are to be passed to each resource on the nodes, and so on.

BOSH *stemcells* are base operating system images on top of which BOSH will layer everything else. There are numerous stemcells maintained on the official BOSH site (*http://bosh.io*).

BOSH is ideal for managing the deployment of complex systems. If something should change, it's trivial to change the deployment manifest, create a new release, and then tell the BOSH director about the new release. It will redeploy the world according to the release.

Why should we use BOSH to release a custom service broker instead of deploying the application with Cloud Foundry itself? After all, isn't the point of developing applications on a platform to be able to use it for deployment? The short answer to this question is that it depends on the virtualized compute resources you intend to manage with your custom broker.

Our service broker is working, through a REST API, to communicate with the Amazon Web Services IaaS directly. Our service broker is not responsible for standing up an S3 instance itself, merely for talking to it.

If our broker only needs to orchestrate with a single IaaS, it is fine to use the HTTP-based APIs of an IaaS to manage its resources. This is similar to what we've done with our Amazon S3 service broker, which is the reason we do not need to create a BOSH release. The benefit of using BOSH is that it is a tool that helps to manage service broker releases that need to orchestrate with the IaaS layer a Cloud Foundry distribution is running on.

The common reason to bundle service brokers in a BOSH release are for the kinds of brokers that need to manage service instances that are composed of large distributed systems. This variety of service broker will need a more fine-grained control of storage devices and network resources provisioned in the IaaS layer. For our S3 broker we do not need to worry about creating a BOSH release, because our broker has no need to communicate with the IaaS layer. Because of this we can operate the broker as a regular application deployment using Cloud Foundry's Cloud Controller API.

Releasing with Cloud Foundry

Let's deploy our service broker to Cloud Foundry. The service broker will need a MySQL instance bound as `s3-service-broker-db`, so provision one before attempting to deploy the application. If you're using PCFDev or Pivotal Web Services, there is a Pivotal-managed MySQL database called `p-mysql`. Interestingly, the plans' specifications are different on Pivotal Web Services and PCFDev. If you're using Pivotal Web Services, the following should work, but you can confirm by inspecting `cf market place` (Example 14-17). At the time of this writing there is also a Pivotal Web Services offering called ClearDB that provides MySQL.

Example 14-17. Provisioning a p-mysql instance on Pivotal Web Services

```
cf create-service p-mysql 100mb s3-service-broker-db
```

If you've compiled the service broker, you need only push it to Cloud Foundry using `cf push` in the same directory as the service broker itself. You'll find a `manifest.yml` file there that describes everything required to run this application (Example 14-18).

Example 14-18. A manifest.yml file that describes how the service broker should be deployed to Cloud Foundry

```
---
applications:
- name: s3-service-broker
  path: ./target/s3-service-broker.jar
```

```
buildpack: https://github.com/cloudfoundry/java-buildpack.git
memory: 1024M
instances: 1
timeout: 180
host: s3-service-broker-${random-word}  ❶
env:
  SPRING_PROFILES_ACTIVE: cloud
  AWS_ACCESS_KEY_ID: replace
  AWS_SECRET_ACCESS_KEY: replace
services:
  - s3-service-broker-db
```

❶ The `${random-word}` token tells Cloud Foundry to generate a random sequence of words to avoid URI collisions. This is particularly useful in a multitenant environment like Pivotal Web Services.

You'll need to customize this `manifest.yml`, providing values for the Amazon Web Services `AWS_ACCESS_KEY_ID` and `AWS_SECRET_ACCESS_KEY`. If you don't want that information hardcoded into the `manifest.yml` (we don't blame you!), tell Cloud Foundry to *not* start the service broker when you do the `cf push`; manually bind the variables, and *then* start the application (Example 14-19).

Example 14-19. The CLI commands for deploying and configuring the Amazon S3 service broker

```
cf push --no-start
cf set-env s3-service-broker AWS_ACCESS_KEY_ID _yourvalue_
cf set-env s3-service-broker AWS_SECRET_ACCESS_KEY _yourvalue_
cf start s3-service-broker
```

You'll need to retrieve the Amazon Web Services credentials from the Amazon Web Services Console. See the Amazon Web Services documentation (*http://amzn.to/2vmUv3L*) for the most up-to-date information on that process.

Our Amazon S3 service broker is now *fully operational* on the platform. We are ready to advertise this service to other applications by registering and enabling the service broker.

Registering the Amazon S3 Service Broker

We must register the service broker. We'll need the URL of the service broker. This is easily had with the `cf apps` call (Example 14-20).

Example 14-20. Returns the state of the Cloud Foundry apps in the current space

```
→ cf apps
Getting apps in org cloud-native-java / space cnj as cnj@...
OK

name               requested state   instances memory disk  urls
s3-service-broker started           1/1       512M   1G    s3-serv..cfapps.io
```

The URL for the application in our example is `http://s3-service-broker-speckled-swallow.cfapps.io`. You'll recall that we configured the service broker with a default username of `admin` and a default password of `admin`. The only other consideration is the visibility of the service. If you're deploying the application to Pivotal Web Services, a multitenant environment you probably don't have administration privileges to, your service broker will only be visible to other applications in the same space. You stipulate as much by tacking on `--space-scoped` to the `cf create-service-broker` call. If you're using PCFDev, on the other hand, then it isn't necessary that you tack on that information. With that information in hand, creating the service broker is easy (Example 14-21).

Example 14-21. Registering the service broker with Cloud Foundry

```
cf create-service-broker s3-broker admin admin \
  http://s3-service-broker-speckled-swallow.cfapps.io --space-scoped
```

The service broker should now be visible in the Cloud Foundry marketplace (Example 14-22).

Example 14-22. Inspecting the Cloud Foundry marketplace

```
→ cf marketplace
Getting services from marketplace in org cloud-native-java / space cnj as cnj@...
OK

service           plans  description
...
s3-service-broker basic  Provides AWS S3 access
...
```

Now that you have a service broker, you'll be able to provision instances of the service and then bind those instances to applications. You very well could end up with a bit of a knot to untie if you want to eventually delete the service broker! You should start with `cf delete-service-broker`, but if that fails, there are two very useful commands worth knowing. `cf purge-service-offering` will recursively delete any instances of a given service (or a specific plan of a given service) if you no longer have a service broker to do it for you. `cf purge-service-instance` will forcefully delete an instance of a given service.

Creating Amazon S3 Service Instances

Now that our S3 broker is running and is registered as a service on PCF Dev's marketplace, we can begin to create service instances to create new S3 storage buckets, as shown in Example 14-23.

Example 14-23. Create the first service instance using the new S3 broker

```
$ cf create-service amazon-s3 s3-basic s3-service

Creating service instance s3-service in org pcfdev-org / space pcfdev-space as <?pdf-cr?>admin
OK
```

If the Amazon Web Services credentials that we set as environment variables on the `s3-broker` application are correct, the command shown in Example 14-24 will succeed. If the command completes without error, that means that a new Amazon S3 bucket and corresponding IAM user were created on the Amazon Web Services account. Before we can see what these resources are, we'll need to create a service binding for a new application deployment that will consume the new Amazon S3 service instance.

If you see a failure after attempting to create a new Amazon S3 service instance, it is because the provided Amazon Web Services credentials were not valid. To fix the issue, make sure that the user with the credentials has the correct resource policies attached for administrating IAM users and managing Amazon S3 buckets. You can configure the policies on the Amazon Web Services console using the *Identity and Access Management* tool.

Consuming Service Instances

When it comes to extending the platform with new services, there should also be a focus on providing developers with an easy way to consume those services in a cloud native application. While a major part of platform engineering is to build services, it is equally important to make those services as easy to consume as possible. To do this effectively, we need to consider the different application runtimes of workloads that will be consuming our new service.

There is a dividing line between implementing functionality in an application and offering that functionality as a service. The rule of thumb is that if you need to implement the same functionality in every application, it should instead be provided a service. We need to take this same view when it comes to writing client libraries to consume new services. For a majority of scenarios for integrating with service instances, there will be an existing client library or SDK available to be used in applications. This will be the case for consuming our Amazon S3 service instances, where we'll be using the Amazon Web Services Java SDK to interact with Amazon S3's storage APIs.

When developing JVM applications to use custom services on Cloud Foundry, platform engineers should take an opinionated view on how application developers consume these services. There is an added benefit to being an opinionated platform engineer: you prevent architecture review boards from having to police the source code of applications to determine the level of compliance with the prescribed standards. We can automate a majority of the compliance in applications by being opinionated about how an application framework integrates with the platform. With Spring Boot we can take the same opinionated approach as an application framework developer by providing Spring Boot starter projects that automatically consume the service instances we provide by extending Cloud Foundry. Spring Boot's auto-configuration is an ideal fit here: we know that Spring Boot applications will all need to talk to our S3 bucket, so we can describe the moving parts central to that integration once, in an auto-configuration, and reuse it everywhere.

To make it trivial for application developers to talk to our Amazon S3 broker, we've created an auto-configuration for the Amazon Web Services SDK's `AmazonS3` client.

The `AmazonS3` depends on a type called `BasicSessionCredentials`, which in turn requires values from a `Credentials` object, all of which is configured for you (using the secure token services facility in AWS to reduce scope of a given token) if you specify the right properties (`amazon.aws.access-key-id` and `amazon.aws.access-key-secret`); Example 14-24.

Example 14-24. Create the first service instance using the new S3 service broker

```
package amazon.s3;

import com.amazonaws.auth.AWSCredentials;
import com.amazonaws.auth.AWSCredentialsProvider;
import com.amazonaws.auth.BasicAWSCredentials;
import com.amazonaws.auth.STSSessionCredentialsProvider;
```

```
import com.amazonaws.regions.Regions;
import com.amazonaws.services.s3.AmazonS3;
import com.amazonaws.services.s3.AmazonS3ClientBuilder;
import com.amazonaws.services.securitytoken.AWSSecurityTokenService;
import com.amazonaws.services.securitytoken.AWSSecurityTokenServiceClient;
import org.springframework.boot.autoconfigure.condition.ConditionalOnClass;
import org.springframework.boot.autoconfigure.condition.ConditionalOnMissingBean;
import org.springframework.boot.context.properties.EnableConfigurationProperties;
import org.springframework.context.annotation.Bean;
import org.springframework.context.annotation.Configuration;

@Configuration
@EnableConfigurationProperties(AmazonProperties.class)
public class S3AutoConfiguration {

    ❶
    @Bean
    @ConditionalOnMissingBean(AmazonS3.class)
    @ConditionalOnClass(AmazonS3.class)
    public AmazonS3 amazonS3(AmazonProperties awsProps) { ❷

      String rootAwsAccessKeyId = awsProps.getAws().getAccessKeyId();
      String rootAwsAccessKeySecret = awsProps.getAws().getAccessKeySecret();

      AWSCredentials credentials = new BasicAWSCredentials(rootAwsAccessKeyId,
        rootAwsAccessKeySecret);
      AWSSecurityTokenService stsClient = new AWSSecurityTokenServiceClient(
        credentials);
      AWSCredentialsProvider credentialsProvider = new STSSessionCredentialsProvider(
        stsClient);
      return AmazonS3ClientBuilder.standard().withRegion(Regions.US_EAST_1)
        .withCredentials(credentialsProvider).build();
    }
}
```

❶ The auto-configuration provides a bean if, and only if, there is not an existing bean of the same type in the application context.

❷ The configuration depends on the custom configuration properties component, AmazonProperties, to resolve the Amazon Web Services access token, secret, and the duration of the token.

A consuming application will need only to add this auto-configuration to the classpath and provide values for two properties, amazon.aws.access-key-id and amazon.aws.access-key-secret.

An S3 Client Application

Let's look at a trivial S3 client REST API. This is a Spring Boot application that depends only on our auto-configuration and `spring-boot-starter-web`. We'll create an S3 service instance (assigning it a logical named `s3-service`) and bind it to our S3 client when it's deployed to Cloud Foundry (Example 14-25).

Example 14-25. Deploy the S3 client

```
cf create-service s3-service-broker basic s3-service
cf push
```

The application is a REST service with two endpoints: `/s3/resources`, which supports HTTP `GET` requests, and `/s3/resources/{name}`, which supports HTTP `POST` requests with multipart file uploads. Upload a file, then check if it exists. Example 14-26 shows the code.

Example 14-26. The S3RestController works with the provisioned S3 service instance

```java
package com.example;

import amazon.s3.AmazonProperties;
import com.amazonaws.services.s3.AmazonS3;
import com.amazonaws.services.s3.model.*;
import org.apache.commons.logging.Log;
import org.apache.commons.logging.LogFactory;
import org.springframework.beans.factory.annotation.Autowired;
import org.springframework.hateoas.Link;
import org.springframework.hateoas.Resource;
import org.springframework.http.ResponseEntity;
import org.springframework.web.bind.annotation.*;
import org.springframework.web.multipart.MultipartFile;

import java.net.URI;
import java.time.Instant;
import java.util.List;
import java.util.stream.Collectors;

@RestController
@RequestMapping("/s3")
class S3RestController {

  private Log log = LogFactory.getLog(getClass());

  private final AmazonS3 amazonS3Client;

  private final String defaultBucket;
```

```
@Autowired
public S3RestController(AmazonProperties amazonProperties,
 AmazonS3 amazonS3Client) {
 this.amazonS3Client = amazonS3Client;
 this.defaultBucket = amazonProperties.getS3().getDefaultBucket();
 log.debug("defaultBucket = " + this.defaultBucket);
}

❶
@PutMapping("/resources/{name}")
ResponseEntity<?> upload(@PathVariable String name,
 @RequestParam MultipartFile file) throws Throwable {

 if (!file.isEmpty()) {
  ObjectMetadata objectMetadata = new ObjectMetadata();
  objectMetadata.setContentType(file.getContentType());
  PutObjectRequest request = new PutObjectRequest(this.defaultBucket, name,
   file.getInputStream(), objectMetadata)
   .withCannedAcl(CannedAccessControlList.PublicRead);
  PutObjectResult objectResult = this.amazonS3Client.putObject(request);
  URI location = URI.create(urlFor(this.defaultBucket, name));
  String str = String
   .format("uploaded %s at %s to %s", objectResult.getContentMd5(), Instant
    .now().toString(), location.toString());
  log.debug(str);
  return ResponseEntity.created(location).build();
 }
 return ResponseEntity.badRequest().build();
}

❷
@GetMapping("/resources")
List<Resource<S3ObjectSummary>> list() {

 ListObjectsRequest request = new ListObjectsRequest()
  .withBucketName(this.defaultBucket);

 ObjectListing listing = this.amazonS3Client.listObjects(request);

 return listing.getObjectSummaries().stream().map(this::from)
  .collect(Collectors.toList());
}

private String urlFor(String bucket, String file) {
 return String.format("https://s3.amazonaws.com/%s/%s", bucket, file);
}

private Resource<S3ObjectSummary> from(S3ObjectSummary a) {
 Link link = new Link(this.urlFor(a.getBucketName(), a.getKey()))
  .withRel("location");

 return new Resource<>(a, link);
```

```
  }
}
```

❶ This endpoint supports file uploads. You can try it out using, for example, `curl` or the PostIt browser plug-in.

❷ This endpoint enumerates all the uploaded resources in the Amazon S3 instance.

The `S3RestController` uses the configured `AmazonS3` client to talk to S3. The auto-configuration requires a valid access key and secret. We can map them to the environment-bound S3 backing service in the configuration properties.

Example 14-27. The configuration for the sample application with two profiles, one for local development and one when deployed on Cloud Foundry with the cloud profile active

```
spring.profiles.active: development
spring:
  http:
    multipart:
      file-size-threshold: 10MB
      max-file-size: 10MB
      max-request-size: 10MB
server:
  port: 8081
---
spring:
  profiles: cloud
  application:
    name: ${vcap.application.name:s3-sample}
amazon:
  aws:
    ❶
    access-key-id: ${vcap.services.s3-service.credentials.accessKeyId}
    access-key-secret: ${vcap.services.s3-service.credentials.accessKeySecret}
    s3:
      default-bucket: ${vcap.services.s3-service.credentials.bucket:bucket}
---
spring:
  profiles: development
  application:
    name: s3-sample-app
amazon:
  aws:
    access-key-id: replace
    access-key-secret: replace
```

❶ Backing service credentials are stored in a JSON structure under an environment variable called `VCAP_SERVICES`. Spring Boot flattens out the JSON structure into keys in the Spring Environment that start with vcap.services.service-id, where service-id is the logical name of the service bound to the application. In this case, we created an instance of the S3 service called s3-service. This configuration dereferences the provisioned access secret and key, as well as the provisioned bucket information, to configure the AmazonS3 client.

Seeing It All Come Together

With both the service broker and the client application deployed, let's put the solution through its paces. First, we'll write a file to S3 by issuing a PUT to /s3/resources/{file-name}, where file-name is the name of the file we'd like to be able to reference later (Example 14-28).

Example 14-28. Write to Amazon S3 with the name test (we've used ellipses to shorten the line length of this listing—substitute the HTTP URI of your deployed Amazon S3 client)

```
curl -v -F file=@/path/to/an/img.png http://s3-sa...cfapps.io/s3/resources/test
```

You should be able to confirm the results by issuing a GET to the /s3/resources endpoint (Example 14-29).

Example 14-29. Reading from Amazon S3

```
curl -v http://s3-sample-app-...cfapps.io/s3/resources
```

Summary

In this chapter we've looked at service brokers, a fundamental part of the Cloud Foundry platform. Service brokers offer a uniform interface to service provisioning and consumption, and simplify the work of operations. Spring Boot's auto-configuration is a nice complement here: it provides a friction-free approach for application developers to plug in provisioned services. The most important aspect of both service brokers and auto-configuration is that they optimize for consistency, which in turn improves velocity.

The service broker paradigm is a powerful one that was born in Cloud Foundry but has seen adoption in other platforms. The Open Service Broker API (*https://www.cloudfoundry.org/open-service-broker-api-launches-as-industry-standard/*) is an initiative to incubate the standardization of service delivery across cloud offerings, bringing service brokers to other cloud offerings. It features the participation of vendors like Google, Red Hat, and IBM, among others.

## CHAPTER 15

Continuous Delivery

We've focused in this book on building production-worthy software. We care very much about shippable software. We've also looked extensively at Cloud Foundry. Cloud Foundry, to quote Andrew Clay Shafer, is "weaponized infrastructure," or *developer-ready infrastructure*, optimized for deploying and running applications. We have looked at how to get applications there, and how to build applications that take full advantage of the platform, once deployed.

In this chapter, we're going to look at the organizational motivations for something like Cloud Foundry and the microservices architecture. We'll look at the practice of *Continuous Delivery* and the application of Concourse, a technology that supports Continuous Delivery pipelines.

Beyond Continuous Integration

Let's take a step back and look beyond software development to software deployment and release. Spring Boot makes it trivial to stand up production-worthy services. It reduces the cognitive (and actual) investment to get working software. It allows organizations to achieve results faster. Many organizations are, mercifully, also using CI (continuous integration) to give developers faster feedback about their code and their tests. What good is something like CI, Spring Boot, test-driven development, and agile software development methodologies if it takes day or weeks or months and countless ITIL tickets to get hardware provisioned and infrastructure deployed? Indeed, what good is any optimization to the act of writing code if the flow of work from concept through production is bottlenecked at any of the subsequent stages in the workflow—testing, operations, etc.?

Nobody builds microservices to then manually deploy them on converged Web-Sphere instances running on hardware that was provisioned on ITIL-requested hardware and infrastructure. This is at best SOA (service-oriented architecture), not microservices. Microservices support agility. They are a part of a value stream, with every step in the value stream contributing to delivering software. You cannot embrace microservices while ignoring this larger context.

> IT delivers software faster than we can dream up changes!
>
> —no businessperson, *ever*

The value stream for most organizations looks something like this: business has an idea, asks product management and user experience and IT to work on it, and— sometime in the hopefully not-too-distant future—it's manifest in the hands of the customer. The *customer* is whoever is sponsoring the effort: it might refer to internal users or external paying customers. Software, in the hands of the customer, should represent *value* to your business or organization. Business would love it if we could streamline and accelerate everything in the value stream, naturally, but the traditional posture from IT is that if we go too fast, we'll introduce errors. This implies that much of the process—the delivery pipeline—is manual, and this is the essence of the problem.

Is your delivery pipeline manual? Do scores of humans sift through code and tediously check for errors? Do deploys require manual, documentation-driven deltas to a production environment? Do deploys happen rarely—once a month, or every three months, or biannually? Does the prospect of *deployment day* fill people with dread? Do deploys require people to log on to bridge lines? Are there war rooms set up that every teammate and their cousin call in to? If any of these are true, they are symptoms of a dysfunctional organization and a broken delivery pipeline.

Continuous Delivery offers a better way forward. Continuous Delivery, as a pursuit, is not a new thing. The idea is simple: automate everything in the value stream as much as possible. In particular, automate everything after the code has been committed so that the path from commit to production is repeatable without human intervention. Some organizations have been doing this, or pretty darned close, for decades.

Continuous Delivery, as practiced today, borrows a lot from the ideas of Lean manufacturing: it ensures the rapid delivery of high-quality products, focusing on the removal of waste and the reduction of cost. It results in cost and resource savings, higher-quality products, and faster time to market.

It may seem paradoxical, but removing tedious and manual processes from the processes *reduces* defects and *increases* quality. Things like software deployments are highly technical, and yet labor-intensive, tedious (boring!) work. This is the most insidious of combinations; humans just aren't built for it. Errors and inconsistencies are bound to crop up. Automation—of *everything*—roots out errors in the process. It results in a delivery process that works the same for staging and production. If there are errors in the process, they can be resolved in staging, saving the organization from trying to debug errors in production.

Automation, in the form of software, is a version-controllable artifact that can help centralize and socialize how deployment works. There no longer needs to be a deployment expert; anybody should be able to grab the bits from version control and run the software to get a version of the application reliably built. As speed of delivery goes up, the cost of fixing defects goes down, because it's conceivable that a new release could be done very soon. Speed de-risks the cost of change, which makes attempting change easier. Change is how a business survives.

Done right, software delivery should be as simple as picking a version of the software from version control and then pushing the equivalent of a big green "Deploy!" button. Some organizations take it a step further, cutting out the "Deploy!" button, and practice *Continuous Deployment*, where the path from a successful git push goes straight to production, assuming all quality gates have been passed.

John Allspaw at Flickr and then Etsy

John Allspaw helped Flickr (and later, Etsy) embrace Continuous Delivery and ship a massive, monolithic application. Etsy's story, detailed in an article in *Network World* (*http://bit.ly/2vnAJ8k*), has been an inspiration for a lot of organizations in the last decade. Allspaw has long championed Continuous Delivery, and talked about the things his organization has done, culturally and technically, to make Continuous Delivery work for them. Both Flickr and Etsy are Software as a Service, delivered online. Allspaw talked a lot (for example, at the 2009 Velocity conference (*http://bit.ly/2rrFnPl*)) about how delivering a web application (which we suspect will be the kind of application most readers of this book will read) changes the approach to delivery.

In a SaaS model, there is no previous version of the software. Refresh the browser and you have the latest installation of the code. The way most organizations use branches —to work on regressions or defects in shrinkwrapped and shipped software—no longer applies. At Etsy, all changes were shipped on master. If there were features that needed to be introduced into the codebase, they lived behind feature flags. These feature flags allow Etsy to deploy features to a percentage of their audience. These features could live in the codebase, collecting information and living in the hot path of actual requests going into the service, where production could then monitor the load of the system. This information informs capacity planning and architectural discussions. By the time the business announces a feature and it's "released," it's an anticlimactic affair; the service has already been up and running happily for weeks or months. If something *does* go wrong, then simply disable the feature with the feature flag, rolling forward.

Etsy quickly learned to automate the movement of code into production, building safeguards in the software and the organization itself to support Continuous Delivery. They didn't set out with a goal of having many deploys a day; they set out to deploy frequently and safely to production.

> You can't deploy ten times a day if you go down ten times a day.
>
> —John Allspaw

Adrian Cockroft at Netflix

Adrian Cockroft helped lead Netflix from a monolithic database and application architecture to a cloud native architecture, starting in 2009. Among the many insights (and all the amazing open source technologies that you'll have no doubt used in reading this book!) that came from Netflix's foray into microservices was the notion that speed of iteration is more valuable than efficiency. The faster an organization can go, the less it matters if a particular service is slower than it could be, because it helps retain a competitive lead. It controls the field. Adrian has talked about this in numerous interviews, such as this one for Scale (*http://bit.ly/2s9NRvY*):

> There's a limit on how big a team you can have to be agile. The limit is probably defined by whatever Etsy is currently doing, because they're the best people at running a very, very agile monolithic app. It's an amazing feat, but most people are saying, *It's amazing, but it's easier to just do things in smaller chunks. It's less efficient, but I care more about speed than efficiency.*
>
> —Adrian Cockroft

Speed is a differentiator. How quickly can you iterate?

Continuous Delivery at Amazon

In his presentation, "DevOps at Amazon: a Look at Our Tools and Processes,"[1] at the 2015 AWS re:Invent conference, Rob Brigham told a compelling story about how Amazon transitioned from a monolithic application to microservices.

Brigham explained that for Amazon, DevOps was any increase in efficiency that reduces the amount of time spent idle in the software delivery life cycle. At face value, that might not be the DevOps epiphany you've been searching for. But for Brigham, this one statement changed the entire world of computing as we know it.

He said that Amazon's delivery life cycle breaks down into two sides: developers and customers. To get features from developer to customer, each change will go through a build, test, and release phase. Once a build is released, the developers can monitor

---

1 DevOps at Amazon: A Look at Our Tools and Processes. 2015. *https://www.youtube.com/watch?v=esE FaY0FDKc*

how the customers are interacting with the new features. This feedback loop is essential, because it gives developers the insights they need in order to determine what they want to work on next.

Brigham said that the feedback loop allows Amazon's developers to guess less often, and to deliver more valuable features that customers enjoy using. He also said that Amazon practices completing one feedback loop as quickly as it can. Continuous Delivery for Amazon originated from speeding up the time that developers spent either building, testing, or releasing code, since this work is invisible in the eyes of the customers. By minimizing the time spent in the delivery phase, Continuous Delivery reduces the time it takes to make a change visible to customers.

The Pipeline

When we talk about Continuous Delivery, we are talking about an automated process —*a pipeline*—that delivers software to a production environment. The pipeline refers, broadly, to the journey software must make make from continuous integration all the way to production. We've heard this alternatively described as "code to cash."

This automated process is called the delivery pipeline. The pipeline makes transparent every aspect of the delivery of value to the customer; business and IT can have coherent discussions about how far along work is in the value stream. It acts as a single funnel through which all changes—hot fixes, new features, regressions—must pass. Both developers and operations can feed into the funnel. It is *critical* that nobody subvert the pipeline! If the pipeline doesn't meet the requirements of all the parties involved, then it can't be trusted and so must evolve. The pipeline is a single visible thing where feedback about the work in flux is visible to all parties so that any errors may be resolved early.

Every pipeline will have a set of basic steps, which takes a change in source code and safely builds and tests it (like you might in traditional continuous integration), before deploying it to production. The steps in the pipeline should be described in an artifact that itself is version-controlled. This artifact might be more software, scripts, or configuration.

Continuous integration is valuable because it forces teams to make the software work somewhere besides their machines. If there are any hiccups in running the code, then those discrepancies must be captured and added to the version-controlled and automated deployment. It should be the first task of a new team to set up the Continuous Delivery pipeline, in iteration #0.

In Continuous Delivery, changes to the software—usually in the form of commits to the code's master branch in a version control system like Git—are funneled through the pipeline. The version control system should have everything required to reproduce the application and its environment. All things except production data should live in version control, even the pipeline definitions themselves. For a modern-day Spring application running on Cloud Foundry, this might mean things like the Maven or Gradle build, the Cloud Foundry `manifest.yml`, and the revision for any configuration in the Spring Cloud Config Server.

Most delivery pipelines will perform the following steps, and possibly more: *build and unit tests, integration tests, release,* and *deployment.*

Build and unit test

In this step, the software is packaged or compiled in a form that all subsequent steps can use. Importantly, there should be very little need for the source code (except perhaps in code quality analysis) beyond this point. As the application moves from one environment to another, the same binary or packaging of code should be used. Here, artifact repositories like JFrog's Artifactory can be useful for storing successful products.

Integration

In this step, the artifact from the previous step is deployed into a production-like environment and then exercised. Cloud Foundry makes it trivial to describe and deploy identical and reproducible environments derived from a concise `.yml` manifest. Here, tests might be more exhaustive and test end-to-end behavior. They might also validate the state of service dependencies in smoke tests. *Smoke testing* is a type of software testing that aims to ensure that the most important functions of an application work. It's entirely possible that human beings will want to do exploratory testing. Once this step is passed, the software moves to the release step.

Release

In this step, an artifact is stamped as releasable. It does not necessarily *have* to be released. It might just sit in an artifact repository, gathering dust. What's important is that it *could* be deployed to production with confidence. If it is deployed automatically, that is Continuous Deployment. If it is not delivered automatically, then that is Continuous Delivery.

Deployment

In this step, the releasable software is promoted to the production environment. It is common for online SaaS applications to pursue zero-downtime deployments using patterns like blue-green deploys.

Testing

Cease dependence on inspection to achieve quality. Eliminate the need for massive inspection by building quality into the product in the first place.

—W. Edwards Deming, "14 Points for Total Quality management" (*http://bit.ly/2vnxQEB*)

Going fast is only fun if it's safe. Nobody would trust a plan that said, "we're going to go faster and just give up all the quality controls! Speed! But no quality! Come what may!"

As a change moves through the pipeline, it must pass through progressively more exhaustive (and slower) quality gates. If at any point a change breaks the pipeline, failing the build, then it must be the priority of the teams involved to restore the build. No new changes must enter the pipeline until it is healthy again. Toyota insisted that any production defects should stop the production line until the defect was fixed. We also must stop the line.

Continuous Delivery is predicated on the use of testing as quality control gates. We talked at length about testing in Chapter 4 as it applies to Spring applications. Broadly, there are four kinds of testing to consider; if you move to Continuous Delivery, you should try to take advantage of as many of them as possible. Brian Marick's "testing quadrants" in Figure 15-1 illustrates the dimensions of testing.

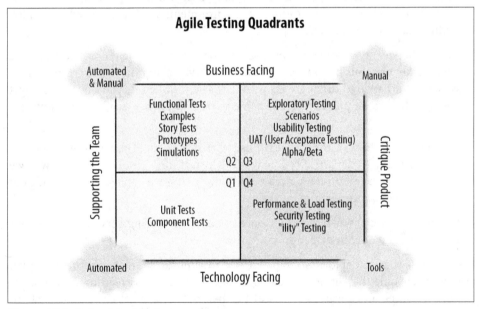

Figure 15-1. Brian Marick's test quadrants

Continuous Delivery for Microservices

One of the most important considerations in software design is modularity. If we think about modularity in the mechanical sense, components of a system are designed as modules that can be changed in the event of a mechanical failure. In the engine of a car, for example, you do not need to replace the entire engine if a single spark plug fails. In software, however, it is common that an entire application be replaced after one small change. Because of this, we should consider ourselves lucky to be building software instead of cars. Some of today's most valuable companies are created using bits and bytes instead of plastic and metal. But despite these advances, there are still some car companies around that can release cars faster than their own software.

Why is it easier to replace a flat tire on a car than to change a module of a software application?

Modularity can also give developers a map for *reasoning* about the functionality of an application. By being able to visualize and map out the complex processes that are orchestrated by an application's source code, developers and architects alike can more easily visualize where to make a change using surgical precision.

An application's source code is a system of connected bits and bytes that is always evolving—one change after another. But as the source code of a system expands or contracts, small changes require us to build and deploy entire applications. To make one small code change to a production environment, we are required to deploy everything else we didn't change.

Shipping changes to production on a shared deployment pipeline is like buying a one-way ticket on a bus bound for "Production City." Taking the bus in a large city is a low-cost alternative to driving your own car. The problem is, you don't exactly get to choose when to be picked up. The same is true when you have one deployment pipeline.

Instead of having to wait for the next bus, what if you could just summon the bus when you're ready to depart? Not a new idea! In fact, this idea changed the way we use technology to travel on-demand by car. Now, what if we applied this same idea to shipping changes to production?

Continuous delivery is like using an on-demand ride-sharing service to ship your changes to production on demand.

When teams share a deployment pipeline for an application, they are forced to plan around a schedule they have little or no control over. For this reason, innovation is stifled—as people must wait for the next bus before they can get any feedback about their changes.

The result of microservices is an ever-increasing number of pathways to push changes to production.

Tools

There are several tools available that help with Continuous Delivery. Tools like Jenkins are still widely used for cloud-based deployments. While there are a few new entrants for release management in the cloud computing era, many will feel comfortable using the tools they are familiar with. The newer tools tend to target different phases of the software delivery life cycle. In this chapter we are going to explore cloud native Continuous Delivery using a tool called *Concourse*.

Concourse

Concourse is a tool that was born ready for the cloud native era. The Concourse toolchain was created at Pivotal. It's a continuous integration tool that allows you to use Docker containers to compose simple or complex deployment pipelines. Concourse differs from tools like Jenkins or Travis in two ways: containers and pipelines.

Containers

Docker revolutionized the way we think about packaging and distributing applications in the cloud. In case you are not yet familiar, Docker was started as an open source packaging tool that would allow you to describe and build an execution environment for your applications as a Linux container. The best way to describe a Linux container is that it *thinks* it's a virtual machine, when it's actually just a filesystem that shares a Linux kernel.

Cloud Foundry largely abstracts away containers using buildpacks, which will intelligently stage your deployment artifacts inside a container without your needing to describe the execution environment. While Cloud Foundry uses its own open source container management tool, Concourse allows you to compose pipelines using Docker containers.

Docker is an ideal choice for running tasks in a composable deployment pipeline. Concourse allows you to create ephemeral build, test, and deployment environments as a pipeline of tasks that will execute inside a Docker container.

Continuously Delivering Microservices

We're going to build two Continuous Delivery pipelines that will use these steps to move code from source code to production. A major part of a delivery pipeline is testing. For this reason, we're going to reuse the code examples from Chapter 4 to build, test, and deploy Spring Boot microservices using Concourse. The testing chapter had two microservices: the *Account Microservice* and *User Microservice* (Figure 15-2).

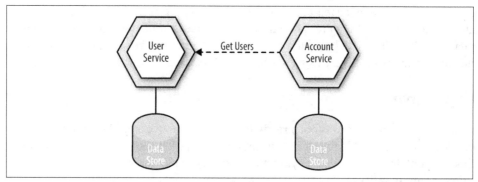

Figure 15-2. The account microservice depends on the user microservice

The benefit of building microservices is that teams can independently deploy features to production. The lack of a shared deployment pipeline is a major benefit to this kind of architecture. But this comes with a cost: responsibility. Teams must make sure that their consumers do not break. This is the subject of continuous integration. With continuous integration, we want to test our microservices early and often, before moving any change to production.

A breaking change can be anywhere from catastrophic (in the case of a data inconsistency) to a minor defect that doesn't break major functionality. Each consumer of a microservice needs to be able to assert their expectations of the service they depend on. We are going to design a Continuous Delivery pipeline that performs continuous integration to ensure that the expectations between consumer and producer remain intact, before a breaking change can go to production.

Installing Concourse

There are multiple ways to install Concourse; the fastest way to get up and running is to use Vagrant. The most up-to-date instructions for installing Concourse with Vagrant are in the Concourse documentation (*http://concourse.ci/vagrant.html*).

Concourse has a CLI tool called fly and a web-based interface for visualizing a pipeline's status. Once you have Concourse up and running and have the fly tool installed, you will be able to set the target to your local Vagrant installation and begin creating pipelines.

To begin using fly, you will need to log in to your Concourse instance. If you're using Vagrant, the URL will be similar to this:

```
fly -t lite login -c http://192.168.100.4:8080
```

Once you have successfully logged in to your Concourse instance using fly, you can begin to create pipelines. There are two simple commands you'll want to know about:

`set-pipeline` and `destroy-pipeline`. In Example 15-1, we see the `set-pipeline` command.

Example 15-1. Create a new pipeline using set-pipeline

```
fly -t lite set-pipeline -p account-microservice -c pipeline.yml \
  -l .pipeline-config.yml
```

Here we create a new pipeline for the account microservice. The `set-pipeline` command takes several parameters, as shown in Table 15-1.

Table 15-1. Set-pipeline parameters

Flag	Parameter	Description
-p	account-microservice	The name of the Concourse pipeline you would like to create.
-c	pipeline.yml	The path to the YAML file that describes the new Concourse pipeline.
-l	.pipeline-config.yml	The path to the YAML file that contains the secrets that will be parameters to your new pipeline.

In Table 15-1, you see the parameters of the `set-pipeline` command from Example 15-1. Note that the parameter value comes from the source code example that comes with this chapter. After executing this command, you'll be able to navigate to the Concourse admin web interface and see the new pipeline that is ready to begin running.

The other useful command that you will need to know is `destroy-pipeline`. Pipelines are immutable, which means that it is perfectly fine to destroy them and recreate them as you see fit. We destroy a pipeline in Example 15-2.

Example 15-2. Destroy an existing pipeline using destroy-pipeline

```
fly -t lite destroy-pipeline -p account-microservice
```

In Example 15-2, you see the command that can be used to destroy the `account-microservice` pipeline that we created in Example 15-1.

Basic Pipeline Design

The basic design of a Continuous Delivery pipeline will include a build, test, and deploy phase.

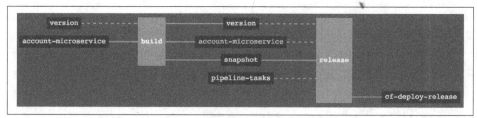

Figure 15-3. Pipeline for the Account Microservice

In Figure 15-3, we see a Concourse pipeline definition for the account microservice. Concourse has three primitives that are used to build a pipeline like the one seen above: resources, tasks, and jobs (Table 15-2).

Table 15-2. Concourse pipeline primitives

Type	Function
Resource	A resource is an input or output of a task.
Task	Tasks belong to a job, building outputs from resources inside a Docker container.
Job	Jobs group together a set of tasks and are the largest building block of a pipeline.

You may have noticed in Figure 15-3 that this pipeline does not have an integration phase. The account microservice doesn't have any consumers yet, but depends on the user service. For this reason, we will start out by designing a simple pipeline that has a build, test, and release phase.

In Table 15-3, you'll find the description of each job in the account microservice's Concourse pipeline. Concourse supports multiple resource types, and they will be defined in your pipeline's definition file. In the example project that is a companion to this chapter, you'll find the account service's source code contains a directory containing the full definition of the Concourse pipeline.

Table 15-3. Concourse jobs for the account microservice

Job	Inputs	Outputs	Description
Build	Current Version, Git Source	Release Artifact, Increments Version	The build job will clone and build the source code of the account microservice and if the unit tests pass, will prepare a new versioned release artifact.
Release	Incremented Version, Git Source, Release Artifact	Cloud Foundry Deployment	The Release job takes the release artifact and deploys the new version to Cloud Foundry.

In Figure 15-4, we see the files that will be inputs into the set-pipeline command that will create the Concourse pipeline for the account microservice. The first file we will explore is the pipeline.yml file, which contains the Concourse pipeline definition.

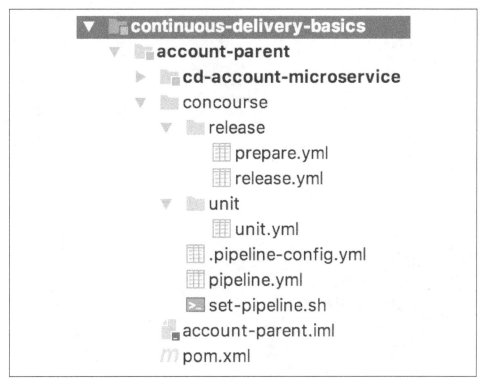

Figure 15-4. Source code directory of the account microservice

In Example 15-3, we see the first part of the Concourse pipeline definition for the account microservice. These are the Concourse resources that will be the inputs and outputs for each job. In the next part of `pipeline.yml`, we will create our job definitions that use the resources defined in Example 15-3.

Example 15-3. The resources of the pipeline.yml for the account microservice

```
# Concourse pipeline definition for the account service.
---
resource_types:
- name: maven-resource
  type: docker-image
  source:
    repository: patrickcrocker/maven-resource
    tag: latest
resources:
- name: account-microservice
  type: git
  source:
    uri:    ❶
    branch: master
```

```
    paths:
    - ./continuous-delivery-basics/account-parent/cd-account-microservice
- name: snapshot
  type: maven-resource
  source:
    url:
    artifact: cnj:cd-account-microservice:jar
    username:
    password:
- name: version
  type: semver
  source:
    driver: git
    initial_version: 1.0.0-RC.0
    uri:
    branch: version
    file: account-microservice
    private_key:
- name: cf-deploy-release
  type: cf
  source:
    api:
    username:
    password:
    organization:
    space:
    skip_cert_check: false
- name: pipeline-tasks
  type: git
  source:
    uri: https://github.com/Pivotal-Field-Engineering/pipeline-tasks
    branch: master
```

❶ The curly braces indicate parameters and secrets that we can inject using `fly`
   `set-pipeline`.

In Example 15-4, we see the jobs and task definitions for the account microservice's
pipeline. In the `build` job we will start by cloning the source code of the account
microservice and use it as an input into the `unit` task. Let's now take a look at the
`unit` task, which will build and unit-test the account microservice using the source
code that was cloned from the Git resource (Example 15-4).

Example 15-4. The jobs and tasks of the pipeline.yml for the account microservice

```
jobs:
- name: build
  max_in_flight: 1
  plan:
  - get: account-microservice
    trigger: true
```

```
  - task: unit
    file: account-microservice/concourse/unit/unit.yml
  - get: version
    params: { pre: RC }
  - put: snapshot
    params:
       file: release/cd-account-microservice.jar
       pom_file: account-microservice/source/pom.xml
       version_file: version/version
  - put: version
    params: { file: version/version }
- name: release
  serial: true
  plan:
  - get: snapshot
    trigger: true
    passed: [build]
  - get: account-microservice
    passed: [build]
  - get: version
    passed: [build]
  - get: pipeline-tasks
  - task: prepare-manifest
    file: account-microservice/concourse/release/prepare.yml
    params:
       MF_PATH: ../release-output/cd-account-microservice.jar
       MF_BUILDPACK: java_buildpack
  - task: prepare-release
    file: account-microservice/concourse/release/release.yml
  - put: cf-deploy-release
    params:
       manifest: task-output/manifest.yml
```

Example 15-5. The unit task that will build and test the account microservice

```
# This task will build and run the unit tests specified in the source code
# of the microservice.
---
platform: linux
image_resource:
  type: docker-image
  source:
    repository: maven
    tag: alpine
inputs:
- name: account-microservice
outputs:
- name: release
run:
  path: sh
  args:
  - -exc
```

```
- |
  cd account-microservice/source \
  && mvn clean package \
  && mv target/cd-account-microservice.jar \
  ../release/cd-account-microservice.jar
```

In Example 15-5, we see the definition of the unit task that will build and unit-test the account microservice. Each task runs inside a Docker container, and will mount input and output volumes, which allows us to pass state along to each task and job in the pipeline. In this example, we are building the JAR artifact of the account microservice only if the tests pass. The result means that the JAR artifact will be the input into the next task, which will prepare a snapshot build and deploy it to a Maven snapshots repository.

For each pipeline you create, you will likely have parameters that contain logins and secrets. When creating a new pipeline, you will be able to supply a configuration file as an input parameter. We've included a set-pipeline.sh script in the account-parent/concourse directory of the example project. In Example 15-6, we see the contents of that script for the account microservice.

Example 15-6. The set-pipeline.sh file creates the account microservice pipeline

```
#!/usr/bin/env bash

fly -t lite set-pipeline -p account-microservice -c pipeline.yml \
  -l .pipeline-config.yml
```

When creating a new pipeline, you will supply your pipeline definition and the configuration file containing your logins and secrets. In Example 15-7, we take a look at the contents of the .pipeline-config.yml file.

Example 15-7. The .pipeline-config.yml configuration file for the account microservice

```
# The Cloud Foundry credentials where the microservice will be deployed
cf-url: https://api.run.pivotal.io
cf-username: replace
cf-password: replace
cf-org: replace
cf-space: replace

# The Maven repository where versioned artifacts will be published
artifactory-url: https://cloudnativejava.jfrog.io/cloudnativejava/libs-release-local/
artifactory-username: replace
artifactory-password: replace

# The git repository containing the microservice source code
```

```
git-source-repository-url: https://github.com/cloud-native-java/continuous-delivery

# The git repository containing the version file
git-version-repository-url: git@github.com:cloud-native-java/continuous-delivery.git
git-version-private-key: |
  -----BEGIN RSA PRIVATE KEY-----
  REPLACE
  -----END RSA PRIVATE KEY-----
```

In Example 15-7, we see the configuration file that contains the configuration parameters for the account microservice pipeline. Before you can run your pipeline, you'll need to update these credentials, or the pipeline will not be able to complete. The first three credentials should be self-explanatory, but the `git-version-private-key` requires a bit more explanation. The `git-version-private-key` is provided to the pipeline so that the deployment task can bump the release version each time the pipeline is run.

In Figure 15-5, we see the `version` branch of the example repository that contains two version files: one for the account microservice and one for the user microservice.

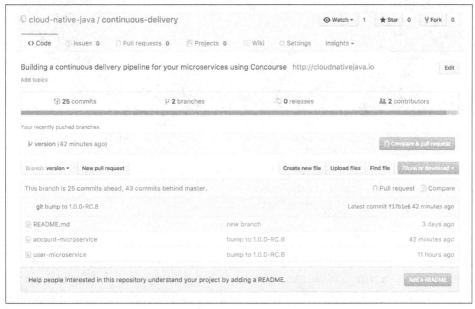

Figure 15-5. The `version` *branch of the example GitHub repository*

Now, each one of these pipelines will run independently, and each time the pipelines pass the test phase, the respective file will be "bumped" from the current version to the new version. This versioning method will give us an event log that we can use to automatically roll back a deployment if and when things go wrong. This is why we need to provide the `git-version-private-key`: so that the pipeline task can increment the version of a microservice each time the pipeline runs.

Now let's start the pipeline from the Concourse admin web interface. Navigate to your Concourse instance's web interface (which will differ depending on your installation) in your browser of choice.

Start pipeline

After navigating to your Concourse web interface, you'll be presented with a side menu that will contain a list of the pipelines you've created. After creating the `account-microservice` pipeline, you'll see that it is ready to be started—highlighted in blue (see Figure 15-6).

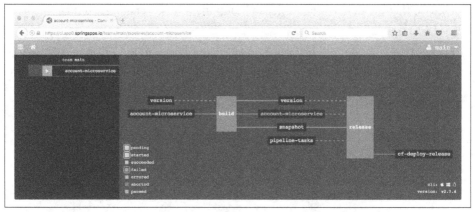

Figure 15-6. The `account-microservice` pipeline is ready to be started

In Figure 15-6, you see the pipeline before it is started. When a pipeline is started, it means that any external triggers—such as a new commit to a Git repository—will cause the pipeline to start running the first task.

Continuous Deployment

Each task in a job can be automatically triggered by a Concourse resource, such as a new commit to a Git repository. In Figure 15-7, the `build` job is highlighted with a pulsating yellow outline. This means that a new commit to the `account-microservice` repository has triggered a new build.

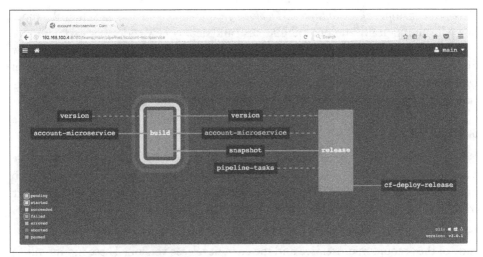

Figure 15-7. The `account-microservice` pipeline starts after a new Git commit

Let's take a look again at the Concourse pipeline definition of the account microservice to see how this works (Example 15-8).

Example 15-8. Snippet from the `account-microservice` pipeline definition

```
resources:
- name: account-microservice ❶
  type: git
  source:
    uri: https://github.com/cloud-native-java/continuous-delivery
    branch: master
jobs:
- name: build
  plan:
  - get: account-microservice ❷
    trigger: true ❸
  - task: unit
    file: account-microservice/concourse/unit/unit.yml
```

❶ Describes the Git resource that will trigger a new build.

❷ Pulls the latest commit on the master branch from Git.

❸ Setting this to `true` means that any new commit will trigger this task.

In Example 15-8, you see a snippet from the `pipeline.yml` file that describes the Concourse pipeline for the account microservice. The snippet shows how you can tell Concourse to automatically trigger a job's task from a new commit to a Git repository.

This is an example of a *Continuous Deployment* pipeline, which means that the pipeline will automatically attempt to build, test, and deploy new code after each commit. This differs from *Continuous Delivery*, in the sense that after each new commit, a new build will be prepared for you but not automatically deployed. The final task will then wait for you to push the button that starts the deployment, which will then tell Concourse to prepare the latest build for a production deployment.

Build and test

When a new build is triggered, a `unit` task will receive the inputs specified in the `pipeline.yml` definition file. If you click on the `build` job in the Concourse web interface, you'll be able to see the status of the build, including a stream of the `stdout` from the Docker container that is executing the build task.

In Figure 15-8, you can see that the build has started with the inputs for the source code of the account microservice and the current release version. These inputs will be passed into the `unit` task, which will build and test the source code of the Spring Boot project using Maven.

Figure 15-8. The first build is triggered with the source code as the input

In Figure 15-9, you can see the stream of output from the Docker container as the Maven build process begins downloading the dependencies of the account microservice.

Figure 15-9. The `unit` task builds and unit-tests the Spring Boot project

Versioned Maven artifact

After the unit tests run and pass, the resulting build can be automatically prepared as a versioned release artifact. As we discussed earlier, this pipeline uses a Maven artifact repository to store versioned artifacts that will be deployed to Cloud Foundry. In Figure 15-10, you see the final state of the build job, which was a success.

Figure 15-10. The build completes and outputs the versioned deployment artifact

If the build fails, you'll be notified of the error and the job will be highlighted in red. In this case, we see that the build and test was a success, and the release artifact was uploaded to the artifact repository with an incremented version.

Deploy to Cloud Foundry

The last step of the `account-microservice` pipeline is to prepare the release to be deployed to Cloud Foundry. In the last job, we built and uploaded a versioned deployment artifact of our Spring Boot application. The `release` task will be triggered by the new version in the Maven artifact repository and kick off a deployment to Cloud Foundry (Figure 15-11).

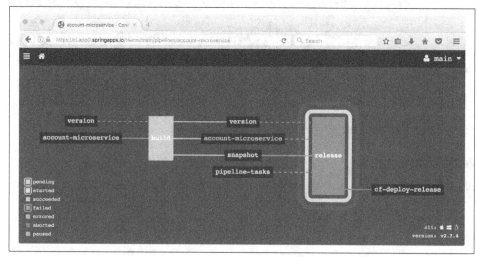

Figure 15-11. After the build task, the new release is deployed to Cloud Foundry

In Figure 15-11, you can see that the `release` job has been started. As a part of this job, the newly published versioned artifact from the `build` job will be prepared to be released to Cloud Foundry. The final output of the `release` job is `cf-deploy-release`. This output will take in a Cloud Foundry manifest file that is created using parameters supplied in the pipeline definition. In Example 15-9, we take a look at what the `release` job plan looks like.

Example 15-9. Release job from the `account-microservice` pipeline definition

```
resources:
# ...
- name: snapshot
  type: maven-resource
  source:
    url:
    artifact: cnj:cd-account-microservice:jar
```

```
      username:
      password:
- name: cf-deploy-release
  type: cf # the Concourse resource for deploying to Cloud Foundry
  source:
    api: # \
    username: # \
    password: # \
    organization: # \
    space: # \
    skip_cert_check: false
# ...
jobs:
- name: release
  serial: true
  plan:
  - get: snapshot
    trigger: true ❶
    passed: [build] ❷
  - get: account-microservice
    passed: [build]
  - get: version ❸
    passed: [build]
  - get: pipeline-tasks # Resource used to create a custom manifest.yml
  - task: prepare-manifest ❹
    file: account-microservice/concourse/release/prepare.yml
    params:
      MF_PATH: ../release-output/cd-account-microservice.jar
      MF_BUILDPACK: java_buildpack
  - task: prepare-release
    file: account-microservice/concourse/release/release.yml ❺
  - put: cf-deploy-release
    params:
      manifest: task-output/manifest.yml ❻
```

❶   A release is triggered by a new version from the artifact repository.

❷   The release can only begin after the build task is passed.

❸   Gets the new version that was output by the build job.

❹   Prepares a custom Cloud Foundry manifest.yml deployment file.

❺   Moves the versioned artifact into a staging release directory.

❻   Deploys the versioned artifact described in manifest.yml to Cloud Foundry.

In Example 15-9, you can find a snippet that describes the release job in the pipe
line.yml definition of the account-microservice pipeline. The release task is

orchestrating a series of complex steps, requiring that each of the inputs passes as an output from the `build` job. The next step is to create a custom `manifest.yml` file, which is required by the CF Concourse resource to describe a new Cloud Foundry deployment. The CF resource called `cf-deploy-release` will be the output of the `release` job, and will deploy the new version of the `account-microservice` to production.

In Figure 15-12, you can see an example of a successfully released version of the `account-microservice`.

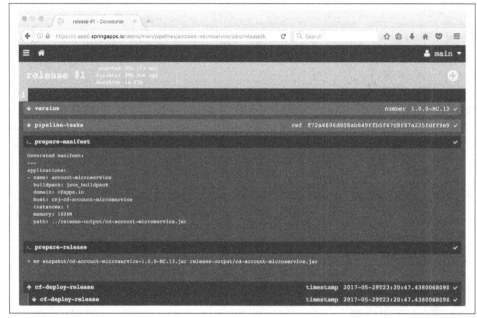

Figure 15-12. The `release` *task successfully prepares a new Cloud Foundry deployment*

 This release was not a zero downtime deployment. You can customize the `release` job to do a zero downtime blue-green deployment by staging the new versioned artifact and then swapping the app's Cloud Foundry route from production to staging.

Continuous Integration

We've explored how to set up a basic deployment pipeline for the account microservice. However, this service did not have any integration testing. Concourse can be used to set up a complex integration environment to do end-to-end testing or basic integration testing using backing services, such as a database. In the next section, we're going to set up a new pipeline for the `user-service`, which the `account-`

`microservice` will depend on. In this new pipeline we're going to explore how to set up an additional `integration` job that will perform consumer-driven contract testing for our two microservices.

Consumer-Driven Contract Testing

Continuously delivering microservices will quickly turn ugly if there are no checks and balances to make sure that teams are not continuously releasing breaking changes. In Chapter 4, we looked at an example of consumer-driven contract testing. Now we're going to iterate on the simple Concourse pipeline we built for the account service, including a consumer-driven testing step to make sure changes do not break consumers. The goal of this new pipeline will be to continuously integrate the *user service* with consumer-driven contract tests that are published by the *account service*.

To do this, we will need to create a source code repository where the *account service* can publish consumer-driven contract stubs for the *user service*. As we discussed in Chapter 4, consumer-driven contract tests are created by consumers of a service dependency. Each of our consumers will be responsible for publishing their consumer-driven contract tests to a designated repository. Let's use the following example.

We are the owners of the *accounts service* and we depend on the *user service*. As consumers, we want to make sure that the *user service* does not release any breaking changes that cause our services to fail. To automate this integration testing, we will publish our consumer tests to a designated repository that is owned by the *user service*. It is then our responsibility as a consumer to publish our consumer-driven tests to an integration repository of the service on which we depend. Otherwise, the *user service* will have no knowledge of our expectations as the *accounts service*.

User Microservice Pipeline

Now let's take the pipeline design we created earlier for the *account service* and modify the recipe to include consumer-driven contract testing for the *user service*. In Figure 15-13, you can see the pipeline for the user microservice.

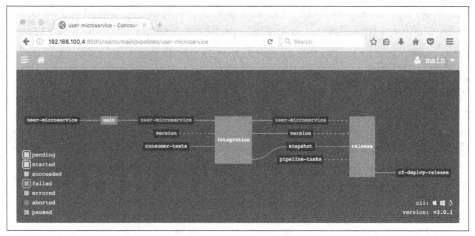

Figure 15-13. The Concourse pipeline for the user microservice

In this service we have an additional pipeline step: the `integration` job. In the integration job, before bundling a new release artifact and uploading it to the Maven artifact repository, a set of consumer-driven tests will be executed against the user microservice.

In Figure 15-14, you can see the source directory of the user microservice.

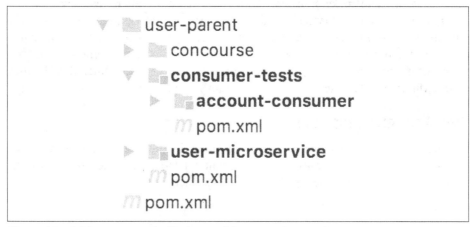

Figure 15-14. The source code directory of the user microservice

For the user microservice we will have an additional directory that will contain a collection of consumer-driven contract tests that are published by consumers. Before that can happen, we need to publish a contract stub from the user microservice that other services can write their tests against.

In Figure 15-15, you can see the consumer-driven contract stub that uses Spring Cloud Contract, which we reviewed in Chapter 4.

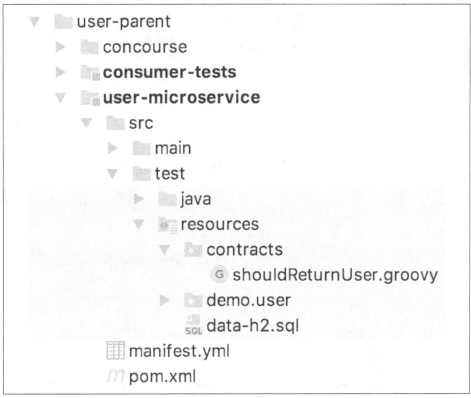

Figure 15-15. A consumer-driven contract stub published by the user microservice

When a user microservice is published, this stub can be used by a service to run an embedded application server that simulates the behavior of the user microservice.

In Figure 15-16, you can see the consumer-driven contract test that is written by the account microservice. The `integration` task in the user microservice pipeline will run each of the consumer tests in this folder to make sure that any new changes will not break consumers. It is the responsibility of each consumer to write these tests, and if a test does not pass, the user microservice will not be able to release the breaking changes to production.

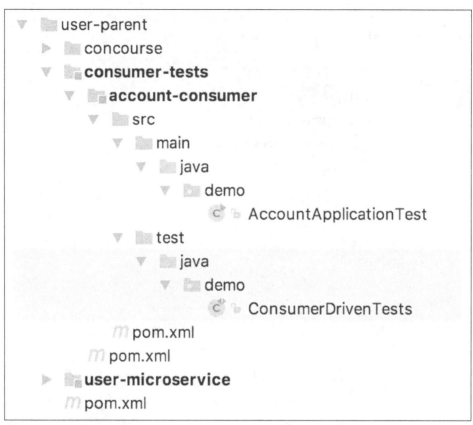

Figure 15-16. The account microservice writes consumer tests against the user microservice

Now let's take a look at the `consumer-tests` task that is a part of the `integration` job in the user microservice's Concourse pipeline (Example 15-10).

Example 15-10. The integration task for the user microservice

```
# This task will run the integration tests and consumer-driven contract tests of
# the user microservice and its consumers.
---
platform: linux
image_resource:
  type: docker-image
  source:
    repository: maven
    tag: alpine
inputs:
- name: consumer-tests
outputs:
```

```
- name: release
run:
  path: sh
  args:
  - -exc
  - |
    cd consumer-tests/user-microservice \   ❶
    && mvn clean install -DskipTests \   ❷
    && mv target/user-microservice.jar \
       ../../release/user-microservice.jar \   ❸
    && cd ../consumer-tests \   ❹
    && mvn clean package   ❺
```

❶ Navigates to the user microservice's Spring Boot application directory.

❷ Installs the user microservice's contract stubs to the local Maven repo.

❸ Stages the JAR artifact to a release output directory for the next task.

❹ Navigates to the consumer tests directory.

❺ Runs all consumer tests against the latest consumer-driven contract stubs.

In Example 15-10, you see the definition of the consumer-tests.yml task included in the concourse directory of the user microservice. In this task, the consumer-driven tests that were written by consumers of the user microservice will be run against any new changes. If one of these tests fails, the pipeline will fail and prevent the user microservice from releasing the changes. By using a Continuous Delivery pipeline to automate these kinds of integration tests, microservice owners must be proactive in resolving breaking changes with consumers before being able to deploy their application to production.

 To make the example snippets easier to read, the folder paths in the examples used in this chapter may differ from the code examples associated with this book. The input resources to a task will use the full path to a microservice. In this book we use monolithic repositories to make things easier to find. For your production microservices, it's not recommended to include multiple microservices in the same Git repository.

Data

We haven't touched on database migration in a blue-green deploy. We can scratch the surface here, as there is no one-size-fits-all solution.

RDBMS schema migration tools like Flyway (*https://flywaydb.org*) and Liquibase (*http://www.liquibase.org*) maintain a manifest in each database of which database schema mutations have been applied, and can deterministically update a schema version to a new version if it determines there is a new one available. If all you ever do is additive—adding new columns and tables and records—then there is nothing to worry about if you need to roll back. You still have all the previous records and schema.

What happens when you deploy a new version of a service, v2, and use Flyway or Liquibase—tools that support versioning schema deltas and migrating existing databases from one version to another—to evolve the schema to version 2.0? What happens if something goes wrong and you've made destructive updates to the schema (for example, changing a column or deleting records)?

You need to take care to consider these issues when designing blue-green deployments. Instead of deleting data, consider using *tombstone* records, where the application logically deletes the record—perhaps by setting a DELETED column to TRUE—but retains the data so that the application may be resurrected by unflagging the tombstone column. If you change a column, can you duplicate the data from the old into a new column, keeping both?

Do whatever you can to make rolling back the code to an earlier version possible, because you never know when something will fail. Practically, though, you don't need to support rolling back to every previous version; just the last one. Teams often give themselves enough wiggle room to roll back to the last known version of a schema, 1. In version 2 the *deprecated* columns and records stay, resident. In version 3, the destruction that should've happened in 1 can be applied, making permanent the migration from 1.

To Production!

> *Software being "Done" is like lawn being "Mowed."*
> —Jim Benson (*https://twitter.com/ourfounder/status/770075137332932608*)

In this book, we've looked at building cloud-native applications. A cloud-native application is one that is destined to run in a cloud platform, and to exploit that paradigm. It is one that, by design, optimizes for ease of iteration and fast feedback; it is never done. A cloud-native application is one that (hopefully) will make many revolutions from concept to production, each time releasing more value to the application's customers. In this chapter, we've looked at how to make the cost of those revolutions as cheap as possible through Continuous Delivery.

## PART V

Appendix

Using Spring Boot with Java EE

In this appendix we'll look at how to integrate Spring Boot applications with Java EE. Java EE, for our purposes, is an umbrella name for a set of APIs and, sometimes, runtimes—*Java EE application servers*. Java EE application servers, like Red Hat's WildFly AS (*http://wildfly.org*)— the application server formerly named JBoss Application Server—provide implementations of these APIs. We'll look at how to build applications that leverage Java EE APIs outside of a Java EE application server. If you're building a brand new application today, you don't need this appendix. This appendix is more useful for those with existing functionality trapped in an application server who want to move to a microservices architecture. For a broader discussion of moving ("forklifting") legacy applications to a cloud platform like Cloud Foundry with minimal refactoring, see Chapter 5.

Spring acts as a consumer of Java EE APIs, where practical. It doesn't *require* any of them. Wherever possible, Spring supports consuming Java EE APIs à la carte, independent of a full Java EE application server. Spring applications should ideally be portable across environments, including embedded web applications, application servers, and virtually any Platform as a Service (PaaS) offering.

Compatibility and Stability

Spring 4.2 (the baseline release for Spring Boot 1.3 and later) supports Java SE 6 or later (specifically, the minimum API level is JDK 6u18, which was released in early 2010). Oracle has stopped publishing updates—save for security fixes—for Java SE 6 and Java SE 7. Consider moving to Java SE 8.

Spring also supports Java EE 6+ (which came out in 2009). In practical terms, Spring 4 is Servlet 3.0+ focused but Servlet 2.5 compatible. Spring Boot, which builds on Spring, works best with Servlet 3.1 or later. Spring Boot's approach to dependencies ensure that you get the latest and greatest, as soon as possible, though you can revert to older Servlet 3.0 generation web servers if you like.

The market consistently favors, by a wide margin, Apache's Tomcat (*http://tomcat.apache.org*) (a project that Pivotal contributes heavily to), Eclipse's Jetty, and Red Hat's Wildfly. Most Java developers don't deploy to full Java EE-compatible containers, and so Spring brings the useful Java EE APIs to the growing majority that aren't running Java EE application servers. Plainly, Java EE offers some very compelling (and entrenched) APIs. The Servlet API, JSR 330 (`javax.inject`) and JSR 303 (`javax.validation`), JCache, JDBC, JPA, JMS, JAX-RS, etc., to name a few, are very useful and, where practical for users, Spring and Spring Boot support them.

As developers move to the cloud, and as a result, to a cloud-native architecture, we see decreasing value in relying on Java EE application servers; the all-or-nothing approach goes against the grain of building cloud-native systems composed of small, singly focused, scalable services.

Some Java EE APIs are very useful, but they're notoriously slow to evolve. This suggests that the benefits of slow-to-evolve, standardized Java EE APIs are best reaped at layers where there is little volatility. JDBC, which provides middleware binding for decades-old SQL-based databases, is an example of a perfectly reasonable API. The Servlet API, which provides a middleware binding for HTTP applications, is also a very capable API. Both JDBC and the Servlet specification are examples of API that don't need to change often.

Except, that is, when they *desperately* do. New development paradigms emerge all the time. As of the middle of 2017, HTTP 2—which offers performance improvements virtually for free—has been supported in most other platforms and technologies for years, but there is no support in the Servlet specification (yet). Developers must use native APIs in the underlying Servlet containers to access this functionality (for the moment). As applications face growing demand and larger datasets, it is no longer acceptable to block threads waiting for input and output when the work could be handled reactively, freeing up precious resources. For reactive programming to work, every link in a request processing chain must support reactivity—from the HTTP Servlet-based request, all the way to the JDBC database. At the moment, neither do. Oracle has suggested that it would like to see reactive programming support in a future JDBC revision, and Java EE 8 will ship with HTTP 2 support. So, eventually, we'll get there.

Software serves a purpose, usually a business purposes, and businesses don't compete by relying on sometimes decades-old, inferior solutions. Embrace standards where, and only where, they make sense.

Let's look at a few commonplace APIs that you'll find work marvelously in Spring Boot applications.

Dependency Injection with JSR 330 (and JSR 250)

Spring has long offered various approaches to providing configuration. Spring doesn't care, really, where it learns about your objects and how you wire them together. In the beginning, there was the XML configuration format. Later, Spring introduced component scanning to discover and register components with stereotype annotations, like @Component, or any other annotation itself annotated with @Component, like @RestController or @Service. In 2006, the Spring Java Configuration project was born. This approach describes beans to Spring in terms of objects returned from methods that are annotated with the @Bean annotation. You might call these bean definition *provider methods*.

Meanwhile, at Google, Bob Lee introduced Guice, which also supports a notion of bean definition provider methods, like the Spring Java configuration project. These two options, along with a few others, evolved independently and each garnered a large community.

Skipping ahead to 2007, 2008, and 2009, and formative days of Java EE 6. The team behind JBoss' Seam that had developed their own dependency injection technology attempted to define a standard, JSR 299 (CDI), to define what it means to be a dependency injection technology. Neither Seam nor JSR 299 looked anything like Spring or Guice, the two most entrenched and popular technologies, *by any stretch*, so Spring founder Rod Johnson and Guice founder Bob Lee proposed JSR 330. JSR 330 defines a common set of annotations for the surface area of dependency injection frameworks *that impact business component code*. This left each dependency injection container to differentiate in the implementations of the engine itself.

JSR 330 is natively supported, of course, by Spring and Guice and, eventually, by JSR 299 implementations. It's so common, in fact, that other dependency injection technologies like Dagger, which is optimized for compile-time code-generation, and mobile environments like Android, also support it. If you absolutely must have portable dependency injection, use JSR 330.

You'll commonly use a few annotations with JSR 330, assuming you have javax.inject : javax-inject : 1 on the classpath, to define, resolve, and inject bean references:

- @Inject is equivalent to Spring's @Autowired annotation. It identifies injectable constructors, methods, and fields.

- @Named is more or less equivalent to Spring's various stereotype annotations like @Component. It marks a bean to be registered with the container and it can be used to give the bean a String-based ID by which it may be registered.

- @Qualifier can be used to *qualify* beans by type (or String ID). This is, naturally, almost identical to Spring's @Qualifier annotation.

- @Scope is more or less analogous to Spring's @Scope annotation and is used to tell the container what the life cycle of a bean is. You might, for example, specify that a bean is session scoped, that is, it should live and die along the lines of an HTTP request.

- @Singleton tells the container that the bean should be instantiated only once. This is Spring's default, but it's such a common concept that it was worth making sure all implementations support it.

JSR 330 also defines one interface, javax.inject.Provider<T>. Business components can inject instances of a given bean, Foo, directly or using a Provider<Foo>. This is more or less analogous to Spring's ObjectFactory<T> type. Compared to injecting an instance directly, the Provider<T> instance can be used to retrieve multiple instances of a given bean, handle *lazy* semantics, break circular dependencies, and abstract containing scope.

JSR 250, which comes from Java EE 5, is *also* supported natively in Spring if the types are on the classpath (they are, in newer versions of the JDK). You may have seen these annotations if you've ever used @javax.annotation.Resource, for example. These annotations are commonly used in EJB 3 code, but I've never really seen them used elsewhere. They can make it easy for developers moving code over from EJB 3 environments where references resolution is signaled with @Resource.

Using Servlet APIs in a Spring Boot Application

Spring Boot auto-configures a web-runtime for you, by default, when you bring in spring-boot-starter-web. This runtime is, in versions of Spring earlier than 5.0, a Servlet container like Apache Tomcat, Red Hat's Undertow, and Eclipse's Jetty.

Spring framework 5.0 and later also support a reactive runtime built on Netty. But we digress.

All are fine choices. Apache Tomcat happens to be the most ubiquitous, but there's no reason not to choose the other implementations if that's your requirement. Spring Boot supports common concerns, like specifying the port with the property server.port, specifying the conttext path with server.context-path, configuring SSL support with server.ssl.*, and enabling GZip compression with server.com pression.*. GZip compression, in particular, takes porous payloads like JSON delivered HTTP and compresses them. Browsers will know how to decompress such resources. This offers a bit of efficiency for large or static payloads, like JavaScript assets or CSS. If you want to compresses all static resources (those that Spring Boot will serve from under `src/main/resources/*`), you need only specify `spring.resour ces.chain.gzipped=true`. If you want to compress dynamic endpoints, such as JSON payloads, you can use the `server.compression.*` properties. Example A-1 shows how to compress all JSON results.

Example A-1. GZip compressing all JSON payloads

```
server.compression.enabled=true
server.compression.mime-types=application/json
```

You can see that this is working by visiting the endpoint without specifying an `accept-encoding` and with an `accept-encoding`. Our sample application contributes a Spring MVC endpoint, under `/mvc/hi`, which returns JSON output. Call that endpoint without an `accept-encoding` header specified, and you'll get raw JSON. Call it with an `accept-encoding` header, specifying `gzip`, and you'll get binary (compressed) data that you'll have to pass to something `gunzip` to read (Example A-2).

Example A-2. Calling the REST endpoint with and without an accept-encoding header

```
> curl http://localhost:8080/mvc/hi
{"greetings":"Hello, world!"}

> curl -H"accept-encoding: gzip" http://localhost:8080/mvc/hi
?VJ/JM-??K/V?R?H????Q(?/?IQT???7

> curl -H"accept-encoding: gzip" http://localhost:8080/mvc/hi | gunzip
{"greetings":"Hello, world!"}
```

There are container-specific properties, too. These properties are, necessarily, inconsistent from one container to another. If you're deploying to Undertow, you might specify `server.undertow.worker-threads=10`, for example, to limit the number of worker threads created. If you're deploying to Tomcat, you might use `server.tomcat.max-threads=10` to cap the number of threads running. If you're deploying to Eclipse Jetty project, then you might use `server.jetty.acceptors` and `server.jetty.selectors` to limit how many acceptor and selector threads Jetty maintains.

Between the common properties and these container-specific properties, you should be able to express most of the configuration you might've before. If on the off chance your needs aren't met, and you want to programmatically customize or interrogate the embedded servlet container engine, then consider an implementation of `Embed dedServletContainerCustomizer`, a callback interface that gives you access to the implementation of the container as Spring Boot is configuring it. Spring Boot supports container-specific callback interfaces as well. These container-specific callbacks are an opportunity to override or contribute configuration for components involved in the development of the application itself.

In Example A-3, we'll dereference the container-specific customizer callbacks and iterate over them. You can contribute your own customizers by adding them to these container instance's collections. There should be a `container#add*` method for the customizer you want access to.

Example A-3. Working with the embedded container in a EmbeddedServletContainerCustomizer

```
package servlets;

import org.apache.commons.logging.Log;
import org.apache.commons.logging.LogFactory;
//@formatter:off
import
    org.springframework.boot.context.embedded.AbstractEmbeddedServletContainer↵
Factory;
import
    org.springframework.boot.context.embedded.ConfigurableEmbeddedServlet↵
Container;
import org.springframework.boot.context.embedded.EmbeddedServletContainer↵
Customizer;
import org.springframework.boot.context.embedded.jetty.JettyEmbeddedServlet↵
ContainerFactory;
import org.springframework.boot.context.embedded.tomcat.TomcatEmbeddedServlet↵
ContainerFactory;
import
    org.springframework.boot.context.embedded.undertow.UndertowEmbeddedServlet↵
ContainerFactory;
//@formatter:on
import org.springframework.stereotype.Component;

@Component
class ContainerAnalyzer implements EmbeddedServletContainerCustomizer {

 private final Log log = LogFactory.getLog(getClass());

 @Override
 public void customize(ConfigurableEmbeddedServletContainer c) {

  this.log.info("inside " + getClass().getName());

  ❶
  AbstractEmbeddedServletContainerFactory base = AbstractEmbeddedServletContainer↵
Factory.class
    .cast(c);
  this.log.info("the container's running on port " + base.getPort());
```

```
  this.log.info("the container's context-path is " + base.getContextPath());

❷
  if (UndertowEmbeddedServletContainerFactory.class.isAssignableFrom(c
  .getClass())) {
  UndertowEmbeddedServletContainerFactory undertow = UndertowEmbeddedServlet↵
ContainerFactory.class
    .cast(c);
  undertow.getDeploymentInfoCustomizers().forEach(
    dic -> log.info("undertow deployment info customizer " + dic));
  undertow.getBuilderCustomizers().forEach(
    bc -> log.info("undertow builder customizer " + bc));
  }

❸
  if (TomcatEmbeddedServletContainerFactory.class
  .isAssignableFrom(c.getClass())) {
  TomcatEmbeddedServletContainerFactory tomcat = TomcatEmbeddedServlet↵
ContainerFactory.class
    .cast(c);
  tomcat.getTomcatConnectorCustomizers().forEach(
    cc -> log.info("tomcat connector customizer " + cc));
  tomcat.getTomcatContextCustomizers().forEach(
    cc -> log.info("tomcat context customizer " + cc));
  }

❹
  if (JettyEmbeddedServletContainerFactory.class.isAssignableFrom(c.getClass())) {
    JettyEmbeddedServletContainerFactory jetty = JettyEmbeddedServletContainer↵
Factory.class
    .cast(c);
  jetty.getServerCustomizers().forEach(
    cc -> log.info("jetty server customizer " + cc));
  }
 }

}
```

❶ It's useful to downcast the container to an abstract base type so that we can do
    more than call various set* methods.

❷ There are container specific implementations for Undertow...

❸ ...and Apache Tomcat...

❹ ...and Eclipse Jetty.

Spring Boot automatically stands up the embedded servlet container and then registers the relevant Spring stack apparatus using the Servlet 3.0 programmatic registration. Spring Boot will register the Spring MVC DispatcherServlet, whatever filters

Spring Security needs, and whatever other machinery is needed for other parts of the Spring ecosystem, as the need arises. It does this all for you so that when you start writing code, *it just works*. You're not required to configure a web.xml or to manage configuration for the container itself. If you're using Spring projects (like Spring MVC), then you're all set. You can also contribute your own servlets or filters, too. Spring Boot will intelligently register any Spring beans (contributed from @Bean provider methods, or annotated with stereotype annotations) of type javax.serv let.Filter or javax.servlet.Servlet as filters and servlets, respectively.

If you want to exert control over how the servlets or filters are registered—their ordering, their URL mappings, parameters, etc.—then you have two further options. You can wrap your servlets in instances of ServletRegistrationBean, and let Spring manage that for you, instead. You can achieve the same for filters with FilterRegis trationBean instances. Suppose we have a javax.servlet.Filter, named Logging Filter (Example A-4).

Example A-4. The oh-so-common logging example, again

```
package servlets;

import org.apache.commons.logging.Log;
import org.apache.commons.logging.LogFactory;

import javax.servlet.*;
import java.io.IOException;
import java.time.Instant;

class LoggingFilter implements Filter {

 private final Log log = LogFactory.getLog(getClass());

 @Override
 public void init(FilterConfig config) throws ServletException {
  this.log.info("init()");
  String initParameter = config.getInitParameter("instant-initialized");
  Instant initializationInstant = Instant.parse(initParameter);
  this.log.info(Instant.class.getName() + " initialized "
   + initializationInstant.toString());
 }

 @Override
 public void doFilter(ServletRequest req, ServletResponse resp,
  FilterChain chain) throws IOException, ServletException {
  this.log.info("before doFilter(" + req + ", " + resp + ")");
  chain.doFilter(req, resp);
  this.log.info("after doFilter(" + req + ", " + resp + ")");
 }
```

```
@Override
public void destroy() {
  log.info("destroy()");
 }
}
```

You can register the instance with a `FilterRegistrationBean` bean definition, specifying initialization parameters, whether the filter should support async operations, which URL paths the filter applies to, and more (Example A-5).

Example A-5. Registering filters and servlets explicitly

```
package servlets;

import org.springframework.boot.web.servlet.FilterRegistrationBean;
import org.springframework.context.annotation.Bean;
import org.springframework.context.annotation.Configuration;
import org.springframework.core.Ordered;

import java.time.Instant;

@Configuration
public class FilterConfiguration {

 @Bean
 FilterRegistrationBean filter() {
  LoggingFilter filter = new LoggingFilter(); ❶
  FilterRegistrationBean registrationBean = new FilterRegistrationBean(filter);
  registrationBean.setOrder(Ordered.HIGHEST_PRECEDENCE);
  ❷
  registrationBean.addInitParameter("instant-initialized", Instant.now()
   .toString());
  return registrationBean;
 }
}
```

❶ We're instantiating an instance of the `Filter` for our own purposes here. There's no reason you couldn't also manage the bean's life cycle as a Spring bean, as well.

❷ Here, we're programmatically specifying initialization parameters. These parameters could in turn come from configuration specified on the command line or from the Spring Cloud Config Server.

Spring will ensure that the `init` and `destroy` methods are called at the appropriate time.

Spring Boot even supports auto-detecting and managing components annotated with Servlet 3.0 annotations @javax.servlet.annotation.WebServlet, @javax.serv let.annotation.WebFilter, and @javax.servlet.annotation.WebListener. Add @org.springframework.boot.web.servlet.ServletComponentScan to a Spring configuration class to activate this support, ideally the same class as the one on which @SpringBootApplication lives. Spring will manage the discovered classes as if the classes had been registered with Spring directly. You don't need to annotate the components with another stereotype annotation like @Component or use a registration bean (Example A-6).

 Obviously, we *don't recommend* writing *new* code as Servlet instances, since you can achieve the same sorts of things with Spring MVC, but if you want to make existing code work, then this might be helpful.

Example A-6. An @WebServlet component that Spring will manage for us

```
package servlets;

import org.apache.commons.logging.Log;
import org.apache.commons.logging.LogFactory;

import javax.servlet.ServletException;
import javax.servlet.annotation.WebServlet;
import javax.servlet.http.HttpServlet;
import javax.servlet.http.HttpServletRequest;
import javax.servlet.http.HttpServletResponse;
import java.io.IOException;

❶
@WebServlet(urlPatterns = "/servlets/hi", asyncSupported = false)
class GreetingsServlet extends HttpServlet {

  private final Log log = LogFactory.getLog(getClass());

  @Override
  protected void doGet(HttpServletRequest req, HttpServletResponse resp)
    throws ServletException, IOException {
    this.log.info("doGet(" + req + ", " + resp + ")");
    resp.setStatus(200);
    resp.setHeader("Content-Type", "application/json");
    resp.getWriter().println("{ \"greeting\" : \"Hello, world\"}");
    resp.getWriter().close();
  }
}
```

❶ You can specify most of the things you'd want to specify in web.xml or in the registration bean in the appropraite Servlet API annotation type.

Building REST APIs with JAX-RS (Jersey)

Spring Boot makes it dead simple to stand up REST APIs using JAX-RS. JAX-RS is a standard and requires an implementation. Example A-7 demonstrates Boot's JAX-RS auto-configuration for Jersey 2.x (*http://bit.ly/2vmlUmk*) in the GreetingEndpoint. The example uses the Spring Boot starter org.springframework.boot : spring-boot-starter-jersey. If you wanted to use an alternative JAX-RS implementation, like REST Easy, it should be straightforward given what we've just learned about registering filters and servlets to get it installed in your Spring Boot application.

Example A-7. The JAX-RS GreetingEndpoint

```
package demo;

import javax.inject.Inject;
import javax.inject.Named;
import javax.ws.rs.*;
import javax.ws.rs.core.MediaType;

@Named
❶
@Path("/hello")
❷
@Produces({ MediaType.APPLICATION_JSON })
❸
public class GreetingEndpoint {

  @Inject
  private GreetingService greetingService;

  @POST
❹
  public void post(@QueryParam("name") String name) { ❺
    this.greetingService.createGreeting(name);
  }

  @GET
  @Path("/{id}")
  public Greeting get(@PathParam("id") Long id) {
    return this.greetingService.find(id);
  }
}
```

❶ JSR 330's @Inject annotation.

❷ JAX-RS's `@Path` annotation is functionally equivalent to Spring MVC's `@Reques tMapping`. It tells the container under what route this endpoint should be exposed.

❸ Spring MVC's `@RequestMapping` provides a `produces` and `consumes` attribute that lets you specify what content-types a given endpoint can consume, or produce. In JAX-RS, this mapping is done with standalone annotations.

❹ The HTTP verb, also otherwise specified in Spring MVC's `@RequestMapping` annotation, is specified here as a standalone annotation.

❺ The `@QueryParam` annotation tells JAX-RS to inject any incoming request parameters (`?name==..`) as method arguments. In Spring MVC, you'd use `@RequestParam`-annotated method arguments, instead.

Jersey requires a `ResourceConfig` subclass to enable basic features and register components (Example A-8).

Example A-8. The ResourceConfig subclass that configures Jersey

```
package demo;

import org.glassfish.jersey.jackson.JacksonFeature;
import org.glassfish.jersey.server.ResourceConfig;

import javax.inject.Named;

❶
@Named
public class JerseyConfig extends ResourceConfig {

  public JerseyConfig() {
    this.register(GreetingEndpoint.class); ❷
    this.register(JacksonFeature.class); ❸
  }
}
```

❶ We register the endpoint using JSR 330, though we could just as easily have used any of Spring's stereotype annotations here. They're interchangeable.

❷ We need to explicitly register our JAX-RS endpoint.

❸ We need to tell JAX-RS that we want to handle JSON marshalling. Java EE doesn't have a built-in API for marshalling JSON (as we discussed above, it'll tentatively be available in Java EE 8), but you can use Jersey-specific *feature* implementations to plug in popular JSON-marshalling implementations like Jackson.

Spring Boot auto-configures the Jersey `org.glassfish.jersey.servlet.ServletCon` `tainer` to listen for all requests relative to the application root. In JAX-RS, message encoding and decoding is done through the `javax.ws.rs.ext.MessageBodyWriter` and `javax.ws.rs.ext.MessageBodyReader` SPIs, respectively, somewhat akin to Spring MVC's `org.springframework.http.converter.HttpMessageConverter` hierarchy. By default, JAX-RS does not have many useful message body readers and writers enabled, out of the box. Our example registers a `JsonFeature` in the `ResourceConfig` subclass to support JSON encoding and decoding.

JTA and XA Transaction Management

Transaction management is a confusing topic for many folks, particularly because there are so many options!

Resource-Local Transactions with Spring's PlatformTransactionManager

Fundamentally, transactions work more or less the same way: a client begins work, does some work, commits the work and—if something goes wrong—restores (*rolls back*) the transaction and resets the state of the underlying transactional resource to how it was before the work began. Implementations across the numerous resources vary considerably. JMS clients create a *transacted* `Session` that is then committed. JDBC `Connection` can be made to *not* auto-commmit work, which is the same as saying it batches work, and then commit when explicitly instructed to do so.

Resource-local transactions should be your default approach for transaction management. You'll use them with various transactional Java EE APIs like JMS, JPA, JMS, CCI, and JDBC. Spring supports numerous other transactional resources like AMQP-brokers such as RabbitMQ (*http://rabbitmq.org*), the Neo4j graph database (*http://neo4j.com/*), and Pivotal Gemfire (*http://www.pivotal.io/big-data/pivotal-gemfire*). Unfortunately, each of these transactional resources offers a different API for initiating, committing, or rolling back work. To simplify things, Spring provides the `Plat` `formTransactionManager` hierarchy. There are numerous, pluggable implementations of `PlatformTransactionManager` that adapt the various notions of transactions to a common API. Spring is able to manage transactions through implementations of this hierarchy.

Spring provides tiered support for transactions. At the lowest level, Spring provides the `TransactionTemplate`. The `TransactionTemplate` wraps a `PlatformTransac` `tionManager` bean and uses it to manage a transaction given a unit of work which the client provides as an implementation of `TransactionCallback`. Let's first wire everything up. We have some things that will be common to the following two examples— a database `DataSource`, a `DataSourceInitializer`, a `JdbcTemplate`, a `PlatformTran` sactionManager, etc.—so we'll define them in a shared Java configuration class. This Java configuration also defines a RowMapper, which is a JdbcTemplate callback interface that maps rows of results to Java objects (Example A-9).

Example A-9. Java configuration for common types in a transactional JDBC service

```
package basics;

import org.springframework.beans.factory.annotation.Value;
import org.springframework.context.annotation.Bean;
import org.springframework.context.annotation.Configuration;
import org.springframework.core.io.Resource;
import org.springframework.jdbc.core.JdbcTemplate;
import org.springframework.jdbc.core.RowMapper;
import org.springframework.jdbc.datasource.DataSourceTransactionManager;
import org.springframework.jdbc.datasource.SimpleDriverDataSource;
import org.springframework.jdbc.datasource.init.DataSourceInitializer;
import org.springframework.jdbc.datasource.init.ResourceDatabasePopulator;
import org.springframework.transaction.PlatformTransactionManager;

import javax.sql.DataSource;

@Configuration
public class TransactionalConfiguration {

    ❶
    @Bean
    DataSource dataSource() {
      SimpleDriverDataSource dataSource = new SimpleDriverDataSource();
      dataSource
        .setUrl("jdbc:h2:mem:test;DB_CLOSE_DELAY=-1;DB_CLOSE_ON_EXIT=FALSE");
      dataSource.setDriverClass(org.h2.Driver.class);
      dataSource.setUsername("sa");
      dataSource.setPassword("");
      return dataSource;
    }

    ❷
    @Bean
    DataSourceInitializer dataSourceInitializer(DataSource ds,
      @Value("classpath:/schema.sql") Resource schema,
      @Value("classpath:/data.sql") Resource data) {
      DataSourceInitializer init = new DataSourceInitializer();
      init.setDatabasePopulator(new ResourceDatabasePopulator(schema, data));
      init.setDataSource(ds);
      return init;
    }

    ❸
    @Bean
    JdbcTemplate jdbcTemplate(DataSource ds) {
```

```
  return new JdbcTemplate(ds);
}

❹
@Bean
RowMapper<Customer> customerRowMapper() {
  return (rs, i) -> new Customer(rs.getLong("ID"), rs.getString("FIRST_NAME"),
    rs.getString("LAST_NAME"));
}

❺
@Bean
PlatformTransactionManager transactionManager(DataSource ds) {
  return new DataSourceTransactionManager(ds);
}
}
```

❶   Define a `DataSource` that just talks to an in-memory embedded H2 database.

❷   Define a `DataSourceInitializer` that runs schema and data initialization DDL.

❸   A Spring `JdbcTemplate` which reduces common JDBC calls to one-liners.

❹   A `RowMapper` is a callback interface that `JdbcTemplate` uses to map SQL `Result Set` objects into objects, in this case of type `Customer`.

❺   The `DataSourceTransactionManager` bean adapts the `DataSource` transactions to Spring's `PlatformTransactionManager` hierarchy.

We can use Spring's low-level `TransactionTemplate` to demarcate transaction boundaries explicitly:

```
package basics.template;

import basics.Customer;
import basics.TransactionalConfiguration;
import org.apache.commons.logging.LogFactory;
import org.springframework.beans.factory.annotation.Autowired;
import org.springframework.context.annotation.*;
import org.springframework.jdbc.core.JdbcTemplate;
import org.springframework.jdbc.core.RowMapper;
import org.springframework.stereotype.Service;
import org.springframework.transaction.PlatformTransactionManager;
import org.springframework.transaction.TransactionStatus;
import org.springframework.transaction.support.TransactionCallback;
import org.springframework.transaction.support.TransactionTemplate;

@Configuration
@ComponentScan
@Import(TransactionalConfiguration.class)
```

```
public class TransactionTemplateApplication {

  public static void main(String args[]) {
    new AnnotationConfigApplicationContext(TransactionTemplateApplication.class);
  }

  ❶
  @Bean
  TransactionTemplate transactionTemplate(PlatformTransactionManager txManager) {
    return new TransactionTemplate(txManager);
  }
}

@Service
class CustomerService {

  private JdbcTemplate jdbcTemplate;

  private TransactionTemplate txTemplate;

  private RowMapper<Customer> customerRowMapper;

  @Autowired
  public CustomerService(TransactionTemplate txTemplate,
    JdbcTemplate jdbcTemplate, RowMapper<Customer> customerRowMapper) {
    this.txTemplate = txTemplate;
    this.jdbcTemplate = jdbcTemplate;
    this.customerRowMapper = customerRowMapper;
  }

  public Customer enableCustomer(Long id) {

    ❷
    TransactionCallback<Customer> customerTransactionCallback = (
      TransactionStatus transactionStatus) -> {

      String updateQuery = "update CUSTOMER set ENABLED = ? WHERE ID = ?";
      jdbcTemplate.update(updateQuery, Boolean.TRUE, id);

      String selectQuery = "select * from CUSTOMER where ID = ?";
      return jdbcTemplate.queryForObject(selectQuery, customerRowMapper, id);
    };

    ❸
    Customer customer = txTemplate.execute(customerTransactionCallback);

    LogFactory.getLog(getClass())
      .info("retrieved customer # " + customer.getId());

    return customer;
  }
```

}

❶ The `TransactionTemplate` requires only a `PlatformTransactionManager`.

❷ A `TransactionCallback` defined with Java 8 lambdas. The body of this method will be run in a valid transaction, and committed and closed upon completion.

❸ The return value could be whatever you want, but I think this is in itself an interesting clue: transactions should ultimately be toward obtaining one valid byproduct.

The `TransactionTemplate` should be familiar if you've ever used any of Spring's other `*Template` implementations. The `TransactionTemplate` defines transaction boundaries explicitly. It's very useful when you want to cordon off sections of logic in a transaction, and to control when that transaction starts and stops.

Use annotations to declaratively demarcate transactional boundaries. Spring has long supported declarative transaction rules, both external to the business components to which the rules apply, and inline. The most popular way to define transaction rules as of Spring 1.2, released in May 2005 just after Java SE 5, is to use Java annotations.

Spring supports declarative transaction management with its `@Transactional` (*http://docs.spring.io/spring-framework/docs/current/javadoc-api//org/springframework/transaction/annotation/Transactional.html*) annotation. It can be placed on a type or on individual methods. The annotation can be used to specify transactional qualities such as propagation, the exceptions to roll back for, etc.

So, what's all this to do with Java EE? Java EE 5, released in 2006, included EJB 3 which defined an annotation-based way to demarcate transaction boundaries with its `javax.ejb.TransactionAttribute` annotation. Spring *also* honors this annotation if it's discovered on Spring beans. The `TransactionAttribute` works well for EJB-based business components, but the approach is a bit limiting outside of EJB-based components. JTA 1.2 defined `javax.transaction.Transactional` as a general purpose transaction boundary annotation, more or less like Spring's `@Transactional` from eight years earlier. Spring *also* honors this annotation, if present.

The configuration to make this work is basically the same as with the `TransactionTemplate`, except that we turn on annotation-based transaction boundaries with the `@EnableTransactionManagement` annotation and don't need the `TransactionTemplate` bean anymore. If you are using Spring Boot, then you don't need to add `@EnableTransactionManagement`; it'll just work if you configure a `PlatformTransactionManager` bean (Example A-10).

Example A-10. Java configuration for a simple @Transactional-based application

```
package basics.annotation;

import basics.Customer;
import basics.TransactionalConfiguration;
import basics.template.TransactionTemplateApplication;
import org.apache.commons.logging.LogFactory;
import org.springframework.beans.factory.annotation.Autowired;
import org.springframework.context.annotation.AnnotationConfigApplicationContext;
import org.springframework.context.annotation.ComponentScan;
import org.springframework.context.annotation.Configuration;
import org.springframework.context.annotation.Import;
import org.springframework.jdbc.core.JdbcTemplate;
import org.springframework.jdbc.core.RowMapper;
import org.springframework.stereotype.Service;
import org.springframework.transaction.annotation.EnableTransactionManagement;

@Configuration
@ComponentScan
@Import(TransactionalConfiguration.class)
@EnableTransactionManagement
❶
public class TransactionalApplication {

  public static void main(String args[]) {
    new AnnotationConfigApplicationContext(TransactionTemplateApplication.class);
  }
}

@Service
class CustomerService {

  private JdbcTemplate jdbcTemplate;

  private RowMapper<Customer> customerRowMapper;

  @Autowired
  public CustomerService(JdbcTemplate jdbcTemplate,
    RowMapper<Customer> customerRowMapper) {
    this.jdbcTemplate = jdbcTemplate;
    this.customerRowMapper = customerRowMapper;
  }

  // @org.springframework.transaction.annotation.Transactional
  ❷
  // @javax.ejb.TransactionAttribute ❸
  @javax.transaction.Transactional
  ❹
  public Customer enableCustomer(Long id) {

    String updateQuery = "update CUSTOMER set ENABLED = ? WHERE ID = ?";
```

```
jdbcTemplate.update(updateQuery, Boolean.TRUE, id);

String selectQuery = "select * from CUSTOMER where ID = ?";
Customer customer = jdbcTemplate.queryForObject(selectQuery,
 customerRowMapper, id);

LogFactory.getLog(getClass())
 .info("retrieved customer # " + customer.getId());
 return customer;
 }
}
```

❶ @EnableTransactionManagement turns on the transaction processing. It requires
    that a valid PlatformTransactionManager be defined somewhere.

❷ You could use Spring's @org.springframework.transaction.annotation.Trans
    actional...

❸ ...or EJB's @javax.ejb.TransactionAttribute...

❹ ...or JTA 1.2's @javax.transaction.Transactional.

Prefer Spring's @Transactional variant. It exposes more power than the EJB3 alternative in that it is able to expose transactional semantics (things like transaction suspension and resumption) that the EJB-specific @TransactionAttribute (and indeed
EJB itself) don't expose, and doesn't require an extra JTA or EJB dependency. It is nice
to know that it will work, either way, however.

These examples require only a DataSource driver and org.springframework.boot :
spring-boot-starter-jdbc.

Global Transactions with the Java Transaction API (JTA)

Spring makes working with *one* transactional resource easy. But what is a developer
to do when trying to transactionally manipulate more than one transactional
resource, e.g., a *global transaction*? For example, how should a developer transactionally write to a database *and* acknowledge the receipt of a JMS message? *Global* transactions are the alternative to *resource-local* transactions; they involve *multiple*
resources in a transaction. To ensure the integrity of a global transaction, the coordinator must be an agent independent of the resources enlisted in a transaction. It must
be able to guarantee that it can replay a failed transaction, and that it is itself immune
to failures. JTA (necessarily) adds complexity and state to the process that a resource-
local transaction avoids. Most global transaction managers speak the X/Open XA
protocol (*http://en.wikipedia.org/wiki/X/Open_XA*) which lets transactional resources
(like a database or a message broker) enlist and participate in global transactions. The

Java EE middleware for the X/Open protocol is called JTA (*http://en.wikipedia.org/wiki/Java_Transaction_API*).

For our purposes, it suffices to know that JTA exposes two key interfaces—the `javax.transaction.UserTransaction` (*http://docs.oracle.com/javaee/7/api//javax/transaction/UserTransaction.html*) and `javax.transaction.TransactionManager` (*http://docs.oracle.com/javaee/7/api//javax/transaction/TransactionManager.html*).

The `UserTransaction` supports the usual suspects: `begin()`, `commit()`, `rollback()`, etc. Clients use this object to begin a global transaction. While the global transaction is open, JTA-aware resources like a JTA-aware JDBC `javax.sql.XADataSource`, or a JTA-aware JMS `javax.jms.XAConnectionFactory`, may *enlist* in the JTA transaction. They communicate with the global transaction coordinator and follow a protocol to either atomically commit the work in all enlisted resources or roll back. It is up to each atomic resource to support, or not support, the JTA protocol, which itself speaks the XA protocol.

In a Java EE container, the `UserTransaction` object is *required* to exist in a JNDI context under the binding `java:comp/UserTransaction`, so it's easy for Spring's `JtaTransactionManager` to locate it. This simple interface is enough to handle *basic* transaction management chores. Notably, it is *not* sophisticated enough to handle subtransactions, transaction suspension and resumption, or other features typical of modern JTA implementations. Instead, use a `TransactionManager` instance, if it's available. Java EE application servers are *not* required to expose this interface, and rarely expose it under the same JNDI binding. Spring knows the well-known contexts for many popular Java EE application servers, and will attempt to automatically locate them for you.

Often, the bean that implements `javax.transaction.UserTransaction` *also* implements `javax.transaction.TransactionManager`!

JTA can also be run outside of a Java EE container. There are numerous popular third-party (and open source) JTA implementations, like Atomikos and Bitronix. Spring Boot provides auto-configurations for both (*http://docs.spring.io/spring-boot/docs/current/reference/htmlsingle//#boot-features-jta*). Atomikos (*http://www.atomikos.com*) is commercially supported and provides an open-sourced base edition. Let's look at an example—in `GreetingService`—that uses JMS to send notifications, and JPA to persist records to an RDBMS as part of a global transaction (Example A-11).

Example A-11. An example service that works with both a JDBC and a JMS resource through JTA

```
package demo;

import org.springframework.jms.core.JmsTemplate;

import javax.inject.Inject;
import javax.inject.Named;
import javax.persistence.EntityManager;
import javax.persistence.PersistenceContext;
import java.util.Collection;

@Named
@javax.transaction.Transactional
❶
public class GreetingService {

 @Inject
 private JmsTemplate jmsTemplate; ❷

 @PersistenceContext
 ❸
 private EntityManager entityManager;

 public void createGreeting(String name, boolean fail) { ❹
  Greeting greeting = new Greeting(name);
  this.entityManager.persist(greeting);
  this.jmsTemplate.convertAndSend("greetings", greeting);
  if (fail) {
   throw new RuntimeException("simulated error");
  }
 }

 public void createGreeting(String name) {
  this.createGreeting(name, false);
 }

 public Collection<Greeting> findAll() {
  return this.entityManager.createQuery(
   "select g from " + Greeting.class.getName() + " g", Greeting.class)
   .getResultList();
 }

 public Greeting find(Long id) {
  return this.entityManager.find(Greeting.class, id);
 }
}
```

❶   We tell Spring that all public methods on the component are transactional.

❷ This code uses Spring's `JmsTemplate` JMS client to work with a JMS resource.

❸ This code uses the `spring-boot-starter-data-jpa` support so can inject a JPA `EntityManager` with JPA's `@PersistenceContext` annotation as per normal Java EE conventions.

❹ This method takes a boolean that triggers an exception if `true`. This exception triggers a rollback of the JTA transaction. You'll only see evidence that two of the three bodies of work completed after the code is run.

We demonstrate this in `GreetingServiceClient` by creating three transactions and simulating a rollback on the third one. You should see printed to the console that there are two records that come back from the JDBC `javax.sql.DataSource` data source, and two records that are received from the embedded JMS `javax.jms.Destination` destination (Example A-12).

Example A-12. Putting our transactional service through its paces

```
package demo;

import javax.annotation.PostConstruct;
import javax.inject.Inject;
import javax.inject.Named;
import java.util.logging.Logger;

@Named
public class GreetingServiceClient {

 @Inject
 private GreetingService greetingService;

 ❶
 @PostConstruct
 public void afterPropertiesSet() throws Exception {
  greetingService.createGreeting("Phil");
  greetingService.createGreeting("Dave");
  try {
   greetingService.createGreeting("Josh", true);
  }
  catch (RuntimeException re) {
   Logger.getLogger(Application.class.getName()).info("caught exception...");
  }
  greetingService.findAll().forEach(System.out::println);
 }
}
```

❶ We haven't seen `@PostConstruct` yet. It's part of JSR 250, and is semantically the same as Spring's `InitializingBean` interface. It defines a callback to be invoked *after* the beans dependencies—be they constructor arguments, JavaBean proprties, or fields.

 Spring Boot will automatically set up JPA based on the configured `DataSource`. This example uses Spring Boot's embedded `Data Source` support (*http://docs.spring.io/spring-boot/docs/current/refer ence/htmlsingle//#howto-configure-a-datasource*). If an embedded database (like H2 (*http://www.h2database.com/html/main.html*), which is what we're using here, or Derby and HSQL) is on the classpath, and no `javax.sql.DataSource` is explicitly defined, Spring Boot will create a `DataSource` bean for use.

Spring Boot makes it dead simple to set up a JMS connection, as well. Just like the embedded `DataSource`, Spring Boot can also create an embedded JMS `Connection Factory` (*http://docs.spring.io/spring-boot/docs/current/reference/htmlsingle//#boot-features-hornetq*) using Red Hat's HornetQ (*http://hornetq.jboss.org*) message broker in embedded mode, assuming the correct types are on the classpath (`org.springfra mework.boot : spring-boot-starter-hornetq`) and a few properties are specified (Example A-13).

Example A-13. The configuration to configure an embedded JMS ConnectionFactory

```
spring.hornetq.mode=embedded
spring.hornetq.embedded.enabled=true
spring.hornetq.embedded.queues=greetings
```

Add the requisite Spring Boot starters (`org.springframework.boot : spring-boot-starter-hornetq`) and HornetQ support (`org.hornetq: hornetq-jms-server`) to activate the right auto-configurations. If you wanted to connect to traditional, non-embedded instances, it's straightforward to either specify properties like `spring.data source.url` and `spring.hornetq.host`, or provide `@Bean` definitions of the appropriate types.

This example uses the Spring Boot Atomikos starter (`org.springframework.boot: spring-boot-starter-atomikos`) to configure Atomikos and the XA-aware JMS and JDBC resources.

In today's distributed world, consider global transaction managers an architecture smell (*http://www.eaipatterns.com/ramblings/18_starbucks.html*). Distributed transactions gate the ability of one service to process transactions at an independent cadence. Distributed transactions imply that state is being maintained across multiple services when they should ideally be in a single microservice. Ideally, services should share state not at the database level but at the API level, in which case this whole discussion is moot: REST APIs don't support the X/Open protocol, anyway! There are other patterns for state synchronization that promote horizontal scalability and temporal decoupling, centered around messaging. You'll find more on messaging in our discussion of messaging and integration.

Deployment in a Java EE Environment

Our examples in this appendix have used the Red Hat Wildfly application server's **awesome** Undertow embedded Servlet engine (*http://undertow.io/*) instead of (Spring Boot's default) Apache Tomcat. You can also use Jetty, if you want. To use either alternative, define an explicit dependency for `org.springframework.boot: spring-boot-starter-tomcat` and then set its `scope` to provided. This will have the effect of ensuring that Tomcat is *not* on the classpath, even if one or many other dependencies bring it in transitively. Then, add a dependency for `spring-boot-starter-jetty` or `spring-boot-starter-undertow`. The contribution for Undertow, in particular, originated as a third-party pull request, but the authors really enjoy it because it's very quick to start up. Your mileage may vary.

Though our examples have used a lot of fairly familiar Java EE APIs, it's still just typical Spring Boot, so by default you can run this application using `java -jar your.jar`, or easily deploy it to process-centric platforms-as-a-service (*http://en.wiki pedia.org/wiki/Platform_as_a_service*) offerings like Heroku or Cloud Foundry (*http://cloudfoundry.org*).

If you want to deploy it to a standalone application server (like Apache Tomcat, or Websphere, or anything in between), it's straightforward to convert the build into a `.war` and deploy it accordingly to any Servlet 3 container. In most cases, it's as simple as changing the packaging of the Maven build to `war`, adding a Servlet initializer, and making `provided` or otherwise excluding the Spring Boot dependencies that provide Servlet container (like `spring-boot-starter-tomcat` or `spring-boot-starter-jetty`) that the Java EE container is going to provide. If you use the Spring Initializr (*http://start.spring.io*), then you can skip these steps by choosing `war` from the *Packaging* drop-down.

If you're converting an existing fat-jar-based Spring Boot application, you'll need to add a Servlet initializer class. This is the programmatic equivalent of `web.xml`. Spring Boot provides a base class, `org.springframework.boot.context.web.SpringBoot ServletInitializer`, that will stand up Spring Boot and relevant machinery in a standard Servlet 3 fashion. Note that any embedded web-container features—like SSL configuration, HTTP resource compression, and port management—will not work when applications are deployed thusly.

```
package demo;

import org.springframework.boot.builder.SpringApplicationBuilder;
import org.springframework.boot.web.support.SpringBootServletInitializer;

public class GreetingServletInitializer extends SpringBootServletInitializer {

  @Override
  protected SpringApplicationBuilder configure(SpringApplicationBuilder builder) {
    return builder.sources(Application.class);
  }
}
```

If you deploy the application to a more classic application server, Spring Boot can take advantage of the application server's facilities, instead. It's straightforward to consume a JNDI-bound JMS `ConnectionFactory`, JDBC `DataSource`, or JTA `User Transaction`.

Summary

We would question a lot of these APIs. Do you really need distributed, multiresource transactions? JPA's a nice API for talking to a SQL-based `javax.sql.DataSource`, but Spring Data repositories include support for JPA, of course, and go further. They simplify straight JPA considerably. They *also* include support for Cassandra, MongoDB, Redis, Riak, Couchbase, Neo4j, and an increasingly long list of alternative technologies. Indeed, even if your goal is to use an ORM with SQL and an RDBMS, you still have a lot of great choices. See, for example, the relevant options for MyBatis (*http://bit.ly/2vnpUmP*) and JOOQ (*https://www.jooq.org*), both of which are featured as options on the Spring Initializr (*http://start.spring.io*). Hopefully lower-level APIs are a stopgap on the road to a microservice architecture, not the destination itself.

In the context of microservices, Java EE goes against the grain of what a modern microservice architecture needs. Microservices are about small, singly focused services with as few moving parts as possible. Some modern application servers can be very tiny, but the principal is the same: why pay for what you don't need? Why go so far to decouple your services from each other only to be satisfied with unneeded coupling of the infrastructure that runs the code?

Application servers were built for a different era (the late 1990s) when RAM was at a premium. The application server promised application isolation and monitoring and consolidated infrastructure, but today it's fairly easy to see it doesn't do a particularly good job of any of that. An application server doesn't protect applications from contention from other applications beyond the class loader (and even there, not particularly well, hence the need for modules (Project JigSaw in Java 9) and technologies like OSGi). It can't isolate CPU, RAM, filesystems, and even in the JVM itself, one component can starve others of resources. Instead, let the operating system provide the requisite isolation. The operating system cares and knows about processes, not application servers and class loaders.

It's very common to see applications with the application server configuration (or even the application server itself!) checked into source control systems alongside the application. This (worrisome) approach implies that few are still trying to squeeze RAM out of their machines by colocating applications on the same application server. They do this because they want to build-and-bake a single image, with all of the configuration for the application server configured along with the application. Why the artificial separation? If there is no chance that an application will ever be deployed into any other application server, why treat the two artifacts (the application and the server) as two physically separate things?

Many developers use the application server (or web servers like Apache Tomcat, to which Pivotal is a leading contributor) because it presents a consistent operations burden. Operations know how to deploy, scale, and manage the application server. Fair enough. Today, however, the container of choice is a container technology like Docker or the Warden technology that powers Cloud Foundry. Containers expose a consistent management surface area for operations to work with. What runs inside is entirely opaque.

Containers, and clouds, only care about processes. There's no assumption that your application will even expose an HTTP endpoint. Indeed, there's often no reason that it should. There's nothing about microservices that implies HTTP and REST, common though it is. By moving away from the application server and moving to .jar-based deployments, you can use HTTP (and a Servlet container) if and only if it's appropriate. We like to think of it like this: what if the protocol *du jour* was FTP, and not HTTP? What if the whole world accessed services exposed through an FTP server? Does it feel just as architecturally unassailable to deploy our applications to an FTP server? No? Then why do we deploy them *into* HTTP, EJB, JMS, JNDI, and XA/Open servers?

In this appendix we've seen that Spring plays well with Java EE services and APIs, and that those APIs can be handy, even in the world of microservices. What we hope you'll take away is that there's no need for the Java EE application server itself. It's just going to slow you down.

Index

Symbols

@ActiveProfiles annotations, 291
@Aggregate annotations, 409
@AggregateIdentifier annotations, 409
@AllArgsConstructor annotations, 286
@Around annotations, 51
@Aspect annotations, 50
@AutoConfigureStubRunner annotations, 123
@Beans annotations, 78
@BusConnectionFactory annotations, 90
@CommandHandler annotations, 405
@Component annotations, 48, 277
@Configuration classes, 45, 327
@ConfigurationProperties type, 81
@ControllerAdvice annotations, 164
@Data annotations, 286, 520
@DataJpaTest annotations, 107
@Document annotations, 302
@EnableBinding annotations, 347
@EnableCaching annotations, 327
@EnableDiscoveryClient annotations, 201, 249
@EnableJpaAuditing annotations, 298
@EnableOAuth2Client annotations, 259
@EnableOAuth2Sso annotations, 261
@EnableResourceServer annotations, 254, 256
@EnableRetry annotations, 395
@EnableZuulProxy annotations, 224
@EventListener annotations, 410
@EventSourcingHandler annotations, 410
@ExceptionHandler annotations, 163
@ExportMetricWriter annotations, 465
@Gateway annotations, 349
@GeneratedValue annotations, 294
@GetMapping annotations, 54

@Input annotations, 346, 350
@JsonTest annotations, 103
@LoadBalanced annotations, 205, 220
@MessagingGateway annotations, 349
@MockBean annotations, 98
@NoArgsConstructor annotations, 286
@OneToMany annotations, 294
    parameters, 297
@Output annotations, 346
@PathVariable annotations, 153
@Primary annotations, 90
@PropertySource annotations, 75
@Query annotations, 299
@Recover annottions, 395
@RefreshScope annotations, 87
@Repository annotations, 277
@RequestBody annotations, 153
@RequestMapping annotations, 153
@RestClientTest annotations, 109
@RestController annotations, 54
@RunWith annotations, 95, 98
@Scheduled annotations, 365
@SpringBootApplication annotations, 95
@SpringBootConfiguration annotations, 95
@SpringBootTest annotations, 95, 102
    working with servlet container in, 102
@StepScope annotations, 361
@TargetAggregateIdentifier annotations, 406, 409
@Transactional annotations, 52
@Value annotations, 75, 361
@WebMvcTest annotations, 106

599

A

AbstractMongoEventListener, 306
access tokens, 254
    exchanging for a Principal, 256
    obtaining with password grant type using curl, 257
    propagating across Feign invocations, 256
AccessDecisionManager, 244
AccountRepositoryTest class, 108
Activiti, 377-391
    Alfresco's Activiti project, 378
    metadata tables in MySQL, 379
Actuator (see Spring Boot Actuator)
adapters, 334
admin processes (in twelve-factor methodology), 20
Advanced HTTP Client, 184
Advanced Message Queuing Protocol (see AMQP)
aggregates, 400
    Axon, 408, 417
aggregators, 334
agility, 7
    definition of agile, 7
Allspaw, John, 543
Amazon
    continuous delivery at, 544
    history of, 1
    platform, 4
Amazon S3 (Simple Storage Service)
    simple service broker, 516, 521
        registering, 532
Amazon Web Services (AWS), 2
    documentation, 532
    evolution of, 5
Amazon Web Services Java SDK, 521
AMQP (Advanced Message Queuing Protocol), 137, 413
    configuring AMQP components in Complaints API, 414
    setting up AMQP message listener container, 415
annotation-driven caching, 329
AnnotationConfigApplicationContext, 73
Apache Cassandra, 8
Apache Commons Logging, 479
Apache Kafka, 331
Apache Tomcat DBCP, 283
App Dynamics, 484

AppDeployer, 418
application forklifting, 125-145
    migrating application environments, 126
        containerized applications, 129
        using custom buildpacks, 127
        using out-of-the-box buildpacks, 126
    soft-touch refactoring to get applications to the cloud, 129-145
        cloud filesystems, 140
        distributed transactions using XA/Open protocol and JTA, 137
        email, 143
        HTTP sessions with Spring Session, 134
        HTTPS, 143
        identify management, 144
        JMS (Java Messsage Service), 137
        talking to backing services, 130
    using Amazon S3, 516
application logging (see logging)
application.properties or application.yml file, 86
application/hal+json content type, 166
application/vnd.error content type, 164
application/x-protobuf media type, 160
ApplicationContext object, 73
    in Spring Boot testing, 95
    listening for events, 471
    mocking selected components in a test cless, 98
    refreshing multiple instances with Spring Cloud Bus, 90
ApplicationEventPublisher, 473
ApplicationRunner, 377
ApplicationTests class, 95
AppsManager, 505
Asciidoctor, 176
    Maven plug-in, 179
aspect-oriented programming (AOP), 50
Assert class, 44
asynchronous operations, returning status of, 519
at-least-once semantics, 400
at-most-once semantics, 400
audit events, 473-477
AuditEventRepository, 476
auditing
    with JPA, 297
    with MongoDB, 306
AuditListener, 476

messaging endpoints, 333-335
event-driven architectures, SEDA, 418
events
    distribution in Axon via AMQP, 413
    in Complaints API (example), 411
    mirror imaging commands in CQRS, 411
eventual consistency, 114, 399
exceptions in Spring Retry, 396
execution environment, handling of logs in, 20
Executor object, 365
expectations, 120

F

Facebook clients, 239
fault tolerance in Spring Batch jobs, 358
Feign library (Netflix), 220-222
field injection, 101
Fielding, Roy
    hypermedia tenet, 165
    REST, 149
files, Spring Integration inbound File adapter, 337
filesystems (cloud), 140
filters, 334
    implementing ZuulFilter or javax.serv-let.Filter, 227
    javax.servlet.Filter
        dynamically white-listing requests into edge service, 228
        Spring Security installed as, 245
    Zuul, 223, 223
        custom rate-limiting filter, 235
        default types, 234
Firefox Poster plug-in, 181
FlatFileItemWriter, 363
Flickr, 543
follow-up (incident response), 450
foreign keys, 297
forklifted applications (see application forklift-ing)
friend access, 44
FUSE-based filesystems, 140

G

gateways, 334
    messaging gateway producer implementa-tion, 348
gauges, 455
GaugeService, 458

generic types
    capturing parameters in class literals, with type token pattern, 219
    retaining type parameters, 190
Git repositories
    for Spring Cloud Config Server, 85, 85
        security, 87
    surfacing information about, with /info endpoint, 469
Google Chrome Advanced HTTP Client exten-sion, 183
Google Protocol Buffers, 158
    REST service serving application/x-protobuf media type, 160
    schema for Customer message, 158
    script to generate Java, Ruby, and Python clients, 159
Gradle projects, 22
    wrapper script in Spring Initializr, 24
Grafana, 465, 466
    dashboard, 467
GrantedAuthority type, 244
graph databases, 309
graphing time series data, 465
Graphite, 466
Graphite Composer, 466
    dashboard, 467
GridFsTemplate, 140
Groovy DSL, 120

H

HAL (Hypertext Application Language), 166, 190
HATEOAS, 150
    (see also Spring HATEOAS)
Hazelcast, 134
HEAD method, 153
health checks, 470-473
    HealthIndicator, 471
    output of default /health endpoint for an application, 470
health monitoring, 507
HealthIndicator, 471, 504
Heroku cloud platform, 14
    buildpacks, 127
    Java buildpack, 128
histograms, 461
    distribution of file upload sizes, 461
historical data, 453

Google Protocol Buffers client, 160

About the Authors

Josh Long is a Spring Developer Advocate, an editor on the Java queue for InfoQ.com, and the lead author on several books, including Apress' *Spring Recipes*, 2nd Edition. Josh has spoken at many different industry conferences internationally including TheServerSide Java Symposium, SpringOne, OSCON, JavaZone, Devoxx, Java2Days, and many others. When he's not hacking on code for SpringSource, he can be found at the local Java User Group or at the local coffee shop. Josh likes solutions that push the boundaries of the technologies that enable them. His interests include scalability, BPM, grid processing, mobile computing, and so-called "smart" systems. He blogs at *blog.springsource.org* or *joshlong.com*.

Kenny Bastani is a Spring Developer Advocate at Pivotal. As an open source contributor and blogger, Kenny enjoys engaging a community of passionate software developers on topics ranging from graph databases to microservices. Kenny is also a regular speaker at industry conferences such as OSCON, SpringOne Platform, and GOTO. He maintains a personal blog (*http://kennybastani.com*) about software architecture, with tutorials and open source reference examples for building event-driven microservices and serverless architectures.

Colophon

The animal on the cover of *Cloud Native Java* is a blue-eared kingfisher (*Alcedo meninting*). This bird is found in Asia, from the Indian subcontinent to Southeast Asia.

The blue-eared kingfisher inhabits shaded forests, where it hunts in small streams and pools. Blue-eared kingfishers eat crustaceans, dragonfly larvae, and fish, perching on branches over densely shaded streams and diving to catch their prey. It has a dark crown with darker underparts. Its lack of an ear stripe differentiates it from the common kingfisher, which inhabits more open habitats. Adult males have dark bills; the bottom half of females' beaks are red.

Many of the animals on O'Reilly covers are endangered; all of them are important to the world. To learn more about how you can help, go to *animals.oreilly.com*.

The cover image is from *English Cyclopedia*. The cover fonts are URW Typewriter and Guardian Sans. The text font is Adobe Minion Pro; the heading font is Adobe Myriad Condensed; and the code font is Dalton Maag's Ubuntu Mono.

Learn from experts.
Find the answers you need.

Sign up for a **10-day free trial** to get **unlimited access** to all of the content on Safari, including Learning Paths, interactive tutorials, and curated playlists that draw from thousands of ebooks and training videos on a wide range of topics, including data, design, DevOps, management, business—and much more.

Start your free trial at:

oreilly.com/safari

(No credit card required)

CPSIA information can be obtained
at www.ICGtesting.com
Printed in the USA
JSHW012258060121
10762JS00002B/70

9 781449 374648